U.S.
THE INTERIOR
7
10
10
9
8
7
38 S.&W. SPECIAL CTG.
YARDAGE
CASE: Make Length
PRIMER: Make - Lot Number - Other Info.
Cartridge Overall Length
ROUNDS FIRED

# The K-Frame Revolver

# The K-Frame Revolver

## The S&W Phenomenon

## Volume II

## Timothy J. Mullin

produced and edited by R. Blake Stevens

Collector Grade Publications
INCORPORATED

2013

# The Collector Grade Library, 1979 - 2013

**• = In Print and Available**

*American Beauty: The Prewar Colt National Match Government Model Pistol* (1999) by Timothy J. Mullin
- *Backbone of the Wehrmacht - The German K98k Rifle, 1934 - 1945* (1991; 1993; 2001; 2013) by Richard D. Law

*The Belgian Rattlesnake - The Lewis Automatic Machine Gun* (1998) by William M. Easterly
- *The Black Rifle - M16 Retrospective* (1987; 1992; 2004) by R. Blake Stevens and Edward C. Ezell
- *Black Rifle II - The M16 Into the 21st Century* (2004) by Christopher R. Bartocci

*The Bren Gun Saga* (1986; Revised and Expanded Edition, 1999) by Thomas B. Dugelby
*The Browning High Power Automatic Pistol* (1984; Expanded Edition 1990) by R. Blake Stevens
- *The Browning Machine Gun, Volume I: Rifle Caliber Brownings in U.S. Service* (2005) by Dolf L. Goldsmith
- *The Browning Machine Gun, Volume II: Rifle Caliber Brownings Abroad* (2006) by Dolf L. Goldsmith
- *The Browning Machine Gun, Volume III: Supporting the Rifle Caliber Brownings* (2007) by Dolf L. Goldsmith
- *The Browning Machine Gun, Volume IV: Semper Fi FIFTY!* (2008) by Frank Iannamico and Dolf L. Goldsmith
- *Colt's New Service Revolver - "A Particularly Strong, Heavy Weapon"* (2009) by Timothy J. Mullin

*Crown Jewels: The Mauser in Sweden - A Century of Accuracy and Precision* (2003) by Dana Jones
- *Death from Above - The German FG42 Paratroop Rifle* (Expanded Edition 2007) by Thomas B. Dugelby and R. Blake Stevens
- *Desperate Measures - The Last-Ditch Weapons of the Nazi* Volkssturm (2005) by W. Darrin Weaver
- *The Devil's Paintbrush - Sir Hiram Maxim's Gun* (1989; 1993; Expanded Edition 2002) by Dolf L. Goldsmith

*EM-2 Concept & Design - A Rifle Ahead of Its Time* (1980) by Thomas B. Dugelby
- *The FAL Rifle* (2011 Classic Edition of the three-volume *FAL Series*) comprising:
  - *North American FALs* (1979; 1989) by R. Blake Stevens
  - *UK and Commonwealth FALs* (1980; 1989) by R. Blake Stevens
  - *The Metric FAL* (1981; 1989) by R. Blake Stevens and Jean E. Van Rutten
  - *The FAL Series Index* (1989) by Eino Sierpe and R. Blake Stevens
- *The FN49 - The Rifle That Ran Out of Time* (2011) by R. Blake Stevens
- *Full Circle - A Treatise on Roller Locking* (2006) by R. Blake Stevens

*The Gas Trap Garand* (1999) by Billy Pyle
- *German Universal Machineguns Volume II: From the MG08 to the MG3* (2012) by Folke Myrvang

*The Grand Old Lady of No Man's Land - The Vickers Machinegun* (1994) by Dolf L. Goldsmith
- *The Great Remington 8 and Model 81 Autoloading Rifles* (2003) by John Henwood

*The Guns of Dagenham - Lanchester, Patchett, Sterling* (1995) by Peter Laidler and David Howroyd
- *Hitler's Garands - German Self-Loading Rifles of World War II* (2001) by W. Darrin Weaver
- *Honour Bound - The Chauchat Machine Rifle* (1995) by Gerard Demaison and Yves Buffetaut
- *Inglis Diamond: The Canadian High Power Pistol* (2001) by Clive M. Law
- *Kalashnikov: The Arms and the Man* (2001) a Revised and Expanded Edition of *The AK47 Story* by Edward C. Ezell
- *The K-Frame Revolver - The S&W Phenomenon Volume II* (2013) by Timothy J. Mullin
- *The Last Enfield - SA80: the Reluctant Rifle* (2003) by Steve Raw
- *MAGNUM: The S&W .357 Magnum Phenomenon* (2012) by Timothy J. Mullin
- *The Mauser Archive* (2007) by Jon Speed

*Mauser: Original Oberndorf Sporting Rifles* (1997) by Jon Speed, Walter Schmid and Reiner Herrmann
- *Mauser Pistolen: Development and Production, 1877 - 1946* (2008) by W. Darrin Weaver, Jon Speed and Walter Schmid

*Mauser Smallbores: Sporting, Target & Training Rifles* (1998) by Jon Speed
- *MG34 - MG42: German Universal Machineguns* (2002; 2012) by Folke Myrvang

*Modern Military Bullpup Rifles - The EM-2 Concept Comes of Age* (1984) by Thomas B. Dugelby
- *More On THE FABLED FAL* (2011) by R. Blake Stevens

*The '03 Era - When Smokeless Revolutionized U.S. Riflery* (1994) by Clark S. Campbell
- *Pistole Parabellum: History of the "Luger System"* (2010) by Joachim Görtz and Geoffrey L. Sturgess
- *Proud Promise - French Autoloading Rifles, 1898 - 1979* (1995) by Jean Huon
- *Rock in a Hard Place - The Browning Automatic Rifle* (2000) by James L. Ballou
- *Sniper Variations of the German K98k Rifle* (1996) by Richard D. Law
- *Sturmgewehr! From Firepower to Striking Power* (2004) by Hans-Dieter Handrich

*The SPIW - The Deadliest Weapon that Never Was* (1984) by R. Blake Stevens and Edward C. Ezell
- *The Sten Machine Carbine* (2000) by Peter Laidler

*Thompson: the American Legend - The First Submachine Gun* (1996) by Tracie L. Hill
*U.S. Rifle M14 - From John Garand to the M21* (1983; 1988; 1991) by R. Blake Stevens
- *The Ultimate Thompson Book* (2009) by Tracie L. Hill
- *WAR BABY! The U.S. Caliber .30 Carbine* (1992; 1998; 2001) by Larry L. Ruth
- *WAR BABY Comes Home - The U.S. Carbine Volume II* (1993; 2001; 2011) by Larry L. Ruth
- *WAR BABY III - The U.S. Carbine Into the 21st Century* (2013) by Larry L. Ruth


**ISBN 0-88935-577-0**

**Published by Collector Grade Publications Incorporated**
**PO Box 1046, Cobourg, Ontario K9A 4W5 Canada**
**Printed and Bound in Canada**

# *Acknowledgements*

## The Author's List

Even though my name appears as the author, this book represents the combined efforts of many people who have done much to ensure the authenticity and improve the scope of what you are about to read. While I accept all criticisms for any faults which should appear herein, much of the credit for the success of this project is rightly due to the assistance and encouragement of the following individuals:

- R. Blake Stevens, my most remarkable editor, who always does such an excellent job of taking my manuscript and, by adding his own contributions and those of others, turns it into a most interesting and useful book, far ahead of anything previously written on its subject, and one that I would be eager to buy and read if I saw it for sale.
- My secretary, Debbie Gallop, who has prepared numerous drafts of my material over the many years it took to be brought to completion, and helped me to keep it organized. During this lengthy process I am certain she has learned more about K-frame Smith & Wessons than she ever wanted to know.
- My friend Leroy Thompson, who took many of the photos we have used in this book, as well as providing invaluable counsel over a long period of time as we discussed the issues to be presented.
- My friends Judge Shawn McCarver, famed lawman Chief Edward Seyffert, Lt. Col. William Terhune, and Dr. Michael Pernoud, who have kindly participated in countless discussions about the issues to be covered, and whose comments and guidance have done much to improve the end result. Karlyn and Hugh May, both long-time Smith & Wesson collectors, have also been of great assistance.
- Others who have allowed me to photograph weapons from their collections, or who have supplied photos and/or background information, include Martin Floyd, David Menendez, Jr., and Patrick Quinn, Graphic Designer at Rock Island Auction Co.

Many others have also assisted in making this book possible, even if they made no other contribution than patiently listening to me talk about the project, and encouraging me to see it through to its completion. I wish to extend my sincere thanks and appreciation to all of these people for their gracious co-operation.

In addition, no book which even mentions the name "Smith & Wesson" would be complete without an acknowledgement to Roy Jinks, the official S&W historian, who enjoys access to all the factory records and material and indeed has over the years acquired a goodly portion of these historical documents and artifacts as his personal property. All of his books and articles about Smith & Wesson products are thus worthwhile in helping the reader get a good grip on the configurations of the various models and the timeline of their introduction. While he has made no specific contributions to this present study, Mr. Jinks has written separate chapters about K-frame revolvers in several of his books. These contain much of interest to anyone researching these arms, as they detail with thoroughness the various engineering changes made over time, and also the various options and alternatives available throughout each period. All of us who are interested in Smith & Wesson handguns owe Mr. Jinks our deepest appreciation.

## The Editor's List

In addition to the above, the editor would like to thank the following kind people who have also contributed generously to this book, and who thus merit individual mention:

- Lt. Col. (ret.) Matti Chemed, curator of the light weapons collection at the Israel Defense Forces Museum in Jaffa/Tel Aviv, Israel, for permitting the use of his article describing the history of the Israeli Model 1952 9mm revolver, and allowing photography of the specimens held by the Museum.
- Gaston Comeau, a Canadian specialist collector with many years of experience working as the manager of a large Toronto sporting goods concern which distributed Smith & Wesson products. Gaston's excellent collection of S&W arms and documentation has been the source of a great deal of the material used herein, including the little-known story of the S&W revolvers assembled in Canada during the 1970s.
- Bill (Dr. William R.) Cross, of Newburgh, Indiana, for information on and photographs of some rare cased and/or exquisitely engraved Combat Magnums from his collection.
- Per Dahlen, a technical consultant for Saab Arms Engineering, Land Division in Östersund, Sweden, for details and photographs of S&W revolvers used by the Swedish Air Force.
- Jim Fisher, of Vaughn, Montana, for photographs of and information on several rare S&W models from his prizewinning collection.
- Jean-Marc Grand, of Rosny, France, for photos of a number of variations of 9x19mm military ammunition of French manufacture.
- Chad Gripp, of Sheffield, Illinois, for photographs of and information on several rare Alvin White-engraved presentation S&Ws from his collection.
- Carl Heinrich, who operates the Washington Basic Police School in Reno, Ohio, who has supplied some interesting period photographs of police useage of a number of K-frame variations from his collection.
- Reiner Herrmann, of Dorzbach, Germany, an arms expert and author who has supplied images and details concerning markings on, and modifications to, Smith & Wesson .38/200 and Victory Models used by various police agencies in the postwar Allied zones of occupied Germany.
- Jean Huon, of Rambouillet, France, for supplying images of the unique French police S&W with side safety, as well as an unofficial 'take' on the motivation for this program.
- Jean-François Legendre, of Saint-Louis, France, for supplying detailed images of the unique French police S&W with a manual safety mounted on the sideplate. The images shown were taken from a sample Model 12 revolver with a 2" barrel, held in the Forensics collection of IRCGN, France.
- John M. Miller, of Marietta, Ohio, who has supplied documentation from his impressive collection and photographs taken by his daughter-in-law,

Tricia W. Miller, of the USAF M13 Lightweight revolver and several types of ammunition used in the K-frame by the U.S. military.

- James Mock, of Los Angeles, California, one of whose major collecting interests concerns the U.S. carbines that were provided to various official agencies after WWII, who has provided some interesting material concerning S&W M&P revolvers that were issued to police in the American zone of postwar Germany.
- Jeff Moeller, of London, Ohio, who has supplied photographs of a number of arms, ammunition boxes, holsters and other rare accessories from his impressive collection which help illustrate the story of post-WWII U.S. military use of Colt, S&W and Ruger revolvers.
- Rick Nahas, of Manassas, Virginia, co-author of the *Standard Catalog of Smith & Wesson*, who has been specializing in alloy-frame S&Ws since 1985. Rick has kindly supplied an image of the USAF medallion as found on the stocks of some M13 "Lightweight" revolvers, and has also provided information on and images of the recent Scandium-aluminum-alloy-frame .38 Special +P Model 315 Nightguard, the only "Sc" model made on the K frame. Introduced in 2008, too late for inclusion in the 3rd Edition of the *Standard Catalog*, this model was discontinued in 2010.
- Mike Pacella, of Gap, Pennsylvania, one of the few S&W collectors specializing in (among other things) the pre-war 2" M&P, who has kindly provided some excellent photos from his impressive collection of "snubbies".
- Charles W. Pate, who has granted us permission to use excerpts from the official U.S. Navy documentation which appears as Appendix F in his fine reference *U.S. Handguns of World War II - The Secondary Pistols and Revolvers*, concerning the fatal accident caused by a dropped Victory Model revolver in 1944, which led to the development and adoption of the definitive rebound slide hammer block safety, which remains in use in S&W revolvers to this day.
- Josef F. Rothmuller, an accredited Austrian-Canadian Master gunsmith, who was employed from January 8, 1972 through December 11, 1979 as the Service Manager of Smith & Wesson Law Enforcement Equipment (Canada) Ltd., where he was in charge of the revolver assembly program at their office and shop in Mississauga, Ontario. Mr. Rothmuller has kindly shared his recollections and some photos and documentation from this period, which we have used to illustrate the section on the Canadian-assembled S&Ws which appears in Chapter Thirty-Two.
- Lt. Col. (ret.) Bernie Schecter, former head, Israeli Police Weapons Identification Lab, Jerusalem, for compiling and translating information on the Israeli 9mm Model 1952 revolver, and taking and supplying photographs of the specimens held at the IDF Museum in Jaffa/Tel Aviv.
- Dave Terbrueggen of Jacksonville, Florida, an inveterate collector of Smith & Wessons (among other things) for 42 years. Dave has kindly provided a number of excellent photographs of standard and unusual K-frame revolvers from his extensive collection.

Several other kind people who have assisted in making this book as complete, attractive and authoritative as possible are as follows:

- David Carroll
- the late Ray Cheely
- Michael Chiapputo (photography)
- Brian Chavez (photography)
- Timothy Comeau (IT and computer expertise)
- Wolfhart Fritze
- Paul Goodwin (photography)
- George Hall
- IRCGN Forensics Collection, France
- Richard Jones, Editor, *Jane's Infantry Weapons*
- Charles Kramer
- Clive M. Law
- Metropolitan Police Service Forensic Firearms Unit
- Ian Patrick, voluntary archivist, Royal Armouries Library
- Greg Pfeiffer <www.britishguns.com>
- Arastou Rafizadeh
- John Ross
- Mara Schecter
- Mike Spradlin (photography)
- Mark Terry <www.facsimiledustjackets.com>
- Larry Wack <www.historicalgmen.squarespace.com>
- Michael Wozniak

## Comments; Questions?

The author welcomes comments, additional information and criticisms from readers of both volumes in this series. He may be contacted as follows:

Timothy J. Mullin
7912 Bonhomme Ave Suite 303
Clayton, MO 63105, USA

<tjmullin@sbcglobal.net>

Uncredited illustrations are from the author's collection.

# *Table of Contents*

## Part II: The Golden Age

**Part III: A K-Frame Retrospective**

# *An Appreciation*

## John Chapman Henwood

### January 4, 1932 - October 2, 2011

John Henwood, in a photo taken of him at his desk in December, 2004. courtesy Mrs. Katherine Henwood

Despite the importance and longevity of the K-frame S&W, it appears that until now only one book has been written exclusively about this model, and even that enjoyed rather limited circulation. This is the now out-of-print title *America's Right Arm - the Smith & Wesson Military and Police Revolver,* which was self-published by the late John Henwood in 1997.

At the outset of this project my editor Blake Stevens and I discussed making a fresh start and establishing for ourselves the chronological facts concerning the various K-frame models and changes. However we soon came to the conclusion that the research in this area which John had conducted for use in his book *America's Right Arm* was exemplary, and could hardly be improved upon. Therefore, rather than going through this whole process again, we have asked Mrs. Katherine Henwood, John's widow and heir, for permission to use, and credit, information from John's original timeline in our book. She has graciously acceded to this request, and for this we offer her our heartfelt thanks.

John printed only a limited number of copies of his book, and it appears that he also did much of the marketing himself. Understandably, this means that it was not as well known or widely distributed as it might have been, and we are glad to have the opportunity to insure that everyone who buys this book will be well aware of his significant contributions to this important story.

John also wrote and self-published two other books, one titled *The Forgotten Winchesters: A History of the Models 1905, 1907, and 1910 Self-Loading Rifles* (1995), and the other titled *The 8 and the 81: A History of Remington's Pioneer Autoloading Rifles* (1993). Both exhibit John's pleasant style of writing, and benefit from his characteristically thorough research methodology.

John's study *The 8 and the 81* was expanded and republished by Collector Grade as *The Great Remington 8 and Model 81 Autoloading Rifles* in 2003.

# *Dedication*

To Eleanor - no one could want a better wife and partner.

And to my daughter Catherine, who has grown into a fine young woman, and Matthew Cort, my son-in-law, with whom I have entrusted her.

# *Foreword*

## On Patrol, On the Range, In the Field - Tomorrow's Collectible Today

This is a well-informed discourse by a professional self-defense expert covering all aspects of the K-frame revolver, the tried-and-true cornerstone product of the prestigious American armsmaking firm Smith & Wesson, Inc. of Springfield, Massachusetts.

From its antecedent .32 caliber Hand Ejector model, introduced in 1896, through well over a century of production, S&W K-frame revolvers have long been recognized as the most perennially popular sidearms in the company's long history, with production totals in excess of the quantities of all other S&W models combined.

## The Series Concept Explained

In Volume I of this series, titled *MAGNUM - the S&W .357 Magnum Phenomenon* (2012), we have discussed the history of several Colt and S&W models (including the K-frame) which were instrumental in leading to the introduction of the S&W .357 Magnum in 1935. The K-frame history detailed here in Volume II necessarily proceeds through largely the same timeframe, and indeed the stories occasionally overlap and combine, or at least run parallel to each other, as for instance when the Magnum chambering was introduced in the K-frame revolver in December, 1955.

To facilitate references to earlier material, the page and figure numbering in this book continue on from where Volume I left off, and a comprehensive Index to both volumes appears in the back of this book.

## An Invitation to "Collect the Uncollected"

As the late John Henwood proclaimed in Chapter Fifteen of his 1997 book *America's Right Arm*, titled "Collecting the M&P",

> *It seems a bit strange, writing a chapter on collecting an (as far as the author can tell) uncollected revolver. Although manufactured with only the most minor of changes for almost one hundred years, having been a favorite with law enforcement and military organizations, and the most popular home- and personal-defense weapon ever mass-produced, it seems odd that nobody collects them. Maybe they are too popular to appeal to collectors; after all, there are over 5,000,000 out there to choose from . .*

Fortunately, however, as we discovered during the research phase of this book, there are indeed a number of advanced collectors who have long specialized in one or another aspect of the K-frame revolver, and photos and details of some of their prizes have done much to improve the authority and scope of this study.

With most Colt Single Actions, Lugers and S&W Registered Magnums now well beyond the reach of many, here is a stunning gazeteer of a fine, precision product, reflecting all the traditions of American manufacturing quality and durability, and available in an almost infinite variety of models and versions.

Many of these are still being made today, and most are still eminently affordable.

# Introduction

The K-frame Smith & Wesson revolver is one of the most popular and prominent handguns ever made. To date, roughly eight million examples have been manufactured, which as noted is more than the production total of all other S&W models combined.

Everyone, it seems, owns at least one K-frame. They have been used all over the globe for over a century now by all manner of people, and many models based on the medium-sized K-frame remain in production to this day.

K-frame S&Ws have proven to be exceptionally versatile throughout this unprecedentedly long period. Fixed-sight M&P versions have provided much peace of mind to those who carried them as duty guns or who kept one handy for home protection, while the adjustably-sighted target models have performed with great reliability and precision in matches fired by a vast number of target shooters. Both types have proven themselves over time to be dependable companions in wild and dangerous places.

## Smith & Wesson - A Little Family History

The history of Smith & Wesson started in the 1850s with the partnership of Horace Smith and Daniel B. Wesson. Both men came from a machining and gun-making background, and started their business at an ideal time. The need for defense weapons was clear and apparent to all, and made even more so by the events leading up to the beginning of the Civil War in the United States, which is still known as "The War of Northern Aggression" by many of my acquaintance.

224 (right). A steel engraving of Daniel Baird Wesson (1825 - 1906) featured in the booklet *Advance Sheets of Biographical History - Ideals of American Life, Containing Biography of Daniel Baird Wesson*, published by the Massachusetts Biographical Society in 1909, wherein Mr. Wesson is described as follows: "Mastership in the invention, development and perfection of modern small arms, during an active business career of over half a century, made Daniel B. Wesson notable."

Gaston Comeau collection

# Notes on the Model 1 Tip-Up Revolver

225. A professional photograph taken shortly after the opening of the new Smith & Wesson factory at no. 6 Stockbridge St., Springfield, Massachusetts, which was completed in March, 1860.

Note the curious workmen watching the cameraman set up his equipment from a number of open windows.

Gaston Comeau collection

In 1858, Smith & Wesson introduced a nice little .22 rimfire tip-up revolver with a seven-shot capacity which people today would view as a toy, but in a world where most handguns were using loose powder and lead balls set off by separate percussion caps, the weather resistance and certainty of the self-contained cartridge used in this first Smith & Wesson revolver were met with great enthusiasm. In a day and age before antibiotics and x-ray equipment, plus little in the way of anesthetics, being shot, even by a .22 short, was not something to be taken lightly. While a cap-and-ball revolver (most likely to be .31 or .36 caliber, not the heavy .44 Dragoon model) fired a larger projectile, the actual power level difference was not that great. The reliability of the self-contained .22 also was much more comforting than the slight extra power that the Colt (or other make) cap-and-ball revolver might offer. After all, ask yourself today if given a choice

226. An early colored postcard view of the Wesson House, described as "The splendid mansion on Maple St."
Gaston Comeau collection

between a .22 cartridge revolver or a cap-and-ball, which would you use as your carry gun? I think we all know the answer when we think about it in those terms.

The following brief excerpt is from *Advance Sheets of Biographical History - Ideals of American Life, Containing Biography of Daniel Baird Wesson*, published by the Massachusetts Biographical Society in 1909:

> *Experimenting and testing his ideas incessantly, Mr. Wesson at length succeeded in perfecting a revolver—the peculiarity and merit of which consisted in the fact that the chambers ran entirely through the cylinder . . Mr. Wesson joined again with his old partner, Mr. Smith. They hired premises on Market Street in Springfield, in 1857, and with twenty-five workmen began operations. In 1860, success having attended their efforts, they built a large factory on Stockbridge Street, where owing to the heavy demand for their weapon starting during the Civil War, they came in time to employ six hundred workmen. The government, it is true, supplied only the old-fashioned arm with percussion caps; but the public with less conservatism and more wisdom demanded the improved weapon . .*

The partnership continued until July, 1873, when Horace Smith retired, having been bought out by Wesson. The company continued to be run by Daniel B. Wesson until he brought in his two sons in 1883. D. B. Wesson continued to be the driving force in the business until his death in 1906, having overseen the development of products that would continue to be staples of the firearms industry to this day, including of course the K-frame revolver and the .38 S&W Special cartridge.

227. Another period postcard, showing a panoramic view of Springfield, Massachusetts with the Smith & Wesson factory on Stockbridge St. in the foreground and the Wesson House (fig. 226) centered on the horizon.
Gaston Comeau collection

## Wessons In Charge Until 1946

Wesson family members remained in charge of the company until 1946, and it must be acknowledged that perhaps these later scions were not as sharp or as hardworking as their predecessors. Of course, they did have to deal with the peremptory takeover of their plant by the U. S. government at the end of World War I; then the Great Depression, along with the anti-gun Roosevelt administration; and then the exigencies of World War II—so perhaps we should not be too harsh. They did come up with some fine handguns, among which were the exceptionally accurate K-frame Masterpiece Target models in .22 rimfire and .38 Special, along with the fine N-frame Third Model Hand Ejector series, and, of course, the .357 Magnum.

In August, 1946, with both plant and management pretty well worn out by the stress of all-out wartime production, then-president Harold Wesson died, and the general superintendent, Carl R. Hellstrom, was installed as the first non-family president. Mr. Hellstrom rejuvenated the company and, by the late 1940s, had Smith & Wesson back in full production, replacing Colt's as the primary revolver maker in the world. The company introduced a lot of very interesting innovations under Mr. Hellstrom's management, not the least of which were the K-frame revolver chambered for the .357 Magnum cartridge, and the short action in the same frame size.

## Under New Management

In fact it was likely this success that caused Smith & Wesson to become a target for corporate takeover when, in 1965, a conglomerate based in Bangor, Maine called Bangor Punta Alegre Sugar Corp. paid $22.6 million to gain control.

The company remained a division of Bangor Punta until January, 1984 when the Lear Siegler Corp. acquired Bangor Punta, and new corporate masters took control of Smith & Wesson. It might be noted that often the people in charge of these corporate entities were not "gun people" but rather businessmen attracted to high profits. As a consequence, quality control often suffered during these times, and many revolvers produced during this period had to be returned by owners for proper fitting. This was a source of frustration for many, although it must be said that if an arm was sent back as defective, it was repaired and returned in excellent working condition.

In December, 1986, leveraged buyout specialists Forstmann Little & Company led a group that took Lear Siegler private in a $2.1-billion LBO, with the new company called Lear Siegler Holdings Corporation. As was typical, the new company sought to sell off assets to pay down the debt, and Smith & Wesson was identified as a non-core business enterprise. As a consequence, in July, 1997, the UK-based conglomerate F. H. Tompkins PLC (later called Tompkins PLC) paid $112 million to purchase Smith & Wesson.

While most of us would not be too surprised to hear that the new British management obviously knew little about guns and failed, as we shall see, to understand the U. S. gun culture, we have to acknowledge that they did invest in a lot of fine new CNC machinery during their period of tenure, and had it installed in the plant. This permitted a significant reduction in the amount of expensive handwork traditionally needed to complete each arm, although the quality of the weapons being produced did not diminish, so that today a K-frame revolver is both cheaper to buy and actually better made than its pre-WWII brothers.

During the time Tompkins PLC owned Smith & Wesson, all U.S. firearm manufacturers came under assault by the federal government at a variety of levels. Smith & Wesson was facing dozens of lawsuits aimed at imposing strict liability on gun manufacturers, which of course was really an attempt to limit gun sales. Rather than attempting to solve the problem with legislation, which is what ultimately nipped this insidious behavior in the bud, apparently the British thought that they could deal with the situation and, in March, 2000, they entered into an agreement with the U.S. government that involved safety standards, design, and distribution issues. The gist of this agreement (which is available on line, by the way, and runs some eighteen small-print pages), is that ultimately Smith & Wesson would be out of the business of selling modern weapons to anyone but the government. No doubt had they proceeded with this settlement, the company, at the time still owned by the British firm Tomkins PLC, would have followed in the footsteps of another famed English gun manufacturer, Webley & Scott, which allowed themselves to be put out of business by the government. News of this ill-advised agreement was met with great hostility by the buying public, and a boycott of the company's products resulted in a forty percent slide in sales.

Amusingly, the boycott was so successful and devastating to the Clinton Administration's plan to hobble gun rights that the Federal Trade Commission's Anti-Trust Division launched an investigation, targeting gun rights groups and firearms dealers whom they suspected of conspiring to undercut the Clinton Administration's policies. They were, of course; but as this happens to be a constitutionally protected activity, the investigation was dropped in 2003.

The ultimate effect of this crippling boycott was that on May 11, 2001, just like their ancestors had left North America some two centuries earlier, Tompkins PLC sold off

Smith & Wesson to Saf-T-Hammer Corp. for $15 million, plus the assumption of $30 million in debt. (You will recall that Tomkins had paid $112 million for the company only four years earlier, so the boycott cost them a very substantial sum.)

The only thing that was lacking was the money to make it happen. According to Securities and Exchange filings at the time, Saf-T-Hammer Corp., formerly known as De Ora Mines, Inc. of Nevada, had assets of only $321,378 as of April 30, 2001; but the corporation claimed, as its main asset, to hold designs involving childproof safety devices that could be fitted to handguns, which appeared to be a good fit for all parties concerned and were indeed later incorporated into the basic S&W revolver design.

By virtue of paying two individuals $250,000 each, plus stock warrants for 354,725 shares, redeemable at one dollar per share, an investor named Colton Melby, who also happened to be a director of Saf-T-Hammer Corp., was induced to lend the company five million dollars to cover the first instalment of the $15 million purchase price. In addition to his note for the five million, he got a stock warrant for 7,094,500 shares, redeemable at forty cents per share if exercised by May, 2007. Mr. Melby's loan was used to pay off the initial five million at the closing of the deal, with the additional ten million to be paid by May, 2002, along with the debt assumption as indicated.

Among the first acts of the new management was to renounce the agreement made with the federal government, upon which the boycott was dropped, and sales once again boomed. Of course it did not hurt that the "shall issue concealed carry" mandate was then being generally adopted in the United States, and that the "war on terror" had begun. Perhaps more than anything else, the recognition of how important the individual customer was to the economic health of the corporation was made clear to all.

By the way, at the time of writing this in April, 2013, S&W stock is selling for $8.54 per share. On April 9, 2003, the earliest relevant date we have located, it was $1.51 a share. In May, 2007, when Mr. Melby's stock option expired, it was selling for $14.08 which, assuming he exercised his option then, translated into a tidy profit of ninety-seven million dollars, in addition to getting his initial five million back.

One could certainly say that, with sales down forty percent, an effective boycott in place, and the world buying Glock and Beretta pistols, things had looked a bit grim over in Springfield when the transaction took place—but then as Lord Rothschild said, the time to buy is "when blood is running in the streets".

## More on Saf-T-Hammer Corp., and Smith & Wesson Today

As noted, the major asset of the acquiring corporation was a series of patent rights for safety units that could be installed in handguns. The fact that these types of designs had been around for decades in one form or another and were always shunned by the knowledgeable did not mean that some people did not like them. Certainly a portion of the "deal" made with the U.S. government was to make handguns safer by making them less capable of being inadvertently fired, and after acquiring the company, Saf-T-Hammer Corp. effectively installed their design in all the S&W models that did not already have a safety system. Thus the classic Centennial models, (M40/42), which had a grip safety, were exempt from the program, but everything else was modified to include the new key safety. These soon became known among Smith & Wesson shooters as "wind-up key" models. Many people shunned the new design while some simply dismantled the lock mechanism for fear it might inadvertently engage, thus tying up the revolver at a critical moment. Others learned to live with the key safeties, and found that they seemed to work fine, and did not engage inadvertently.

The big advantage was that this allowed Smith & Wesson to sell into some markets that otherwise would have remained closed, since a few states had enacted radical laws banning weapons without locks from being sold.

It is most interesting to consider, as we do in this book, how safety features on Smith & Wesson revolvers have been a recurring theme over the years. Obviously, right from the beginning everyone connected with the newly-developed Hand Ejectors was familiar with the danger of a weapon firing if dropped with a cartridge under the firing pin, as many a person had been shot when dropping his Colt Single Action or saddling a horse when a stirrup tripped the hammer. We have documented the repeated efforts by Smith & Wesson to ensure that their revolvers were free from this hazard, with the most recent modification being added in 1944 in response to the incident of a sailor who was fatally shot by his dropped Victory Model during WWII.

However, the new key-lock safety system was not intended to address the problem of inadvertent firing, but rather to guard against intentional firing by unauthorized persons. Surely no one wants to see an inquisitive child of tender years gain access to a loaded weapon without supervision, nor do we want to see one in the hands of some mentally challenged person who might inadvertently or intentionally cause harm, and if utilized the key-lock system would definitely preclude such occurrences.

Nevertheless a revolver is first and foremost an item of personal security equipment, and it may not be possible to insert a small key into a small hole in a sufficiently prompt and positive manner as part of a response to a crisis. Additionally, people being people sometimes forget to unlock items even when putting them on. The holsters for the SIG P229 pistols issued to the U.S. Secret Service have a hole, designed to take a padlock, which agents can insert through the holster and the trigger guard of the pistol, rendering it "safe" when taken off at home. Agents on duty have been spotted with padlocks in place on their holstered weapons. How much more likely is it that a small metal flag poking slightly upwards beside the hammer will be missed when holstering a weapon? I say this as someone who has seen police officers carry empty weapons on duty, or weapons still loaded with short-range plastic training ammunition.

# Part I: The First Million M&Ps

*Chapter Twenty-Five*

# Developments Prior to WWI

## The I-Frame .32 Hand Ejector, Model 1896

228. Right side view of the Model 1896 .32 Hand Ejector revolver, along with a depiction and description of the .32 S&W Long cartridge, as shown on page 32 of the 1902 S&W catalog.

As shown in fig. 233, the cylinder legend is actually upside down and backwards when viewed from this side.
Compare with fig. 233: the drawing does not depict the top screw in the sideplate. Gaston Comeau collection

Smith & Wesson's first solid-frame, side-ejecting revolver was introduced in 1895, and was featured in the 1902 catalog as the Model 1896. It was built on what was known as the "I" frame, which was slightly smaller than the later K frame.

Several features of the mechanism of the early I-frame revolvers were unique and short-lived. In the Model 1896 the cylinder stop, copied from that of the original tip-up S&Ws, was a tempered spring-steel component (part no. 315, fig. 230) located in a longi-

SMITH
&
WESSON
SPRINGFIELD
MASS

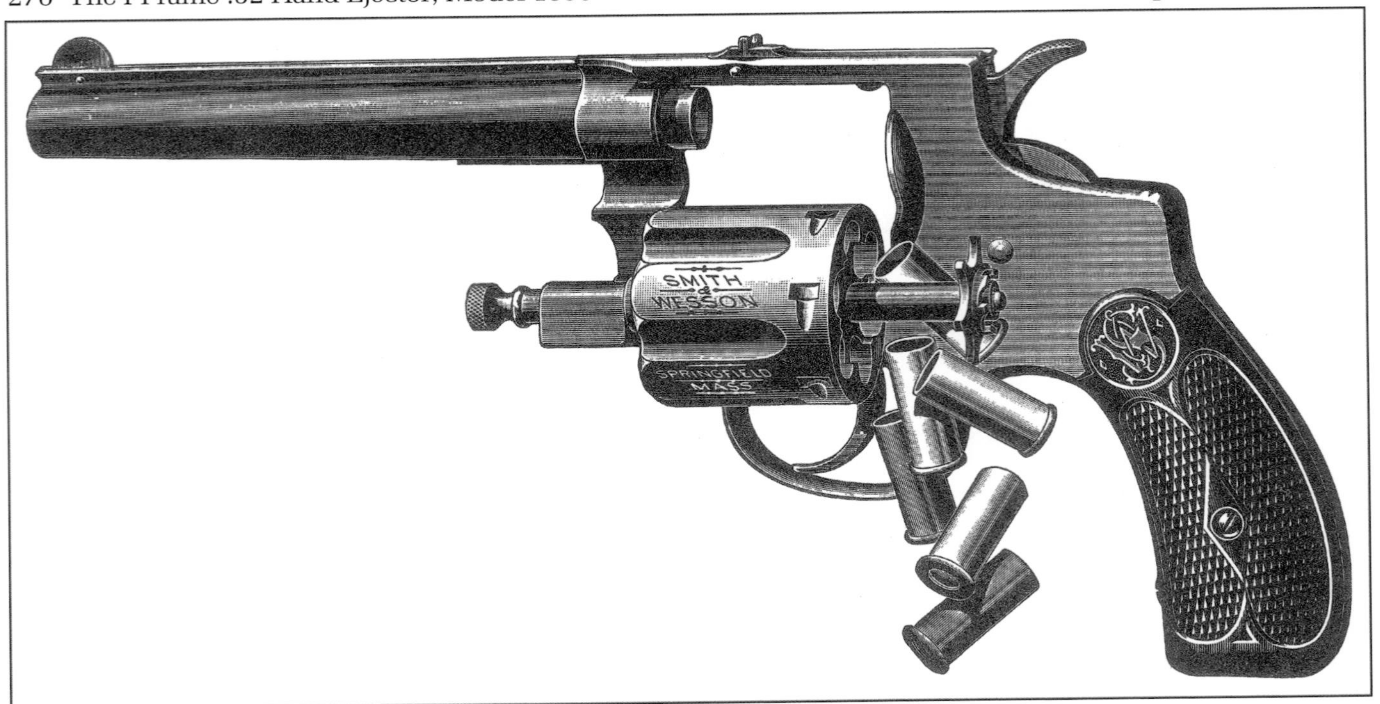

229. Left side view of the Model 1896, also from the 1902 catalog, showing the cylinder open and the ejector rod pushed to the rear, with the spent cartridges being ejected.
Gaston Comeau collection

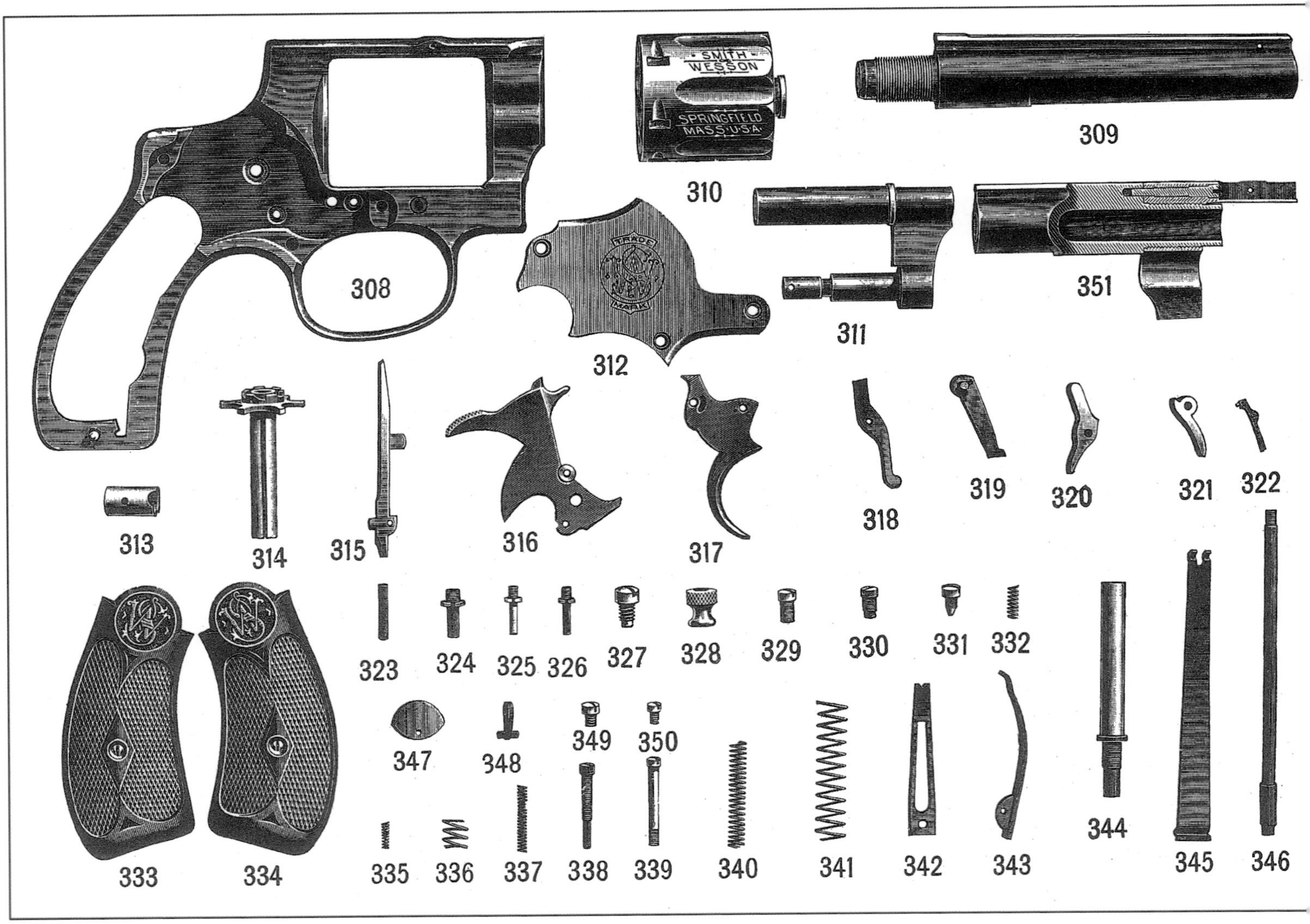

SMITH
WESSON
SPRINGFIELD
MASS·U·S·A·
TRADE
MARK
308
309
310
311
312
351
313
314
315
316
317
318
319
320
321
322
323
324
325
326
327
328
329
330
331
332
333
334
335
336
337
338
339
340
341
342
343
344
345
346
347
348
349
350

231. Left side view of an actual deluxe example of the Model 1896, nickel plated and fitted with pearl stocks.
Gaston Comeau collection

tudinal slot in the top strap, and incorporating the rear sight. The rear quill-like portion of this component is split lengthwise, so that when the hammer is cocked, either manually or by pulling the trigger in double action, a projection on top of the hammer lifts the cylinder stop briefly to free the cylinder so that the hand can begin to rotate it. As the hammer falls, the pointed front end of the hammer projection slips through the slot, momentarily spreading the two halves of the stop.

## Marking the Model 1896

On the Model 1896 the familiar S&W trademarked logo appeared on the sideplate, while all other markings were roll-stamped between the flutes around the circumference of the cylinder in six portions, reading as follows:

SMITH
—&—
WESSON

SPRINGFIELD
MASS

U.S.A.
PATENTED

JULY 1, 84
APRIL 9, 89

MARCH 27, 94
MAY 29, 94

MAY 21, 95
JULY 18, 95

230 (previous page). Page 61 of the 1902 catalog shows the Model 1896 completely disassembled and all the components numbered.

Of interest is the section drawing (no. 351), which is described on page 62 of the catalog as follows: "Section of barrel showing dowel screw [part no. 338], which must be removed before the barrel can be unscrewed."
Gaston Comeau collection

# The Original Hammer Safety

Patent no. 520,468, titled "Revolver-Lock Mechanism", was applied for on January 28, 1894 and granted to Daniel B. Wesson on May 29, 1894, this being one of the patent dates roll-marked on the cylinder of these arms. This patent claimed several "improvements in revolvers", the most important of which was an early rebounding hammer. This appears to have been the first in an interesting series of attempts to provide a positive hammer safety in the basic Smith & Wesson Hand Ejector revolver design. This mechanism is described in excerpts from the patent disclosure as follows:

> *. . In the construction of rebounding lock mechanism for arms of the class herein shown and described . . no means have usually been provided for preventing the accidental movement of the hammer against a cartridge acting after the hammer shall have rebounded, whereby the hammer is rigidly retained in a retired position relative to any cartridge which may move in front of it, until the trigger shall have been again operated to fire the arm. The absence of such provision for retaining the hammer in said retired position leaves the latter dependent upon some spring action to hold it away from a cartridge, and, consequently, a force inadvertently exerted against the hammer capable of overcoming said spring action might drive the hammer [forward] and produce an accidental discharge of the arm. To provide against the danger of such accidental discharge of the arm and to surely and rigidly maintain the hammer thereof in what may be termed a "safety-position", the below described improved mechanism is provided.*
>
> *The hammer, 2, is pivoted in the usual manner at 5 in the arm . . [Upon firing] the immediate action of [the main spring, 9] against the [hammer stirrup] causes the upper extremity of the hammer to be instantly retired rearwardly away from the cylinder, as illustrated in [patent] Fig. 1 . . This last described action of the hammer is what is termed the rebound thereof, but were there nothing to prevent it it will be clearly understood that a blow upon the rear edge of the hammer, while held in the position shown in Fig. 1, by the action of the main spring, only, the hammer may be driven forwardly against a cartridge in the cylinder . . with sufficient force to explode [it] accidentally. To provide against said accidental movement of the rebounding hammer a catch-lever, 10, is pivoted below the latter having a catch-notch, 11, thereon which is adapted to automatically engage with the . . notch, 6, on the lower end of the hammer, when the latter shall have been, by said reaction of the main spring, 9, brought to the rearward position shown in Fig. 1. A spring, 12, acts under said lever to so engage it.*

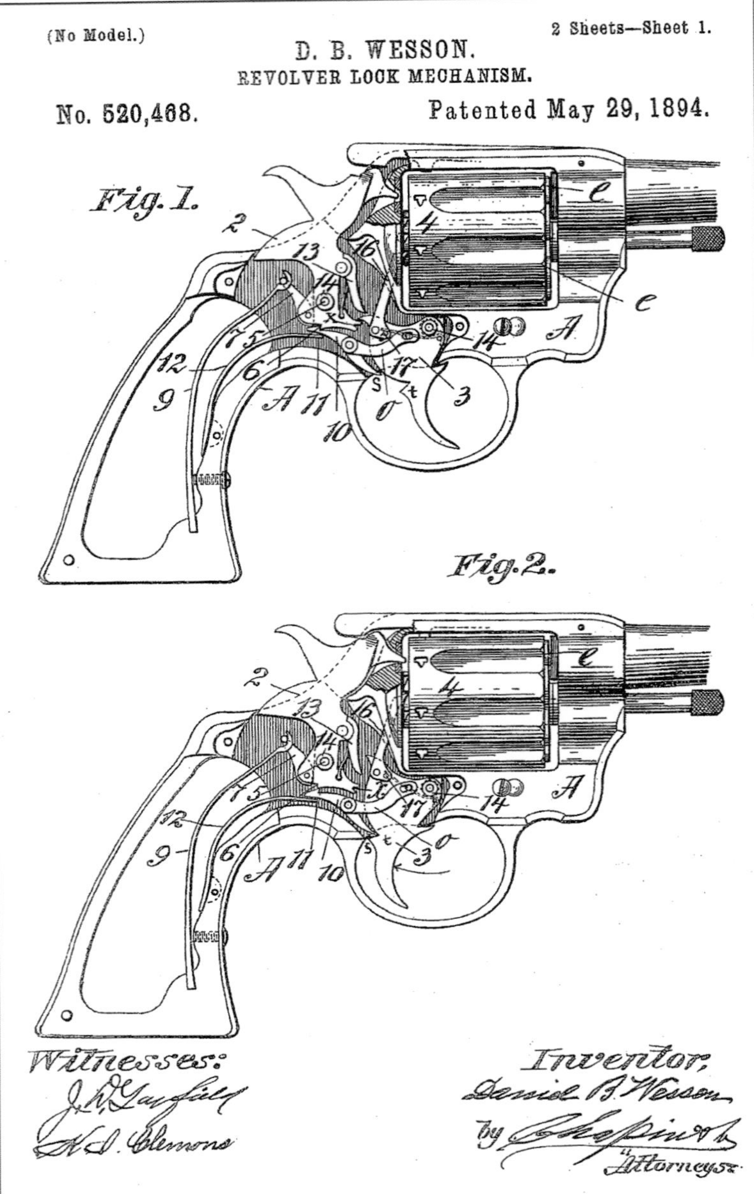


232. Sheet 1 of 2 sheets of drawings from U.S. patent no. 520,468, granted to Daniel B. Wesson on May 29, 1894, covering the features of the original hammer safety mechanism as fitted to the Model 1896 and Model 1899 Hand Ejector revolvers.

In keeping with the deliberately misleading obfuscation common to many patents of those days, the shape of the frame is strongly reminiscent of the Colt design - but note the outline of the cylinder stop, mounted in the top strap.

U.S. Patent Office

*. . By reference to Fig. 2, it is seen . . that when the cartridge is so struck, the notch, 6, on the hammer may be slightly back of the notch, 11, in the lever, 10, but the said rebound of the hammer brings it, relatively to said notch in lever, 10, to the position shown in Fig. 2, so that the said notches, 6 and 11, are in coinciding positions, and will co-engage as in Fig. 1, when the trigger is released and swings to the position shown in the last-named figure . .*

This initial hammer safety was not completely successful, and a number of further improved designs were introduced over time in an attempt to ensure a positive hammer safety. In fact, as we shall see, it appears that no other feature of the basic S&W Hand Ejector revolver was the subject of so many revisions.

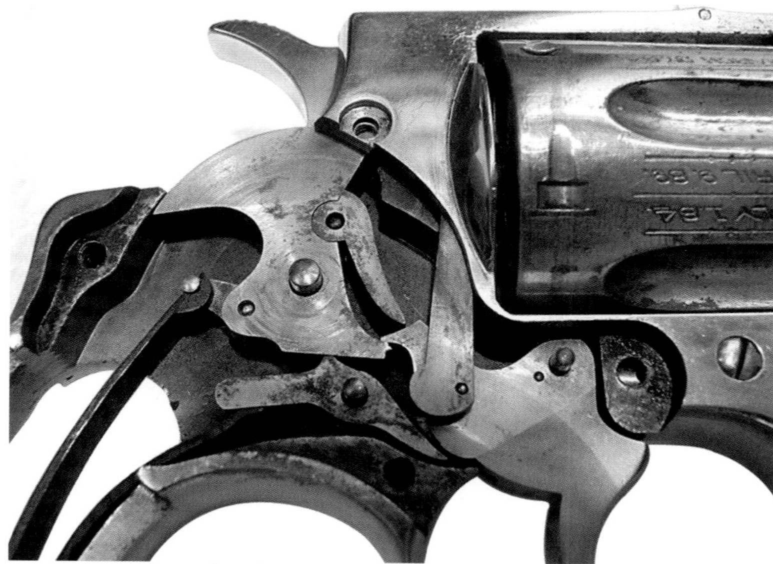

233. Right side closeup of a typical Model 1896 Hand Ejector revolver with the sideplate removed to show the mechanism, which embodies the catch-lever and its separate spring, shown in the two patent drawings in fig. 232. Note the sideplate is actually held on by four screws.
Gaston Comeau collection

## Summing Up the I-Frame Hand Ejector

John Henwood and others record the development of several improved versions of the I-frame Model 1896, which comprised an initial Model 1903, wherein the cylinder stop was relocated more conventionally to below the cylinder, and a total of five further models listed as First through Fifth Changes to the Model 1903. Henwood sums up this early series of Hand Ejector models as follows:

*. . these early double-action revolvers were less than totally satisfactory, the mechanism requiring a number of years of additional development and refinement before it was trouble-free.*

# The M1892-Series .38 Colt Revolvers

## Leaving Room for Improvement

Meanwhile, as discussed in my earlier Collector Grade title *Colt's New Service Revolver* (2009) and in Volume I of this series, the Colt's Patent Firearms Manufacturing Company had developed their own simultaneous side ejector revolver, in .38 Long Colt caliber. This was in response to a demand from the U.S. military which, in the 1890s, had recognized the need for a more modern arm to replace their aging M1873 .45 caliber single-actions. The large-bore revolver remained supreme in England right through World War I and beyond, but in the U.S. and many European armies, double-action revolvers in smaller calibers were rapidly replacing the large-bore black-powder revolvers which had been adopted as the first step after discarding the percussion system.

Colt's moved into the field of small-bore military revolvers with its Model 1892 and subsequent variations on this theme. A typical example of a Colt double-action revolver from this period, actually the improved model purchased under the 1895 Navy contract, appears in fig. 1.

Smith & Wesson models from this time were typically well made, but their top-break design was such that they could hardly crack the military market. The solid-frame, side-ejecting Colt M1892 revolver, chambered for the .38 Long Colt cartridge, was also well made, and early reports in the press of the day were positively glowing with accounts of how pleasant they were to shoot, and how accurate. Had they been sold to Sweden or a similar nation's army, they might well have been perfectly acceptable, but as discussed in several books, the U.S. Army was soon to encounter a very formidable foe in the Philippines, where it was found that the 150-grain .38 caliber Long Colt bullet loafing along at 750 fps or so was simply not up to the task.

In his excellent book *A Study of Colt's New Army and Navy Pattern Double Action Revolvers 1889 to 1908*, author Robert Best states:

> . . *Reports from the war zone in the Philippine Islands indicated that the current .38 caliber round was underpowered. Colt Army revolvers with their low powered .38 Long Colt cartridges, received a bad reputation for failing to stop Philippine rebels in close quarter fighting. There were many reports of rebels being hit multiple times by .38 caliber bullets and killing the U.S. soldier who shot them before the rebel was himself killed.*

In *U.S. Military Automatic Pistols, 1894 - 1920*, author Edward Scott Meadows sums up this issue as follows:

> . . *actual combat experiences during the Philippine Insurrection proved that the .38 caliber cartridge had inadequate stopping power against an adversary such as the fanatical Moro tribesmen who were encountered there. The records are full of first hand, eyewitness accounts to this effect.*

Additionally it was found that the M1892 and subsequent Colt revolvers in that series, while better than earlier Colt double-action revolvers (such as the M1877) as far as field reliability was concerned, were still not as dependable as might be wished. Many developed timing problems and similar defects, sidelining the weapons just when they were needed the most.

# Introducing the S&W "Military" Model of 1899

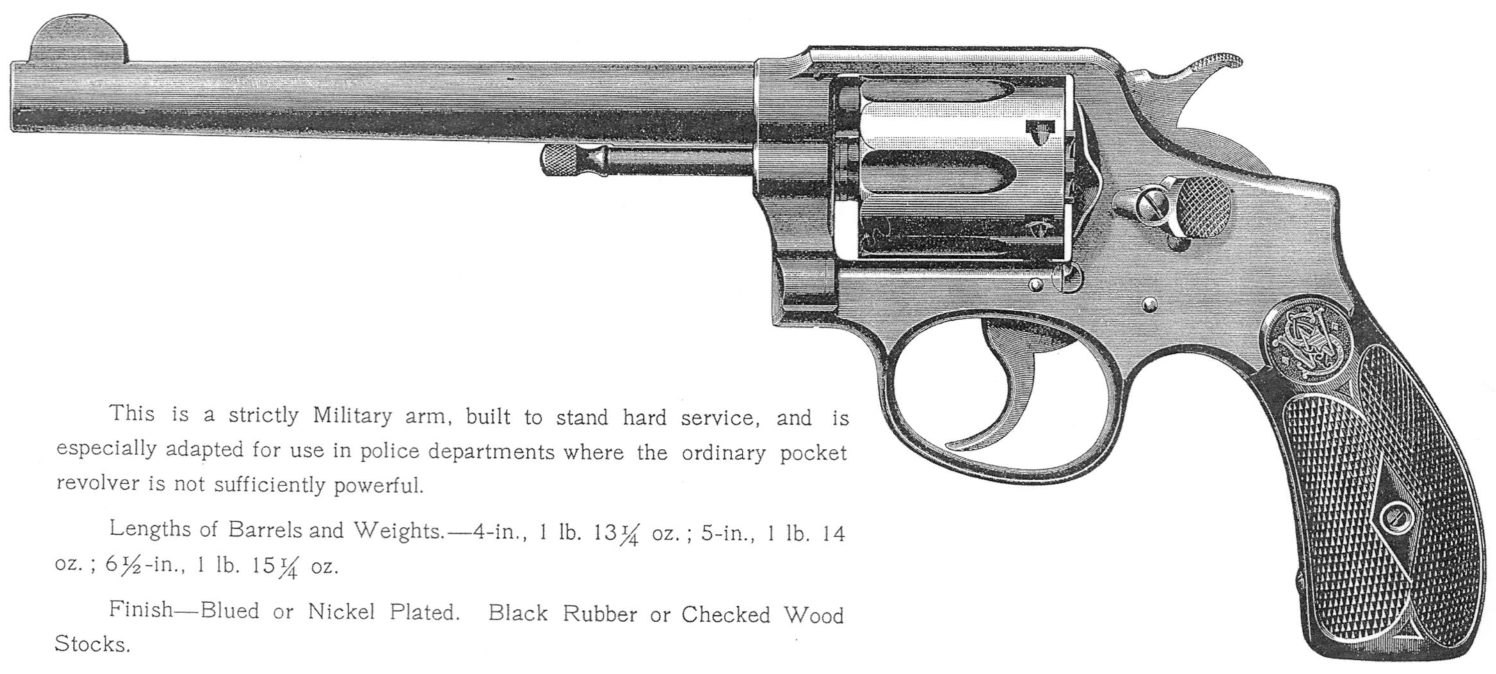


234. Page 35 of the 1902 S&W catalog introduces the ".38 Military" Model 1899. This image also appears as fig. 3. Note the absence of the cylinder stop spring screw in front of the trigger guard, which did not appear until the cylinder stop assembly was improved in the Model 1905.
Gaston Comeau collection

# .38 MILITARY.

The ammunition adapted to this arm is the .38 Smith & Wesson Special, United States Service Cartridge (listed as .38 Long Colt), and the .32 Winchester Repeating Rifle Cartridge.

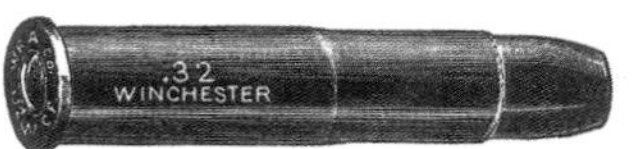


The .38 Smith & Wesson Special contains 21½ grains of powder, and 158 grain solid base bullet. Penetration, 8½ ⅞-in. pine boards. This is a very powerful charge and extremely accurate. Gallery charge, 6 grains of powder and 70 grain round ball, loaded in same shell.

The Regular .38 United States Service Cartridge (listed as .38 Long Colt) is used in the same revolver and is very accurate but not so powerful as the Special. It contains 18 grains of powder and 150 grain hollow base bullet. Penetration 6½ ⅞-in. pine boards.

The .32 Winchester is the regular Winchester Repeating Rifle Cartridge. It is very accurate and powerful and gives good results up to 200 yards. It contains 20 grains of powder and 115 grain bullet. Penetration 6½ ⅞-in. pine boards.

235. Page 34 from the 1902 catalog, depicting and describing the three cartridges adapted to the Model 1899 Hand Ejector revolver. Gaston Comeau collection

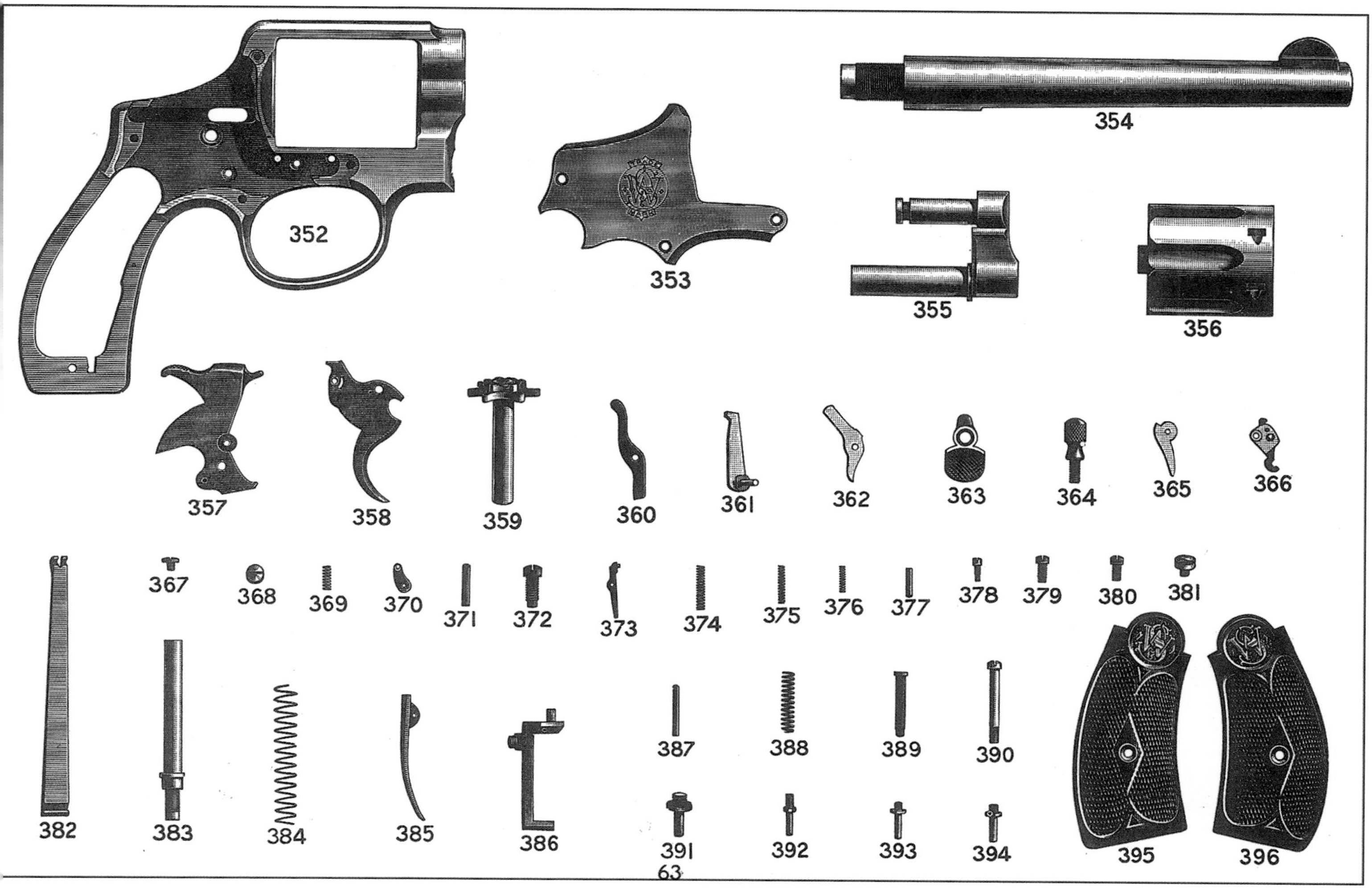

237. Right side view of a typical civilian version of the Model 1899 Hand Ejector revolver, with blue finish, round butt, checkered hard rubber grips with S&W monogram, and a 6½" barrel.

The legend roll-stamped on top of the barrel reads "SMITH & WESSON SPRINGFIELD MASS. U.S.A. PAT'D JULY 1.84/APRIL 9.89. MAY 21.95. JULY 16.95. AUG 4.96. OCT 4.98." courtesy Rock Island Auction Co.

236 (previous page). Page 63 of the 1902 catalog shows the Model 1899 completely disassembled, with all the components numbered.

The "dowel screw" (fig. 230) has been done away with, although there is still no lug under the barrel to secure the front of the ejector rod, and the arm is now fitted with a cylinder latch assembly (parts nos. 363, 375, 377, 378 and 386). Gaston Comeau collection

238. Right side view of another civilian Model 1899, serial no. 11561, with the sideplate removed.

This revolver was shipped on March 14, 1901 to Marcus Hartley & Co. in New York City, and has a history of law enforcement use in western Pennsylvania.

Compare with fig. 252: note the absence of "chafing pins" on the hammer and trigger. private collection

By 1899, Daniel B. Wesson and his designers had developed a new revolver in a slightly larger frame size, soon to be known as the K-frame, which they named the .38 Hand Ejector Military, Model 1899. It was chambered to accept both the .38 Long Colt service cartridge as well as the newly-designed Smith & Wesson .38 Special.

Weighing 158 grains, the .38 Special bullet was 8 grains heavier than the 150-grain .38 Colt bullet, and its slightly longer case, (1.120 - 1.168" compared to the 1.012 - 1.053" case length of the inside-lubricated Army version of the .38 Long Colt round) held 21½ grains of black powder versus 18 grains for the Colt load. Thus the more powerful Smith & Wesson .38 Special cartridge produced measurably greater velocity and penetration.

This first S&W Military model was manufactured from 1899 until 1902, with separate serial number ranges for the two available chamberings, .32-20 (.32 WCF) and .38 Special. The .32-20 models were numbered from 1 to 5311, while the .38 models were numbered from 1 up to 20975, indicating the almost four times greater popularity of the larger chambering.

The Model 1899 was available commercially in blue or nickel finish, and in 4, 5, and 6 ½-inch barrel lengths. Checkered hard rubber or walnut grips were available, with a "U"-shaped fixed rear sight as standard and adjustable target sights optional.

This first model of what was to become the most popular revolver in the world (at least as pertains to numbers produced, if not the most well known to a wide audience – that of course is likely to be the Colt Model 1873 Single Action Army) lacked the barrel lug that provided a front lock or support for the cylinder extractor rod. This was later to become a distinctive feature of Smith & Wesson revolvers, much touted in their literature to the point where it became almost synonymous with the Smith & Wesson product.

## Improvements Incorporated in the Model 1899

### Hardened Steel Cylinder Shims

In addition, unlike the Colt, the S&W Model 1899 had some interesting machining and manufacturing aspects. For instance, hardened steel shims were installed in the cylinder slot stops to prevent wear. Page 5 of the 1902 S&W factory catalog describes the rationale for these hardened shims as follows:

> *. . The accuracy of a Revolver depends in a large measure upon the perfect alignment of cylinder and barrel. In no other Revolver is this important feature accomplished and maintained to the degree of perfection found in the Smith & Wesson arms.*
>
> *To secure this result the stop and stop-notch, which arrest the momentum of the cylinder and hold it in position during discharge, must be accurate and substantial. In all double-action Revolvers notches made in the soft steel of the cylinder, without being reinforced, would soon wear and spread so as to seriously impair the alignment and result in shaved bullets, which is fatal to accuracy, if nothing worse. To overcome this wear and spread, a piece of hardened steel is fitted into the side of the notch which comes in contact with the stop, when the motion of the cylinder is checked .*
> .

239. An illustration from page 5 of the 1902 S&W catalog, captioned "Section of Cylinder, showing Hardened Steel Shims, unfinished." Gaston Comeau collection

## Installing the Patented Shims

Excerpts from patent no. 401,087, applied for on January 31, 1889 and granted to Daniel B. Wesson on April 9, 1889, describe these shims and how they were inserted in the cylinder notches, as follows:

> . . *In practice the said cylinder of the arm is made of soft or untempered steel, and after the stop-notches have been cut therein in the usual way the recesses in the cylinder which are to receive said abutment-blocks are cut by a mill or other suitable tool, and said blocks* **g**, *having been made to fit very tightly in said slots, are then forced into and thereby rigidly secured in the latter in the positions shown in [patent] fig. 2; or the catch-block in the cylinder and the block may be formed as shown in fig. 5* . . .

These shims must have been an expensive nightmare to install, and their use was discontinued late in production of the Model 1905 Second Change, discussed below.

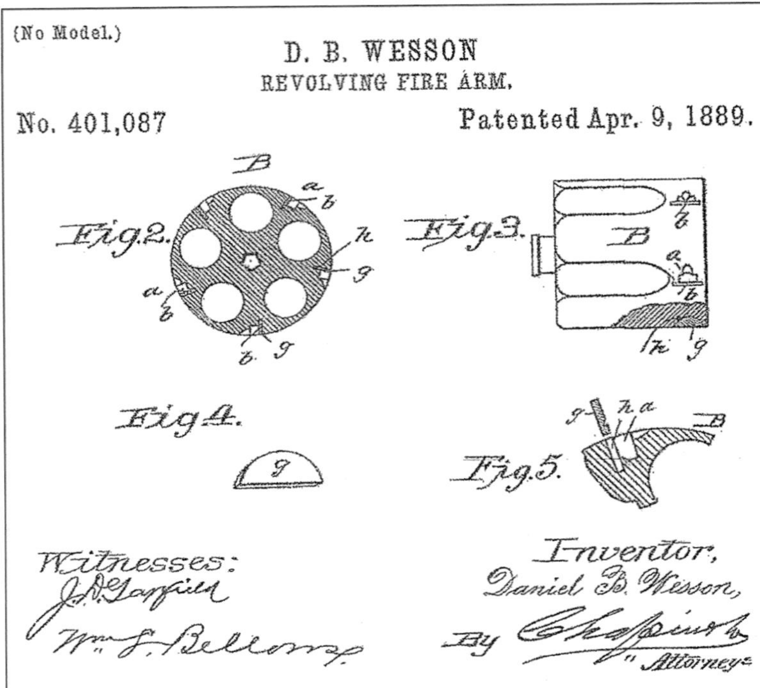


240. Excerpts from the page of drawings from patent no. 401,087, granted to Daniel B. Wesson on April 9, 1889, showing a cross section and side views of the cylinder (patent figs. 2 and 3), a hardened steel shim (patent fig. 4) and the method of its insertion in one of the slots cut into the cylinder (patent fig. 5). U.S. Patent Office

## Hardened Steel Collars in the Frame

In addition to the hardened cylinder lock shims, the 1902 S&W catalog describes another feature of the mechanism of the Model 1899, as follows:

> . . *Another feature which is found in no other Revolver and illustrates the thoroughness of manufacture is the steel bosses, or collars, fitted into the frame to keep the hammer, trigger, etc., from coming in contact with the sides of the frame. These reduce the friction to a minimum and insure the smooth working qualities for which these Revolvers are celebrated. These bosses are to a Revolver what the jewels are to a watch, and add greatly to its durability.*

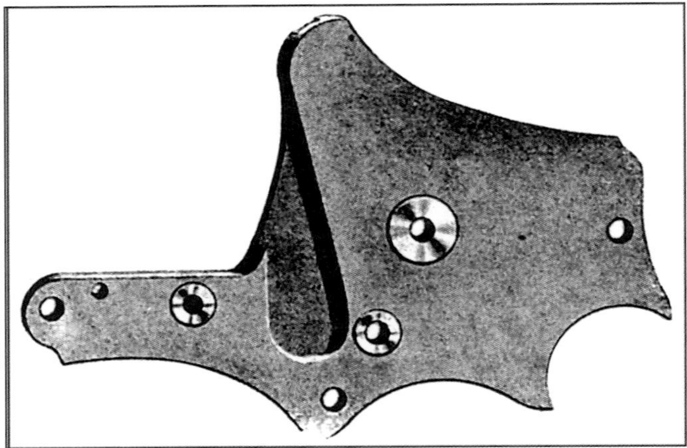

241. Illustration from page 6 of the 1902 S&W catalog, captioned "Side Plate of Military Revolver Showing Raised Steel Bosses." Gaston Comeau collection

### The Patented Cylinder Latch

Along with the redesigned cylinder stop, now located in the frame below the cylinder, the now-familiar cylinder latch was first introduced. As well as providing a convenient means of opening the cylinder, another feature was built into the cylinder latch which was the subject of patent no 635,705, applied for on August 18, 1899 and granted to Joseph H. Wesson, D. B. Wesson's middle son, who had been admitted into the firm in 1887, and John L. Hobbs, on October 24, 1899.

Interestingly, in what was probably a deliberate obfuscation in the patent, the cylinder latch is shown as being operated by pulling it to the rear in order to open the cylinder, and the language of the patent makes this clear. This required a stud (34, patent fig. 5) on the sliding cylinder latch 20, and alterations to the hammer and frame (shown in patent figs. 6 and 7) to accommodate this notch. This rather complicated design was perhaps merely a patent obfuscation, and it appears that the long-established method of pushing the cylinder latch forward to open the cylinder was incorporated right from the very beginning in actual Model 1899 production.

Nevertheless, the patented safety principle remained the same, in that when the cylinder is open the hammer is blocked and the arm cannot fire. This is described in an excerpt from the patent disclosure as follows:

> . . *an improved construction of certain lock parts of revolver-pistols whereby the arm cannot be cocked while the cylinder is misplaced and the firing of the same cannot take place when the cylinder-chambers are not in line position relative to the barrel, thus obviating accidents which might occur* . .
>
> *The side of the frame on which the bolt 20 slides in the groove 21 has a slot through it, letting a screw-stud 26 project through it, whereby the finger-piece 28 for operating the slide from the outside is secured to the bolt by a nut. (Shown in [patent] Fig. 5)* . . *The said safety-bolt 20 and the hammer 31 are provided with coacting means whereby, should said bolt be from any cause prevented from sliding forward to said cylinder-pin-engaging position, when loaded for firing or otherwise, the hammer cannot be operated to explode a cartridge* . .

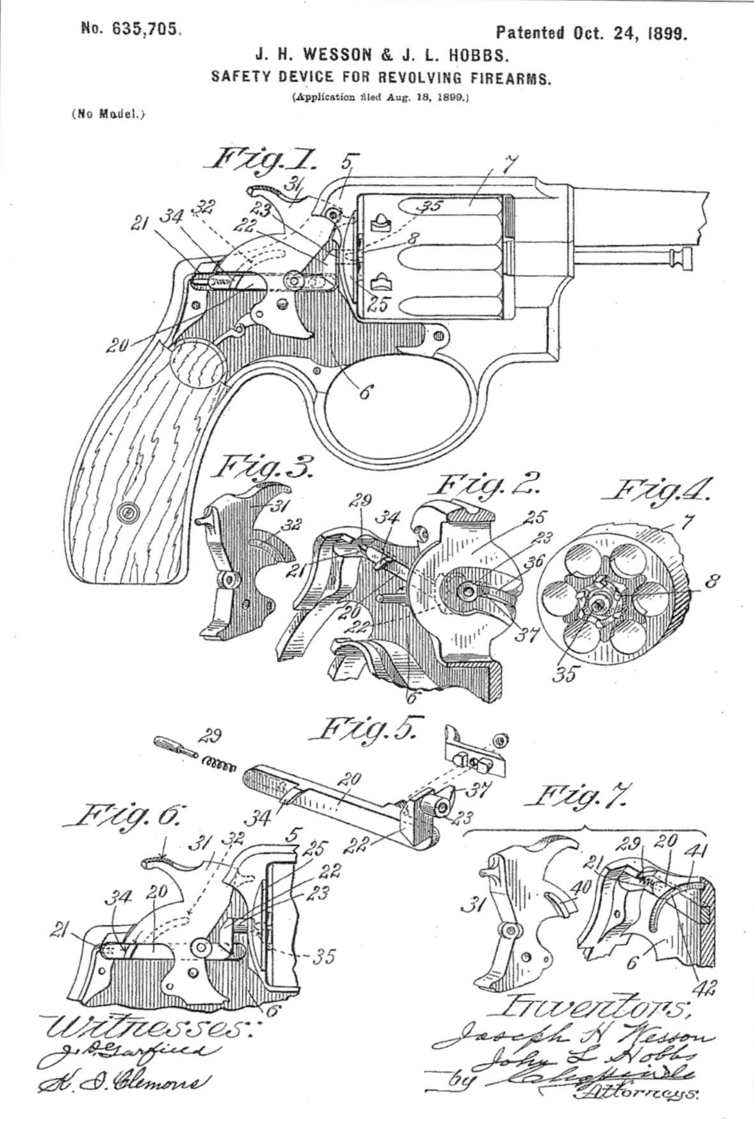


242. The sheet of illustrations from patent no. 635,705, granted to Joseph H. Wesson and John L. Hobbs on October 24, 1899, illustrating the form of the cylinder latch which in the drawings is configured to be pulled to the rear to open the cylinder.

The safety principle, whereby the arm cannot be fired when the cylinder is open, is clearly shown.

U.S. Patent Office

# Military Adoption of the Model 1899

## The U.S. Navy .38 Double Action Model

Justifying its "Military" name, quantities of the Model 1899 .38 Hand Ejector were purchased by both the U.S. Navy and Army.

One thousand Model 1899 revolvers were ordered by the U.S. Navy on June 25, 1900, with factory serial numbers running from 5001 to 6000. These guns were blued, fitted with 6" barrels and plain walnut stocks, and did not have the patented steel shims in the cylinder notches. They were chambered for the ".38 Service" (.38 Long Colt) cartridge, and bore Navy numbers in a separate series from 1 to 1000.

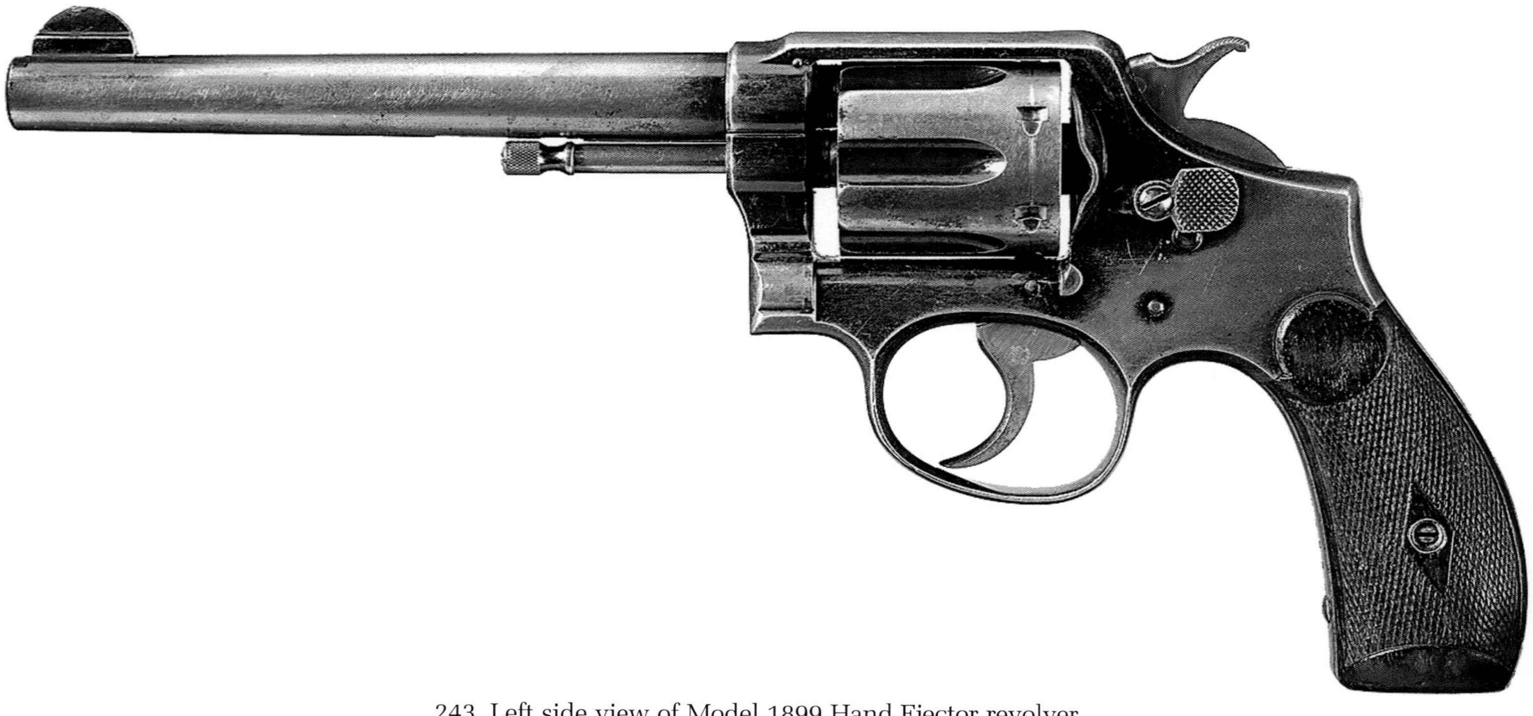

243. Left side view of Model 1899 Hand Ejector revolver serial no. 5930, one of 1,000 purchased by the U.S. Navy on June 25, 1900. courtesy Rock Island Auction Co.

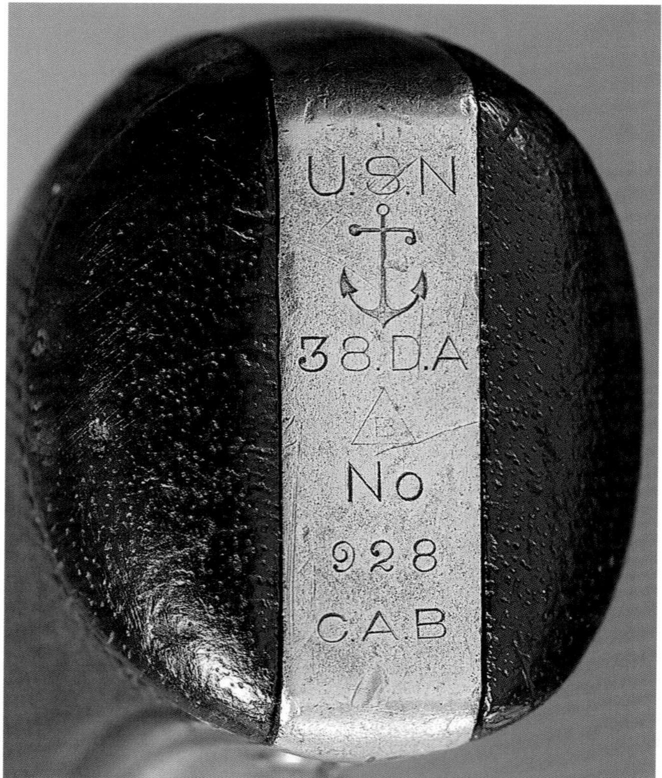


244. Closeup of the bottom of the round butt of the above revolver, showing Navy markings and number 928.

The initials "C.A.B." are those of Naval Inspector Lt. C. A. Brand. courtesy Rock Island Auction Co.

SMITH & WESSON
A BANGOR PUNTA COMPANY
SPRINGFIELD, MASS. 01101

PLEASE ADDRESS ALL COMMUNICATIONS TO THE COMPANY

May 22, 1984

Dear

The revolver about which you inquired in your letter of recent date is the .38 Hand Ejector, Military & Police Model. This model was introduced in 1899 and designed to fire the .38 S&W Special Cartridge. It has been in continued production since it was originally introduced. However, during the past years many design improvements have been made to this model to improve the revolver's function. The collector has classified all of the improvements which occurred before 1945. Therefore, your revolver is classified as the .38 Hand Ejector, Military & Police First Model. This was the original design of our famous M&P Revolver, which was introduced in 1899 and produced until 1902, with a total production of 20,975 revolvers. These revolvers were produced between sdrial numbers 1 and 20975 of the .38 Hand Ejector series. The current production model of this series is known as the Model 10.

We have researched our company records and they indicate that your revolver, serial numbered 5930, was shipped from the factory on September 29, 1900 to the United States Navy, at Brooklyn, New York.

We hope that this information will be useful, as well as interesting to you.

Sincerely,

SMITH & WESSON

Roy G. Jinks
Manager of Consumer Relations
Historian

RGJ/dsg

245. S&W factory letter covering this revolver, which was shipped to the Brooklyn Navy Yard on September 29, 1900. courtesy Rock Island Auction Co.

## The U.S. Army Model 1899

246. Left and right side views of the U.S. Army version of the Model 1899 Hand Ejector revolver.

Note the barrel markings "S.&W. .38 MIL.", and the lanyard swivel.

The inspector markings "K.S.M." on the left rear of the frame and on the right grip stand for Kelly S. Morse, an Army inspector from 1893 to 1915. The inspector markings "J.T.T." on the left grip stand for Ordnance Captain John T. Thompson, later of Tommy Gun fame, who was an Army inspector from 1896 to 1902.

Marty Floyd collection

An additional 1,000 Model 1899 revolvers, chambered for the .38 Long Colt service cartridge and fitted with lanyard swivels, were sold to the Army on April 20, 1901, numbered in the 13000 - 14000 range.

The Army also chose blued examples with 6-inch barrels and walnut grips, and had their own special military nomenclature and numbers stamped on the butts in addition to the standard factory serial numbering.

247 (left). Underside closeup of the Model 1899 Army revolver in fig, 247, showing markings.
Marty Floyd collection

# The Improved Model of 1902

## Adding the Front Cylinder Pin Locking Lug

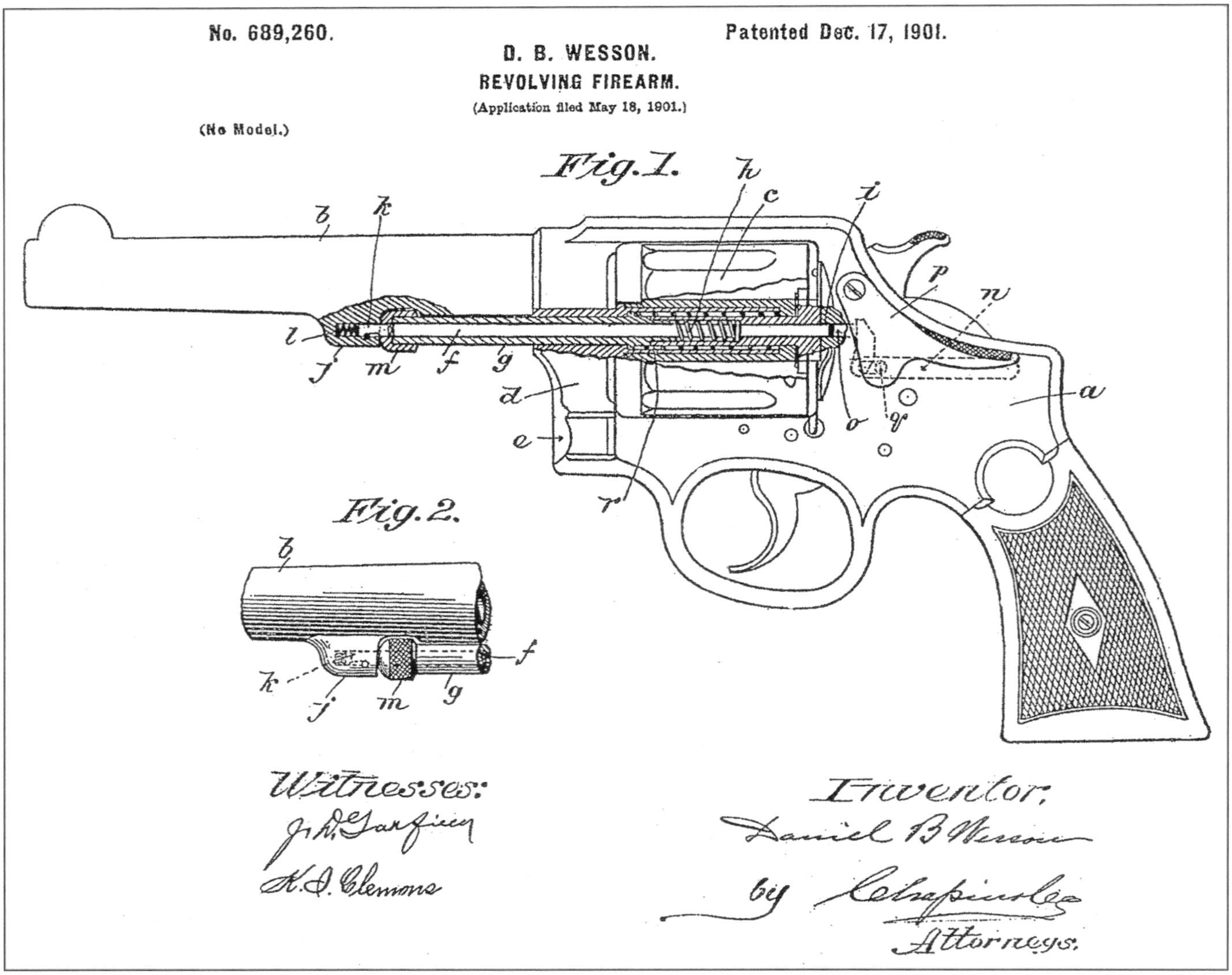

No. 689,260. Patented Dec. 17, 1901.

D. B. WESSON.
REVOLVING FIREARM.
(Application filed May 18, 1901.)

(No Model.)

Fig. 1.

Fig. 2.

Witnesses:

Inventor:
Daniel B. Wesson
by
Attorneys.

In 1902 the Military model of 1899 was replaced by a second, improved model. This was basically the same round-butt revolver, except the now-familiar front cylinder pin locking lug was made integral in the barrel forging.

U.S. patent no. 689,260 covering the barrel lug feature, titled "Revolving Firearm", was applied for by Daniel B. Wesson on May 18, 1901 and granted on December 17, 1901. Interestingly, this patent was granted exactly 14 days after the patent for the much more complicated triple-lock enclosed ejector rod (fig. 10).

Excerpts from the patent disclosure covering the front locking lug explain its purpose and function as follows:

> *[In] "solid frame" revolvers, in which the cylinders swing out to one side of the frame . . . the improvement in means for securing the cylinder . . [so] that the axis of the chambers when in firing position will register accurately with the axis of the barrel . .*
>
> *The essence of this invention lies in the provision of means for locking the cylinder at opposite ends thereof in the frame . .*
>
> *At the forward end of the extractor-stem [fig 248] a lug* j *is formed on the barrel, and this is bored out in axial alinement with the center-pin* f *for the reception of a bolt* k, *which by a spring* l *is forced toward the end of the center-pin in the extractor-stem* g *. . The forward end of the extractor-stem* g *is provided with a head* m, *having a spherical-shaped end thereon, the purpose of which is to crowd the bolt* k *back into its recess in the lug* j *when the cylinder is swung into the frame, it being obvious that the bolt* k *will shoot outwardly as soon as the end of the extractor-stem is withdrawn from in front of the lug* j *. .*

## To Lug, or Not to Lug?

Whether securing the cylinder at both front and rear ends is necessary has always been somewhat of a debate. Smith & Wessons have the front locking feature and Colt revolvers do not, although they seem to get along fine without it, and as John Henwood points out, there is a reason for this:

> *. .While it is true that Colt revolvers get along without this front cylinder lock, you must remember that Colt cylinders turn clockwise. Accordingly the Colt revolver hand is pushing the cylinder more tightly into place as the gun is cocked. S&W cylinders turn counter-clockwise, and thus are being pushed out of position by the hand; the front lock prevents this.*

As for the S&W side of the story, their comments, as they first appeared in the 1925 factory catalog, read as follows;

> *. . Though solid-frame revolvers had been made before, the Smith & Wesson Military and Police Model was the first and is today the only arm of this type in which the cylinder is locked in perfect, permanent alignment with the barrel by hardened steel bearings at each end - exactly like a pulley perfectly supported between two bearings . .*

248 (previous page). The drawings from patent no. 689,260 covering the barrel lug and front locking pin for the extractor rod, granted to Daniel B. Wesson on December 17, 1901 and described in the patent disclosure reprinted above.
U.S. Patent Office

Such things are of course mud collectors and do make adjusting the barrel gap on a Smith & Wesson more difficult than on a Colt. Still, Smith & Wesson users like it, so I suppose the Springfield supporters are willing to put up with the few acknowledged drawbacks to gain the advantage of increased strength and more perfect alignment in lockup. I personally prefer Smith & Wesson revolvers to Colt products, but I admit this is a prejudice with little or no legitimate basis. I like blondes, too, but am married to a brunette whom I would not swap off for any blonde, and so it goes, I suppose.

On the subject of the barrel lug, McHenry and Roper, writing in *Smith & Wesson Hand Guns* in 1944, made the following interesting observation:

> *. . The forward lock [on the S&W hand-ejector revolver] was in addition to the usual rear lock and supplied a more rigid brace for the cylinder. Perhaps pride has dissuaded the Colt Corporation from adding the forward cylinder lock to their hand-ejector revolvers. At any rate they have never done so, although the patent has expired long since.*

## A Review of the Early Hammer Safety Mechanisms

In common with the first S&W Hand Ejector, the I-frame Model 1896, both the Models 1899 and 1902 utilized a separate flat trigger spring in the butt operating a patented "trigger lever" to return the trigger and hammer (figs. 233 and 238). As discussed on pages 278 and 279, this mechanism incorporated a "catch lever" and a "catch notch", which was intended to act as a positive hammer safety.

This mechanism was replaced by the rebound slide in the Model 1905, discussed below, which was itself the second of the several hammer safety mechanisms which have appeared in the mechanism of the Smith & Wesson revolver over the years.

A further patent, no. 824,197, applied for on March 5, 1908 and granted to Elmer E. Neal on June 26, 1906 and assigned to Smith & Wesson, covers a novel but complex method of sleeving the hammer to guard against an accidental discharge of the arm caused by a blow to the hammer. This might have qualified as yet a further type of hammer safety, but it appears that while this patent was purchased by Smith & Wesson, the device was never used by them.

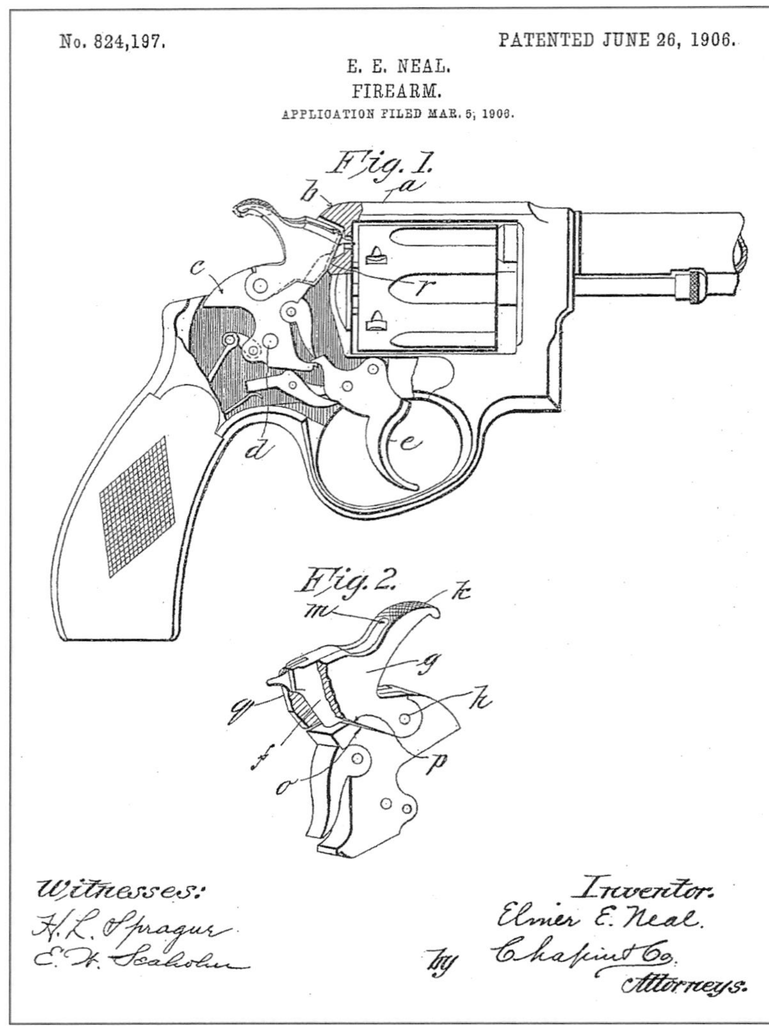


249 (right). The sheet of illustrations from patent no. 824,197, granted to Elmer E. Neal on June 26, 1906 and assigned to Smith & Wesson, covering Neal's proposed hammer sleeve safety, which it appears was never used.
U.S. Patent Office

## "Chafing Pins" in the Hammer (and Later, the Trigger)

The 1909 S&W catalog (figs. 5 and 6) speaks of the further addition of "hardened steel pins inserted in the hammer and trigger to keep these parts from coming in contact with the sides of the frame". John Henwood calls these "chafing pins", and notes that they were first added through the sides of the hammer in 1902. Later, in November, 1904, one similar pin was added to the trigger. Both components are shown with these pins installed in fig. 252.

The original hammer pins were the subject of patent no. 684,331, applied for on March 25, 1901 and granted to Daniel B. Wesson on October 8, 1901, wherein their purpose was described as follows:

> *. . This invention relates to firearms, and has for its object the provision of means for preventing friction between the side of the hammer and the frame of the arm, and it is particularly applicable to revolvers of the self-cocking type. It not infrequently happens that for one reason or another the hammer will bear on the frame to such an extent as to render the cocking operation difficult and prevent, at any rate, the smooth working of the arm . . To prevent the contact of the hammer with the sides of the frame on one side and with the side plate on the other, I provide, preferably at two points on the hammer, points of contact between the hammer and the inner surface of the frame and side plate, these two points being so located that they will be at all times within the frame of the arm during the swing of the hammer, and they are preferably provided by drilling holes through the hammer-body parallel with the pivot of the ham-*

*mer . . In these holes in the hammer pins* c *are tightly driven and the outer ends cut off at such a point beyond either side of the hammer as will . . permit the latter to swing as closely as possible in the frame without touching it, the ends of these pins only bearing on the frame.*

*The ends of the pins projecting from each side of the hammer are rounded off smooth, as shown in [patent] fig. 3, and they are preferably hardened . . In practice the projecting ends of the pin* c *are so close to the side of the hammer as to be scarcely discernible to the touch . .*

The description of the action included in the 1909 catalog adds these "chafing pins" to the earlier claim made in the 1902 catalog so that they, along with the hardened steel collars in the frame, are "to a revolver what jewels are to a watch . ."

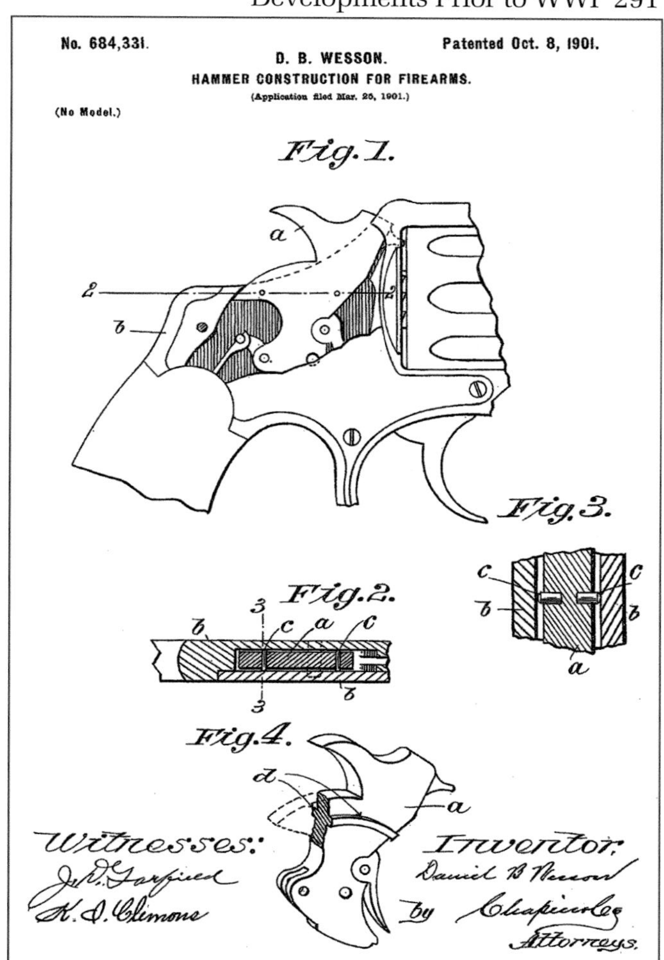


250 (right). The sheet of drawings from patent no. 684,331, granted to Daniel B. Wesson on October 8, 1901, covering the "chafing pins" inserted in the hammer to prevent the contact of the hammer with the sides of the frame.

As shown in fig. 252, a similar pin was later installed in the trigger as well, before being discontinued altogether late in production of the Second Change version of the Model 1905 M&P. U.S. Patent Office

## A Commercial Model 1902

251. Left side view of a well-traveled commercial Model 1902 with 5" barrel, serial no. 20994, shipped on May 1, 1902 to the Norvell Shapleigh Hardware Co.

Purchased by the L. and N. Railroad, and used to arm train crews in order to deter thieves from breaking into boxcars to steal merchandise.

Inset: L. and N. Railroad Sergeant of Police badge no. 3448, vintage 1900 - 1910. private collection

252 (left). Right side closeup of Model 1902 serial no. 20994 with sideplate removed, showing early mechanism with chafing pins in hammer and trigger.
Compare with fig. 238. private collection

## Details of the Second Model Commercial Versions

Commercial versions of the Second Model (the Model 1902) revolver were available in .38 Special and .32-20 chamberings. The serial number range of the .32-20 version ran from 5312 to 9811, while the numbers on the more popular .38 Special second model ran from 20976 to 33803. Nickel was a no-cost option to the normal blue finish, and 4, 5, 6, and 6½ inch barrels were offered. Butts remained round, fitted with stocks of hard rubber or walnut. Service fixed sights and adjustable target-style sights were available. Given the small numbers produced, some variations of this model are pretty rare today.

## Model 1902 "First Change"

The factory did not distinguish between the initial Model 1902 and the version collectors have dubbed the Model 1902 "First Change", which was introduced in 1903 and produced until 1905. This was still a round butt revolver similar to the Model 1902, except the barrel diameter was enlarged to add strength, and, of course, the frame diameter at the barrel hole was also enlarged to accommodate the larger barrel. A clearance cut was milled along the bottom rear portion of the barrel to allow clearance between it and the extractor rod (fig. 253).

The serial number range of the .32-20 version of the Model 1902 First Change ran from 9812 to 18125, while the .38 Special version serial numbers ran from 33804 to 62449, which was a pretty good run for the two years this model was in production.

The Model 1902 First Change was available in 4, 5, and 6½-inch barrel lengths, the 6-inch option having been dropped. Blue and nickel finishes remained optional at the same price, and the revolver was chambered for .38 Special, the specific .38 Long Colt chambering having been dropped as unnecessary, as these cartridges would fit in cylinders dimensioned for the .38 Special.

## A Shipment to the U.S. Revenue Cutter Service (Coast Guard)

Information from Carl Heinrich reveals that Model 1902 serial no. 20765, originally fitted with a 6 or 6½" barrel, was part of a 50-gun order shipped on March 13, 1902 to Capt. Russell Glover of the U.S. Revenue Cutter Service at Baltimore, Maryland. The U.S.R.C.S. became the U.S. Coast Guard in 1915.

This gun, which bears no military markings, still has the original military-style checkered "diamond" wood stocks with no S&W medallions.

This revolver was sold as surplus during the 1920s and ended up in northern West Virginia, probably as a coal company guard gun. At some point the barrel was professionally shortened to 4½", the front sight reset, and the gun reblued. The name "Ben C. Beam" is scatched on the underside of the barrel, and several other places on the frame.

253. Left side view of Model 1902 serial no. 20765, originally fitted with a 6 or 6½" barrel, was part of a 50-gun order shipped on March 13, 1902 to Capt. Russell Glover of the U.S. Revenue Cutter Service at Baltimore, Maryland. The U.S.R.C.S. became the U.S. Coast Guard in 1915.

Compare with the U.S. Navy model shown in fig, 254: this gun has the "First Change" enlarged frame while the Navy model is in the original Model 1902 configuration. private collection

## The U.S. Navy Orders 1,000 Model 1902s

254. Left side view of Model 1902 serial no. 25766, shipped on February 28, 1903 to the U.S. Navy at the Brooklyn Navy Yard. The original barrel was later replaced with a 1906-vintage commercial barrel. private collection

255. Closeup of the front grip strap of the Navy Model 1902 in fig. 254, showing placement of the S&W serial number.
private collection

256. Closeup of the butt of the Navy Model 1902 in fig. 254, showing Navy markings. The "S with arrow" in the center is an acceptance mark, while the initials "J.A.B." are those of Naval Inspector Lt. John A. Bell.
private collection

257. Right side view of another U.S. Navy Model 1902 Hand Ejector revolver. The Navy markings resemble those shown above except the Navy number is "1890".
The checkered wood "diamond" stocks have no S&W medallions. courtesy Rock Island Auction Co.

In August, 1902, the U.S. Navy ordered 1,000 Model 1902s with 6-inch barrels in .38 Long Colt caliber, factory serially numbered from 25001 through 26000 on the front grip strap, and marked on the butt with the typical Navy nomenclature and numbers.

## The Early M&P Popular with Coal Company Guards

258. A mounted employee of the Baldwin-Felts Detective Agency, commissioned as a deputy sheriff of Fayette County, West Virginia, to provide law enforcement services to the Collins Colliery Co, of Glen Jean, West Virginia (note the "C C Co." collar insignia).

These men were well armed, as gunfights and other "misunderstandings" in Appalachian Mountain areas could be as quick and deadly as those out West.

This officer is carrying a Savage Model 1899 rifle and, in addition to a highly polished night stick, he has two round-butt S&W M&P revolvers with 6½" barrels stuck in his belt. Carl Heinrich collection

259 (left). A closeup of the bottom edge of the left hard rubber grip on the revolver shown in fig. 260.

Note the engraved patent date "Jan. 29, 78", which is usually missing if the rubber grips show any wear.

private collection

260. Left side view of Model 1902 M&P no. 31219, a nickel-plated version with a 5" barrel and hard rubber grips, in excellent condition. As shown in fig, 259, the engraved patent date is still visible on the bottom edge of the left grip.

Shipped November 12, 1902 to Schoverling, Daly & Gales, New York City. Stamped "F.C.Co. 6" on the butt, which stands for Fairmont Coal Co. of Fairmont, West Virginia, a subsidiary of the Consolidated Coal Co., once the largest coal mining concern in the U.S.

private collection

## Introducing the Square Butt

John Henwood records that the square butt was first introduced as a no-cost option to the Model 1902 First Change circa November, 1904, at around (.38 Special) serial no. 58000, calling it "probably the most important single change ever made to the M&P revolver."

Rubber or walnut stocks remained optional on round-butt versions, while the square butt was furnished with hand-checkered walnut "standard" or "service" stocks, with uncheckered diamonds surrounding the stock screw and nut.

# The Model 1905 Military and Police

By this time, in addition to the various barrel lengths and optional blue or nickel finish, the Military and Police revolver was available in four basic versions: round butt or square butt, in calibers .32-20 or .38 Special.

## The Introduction of the Cylinder Stop Plunger and Screw

Further mechanical improvements introduced in the Model 1905 included the first appearance of the cylinder stop plunger screw in the front of the trigger guard. Earlier models in the M&P series did not have this visible screw.

This, and the other mechanical changes introduced in the Model 1905 are described by John Henwood as follows:

*. . a new cylinder stop, which moved slightly back-and-forth as it operated; the cylinder stop notches and the frame cut were enlarged to allow this movement, and the shape of the trigger was altered to operate this new stop; a screw, spring and cylinder stop plunger were installed through a hole in the top front of the trigger guard; chafing*

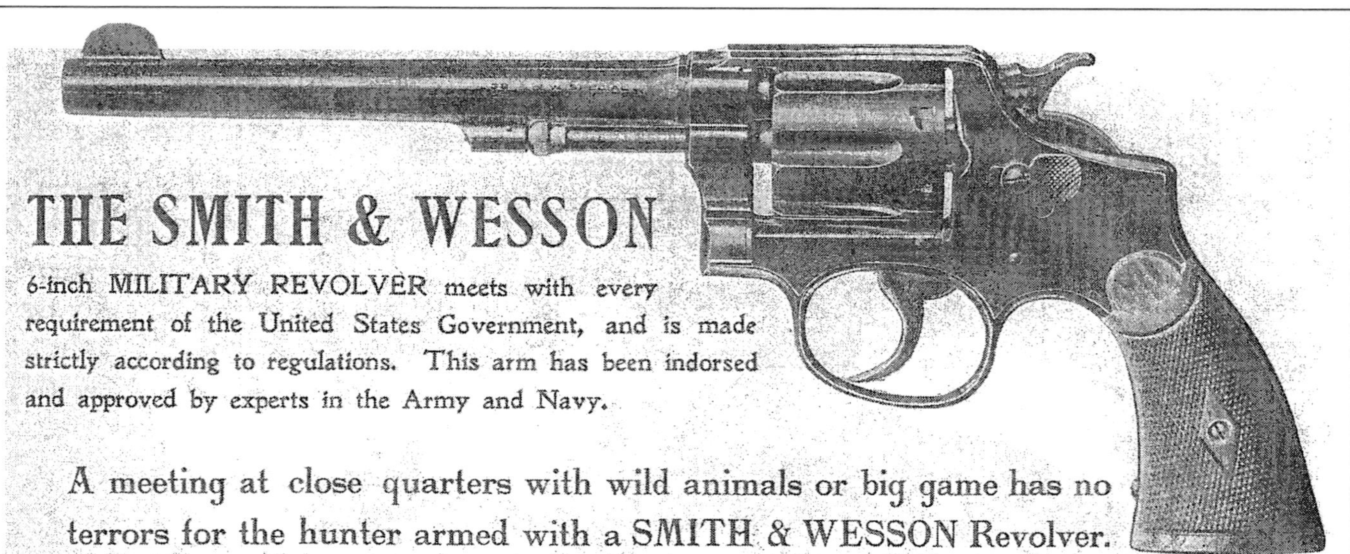


THE SMITH & WESSON MILITARY MODEL 1905

is a powerful, safe, and absolutely reliable revolver; such a gun as a man may trust his life to when trouble comes. It is fitted with the hand ejector which permits quick ejection of empty shells and reloading, and at the same time makes accidental ejection of the loads impossible.

The new stock has that confidence-inspiring feel to the hand. The front cylinder lock used in connection with the regular locking pin absolutely assures that perfect SMITH & WESSON alignment of cylinder and barrel without which accuracy is impossible.

The construction of all working parts is such that all wear is automatically overcome. But one quality of material and workmanship is found in all SMITH & WESSON revolvers; that is the BEST. The best steel for barrel and cylinder. Hardened tool steel bushings in frame and cylinder. Hardened steel pins in hammer and trigger keep these parts from contact with the frame, reduce friction, and make close joints possible. All these features spell durability which together with their accuracy and finish make the superiority of SMITH & WESSON arms everywhere acknowledged.

If you need a Revolver for the protection of your life and property, get a SMITH & WESSON. When you do need a Revolver, the best (SMITH & WESSON) is none too good, regardless of its cost.

All SMITH & WESSON Revolvers have the S. & W. Monogram Trade-mark stamped on the frame. None others are genuine.

Our Catalogue illustrates in detail the various models of Revolvers made under this famous name. Mailed to any address for three cents postage.

SMITH & WESSON

47 STOCKBRIDGE STREET, SPRINGFIELD, MASS.

261. The first printed advertisement for the square butt version of the S&W "Military Model 1905" with 6" barrel, which appeared in the December 14, 1905 issue of the official NRA publication *Shooting & Fishing*.

Note the claim in the second paragraph of small print that these arms featured "Hardened tool steel bushings in frame and cylinder [and] Hardened steel pins in hammer and trigger [to] keep these parts from contact with the frame, reduce friction, and make close joints possible."

The use of these hardened steel "chafing pins" was discontinued late in production of the Second Change version of the Model 1905 M&P.

262. Right side view of an original Model 1905, serial no. 72413 with round butt, hard rubber grips and 4" barrel. The barrel is roll-stamped with the S&W name and address and patent dates in three lines. Note the cylinder stop plunger screw in front of the trigger guard, which first appeared in the Model 1905.

This arm is documented as the service revolver used by the colorful M. Berstrand Couch, or "Frisco Bert", as he often called himself. Couch was a famous Texan and civil servant who started out as a U.S. Customs Inspector in Laredo, Texas, and was eventually promoted to Technical Advisor to the U.S. Consul General in Stockholm, Sweden.
courtesy Rock Island Auction Co.

*bushings were added on each side of the trigger to reduce friction; and the diameter of the cylinder center pin and its locking hole in the center pin bushing were reduced.*

The initial Model 1905 was manufactured for only two years, 1905 to 1906. Serial numbers on the .32-20 version ran from 18126 through 22426, while serial numbers on the .38 Special version ran from 62450 through 73250.

# Model 1905, First Change

A further series of refinements to the Model 1905 were introduced in 1906, prompting collectors to assign the name "Model 1905 First Change" to these models. The Model 1905 First Change was in production during the period 1906 - 1908. Serial numbers of the .32-20 variant ran from 22427 through approximately 33500, while serial numbers of the .38 Special version ran from 73251 to roughly 120000, indicating that the .38 Special chambering continued to outsell the .32-20 by a factor of four to one.

263. Left side view of Model 1905 First Change M&P, serial no. 100264, with 6½" barrel and round butt.

This revolver was used by the Norfolk & Western Railway Co, which operated in Virginia, West Virginia and Ohio. Both hard rubber grips as well as the front edges of the frame and both sides of the barrel at the muzzle show considerable carry wear. The barrel has a slight upward bend which also buckled the top strap of the frame, the result of being used as a pry bar to break boxcar seals or locks, which was the only way the railroad police officers could get into a boxcar "on the road" should it become necessary. private collection

## The Rebound Slide - a Second Attempt at a Positive Hammer Safety

The mechanism in the Model 1905 First Change was altered to incorporate a patented rebound slide, which replaced the earlier "trigger lever" as a means of returning the trigger to its forward position, and also replaced the "catch-lever", which had been the initial attempt at a positive hammer safety.

The rebound slide, which has remained a feature of the S&W action ever since, was a spring-loaded block of hardened steel which reciprocated on a stud inserted through the left side of frame. In manufacture up to and including the models made during WWII, the head of this stud is visible on the left side of the frame.

The rebound slide was the subject of patent no. 811,807, applied for on July 11, 1905 and granted on February 6, 1906 to Joseph H. Wesson, Daniel Wesson's middle son, who had become a partner in the firm in 1887.

Excerpts from the patent disclosure read as follows:

> *. . This invention relates to firearms, the object thereof being to provide construction of so-called "rebounding" mechanism, but in this case more properly termed a "retracting device for the hammer", inasmuch as a positively-moved device is interposed at the proper time between the hammer and the frame to retract the nose of the hammer from the position it occupies at the moment of firing, and which serves as a positive block for the hammer to prevent the latter from being accidentally brought in contact with the primer of a cartridge in the cylinder by some accidental blow.*
>
> *. . the invention consists in mounting a sliding wedge-like member in the frame which is connected by suitable means with the trigger, whereby when the trigger is released after the fall of the*

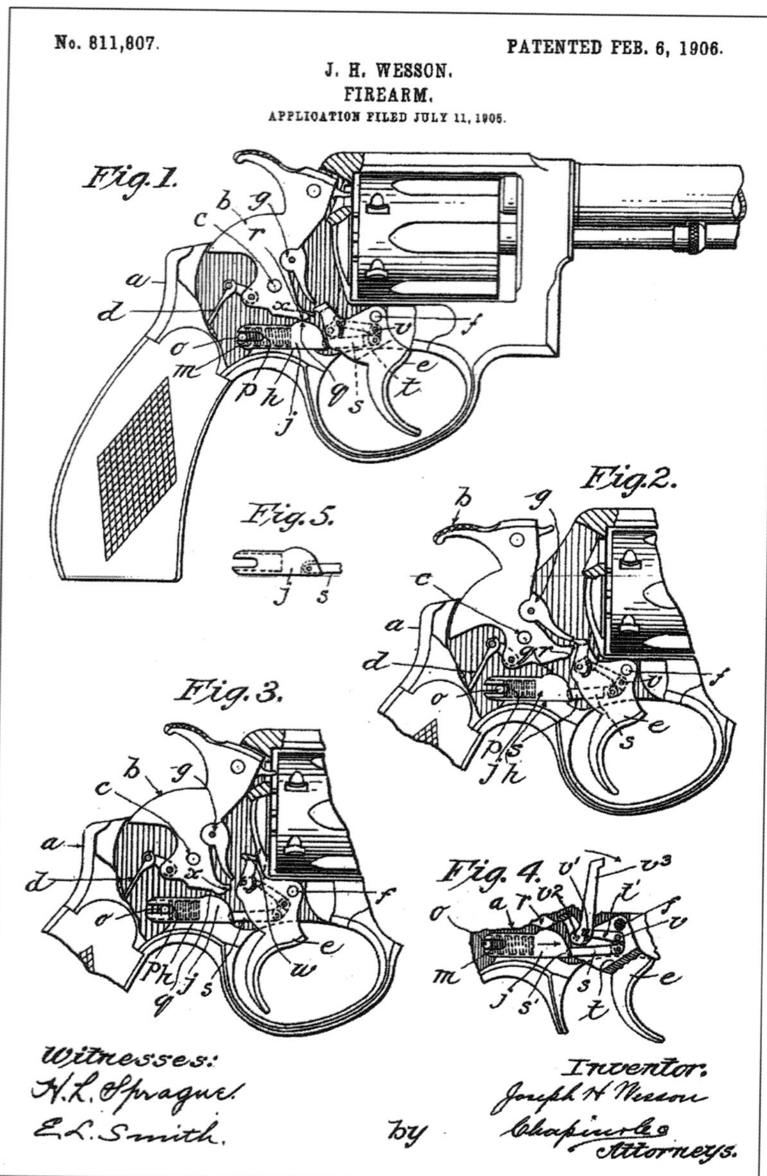


*hammer a suitable spring associated with this sliding member operates to swing the trigger forward to normal position and simultaneously to retract the hammer by pushing said wedge-like member under the lower end thereof forwardly of its pivotal point, which operates to retract the upper end of the hammer and to hold it in retracted position . .*

As noted, when the trigger is in its forward position the rebound slide was intended to act as a hammer block, and thus a safety feature. McHenry and Roper state that "The rebound block of the S&W provides an almost positive hammer safety to prevent forward motion of the hammer if it is struck." However, writing in 1944, they go on to say that "due to the hammer's distance from the center and the possibility of the parts springing under impact of a very hard blow, a second safety block [discussed in Chapter Twenty-Seven] is interposed between the hammer and the frame just below the hammer nose, or firing pin."

264 (left). The sheet of drawings from patent no. 811,807, granted to Joseph H. Wesson on February 6, 1906, illustrating the action of the rebound slide, which has remained a feature of S&W Hand Ejector revolvers ever since.

In the language of the patent, the rebound slide was initially intended to serve as "a positive block for the hammer to prevent the latter from being accidentally brought in contact with the primer of a cartridge in the cylinder by some accidental blow." U.S. Patent Office

# Model 1905, Second Change

For the first time there was an overlapping in production, both First and Second Change models being produced at the same time. As Henwood explains, this was probably done in order to use up First Change parts in an orderly manner. Serial nos. of the .32-20 version ran from roughly 33501 through 42200, and from about 120001 through 146899 for the .38 Special chambering.

Henwood records the major alterations embodied in the Model 1905 Second Change as follows:

*The Second Change . . was introduced in 1907, the year before the First Change was discontinued,*

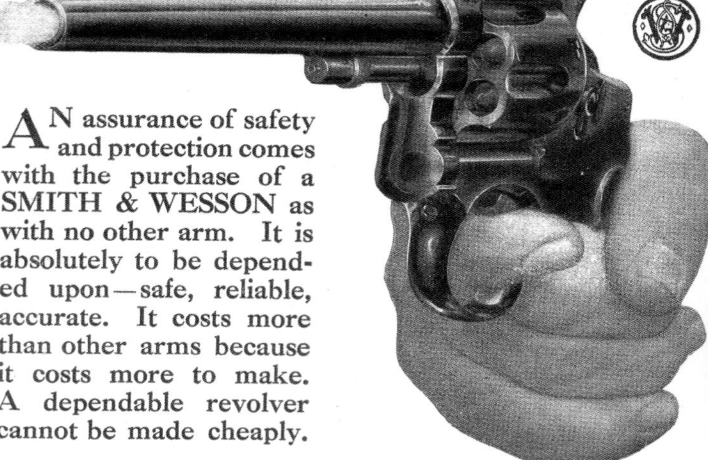

*and continued through 1909. Changes included minor alterations in the rebound slide, the addition of a rib on the bottom of the hammer, and two dowels added to the rear face of the cylinder to keep the extractor in position.*

In addition, the use of hardened steel pins in the cylinder stops was discontinued late in production of the Second Change version of the Model 1905 M&P, which must have been a red-letter day for the fitters in those pre-CNC machine days!

# Model 1905, Third Change

266. An interesting photo dated April 30, 1912, originally hand-captioned "Posse after murderer".

Judging from their dress and demeanor, it would appear that the man at far left is the sheriff and the one at far right is his deputy (or vice versa), with the remaining six probably local men who were signed up for the posse.

From left, the visible firearms are: no. 3 man is armed with a Winchester Model 92 rifle; no. 4 has a S&W M&P in his belt; no. 5 has a Winchester Model 1873; no. 6 has a Model 1878 Colt holstered on his belt, and no. 7 also has a Model 1878 Colt, hanging from his pocket.

The photo was taken in eastern Kentucky - note the muddy terrain typical of an Appalachian spring.

Carl Heinrich collection

The Model 1905 Third Change variation was introduced in 1909, with production through 1915. The alterations were minor, which as Henwood records resulted in a lighter (but longer) double-action trigger pull. The extractor knob, while still larger than the diameter of the rod, was now made in one piece with the extractor rod.

65 (previous page). A Smith & Wesson advertisement epicting the target-sighted version of the Model 1905 econd Change revolver - "guaranteed when standard ctory-loaded ammunition is used, either black or smoke-ss powder" - which appeared in *Everybody's Magazine* 1 1909.

As with other Smith & Wesson advertisements from is early period, this one contains the reminder that "A ependable revolver cannot be made cheaply."

Gaston Comeau collection

Serial numbers in the .32-20 Third Change version ran from 45201 through 65700, and from serial number 146900 through 241703 in the .38 Special variant.

Third Change Model 1905 revolvers were available in 4- or 6-inch barrel lengths, with the 5-inch missing from the lineup. The 6½" barrel length option was also discontinued, never to return in the M&P revolver.

Actually, revolvers with 5-inch barrels are relatively rare, or at least unusual, which is odd since many seem to think it an ideal length, splitting the difference between 4" and 6". However, 5" barrels were not available again on the M&P until the Fourth Change version, introduced in 1915.

The Third Change variation was the last of the M&Ps to be produced without a dedicated hammer block mechanism.

# World War I Disrupts M&P Production

The .38 caliber revolvers purchased by the U.S. military prior to 1920 were basically of two classes. The earliest examples, chambered for the black powder .38 Colt cartridge, which were used either in testing or to arm Army and Navy personnel who otherwise would have had an M1894 Colt; and then some odd-lot purchases to fill the needs of troops until enough of the .45 caliber weapons (whether the M1909 revolver or M1911 self-loader) became available.

Of course the M&P had been in production from 1899 on in various versions, but most of these had been made for commercial sale. From what I can gather, by the time U.S. troops entered World War I in 1917, the .38 revolvers that had been purchased by the military were pretty much restricted to National Guard and stateside duty.

The Fourth Change to the Model 1905 was actually introduced in 1915. However, as discussed on pages 10 through 12, due to war production during the 1914 - 1919 period, first of the .455 version of the .44 caliber Hand Ejector for the British and later the "U.S. Revolver Model 1917" in caliber .45 ACP, nearly all Fourth Change Model 1905 production took place after the end of WWI.

## Model 1917 Production under Government Control

When Smith & Wesson was awarded the contract to produce the M1917 .45 ACP caliber revolver for the military, it appears that they found it impossible to make both the M&P and the M1917 revolver at the same time. Accordingly, they were instructed to discontinue production of the .38 M&P and focus all their time and skill on the .45 caliber model. General Pershing had an announced goal of arming every U.S. soldier deployed to France with a handgun. He meant that to be a .45 caliber handgun, so the M&P line went silent for a period.

During the 1918 – 1919 timeframe the U.S. Ordnance Department went even further, seizing control of the S&W plant and dedicating it to the exclusive production of the .45 ACP caliber M1917 revolver for the government.

## An Eyewitness Comment on the Period of Government Operation

In a letter dated August 28, 1924, addressed to the then-well-known Canadian gun writer and ballistics expert Ashley A. Haines, Roy D. Jones of the S&W Ballistic Department commented on this period of enforced Ordnance Department control, and also mentioned an apparently then-recent seven-week plant closure which, as far as we know, has not been documented before:

*. . I have been anxiously waiting for the factory to reopen, it now having been closed for seven weeks, in order that I might get all of the information you want from the official records. I do not find any of the old catalogs and circulars, all of our stuff having been cleaned out at the time the Government operated the factory for the Model 17 revolver. Nothing has any value to those Ordnance men except winning the war, which was rather hard on all of our old parts and ancient records . .*

*Chapter Twenty-Six*

# Contemporary Evaluations

In factory catalogs the Smith & Wesson Military and Police revolver was initially called simply the "Military" Model, either of 1899, 1902, or 1905. From the available documentation, the first use of the term "Military and Police" was in an advertisement which appeared in the March 23, 1899 issue of *Shooting & Fishing* magazine, discussed below.

As far as the actual factory documentation is concerned, the new arm remained the "Military" model in the S&W catalogs we have available, beginning with the 1902 catalog (fig. 2), until it was called the "Military and Police" in the 1912 Price List.

In any event, (externally, at any rate), by 1906 the arm which we will refer to as the "M&P" had reached the definitive form it was to maintain for the next forty years.

## A Chronicle from *Shooting & Fishing*

I think it is quite interesting to go back and see how this revolver was viewed when it first appeared, as no one at the time could possibly have predicted that it would go on to become the most important police and target revolver of the 20th century. At the time the M&P appeared, the standard target revolver was the Smith & Wesson No. 3 in .44 Russian, and the military issue revolver was the .38 Colt M1894.

### A Brief History of the Official NRA Publications

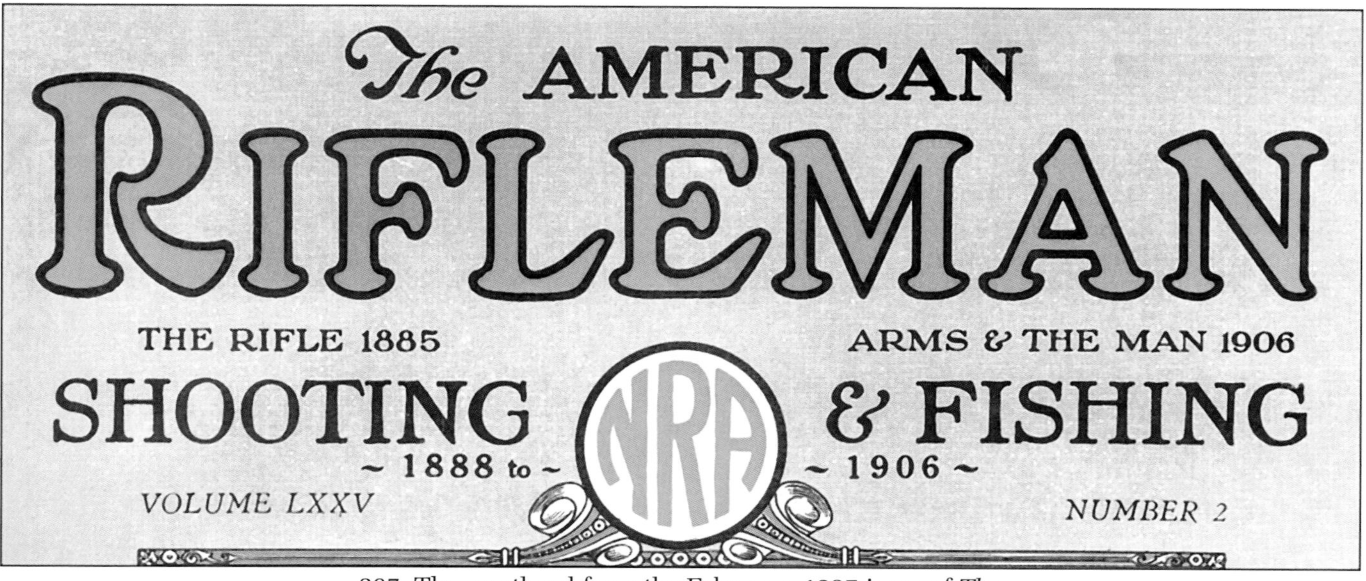


267. The masthead from the February, 1927 issue of *The American Rifleman*.

As shown, throughout the years when this early format was in use, the history of all the official NRA publications was included as part of the title block on each issue.

Gaston Comeau collection

The official NRA periodical of the day was *Shooting & Fishing*, which had superceded the earlier *Rifle* magazine (1885 - 1888) in 1888, and was itself discontinued in 1906, when it was replaced, first by *Arms and the Man* (1906 - 1923) and finally by *The American Rifleman*, from 1923 to date.

I have a complete bound collection of all these early magazines, and I find it rewarding to delve into them from time to time in order to see what sort of coverage was accorded certain developments, such as the new M&P revolver.

## Advertising the "New Model 1896"

The New 1896 Model Smith & Wesson Revolver

SOLID FRAME
SWING OUT CYLINDER
HAND EJECTOR
REBOUNDING LOCK

EXCEPTIONAL STRENGTH, ACCURACY, PENETRATION, AND WORKMANSHIP ARE FEATURES OF THIS REVOLVER

The Smith & Wesson Hammerless Safety The ideal arm for home protection. Cannot be discharged accidentally, safe in the hands of a child and always ready when needed.

The Smith & Wesson Target Pistol Accurate and without equal for target practice. The wonderful scores made by WALTER WINANS last year with the Smith & Wesson Revolver should commend this make to any one wanting the best small arm manufactured.

SEND FOR HANDSOME ILLUSTRATED CATALOGUE SHOWING ALL THE DIFFERENT MODELS.

SMITH & WESSON, 8 Stockbridge St., Springfield, Mass.

268. An advertisement describing the first S&W Hand Ejector, the I-frame Model 1896, which appeared in the March 26, 1896 issue of *Shooting & Fishing* magazine.

The advertisement shown here, along with a descriptive article, both describing the first S&W Hand Ejector, the Model 1896, appeared in the March 26, 1896 issue of *Shooting & Fishing* magazine.

Portions of this interesting article are excerpted as follows:

### *A New Smith & Wesson Revolver*

*. . A few years ago the Colt Patent Fire Arms Co., of Hartford, Conn., introduced a radical departure in revolvers by presenting a revolver with a cylinder mounted upon a crane and pivoted in the frame below the cylinder, set so that on drawing the cylinder latch to the rear the cylinder swung to the left and downward out of its seat in the frame . . We think the Ordnance report of the U.S. Government will sustain us in expressing an opinion that the solid frame of the Colt revolver caused it to be recognized as a better arm for military purposes than the beautifully made and extremely accurate Smith & Wesson revolver, solely because the latter arm had not a solid frame.*

*But revolvers with solid frames make loading a slow process, and mechanical ingenuity was directed toward producing an arm which had a solid frame, but could be loaded and the shells extracted in an expeditious manner. To do this it was necessary to devise a system whereby the cylinder could be swung from the frame, the exploded shells speedily ejected, and the arm reloaded . .*

*The [Colt] system did not find favor among many at first. It had some defects, but they were largely overcome, and the system has grown in favor. At the present time the U.S. Army, the Navy, and many of the volunteers are equipped with [Colt] revolvers of the swinging cylinder type.*

*This system, by its popularity, has caused the old type of [single action] Colt revolver and the Smith & Wesson [top break] revolver to be regarded in military circles as obsolete . .*

*. . One accustomed to handling the Colt revolver may perhaps at first consider the [Smith & Wesson Hand Ejector] mechanism somewhat awkward, as . . one pulls [the cylinder pin] for-*

*ward with the thumb and forefinger, at the same time pressing the second and third fingers on the cylinder, which swings it out of the frame . .*

*So far as the fitting of the parts, the arm seems faultless. It is beautifully made, like all Smith & Wesson products. It is double action . . .32 caliber, and made to take the self-lubricated cartridge, the invention of Mr. D. B. Wesson . .*

*We think it unfortunate that the .32 caliber was chosen for this new revolver. [It] is, in our opinion, best suited for target practice, and is far below the .38 caliber in effectiveness; and a revolver for defense, of less caliber than .38, in our opinion rapidly loses its value as a practical weapon . .*

## First Mention of the Model 1899 - March 9, 1899

Given the general understated conservatism of the times, the early articles dealing with the M&P were few in number, and actually quite minimal in coverage.

The first mention of the new .38 Special caliber Model 1899 Hand Ejector revolver is in a brief descriptive article which appeared on page 430 of the March 9, 1899 issue of *Shooting & Fishing* magazine (fig. 269). This records the first sample of the new revolver being received by the W. Robinson Co. of 79 Chambers St., Smith & Wesson's New York City distributors, where it was made available for viewing by interested individuals.

Smith & Wesson's latest model revolver has made its initial bow before the audience of sportsmen. Mr. Robinson, local agent for the firm, received the first one of this model to be sent to this town, and the writer happened to be in his place last Saturday when the case containing it was opened. It is something like the model 1896, and yet very different. The first thing one notices is that the frame is absolutely solid; next, that the barrel has no rib along its top, and third, that the arm fits the hand snugly. It is double action, and has a swing out cylinder that may be operated very rapidly, in this wise: After one has fired six shots—or one, for that matter—if he desires to reload, he simply pushes a small catch forward with the right thumb, gives the arm a slight jerk to left, and the cylinder tips out. This is performed with the right hand and without moving it save for the slight motion of the thumb in pushing the catch forward.

This revolver takes the .38 special or military cartridge and is of holster size, having a substantial frame and long barrel. The front sight is a part of the barrel, and the rear sight is a notch in the end of the solid frame, which is slightly grooved along its upper surface. The exquisite workmanship for which Smith & Wesson arms are noted is seen on the new model, but it impresses one with its durability and strength, and will no doubt prove to be what it was intended for—a serviceable military revolver.

269 (right). The brief descriptive article which appeared on page 430 of the March 9, 1899 issue of *Shooting & Fishing* magazine. This was the first mention of the new .38 Special caliber Model 1899 Hand Ejector revolver.

## The Advent of Smokeless Powder Loads for the .38 Revolver

Page 451 of the July 3, 1902 issue records that the noted marksman C. S. Axtell, who by 1908 had become the president of the U.S. Revolver Association, was using a target-sighted M&P model to shoot targets that were apparently used as "giveaways" by the factory while the revolver was displayed at the Fifth Annual Sportsmen's Exposition, held at Madison Square Garden in New York City. Another article on the same page contains a report of the new revolver being shot with smokeless powder loads. Since both the .38 Long Colt and .38 Special rounds were initially introduced as black powder cartridges, it is very interesting to see the M&P adapted to smokeless powder loads so soon after its release.

An excerpt from this article reads as follows:

*. . 8 grains of Laflin & Rand smokeless sporting rifle powder is used in the .38 caliber, and this charge corresponds to the service load of black powder. The powder is absolutely smokeless, the recoil is reduced, and the report much less. The cartridge is known as the .38 Long Colt, and while it is not yet on the market, it will be ready for sale very soon.*

With smokeless loads now available, it quickly became apparent to many that the M&P revolver was a very accurate weapon. Over the next several years *Shooting & Fishing* magazine ran numerous articles which included reproductions of groups shot with the M&P that would rival anything being shot today by the finest marksmen with the best target weapons.

Page 38 of the April 27, 1899 issue was the first such article I found in my collection, but many others followed, displaying groups submitted by readers showing fine work with the M&P.

## First Advertisement - March 23, 1899

As noted, the "New Military and Police Revolver" first appeared, along with other models, in an advertisement on page 476 of the March 23, 1899 issue (fig. 270), which discussed the results of some important shooting matches of the day, all of which had been won by S&W revolvers. The M&P itself won the Military Revolver Championship, held in New York City, with a score of 274 out of a possible 300.

270 (right). The first advertisement mentioning the "New Military and Police Revolver", which appeared, along with a list of matches won by other models, on page 476 of the March 23, 1899 issue of *Shooting & Fishing*.

## First Exclusive Mention - May 11, 1899

Finally realizing that they had a real winner in the Model 1899 revolver, S&W ran an advertisement for that model exclusively titled "A Full Hand", which appeared on page 78 of the May 11, 1899 issue (fig. 271). A subsequent advertisement ran on page 518 of the October 12, 1899 issue.

Nor was the M&P restricted to match shooting at 50 yards or less, for on page 507 of the April 5, 1900 issue, an article detailing work at 100 yards was published. The photo illustrating the man-sized target shows a good group made at 100 yards offhand, one-hand hold, with which most of us would be very pleased today.

Readers of the period also inquired about the relative use of target-sighted models and the availability of the model in .32-20 chambering, and the responses were printed on page 238 of the June 5, 1900, issue and page 499 of the October 4, 1900, issues respectively.

271. The first advertisement mentioning the Military & Police revolver exclusively, which appeared on page 78 of the May 11, 1899 issue of *Shooting & Fishing*.

## The End of an Era - Phasing Out the Last Single Actions

An article which appeared on page 223 of *Shooting & Fishing* magazine for July 4, 1901 (fig. 272) noted that the old .45 Colt single actions were finally being recalled from the last U.S. field artillery batteries which then had them on issue, and I note no weeping or gnashing of teeth as occurred in the 1980s when the Beretta M9 in 9x19mm officially replaced the venerable M1911A1 .45 ACP pistol.

Interestingly, on page 50 of the October 31, 1901 issue, it was noted that only native troops in the Philippines, which was then undergoing pacification by U.S. troops in the aftermath of the Spanish-American War, were to retain the .45 single-actions, everyone else being issued .38 caliber double-action Colts.

**PASSING OF THE .45 CALIBER REVOLVER.**

The old .45 caliber revolver was for many years the ideal weapon for the army and frontiersmen. It was a weapon of undoubted power and effectiveness, but the persons who could handle this weapon skillfully were comparatively few. Several years ago it became apparent that a revolver of this caliber and power was not liked by United States army officers. Its excessive recoil made practice with it dreaded by most officers. The revolver itself was probably the best military revolver in existence, but the cartridge for it was far from satisfactory; its excessive power almost made the arm useless. The Colt .45 caliber United States army revolver was gradually withdrawn from the United States army, the Colt .38 caliber taking its place, and while the former is a more effective weapon in the hands of those who can handle it skillfully, the latter, on account of its greater accuracy and the ability of most men to shoot it accurately, is vastly superior.

The .45 caliber revolver was retained in some of the light batteries until recently, but on June 19 general orders were issued from the headquarters of the army which say: "By direction of the secretary of war, commanding officers of batteries of field artillery will submit timely requisitions to the chief of ordnance of the army for .38 caliber Colt revolvers, pistol holsters, revolver cartridge belts (woven), and ammunition to replace the .45 caliber Colt revolvers, pistol holsters, and ammunition now in use in these organizations, and upon receipt of the new equipment will turn the .45 caliber revolvers in to the Springfield armory, Springfield, Mass.; the pistol holsters to Rock Island arsenal, Rock Island, Ill., and the ammunition to Frankford arsenal, Philadelphia, Pa."

272 (right). An article which appeared on page 223 of the July 4, 1901 issue of *Shooting & Fishing* magazine, announcing that the old .45 Colt single action was finally being recalled in favor of new .38 caliber double-action Colt revolvers, and giving instructions for the disposition of the earlier arms and accouterments.

## Introducing the Model 1900 Luger Pistol

As an aside, the first advertisement for the .30 caliber Luger pistol appeared on page 15 of the October 17, 1901 issue (fig. 273), where it was priced at $25.00 for the weapon and $2.50 per hundred for the cartridges. The same ad with the claim "116 shots in a minute" ran again on May 11, 1902.

By the way, gold was $20.00 an ounce then, so multiply those figures by 80 – 90 times to get today's values. It makes today's Glock 17 pistol and Wal-Mart ammunition prices look really good, even if they are a lot higher than just a few years past.

**LUGER AUTOMATIC**

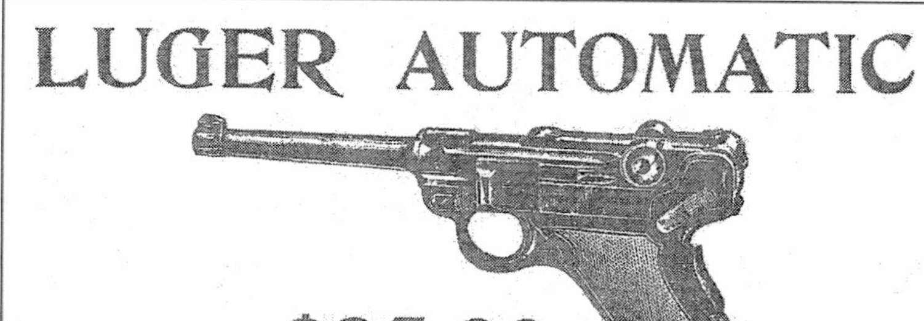

**$25.00**

.30 Caliber Smokeless Cartridges, $2.50 per hundred.

NOW READY FOR DELIVERY.

**Schoverling, Daly & Gales,**

**302-304 Broadway,** Corner Duane Street, **NEW YORK.**

Agents Walsrode Powder, Daly Guns, Sauer-Mauser Rifles.

273 (right). The first advertisement for the Model 1900 .30 caliber "Luger Automatic" appeared on page 15 of the October 17, 1901 issue of *Shooting & Fishing*.

## Publicity Means Police Use Is On the Rise

The publicity being accorded the S&W M&P revolver was finding its mark, and police departments around the country were soon rearming with them. Not only that, but some were even shooting them competitively! Reports of matches between officers in the same or different departments were soon a commonly seen feature in *Shooting & Fishing* magazine, as were articles dealing with the issue of training officers in how to operate these revolvers and shoot them safely and accurately.

Page 27 of the April 17, 1902 issue discusses a match between Chicago and St. Louis police officers, with both using M&P revolvers. A later article on page 17 of the April 16, 1903 issue details St. Louis Police Department practice and a course of fire with the M&P revolver.

## "Improved Ammunition for Revolvers"

Page 226 of the July 3, 1902 issue contains a further article praising the properties - and accuracy - of smokeless powder loads in the S&W .38 Hand Ejector, indicating that the days of those difficult-to-shoot big-bores and dirty black powder loads, if not completely gone, were at least numbered. This interesting article is excerpted as follows:

*. . A few years ago all revolvers makers and perhaps all ammunition makers unhesitatingly declared that smokeless powders would probably not be applicable to revolvers, but gradually improvements have been made until these powders have been produced which have greatly lessened the recoil, reduced fouling to a minimum, and as a natural consequence increased accuracy is secured.*

*. . A fine example of the accuracy of smokeless powder ammunition of today in a modern military revolver has been sent to us in the form of a target [fig. 274] shot from a Smith & Wesson New Military .38 caliber revolver, charged with U.M.C. factory ammunition, containing Laflin & Rand Bullseye smokeless powder. The shooting was done by the well-known expert, C. S. Axtell, at a range of 57 feet. The group contains ten shots.*

*Mr. Axtell informs us that the recoil of this cartridge is so surprisingly light that he hardly sees the need of a reduced gallery charge for fine target work . . The cleanliness of this ammunition, Mr. Axtell adds, is remarkable. With it the barrel was as clean after 100 shots as after the first. He says further that when he shoots black powder in his revolver he usually concludes his shooting with one charge loaded with Bullseye smokeless powder to clean the barrel of his revolver. He says it does the work better with one shot than twenty minutes' work with a good brush.*

274 (right). A reproduction of the target mentioned in the quote at left, showing the 10-shot group shot at 57' by C. S. Axtell, using a "Smith & Wesson New Military .38 caliber revolver, charged with U.M.C. factory ammunition, containing Laflin & Rand Bullseye smokeless powder."

The development of smokeless powder loads for revolvers and semi-automatic pistols—many of the latter deriving from the creative mind of John M. Browning—prompted many articles dealing with the increased power and accuracy of such loads. An interesting article about penetration of such loads appeared May 22, 1902, on page 106, and a further article illustrating how accurate smokeless loads were appeared on page 226 of the July 3, 1902 issue. Groups at almost 20 yards measured one inch for six, and five-eighths of an inch for five shots, both fired offhand. Can you do better? I cannot.

## More on the Policeman's Lot

Some things involving handgun use by the police never change, as the following excerpts from the article on page 289 of the July 24, 1902 issue clearly illustrate:

*. . The interest taken in revolver shooting by the police of different cities has been given some consideration in* Shooting & Fishing, *and surprise has*

*been expressed that their interest in this subject was not greater . .*

*The reasons that tend to shape matters as they are are not few. In the first place municipalities do not attempt to consider the police department as much a military organization as they should, and so do not consider the need of drill in shooting, and do not make the ability to make a good score with the revolver as an essential point in a good policeman. They do not provide the three most important factors, time, ammunition and a place for practice . .*

*In the majority of cases the patrolman is not furnished with either revolver or ammunition, but has to pay the market price for same. This makes some patrolmen think they ought to take better care of their revolvers than to be hanging around a range. Of course, such men have no love for the sport, but they have a right to care for their propoerty as they think best . .*

Anyone working in the field of police training today may be heard saying essentially the same things, more than a century later.

## Colt's New Army Revolver - in .38 Special

Meanwhile, things were proceeding at the Colt plant over in Hartford, Connecticut. By this time it was generally known that the Colt Model 1894, which took a black powder cartridge, was prone to some reliability issues. On page 40 of the October 13, 1904 issue of *Shooting & Fishing*, Colt's ran an advertisement for their new Army Revolver, chambered for the .38 S&W Special cartridge. On page 10 of the November 17, 1904 issue, a test of the target-sighted version, called the Officer's Model, was reported on by Samuel Fort, who was to become a well-known gun writer in the 1920s and 1930s.

## Introducing the Ideal "Wadcutter" Bullet

Page 40 of the October 27, 1904 issue of *Shooting & Fishing* reviewed a new bullet for the .38 Special. This was the square-faced load we have all come to call "the wadcutter". Over the next century, this would become the standard bullet for formal target shooters throughout the world.

An excerpt from this article describing the new bullet design is as follows:

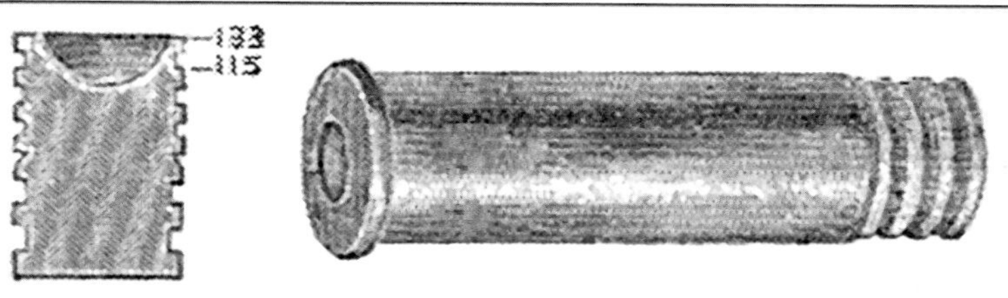


275. Illustration of the .38 Special cartridge showing a sectioned view of the new "wadcutter" bullet design, introduced in 1904 by the Ideal Mfg. Co. of New Haven, Conn.

*The Ideal Mfg. Co., of New Haven, Conn., has just brought out a new bullet for the .38 S&W Military and Colt .38 caliber Officer's model revolvers as per illustration [fig. 275]. In design it is similar to the British Man-stopper, inasmuch as both have a cavity in the front end . .*

*The Ideal bullet has a flat base and is made sufficiently large in diameter (.360 of an inch) to insure a perfect fit in the barrel without any upsettage. . .*

*These bullets cut a clean full-sized hole in the target, thus obviating disputes in count as to whether the ring on the target is cut or not . .*

## A Look Inside the S&W Cylinder

In addition, a partially cross-sectioned view of a Smith & Wesson cylinder was featured, and it and the new bullet design were further described as follows:

*The forward portion [of the bullet] that projects beyond the muzzle of the shell is .358 of an inch in diameter, which is the same size as the smaller portion "a" of the chamber of the cylinder as shown in [fig. 276]. This illustration shows cylinder with a portion cut away, so as to show the inside formation of the chamber in which the loaded cartridge sits. It is claimed that with the bullet fitting snugly in the shell and the shell left straight at the muzzle, not crimped, the bullet will not be mutilated, scraped or deflected by the turned-in edge of the shell when passing out. The bullet and shell . . are placed in the chamber, the shell fitted in the portion "b" and the forward portion of the bullet . . pressed into the chamber "a". Shell and bullet must then certainly be in perfect alignment, which tends to secure accuracy . .*

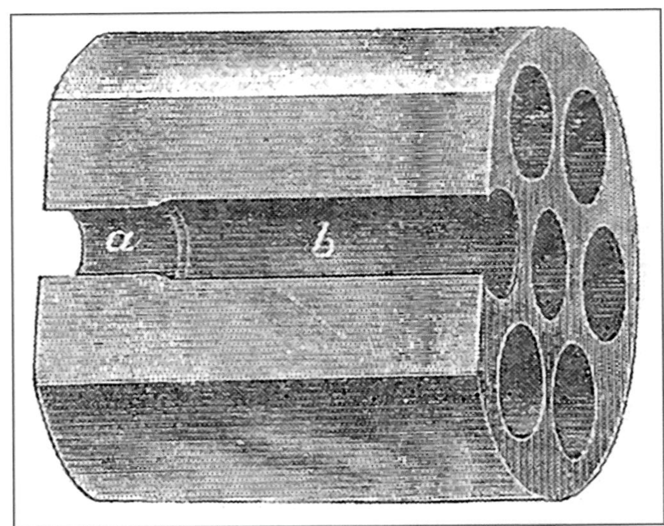


276 (right). Diagrammatic left side sectioned view of a S&W cylinder showing reduced diameter "a" into which the bullet is pressed so that "Shell and bullet must then certainly be in perfect alignment, which tends to secure accuracy . ."

# More on the Trouble in the Philippines

## Stopping Power Becomes a Hot Issue

But while all was well on the ranges at home, trouble was brewing in the Philippines. You will recall that the military had withdrawn the last .45 Colts from U.S. troops by 1901 in favor of the .38 Long Colt caliber Colt double-action Model 1894, which was now called upon to enforce a program of pacification against men who had fought the Spaniards for many generations and who also embraced a different faith than the foreigners, whether Spanish or American, as they continued their campaign for independence. While it is often forgotten today in the warm memory of Theodore Roosevelt's victory in the short 90-day war in Cuba, many were then strongly opposed to the occupation of the Philippines, thinking it un-American to embrace an imperialist policy as the Europeans had done. Among these groups, large numbers of Civil War veterans opposed such overseas military adventurism.

None of this of course had any effect on the man at the short end of the stick who was in a National Guard unit shipped overseas as he walked up a trail only to be attacked at short range by an individual who thought if he could kill the infidel he would go to heaven and be rewarded with 72 virgins. (This sounds familiar, doesn't it?) That U.S. soldier would soon find that his pleasant-to-shoot, accurate and lightweight .38 Colt revolver had some real shortcomings.

Starting in April, 1905, *Shooting & Fishing* carried a number of articles about the need for increased stopping power in revolver cartridges. Noting that the current service revolver cartridge was insufficient, a number of alternatives were discussed, ranging from going back to the black-powder .45 again; adopting the .44 Russian with smokeless loads; improving the bullet design of the .38 to give it a flat tip; or considering the adoption of really big-bore double-barrel 12- or 20-gauge pistols such as the British had used in the Sudan when facing similarly motivated adversaries.

Most agreed that the saber was worthless and should be discarded, and many recalled their experiences during the Civil War, which are really quite interesting. My favorite was the suggestion of issuing a brace of handguns. Interestingly enough I had suggested this very thing to a colleague on his way to Afghanistan only months earlier, and a Government Model on the hip and a Smith & Wesson Model 60 in my left breast pocket was always my choice of equipment when I was in the Army.

Page 350 of the April 9, 1906 issue dealt with the possibility of using the better (flat-nosed) bullet in the .38 revolver to obtain better stopping power, which more critically shows this to be a very accurate load. This may come as no surprise to all of us familiar with target-grade wadcutter ammunition today, but nevertheless the recorded results were really very good. I would also note that as a kid before Super Vel ammunition came out—in about 1965, if I recall—my defense loads of choice for my .38 Chief Special three-inch were either 200-gr. Super Police loads or a hollow-base wadcutter I loaded with the bullets reversed, so the large hollow cavity became the nose. It is comforting to know that people were already advocating this back in 1906.

## Reverting to .45 Caliber

Happily for members of the U.S. military the unfortunate experiences in the Philippines were remembered, so that even when pacification duties were over, the demand for .45 caliber handguns remained. This, coupled with John Browning's intellect and skill, gave us the M1905, later modified in stages to become the definitive Government Model self-loader of 1911, and later the M1911A1.

However, as we shall see, the military keeps tracking back to the side of accuracy, light recoil, and easy-to-shoot handguns, as witness the Victory Model during WWII, the Combat Masterpieces during the Korean and Vietnam Wars, and the Beretta 9mm handguns of today. In the face of this, those at the sharp end who can manage it keep digging up old out-of-fashion big-bore weapons to carry.

# The M&P in Law Enforcement

While the "military" part of the M&P revolver name had effectively hit a dead end in the U.S. by 1905, when it was determined that any new service weapon would be in not less than .45 caliber (at least until things got really critical in 1941), it was not so with the "police" part of the name.

Law enforcement agencies in the U.S. had really started to embrace the .38 Special revolver even before World War I. Before the M&P became the most popular choice, police departments were using a wide variety of .32 and .38 Smith & Wesson top-break revolvers, or early Colt and S&W swing-out-cylinder models in the same chamberings. As the 20th century went on, more and more of these small-caliber revolvers went onto the discard pile, so that by the mid-1920s the M&P in .38 Special or the Army Special/Official Police Colt with between a four- and six-inch barrel was what people thought of when they said "duty revolver".

Of course there were exceptions, where Colt Single Actions or Government Models were seen and, from time to time, smaller-framed revolvers in .38 Smith & Wesson (rarely .32) were found, but these were noteworthy by their rarity. By the time the Jazz Age arrived, the mid-frame Smith & Wesson and Colt .38 revolvers were standards.

Colt's seemed to have been more active in promoting their products during this period, and no doubt the staunch presence of the justly-famed J. Henry FitzGerald helped appreciably in this endeavor.

It was also a time when most police shooting courses were fired in the single-action target style rather than using the self-cocking feature of the double-action revolver. As everyone who has shot one knows, the single action on Colt revolvers is always easy to cock, and quite crisp. The double action "stacks" terribly, however, unlike that of the Smith & Wessons, but if you do not use this mode of shooting then it makes no difference.

*Chapter Twenty-Seven*

# The M&P Through 1920

## Early Problems with Imitations

277. An early S&W advertisement circa 1902 which sums up the firm's message in a few well-chosen words - "No! A Smith & Wesson Revolver is good enough - No cheap substitutes, please." Gaston Comeau collection

278. A further advertisement which appeared in *Cosmopolitan* magazine in 1903, taken from a painting by G. W. Peters, titled "At Bay".

The gun shown is an early top-break, but the message is clear: "when it comes to a question of 'My life or his', the revolver needed is a Smith & Wesson."

Gaston Comeau collection

The problems created by cheaply-made imitations of Smith & Wesson revolvers, which were to come to a furious head in the years following WWI, are discussed in Chapter Twenty-Eight. But ever since the turn of the century S&W had been aware of the problem, and stressed the quality and reliability of its products in its advertising, repeating the fact that only genuine Smith & Wesson bore the firm's recognized trade mark monogram.

## The 1917 "Catalog D"

279. The color cover of the S&W Catalog D, from 1917, taken from the painting of a literal cliffhanger by artist Philip Lyford. Gaston Comeau collection

SPECIAL NOTICE

Our Trade-Marks  SMITH & WESSON

None but genuine Smith & Wesson arms bear these trade-marks—which are registered throughout the world—and we caution the trade about handling imitations of our goods.

Manufacturers of spurious arms in imitation of ours have copied our designs and have used trade-marks bearing a sufficiently close resemblance to ours to mislead unwary purchasers, and have used the name "Smith & Wesson" in such manner as to lead customers who are unable to read the English language to infer that the arms are of our make.

We shall protect our interests to the fullest extent, and take this opportunity of informing the trade of our intentions in this direction, so that if anyone should meet with losses arising from confiscation of imitation goods in their hands, we do not wish to be censured in any way.

At the same time, we rely upon the support of our friends and clients in meeting this class of competition, which undoubtedly is equally as dangerous to them as to us.

In the selection of a revolver the first considerations should be quality, precision, security, reliability and the reputation of the manufacturer—cost is of much less importance—the legend SMITH & WESSON is an absolute guarantee of superiority and confidence.

Be sure, when making a purchase, that the appearance and finish of the arm correspond exactly to the illustration and description found in this catalog; and that it bears our name, SMITH & WESSON engraved in the barrel and our monogram on the stocks.

SMITH & WESSON,
Springfield, Mass., U. S. A.

280. A "Special Notice" which appeared on the inside of the cover of the 1917 Catalog D, indicating that the firm was well aware of the problems being engendered by "Manufacturers of spurious arms in imitation of ours", and enjoining purchasers to be sure they were purchasing a genuine Smith & Wesson. Gaston Comeau collection

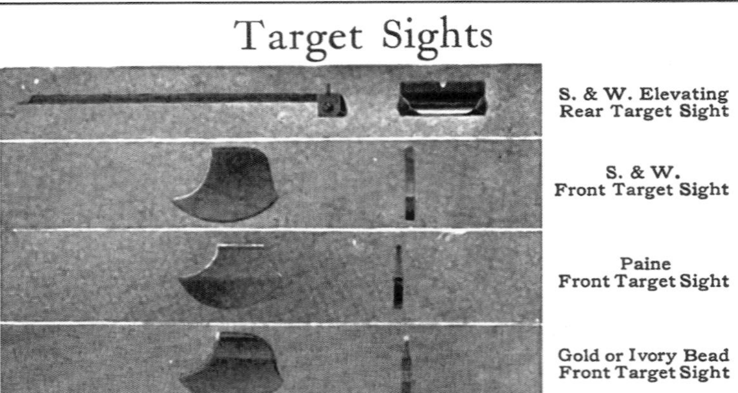

Target Sights

S. & W. Elevating Rear Target Sight

S. & W. Front Target Sight

Paine Front Target Sight

Gold or Ivory Bead Front Target Sight

These Target Sights can be furnished at an extra charge on either of the following models:

Perfected Hand Ejector Model .22 Cal.
Military and Police .38 Cal., either Round or Square handle
Hand Ejector Model. 32 Cal.
Military and Police .32 W. C. F., Square Handle
Military Model .44 Cal.

281 (left). A section headed "Target Sights" taken from page 15 of the 1917 catalog, illustrating and describing the earliest type of screw-adjustable rear sight, above, and the various types of front sight blades which were available on several models, including both the round- and square-butt versions of the Military and Police revolver.
Gaston Comeau collection

# No Record of Combat Use in WWI

As the world went to war in 1914 and Smith & Wesson started making lots of .455 caliber revolvers for the British to help arm "Kitchener's New Army", no doubt the supply of new M&P revolvers was reduced, although it appears that some production did continue throughout the early years before America's entry into the war in April, 1917.

Most of these M&Ps were seemingly sold through commercial channels, not for military export orders, but doubtless some were taken abroad by individuals who subsequently used them in combat. Curiously, however, I have never run across any books written by English-speaking (or writing at least) veterans who mention using a .38 M&P revolver during World War I. I am certain that some must have shown up on the front lines, but oddly enough, to the best of my knowledge, no one has mentioned this. People like McBride and others discuss Webley .455s, Smith & Wesson .455s, and Colt .45 autos, as well as 9mm Lugers and .30 caliber Mausers, but no .38 M&P revolvers.

## The Smith & Wesson Target M&P - "The Gun that Won" in 1919

The
**Individual Inter-Allied Pistol Match**
*Won by* Michael Kelly
*Master Engineer, Senior Grade*
*7th U. S. Engineers*
*5th Division, U. S. Army*

**with an S. & W. — .38 Cal. Military & Police Revolver, with target sights, was held at LeMans, France, June 27th, 1919. Supremacy in skill with side arms was contested by a large field of shooters selected from the armies of the**

| | |
|---|---|
| UNITED STATES | CANADA |
| FRANCE | BELGIUM |
| PORTUGAL | ROUMANIA |
| ITALY | GREECE |

**When it was decided to hold these Matches, the Ordnance Department at Washington, realizing the advisability of equipping the representatives of our army with the most accurate side arms that could be produced ordered us to send fifty of our .38 Cal. Military & Police Model Revolvers, fitted with target sights, to the American Expeditionary Forces in France. The result proved the wisdom of this selection.**

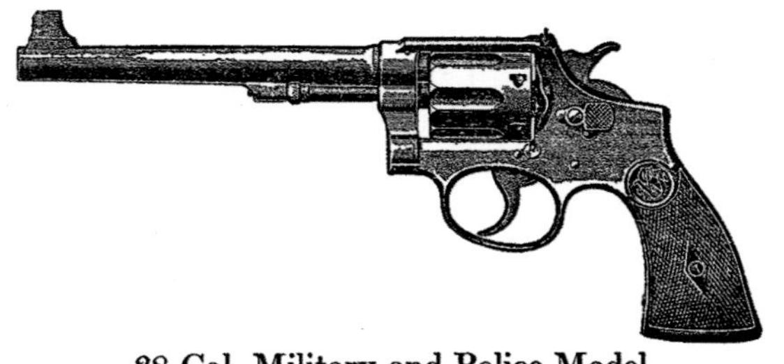

.38 Cal. Military and Police Model
"The Gun that Won"

**The following is what Mr. Kelly has to say regarding it:**

***"The Smith & Wesson Revolver excels in style and appearance, and best of all in accuracy."***

***Respectfully yours,***

***Michael Kelly, A. E. F., France***
***Winner of the***
***Individual Inter-Allied Pistol Match***

282. The inner two pages of a four-page folded brochure describing the "Individual Inter-Allied Pistol Match", held at Le Mans, France on June 27, 1919.

As shown, this event was won by an American, firing one of the 50 target model M&Ps which the Ordnance Department had ordered shipped to the A.E.F. in France.
Gaston Comeau collection

By the summer of 1919 the war had been over for six months, but many Allied troops had not yet been returned to their home countries. With these idle men presumably in need of some supervised diversion, an interesting event known as the "Inter-Allied Pistol Match" was held in June, 1919 in Le Mans, France. The inner two-pages of the four-page self-congratulatory brochure issued by Smith & Wesson to celebrate the outcome of this event is reproduced here.

## The Government "Dumps" Model 1917s in the Aftermath of WWI

As John Henwood records it,

> *. . With the war over, the U.S. Government took a step which was to have repercussions following World War II . . During the 1920s and 1930s, acting through the Director of Civilian Marksmanship, the Army sold many thousands of 1917 revolvers to qualifying members of the National Rifle Association. At the time, Smith & Wesson was selling the commercial model for $36.75; the D.C.M. price was $16.15, plus a small packing and handling charge. The firm neither forgot nor forgave what they considered to be "dumping".*

# The Model 1905, Fourth Change

As noted, the .38 Hand Ejector M&P Model 1905 Fourth Change had been released in 1915, but due to the disruption in commercial production caused by war work, it appears that almost all were made after the war. The Model 1905 Fourth Change M&P remained in the line until commercial production was once again curtailed in favor of war work during World War II when, as discussed in Chapter Thirty, this model served as the basis for both the British .38/200 and the U.S. Victory Model revolvers.

In addition to the rebound slide, the Fourth Change incorporated the initial style of direct hammer block, mounted in the sideplate, called the "wing style" (Jinks) or "side-swing" (Henwood) hammer block.

Other improvements introduced in the Fourth Change M&P included the introduction of heat treated cylinders in 1919, at about serial no. 81287 in the .32-30 guns and around no. 316648 in .38 Special models. In addition, the "chafing pins" in the hammer and trigger were discontinued, replaced, as Henwood records, by slightly raised "hubs" or "bosses" surrounding the pivot studs in the frame and sideplate.

Serial numbers in the .32-20 version of the Fourth Change M&P ran from 65701 through 144684, this last number being reached in 1940, at which time the .32-20 chambering was discontinued.

Serial numbers of the Fourth Change .38 Special version started at circa 241703 and ran until a new series of serial numbers was established for the Victory Model during WWII.

283. The cover of S&W Catalog D-1, issued in August, 1919.

Note the prominent use of the phrase "The Gun that Won", recalling the win in the "Individual Inter-Allied Pistol Match" the previous month in Le Mans, France.

Gaston Comeau collection

## Introducing the "Side-Swing" Hammer Block

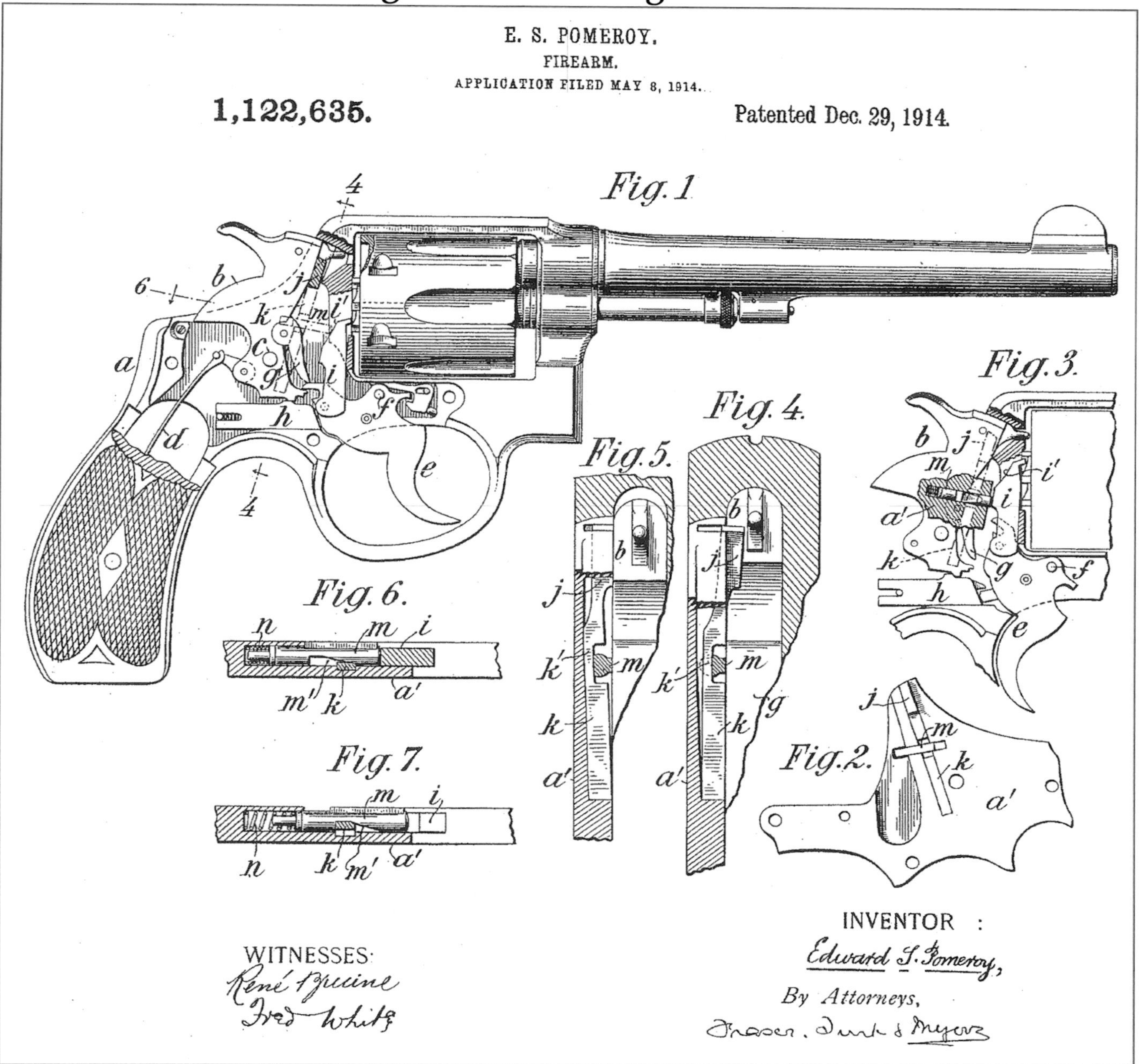


284. The sheet of drawings from patent no. 1,122,635, covering the "side-swing" hammer block, granted to S&W plant superintendent Edward S. Pomeroy on December 29, 1914 and assigned to Smith & Wesson.

This initial version of the "side-swing" hammer block was activated by a spring-loaded "sliding pin" (*m*, patent fig. 2), mounted in the sideplate. The pin itself was activated by the hand, as described in the patent disclosure and shown in patent figs. 4 through 7.

U.S. Patent Office

John Henwood notes that "Third change M&Ps were the last made without an automatic hammer blocking mechanism, which prevents the revolver's firing unless the trigger is held to the rear." He also states that while it is impossible to pinpoint exactly when a given change was introduced, square-butt fixed-sight M&Ps were fitted with the "side-swing" hammer block starting in April, 1915 and target models starting in June, 1926, while round butt guns were not so fitted until July, 1926.

Invented by S&W plant superintendent Edward S. Pomeroy and assigned to Smith & Wesson, the initial sideplate-mounted "side-swing" hammer block was granted U.S. patent no. 1,122,635 on December 29, 1914. Excerpts from the patent disclosure read as follows:

> *This invention relates particularly to revolvers of the self-cocking type, its object being to provide a safety device to prevent the hammer being accidentally brought into contact with the primer of a cartridge, as might happen from receiving a blow against the hammer. To this end a positive lock or chock-piece is provided which is pressed laterally by a spring, so that upon the rebound or partial retraction of the hammer after firing, it enters in front of the hammer, filling the space between the hammer and frame, so that it offers an obstacle to the further forward movement of the hammer until retracted by the cocking movement.*
>
> *. . . the safety lock comprises a laterally movable block* j *which after the retraction of the hammer enters between the front face of the hammer and the rear face of the frame, and positively prevents any forward movement of the hammer. This block* j *is mounted on a spring arm* k *which is seated in a groove in the usual detachable cheek plate* a'*, its location therein being shown in [patent] Fig. 2 and in the transverse sections Figs. 4 and 5, its lower end being fast in the groove, and its upper portion free to move laterally therein. Such lateral motion is imparted to it by means of a sliding pin* m*, shown best in Figs. 6 and 7, which moves in a transverse groove in the cheek plate crossing the groove containing the spring* k*. This pin* m *has an inclined or wedging face* m' *which engages within a notched portion* k' *of the spring, so that as the pin is pressed back against the stress of its spring* n *this wedging face presses outwardly against the spring* k *and moves it from the locked position shown in Fig. 4 to the unlocked position shown in Fig. 5. The end or head of the pin* m *bears against the rear face of the hand* i*, as shown in Figs. 3 and 6, so that its spring* n *serves both for restoring the pin* m *and for pressing the hand* i *into engagement with the cylinder ratchets. As the hand is moved up or down by the movement of the trigger* e*, its rear face moves against the head of the pin* m*, and the wedge portion* i' *of this face has a cam action against the pin, whereby as the hand rises the pin is pressed rearwardly, and as the hand descends the pin is released and permitted to move forwardly. The movement thus imparted to the pin is in turn communicated to the spring* k*, and hence moves the safety block* j *into or out of the safety position . . .*

## Two Versions of the "Side-Swing" Hammer Block

285. Right side closeup of .32 WCF Target Model M&P serial no. 96878 with sideplate removed, showing the configuration of the hand used in conjunction with the early style "side-swing" hammer block.
Gaston Comeau collection

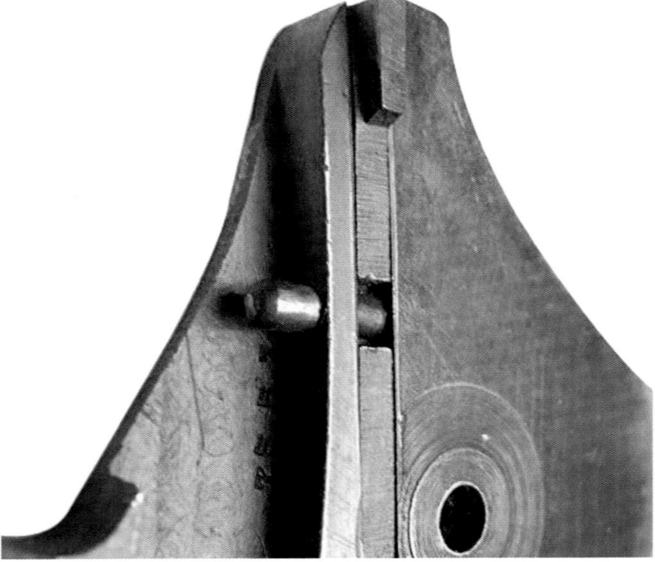

286. Inside closeup of the sideplate of M&P no. 96878, showing the spring-loaded hammer block plunger (the "sliding pin", *m* in patent fig. 2, above), mounted in the sideplate, which is cammed rearwardly by the hand to withdraw the hammer safety. The spring-loaded hammer block plunger also acts as the hand spring.
Gaston Comeau collection

287. Right side closeup of .38 Special Target Model M&P serial no. 670727 with sideplate and cylinder removed, showing the configuration of the hand used in conjunction with the later style "side-swing" hammer block.
Inset: rear closeup of the hand (arrow), showing wedge-like cam surface. Gaston Comeau collection

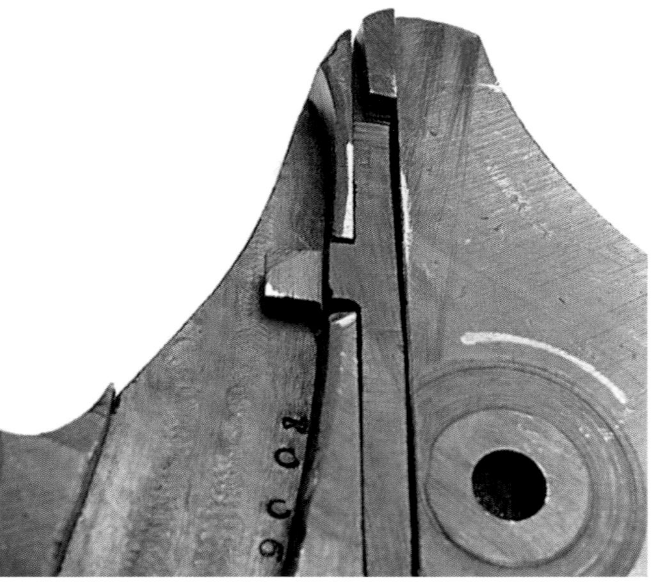

288. Inside closeup of the sideplate of M&P no. 670727, showing the tab added to the front of the hammer safety. Gaston Comeau collection

The initial version of the "side-swing" hammer block resembled that shown in the patent illustrations, and was activated by a spring-loaded "sliding pin" (*m*, patent fig. 2, above), mounted in the sideplate. The pin itself was activated by the hand, as described in the patent disclosure and shown in patent figs. 4 through 7.

The "side-swing" hammer block was later simplified, albeit at the cost of a more complex hand assembly, which now required its own spring and lever, mounted inside the trigger.

The sliding pin and its spring housed in the sideplate were eliminated, and the arm of the hammer block itself was modified with an added front tab. The action of forcing the nose of the hammer block out of the path of the hammer was then accomplished by a wedge-like cam extending from the rear edge of the hand (inset, fig. 287), which contacted the hammer block tab as the hand was raised, forcing the hammer block back into its recess in the sideplate.

## The "Police" Portion of the M&P Name Gains Credence

By 1920 the popularity of the Smith & Wesson .38 Special M&P revolver in police circles meant that it had truly begun to overshadow the top-breaks of old. True, the M&P had not been a resounding success in the military arena, but among police and civilian shooters, it was soon viewed as both a viable self-defense weapon and a very accurate target arm. It shot a smokeless cartridge, and while the bullets were smaller and thus cut a smaller hole in a target, which might cost a shooter some points that would be grabbed by the bigger .44 bullets shot from a No. 3 Smith & Wesson, the previous target shooter's standard, the smokeless powder made shooting indoors much more pleasant, more rounds could be fired without cleaning, and a target model M&P was every bit as accurate as a No. 3. In fact, it was every bit as accurate as any revolver made today.

The .38 Special cartridge might not be as effective a manstopper as the military .45, but it was easier to shoot for the typically ill-trained police officer (then as now, of course), and it was a definite improvement over the top-break .32s and .38s previously seen (or unseen) in the hip pockets of officers of the late 19th century. Also by 1920, changing fashions and tastes permitted the uniformed officer's handgun to be seen holstered on his belt, and this further aided and abetted the acceptance of the M&P revolver as an official police sidearm.

# The M&P in Demand for Home Defense

The home defense crowd always seems to be divided into two camps. The first group will be happy with some tired old weapon bought cheap, as they do not want to invest much money in the project; while the other, made up of alert and responsible citizens, want what the police have and use.

For the first batch of users in the pre-1920 timeframe, a lot of cheap .32 and .38 top-breaks of low quality were available, then as even now. However it seems there were quite a few who followed the example of the police, as more and more Smith & Wesson M&P revolvers were sold commercially during the period. This of course is the very reason that to this day we are still finding early-production revolvers in nearly new-in-the-box condition. Bought at the local hardware store in those pre-1968 Gun Control Act days when most such stores sold firearms the same way they sold any other merchandise, such home defenders put them away or gave them to spinster sisters, widowed mothers, or young ladies to whom they were engaged who hid them, still in the box, under their stockings where they tended to stay undisturbed for the next several decades. I found just such a weapon among my widowed aunt's effects when she died in 1961, and it was a surprise to all of us. My guess is that it had been there since the Czar was on the throne in Russia.

# The Groundswell Continues

Besides the target shooters who were gravitating to the M&P revolver, typically but not always the target model; the police, who since the turn of the century had preferred a swing-out cylinder, solid-frame revolver to a top-break (which had gone out of fashion along with tall police helmets and billy clubs at the waist); and the more alert home defenders who copied the cops, there were outdoorsmen who also went to the M&P, mainly but not always because it was also available in .32-20 WCF.

While the .38 Special was perennially the more popular chambering, most outdoorsmen who bought the M&P seemed to prefer the flat-shooting, light-recoiling .32-20 WCF model. These are interesting enough, although somewhat rare today and always priced high, in my opinion, given the well-worn condition in which they are usually found, and their rather specialized usefulness.

289. Right side closeup of an early nickel-plated M&P chambered for the .32-20 cartridge, showing caliber marking.
Note the large extractor knob.

However, if you did not haunt places where big bears tended to walk about, the .32-20 caliber certainly made an excellent choice. Its flat-shooting ballistics made the issues of range estimation and bullet drop much easier; the cartridges were less bulky and a little lighter to carry; and the flat-tipped bullets were pretty good on game animals. With proper placement, game the size of a whitetail deer could be harvested.

While most are the longer-barreled variants, some four-inch .32-20 models are seen, as apparently there were always enough men who thought a four-inch could be carried more readily in the top of bib overalls.

# The M&P: Well Poised for the "Brave New World"

After the end of the "War to End Wars", as the United States encountered the industrialization and (even worse) Prohibition of the brave new postwar world of the 1920s, the Smith & Wesson M&P was well poised to be the logical choice for all possible groups of revolver users. We shall continue the discussion of its history during the next ten or so years in the following chapter.

*Chapter Twenty-Eight*

# The M&P During the Roaring Twenties

## America Rises in the Aftermath of WWI

In 1914 the United States had been a rather isolated, rural nation with few big cities, protected on both coasts by wide oceans, and espousing a political philosophy which echoed Founding Father George Washington's warning to "beware of foreign entanglements".

By the time World War I had ended in 1918, however, the country was much different. Wartime contracts for food and munitions had created great wealth for many American farmers and industrialists. Unlike the European powers, where an entire generation of young men had been annihilated by four years of grinding war, the United States had sustained relatively few casualties. Also, since the U.S. had not entered the war until April, 1917, there was not the same sense of exhaustion, either on public morale or from a physical and economic standpoint. In fact, by 1919 the United States had emerged as one of the world's leading nations, while the nations of Europe were never to regain such status.

## Crime and Prohibition

For reasons that can be debated, the United States then passed the 18th Amendment, which prohibited the manufacture, distribution, and sale of intoxicating liquor. The familiar corner saloon, long the refuge of working men, was gone, along with the free lunch, soon to be replaced by the shadowy speakeasy. Prohibition proved to be a boon to the underworld, which had no scruples about selling an illegal product to willing buyers for a considerable profit.

Crime had always existed, of course, but this new sellers' market for illegal alcoholic beverages enriched and empowered a large number of violent, organized criminals. Moreover, since big money brings its own temptations, it also greatly increased the numbers of "bent" police officers and other public officials who were "on the take".

As the twenties went on, the police departments in most large cities, which were heavily involved in politics, expanded to meet the demands caused by burgeoning urbanization and the public perception that crime had greatly increased. Naturally all of these officers had to be armed, which led to the vastly increased use of the Smith & Wesson M&P revolver as a police sidearm during the 1920s.

# The M&P Becomes the Ideal Duty Revolver

While top-breaks and weak side-openers in small calibers had been normal police weapons prior to 1899, during the 1920s more forward-thinking departments started adopting the M&P and its Colt competitor, the Army Special. Officers coming new to the job likewise tended to shun the old top-breaks chambered for weak cartridges. The old-time long coat, so favored as it allowed the officer to project an unarmed appearance, also started to disappear, replaced by holstered belt guns, both in urban departments and rural sheriffs' offices, where for decades they had been hidden from view if indeed carried at

290. Left side view of a pre-1921 .38 Special M&P used by the St. Louis Police Department.
Inset: closeup of the back strap showing hand-stamped property mark with Police Department issue no. 1008.

all. The M&P of course made for a nearly ideal belt gun, then just as it still does today. Not too heavy; not too big; but still strong enough to meet the demands of police service, reliable in the extreme even if ignored (as were many officers' weapons) and powerful enough yet easy enough to shoot for most purposes. Even if it did fail the stopping power test from time to time, it was certainly better than the old .32s commonly used before.

During this period, which pre-dated the general use of automobiles by police patrolmen, the M&P with the six-inch barrel length was most commonly seen. It weighed but little more than the four-inch model, and for many it was easier to shoot. Because it was used by the police, it was also bought by many non-law enforcement civilians who wished to have a firearm for home or business protection. The factory at the time offered the M&P in four- and five-inch lengths also, but a "gun show census" of items for sale points to a preponderance of six-inch models, with five-inch models being next. But then, perhaps some people sold their six-inch models and held onto their shorter examples for practical use in the future.

Nickel-plated examples from this era seem to be especially common today, mostly with peeling finishes to be sure, the sign of much use and some neglect, I fear. Of course for a weapon worn on the belt in all sorts of weather, the nickel finish makes good sense. Until stainless steel became a common material from which to make revolvers, I always had all my serious Smith & Wesson revolvers nickel-plated at the factory for use in the humid Midwest.

# Relocating the S&W Monogram

## Catalog D-2 (1921)

In a further attempt to protect the genuine S&W product and guard against the influx of cheap imitations, it was announced on the inside of the cover of factory catalog D-2, dated January 1, 1921, that the S&W gold monogram would no longer appear on the wood stocks, and the trademark logo would be relocated to the left side of the frame, where it could not be easily removed.

As discussed below, however, this was not nearly enough, and further, tougher measures were needed to stem the tide of these cheap European "lookalikes".

291. The cover of S&W factory catalog D-2, dated January 1, 1921. Gaston Comeau collection

## Monograms

We have discontinued the policy of placing the gold S. & W. Monograms in the Wood Stocks and hereafter all of our arms will be marked with the S. & W. Monogram on the Frame as we feel this to be a far better place for this identifying Trade Mark.

It cannot easily be removed from the frame, which is the case when Stocks are changed, and then again in omitting the Monograms from the Wood Stocks it enables us to build them much fuller at this point, thereby giving the User a better hand hold.

292. The notice headed "Monograms" which appeared inside the cover of catalog D-2, announcing the relocation of the S&W logo from the wood stocks to the left side of the frame, Gaston Comeau collection

293. A nickel-plated .38 Special M&P with 6" barrel, produced after the implementation of the above notice. Note the absence of the monogram on the walnut stock, and the logo on the left side of the frame. courtesy Rock Island Auction Co.

294. Left side view of a 4" blued M&P with round butt, also exhibiting the small logo on the frame.

This example is fitted with checkered hard rubber grips, which were molded with the S&W monograms as an integral part of the design. Dave Terbrueggen collection

# Improving the "Service" Sights

## Catalog D-3 (1923)

### Our Improved Service Sights

**The cuts on this page illustrate the improved SERVICE SIGHTS, PATRIDGE TYPE, with which our Square Butt Military & Police Models, the .38 and .32/20, are now furnished.**

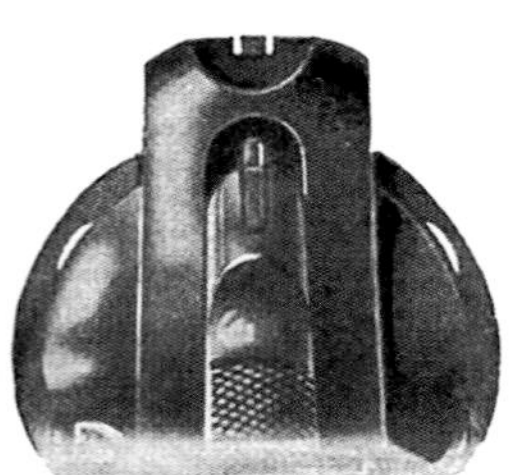

Fig. 1

Fig. 1 shows the proper position of the FRONT SIGHT as it should be seen through the REAR SIGHT notch at time of firing.

Note the flat tops of both sights and the sharply defined vertical sides.

Fig. 2 is a slightly enlarged view of the REAR SIGHT, showing its perpendicular rear face, shaded and protected by the semi-circle.

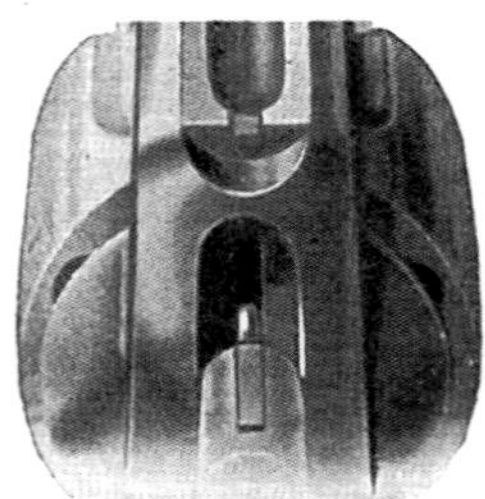

Fig. 2

These *fixed sights*, which cannot be injured, have been proved by careful tests to give practically all the advantages of the special Target Sights.

They make it possible to obtain far greater accuracy than either the thin blade or the bead types.

# The Scourge of "Those Spanish Imitations"

The increasing popularity of the S&W K-frame revolver during the early to mid-1920s was proving to be somewhat of a two-edged sword, as imitators did their best to flood the market with cheap European "lookalikes".

The major foreign competition came from Spanish revolver manufacturers. During WWI, when France was very short of handguns, the government of France had gone across the border to Spain and bought lots of handguns. Most of these were cheap, "Ruby"-style blowback 7.65mm (.32 ACP) self-loaders, which were made by a myriad of home-based manufacturers, all to a similar rudimentary design. But in addition to these, the French also bought Spanish-made revolvers chambered for their 8mm Lebel cartridge, which is similar to the .32-20 WCF. These revolvers had swing-out cylinders and hand ejection, and looked rather like Smith & Wessons chambered in .32 Smith & Wesson Long, but chambered for the 8mm Lebel cartridge pistol instead.

At the conclusion of the war, a couple of U.S. firearms dealers went to Spain and persuaded the manufacturers of these revolvers to begin copying the M&P revolver, chambered for .38 Special or .32-20 WCF, for sale in the U.S.

These Spanish revolvers were made of softer steel, which did not hold the tolerances of the fine Springfield product. But working on the theory that many people could not tell the difference, especially if English was not their primary language, or if they were less than knowledgeable about weapons, the Spanish copies had markings on them which, while not actually copying those of genuine Smith & Wessons, certainly at first glance could appear to be so to the less sophisticated. The blue finish was always quite highly polished, so at a quick glance they really looked good. Barrels typically were marked in small letters stating that the weapon took the Smith & Wesson .38 Special cartridge, with large letters emphasizing the "Smith & Wesson" portion of this identifier. The grips had brass inserts with an intertwined design that looked very much like the Smith & Wesson logo unless it was carefully examined. All in all, therefore, it was quite clear that these revolvers were intended to gull the purchaser into thinking he was buying a legitimate Smith & Wesson product. Naturally they could be sold at a substantially lower price, and still yield a good profit for the retailer.

:95 (previous page, left). The cover of S&W factory catalog )-3, dated March, 1923. Gaston Comeau collection

:96 (previous page, right). Page 13 from the 1923 catalog )-3, depicting and describing the improved Service (fixed) ights. Gaston Comeau collection

Apparently these weapons deceived enough people that sales of genuine Smith & Wessons began to be impacted to a degree. More critically, the poor quality of these weapons, along with their close approximations to the real thing, began adversely affecting the reputation of the U.S.-made product, which was even worse as far as Smith & Wesson was concerned. Certainly the Spanish revolvers could not compete with genuine Smith & Wessons in quality, but nor could Smith & Wesson compete against the price of the Spanish product; but when the poor reputation garnered by the Spanish imports began tarnishing the real thing, something had to be done.

A brief excerpt from *Smith & Wesson Hand Guns* by McHenry and Roper gives some background to the situation, as follows:

> *Smith & Wesson, Colt and other top-notch American manufacturers always had to contend with cheap imitations of their products as quickly as patents expired; but cheap domestic revolvers never were as troublesome as the Spanish imitations which flooded the country in the early 1920s . .*
>
> *Return of our expeditionary forces in late 1918 and 1919 probably helped the American public become more "gun conscious" than it had been since frontier days. People who had never before owned firearms began to want pistols and revolvers, and as is always the case, demand creates supply.*
>
> *New lines of revolvers began to appear in show windows of the cheaper stores. To the casual observer they seemed to be Smith & Wessons and Colts, and as the price was low, many were sold.*
>
> *. . Smith & Wesson did not realize immediately how much the Spanish imitations were hurting their business. When they did, some time was required to learn who was at the bottom of the import business. Three firms were found to be responsible: Aaron Newmark, doing business as the Paramount Trading Company; E. E. Glick, operating under the revealing title of Import Trading Company; and an individual named J. L. Galef . .*

Excerpts from then-Major J. S. Hatcher's article entitled "Those Spanish Imitations", which appeared

297. Left and right side views of a typical Spanish imitation of a Smith & Wesson M&P revolver. Other than the cylinder latch, most features are intentionally very similar to those of the genuine product.

298. Left side closeup of the barrel of the above Spanish imitation, with wording reading "FOR .38 SPECIAL AND U.S. SERVICE CTG."

Note the Spanish Lion proof of the Eibar Proof House (far right), described by Wirnsberger as used from 1923 to 1929 as the single and final proof for self-loading pistols and revolvers. courtesy NRA National Firearms Museum

in the April 1, 1923 issue of *The American Rifleman* further confirm the extent of this problem in detail, as follows:

*A glance into the window of almost any pawnshop or second-hand store will show a glittering array of revolvers which apparently are new Colts and Smith & Wessons. A closer scrutiny may reveal some markings that will perhaps seem a little peculiar, such as the legend "For .32 Caliber United States Service Cartridges", that I noticed the other day . . the fact that the United States has no .32 caliber service cartridge does not detract from the value of the lettering, but adds to it, for it shows that the gun is one of the many Spanish counterfeits with which this country has been flooded for some time.*

*. . They come in various calibers, .32-20 and .38 being the most popular; but I have seen .22s also, in the Smith & Wesson type. In many cases the imitations are so faithful as to appearance that experts in the big factories cannot tell the genuine from the counterfeit without examining the markings. When the distinctive monograms on the stock are closely imitated, and small structural details, such as the cylinder latch, are copied exactly, all that is needed to convince the average man that he is buying a genuine American-made weapon of standard make is the inscription on the side of the barrel,*

"FOR **SMITH & WESSON** CTG."

*Of course, a very careful and well-informed purchaser might detect the name of the place of manufacture, which is required by law to be stamped on the gun; but this mark "Spain" is small, and often cleverly placed so as to elude the eye of the unwary.*

McHenry and Roper continue:

*. . Since patents covering the imitated Smith & Wesson revolvers had all expired, infringement suits were out of the question, and it was decided to bring injunction suits against the importers for unfair competition in trade . .*

*Action was brought in the United States District Court for the Southern District of New York and came up before Hon. Learned Hand, U. S. District Judge. On March 27, 1922, he handed down his decision . .*

Judge Learned Hand's decision, along with further comments from Major Hatcher in his April 1, 1923 *American Rifleman* article, are as follows:

*. . The degree to which the imitation of the genuine product extends may be imagined from the following remarks from an opinion by Judge Learned Hand:*

*"There appears to me not the slightest question that all the infringing revolvers were deliberately made for the purpose of imitating a model of the plaintiff's. In the case of Galef & Newmark they correspond in dimension even by gauge, a coincidence wholly impossible in the absence of conscious imitation. In the case of Gluck, the visual similarity is as complete . . The lettering along the top of the barrel, except in the case of Exhibit Number 1 in Newmark's case, is either a plain fraud, e.g., in Galef's revolvers, or merely fatuous nonsense. That upon the side of the barrel is little better, and serves no real purpose . ."*

*That even factory experts themselves may be fooled by appearance is clearly shown by the fact that when I wrote to Smith & Wesson for a photo of one of these guns they replied, "Photographs would be useless because we ourselves have to look for very small details in order to distinguish them. It is not until one takes off the side-plate or looks down the barrel that he realizes that all is not gold that glitters. Also the Brinell tests very quickly show by less than 50 per cent of the resistance of our own metal . . I have shot one or two of them, but do not care to take a chance with many, particularly after testing one cylinder which in our gun runs to 82 test and in this one ran from 22 to 28 Brinell."*

*I have examined a number of these guns, and have done some shooting with them. On the outside they look good, especially at a short distance . . The Smith & Wesson types have the gold monogram similar to those formerly seen on the genuine product, and though on close examination the letters are found to be different, the effect is the same . . However, on looking inside . . I find that the resemblance ceases. The shape of the pieces is the same, to be sure, as the guns are copies throughout; but a big difference is immediately apparent in finish and material. To notice this difference, it is really necessary only to raise the hammer and look at the hammer-nose. Instead of the regular shape and glass-smooth surface that is seen on the Smith & Wesson, we find on the imitation that this part, which is normally hidden from sight, is most crudely shaped up with a coarse file. In many cases the point is so sharp that punctured primers are sure to result. The same*

1430 ESTABLISHED 1871 Blish, Mize & Silliman Hardware Co. ATCHISON, KANS.

## SMITH & WESSON REVOLVERS AND PISTOLS

### MILITARY AND POLICE MODEL REVOLVER

**.38 Caliber, Round Butt**

Blued steel solid frame, checkered rubber stocks, double action swing-out cylinder, safety hammer blocks, six shots. For .38 Caliber S. & W. Special cartridges.

| Nos. | 448B | 458B | 468B |
|---|---|---|---|
| Length barrel, inches | 4 | 5 | 6 |
| Length overall, inches | 8⅞ | 9⅞ | 10⅞ |
| Weight, ounces | 28¾ | 29½ | 30½ |
| Each | $51.20 | 51.20 | 51.20 |

Nickel plated finish can be furnished from factory at same prices. If wanted substitute N for B in the catalog numbers.

### MILITARY MODEL REVOLVER

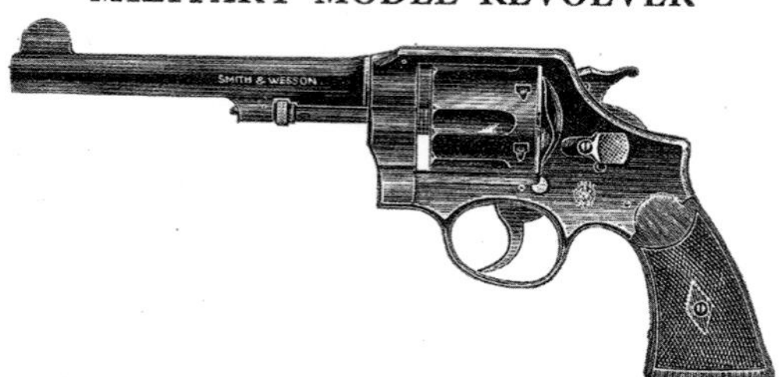


**.44 Caliber, Square Butt**

Blued steel solid frame, checkered walnut stocks, double action swing-out cylinder. Six shots. For .44 Caliber S. & W. Special cartridges Can be furnished with Target Sights at additional cost.

| Nos. | 554B | 564B |
|---|---|---|
| Length barrel, inches | 5 | 6½ |
| Length overall, inches | 10¼ | 11¾ |
| Weight, ounces | 37 | 38 |
| Each | $56.00 | 56.00 |

Nickel Plated finish can be furnished from factory at same price. If wanted substitute N for B in the catalog number.

### U. S. ARMY MODEL 1917 REVOLVER

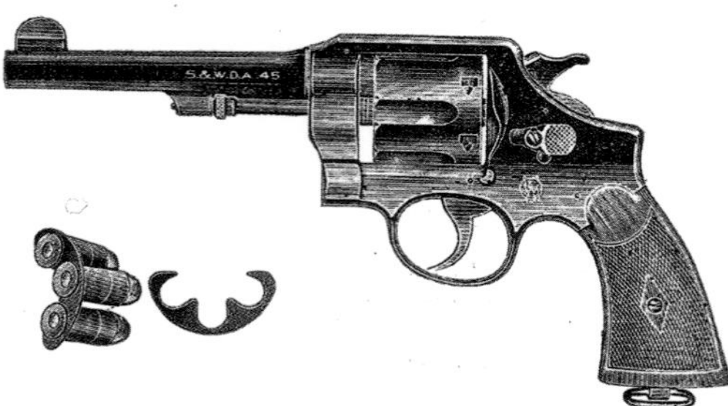

**.45 Caliber, Square Butt**

Same as Military Model, except for caliber and length of barrel. Blued steel solid frame, checkered walnut stocks, double action swing-out cylinder. Six shots. For .45 Auto Pistol cartridges in clips or .45 Auto Rim cartridges without clips.

**No. 455B**—.45 Caliber, Square Butt U. S. Army Model 1917. Length of barrel 5½ inches, length over all 10¾ inches. Weight 36¼ ounces.................................Each, $58.80

**No. 455CC**—Extra Cartridge Clips................Per Pair, .12

### HEAVY FRAME TARGET MODEL REVOLVER

**.22 Caliber on a .32 Caliber Frame**

Blued Steel Solid frame, checkered walnut stocks, double action swing-out cylinder, Target sights, six shots. For .22 Short and Long Rifle cartridges, .22 Extra Long and .22 Marksman Long Rifle.

**No. 2211B**—.22-32 Caliber Heavy Frame Target Model. Length of barrel 6 inches, length over all 10½ inches. Weight 22¾ ounces.............................................Each, $52.80

### STRAIGHT LINE SINGLE SHOT PISTOL

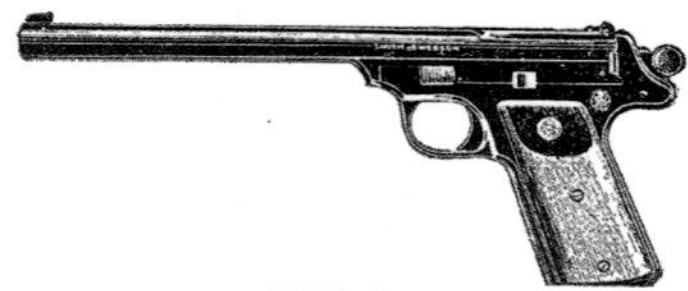

**.22 Caliber**

This Straight Line Single Shot Pistol is a practical weapon for the sportsman, fisherman and trapper, as well as an extremely accurate arm for target shooting. Straight line trigger and hammer. Walnut stocks. Adjustable rear and Partridge front sights. Furnished in pressed steel case with cleaning rod and screw driver. Blue finish only.

**No. 22SL**—Shoots .22 Long Rifle cartridges. Length of barrel 10 inches. Length overall 11⅛ inches...................Each, $56.00

### SPANISH HAND EJECTOR

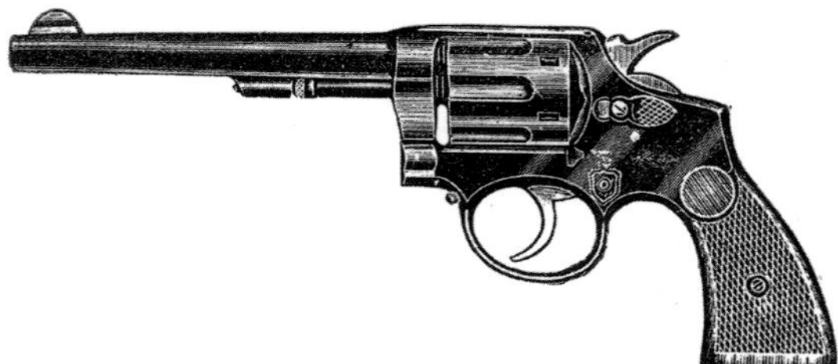

**Made in Spain**

Blued steel solid frame, checkered walnut stocks, double action swing-out cylinder, safety hammer block, New Patridge type sights. Six shots.

**.32-20 Caliber, Square Butt**
Uses .32-20 caliber cartridges.

| Nos. | 3142N | 3142B | 3152N | 3251B |
|---|---|---|---|---|
| Length barrel, inches | 4 | 4 | 5 | 5 |
| Length overall, inches | 9⅛ | 9⅛ | 10⅛ | 10⅛ |
| Weight, ounces | 30½ | 30½ | 31¼ | 31¼ |
| Each | $23.50 | 23.50 | 23.50 | 23.50 |

**.38 Caliber, Square Butt**
Uses .38 Caliber S. & W. Special Cartridges.

| Nos. | 3158N | 3158B |
|---|---|---|
| Length of barrel | 5 | 5 |
| Length overall, inches | 10⅛ | 10⅛ |
| Weight, ounces | 30 | 30 |
| Each | $23.50 | 23.50 |

**.32 S. & W. Caliber**
Uses .32 S. & W. and .32 S. & W. Long cartridges.

| Nos. | 3042N | 3042B |
|---|---|---|
| Length barrel, inches | 4 | 4 |
| Length overall, inches | 8¾ | 8¾ |
| Weight, ounces | 16 | 16 |
| Each | $23.50 | 23.50 |

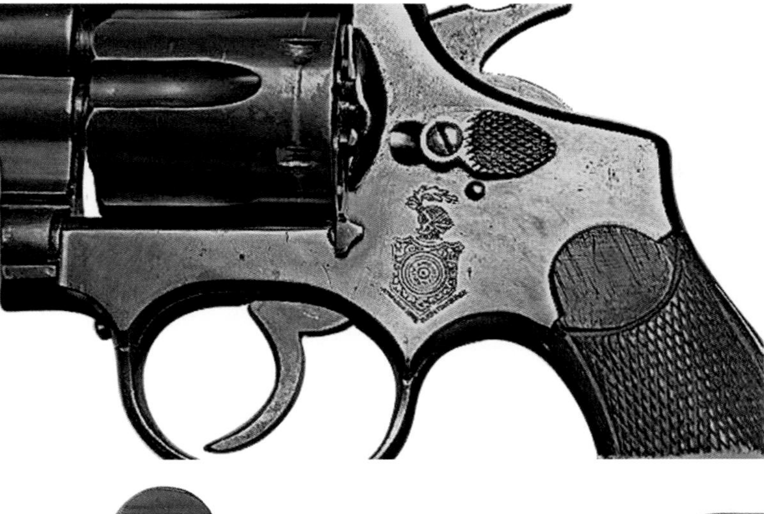

300 (left). Left side closeup of a Spanish imitation bearing the trademarked crest of the importers, J. L. Galef & Son Inc., of 85 Chambers St., New York City (shown enlarged in fig. 569).

Ironically, Smith & Wesson's New York distributors, the W. Robinson Co., was just a few doors down at no. 79.

courtesy NRA National Firearms Museum

301. Left side view of another Spanish M&P lookalike. The hammer spur is probably the result of a repair, while the cylinder latch and other features closely resemble those of the genuine article, although the quality is very poor.

Note the brass medallion in the grip, with intertwined "T.A.C." design resembling the S&W logo.

courtesy NRA National Firearms Museum

*character of work is apparent throughout the whole mechanism. If the cylinder fails to line up with the barrel by a sixteenth of an inch or so, or the barrel is on one angle and the cylinder on another, what does it matter to the maker in Spain or Germany? He doesn't have to worry about the reputation of his product. He is selling on Colt's reputation, or Smith & Wesson's, which are excellent at present, but probably will suffer severely if the undiscriminating public blames them for the performance of these thousands of pot-metal counterfeits . .*

*Besides just poor shooting, there are possibilities for more serious trouble. Many of these Spanish guns are being sold in the .32 Winchester caliber. Now the .32 W.H.V. [rifle cartridge] is not exactly safe in any revolver, but the Smith & Wesson people are now making a heat-treated cylinder that will hold this cartridge if it is accidentally used; but I can think of no better suicide combination*

299 (previous page). A contemporary catalog page from the Blish, Mize and Silliman Hardware Co. of Atchison, Kansas, listing the "Spanish Hand Ejector" on the same page as Smith & Wesson revolvers and pistols.

Compare with fig. 300 - note the Galef crest on the frame of the Spanish revolver.

The round butt M&P lists for $51.20, the square butt version for $56.00, while the Spanish imitation, in either .32-20 or .38 Special, costs only $23.50.

Gaston Comeau collection

302. Top closeup of the barrel of the "T.A.C." revolver, showing markings reading "BEST AMERICAN CARTRIDGES ARE THOSE THAT FIT BEST THE T.A.C. REVOLVER".

Markings on the left side of the barrel, just visible here, read "38 LONG CARTRIDGE".

According to Judge Learned Hand's decision, reprinted above, the lettering along the top of the barrel "is either a plain fraud . . or merely fatuous nonsense. That upon the side of the barrel is little better, and serves no real purpose . ." courtesy NRA National Firearms Museum

*than the Spanish .32-30 gun and the W.H.V. cartridge. All that the newspapers would say is "A Smith & Wesson exploded."*

*. . Readers of this magazine can do much to discourage this trade in counterfeits if they will bear in mind and impress on others the following facts:*

*These imitations were designed for the express purpose of cheating the purchaser; the man who sells one of them to a would-be marksman is . . palming off on his customer a weapon that is useless for target practice, and the dealer who carries this line at all is doing an injury to his own future business by helping bring the pistol and revolver into general disrepute and thus paving the way for objectionable anti-firearms laws.*

## A Genuine S&W, Submitted to the Court

## "Few Spanish Revolvers Worthy of American Ownership"

The 1968 revision of W. H. B. Smith's *Book of Pistols and Revolvers* by Joseph E. Smith sums up the Spanish copies as follows:

> *All Spanish revolvers of this type are imitations or modifications of Colt or Smith & Wesson designs. The best of them are good; the worst are positively dangerous. In those which are made of fair-quality forgings, the fitting and tolerances are poor. Some were made from castings which frequently blow up when used with standard U. S. ammunition. While there are some Spanish automatic pistols of reasonably reliable quality . . there are few Spanish revolvers worthy of American ownership.*

## The Flip Side - Not All Spanish Copies are Bad

304. Left side view of a Spanish M&P copy in .32 WCF caliber, manufactured by Crucelegui Hermanos in Eibar, Spain.

As the owner explains, below, "this one is well made, works great, always has, and I suspect will for quite a long time." Greg Pfeiffer collection

The phrase "the best of them are good" in the above quote sets us up for the following comments, written for us by Greg Pfeiffer, proprietor of the interesting website www.britishguns.com, concerning his own Spanish S&W copy—in .32-20 caliber, no less—which we have paraphrased as follows:

03 (previous page). Left side view of a genuine S&W M&P, ubmitted on March 22, 1922 as an exhibit to establish for e court just what a real Smith & Wesson looked like, and ow deviously the copies were designed to be easily onfused with the real thing by a gullible consumer.

Note the gold inlaid inscription. This revolver bears no erial number.

courtesy NRA National Firearms Museum

> *Spanish pistols only half deserve derision. I have this old Spanish copy of a Smith & Wesson, a .32-20 revolver made by Crucelegui Hermanos in Eibar, Spain. Although there are some Spanish guns you should pass on, this one is well made, works great, always has, and I suspect will for quite a long time. The finish is worn badly and the hammer spur had broken off at one time, and seems to have been repaired by a blacksmith. I am uncertain of its age [but the] Crucelegui Brothers, one of many companies consumed by the Spanish Civil War, quit making revolvers around 1936.*
>
> *Crucelegui Hermanos began by making Velo Dog-style guns, which were used by cyclists to deter*

305. Right side closeup of the .32 WCF caliber Crucelegui Hermanos revolver, showing "Trade Mark" legend on the receiver and in the grip medallion, clearly intended to resemble the genuine S&W logo. Greg Pfeiffer collection

306. Right side closeup with sideplate removed, showing the cleverly designed amalgam of Colt and S&W components.

The Colt type mainspring presses down on the rebound lever as the hammer is cocked. There is no hammer safety as such, but the arm of the rebound lever tucks under the rear of the hammer to impede its forward movement unless the action is cocked. Greg Pfeiffer collection

*wild dogs. They were never thought of as being junk guns, and most were well made. The Basque region of Spain where almost all the guns were made has a metalworking history that goes back forever—if any Roman Legionaires were still around you could ask them what they thought of Spanish steel.*

*WWI seemed to be the cause of Spanish quality problems. The warring powers got themselves into a lot bigger war than they were meaning to, and they had a serious need for firearms, more than they could themselves turn out. Britain and France turned to other countries (not involved in the hostilities) and one of those countries was Spain. Little shops in the Basque area were asked to produce handguns, and once accepted, were given huge orders to fill, far beyond the capacity of shops that each employed only a few craftsmen. The war's demand for guns led to a choice between quantity and quality, and also brought unscrupulous characters into the gun business. Spanish quality eventually hit bottom trying to meet the demands of the war.*

*By 1916, the British had dropped all Spanish contracts because of the number of rejected guns, however they dropped S&W's contracts as well six months later, and Colt's a couple of months after that, mainly because by that time their home industries were catching up.*

*After the war was over, the low-end Spanish guns started flowing to America, a country better off than most. The ability of Spain to make decent guns was always there—no one talks badly about Star or Astra pistols.*

## The Spanish Civil War Helps Stem the Flow of S&W "Lookalikes"

While injunction lawsuits stopped the importation of the cheap Spanish counterfeits to a great extent into the United States, they of course had no direct effect in Latin America, which was always a big market for Smith & Wesson, and this problem lingered on as a thorn in the side of the Smith & Wesson company for a number of years.

Ironically, what probably helped more than anything was the Spanish Civil War, which effectively caused weapon exports from Spain to cease, and as noted above by Greg Pfeiffer, spelled the demise of a number of Spanish arms companies. This, combined with the effects of the worldwide Depression, which limited demand for virtually all products, eventually had the greatest impact.

# More Events and Examples from the 1920s

## Grooving the Target Model Trigger and Grip Straps

Fixed "service" sights were standard, of course, but right from the introduction of the S&W Hand Ejector, adjustable target sights had been available as an extra-cost option. Target models of the M&P, with well-made and fairly rugged adjustable sights, were popular mostly with target shooters (no surprise there) and outdoorsmen (again no big surprise, since they might well use various loads necessitating sight changes).

Starting on August 14, 1923, the target models had grooved front and back straps to assist in maintaining a firm hold, and the trigger was likewise grooved to improve control.

## A Texas Ranger M&P

307. Left side view of a well-used 5" M&P, serial no. 443571, shipped to Belknap Hardware Co. in Louisville, Kentucky on January 26, 1924 and documented as being owned by Albert R. Mace (1872 - 1938), who was an active Texas lawman for a number of years and served two tours of duty with the Texas Rangers in the 1920s.

The front sight has a brass insert, and the gun shows much wear from holster carry.

Inset: a 1920s-period Texas Ranger badge. The center of the star is dished from wallet carry. private collection

## Illustrating the Scarcity of .38 Special Ammunition

The .38 Special is by far the most popular centerfire revolver chambering today, and we are all used to seeing these cartridges available in a wide variety of loadings anywhere ammunition is sold. But it was not always so, and I recently came across an article that I believe reflects the fact that neither the .38 Special cartridge itself, nor the M&P revolver that shot it, were by any means common by the time the 1920s rolled around.

The .38 Special had first appeared in 1899, along with the M&P revolver, and the shorter .38 Long Colt load had preceded it by a number of years. Yet, in an article which appeared on page 5 of the August 1, 1925 issue of *The American Rifleman*, J. V. K. Wagner, a noted gun writer of the day, shows how rare both these cartridges still were, as follows:

> *. . It was in the latter part of 1919 that I first realized the importance of this advantage [availability of cartridges]. I was then working in a Northern Wisconsin lumber mill and had with me an S&W Military & Police square butt revolver shooting the .38 Special cartridge. I had not followed my usual practice of buying a large amount of ammunition before going into the country, and soon depleted my small supply.*
>
> *Then the trouble began. I'd go into one of the few small general stores in that country and ask for .38 revolver cartridges. I didn't care if they were .38 S&W Special or Colt Special, .38 Long Colt or .38 Short Colt cartridges: just something I could use in my revolver. Always the storekeeper would bring out a box of .38-40s . . I could get nothing to shoot in my gun, and the storekeepers were unwilling to order cartridges for loggers because of their transitoriness unless paid in advance.*
>
> *That Smith & Wesson revolver was a splendid arm, killing two deer and much smaller game, but I've never carried a revolver chambered for the .38 S&W Special cartridge since that time except on short trips near home.*

These paragraphs and the article in general raise a number of interesting points for those of us living in the second decade of the 21st century, less than 100 years later. First, Wagner noted how he could easily find .38-40, .44-40 and .45 Colt cartridges, and yet, 20 years after the introduction of the .38 Special cartridge, it was still so rare that small stores which might commonly be called upon to sell ammunition of all kinds did not even stock one box. I could see a similar thing happening today to someone looking for .357 SIG ammunition in little stores in the hills of Idaho. We all know how rare (and expensive) that ammunition is, unless you are associated with a police agency or living in a big city.

Secondly, it is interesting that an experienced hunter and shooter like Wagner thought a 158-gr. RNC .38 Special round was adequate for deer. I would think it a bit light, myself.

Thirdly, the problems associated with ordering goods in general in that era is illustrated. There were no overnight deliveries; no direct shipping to your home; no telephone, internet, or credit card purchases. You placed your order, the storekeeper mailed it in to the distributor, it got shipped by rail to the nearest railhead, picked up, likely by a horse-drawn wagon, and brought in with the rest of the supplies. A slow process, obviously.

Lastly, the migratory lifestyle common to many at the time is illustrated here. Wagner could not count on being in the area long enough to pick up ammunition that might take several weeks to arrive, and did not want to pay for it and risk not being able to show up to claim it. For his part, the storekeeper had no call for .38 Special ammunition, and was accordingly not willing to risk investing in it unless it was paid for in advance, since he might never have another customer who would want it. Obviously no one had asked for it before, for if commonly requested, it would have been on hand. No doubt such a store routinely stocked many items, including axes, wool socks, tobacco, and whiskey—just no .38 Special ammunition.

## The Return of the Single Action?

As discussed, the Smith & Wesson M&P revolver was first released in 1899, and a small number were sold to the U.S. Navy and Army prior to WWI, but no large military orders for this model had been forthcoming during this period.

While the double-action Colt .38 revolver had been greeted by everyone as an improvement over the old .45 caliber Single Action, it soon became apparent that when used as a weapon, rather than merely a badge of office or a remote paper-punching device, the .38 Colt and its cartridge had some serious drawbacks. By 1902, military campaigns had shown that the caliber was a little too small, and by 1906, according to reports such as we have reprinted in the last chapter from the then-pre-eminent periodical *Shooting & Fishing*, most military people wanted a new .45 caliber weapon.

According to the literature I have read, by 1906 the military caliber debate was over for the most part, with the choice being limited to either a .45 caliber double-action revolver or a .45 caliber self-loader. When the Ordnance Department opted definitively for a .45 caliber self-loader, this ended the entire debate.

Of course, individuals continued to write about how important it was to place shots accurately, and how much easier it was to do so with the easy-shooting and light-recoiling .38 caliber revolver. Also, after the flat-tipped bullet we call the wadcutter was developed, many comments appeared about how this bullet would help increase stopping power in the .38 revolver.

Interestingly enough, while the Colt M1873 shooting black powder loadings of the .45 Colt cartridge had proven itself useful against Moslem attackers, there does not seem to have been any real call for its return after it was withdrawn. I say interestingly enough because by the mid-1920s, many thoughtful firearms experts were stating that in their opinion the best self-defense tool was exactly that weapon—with a shorter barrel than 7½ inches, of course. Before you roll your eyes and mutter, remember that a 4¾-inch Single Action in .45 ACP was the duty weapon of General Wainwright, the last Commander of U.S. Forces in the Philippines before it fell to the Japanese. General George Patton carried a .45 Colt-chambered example in WWI and later in WWII as well, and noted firearms expert Jeff Cooper also carried one when he went off to war in 1942, leaving his loaded .38 Super Colt at home with his wife.

## Catalog D-4 (1925): Adding "Made in U.S.A."

308. The cover of S&W factory catalog D-4, issued in February, 1925. Gaston Comeau collection

SPECIAL NOTICE

Our Trade-Marks  SMITH & WESSON

None but genuine Smith & Wesson arms bear these trade-marks - which are registered throughout the world - and we caution the trade about handling imitations of our goods.

Manufacturers of arms in imitation of ours have copied our designs and have used trade-marks bearing a sufficiently close resemblance to ours to mislead unwary purchasers, and have used the name "Smith & Wesson" in such manner as to lead customers who are unable to read the English language to infer that the arms are of our make.

We rely upon the support of our friends and clients in meeting this class of competition, which undoubtedly is equally as dangerous to them as to us.

In the selection of a revolver the first consideration should be quality, precision, security, reliability, and the reputation of the manufacturer - cost is of much less importance - the legend SMITH & WESSON is an absolute guarantee of superiority and confidence.

Be sure, when making a purchase, that the appearance and finish of the arm correspond exactly to the illustration and description found in this catalog; and that it bears our name, SMITH & WESSON engraved in the barrel and our monogram on the frame. After this date the words "Made in U. S. A." will appear on all our arms.

SMITH & WESSON, Inc.,
Springfield, Mass., U. S. A.

February, 1925.

309. The "Special Notice" printed on the inside of the back cover of catalog D-4, issued in February, 1925, announcing that the words "Made in U.S.A." would appear on all S&W arms after this date. Gaston Comeau collection

Two catalogs were issued in 1925 - the small pocket-sized Catalog D-4, shown here, dated February, 1925, and a more complete catalog in a larger format in December. In addition, Catalog D-4 contained the announcement that henceforth all Smith & Wessons would be marked "Made in U.S.A."

310. Right side view of a nickel-plated M&P with carved ivory steer horn grips, once owned by Charles Winstead, a well-known FBI agent who shot John Dillinger in 1934. Note the legend "MADE IN U.S.A." on the frame.

Winstead did not use this aftermarket-engraved example in the Dillinger encounter.

## Target Models Available in Blue Finish Only

S&W offered the target models in blue finish only. The reason for this is as stated in a letter from the factory dated June 17, 1925, signed by the manager of the S&W Service Department, Walter Roper (fig. 311), which explains "All of our target model revolvers are regularly finished in blue, and while we can furnish a target arm finished in nickel, as you specify, this necessitates the removal of the blue finish and refinishing in nickel and adds $5.58 to the regular cost."

I have never seen a nickel finish on a target model, which notwithstanding the extra cost is odd when one considers that target shooters of three decades earlier often had various finishes other than blue applied to their Smith & Wesson No. 3 .44 Russian caliber revolvers. Perhaps it is just a fashion thing, as a nickel-plated target-sighted revolver (with black sights, of course) certainly would be appreciated by me, but then I have a number of adjustable-sighted K-frames which have a factory nickel finish.

SMITH & WESSON
SPRINGFIELD, MASS.

June 17, 1925

Mr. M. E. Wilkerson
c/o Police Department
Indianapolis, Indiana

Dear Sir:

All of our target model revolvers are regularly finished in blue, and while we can furnish a target arm finished in nickel, as you specify, this necessitates the removal of the blue finish and refinishing in nickel and adds $5.58 to the regular cost.

We are very glad to quote you our special police price on our .38 Special Calibre Military & Police Target Model with 6 inch barrel, i. e., $25.70 plus postage charges or $26.02 in all, when finished in blue as regularly furnished; however, if you wish this revolver finished in nickel the cost will be $31.83 plus postage or $32.15 in all.

We shall be glad to receive your order and assure you it will receive our very best attention.

Yours very truly,

SMITH & WESSON, INC.

W. F. Roper

W.F.Roper/T

311 (right). A letter from S&W Service Manager Walter F. Roper dated June 17, 1925, explaining to a police customer why the Target Model M&P was not normally available in nickel finish. Gaston Comeau collection

## A Personalized M&P for the N.Y. State Police

312. Right side view of a blued M&P, serial no. 499424, with 4" barrel and plain pearl grips, which were probably an aftermarket addition. Shipped to E. K. Tryon Co., Philadelphia, Pennsylvania, on August 12, 1926.

Note above and in the inset the engraved legend "A Gigliotti, Geneva, N.Y." on the sideplate. Anthony Gigliotti was a member of the Geneva, N.Y. Police Department from 1925 to 1949. He started as a patrolman and retired as a sergeant.

The wear pattern indicates that this gun was probably carried in an Audley style holster (fig. 742), which was popular with the N.Y. State Police. private collection

## Stressing "Protection" (1927)

An S&W advertisement from 1927 stressing protection is depicted in fig. 313. The six points in tiny type in the center of the text block are well worth reading but are very small, so they are reprinted as follows:

1. *The revolver has a place in the hands of the law-abiding public.*
2. *A thug would rather attack an unarmed pedestrian, motorist or householder than an armed one.*
3. *To prohibit the manufacture and sale of revolvers in order to prevent crime would be equivalent to prohibiting the manufacture and sale of automobiles to put an end to automobile accidents.*
4. *The use of a revolver or any form of concealed weapon in commiting a crime should demand an increased sentence, with no possibility of probation or suspended sentence.*
5. *A swift, sure punishment for crime is the only proper means for reducing crime.*
6. *The 2nd Amendment to the Constitution of the United States means just what it says: "The right of the people to keep and bear arms shall not be infringed."*

*That is why we are proud of the high traditions of public service that have been handed down from generation to generation in this Company. In times of national danger it has enabled us to do our part in protecting the Nation as a whole, and in times of peace it has enabled us to protect the individual.*

*The revolver is an effective instrument in the promotion of law and order. It is an invaluable factor in the conservation of life and property and creates a feeling of security*

# PROTECTION

Thundering tons of traffic come to a stop. The most dangerous crossing in town is robbed of its power to harm the tiniest pedestrian . . . protection at hand . . . what a feeling of security it creates and how well even the youngest sense it . . . how consciously apprehensive we all are in its absence.

The same children, wives, and mothers who need protection on the highways also need protection in the home. There may be only one time in their lives when this need will be urgent, but to be able to fulfill the need at that critical moment is vital.

1. *The revolver has a place in the hands of the law-abiding public.*

2. *A thug would rather attack an unarmed pedestrian, motorist or householder than an armed one.*

3. *To prohibit the manufacture and sale of revolvers in order to prevent crime would be equivalent to prohibiting the manufacture and sale of automobiles to put an end to automobile accidents.*

4. *The use of a revolver or any form of concealed weapon in committing a crime should demand an increased sentence, with no possibility of probation or suspended sentence.*

5. *A swift, sure punishment for crime is the only proper means for reducing crime.*

6. *The 2nd Amendment to the Constitution of the United States means just what it says: "The right of the people to keep and bear arms shall not be infringed."*

*That is why we are proud of the high traditions of public service that have been handed down from generation to generation in this Company. In times of national danger it has enabled us to do our part in protecting the Nation as a whole, and in times of peace it has enabled us to protect the individual.*

The officer at his post and his brother guardians of the peace can furnish protection in only one place at a time. Quick and fearless in responding to emergency calls, the fact remains that the guardian of the law is generally called after the law-breaker has swept upon his prey. Do you want revenge or . . . protection?

Banish fear. The safest, most dependable revolver for home defense. Smith & Wesson originated the safety idea in firearms over 40 years ago. The .32 and .38 caliber S & W Safety make accidental discharge by adult or child impossible.

*Our Descriptive Booklet E may interest you—it will be sent free upon request.*

**SMITH & WESSON**

SPRINGFIELD, MASS., U. S. A.

THE · REVOLVER MANUFACTURER

# A Factory-Marked Series for the St. Louis Police

314. Left and right side views of a 5" barreled square-butt M&P, serial no. 395204, police No. 13. This was one of 100 similarly marked revolvers which were supplied to the St. Louis Police Department in 1927.

Inset, below, is the property mark roll-stamped on the backstrap of this revolver at the factory.

Note the engraved intertwined intials "WA" on the sideplate.

13 (previous page). A Smith & Wesson advertisement rom 1927 on the theme of Protection.

The tiny block of text in the center is reprinted on page 37. Gaston Comeau collection

315. Left side view of another St. Louis P.D. square-butt, 5" M&P revolver, serial no. 531350.

Inset: closeup of the backstrap showing factory roll-stamped police marking, showing police no. 568.

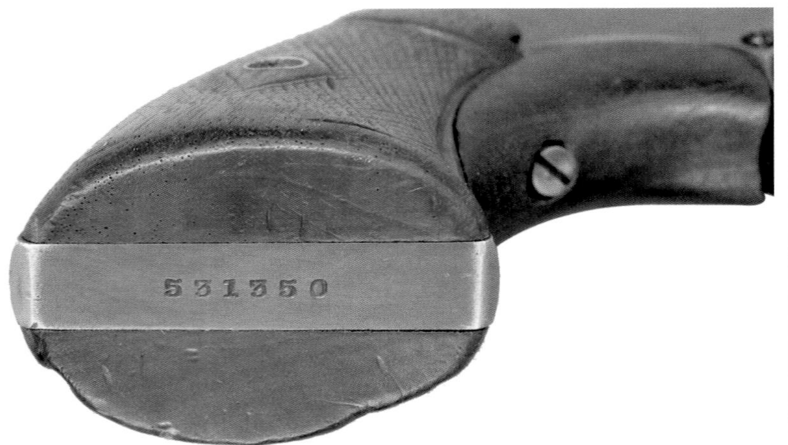


316. Underside closeup of the grip showing serial no, 531350, well-worn grips and added wood grip adapter.

BOARD OF POLICE COMMISSIONERS
CITY OF ST. LOUIS
MISSOURI

MEMBERS:
ALLEN C. ORRICK, PRESIDENT
FRANK L. MAGOON, VICE-PRESIDENT
ARTHUR J. FREUND, PURCHASING MEMBER
HENRY KORTJOHN, JR., TREASURER
VICTOR J. MILLER, MAYOR, EX-OFFICIO MEMBER

E. H. BARTELSMEYER, SECRETA

December 14, 1927.

Mr. W. F. Roper,
Smith & Wesson Mfg. Co.,
Springfield, Mass.

Dear Sir:-

This to acknowledge receipt of shipment of four boxes containing one hundred .38 Smith & Wesson revolvers which you engraved for us.

We have forwarded you today by prepaid express another shipment of four boxes containing one hundred .38 Smith & Wesson 5-inch square revolvers, which kindly engrave on the back of the grip, as follows:

"Police Dep't. St. Louis, Mo."

We also request that you thoroughly grease each gun and wrap same in paper. When you have completed the engraving of this shipment, kindly return by express collect.

Very truly yours,

BOARD OF POLICE COMMISSIONERS,

per E. H. Bartelsmeyer

Secretary.

VW.

317 (left). A letter from the Board of Police Commissioners for the City of St. Louis dated December 14, 1927, acknowledging receipt of 100 .38 M&P revolvers which the S&W factory had roll-stamped with a property mark, and ordering the marking of a further series of 100 square-butt M&Ps with 5" barrels.

Judging from the revolver depicted above, police no. 568, it would seem that this process was repeated a number of times in the course of arming the entire department.

## The S&W Barrel Rifling Process

Under the date of September 22, 1928, the Chief of the St. Louis, Missouri Police Department, Joseph A. Gerk, wrote on Department of Police letterhead to Smith & Wesson asking for details of the barrel rifling process then in use on S&W revolvers, as follows:

> *. . We are seeking further information for use in our Bureau of Forensic Ballistics . . and the particular information we desire is: Are all the grooves in a revolver, or pistol, barrel cut at one time, or is each groove cut separately? If the cutting of each groove is a separate and distinct operation, how many grooves can be cut before the tool used in cutting it must be resharpened; or how often is the tool sharpened to cut one groove?*

S&W received this letter on September 25, and replied as follows in a handwritten note appended to the bottom of Chief Gerk's letter, as follows:

> *We are glad to give to you the information regarding rifling of pistol barrels as requested in your letter of Sept. 22.*
>
> *The rifling is done by a single-bladed tool - which cuts each groove one after another, the barrel being indexed from one groove to another. Several cuts on each groove are necessary to reach the desired depth. A rifling tool will cut the rifling in perhaps 3 or 4 barrels before requiring resharpening. Another operation which should be mentioned is the lappery, which consists of moving a lead plug which has been cast into the barrel, back and forth with an abrasive . . This . . makes the barrel smooth.*

## M&P Popularity Still on the Rise at Decade's End

At the close of the 1920s, no doubt many business and home owners still depended on their top-break .32 or .38 revolvers. As far as law enforcement duty guns were concerned, oddities such as self-loading pistols, from the Colt Model 1903 .32 ACP to .45 Government Models (along with .30 caliber or 9mm Lugers) were occasionally used, but what was encountered most commonly was the Smith & Wesson M&P .38 Special revolver, or a Colt Army Special/Official Police in the same chambering.

Meanwhile, articles in periodicals of the day which dealt with handguns seemed mainly to be interested in the target versions of existing weapons, the fixed sight models apparently being too common to be interesting.

SMITH & WESSON
SPRINGFIELD, MASS.

PLEASE ADDRESS ALL COMMUNICATIONS TO THE COMPANY.

August 21, 1928.

Mr. J. Tenney Spofford,
42 Williams St.,
Malden, Mass.

Dear Sir:

The finest tool for the most fascinating sport and the most trustworthy protection - all in one gun - that's what you get when you buy a modern Smith & Wesson revolver.

Whether you select the record holding 22 Heavy Frame Model for super-accurate target and small game shooting, the Military & Police 38 Special Caliber with its record for both regulation and 300 yard target work and as a field arm or the big equally accurate 44 Special Caliber Military Model - you will find that you will do better shooting than you ever thought possible with a hand gun.

If you want an arm to be carried in the pocket for protection, no gun has ever given the positive, safe, trouble free service supplied by the Safety Hammerless; it is a gun you can trust implicitly.

You will find each of our arms fully described in the catalog we are enclosing but we want you to ask any questions you may wish about either guns or ammunition, as it will be a real pleasure to help you select a revolver.

Very truly yours,

SMITH & WESSON, INC.

Walter F. Roper

W.F.Roper/M.T.

318 (right). The form letter, sent out over the signature of Service Manager Walter F. Roper, to anyone who requested a S&W catalog. This example is dated August 23, 1928. Gaston Comeau collection

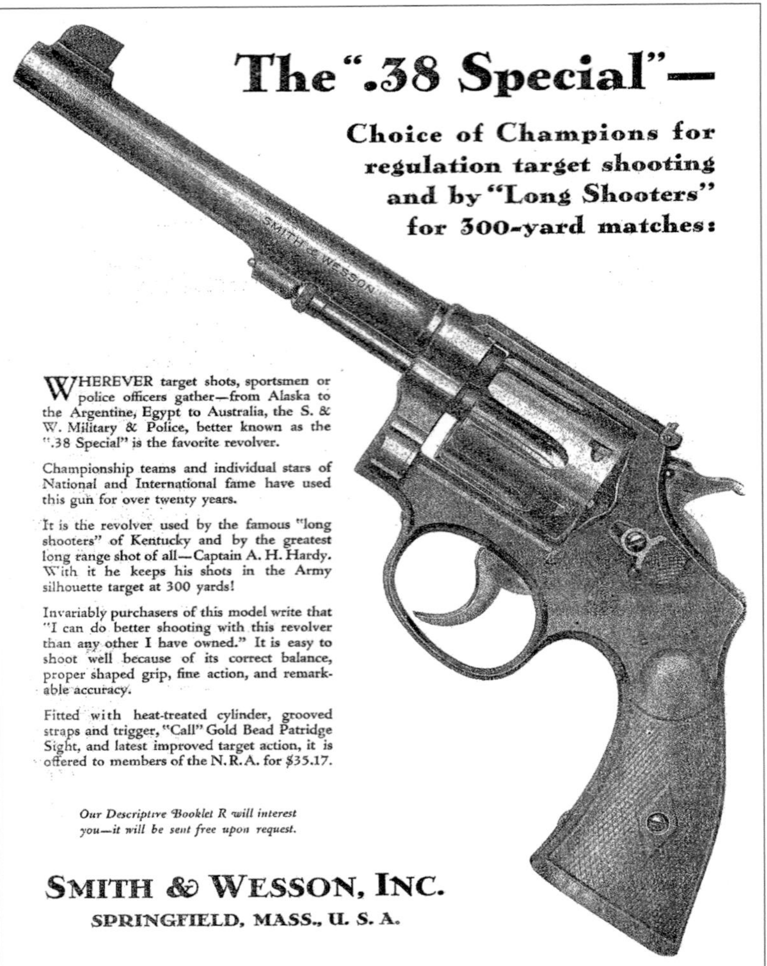
The ".38 Special"—

Choice of Champions for regulation target shooting and by "Long Shooters" for 300-yard matches:

WHEREVER target shots, sportsmen or police officers gather—from Alaska to the Argentine, Egypt to Australia, the S. & W. Military & Police, better known as the ".38 Special" is the favorite revolver.

Championship teams and individual stars of National and International fame have used this gun for over twenty years.

It is the revolver used by the famous "long shooters" of Kentucky and by the greatest long range shot of all—Captain A. H. Hardy. With it he keeps his shots in the Army silhouette target at 300 yards!

Invariably purchasers of this model write that "I can do better shooting with this revolver than any other I have owned." It is easy to shoot well because of its correct balance, proper shaped grip, fine action, and remarkable accuracy.

Fitted with heat-treated cylinder, grooved straps and trigger, "Call" Gold Bead Patridge Sight, and latest improved target action, it is offered to members of the N. R. A. for $35.17.

*Our Descriptive Booklet R will interest you—it will be sent free upon request.*

SMITH & WESSON, INC.
SPRINGFIELD, MASS., U. S. A.

319. An S&W advertisement for the target version of the M&P, aimed at "target shots, sportsmen or police officers", which appeared in the August, 1928 issue of *The American Rifleman*.

320. Pittsburg, Pennsylvania motorcycle officer George H. Wood, shown carrying a square-butt Smith & Wesson M&P in a cross-draw western-style holster. Judging from the length of the holster body, the barrel length is most likely 6 inches.

The "3" on his collar indicates the Third District (Precinct), while the design of the badge on his blouse pocket was adopted in the late 1890s, and continues in use today.

Almost out of sight to the right of his Sam Browne belt buckle can be seen extra .38 Special rounds, carried in exposed loops.

This photograph was taken in 1929, during the period when Pittsburg Police Department officers could carry the revolver of their choice. Most PPD officers chose Colt Army Special or Official Police .38s but, untypical of what is usually seen in period PPD photos, Wood chose an M&P.

Carl Heinrich collection

*Chapter Twenty-Nine*

# Tough Times

## The Stock Market Crash and the Depression

### The "Trickle-Down" Effect

For an event that really involved very few people at the time, the stock market crash of 1929 had a substantial influence over the entire next generation of citizens, both in America and all over the world. While no doubt there were some average citizens who were involved with the stock market, it seems that most people at the time were not. My grandfather on my mother's side was laid off during the Depression, but no one on that side of the family had ever bought a share of stock, and the plunging markets had no direct bearing on them. Most people in the United States at the time were that way, I am certain, but when the Federal Reserve froze credit, as they did, which action many of course attribute to a great extent to the crash, many businesses could not operate. When those businesses stopped operating, it had the typical trickle-down effect so commonly experienced by everyone over the last few years.

But in the early 1930s, the unemployment benefits and various welfare programs that many rely upon today were simply unheard of. When orders for steel dried up and Grandpa Fleming was laid off as a tool and die maker at the St. Louis area steel mill, he had only his savings to fall back upon to support his wife and four children.

While many lay people had the image that a bank kept all of its deposits in a pile in the back room (I used to think this as a kid, so who can blame them), this of course was and is not true. Instead the banks loaned this money out, as well as the capital invested by the bank's stockholders. As long as the loans the bank made were repaid with interest in a timely fashion, all went well, and the bank made enough to cover expenses and pay a dividend to its investors. But when loan payments were not made, and the collateral held fell below the value of the loan, the difference was made up from invested capital first, and then with depositors' money.

Of course, when a man is laid off with nothing coming in (especially if he thinks the bank may not have enough to cover its deposits), he will go down right away and attempt to withdraw all of his money, and keep it at home instead. Multiply this by hundreds of thousands of anxious depositors and you have a bank run, then a closed bank until all the loans could be sold off, a process which often took years and resulted in substantial losses. Many banks failed during this period, and thus the savings, that the frugal or concerned had set aside for just this type of exigency, disappeared. There was also no Federal Deposit Insurance to cover those deposits which the bank could not repay.

### Economics 101: Handguns in a Depression

Handgun manufacturers face two problems in such a depressed economic climate. First, handguns are not considered a necessity by most (and those that already exist last a long time and thus do not need to be regularly replaced, unlike some products), and second, they are rather complicated to make. This means that it takes a long time to train a worker to perform the functions necessary to produce a quality product. Once trained, you want to keep him in your employ, since it will take a lot of time and expense to replace him. Of course there are not a lot of other jobs around for him to go to, so that helps somewhat, but skilled workers are always in greater demand than unskilled ones, so even if that skilled handgun maker has to take a lower-paying job elsewhere, at least he is still working, unlike those with fewer skills.

# The M&P Revolver in the 1930s

It is with these observations in mind that we can discuss the M&P revolver during the 1930s. Please also keep in mind that most economic downturns (depressions or recessions) in U.S. history prior to 1929 typically lasted two to four years. The peculiar nature of the post-1913 world (after the advent of the Federal Reserve) and the post-1932 world, affected as it was by FDR's economic policies which imposed many restrictions on business and extended the Depression, which had begun with the stock market crash of 1929, right into the 1940s.

Roosevelt's "New Deal" took a lot of capital from the market to fund government programs which were not economically productive, but rather advanced a social agenda so beloved by "New Dealers" of the era. It was only with the outbreak of WWII in 1939, when many foreign orders began coming in from Europe, that much of the "New Deal" anti-free market legislation was moderated.

Meanwhile, predictably, over at Smith & Wesson, handgun sales went down, and so did production. For collectors today this makes for rarity, especially in certain models, and wonderful quality in all the examples made during this period. As demand was light, there was plenty of time for the workers to turn out a superior product. The factory had an incentive to make a good product to sell to the discerning consumer, as this kept those oh-so-difficult-to-replace workers from leaving.

Remarkably, however, as discussed below, despite the severely depressed economic conditions which prevailed, both Colt's and Smith & Wesson took it upon themselves to introduce major new models during this period.

## Dealing with Motorized Bandits

As if the effects of the Depression were not enough to worry about, during the late 1920s and early 1930s infamous gangs of robbers roamed around the country, terrorizing and pillaging seemingly at will. These outlaws went from town to town robbing banks, much like the James brothers in the post-Civil War era, only now they were driving (often stolen) automobiles instead of horses, and were thus much more mobile and able to range much farther afield. They also tended to be armed with the best that could be stolen from the local police or National Guard armory. This meant Thompson sub-machine guns, .45 ACP Government Model automatic pistols, and Browning Automatic Rifles. Bulletproof vests, stolen from the police or (rarely but occasionally) purchased, also helped lengthen the odds in favor of the motorized bandit.

The police of the day were mostly localized, with a limited range of authority, and were initially not well enough equipped, trained, or prepared to handle such a threat. It was to take several years for them to get up to speed with improved tactics that would involve settling jurisdictional issues, the development and routine use of mobile police radios, and the availability of more powerful weaponry.

Obviously firearms themselves were not going to solve this problem, but some developments could help. For example, the problem associated with bulletproof vests being worn by criminals was one that better handguns could and did help counter. It was only after a chance high shot from a policeman's .38 revolver hit a certain criminal in the head that his body was discovered to be clad in a bulletproof vest, which had absorbed all the .38 Special rounds aimed at his torso. Since lucky head shots could not be depended upon, the way ahead clearly required ammunition with better penetration.

## The Advent of the Colt .38 Super Auto Pistol

Over at the Colt plant, they rechambered their Government Model for the old .38 Auto cartridge. Everyone had always liked the penetration of the .38 Auto, and now Colt added a little powder to increase velocity, and the resulting ".38 Super" automatic (fig. 20) was officially released on January 3, 1929.

The full-metal-jacket 130-grain slug of the Colt .38 Super, going substantially faster than the .38 Special, gave much greater penetration, and many police departments flocked to it. In my home town area, a local suburban department, the Shrewsbury Police, was the first department in the U.S. to adopt the .38 Super Colt, and in St. Louis itself, the Metropolitan Police organized a "Flying Squad" of motorized officers to handle high-risk, violent offenders, arming them with .38 Super autoloading pistols also (nicely roll-marked with an issue number and letters "St.L. M.P.D.", making them highly sought-after collectors' items today).

## S&W Counters with the .38/44 Heavy Duty

However, coming as it did on the rather touchy Government Model platform, the .38 Super automatic was not the best weapon for many law enforcement officers, and numerous accidents were attributed to its design. The boys at Springfield of course were, with few exceptions, revolver men, and as detailed in Volume I, in April, 1930 Smith & Wesson introduced their .44 caliber N-frame revolver rechambered to shoot high-pressure, high-velocity .38 Special loads that experimenters such as Elmer Keith had come up with, which gave greater penetration. These loads shot a 158-grain bullet (the standard .38 Special bullet weight) at 1,150 fps, rather than the 800 fps of the normal M&P loads. Naturally, since this cartridge could be inserted in the chambers of earlier revolvers, pressures had to be kept low enough to avoid danger, so while not comfortable to shoot in an M&P revolver, the more powerful .38/44 loads would not destroy them.

Of course the Colt .38 Super projectile was hitting 1,300 fps and weighed 130 grains, but it was a fully-jacketed bullet, much more likely to penetrate a ballistic vest of the day than was the 158-grain lead bullet used in the Smith & Wesson .38/44 Heavy Duty. There were some bullet variations which offered a sharper nose to the projectile that were advertised as producing better penetration, particularly in car bodies.

The .38/44 was still not quite in the same league as the .38 Super Colt automatic, but it was a double-action revolver and as such it was safer for the average officer to handle and carry, even though the N-frame Heavy Duty made for a greater burden on his belt than a standard M&P.

# The K-22 Outdoors-Man's Revolver

321. Left side view of an early K-22 Outdoors-Man's revolver, serial no. 634726, with target sights, grooved trigger, and a 6" round barrel. Introduced in 1930, the K-22 was the first .22 caliber S&W built on the K frame of the .38 M&P model.
Dave Terbrueggen collection

It is interesting that S&W president Harold Wesson chose to introduce the new .22 caliber "Outdoors-Man's" revolver in January, 1931, just as the effects of the Depression were sinking so pervasively into the economy at large. But, however straitened the times, this new target model .22 caliber revolver, built on the M&P K-frame, was admirably designed to stand the tests of time and adversity, and the K-22 went on to become one of the most popular and long-lived arms in the entire S&W catalog.

## The Four-Page "K-22" Brochure

SMITH & WESSON
SPRINGFIELD, MASS.

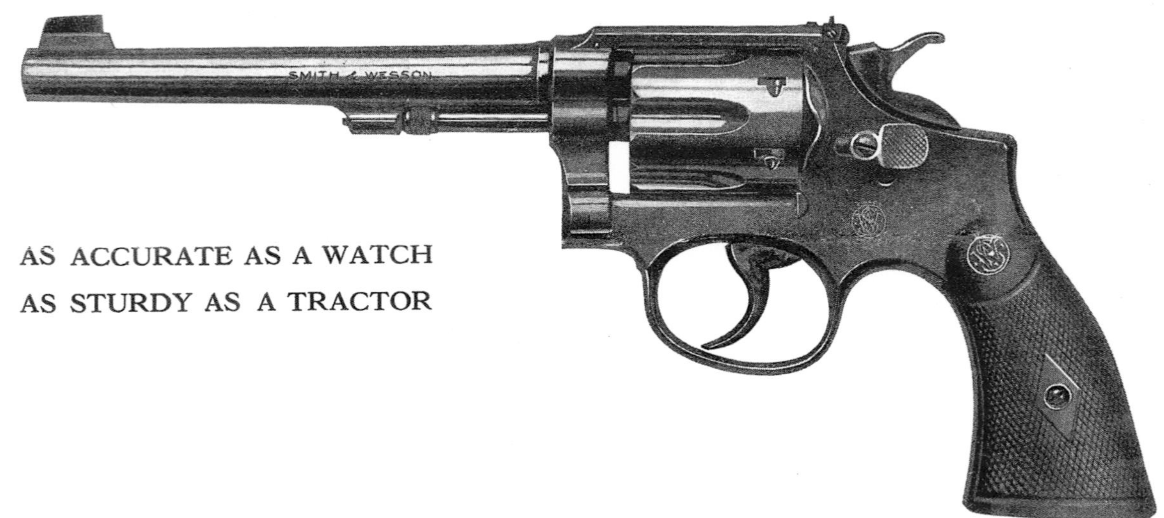


AS ACCURATE AS A WATCH
AS STURDY AS A TRACTOR

# THE "K-22" OUTDOORS-MAN'S REVOLVER

*Introduction* This revolver has been produced to meet the demand of the outdoors man for a full sized, well balanced, correctly sighted revolver of the highest grade; with sufficient weight, and comfortable, well-fitting grip to assure steady holding and perfect let-off, and using the inexpensive but efficient .22 Long Rifle cartridge. It is made with a frame similar to that of our famous .38 Military and Police Target Revolver that has been the choice of the best revolver shots of the world for the past twenty-five years, and it will be found just as efficient, accurate, and durable as that celebrated weapon.

## THE "K-22" OUTDOORS-MAN'S REVOLVER

*Uses* Colonel Townsend Whelen has said of this revolver: "The K-.22 will be found to be the most generally useful hand arm that any outdoors man can own. It deserves to be a constant companion at home and on all kinds of vacation trips at every season of the year. It is excellent for hunting all kinds of small game, for serious target practice, for fancy shooting, or for shooting just for fun. The fisherman will find interesting use for it along the shore; the hunter of big game will find that it will bag grouse and ducks for the pot without expense, noise, or weight, and the vacationist will find much pleasure in its use on all kinds of targets. Trappers and the professional guide will find it to be just the weapon they have been looking for as it is accurate enough to surely hit large animals in the brain or to kill small animals and birds for the pot or trap meat at extreme revolver range, and it will kill all small fur bearing animals without injuring the pelts. It is also particularly indicated for the shooter who desires to train himself to the highest degree of expertness with the revolver because the ammunition is so cheap that the large quantities required to produce results do not represent a serious drain on anyone's resources; the revolver and cartridge are accurate enough to respond to every particle of skill any shooter can develop and it has the fit, feel, balance, pull, and weight of the best large caliber revolvers."

## THE "K-22" OUTDOORS-MAN'S REVOLVER

*Specifications* This revolver is made only on the following specifications:

CALIBER: .22.
FRAME: .38 M. & P. target.
LENGTH OF BARREL: 6 inches only.
NUMBER OF SHOTS: 6.
SIGHTS: Call gold bead front, Patridge square notch rear, adjustable for windage and elevation. Other sights can be fitted on request.
DISTANCE BETWEEN SIGHTS: 7⅛ inches.
TRIGGER PULL: 3 to 4 pounds.
FINISH: Smith & Wesson blue.
STOCKS: Checked Circassian walnut with S. & W. monogram.
STRAPS AND TRIGGER: Grooved to prevent slipping.
WEIGHT: 35 ounces.
CARTRIDGE: Any .22 Long Rifle.
ACCURACY AT 50 YARDS: 1½ inch circle.
ACCURACY LIFE: At least 100,000 rounds.

## THE "K-22" OUTDOORS-MAN'S REVOLVER

*Cylinder* The cylinder of the K-.22 Outdoors-man's Revolver is of heat-treated nickel steel, and presents a very radical improvement in revolver design. The chambers for each cartridge are recessed at the rear so as to accommodate the head and rim of the cartridge, the head being flush with the rear surface of the cylinder, and the rear surface of the cylinder in turn is flush with the frame. This makes the safest cylinder construction and design ever placed upon a revolver. Of necessity the head and rim of all .22 caliber rim fire cartridges must be made very thin, and occasionally this rim or head bursts, and there is an escape of intensely hot gas. At the present time .22 Long Rifle cartridges with greatly increased velocity, pressure, and killing power are being produced, and the demand for them shows that they are with us to stay. In an ordinary revolver a burst head with these Hi-Speed cartridges is a very serious matter, and the shooter's hand is liable to be injured; with the "K-.22" revolver the recessing of the cartridge heads in the cylinder absolutely precludes that the fingers will be cut or burned by escaping gas, or that the adjacent cartridges in the cylinder will be discharged, or that the weapon will be injured in the slightest.

## THE "K-22" OUTDOORS-MAN'S REVOLVER

*Ammunition* The "K-.22" revolver will function satisfactorily with any standard make of .22 Long Rifle cartridge, of either the regular or the high velocity types. Many makes and varieties of this cartridge are sold. Occasionally some one of these may not give especially good results; the remedy is merely to change the make or type.

## THE "K-22" OUTDOORS-MAN'S REVOLVER

*Hi-Speed Cartridges* The "K-.22" Outdoors-man's Revolver will be found to be perfectly safe with the varieties of .22 Long Rifle cartridges having high velocity, flat trajectory and increased killing power, and known as "Hi-Speed," "Super X," etc., and is in our opinion the only revolver at present made which is safe with these cartridges. We expect that the details of the cylinder described above, which make it safe, will later be largely copied in other revolvers. For many uses, particularly in hunting, the use of these high velocity cartridges is a decided advantage. The muzzle velocity given by the ordinary .22 Long Rifle cartridge in a revolver with 6-inch barrel is only 815 feet per second, and complaints are often heard that the killing power is not sufficient for small game. But the muzzle velocity of the "K-.22" revolver with the new high velocity cartridges is approximately 1,000 to 1,100 feet per second, or the same as that of the .22 caliber rifles that have been used successfully for small game hunting for over 50 years.

## THE "K-22" OUTDOORS-MAN'S REVOLVER

*Burnished Chambers* The chamber of an ordinary firearm is reamed, and, if the cross sectioned chamber be examined under a magnifying glass, cross tool marks more or less deep can be seen in the surface. These make extraction difficult and provide lodgment for fouling which will cause rust in time. The chambers of all Smith & Wesson revolvers, including the "K-.22," are reamed rather small and are then burnished longitudinally to exact size, giving a perfectly smooth, mirror-like surface and insuring extremely easy extraction as well as freedom from rust. Fired cartridge cases almost drop from the chambers. Smith & Wesson are the only manufacturers using burnished chambers, and this is the first time in the history of firearms manufacturing that this patented process has been applied to .22 caliber arms.

2 (previous page). Page 1 of the 4-page factory brochure sued to describe the new K-22 Outdoors-Man's .22 cali-r K-frame revolver. Gaston Comeau collection

323. Page 2 of the 4-page brochure on the K-22 Outdoors-Man's revolver. Gaston Comeau collection

## THE "K-22" OUTDOORS-MAN'S REVOLVER

*Sights* Each individual varies in the way he holds and aims a revolver, and each make of ammunition shoots to a slightly different spot. A fixed sight revolver will not consistently shoot correctly enough for any individual to hit very small objects with it except by mere chance. It is extremely important in an outdoors-man's revolver, intended for small game which presents a small target, and also for fine target shooting, that the shooter be able to easily make those small changes in both elevation and windage that are so necessary from time to time to keep the revolver sighted so that the bullets will strike exactly where he aims. The "K-.22" revolver has a rear sight that is adjustable both vertically and laterally with a small screw-driver. The adjusting screws are so threaded that one turn will change the point of impact one inch for each 10 yards of range. Both sights are simple, strong, and sturdy, and there is not the least liability of their getting injured. Their adjustment cannot be moved except intentionally with a screw-driver.

Ordinary revolver sights are so shaped that they soon become bright from holster wear. In aiming outdoors the sun reflects on these bright surfaces, they glisten, accurate aim cannot be taken, and the sights look differently so that they are not lined up the same way, causing a serious change in where the bullet strikes. The sights on the "K-.22" revolver present dull, black, perpendicular surfaces to the eye that do not wear bright, and are not affected by light. One sees a clear-cut, never changing silhouette of the sights. They are the most accurate revolver sights known. The Call front sight has a circular gold bead sunken on its rear surface, and shows up clearly and distinctly against any game or background. Holding a burning match to it for a second blackens it for target shooting, after which a rub with the thumb makes it bright again. If so desired the "K-.22" will be furnished with regular Patridge front sight.

## THE "K-22" OUTDOORS-MAN'S REVOLVER

*Trigger Pull* The trigger pull of this revolver is crisp and sharp without drag or creep and is adjusted at the time of assembling to a pull of between 3 and 4 pounds. The Smith & Wesson system of lock work has as its basis a hammer and trigger treated to produce a notch and engaging point so hard as to remain unchanging and free from wear after years of use; and so efficiently is this carried out that both hammer and trigger are capable of cutting plate glass. The superiority of this system over one in which the parts can be attacked with a common file must be apparent to everyone and need not be enlarged upon. This pull will not change in a lifetime and is exactly right for the best control of the trigger squeeze in both slow and rapid firing.

## THE "K-22" OUTDOORS-MAN'S REVOLVER

*Stocks, Straps, and Trigger* The stocks are of imported Circassian walnut, finely checked, and bear a chrome-plated "S. & W." monogram. The front and rear straps are sharply grooved, as shown in the cut, and the front of the trigger is also grooved. The checking and the grooving cause the hand to stick tight with no tendency to slip, and neither will the forefinger slip on the trigger. It is the most secure and comfortable grip ever placed on a revolver.

Note:—The cut showing the grooved tang is of the .38 M. & P. Target model and is used to show the similarity of the two models. The head space and charge holes are of course for the .38 S. & W. Special Cartridge.

324. Page 3 of the 4-page K-22 Outdoors-Man's revolver brochure. Gaston Comeau collection

## THE "K-22" OUTDOORS-MAN'S REVOLVER

*Revolver Marksmanship* Our many years of experience as revolver manufacturers has taught us that it is extremely rare that anyone becomes a good revolver shot unless he has the assistance of a competent instructor, or unless he studies and follows a good instruction manual. Those who do not master the basic principles of good revolver shooting usually fail utterly in their efforts to shoot exceptionally well. We have prepared an excellent instruction manual entitled, "Burning Powder." With intelligent practice directed by it anyone can quickly become an excellent revolver shot. We will be glad to send this manual without charge to any user of Smith & Wesson revolvers if, in requesting it, they will mention the model and number of their revolver.

## THE "K-22" OUTDOORS-MAN'S REVOLVER

*Care of the Revolver* This is the easiest revolver on the market to care for because, when .22 Long Rifle ammunition of standard American makes, loaded with non-corrosive priming, smokeless powder, and lubricated lead bullets is used exclusively, the bore and chambers absolutely do not have to be cleaned. The fouling of these cartridges is as good a rust preventive as any known oil or grease. All that is necessary is to rub the exterior of the revolver after use with an oily rag to remove perspiration and powder smudges, and to occasionally place a few drops of thin oil on the lock and working parts. When cartridges loaded with Lesmok powder or ungreased bullets are used the revolver should be cared for as directed in our general catalogue.

## THE "K-22" OUTDOORS-MAN'S REVOLVER

*Caution* The extreme dangerous range of the "K-.22" revolver when using the new high velocity ammunition is 1,400 yards, nearly a mile, the barrel being elevated at an angle of 30 degrees.

## THE "K-22" OUTDOORS-MAN'S REVOLVER

*Purchase* We prefer to distribute our revolvers through regular dealers in firearms. If, however, you cannot obtain our arms from your local dealer we will accept your order for the "K-.22" Outdoors-man's Revolver, and give it prompt and careful attention.

Price, $37.25

*Special prices to officers of the Army, Navy, Police Departments, and members of the U. S. R. A. and N. R. A.*

SMITH & WESSON
SPRINGFIELD, MASS.

325. Page 4 of the 4-page factory brochure on the K-22 Outdoors-Man's revolver. Gaston Comeau collection

## Julian Hatcher Greets the New K-22 in *The American Rifleman*

Then-Major Julian S. Hatcher greeted the new arrival in an enthusiastic article published in the March, 1931 issue of *The American Rifleman*, which is excerpted as follows:

### *A New Revolver of Advanced Design*

*. . Most of our readers are well aware of the recent developments in .22 caliber ammunition, all trending toward higher velocity. The past season witnessed the introduction of a new type of .22*

326. Left and right side views of another early K-22 Outdoors-Man's revolver, serial no. 638567.

This arm is fitted with the Wesson grip adapter (fig. 682), which as discussed further in Chapter Thirty-Seven is much more rarely seen in the K-frame size than dimensioned for the larger N-frame. Gaston Comeau collection

*caliber cartridge called Hi-Speed. The ordinary .22 caliber long-rifle cartridge gives a muzzle velocity of 1,100 f.s. in rifles, but the new Hi-Speed ammunition boosts this up to 1,400 f.s. While this is excellent for the rifle-user, it has up to date been of no advantage to the revolver-shooter because the makers of the cartridge recommended it only for use in the highest-grade target rifles.*

*. . With revolvers and single-shot pistols in which the head of the cartridge is out in the open ., . there have been cases in which the cartridge heads have burst, allowing gas to escape and burn the hand of the firer severely. In some cases particles of brass have been blown into the firer's finger.*

*. . Smith & Wesson decided that . . it was possible for a new gun to be made which would be safe for these cartridges . . and the new K-22 Outdoorsman's Revolver has been made in this way. Safety for use with Hi-Speed cartridges has been accomplished by . . counterboring or recessing each chamber at the rear to give space for the head of the cartridge. The cartridge head is thus entirely enclosed in the metal of the cylinder and there is no chance for it to burst, as it is supported all around . .*

*The firing pin of this revolver is also designed for additional safety against punctured primers. The firing pin, instead of being attached to the hammer as is common revolver practice, is built into the frame of the gun in such a way that gas cannot escape past it . .*

*[The] new Outdoorsman's revolver . . is a .22 caliber cartridge revolver on the frame of the famous Smith & Wessen [sic] Military and Police, which is, as all our readers are aware, a full-sized military type of revolver of .38 Special caliber . .*

*The K-22 has a rear sight that is adjustable both vertically and laterally with a small screwdriver which is furnished with the gun. The adjusting screws are so threaded that one turn will change the point of impact 1 inch for each 10 yards of range . .*

*. . the gun is an exact duplicate in size, grip, weight, and appearance of the regular .38 Special*

*Military and Police [although] its main field of usefulness is the shooting that can be done with it on its own account without any thought of the large-caliber guns. In revolver-shooting as a sport there is no need for a large-caliber gun; the greatest sport can be obtained from the .22. For nearly every kind of practical work it is superior to the larger-caliber guns; and, in fact, for almost any use that the outdoorsman may want a revolver for, the .22 will be found to be the ideal caliber . . Moreover, the .22 has a clean bill of health before the public, as it is decidedly not the type of gun that the criminal element would want.*

*For the sportsman, the outdoorsman, the target shot and the plain gunbug, the advent of the K-22 is a most attractive milestone in revolver progress.*

## Illustrating Some Features of the K-22 Oudoors-Man's Revolver

### *No* Hammer Safety On This Model!

327. Right side closeup of K-22 Outdoors-Man's revolver serial no. 638567, with sideplate removed.

Compare with figs. 285 and 287: note the redesigned hand, with pin to contact the hand lever, which along with the hand lever spring is located inside the trigger.

There is no hammer safety on this model.

Gaston Comeau collection

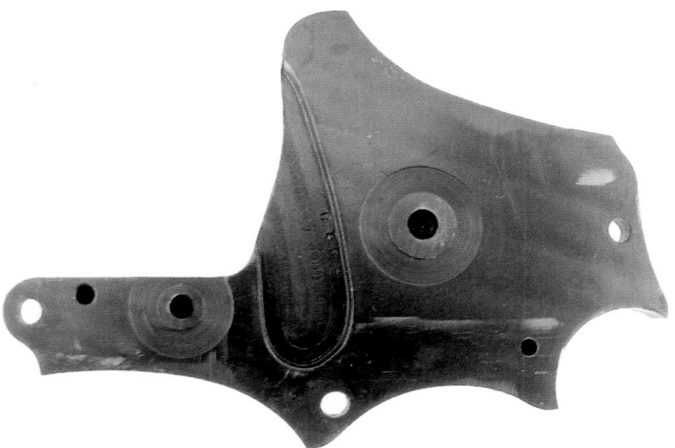

328. Inside view of the sideplate from the K-22 revolver shown at left.

Compare with figs. 286 and 288: note there is no cutout for the "side-swing" hammer safety.

Gaston Comeau collection

329. Closeup of the back of the trigger of the above K-22 Outdoors-Man's revolver, showing marking "REG. U.S. PAT. OFF."

As noted on page 4 of the Magnum brochure (fig. 43), "The glass-hard, tough-cored hammer and trigger . . have been accepted by the United States Patent Office as a *recognized trade-mark.*" Gaston Comeau collection

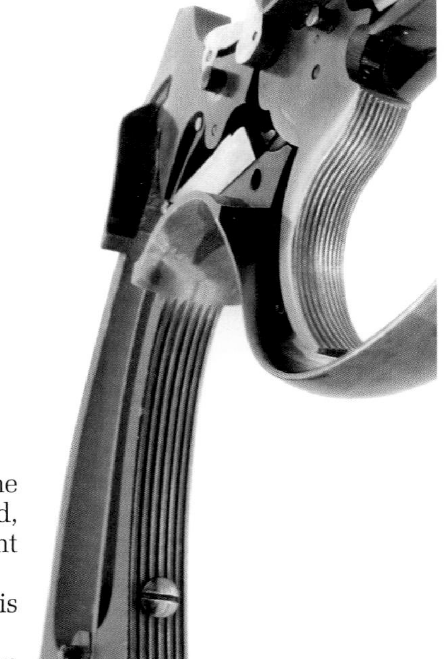

330 (right). Closeup of the K-22 with grips removed, showing the grooved front strap and trigger.

The back grip strap is similarly grooved.

Gaston Comeau collection

331. Rear closeup of the K-22 cylinder, made of heat-treated nickel steel, showing serial number.

Note the recesses around each chamber, described in the brochure (fig. 223) "so as to accommodate the head and rim of the cartridge". As noted, this was an especially important safety feature when shooting high-speed rimfire cartridges. Gaston Comeau collection

332. Closeup of the K-22 square blade front sight, fitted with the optional flush-mounted Call gold bead. Gaston Comeau collection

## A Commercial K-22 with Service Sights, as Made for the Coast Guard

333. Left and right side views of a prewar commercial K-22, serial no. 657626, fitted with standard service sights, a 6" barrel, and a lanyard swivel.

Identical to the series of 25 shipped to the U.S. Coast Guard in Curtis Bay, Maryland in 1935, this is one of five commercial examples produced, and the only one known to exist today.

Inset. right: a portion of the bottom of the red shipping box, showing serial number and notation "Reg" (for fixed sights). Jim Fisher collection

## The Little-Known Earlier History of the K-22

Interestingly, it appears that an attempt had been made to introduce an initial version of a Smith & Wesson .22 caliber revolver built on the M&P frame considerably earlier than 1931, although for the reasons described below, it was not a success.

Walter F. Roper, later well known for the excellent custom pistol and revolver grips his company manufactured and sold, was for some years the Service Manager at Smith & Wesson. He was also an expert shooter, and the author of several well-received books and articles. Mr. Roper discussed the little-known early history of the K-22 revolver in an article published in the May, 1944 issue of *The American Rifleman* and in at least one of his books. These make interesting reading for several reasons.

First, excerpts from his 1944 *Rifleman* article, titled "The Old and the New", are as follows:

> *. . This is the story of . . how, for some twenty years, one little mistake deprived handgunners of the heavy-frame .22 revolver.*
>
> *Back in 1920 . . we [had] the "Any Revolver" Match which was usually shot with a .22 caliber gun. The only guns available then were the rather light Colt Police Positive and the Smith & Wesson .22-32. Using these guns, shooters had difficulty in making scores equal to those possible with the heavier guns shooting the .38 Special cartridge. In spite of this . . the .22 Long Rifle cartridge was still believed to be tops in accuracy and the demand became general for a.38 size gun shooting the .22 cartridge.*
>
> *At that time the writer became connected with Smith & Wesson and one of the first things I remember there was being handed what looked like a round-butt Model K target revolver. My Chief, Mr. David Reddie, remarked, "Sometime you might like to try this gun. Maybe you can discover why it doesn't shoot as it should." By the time he had finished that remark, I had discovered that the gun was not a .38 but a .22 on the .38 Military and Police frame; in other words, exactly the gun I, and many other shooters, had been wanting! Yes, there it was, the first heavy-frame .22 caliber revolver. And except for the round butt, the plain cylinder—and one other thing—it was exactly like the K-22, now famous but destined to be only a dream for many years!*
>
> *Mr. Reddie then proceeded to tell me the history of the gun. Some ten years earlier—about 1910 or 1912—a number of Army officers had persuaded Smith & Wesson to build a small lot of these .22 caliber guns on the .38 Military and Police frame . . the guns were made and sent to the officers and, regardless of what happened later, I'll bet they never saw anything in the handgun line more beautiful, judging from the sample I tried.*
>
> *Reports on the shooting qualities of the gun, however, were not so good. Flyers were frequent. Finally, as I remember the story, Smith & Wesson had the guns returned and, except for the sample Mr. Reddie gave me, they were all destroyed.*
>
> *. . Well, to me, that gun seemed the most beautiful revolver I had ever seen! But it had to be scrapped! Not without reason, either. I proved that to my own satisfaction by shooting it. It threw too many flyers to be a first-class target revolver. But whether those flyers were due to the long jump between cylinder and barrel, or to some other cause I wasn't sure.*
>
> *. . one day, while cleaning the gun, I noticed that the cleaning rod seemed to revolve too fast. Why? I made some measurements and found that the rifling in that .22-38 barrel was one turn in ten inches!*
>
> *How it came to be made that way I have no idea. I knew, and certainly Smith & Wesson knew, that one turn in about sixteen inches was correct for the .22 Long Rifle bullet, yet the gun was made with one turn in ten inches. I have no doubt whatever that the ten-inch twist was the cause of the flyers that caused the abandonment of an otherwise fine gun—the first of the heavy-frame .22s.*
>
> *The K-22, which came out some eleven years later, was rifled with a twist of one in fifteen inches. At that time, however, the Straight Line Pistol was being developed and the heavy-frame .22 revolver was laid aside again. Not until the early '30s was this type of revolver again considered and the present K-22 made . .*

It is interesting to compare this story, where the reason for the wrong rifling twist was, in Mr. Roper's words,"probably entirely unknown to the officials of the concern", with the following excerpts from his book *Pistol and Revolver Shooting,* which first appeared one year later in 1945. These make it clear that the one-in-ten twist was indeed standard in the .22-32 revolver, which had been available since 1911:

> *. . A usual experience with the .22-32 of that time was to make a number of very satisfactory, closely grouped shots, and then have the next, although apparently as perfectly held and let off as the others, print anywhere from 3 to 6 inches away*

*from the group made by the previous shots. Just as now, however, shooters were experimenters . . My own experiment was a new regulation-weight barrel, rifled to rotate the bullet once in 16 inches instead of the one turn in 10 inches that was then standard in the .22-32. This barrel eliminated the very wide shots thrown by the regular gun, but the light weight of the gun made it difficult to hold well . .*

*Even before 1914 the need for a larger and heavier .22 revolver was recognized . . and a forerunner of the S&W K-22 had already been built . . This old gun looked exactly like the present-day K-22 except for the round butt.*

*This early K-22 did not produce the accuracy hoped for [and] the fact that the barrel was rifled to spin the bullet one turn in 10 inches probably had much to do with it . . the different rifling—one turn in 15 inches—was, I believe, responsible for most of the improvement over the old gun. It is interesting to find . . that Smith & Wesson made a real effort many years before the modern heavier-frame .22 revolver became an established fact, to produce just such a gun . .*

334 (right). Page 12 from the 1919 S&W catalog, depicting and describing the .22-32 revolver, which had been available since 1911 with 1-in-10 rifling.

Considered a heavyweight in its day, the .22-32 weighed 22¾ oz., while the new K-22 Outdoors-Man's revolver weighed 35 oz. Gaston Comeau collection

## 22/32 Heavy Frame Target Model

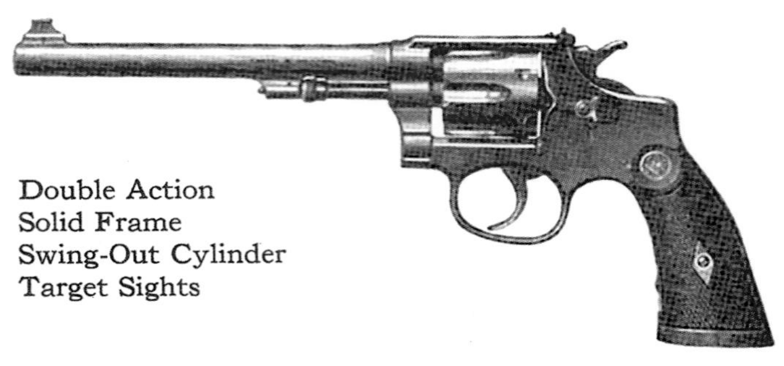

Double Action
Solid Frame
Swing-Out Cylinder
Target Sights

### Description

| | |
|---|---|
| Calibre | .22 |
| Length of Barrel | 6 inches |
| Length over all | 10½ inches |
| Finish | Blued |
| Stock | Circassian Walnut, Checked |
| Weight | 22¾ ounces |
| Ammunition | .22 Short, Long Smith & Wesson and Long Rifle Cartridges<br>22 Ex Long<br>22 NRA Long Rifle |
| Number of Shots | Six |

This arm is regularly furnished in Blued Finish only; if desired in Nickel Finish it can be supplied at additional cost.

Page 12

# Differing Philosophies - Colt's versus S&W

Historically, Colt revolvers competed with comparable Smith & Wessons for the same market share, and it is interesting to compare the widely diverging philosophies that governed the design and manufacture of the two companies' products. Now, as then, the internal moving parts in Smith & Wesson revolvers are case-hardened to prevent excessive wear, thus making these components stay within specification longer. It appears that this process was first described in detail in the 1931 75th Anniversary catalog, as follows:

*. . In all Smith & Wesson arms the hammer notch and trigger point are glass hard. This non-wearing surface is responsible for the crisp, unchanging trigger pull for which Smith & Wesson arms are noted.*

*To obtain this action and avoid the brittleness of hardened tool steel we convert the surface of the low carbon manganese steel from which the hammer and trigger are made into glass hard high carbon steel by the process of case hardening.*

Conversely, in a Colt revolver, the components are intentionally softer and more malleable. As Colt representative J. Henry Fitzgerald famously said, "I can take any Colt revolver and make it pass new inspection." In a Colt revolver a worn hand, for example, can be elongated by judiciously tapping it with a metalworking hammer to restore proper timing, whereas hammering a hardened Smith & Wesson part will simply shatter it.

On the flip side, of course, the glass-hard Smith & Wesson components are likely to stand up much longer in use than their softer Colt counterparts. Their only potential disadvantage is that once they do become worn, field repairs, other than replacement, are out of the question.

## Two Factory Takes on S&W Trigger Pull Adjustment

Interestingly, the 1931 S&W catalog goes on to open the door on an ill-advised permissiveness regarding the issue of trigger pull adjustment, as follows:

> *. . Adjustment of the trigger pull in a Smith & Wesson can only be made with a very fine oil or india stone and this should never be attempted, except by an expert gunsmith or preferably by sending the arm to us for the change desired.*

Factory approval of this owner-mandated method of, and responsibility for, trigger pull adjustment proved to be very short-lived, which the 1935 80th Anniversary catalog explicitly reversed, as follows:

> *. . In obtaining the desired weight of trigger pull it is done at our plant by matching hammers and triggers; we do not stone as this will not give the quality of pull we demand. We make no charge for such adjustments on arms sent in to us.*

# Adding the 2" Barrel Length

The standard barrel lengths available for the M&P during the period were initially 4, 5, and 6 inches. Excerpts from *Smith & Wesson Hand Guns* by McHenry and Roper provide some interesting background to the introduction of the 2" barrel length in Smith & Wesson revolvers, as follows:

> *In the early nineteen-twenties, [Colt] began to produce a short-barreled revolver at the behest of the Post Office Department. A gun was needed for railway service men which would be convenient for pocket carrying but husky enough to qualify as a man-stopper. The Colt weapon designed to meet these specifications had a two-inch barrel and . . was known as the "Bankers' Special". A little later, snub-barreled Colt Police Positive Specials were turned out under the nomenclature of "Detective Special".*
>
> *Considerable demonstrating—much of it by the well known J. R. [sic] Fitzgerald . . was needed to convince the sleuths that accurate shooting could be done with such stubby affairs. "Fitz" insisted that his prospects do the shooting and soon convinced them that the short barrel was not fatal to accuracy . .*

Published accounts differ as to just when Smith & Wesson followed suit. John Henwood states that "The 2-inch barrel was introduced during 1933", while McHenry and Roper state as follows:

> *Smith & Wesson did not succumb to the fad for short-barreled revolvers until 1936, when the firm brought out what was termed the "S&W .38/32 2"", later christened the "Terrier" which was simply the round butt Regulation Police Model with a two-inch barrel [in caliber .38 S&W] . . The corporation produced its round butt .38 Military & Police model with a two-inch barrel in 1938.*

However, according to Mike Pacella, an advanced collector of Smith & Wessons and prewar 2" K-frame models in particular, the round-butt 2" M&P first appeared in the 1934 price list, in blue or nickel finish, with hard rubber grips only. The earliest known shipping date was for serial no. 626xxx, shipped in January, 1934.

Interestingly, the 2" M&P with the earliest known serial number, no. 597812, was not shipped until September, 1935, indicating right from the outset that the sequence of serial numbers on the prewar 2" model is no guarantee of shipping order. The earliest known square-butt 2" M&P was shipped in September, 1937.

## Some Prewar "Snubbie" Statistics

Mike Pacella, who specializes in prewar 2" M&Ps, has gathered some interesting statistical information about the relative popularity of the features offered on the 2" M&P model, as follows:

round butt blue: . . . . . . . . . 71%
round butt nickel: . . . . . . . . . 24%
square butt blue: . . . . . . . . . . 3%
square butt nickel: . . . . . . . . . 2%

Of the round butt guns, only 29% were ordered with walnut grips, the remainder with hard rubber.

335. Left and right side views of two typical early M&P revolvers with 2" barrels.

Above: blued finish; below: nickel finish. Both are the more popular round butt models, fitted with hard rubber grips. Mike Pacella collection

336 (left). Right side view of a unique K-22 revolver with 2" barrel and fixed sights, owned by Col. Rex Applegate, the noted close-quarter battle trainer and author.

The factory letter states that this "K-22 Outdoorsman Special Production Variation", serial no. 657624, was originally put in the Smith & Wesson Office showcase on January 17, 1944, then removed and the serial number was assigned and it was shipped on a no charge basis under the Smith & Wesson memo accounts to Lt. Col. Rex Applegate, Laredo, TX, on June 25, 1946.

Jim Fisher collection

## The Advent of the .357 Magnum

Early in 1935, after a few years of production of the fixed-sight .38/44 Heavy Duty (fig. 23) and its adjustably-sighted counterpart, the Outdoorsman (figs. 28 and 29), the .357 Magnum appeared (fig. 38). This story is fully discussed in Volume I of this series.

All of the previous comparisons became moot when the .357 Magnum was released, and more critically the sway of the motorized bandits was countered with better radios, autos, and jurisdictional resolutions, finally coming to a somewhat loud end in 1938 with the destruction of the Brady Gang by the FBI in a Maine shootout (Volume I front endpaper and pages 78 - 80). Famed FBI Agent Walter Walsh used his Smith & Wesson .357 Magnum to kill one of the bandits, after he was shot in the chest at a range of two to three feet. He had to shoot through a glass panel in a door to do it, so maybe that extra penetration helped out after all.

## The M&P (and Its Colt Counterpart) Soldier On

Sales of the fixed-sight .38/44 Heavy Duty, typically in five-inch but also available both longer and in four-inch barreled versions, along with the target-sighted variation known as the Outdoorsman, no doubt cut into the sales of the M&P revolver—perhaps not as much as might appear at first blush since a person buying one very likely already had an M&P (or a comparable medium-frame Colt) and would not have needed another one, whereas the Heavy Duty (or Outdoorsman) was seen as an improvement, and thus the buyer was willing to accept the extra weight and expense in exchange for more powerful performance.

I have little doubt that many of the individual owners of such weapons who bought and carried them (as opposed to bulk agency purchases) rapidly found that they disliked the heavy drag on their belts and, since the likelihood of actually confronting a motorized, bulletproof-vest-wearing bandit was pretty low, they went back to their M&P revolvers. You have to be pretty dedicated and have a pretty seriously-considered need to pack your Heavy Duty seven days a week, ten to twelve hours a day. Try as I might to convince myself that a .38 caliber N-frame four-inch was a good carry gun, I find myself always asking myself, is it really better than a K-frame, which is both lighter to carry and more nimble in my hand as I draw it from my holster to engage a target? That extra bulk and the extra seven or so ounces of weight have always created a problem for me, and likely it was the same for a lot of shooters who acquired a .38/44 Heavy Duty in the 1930s.

Thus, as the '30s went on, the medium-frame Colt Army Special (introduced in 1908 and renamed the Official Police in 1927) and the M&P continued to compete for the police market, mostly in .38 Special, although occasionally in .32-20. Some people liked the .32-20 for its penetration (better for shooting through moonshiners' barrels, according to one officer of the period), and others liked the light felt recoil. An old Bureau of Investigation friend of mine carried such a four-inch model during the 1920s while he was with the Bureau. He continued to do so well into the mid-1970s, in fact.

337. Left side view of a much-traveled M&P, serial no. 654498, which was originally shipped as a standard 4"-barreled revolver to Powell & Clement Co., Cincinnati, Ohio on October 25, 1935 for delivery to the Kentucky Highway Patrol. This was the model first issued to their road patrol units. The KHP became the Kentucky State Police in 1948.

In 1951 this revolver was returned to Smith & Wesson and fitted with a 2" barrel salvaged from serial no. C 104279 (which had been shipped by the factory directly to the KSP on June 20, 1950 and later damaged). No. 654498 was then refinished, marked with a star after the original serial number, and returned to duty, where it was carried by a plain-clothes KSP arson investigator.

The original KSP rack number "20" is electro-pencilled on the butt, and this gun came with the Tyler 'T' grip when it was later sold as surplus. private collection

Fit and finish were at the height of quality for all Smith & Wesson products, including the M&P, during the 1930s. Design features remained rather static, which makes sense, for why change something that works well; and with no incentive to cut hand labor, many of the improvements that later helped so dramatically to control costs and increase production were not yet envisaged. Therefore the M&Ps that had come off the line as the Jazz era ended were pretty much the same as the ones that greeted the arrival of WWII.

# The Rare Prewar K-32

John Henwood records the story of the prewar K-32 as follows:

> *In 1938 Smith & Wesson produced another new target revolver, the K-32. Identical to the .38 Hand Ejector Target Model, it was chambered for the .32 S&W Long cartridge. Manufactured for only two years, just 94 were sold. This model is now known to collectors and the "K-32 First Model", and was furnished with square butt, blue finish, and a 6-inch barrel. Some (if not all) were furnished with the same new [micrometer] rear sight used on the Second Model K-22. Presumably at least the later guns would have been furnished with the new*

338. Right side view of the rare prewar K-32 First Model, serial no. 677296, which was introduced on April 15, 1938 and manufactured until 1940. Only 94 of these were sold before the war. Gaston Comeau collection

*Magna stocks. K-32s were numbered in the .38 Hand Ejector serial number block between about no. 690000 and 1000000.*

*The K-32 was intended to appeal to the competitive target shooter, offering reduced recoil, leading to faster recovery time between shots, when compared to the .38 Special used in the K-38. The .32 caliber wadcutter bullet proved to be considerably more affected by wind than the heavier .38 wadcutter. Practically speaking, this restricted its use to indoor ranges, and in those depression days few shooters could afford the luxury of one centerfire competition revolver for outdoor use, and another for use indoors. The K-32 was revived following World War II [see Chapter Thirty-One], but it was soon discontinued again.*

339 (right). The S&W factory letter dated May 18, 1981 concerning K-32 First Model serial no. 677296, which was shipped to a well-known Toronto hardware concern in 1941. Gaston Comeau collection

**Smith & Wesson**
a BANGOR PUNTA Company

May 18, 1981

Gaston Comeau

Dear Gaston:

We received your inquiry of recent date in reference to a Smith & Wesson K-32 revolver. This model was originally introduced during the 1930's as a special order target revolver manufactured on a .38 Military & Police frame.

These early K-32s are officially known as the K-32 First Model. They were introduced by the company on April 15, 1938, and manufactured until 1940. The demand for this revolver was extremely small and only ninety-four units were completed. It was temporarily discontinued to allow the factory to start full war-time production.

Smith & Wesson reintroduced its famous K target series at the close of World War II. Included in this group was a newly designed K-32 called the K-32 Masterpiece.

Production on the new K-32 Masterpiece began on July 22, 1947, at serial number K2137. This revolver differed from the First Model in that it incorporated a ribbed barrel, micrometer adjustable rear sight, and a new shorter action.

The K-32, or Model 16 as it was later known, was produced by Smith & Wesson until June, 1973. At that time it was officially discontinued and a total of only 3630 were manufactur

Research of company records indicate serial number 677296 to be a K32 revolver which was shipped from our factory on February 6, 1941, to Aikenhead Hardware Company of Toronto, Canada. The box you described is correct for this model.

We hope the information we have provided will interest you.

Sincerely,

SMITH & WESSON

R. G. Jinks

R. G. Jinks
Services Operation Manager
Historian

RGJ/gmc

2100 Roosevelt Avenue
Springfield, Massachusetts 01101 USA
Telephone (413) 781-8300
TELEX 95-5465. CABLE-WESSON SPM

340. Prewar First Model K-32 serial no. 677296 in its original box with all accessories—bore brush, mop, screwdriver, tissue paper, instruction sheet, etc.—just as it was shipped.

As further discussed in Chapter Forty-Three, this is the distinctive "patent" or "display" box with hinged lid and beveled front corners. Made of cardboard covered with maroon paper, and marked at the bottom of the lid "This Container Patented Dec. 28, 1920".

Gaston Comeau collection

*Chapter Thirty*

# The M&P Goes to War

As we have seen, comparatively very few Smith & Wesson Military & Police revolvers had been adopted by U.S. military organizations prior to 1940. As discussed in this chapter, it was Adolf Hitler who really put the "Military" in the M&P name.

# The S&W 9mm Light Rifle

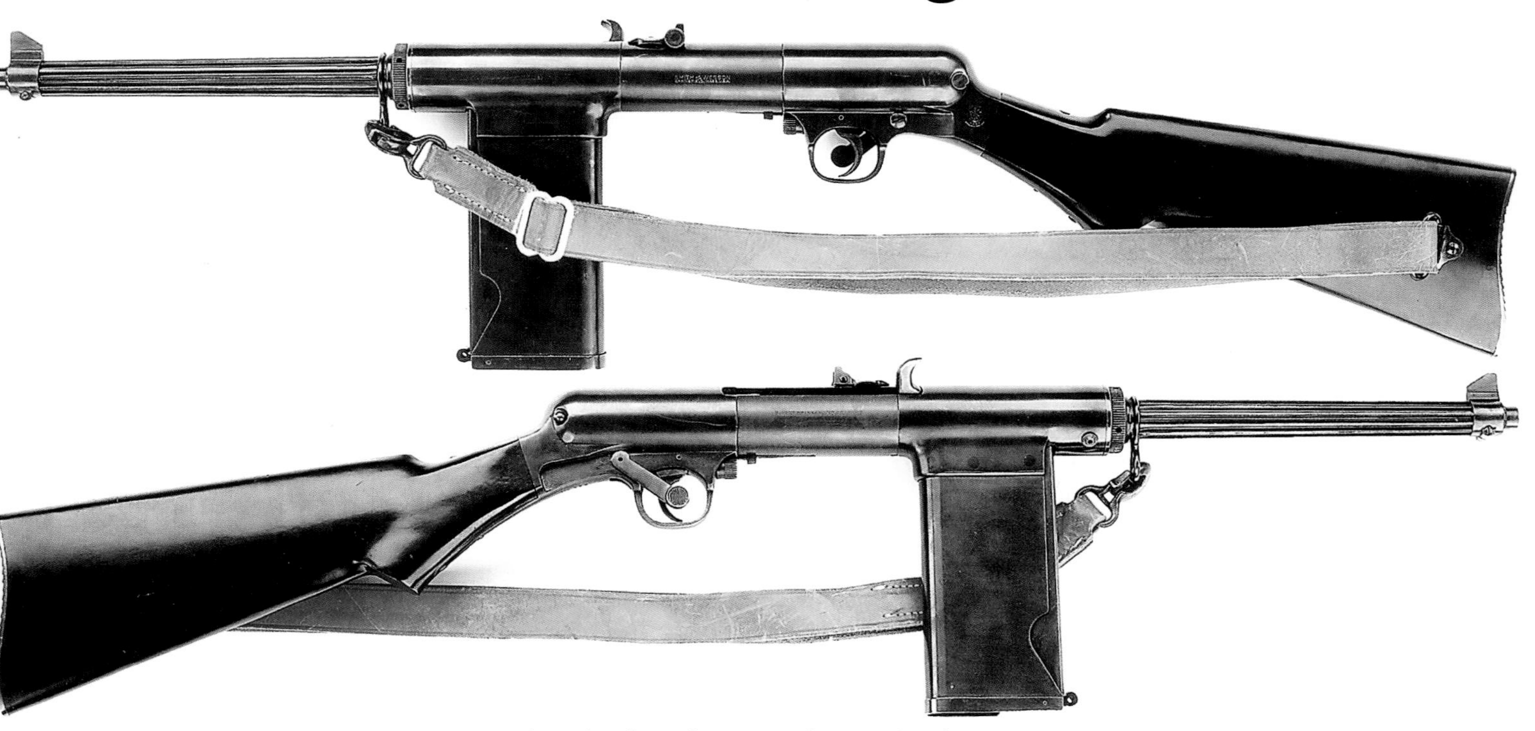

341. Left and right side views of 9mm Smith & Wesson Light Rifle serial no. 541, shown fitted with a 20-round magazine and a genuine S&W tan leather sling.
courtesy George Hall

## The Accepted Version of the Story

An excerpt from the text which appeared on a 1995 Smith & Wesson calendar briefly explains the history of the Smith & Wesson 9mm Light Rifle as it has generally become accepted:

*The Depression found Smith & Wesson with plummeting sales and on the edge of bankruptcy. When the demand for firearms increased again in 1939, S&W agreed to produce a military light rifle in 9mm for the British Government. The development of this rifle was assigned to S&W plant superinten-*

342. Left side closeup of the Smith & Wesson Light Rifle, showing company identification stamped on the side of the receiver tube.
Note the grooved trigger. courtesy Charles Kramer

*dent E. S. Pomeroy. In 1940 they supplied the British Government with samples for testing. Called the 1940 9mm Light Rifle, it was a complete failure, and so embarrassed its designer that Mr. Pomeroy retired. S&W firearms designer Joe Norman took on the challenge, but in the interim the British lost interest . .*

Thus, the story goes, 1940 found Smith & Wesson with a worthless rifle and owing the British a million dollars which had been advanced in prepaid development funds. (This may not sound like much now, but it is the equivalent of $15-25 million in today's money.) Added to the other problems of failing sales which the Depression had generated, this was a crushing debt which the company had little or no hope of repaying.

# Some Recently Discovered Facts

Ian Patrick, a voluntary researcher at the Royal Armouries Library in Leeds, has recently compiled a chronology of events taken from actual surviving documents, which sheds new light on the Light Rifle program from the British standpoint. Some of the interesting facts he has uncovered are excerpted as follows:

First, according to Roy Jinks' *History of Smith & Wesson*, the design of the Light Rifle was completed on June 28, 1939. Then, according to Ordnance Board Proceeding No. 3678, the president of the American Equities Corporation, representing Smith & Wesson, wrote to the U.K. military attaché in Washington on October 24, 1939, offering this new weapon for possible British military use. This seems to be the first the British had heard of the Light Rifle, which they referred to as the "Smith & Wesson 9mm Self-Loading Carbine", and there is no evidence that it was designed at the request of the British.

On November 12, 1939 the Ordnance Board was advised of the offer from Smith & Wesson, and requested full particulars, including drawings, and a sample carbine for examination.

Meanwhile, a trial of the Light Rifle, fitted with its original wooden stock, was held at Aberdeen Proving Ground in November, 1939. The results were described as inconclusive, but it was requested that a .45 ACP caliber version be submitted for trial.

Then, samples having been sent from the factory and received in England, a trial of both a semi-automatic and a selective-fire version of the S&W 9mm carbine was carried out in Britain on May 20, 1940, using Winchester (U.S.) and ICI (British) ammunition. Functioning, on the whole, was good, and the carbines were considered to have passed this initial acceptance test.

The report did not mention any breakages, but stated that two failures to feed had occurred, caused by a weak magazine spring. The letter covering the reports stated that this weakness had been pointed out to Mr. Wesson, indicating the possibility that Harold Wesson himself had attended these trials.

In addition, the fact that the chamber could not be inspected by the firer was pointed out, and magazine changing was described as "not very simple". The cyclic rate on full-auto fire was 1,200 rpm, which was considered too high.

In late May, 1940 a contract for 4,000 fully-automatic S&W Light Rifles was apparently placed by the Swedish government, with the initial 2,000 to be delivered by July 18, 1940, and the balance by October. No evidence exists that any deliveries were made against this contract.

On June 27, 1940, the British placed a production order with Smith & Wesson for 22,000 Light Rifles at a cost of $85 each. This seems compatible with the one million dollar advance which Jinks' *History of Smith & Wesson* indicates was made by the British government.

On August 2, 1940 the British Director of Artillery (DofA) stipulated that the first 2,000 of the ordered Light Rifles were to be the semi-automatic version, and from serial no. 2001 on the rest would be selective-fire. Parts to convert the semi-automatic carbines to selective-fire would follow.

On August 12 the Admiralty (Royal Navy) ordered 2,000 "S&W self-loading carbines", apparently from the Ministry of Supply.

## The Detachable "Butt, Mk. II"

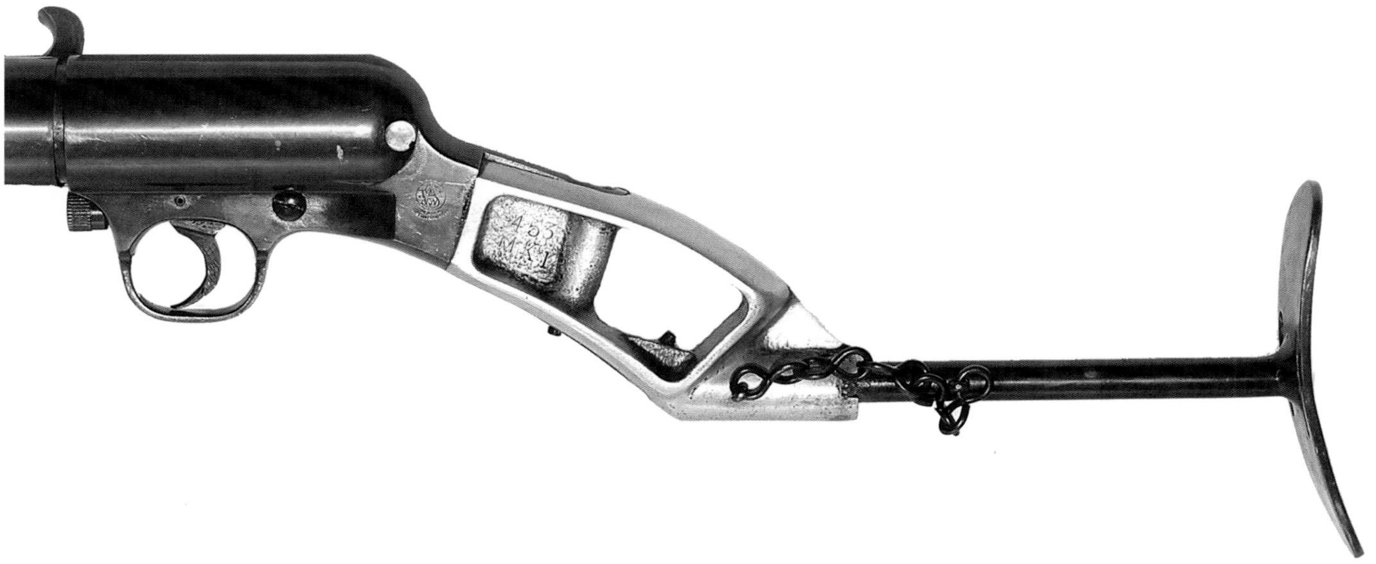

343. Left side closeup of a Smith & Wesson Light Rifle fitted with the British-designed detachable "Butt, Mk, II", developed for paratroop use. courtesy Richard Jones

On August 23, 1940 the Armaments Design Department (ADD) commenced design of an alternative butt for the carbine. Called the "Butt Mk. II", this consisted of a cast aluminum pistol grip, into which a detachable steel tube ending in a butt plate was fitted.

While not a folding stock, this was apparently designed in accordance with a requirement for a detachable butt, associated with the formation of British paratroop forces.

## Patenting the Light Rifle

### U.S. Patent No. 2,213,348

The first of a total of three U.S. patents, no. 2,213,348, was granted to E. S. Pomeroy and assigned to Smith & Wesson on September 3, 1940, titled "Fire Control Mechanism for Firearms". The following excerpts from the disclosure make it clear that right from the outset, the arm was intended to be capable of selective full- and semi-automatic fire:

> *This invention relates to the control mechanism of automatic firearms and more particularly to trig-*

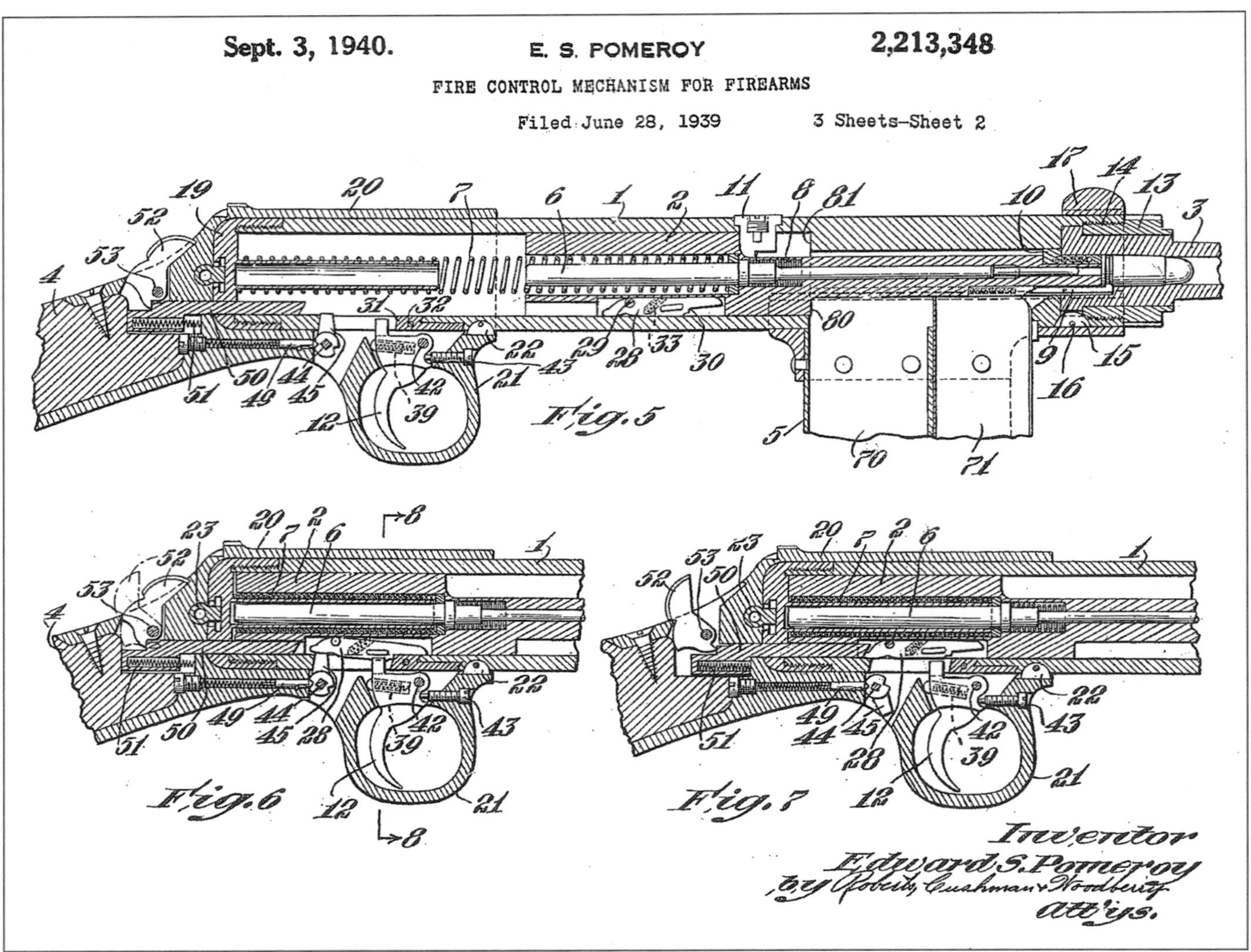


344. Sheet 2 of 3 sheets of drawings from the first Light Rifle patent, no. 2,213,348, granted to E. S. Pomeroy and assigned to Smith & Wesson on September 3, 1940.

The selective-fire control lever is shown as patent no. 52.

U.S. Patent Office

*ger mechanism and means for rendering firearms either full-automatic or semi-automatic . .*

*. . For full-automatic operation the firearm is provided with a member* **50** *which slides forwardly and rearwardly immediately behind the cocked position of the sear* **28**, *the member being normally held in retracted position by means of a spring* **51** *but being movable to forward operative position by means of a control member* **52** *pivoted in a recess in the frame* **20** *on a pin* **53** *to swing from the semi-automatic position shown in [patent figs. 5 and 6] to the full-automatic position shown in broken lines in [patent fig. 6] and in full lines in fig. 7.*

Further details describe the unusual configuration of the magazine, as follows;

*. . As shown in fig. 5 the fore-grip is divided into two compartments* **70** *and* **71**. *The rear compartment* **70** *is open at the bottom and serves merely as a passageway through which empty cartridge cases are ejected downwardly. The forward compartment* **71** *contains the magazine* **72** *comprising the usual follower and follower spring for feeding the cartridges which are disposed in staggered relationship. The magazine may be removed from the open side of the fore-grip by pressing the detent . .*

## U.S. Patent No. 2,216,022

A second patent, dated September 24, 1940, also granted to Mr. Pomeroy and assigned to S&W, was not illustrated, and was concerned merely with improvements in the method of attaching the barrel of the Light Rifle to the receiver.

## U.S. Patent No.2,231,978

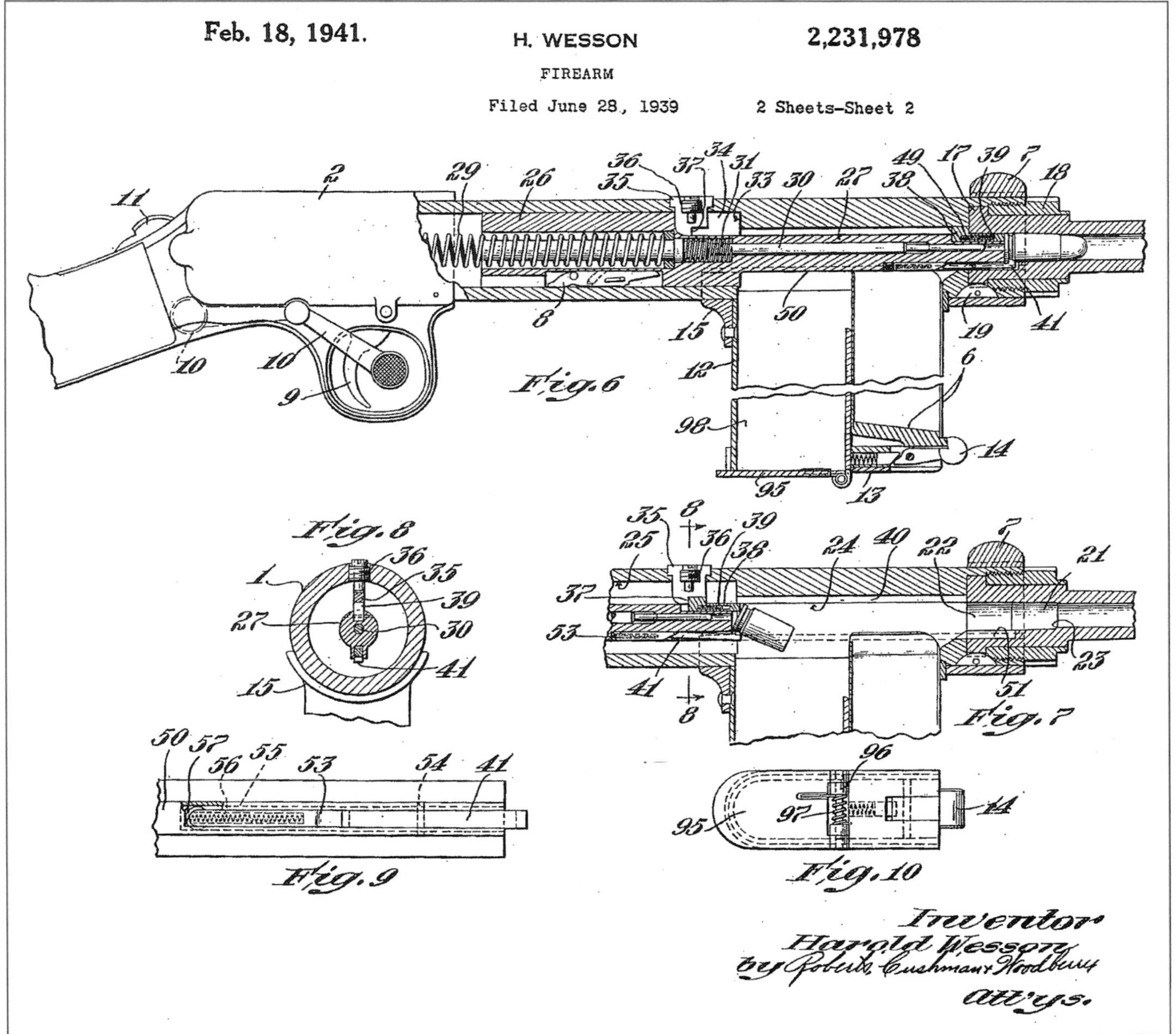


345. Sheet 2 of 2 sheets of drawings from Light Rifle patent no. 2,231,978, granted to Harold Wesson and assigned to Smith & Wesson on February 18, 1941.

The selective-fire control lever is shown as patent no. 11.

As described in the excerpts from the disclosure, this version was rendered even more complicated by the spring-loaded hinged cover on the bottom of the rear portion of the magazine well, into which the empty cartridge cases were ejected. U.S. Patent Office

The third Light Rifle patent was granted to S&W president Harold Wesson and assigned to the company on February 18, 1941. Excerpts from the patent disclosure read as follows:

> *This invention relates to firearms of the automatic type and more particularly to low-power firearms in which the bolt recoil is resisted only by the recoil spring and the inertia of the moving parts . .*
>
> *. . According to the present invention the firing chamber* **21** *is not located in the usual position at the extreme rearward end of the barrel but is separated from the rear end of the barrel by a throat portion* **22** *whose diameter approximates the maximum diameter of the cartridge case . . As shown in [patent] figs. 6 and 7 the firing chamber is slightly tapered and is provided at its forward end with a shoulder* **23** *against which the cartridge case seats.*
>
> *. . The modified fore-grip shown in figs. 6 and 10 includes a cover for the opening* **90** *in the bottom* **13** *of the fore-grip, the cover being hinged to the bottom at* **98** *and held in closed position by the spring* **97**. *With this construction the empty cartridge cases accumulate in the rear chamber* **98** *of the fore-grip until the cover* **95** *is depressed to dump the contents . .*

## Further British Trials

Meanwhile, a note from the Superintendent of the Experimental Establishment at Pendine (SEE(P)) dated September 10, 1940, concerns exploratory trials of a fully automatic Light Rifle provided by DofA. Two butts were sent with the weapon: a wood version, described as the "normal" butt (shown on page 686 of the Nelson and Lockhoven classic *The World's Submachine Guns [Machine Pistols] Volume I*) and the detachable "Butt Mk. II".

On October 18, 1940 it was reported that "carbine number 6 and carbine number 7, recently received from the USA, had plastic butts." A rough usage trial confirmed that the plastic was a satisfactory substitute for wood.

Further accuracy trials were held later in October, 1940, the trials report concluding that the general results were very satisfactory. However, in November, the report of automatic fire trials concluded that the cyclic rate was excessive; automatic accuracy was unsatisfactory; and the reliability and endurance of the carbines "left much to be desired."

The final Light Rifle trial to be conducted in the U.K. was held on December 11, 1940, wherein endurance and reliability were again considered unsatisfactory.

Nevertheless, according to Chapter 5 of the Revised Edition of *Smith & Wesson, 1857 - 1945* by R. J. Neal and R. G. Jinks, a total of 833 carbines were shipped in three groups to the U.K. in April, 1941, with serial numbers in the range 1 - 1010.

## Summing Up the Light Rifle Program

A letter from Smith & Wesson (presumably signed by the historian) to a private individual, now held in the MoD Pattern Room archive, states that production was terminated on April 16, 1941 after approximately 860 Light Rifles had been manufactured.

There is no indication of a British document officially rejecting the Light Rifle design, although no more were produced.

Most if not all of the 833 examples in the U.K. were passed on to the Royal Navy. The Chief Inspector of Naval Ordnance (CINO) reported in July, 1942 that many of the plastic butts had broken, and that the ADD was requested to design a wooden replacement, capable of accepting the original butt plate.

It appears that this request was not pursued: the Admiralty published a manual titled "Notes on the Smith & Wesson 9mm Self-Loading Carbine" on April 9, 1943, which was amended on October 14, 1943 to include a note on how easily the plastic butts could be damaged.

To sum up, it appears that

1. The British did not specifically order the development of the S&W Light Rifle;
2. Although it appears that he accepted full responsibility for the failure of the project, Mr. Pomeroy was not the only designer, as the latter patent quoted above was granted in the name of company president Harold Wesson;
3. There is no evidence that the British officially rejected the Light Rifle, available stocks of which apparently remained in Royal Navy inventory throughout the war.

4. It appears that the selective-fire version of the Light Rifle did not progress beyond the trials stage, and no mention of the improved Mark II version has been found in any surviving British document, nor has an example been found in the U.K. The *History of Smith & Wesson* states that only 200 of the Mark II version were manufactured.

## Some Later Light Rifle Correspondence - from 1944

SMITH & WESSON
SPRINGFIELD 2, MASS.

PLEASE ADDRESS ALL COMMUNICATIONS TO THE COMPANY

March 3, 1944

Mr. M. L. W. Johnson
15 Fairview Street
Willimantic, Connecticut

Dear Mr. Johnson:

We are writing to acknowledge your letter of February 29, and though we did prepare an instruction booklet for the 9 mm. Light Rifle which we manufactured for the British Government, we believe that information on this gun is still restricted and we are afraid that we are not at liberty to release detailed data.

In general, the 9 mm. Rifle was a straight blowback design with a 9-3/4" barrel and weighing 8 lbs., 14 ozs., with loaded magazine.

Two types were manufactured and designated as the Mark I and Mark II. Essentially they were the same gun though many details of the design were changed.

Originally the 9 mm. Light Rifle was developed experimentally by Smith & Wesson in 1916 but at that time there was very little military interest in this particular type of weapon and it was not until the present war that light semi-automatic and automatic arms became generally used.

We manufactured this gun for the British in 1940 and 1941, it finally being taken out of production when the demand for sidearms became so important that it was necessary for us to devote our entire facilities to revolvers.

We are sorry that we cannot send you more complete information, but hope that the above will be of interest.

Sincerely yours,
SMITH & WESSON, INC.

David H. Murray
Sales Manager

346. The reply from S&W Sales Manager David Murray, dated March 3, 1944, to Mr. Johnson's first letter of February 28, briefly describing the Light Rifle but declining to supply any detailed information.
Gaston Comeau collection

SMITH & WESSON
SPRINGFIELD, MASS.

PLEASE ADDRESS ALL COMMUNICATIONS TO THE COMPANY

April 28, 1944

Mr. M. L. W. Johnson
15 Fairview Street
Willimantic, Connecticut

Dear Mr. Johnson:

We have just received your letter of April 26, and are afraid that we will have to give you a rather disappointing reply.

Our sub-machine gun was manufactured in 9 mm. only, and no model was made up for the .45 Colt Automatic cartridge. Also, when this gun went out of production, all work in process was disposed of, and we do not have any material on hand at the present time.

As far as making up special magazines for you is concerned--unfortunately, the press of our military contracts keeps our machine shop overcrowded as it is, which means there is practically no chance that we could undertake any special work during the war.

In regard to stocks--these, too, were sold for scrap when the gun was taken out of production, and the only samples we have left are on the model guns we have to keep for our own records.

We regret exceedingly that we cannot give you a more favorable reply, and certainly wish that the 9 mm. hadn't been cleaned out so thoroughly when production was stopped.

Sincerely yours,
SMITH & WESSON, INC.

David H. Murray
Sales Manager

347. Mr. Murray's reply, dated April 28, 1944, to Mr. Johnson's second letter of April 26.
Gaston Comeau collection

Three letters from the Gaston Comeau collection, two from Smith & Wesson and one from an interested would-be inventor of "a new light sub-machine gun", provide a few further details concerning the 9mm Light Rifle.

The letter which obviously began this exchange, written to the firm by a Mr. M. L. W. Johnson of Willimatic, Connecticut, on February 29, 1944, has not come to hand, but the reply from S&W Sales Manager David E. Murray, dated March 3, is reproduced in fig. 346.

Interestingly, according to this letter, the Light Rifle was originally "developed experimentally in 1916", which would perhaps help to explain the anachronistically costly and overbuilt construction of the WWII version.

Mr. Johnson responded to Mr. Murray's first letter on April 26, 1944, asking whether the Light Rifle had ever been produced in .45 ACP caliber, and, if so, whether any spare .45 caliber magazines were available which he might have. Failing this, he asks, ingenuously, "If not, do you think that your shop could make up a few of same for me?" Interestingly, in this letter Mr. Johnson goes on with some further information he had gleaned from an unmentioned source, as follows:

> . . *I noted, with interest, that your arm was furnished with a bakelite plastic stock transfer-*

*molded by the Shaw Insulator Company. Have you any extra one of these that I could purchase for examination and tests?*

It appears that S&W's reply to this letter, also from the long-suffering Sales Manager David Murray (fig. 347), brought this correspondence to an end.

# The "S & W Pistol No. 2" Saves the Day

Instead of concluding an armistice with the Nazis, as the French had done, the British chose to fight on alone. To do this they needed arms, including revolvers, lots of revolvers. Since the British had adopted the .38 Smith & Wesson caliber (which they called the ".38/200") Enfield revolver in the late 1930s to replace their earlier Webley Mk VI .455 service revolvers, they agreed to take similarly chambered M&P revolvers from Smith & Wesson at a fixed rate, which would allow the million-dollar debt engendered by the failed Light Rifle project to be paid off in revolvers, not cash.

A speech given by David Penn, then the Keeper of the Department of Exhibits and Firearms at the Imperial War Museum, titled "American Handguns in British Service: Smith & Wesson and Their Competitors" was reprinted in Volume 26 Number 4 of the Smith & Wesson *Collector's News*, published in the winter of 1992. Mr. Penn's speech contains the following interesting statement which contradicts yet another part of the story as it is popularly held:

*. . It has often been said that the failure of the Light Rifle, in which the British Government had invested $1,000,000, resulted in revolvers being accepted in lieu. This is a misleading view, as the British had decided to buy Smith & Wesson Military & Police revolvers in quantity in .38 Smith & Wesson caliber well before the Light Rifle was rejected. The price was, however, fixed at a rate that would allow Smith & Wesson to pay off the advance . .*

This was found to be an ideal solution for all concerned. Commercial production was cut sharply at the factory, and all efforts were directed toward producing .38/200 caliber M&P revolvers for the British.

## Background on the .38/200 Cartridge

John Henwood records the early development history of the British .38/200 cartridge as follows:

*. . Since the 1920s the British had been conducting a series of trials seeking an improved service pistol cartridge. By 1929 they had settled on a cartridge using the .38 S&W case, but loaded with a 200-grain round-nosed bullet. This they called the ".380 Revolver cartridge Mark I". Their tests indicated that this combination was as effective as the old .455 Webley manstopper, when loaded with the hemispherically-nosed 200-grain lead bullet. Official German protests about the "inhumanity" of the lead bullet resulted in the adoption (in 1937) of a jacketed bullet, weighing 178 grains, and having a long, tapered nose with a rounded point: the .380 Revolver cartridge Mark II. This cartridge proved far less successful than the earlier version, the usual complaint being that it lacked stopping power.*

## The Chicken, or the Egg?

In the standard reference work *Centerfire American and British Pistol and Revolver Cartridges*, authors H. P. White and B. D. Munhall record some further details of the origins of the original 200-gr. bullet used in the Mark I version of this round, and what was then known about its relationship to the Western Cartridge Company's "Super-Police" loading of the .38 S&W cartridge, as follows:

*. . The .380 Revolver Mark I cartridge is identical to the "Super-Police" loading of the .38 Smith & Wesson round which we believe originated in the U.S. in the late 1920s.*

*. . Toward the end of the 1920s, the British Army was experimenting with .38 caliber revolvers in hopes of developing a lighter weapon than their standard .455. These efforts were responsible, at least in part, for the firm of Webley & Scott introducing, in 1929, their .38 Mark IV Revolver chambered for the .38 Smith & Wesson cartridge, or, as they called it, the "Webley Special". It was loaded with a 200-grain solid lead bullet. Our research*

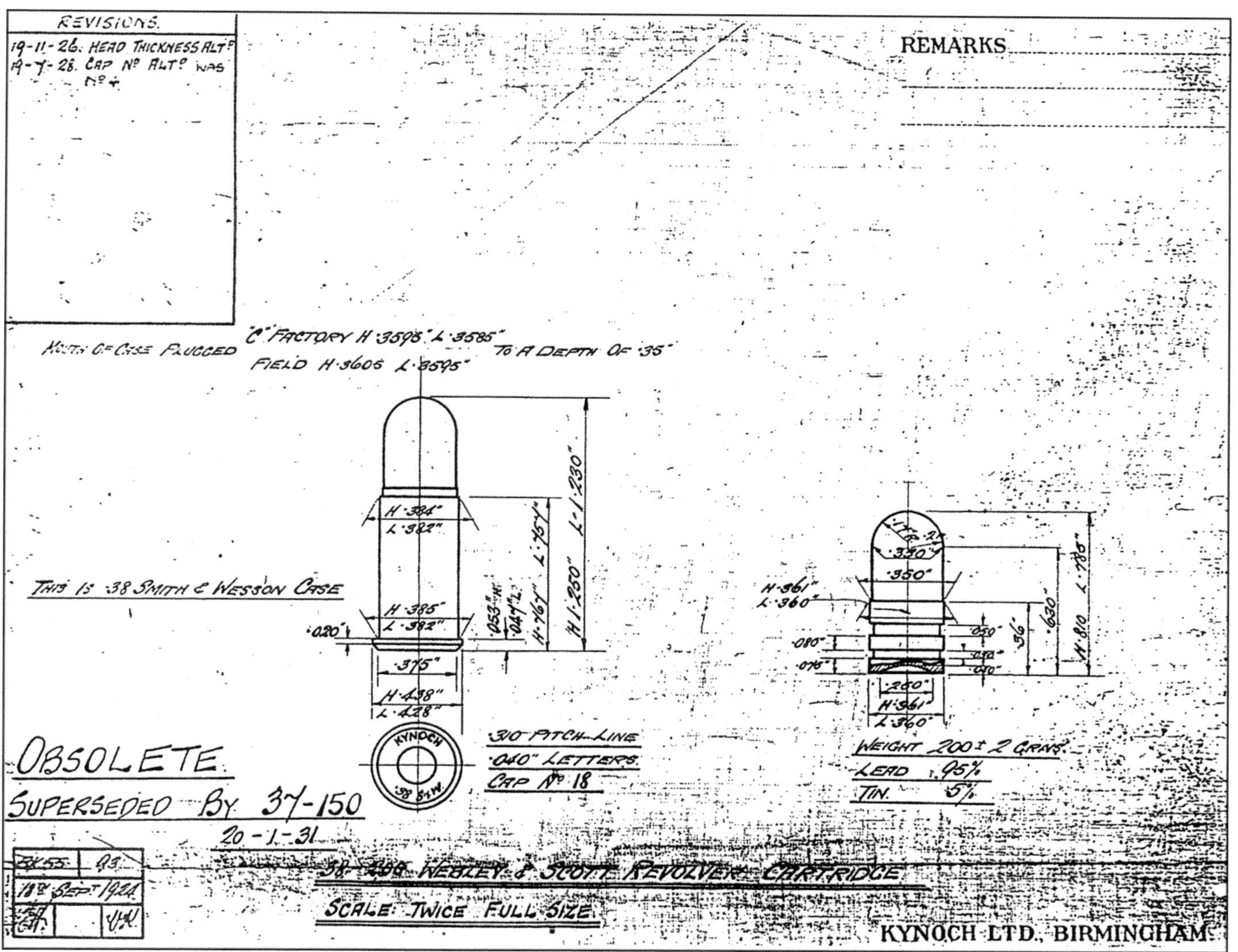


348. A drawing of the ".38-200 Webley & Scott Revolver Cartridge" by Kynoch, Ltd. of Birmingham, dated 18 September, 1924. This would seem to settle the issue once and for all regarding which version came first in favor of the Webley cartridge. MoD Pattern Room Library, courtesy Ian Patrick and Richard Jones

*fails to divulge whether Webley copied the Western Cartridge Company's ".38 Super-Police" round or whether the situation was reversed. We know Western was advertising its 200-grain .38 Smith & Wesson ammunition as early as February of 1929.*

The above drawing of the ".38-200 Webley & Scott Revolver Cartridge" by Kynoch, Ltd. of Birmingham, dated 18 September, 1924 would seem to settle the issue once and for all regarding which version came first in favor of the Webley cartridge.

## Genesis of the Enfield No. 2 Mark I Revolver

A further excerpt from *Centerfire American and British Pistol and Revolver Cartridges* details what was then known concerning the history of the British pistols (revolvers) made and used before the advent of the S&W .38/200 program, as follows:

*. . We are also in doubt as to whether or not the British Government officially adopted the Webley .38 Mark IV Pistol. We know that the British Army must have been using some of them at an early date, as evidenced by the fact that the British Government Arsenal at Woolwich was making the ammunition as early as 1932 . .*

*About 1937 the British Army did adopt a revolver of their own design, closely patterned after the Webley Mark IV. This was the Enfield No. 2 Mark I arm which is officially known as the "Pistol No. 2 Mark I .38 inch" . .*

## A Bald Appropriation

The following notes, excerpted from the 1988 book *Webley Revolvers* by Gordon Bruce and Christian Reinhart, provide a much more precise timetable for the events described above, and indicate in no uncertain terms that the "Pistol, Revolver No. 2 Mark I" was in fact purely and simply appropriated by the British government from the commercial Webley Mark IV design:

*Development of the Mark IV .38 commenced during 1921, when Webley & Scott proposed a number of design alterations on the Mark III revolver. These changes were undertaken in response to War Office recommendations for a smaller and lighter weapon to replace the existing .455 Webley [Mark VI] Service Revolver. The intention had been to provide a calibre .38 weapon with the "stopping power" equivalent to that of the .455 model . .*

*. . Following a series of firing trials with the new weapon at the School of Musketry, Hythe, more alterations were made to the construction in the summer of 1922. The stock had been considered rather small for the average hand [and] it was recommended that Mark VI stock-plates should be fitted, and the hammer thumbpiece should be made wider to assist in cocking. Development of the .38 model thereafter took precedence over further modifications to the .455 revolver.*

*Cartridges supplied by Webley & Scott for use in the new model were composed of Smith & Wesson cases, charged with 2.8 grains of Neonite, and a special 200-grain bullet.*

*There followed a period of more testing and amendments before the War Office decided to adopt a calibre .38 design to replace the .455 model in October, 1926. Drawings of the new Webley revolver were duly prepared for manufacture to begin. By that time, however, a certain amount of friction had developed between the Webley & Scott management and Government officials with the result that future production of the new .38 Service Revolver was allocated to the Royal Small Arms Factory at Enfield. The weapon then became officially known as the Pistol, Revolver No. 2 Mark I.*

*. . Webley & Scott later claimed compensation for patent infringements and other expenses but the matter was not resolved until 1931 with an award of just 1,200 Pounds. Webley & Scott offered the Mark IV revolver to the commercial market as a Police & Military Model in barrel lengths of 3", 4" or 5". There was also a Target Model with 6" barrel . .*

*The Webley Mark IV revolver proved to be a very successful design and was supplied to various police and armed forces throughout the world . . mostly . . within the British Empire.*

## Official Wartime Production at Webley & Scott of Both the Webley Mark IV and the Enfield Pistol, Revolver, No. 2 Mark I

Fighting for their lives against the might of Nazi Germany, the British needed every revolver they could get, and as the above account continues, the Webley Mark IV itself saw service in substantial numbers during World War II:

*. . Despite the fact that its components differed from those of the [Enfield] Pistol, Revolver No. 2 Mark I, the War Office (via Ministry of Supply) placed contracts for the Webley Mark IV version to fulfil urgent requirements . . Official records show that Webley & Scott provided more than 100,000 Mark IV .38 revolvers to the British Government [from May, 1940 through November, 1944].*

*(In typical Ministry fashion, the Mark IV was finally approved as an official Government weapon on 20 September, 1945.)*

*It is interesting to note that the Webley & Scott factory even produced the Pistol, Revolver No. 2 Mark I at certain stages of the war. In 1940, the British Government ordered 10,522, and another 54,000 in 1942 . .*

*No doubt this had been very welcome business and it must have been gratifying for the firm to realise that it was not forgotten—although a far cry from being sole contractors, as had been the case during the period from 1887 to 1928 . .*

349. Left and right side views of Webley Mark IV .38 caliber revolver, serial no. 76248, manufactured for British service use during WWII. As noted, Webley & Scott provided more than 100,000 Mark IV .38 revolvers to the British government from May, 1940 through November, 1944.

Note the rough milling marks which have not been polished out of the "WAR FINISH".

Greg Pfeiffer collection

## Double-Action Only: the Enfield "No. 2 Mark I*"

In their book *.380 Enfield No. 2 Revolver,* authors Mark Stamps and Ian Skennerton describe the development of the double-action-only Mark I* and Mark I** versions of the Enfield No. 2 Mark I revolver as follows:

*The Mark I* and I** variations are readily distinguished from the parent model as they have no cocking spur on the hammer. Without the thumb-cocking single action spur and sear notch, these revolvers can therefore be operated by trigger action only. The Mk. I* and I** hammers have no thumbpiece or full-cock bent. The double-action*

350. Right side view of the double-action-only Enfield No. 2 Mark I* revolver, with black painted wartime finish and plastic grips. Note the distinctive spur-less hammer.

By the summer of 1938, this was the only version of the Enfield revolver approved for British service use.

*only characteristic also required a lightened mainspring which was designated "Spring, main, Mark I*" . .*

*Conceived before the war during the development and trials period of the No. 2 Mk. I revolver, the Mk. I* was a special requirement for the Armoured Corps who complained of "hang ups" with the hammer thumb-spur on interior equipment and fittings, especially in the circumstances of hasty exit and entry of the armoured fighting vehicles. The June, 1938 approval date of the Mark I* is also interesting as government small arms contract records list an order dated 29th April, 1936 for 4,600 of the Mark I* models, more than two years before its official approval per the List of Changes . .*

By the List of Changes entry approved in June, 1938, the No. 2 Mark I* (and the later Mark I** model, involving a further internal simplification) were adopted as the only versions of the No. 2 pistol approved for manufacture, indicating that the double-action-only model was thenceforth intended for use by all units of the armed forces, not just the Armoured Corps. An excerpt from this 1938 List of Changes entry confirms this, as follows:

*. . Mk. I No. 2 pistols will be converted to Mk. I* pattern as and when they are passed through Ordnance Factories for repair.*

*. . the Mk. I pattern is hereby declared obsolescent . .*

## Carl Hellstrom Takes Over as S&W General Superintendent

Meanwhile, back in Springfield, when E. S. Pomeroy retired in the wake of the failed Model 1940 Light Rifle program, Carl R. Hellstrom, previously an independent consulting engineer, was called in and offered the vacated position of general superintendent of the S&W factory.

In an excerpt from his own account, published in *Smith & Wesson, The Story of the Revolver*, Hellstrom, who was later the first non-Wesson family member to become president of the firm, recalled,

*. . As a result of the Dunkirk evacuation, the company had received substantial orders for revolvers from the various British Dominions, and England herself was sorely in need of a large quantity of this type of arms. Arrangements were made to pay back the British advance by supplying revolvers at a fixed rate, and ways had to be found to produce guns in quantities heretofore undreamed of. At the same time, production economies had to be effected under the fixed price contract . .*

*Our success in pulling out of this desperate period is a monument to cooperative efforts among men [although] the obstacles to normal production seemed insurmountable at first. We had no drawings or tool catalogs, all work being done to templates or models. No fixed tolerances could be established, and all threads and tapers were nonstandard . . As a result, we were forced to make our own tools, and we were, I believe, at that time the most self-sufficient plant in the country . .*

# Development and Production History of the S&W .38/200 Revolver

## Barrels Remain Dimensioned for the .38 Special

Some further interesting technical details of this program, as recorded by McHenry and Roper, are as follows:

*. . On account of the urgent need, there was no time for Smith & Wesson to design a new revolver [and] the question considered was which of the firm's existing models came the closest to meeting the British specifications with the least possible modification . .*

*It was but natural that the lot should fall upon the tried and true Military and Police model, designed to shoot the .38 Special cartridge. The job of adapting it to the shorter .38 Super Police cartridge was not as difficult as one might suppose. The bullet diameter is a hair's breadth or so larger than that of the .38 Special [groove diameter .360" compared to .357" for the .38 Special], but not enough but what it could be fired through the barrel with perfect safety . .*

*The chambering of the cylinders had to be enlarged, for the taper of the .38 cartridge is sharper than that of the Special, but this was a minor operation . .*

Excerpts from John Henwood's *America's Right Arm* pick up the story as follows:

*. . This new model, known to collectors as the ".38/200" or ".38/200 British Service Model", was officially named the "Pistol, Revolver, Smith & Wesson, .38-in., No. 2" by the British. (In British military usage all handguns are "pistols".) It was similar to the .38 Hand Ejector Model of 1905, Fourth Change, except for the caliber . .*

*The .38/200 was placed in production during March, 1940 and was numbered in the .38 M&P serial number block. During September of that year all other production was cut sharply, and the factory concentrated on this model alone. By February, 1941 production has increased to the point that some commercial M&P production was revived. Several minor mechanical changes were made to speed production; these were retained in the post-war civilian guns as well. The yoke retaining plunger and the bolt plunger retaining screw, for example, were dropped, while the extractor rod head was reduced in size.*

## Initial Orders - from the Union of South Africa

According to Charles Pate, "The earliest WWII guns, those going to the Union of South Africa, appear in factory shipping records at approximately serial no. 612000." A later example from this series, serial no. 690472, appears as fig. 351.

A telegram dated June 1, 1940 (fig. 352), sent from the British Purchasing Commission (BPC) to the British Military Staff in Washington, D.C., confirms that a later shipment of Smith & Wesson .38/200 caliber revolvers destined for South Africa had been effectively hijacked en route by the BPC, and diverted to the U.K.

351. Left side view of a 4" S&W M&P with prewar bright blue finish, serial no. 690472, fitted with a lanyard loop, as sent to the Union of South Africa.

Inset, left; the South African 'U' and Broad Arrow property mark, along with an inventory number, stamped on the rear knuckle of the frame.

Gaston Comeau collection

YOUR BS 3368 - FILE S 4/15/3.
WE HAVE OBTAINED FOR IMMEDIATE DELIVERY AFTER ISSUANCE OF EXPORT LICENSES, APPROXIMATELY 12,300 REVOLVERS AND PISTOLS WITH AN ADDITIONAL 3,500 TO BE DELIVERED OVER THE NEXT THIRTY DAYS. REMAINDER OF 20,000 CAN BE DELIVERED IN JULY. ABOUT ONE-HALF OF THE QUANTITIES TO BE DELIVERED ARE .38 CALIBRE SMITH AND WESSON REVOLVERS CHAMBERED FOR 38-200 SMITH AND WESSON, OR .380 OR MARK 1 I.C.I. BRITISH AMMUNITION. PLEASE NOTE THAT THESE REVOLVERS HAVE BEEN DIVERTED FROM AN ORDER FOR SOUTH AFRICA, AND ACCORDINGLY WE HAVE NOT HAD OPPORTUNITY TO DEVELOP AMMUNITION PRODUCTION HERE. WE ARE HAVING DIFFICULTY SECURING THIS AMMUNITION FOR IMMEDIATE DELIVERY. CAN THIS STANDARD BRITISH AMMUNITION BE SUPPLIED UPON RECEIPT OF THESE GUNS IN ENGLAND, IF WE REPLACE THIS AMMUNITION FROM THE UNITED STATES LATER?

ENDS JUNE 1/40 11 AM

352. The telegram, dated June 1, 1940, sent from the British Purchasing Commission (BPC) to the British Military Staff in Washington, D.C., confirming that a shipment of Smith & Wesson .38/200 caliber revolvers destined for South Africa had been effectively hijacked en route and diverted to the U.K. MoD Pattern Room Library, courtesy Ian Patrick and Richard Jones

## Standardizing the 5" Barrel and Smooth Wood Grips

353. Left and right side views of an early .38/200 revolver, serial no. 885317, with 5" barrel. The finish is a "brushed" (matte) blue, while the stocks are plain with no medallions and the lanyard loop is fitted.

This example has the "United States Property" marking on the top strap, indicating it was shipped as part of the Lend Lease program, although it does not bear any British or other property or proof marks.

Gaston Comeau collection

Originally the .38/200 came off the line variously fitted with four-, five-, and six-inch barrels, with checkered wood grips and commercial-level bluing.

By this time, however, Hitler's *Wehrmacht* had overrun France and Belgium and, from a mere twenty miles or so away across the English Channel, German forces were impatiently awaiting the order to launch "Operation Sea Lion", the planned invasion of Britain. In response to demands for faster, more economical production, and in addition to the mechanical changes noted above, the S&W factory substituted plain wood grip panels, stuck mainly to five-inch barrels, and soon adopted a quickly-applied flat sandblasted and "Black Magic" phosphated finish.

354. Right side view of a classic example of the British-issue .38/200 revolver, with 5" barrel, phosphated finish, and British proofs and property markings. Note the domed rear sideplate screw, used in place of the normal flat-headed screw in this location in the interests of simplification and speedy production. courtesy Rock Island Auction Co.

Inset: a typical box of .380 ammunition, made in Canada, marked "12/CARTRIDGES/REVOLVER/.380 INCH/ MK IIZ (nitrocellulose). Gaston Comeau collection

355. Left side closeup of a typical British .38/200 revolver, showing "United States Property" marking on the topstrap. Note the British proofs on the barrel, and on each chamber of the cylinder. Jeff Moeller collection

356 (right). Closeups of the bottom of the butts of two .38/200 revolvers, showing Ordnance bomb and inspectors' markings.

Left: "W.B." initials of Lt. Col. Waldemar Broberg, found on production from 1940 - 1942.

Right: "G.H.D." initials of Col. Guy H. Drewry, found on production from 1942 - 1945. Jeff Moeller collection

357. A typical British web holster, belt and ammunition pouch, with holster markings dated 1942.

The revolver is a S&W .38/200, although a .38 Webley or Enfield would also fit. Jeff Moeller collection

## An Australian-Issue .38/200

358. Left side view of another typical .38/200, serial no. 817030, with Australian-issue lanyard and cleaning rod.

Note the hand-stamped VEGA SAC CA (Vega, Sacremento, California) importer's marking on the frame above the trigger. After the 1968 Gun Control Act came into effect, such markings were required on all U.S.-made arms which were exported and subsequently re-imported.

Dave Terbrueggen collection

# The .38/200 Issued to Commonwealth Forces, and the French Resistance

John Henwood continues as follows:

*The British parcelled these guns out among the various Empire forces. Of the 586,200 produced, the South Africans received 21,347 with 5-inch barrels and 13,847 with 4-inch barrels between 1940 and 1942. Canada got 18,160 with 6-inch barrels and 1,560 with 4-inch barrels in 1940 - 41. Australia received 8,000 with 5-inch barrels in 1941. This left a bit over 500,000 for the British forces (and the New Zealanders; it is not known how many they obtained, but they adopted it as "standard issue" in 1942), as well as for post-1942 Dominion issue. Probably some went to the Indian Army, and additional shipments to various Commonwealth forces are likely. Apparently those guns going to Commonwealth nations were shipped*

359. A pamphlet found in the plain cardboard box in which the surplus Australian revolver shown in fig. 358 was received.

While the 5" .38/200 version is depicted, it is erroneously described as a "Victory Model".

Dave Terbrueggen collection

*direct, rather than passing through Britain, since they (for the most part) lack British proof marks. A number of British .38/200s were furnished to the French resistance movement, for use in occupied France.*

## Summing Up the British .38/200 Service Revolver

The British .38/200 model was summed up in the 1945 book *Smith & Wesson Hand Guns* by McHenry and Roper as follows:

> *. . 5" barrel—Butt Swivel—Brush-Polish Blue, Bright Polish Blue, and Sand-Blast with Blue and Parkerized finishes have been used—both smooth and checkered stocks have been installed. The .38/200 is a great favorite with the Commandos and men in many other branches of the British Services. This gun has been in production since April 1940, and manufactured in tremendous quantities. It is undoubtedly the most extensively used military revolver ever made.*

John Henwood records further details regarding the .38/200 revolver, as follows:

*. . The price paid for these revolvers escalated somewhat, as wartime inflation took hold. In mid-1940 the price was just under $25 each. (The retail price at the time was $33.) By June of 1941 the price had jumped to $30. Nevertheless, by July, 1941 the British had placed orders for 168,820 .38/200 revolvers, almost $4,500,000 worth.*

### *Serial Numbering*

*The first .38/200s were numbered in the same series as the M&P. When serial numbers reached 1000000 on April 24, 1942, S&W introduced a new series, the "V-prefix" serial number block. .38/200s were numbered in this V-prefix series, starting with #V 1, until about V 40000, when the "Victory Model" was introduced . . Serial numbers are found on the bottom of the butt (this is the official serial number), underside of the barrel, the yoke, the extractor, the inside of the right stock, and the rear face of the cylinder. The .38/200 was discontinued in March, 1945; about 568,200 were produced.*

**[*Two Series of .38/200 Revolvers*]**

*. . there are actually* two *series of .38/200 revolvers. Those which the British paid for (early guns) and those made after the U.S. Lend-Lease Act was passed, which were paid for by the American taxpayer. Thus those guns without the "U.S. Property" marking belong to the British; those having this rollmarking were (supposedly) only loaned to them.*

# More on the Canadian Story

360. Various views of an early Canadian military M&P, serial no. 734706, with 6" barrel, prewar commercial blue finish and checkered stocks with silver S&W monograms.

Inset, above left: enlargement of the 'C' and Broad Arrow Canadian property mark on the sideplate, above the trigger.

Inset, below right: note the absence of a military inspector's marking beside the 'P' proof mark.

Gaston Comeau collection

361. Various views of a later Canadian-issue .38/200, serial no. 931095, with a 5" barrel, finished in charcoal (dull) sandblast blue and fitted with plain stocks and a lanyard swivel.

Inset, above left: an enlargement of the Canadian 'C' and Broad Arrow property mark, as stamped on the sideplate. Other examples exist with the 'C' and Broad Arrow stamped in other locations, such as on the frame at the front of the trigger guard.

Inset, below, right: inspector's initials "W.B." and Ordnance bomb alongside factory 'P' proof on the front of the butt strap. Gaston Comeau collection

The following excerpts from *Canadian Military Handguns, 1855 - 1985* by Clive M. Law give some specifics on the .38/200 revolver purchases made by and for Canada. These were supplied either through the British Purchasing Commission in New York or direct from the factory, which explains why they do not exhibit British proof marks:

> *. . By early 1940, all Canadian purchases for handguns in the United States were administered*

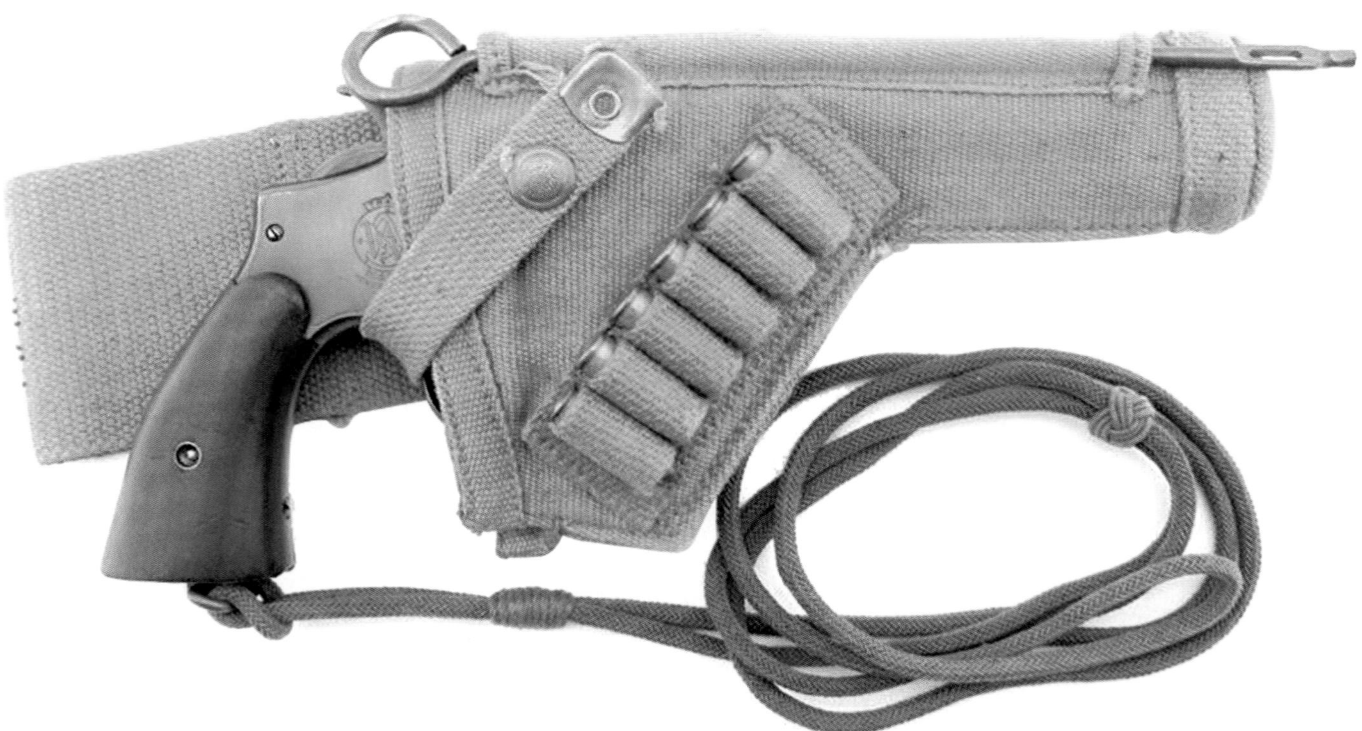

362. The Royal Canadian Armoured Corps pattern web holster, with spare cartridge loops and provision for cleaning rod.
The S&W .38/200 revolver held inside by the safety strap has an issue lanyard attached.
Gaston Comeau collection

*by the British Purchasing Commission in New York . .*

*When Japan attacked the U.S. Navy installations in Hawaii, they in effect closed the doors to both Colt and Smith & Wesson for Canada. The U.S. was now involved in the War and needed all of its arms manufacturing capabilities dedicated to its own mobilization.*

*This situation left Canada in an awkward position as it had no handgun manufacturing capability of its own and Britain's factories were busy trying to meet the needs of the War Office. Canada did manage to make a few more purchases of revolvers. In July, 1942 Smith & Wesson was awarded a contract to supply the Army with 5,100 pistols and, in September, they were asked to supply a further 13,700.*

*Finally, in 1943, the Government of Canada awarded a flurry of contracts for the now standard Smith & Wesson [.38/200] revolver . .*

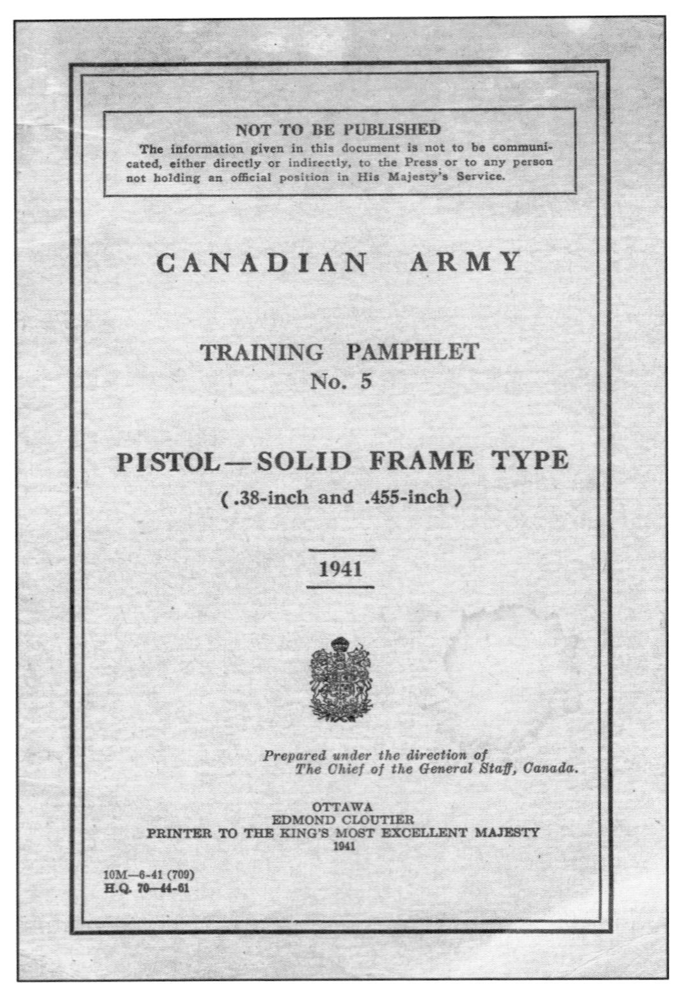

NOT TO BE PUBLISHED
The information given in this document is not to be communicated, either directly or indirectly, to the Press or to any person not holding an official position in His Majesty's Service.

CANADIAN ARMY

TRAINING PAMPHLET
No. 5

PISTOL—SOLID FRAME TYPE
(.38-inch and .455-inch)

1941

*Prepared under the direction of The Chief of the General Staff, Canada.*

OTTAWA
EDMOND CLOUTIER
PRINTER TO THE KING'S MOST EXCELLENT MAJESTY
1941

10M—6-41 (709)
H.Q. 70—44-61

363 (right). The Canadian Army Training Pamphlet No. 5, dated 1941, covering both .38 and .455 caliber revolvers.
Gaston Comeau collection

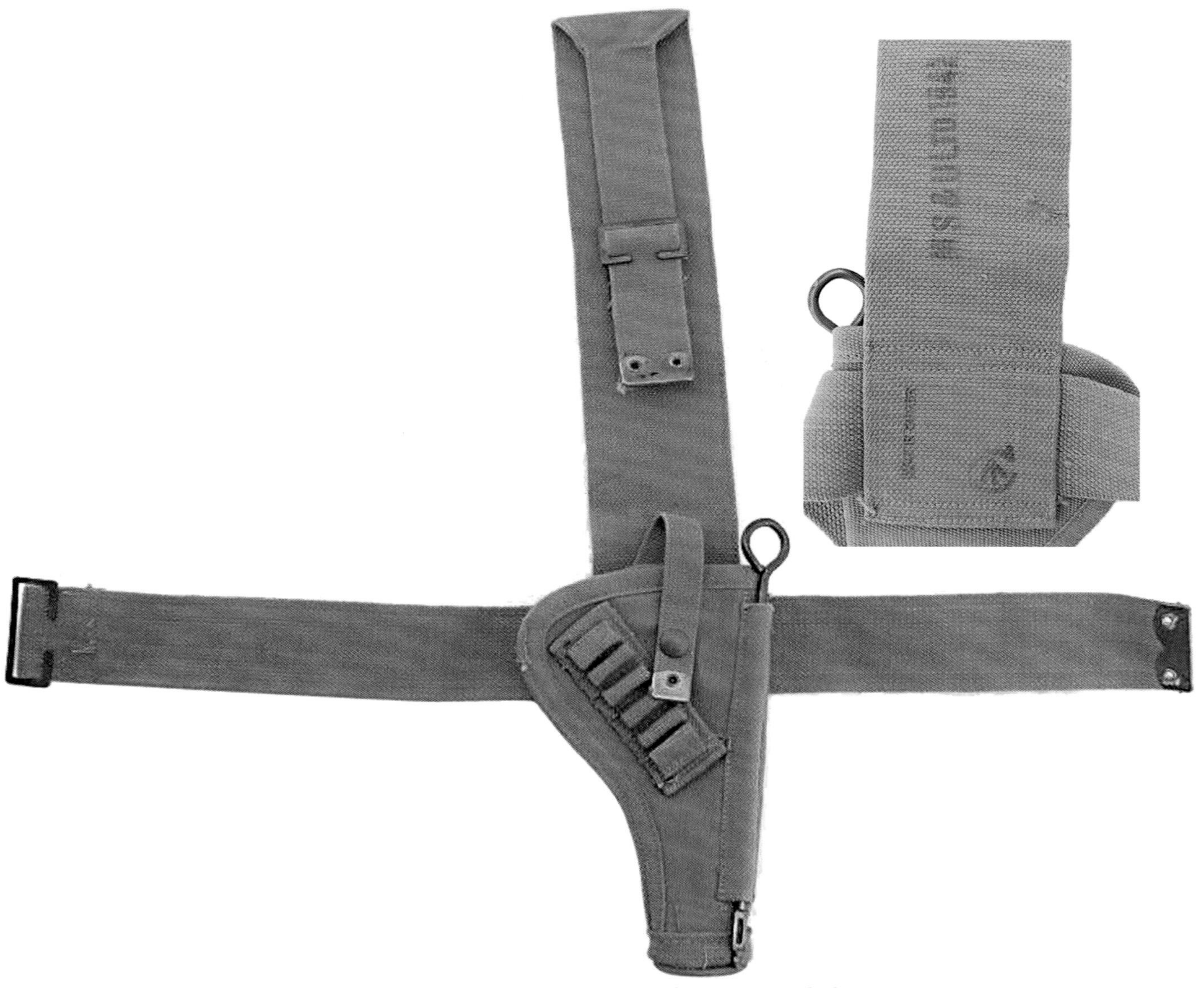

364. The Canadian-issue Armoured Corps web holster, modified for carrying on the leg by tank crew members.
Inset, right: rear closeup of the elongated strap, showing "M S & U LTD. 1942" maker's mark (Montreal Suspender and Umbrella Ltd.), and 'C' and Broad Arrow acceptance marking. Gaston Comeau collection

## Experimental .38/200 Revolvers in 9mm Caliber

Clive Law continues to describe this little-known experimental project as follows:

*An unknown aspect of the use of the .38/200 revolver was an attempt to convert them to fire 9mm ammunition. In early August of 1942, Lt. Col. F. F. Fulton of Canadian Military Headquarters (CMHQ) in London wrote to the Liasion Officer at the British Small Arms Directorate in Cheshunt:*

*". . Consideration is being given by Canadian Army to the modification of Pistols .380" to enable them to use ammunition Sten 9mm . .*

*". . The elimination of one additional type of ammunition supply to field units would . . be extremely desirable, and any suggestions you may have in respect of a suitable form of modification will be appreciated. Approximately 20,000 weapons would be involved."*

365. Left and right side views of a wartime Smith & Wesson .38/200 revolver, serial no. 9, experimentally chambered for the 9mm Parabellum cartridge.
courtesy Metropolitan Police Service Forensic Firearms Unit

366. Underside closeup of the barrel of the above 9mm revolver showing presumed serial number, 9.

Whether this example forms part of the lot of 12 revolvers discussed below is not known, although it is clearly stated that the latter were taken from British Stores, and would therefore be serially numbered and marked in the normal fashion. courtesy Metropolitan Police Service Forensic Firearms Unit

367. Rear closeup of the 9mm revolver with cylinder open, showing the shoulders on which the rimless 9mm cartridges chamber. courtesy Metropolitan Police Service Forensic Firearms Unit

*Ultimately, 12 pistols, six Smith & Wesson and six Enfield, were taken from Stores for modification. The report, delivered in September [1942] is from the Director of Ordnance Services to the Deputy Quartermaster General It states in part that:*

*"Pistol revolver .380 Enfield No. 2 Mk. 1 Registered No. B.7767 on which modifications were carried out to adapt it to take 9mm parabellum ammunition has been tested by an officer of this branch and found to function in a satisfactory manner."*

*. . However, it was felt necessary at this time to invite the comments of the Infantry branch and of the Chief Inspector of Small Arms. In July 1944, the final decision was that "the .38 Pistol is insufficiently strong to withstand extended use with 9mm ammunition." The subject was closed.*

# Meanwhile, Back in Peacetime America . .

## The 1941 S&W Catalog

For most of 1941 the United States was not yet at war, and Smith & Wesson was able to produce one last commercial catalog only months before the Japanese attack on Pearl Harbor.

Some interesting excerpts from this last pre-war S&W catalog read as follows:

### *Foreword*

*Heretofore we have prefaced our catalogues with historical notes setting forth the important part this company and its founders played in the early development of firearms. We have decided to pass that by, for after all, the pioneering efforts of this company in the hand gun field are so well known as to require little comment.*

*Suffice it to say that the three principal offices in the SMITH & WESSON COMPANY are ably filled by WESSONS, all grandsons of the founder, all trained in the factory, and all able and proud to carry on this gun-making industry on the high plane of manufacturing and business ethics which have ruled this company since its inception nearly a century ago.*

368. The maroon cover of the 1941 Smith & Wesson commercial catalog. Gaston Comeau collection

### *Double Safety Features*

The following comments refer to the early "side-swing" hammer block which, in combination with the rebound slide, was at this time considered ample protection against inadvertent discharge. As discussed later in this chapter, however, in response to a fatal accident which occurred in exactly the manner described in the second paragraph below, the "side-swing" hammer block safety was to be replaced by a totally new design only three years later:

*Unless the trigger is pulled intentionally, it is impossible to discharge a modern Smith & Wesson accidentally, as the hammer is prevented from striking the firing pin by* two *safeties—the rebound slide upon which the lower end of the hammer rests, and the solid steel hammer block which lies between the hammer and the frame just below the hammer nose.*

*Even if the arm should fall and strike on the hammer these two safety devices make accidental discharge impossible.*

## The Rare Second Model K-22 "Masterpiece"

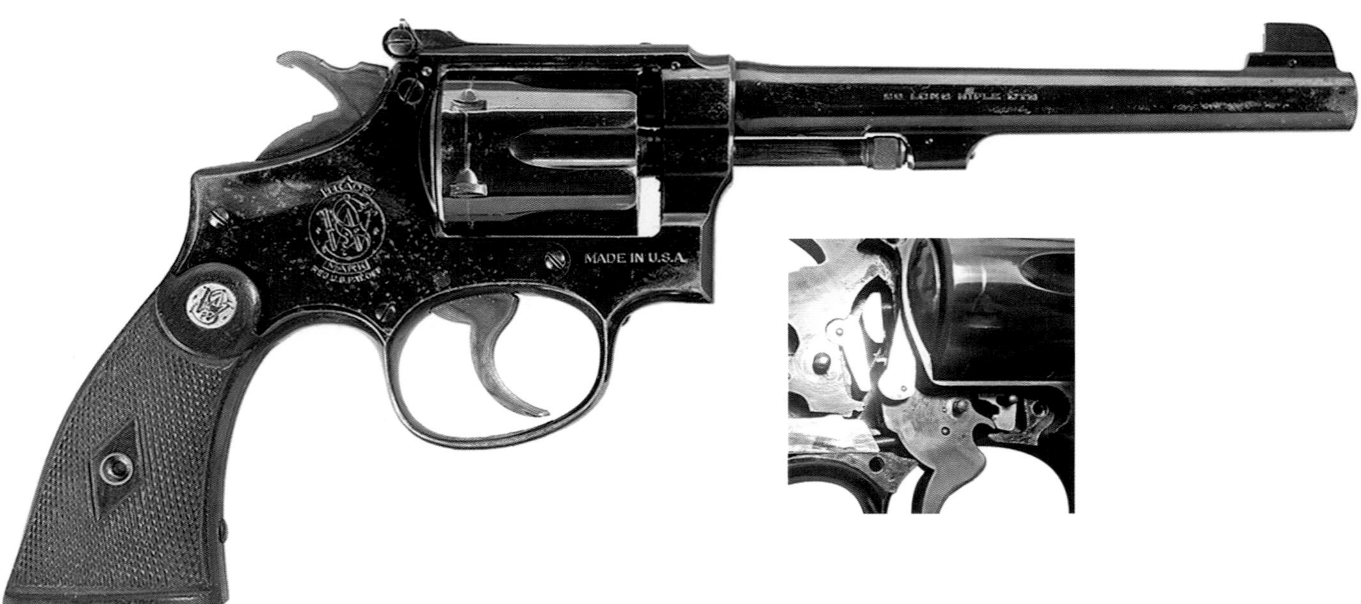


369. Right side view of the Second Model K-22, with short action and micrometer rear sight.

Manufactured from January 25, 1940 to March 12, 1942, the Second Model K-22 is a rare find today in that only 1,067 examples were produced.

courtesy Rock Island Auction Co.

Inset: the "antibacklash" trigger of this model, described on page 387, held back as far as it will go. Compare with fig. 287: note the unique recurved hook on the front of the trigger, which apparently bottoms on the frame to limit trigger movement. Jim Fisher collection

The following further excerpts from the 1941 S&W catalog describe the new short-action K-22 "Masterpiece" revolver:

### *The New K-22 Masterpiece*

#### *For the .22 Long Rifle Cartridge*

#### *Made with the Rugged Precision of a French "75"*

*This .22 caliber, heavy frame revolver, truly a* masterpiece *of the gunmaker's art, makes its bow to the hand-gun fraternity as a worthy successor to the world-famous S&W K-22.*

*A replica of that favorite police veteran, the .38 M&P Target Revolver, the S&W Masterpiece embodies all the time-proved, sure-shooting features of the K-22 plus a number of unique improvements that make for even greater accuracy, speed, and ease of handling. As with its predecessor, the Masterpiece barrel is precision drilled, reamed, and rifled, and the cylinder, with recessed head space, is chambered for the .22 Long Rifle cartridge.*

#### *NEW! S&W Micrometer Sight (Patents Pending)*

*Positive two-point click adjustments for both windage and elevation. One click moves point of impact 1 inch at 50 yards—1/2 inch at 25 yards. Husky construction throughout. Large, strong adjustment screws. Stays put!* Will not shoot loose!

#### *NEW! Speed Lock*

*Shorter! Faster! Easier cocking! Smooth as velvet. Allows grip to remain unchanged during fast fire.*

### *NEW! Built-In Antibacklash Trigger*

*No adjustment screws or gadgets. Trigger travel to rear positively stops when hammer starts to fall.*

### The Hump Back Hammer Is Not an Option on the Short-Action K-22

***This model will be supplied with the standard hammer only. The extreme leverage of the "Hump Back" [hammer] is not needed on this new short action.** [Emphasis in original.]*

## Walter Roper Comments on the S&W K-22 "Masterpiece"

In a further excerpt from his 1945 book *Pistol and Revolver Shooting*, Walter F. Roper welcomes the new K-22 Masterpiece revolver, and also gives credit to the custom gunsmiths whose innovative designs preceded the introduction of the factory-made short action, as follows:

> *. . We now come to the very latest S&W product, the K-22 Masterpiece, first placed on the market in 1939. Comparatively few of these guns were made before the war stopped their manufacture, but it is evident from the experiences of the shooters lucky enough to have obtained one, that S&W has scored a very definite triumph in this new gun. To be perfectly fair, I think at least some of the credit for this better gun should be given to those ingenious gunsmiths like Buchanan, King, Pachmayer [sic], Jesse Harpe, and several others who for years have been building over Colt and S&W revolvers to have a short hammer fall to make cocking in rapid fire easier, and the time of hammer fall less. Smith & Wesson certainly deserve the thanks of shooters for incorporating this most desirable feature in the new Masterpiece, and also for equipping this gun with a real micrometer adjusting sight in which the adjusting screws are self-locking. As a final refinement the action is made so that the trigger moves only the amount required to release the hammer. The Masterpiece is a beautifully made, finely finished revolver with three features shooters have long wanted, and I predict that it will become one of the best liked of all the fine S&W guns.*

John Henwood sums up the Second Model K-22 as follows;

> *This new revolver, the "K-22 Hand Ejector Second Model" as the factory called it, was similar to the [First Model], differing in that it used a new rear sight featuring micrometer adjustments; it also had a shorter hammer throw and an anti-backlash trigger . .*
>
> *. . Known as the "K-22 Second Model" by collectors, only 1,067 were made before war production demands forced a halt to its manufacture . .*

# The U.S. .38 Special Victory Model

Even before the December 7, 1941 Japanese attack on Pearl Harbor which triggered U.S. entry into WWII, it had been decided that M&P revolvers in .38 Special caliber should be supplied to the U. S. government.

The standard U.S. .38 Special Victory Model had a dull phosphated finish, smooth wood grips, and a four-inch barrel. But two-inch models were known, as well as a few examples in other barrel lengths, found no doubt when parts bins were closely examined.

## Victory Model Serial Numbers

John Henwood records that both British .38/200 revolvers and U.S. .38 Special Victory Models were numbered in the same V-prefix series:

> *[Victory Model] Serial numbers start at about #V 40000 (circa May, 1942) and run to #VS 811119 (August 27, 1945) . .*

## A Rare Presentation Victory Model, for General Hatcher

370. Left and right side views of Victory Model serial no. V 3, presented to General Julian Hatcher, Chief of Staff, Small Arms Division, U.S. Army Ordnance Department.
NRA National Firearms Museum collection

## The Timetable of Victory Model Finishes

In a further excerpt from the 1945 McHenry and Roper book *Smith & Wesson Hand Guns*, the Victory Model was described as follows:

> *. . During the summer of 1940, Smith & Wesson went on to war production exclusively and since that time, no guns have been produced for direct commercial sale. Two principal types of revolvers have been manufactured [the .38/200 and the Victory Model], and the various changes in specifications listed below apply to both types:*
>
> 1. *December 4, 1941—Finish changed from bright polish to brush polish.*
> 2. *January 1, 1942—Stocks changed from checkered walnut with S&W monograms to smooth uncheckered walnut without monograms . .*
> 4. *January 1942—April 10, 1942—Finish changed from brush-polish to non-light-reflecting sandblast surface.*
>
> *All wartime production had blue rather than nickel finish. Carbonia Heat Process, Black Magic Chemical Oxide Process, and Parkerizing Process were all used.*

371. Right side views of a pair of .38 Special Victory Models, both with U.S. Navy markings.
Above: 2" barrel, for issue to Navy pilots.
Below: standard Navy-issue version, with 4" barrel.
Jeff Moeller collection

## Ordnance Concerns at Smith & Wesson

A civilian representative of the Ordnance Department, Mr. C. H. Franklin, visited the S&W facility on December 9, 1942 and voiced several concerns as part of a detailed report dated December 10, by which time the Victory Model had been in production for approximately eight months. Excerpts from this report are as follows:

*. . 127 Smith & Wesson .38 Special revolvers rejected by Government Inspection out of a lot of 550 submitted were observed. Barrels were loose, cylinders not properly lined up, in fact much evidence was present that the facility was throwing a considerable burden of manufacturing inspection on the Resident Inspector of Ordnance on the one hand, and giving him insufficient space (in a*

372. Left side closeup of Navy Victory Model showing "U.S. NAVY" marking on top strap of both the 2" and 4"-barreled examples in fig. 371. Jeff Moeller collection

*basement) to house his inspectors, on the other. A check with the Springfield Ordnance District showed that they had been accumulating data over a two week period to bring forcefully to the attention of the facility, showing 23% to 27% rejections per day in Gov't. inspection, and proving definitely that the manufacturer is not doing his job, even after accepting his protests that he loses inspectors as fast as he trains them.*

*The worst part of this situation as the writer sees it is that every time 550 guns are delivered to the Army Inspector of Ordnance, the same quantity is PACKED for the Navy, whose inspector visits Smith & Wesson but once or twice a week, and who, it is reported, resents efforts of the Army inspector to bring this condition to his attention. This can only result in the Navy getting about 25% of their guns in such poor shape that the Army would have rejected them.*

*. . The Springfield Ordnance District Office has contacted the Smith & Wesson Mfg. Co. to immediately do a more thorough manufacturing inspection job. A complete report will be made to the O.C.O.*

373. Left side closeup of 4" Navy Victory Model, showing "PROPERTY OF U.S. NAVY" marking on side of frame. Jeff Moeller collection

## A Brief History of Victory Model Service

Unlike the .38/200 revolvers, which were supplied to British and Commonwealth military forces and used in every theater of the war, Victory Models were only rarely used by the U.S. military. As John Henwood records:

*There were many American fighting men for whom the handgun was a secondary weapon. These men could get along with "less gun" than the M1911 pistol, and in the interests of standardization it was decided that the Navy's aviation forces were to be armed with .38 caliber S&W revolvers . . As it turned out, the Navy received more than enough*

374. A typical .38 Special U.S. Victory Model, shown on top of its plain cardboard shipping carton. This carton which was still sealed when purchased by the present owner, contained the brochure shown below.
Dave Terbrueggen collection

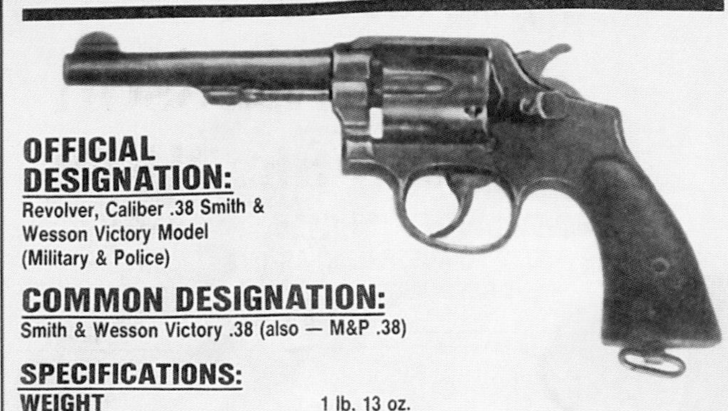

**OFFICIAL DESIGNATION:**
Revolver, Caliber .38 Smith & Wesson Victory Model (Military & Police)

**COMMON DESIGNATION:**
Smith & Wesson Victory .38 (also — M&P .38)

**SPECIFICATIONS:**

| | |
|---|---|
| WEIGHT | 1 lb. 13 oz. |
| LENGTH | 10.2 in. |
| BARREL LENGTH | 5 in. |
| NUMBER OF GROOVES | 5 |
| TWIST | Right |
| SIGHTS | Front — Fixed Blade<br>Rear — Square Notch in Frame Top |
| CALIBER | .38 (.357 in.) |
| CARTRIDGE | .38 Smith & Wesson (.38/200) |
| BULLET | 145 Grain (bullet weight may vary) |
| MUZZLE VELOCITY | 870 f.p.s. |
| MUZZLE ENERGY | 265 ft. lb. |
| EFFECTIVE RANGE | 50–75 yd. |
| OPERATION | Single or double action — revolving cylinder — six shot with hand ejector to extract fired cases from all cylinders simultaneously. |

**AMMUNITION**

Smith & Wesson Victory Model revolvers are chambered for .38 Smith & Wesson cartridges, not .38 Special or other variation. The correct cartridge is also known as .38/200 caliber.

The .38 Smith & Wesson cartridge is a standard, centerfire round that is manufactured by Remington, Winchester and some other commercial factories.

**SAFETY — IMPORTANT INFORMATION**

1. Learn the mechanical characteristics of the gun.
2. Keep the muzzle pointed in a safe direction at all times.
3. Always wear ear and eye protection when shooting. Anyone near the shooter should also wear adequate protection.
4. Make sure the gun is in good condition and the bore is clean and clear before shooting.
5. Keep the gun unloaded when stored or transported to the shooting area.
6. Be sure of your target. Do not shoot at hard surfaces or at water. Target shooting requires that you are certain of proper backstop. Always visualize where the bullet may travel BEFORE you shoot.
7. Do not ford streams, climb trees or fences with a loaded gun.
8. Do not cock the gun or finger the trigger until you are ready to shoot and have determined the course of the bullet.

**ALCOHOL, CONTROLLED SUBSTANCES AND CERTAIN LEGAL MEDICATIONS CAN IMPAIR JUDGEMENT AND MAKE YOU A DANGEROUS SHOOTER. THE LAW AND COMMON SENSE REQUIRE YOU TO BE A RESPONSIBLE SHOOTER.**

375. The two-page brochure describing the .38/200 revolver, which was inside the sealed carton shown above when it was purchased. Dave Terbrueggen collection

# SMITH & WESSON
## .38 SPECIAL CALIBER
# "VICTORY"
## MODEL REVOLVER

### NON-LIGHT-REFLECTING FINISH

No longer need guards risk being spotted by the tell-tale gleam of a highly polished gun. In cooperation with the U. S. Army Ordnance Dept., Smith & Wesson has developed a blued, sandblast finish that does away with light reflection.

Caliber: .38 Special . . . Barrel Length: 4 inches . . . Length Overall: 9⅛ inches . . . Number of Shots: 6 . . . Weight: 30 ounces . . . Sights: Fixed 1/10th-inch service type front sight — square notch rear . . . Stocks: Smooth, unchecked walnut.

### THE CHOICE OF HUNDREDS OF AMERICA'S KEY WAR INDUSTRIES

From coast to coast Smith & Wesson's "Victory" Model Revolvers are on guard today at leading plants. For the rugged, hard-hitting Smith & Wesson — long a favorite with law-enforcement agencies throughout America — has proved ideal equipment to provide the protection every factory in America now needs more than ever before.

### LIGHT 30-OZ. WEIGHT WITH A 266 FOOT-POUND PUNCH!

88 years of experience in filling the exacting needs of top-ranking police departments lie behind the Smith & Wesson "Victory" Model. In its design you'll find the perfect combination of qualities for modern, personal combat — light weight plus a powerful, man-stopping blow even at long ranges.

### COMPACT, SAFE EASY TO HANDLE!

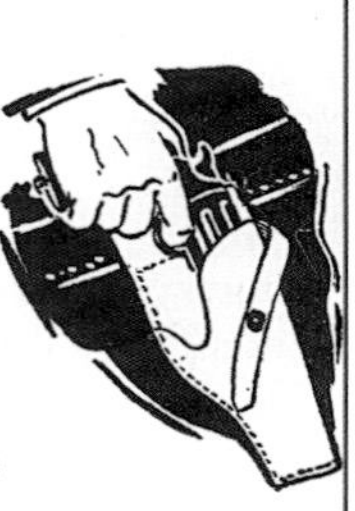

Smith & Wesson's "Victory" Model eliminates the disadvantages of cumbersome, unwieldy arms. Always ready for instant use. Incorporates S&W's famous lockwork design for ultra high-speed double-action shooting. Also two special safety features that positively prevent accidental discharge.

Order from
**DEFENSE SUPPLIES CORPORATION**
**811 VERMONT AVENUE, N. W.**
**WASHINGTON, D. C.**

Although the U. S. Government is now taking our entire output, the War Production Board, by special arrangement, is allocating a limited number of "Victory" Model Revolvers for distribution to peace officers and war plants. Orders should be sent direct to Defense Supplies Corporation — not the factory.

**SMITH & WESSON, INC.**
SPRINGFIELD, MASS.
*"The World's Standard Since 1854"*

377. Left side closeup of a .38 Special Victory Model, showing typical military markings including the Ordnance bomb and the initials of inspector Col. Guy H. Drewry. Jeff Moeller collection

*Victory Models for this purpose, and issued them to other users as well . .*

Other than the small number supplied to Navy aviators, the few issued to Military Police and counter-intelligence organizations, most Victory Models were supplied by the semi-official Defense Supplies Corporation (DSC) for use at U.S. defense factories which, per their government production contracts for war goods, were required to have armed guards on duty protecting their premises. The DSC served as the arbiter of this process, taking delivery of the weapons and supplying them to the corporations as needed to arm their plant guards.

A few Victory Model revolvers were also supplied to local police departments (the New York City Police Department being one well-known recipient of large numbers, which is not surprising, given their likely expansion during the war when New York City was a shipping hub for wartime deliveries). A few were sold to the U.S. Department of Justice to be supplied to the FBI, which also expanded in size during the war, given the emerging need for counter-intelligence work and other security-related issues. All these people needed handguns, and by issuing them M&Ps, standard-issue M1911A1s could be reserved for organizations more likely to be engaged in actual combat.

## U.S. Use of the "Revolver, S&W, M&P, cal. .38 Regular (.38/200)"

John Henwood records that some .38/200 revolvers were issued to U.S. troops, although no one now seems to know exactly how many or why, and continues that these were

*. . Known to the U.S. Army as the "Revolver, S&W, M&P, cal. .38 Regular (38/200)", these are immediately recognizable through their lack of British (or Commonwealth) markings. U.S. Army holsters were made to accommodate either 4- or 5-inch barreled guns . .*

376 (previous page). The S&W brochure advertising the .38 Special Victory Model, which was available to arm guards at war industry plants through the Defense Supplies Corporation. Gaston Comeau collection

## Colts, Too!

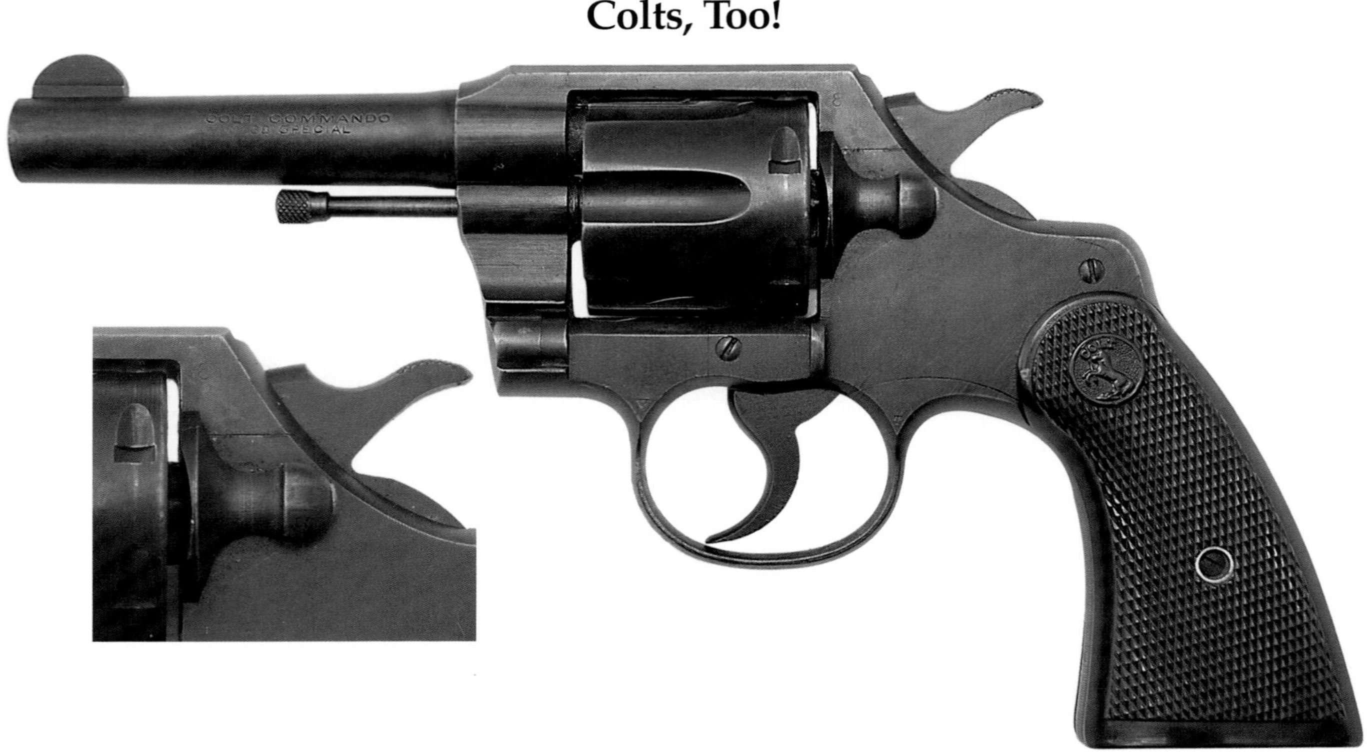


378. Left side view of a typical WWII-era 4" barreled, .38 Special caliber Colt Commando revolver, with dull phosphated military finish and brown plastic grips.

Inset, left: closeup of the Ordnance bomb stamped on the top rear of the receiver.

Quantities of Colt Official Police models with 5" barrels and 2" Detective Specials were also purchased for military use.

Jeff Moeller collection

# The Final Hammer Block Safety

## A Fatal Accident Forces a Definitive Redesign

Despite the repeated efforts of S&W's best and brightest engineers, beginning with D. B. Wesson himself in his patented "Revolver Lock Mechanism" of May 29, 1894 (fig. 232) and following with the various hammer-blocking safeties discussed in earlier chapters which had over time been incorporated into the basic S&W Hand Ejector design, a fatal accident in May, 1944 made further improvement mandatory.

The official records, documented by the U.S. Navy Ordnance Bureau, are included as Appendix F in the fine reference *U.S. Handguns of World War II: The Secondary Pistols and Revolvers* by Charles W. Pate, and excerpts from these documents are reproduced here with the kind permission of the author.

The first excerpt, from a Product Corrections Report from the U.S. Navy Field Service Division, Maintenance Branch, Small Arms Section, addressed to the Industrial Division, Small Arms Branch, Hand Arms & Equipment, dated 6 May, 1944, reads as follows:

***Subject: Malfunction of Revolver, Smith & Wesson, Military and Police, Cal. .38 Special***

*. . The Ordnance Bureau, Navy Dept. has received a report of the death of a seaman resulting from the accidental discharge of a Smith & Wesson Revolver.*

*A revolver (Smith & Wesson, Military and Police, Cal. .38 Special—No. V 95139) fell from the hands of the seaman to a steel deck, which caused the weapon to be discharged, fatally wounding the seaman. This weapon upon careful examination by the Bureau of Ordnance showed no evidence of . . having been altered. Primed cartridge cases were placed in the revolver and were discharged by dropping the weapon.*

*The accident resulted in an investigation of the safety features of the Smith & Wesson revolvers. Ninety (90) revolvers as received from the factory in original grease and wrapping were subjected to the test. The revolvers were mounted in an aluminum frame and pointed towards the ground. A brass weight was permitted to fall upon hammer spur. Despite both safeties, primed cartridges were discharged in thirty-one (31)weapons by a two (2) pound weight falling two and one-half (2 1/2) feet. Only one (1) weapon required a four (4) pound weight falling three (3) feet.*

*. . As a result of these tests the Smith & Wesson Military and Police, Caliber .38 Special Revolver as now being supplied is considered unsafe for issuance to Naval forces. To guard against recurrence of accidents as herein described, instructions are being issued to Naval activities not to carry a cartridge in the chamber under the hammer.*

*Information is requested as to whether the War Department can effect suitable modifications to overcome the malfunctioning herein described or supply a revolver of similar type which still functions satisfactorily. Total issues to date to all Naval activities of Smith & Wesson revolvers are 145,000 . .*

## The Navy Reports on Investigative Trials

On May 29, 1944 a report detailing the results of an investigation into the causes of the accident, and of the discharges produced by dropping weights on the hammer spurs of the test revolvers as detailed above, was added to the file as a First Indorsement. Excerpts from this somewhat face-saving (not to say ass-covering) document read as follows:

*. . Examination of several weapons indicated that the cause for accidental discharge is as follows:*

*a. The Block, Hammer, is harder than the Hammer and Frame of the Revolver;*
*b. When the Hammer spur is struck a sharp blow, the hardened Block, Hammer causes a sufficient indent of both hammer face and frame to permit firing the weapon.*

*It should be noted that the Smith & Wesson Military & Police revolver, Cal. .38 Special is in no sense a Military weapon. It was originally procured by the Navy Contracts as a commercial weapon. The fatal revolver referred to above and those inspected at the Navy Yard . . were produced on Navy contracts.*

*It is not intended to imply that revolvers produced on Ordnance contracts will not fire when dropped so that the hammer spur is struck . .*

## Smith & Wesson Reacts Positively

Carl Hellstrom, writing in *Smith & Wesson, The Story of the Revolver*, briefly describes the company's "take" on the accident recorded above, and the factory's swift reaction to the challenge it presented, as follows:

*. . Some time after the United States entered the war, an accident, resulting in the death of a sailor, brought to focus the danger of issuing side arms to raw recruits. A loaded revolver had been dropped on the deck of a battleship, discharging a cartridge. At an ordnance meeting the following day, in reviewing the long history of accidents, an urgent demand was made upon us to design, within three days, some positive safety device superior to those in use up to that time. It was during the three hectic days and nights which followed that our revolvers became the safest in the world . .*

## Describing the New Hammer Block

Excerpts from further documentation taken from Navy Ordnance Bureau files recap the story and describe the new hammer block design mentioned by Mr. Hellstrom, as follows:

***Report of Test on New Smith & Wesson Hammer Block***

1. *Test was conducted on 1 Sept. 1944 at the Navy Yard Ordnance Laboratory. Two Revolvers, Smith & Wesson Military & Police, Cal. .38 Special, with four-inch barrel, were tested. Both revolvers had the new type of hammer block, operated by the rebound slide movement.*
2. *The purpose of test was to determine whether the new hammer block provides adequate safety in instances where a revolver may be dropped from one deck to another aboard ship, possibly landing on the hammer spur. The current type hammer block, as now manufactured, fails to provide safety under such circumstances.*
3. *The Smith & Wesson hammer block, or safety device, has been subject to criticism for failures to prevent accidental discharge. Some of these failures have been due to the hammer block spring becoming inoperative due to dirt, sand or metal filings becoming wedged between the hammer block and the sides of the plate groove in which it operates.The inherent weakness of this device has been discussed with the manufacturer, and adoption of a more positive device recommended . .*
5. *The writer contacted Mr. Hellstrom, Production Manager of Smith & Wesson by telephone, explaining the necessity for prompt action in changing to an improved safety device. It was suggested that a hammer block having more metal between the hammer and the frame be used, and that this block be supported at both sides of the hammer recess in the frame. Mr. Hellstrom agreed to make up a sample revolver incorporating the proposed changes and deliver the revolver to this office within four days.*
6. *The sample revolver was delivered and approved with only one minor change . . Arrangements were made for five revolvers to be prepared, using the new hammer block. Two were forwarded [to] Springfield Armory, with instructions for testing, and two were used in [our] tests. The fifth revolver was presented to the British for their information, as they also use the Smith & Wesson revolver in the .38-200 Caliber.*
7. *The new hammer block is a larger component than the type now in production. It is operated from a stud added to the upper right side of the rebound slide. An eccentric hole in the bottom of the hammer block provides the camming surface. When the trigger is moved to the rear, whether by cocking the revolver single or double action, the rebound slide moves to the rear, withdrawing the top of the hammer block downward from [an] engaged position between the hammer and face of the frame. The forward face of the hammer requires slight modification to provide adequate clearance for the top of the hammer [block]. An additional cut is required in the sideplate, and a new rebound slide completes the alteration to the new type safety device.*

## Introducing the New Hammer Block

John Henwood records that the new rebound slide-activated hammer block was introduced in December, 1944 at serial number V 767000, and continues as follows:

> *. . When the "side-swing" hammer block was discarded in favor of an improved hammer block in December, 1944, the serial number prefix "V" (used by the factory to indicate a sub-standard wartime exterior finish) was changed to "SV"; frames in production which were already serial numbered, and which received the improved ham-*

379 (following page). Page 1 of a U.S. Navy Bureau Ordnance catalog issued in support of the S&W .38 Spec Military & Police revolver. Jeff Moeller collecti

BUREAU OF ORDNANCE SECTION

# CAL. .38 SPECIAL SMITH & WESSON MILITARY and POLICE REVOLVER

## GENERAL INFORMATION

### FOREWORD

1. **THIS SECTION INCLUDES:** The Cal. .38 Special, Smith and Wesson Military and Police Revolver. In accordance with Cir. Ltr. GV1-45, Smith and Wesson Revolvers are to be issued to flight crews. These side-arms are for aviation personnel only. See Sheet .9631 for side-arms to be used by other Navy Personnel.
2. **REQUISITIONS MUST:**
   - **A.** Name the gun for which the part is needed. Cal. .38 Special Revolver, Smith and Wesson, Military and Police.
   - **B.** Use the Authorized Stock Number as shown in Column 2.
   - **C.** Use the Authorized Nomenclature.
   - **D.** Explain in detail and justifiy all requisitions in excess of Cir. Ltr. GV1-45.
3. **SOURCES OF SUPPLY:** Requisitions are to be submitted in accordance with enclosure (C) of Joint Ltr. BuOrd S31-3(Mn1) and BuSandA No. L 8/S 31 L 4/JJ-2(4) of 9 Feb. 1945. Primary sources of supply are NSD Norfolk and NSD Oakland.
4. **REPAIRS:** Repairs beyond the continental limits may be requested from the nearest Army or Marine Corps Activity with available facilities. Repairs within the continental limits, when deemed advisable, may be made at NSD Norfolk, NSD Oakland, or Navy Yard, New York.
5. **RECONCILIATION OF STOCK RECORDS and STOCK NUMBERS:** All Ordnance Supply Activities are required to reconcile stock records, bin and stock tags with the authorized nomenclature and stock numbers appearing herein. Column 2 shows stock numbers to be used for requisitioning, stock records, storage, issue, and inventory reporting. Stock numbers are Army numbers.
6. **ALTERNATE ITEMS:** In certain cases the Supply Depots are instructed by BuOrd to issue substitutes. These substitutes are to be accepted by requisitioning activities since changes in material and specifications are frequent in order to improve the equipment.
7. **PUBLICATIONS AVAILABLE FROM BUORD PUBLICATION CENTERS:** TM9-1295; SNL B-29.
8. **A LINE THROUGH STOCK NO. INDICATES ITEM IS NOT STOCKED:** Order the available component parts or the next larger available assembly.

## HOW TO USE THE CATALOG

The Cal. .38 Special, Smith and Wesson Military and Police Revolver is composed of assemblies and individual parts.

**COMPONENT BREAKDOWN TABLE** contains:
Assemblies—their Authorized Nomenclature and Stock Number.
Sub-Assemblies—their Authorized Nomenclature and Stock Number.
Item Numbers—for the parts composing assemblies and sub-assemblies.

**PARTS LIST** contains:
Authorized Stock Number
Authorized Nomenclature
Item Number

**ITEM NUMBER**—This is a device used in cataloging to identify individual parts. Item numbers are also used to identify assemblies and sub-assemblies.

**EXAMPLE:** Item 18 is an assembly composed of assemblies 21 and 22, and individual parts, COLLAR 1, PLUNGER 3, ROD 1, SPRING 1, and SPRING 5. →

Item 21 is composed of CYLINDER 1, PIN 7, and RING 1.
Item 22 is composed of BUSHING 3 and EJECTOR 1.

Remember:
**COLUMN 1 = COLUMN 2 = (COLUMN 3 + COLUMN 4)**

| COL. 1 | COL. 2 | COL. 3 | COL. 4 | | | | COL. 5 |
|---|---|---|---|---|---|---|---|
| | | | Parts Making Up Balance of Assy. | | | | |
| Item No. | Stock No. | Sub. Assy. Item No. | Part Name & Item No. | Qty. | Part Name & Item No. | Qty. | Next Larger Assy. |
| **CYLINDER, WITH EJECTOR ASSEMBLY** | | | | | | | |
| 18 | B029-7310292 | 21, 22 | COLLAR 1 | 1 | SPRING 1 | 1 | 2 |
| | | | PLUNGER 3 | 1 | SPRING 5 | 1 | |
| | | | ROD 1 | 1 | | | |
| **STOCK, RIGHT ASSEMBLY** | | | | | | | |
| 19 | B029-7310301 | | ESCUTCHEON 3 | 1 | STOCK 3 | 1 | 12 |
| **STOCK, LEFT ASSEMBLY** | | | | | | | |
| 20 | B029-7310300 | | ESCUTCHEON 1 | 1 | STOCK 1 | 1 | 12 |
| **CYLINDER ASSEMBLY** | | | | | | | |
| 21 | B029-7310290 | | CYLINDER 1 | 1 | RING 1 | 1 | 18 |
| | | | PIN 7 | 1 | | | |
| **EJECTOR ASSEMBLY** | | | | | | | |
| 22 | B029-7310294 | | BUSHING 3 | 1 | EJECTOR 1 | 1 | 18 |

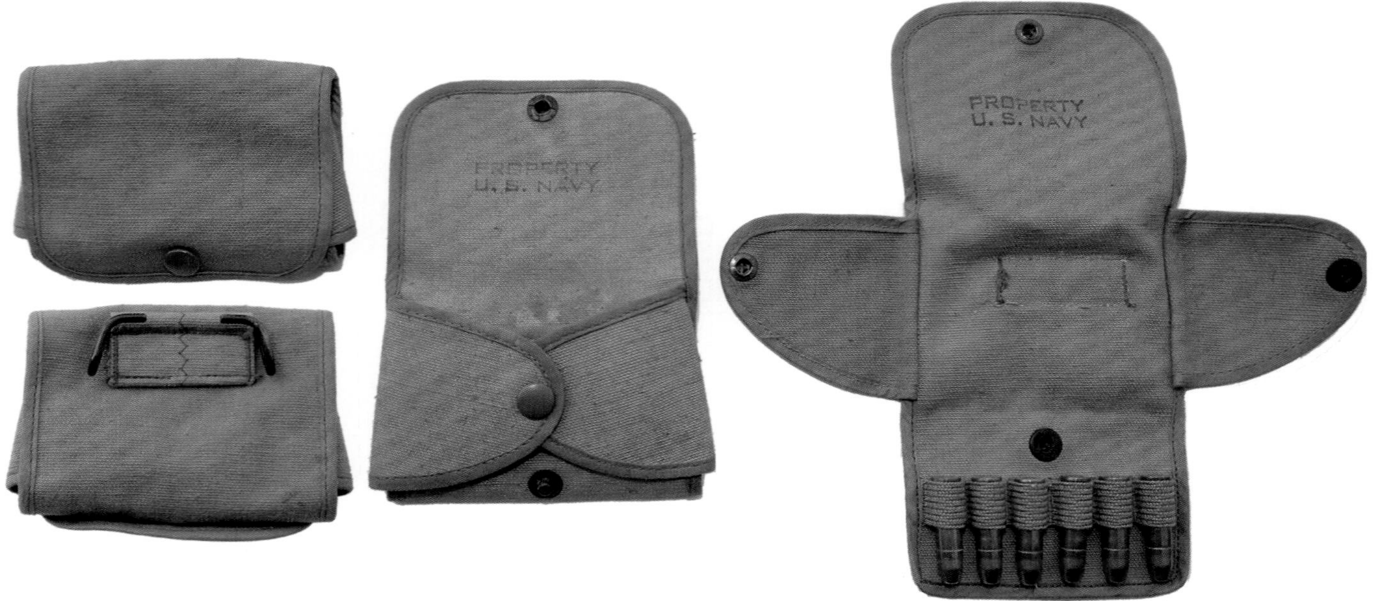


380. Several views of a WWII-era web spare cartridge belt pouch, marked "PROPERTY U.S. NAVY", a remarkably over-engineered piece of kit for just six spare rounds!

On page 6 of the Navy supply catalog depicted in fig. 379, an additional accessory item is described as "POUCH, 1st Aid packet (used with revolver as ammunition carrier)." Jeff Moeller collection

*mer block, had an "S" handstamped in front of the existing serial number, making it read "S V". Later guns are machine-stamped "SV" in front of the lanyard swivel, with the numeric segment of the serial behind the swivel . .*

*Sideplates . . on those "S V" and "SV" revolvers are marked at the top rear corner with a tiny "s" just above the rear sideplate screw . . probably to assist the assemblers in keeping the two types of sideplates straight . . since the two styles of sideplates do not interchange, at least not if a hammer block is to be installed.*

381. Another web carrier with loops for spare cartridges (13 rounds, in this case), which could be slid over the shoulder holster strap for use by Navy pilots. Jeff Moeller collection

## A Late-War Ordnance Timetable on Hammer Safety Reworks

A document from the Jeff Moeller collection is a report, prepared by Ordnance Major Arthur G. Snyder, of a visit to Smith & Wesson on 3 - 4 January, 1945, when existing revolvers from military stores with the earlier "side-swing" hammer safety were being reworked and fitted with the improved hammer safety. After the conversion a small letter 's' was stamped, usually on the sideplate, to indicate the presence of the new safety. This interesting report is excerpted as follows:

*. . The rework program is now under way. At a price of $7 each the facility reworks each weapon. It is then inspected by Ordnance in the same manner as new weapons are inspected. The letter "s" for serviceable is stamped upon each reworked revolver that is accepted.*

*The facility function fires, targets and proof-fires (one cylinder) each weapon under Ordnance surveillance. A personal check of this test firing was made. It revealed that the guns were satisfactorily targeted and that they met accuracy requirements with ease. It was stated by the RIO [Resident Inspector of Ordnance] that the facility does a 100% final inspection with approximately 40% rejections. Upon a visit over a year before the writer had found that such "screening" was at that time being done by Ordnance. At the present time Ordnance final inspection rejects about 6% which are then reworked by Smith & Wesson. The ratio of facility to Ordnance inspectors is approximately three to one.*

*On 30 December [1944] the plant stopped shipping .38 Special Revolvers with the old style hammer. The facility has promised the District 4,000 of the 4-inch barrel revolvers for the Navy for January. It was stated that the new hammer was expected to be placed in the .38/200 Revolver for the British during March [1945] . .*

*The estimated January [1945] production of the Cal. .38/200 revolver is 7,500 . .*

*The RIO raised a question regarding the proofing of spare barrels and cylinders stating that they were not being proofed. A check with the Operating Branch has revealed the fact that such requirements were not in the 1917 Cal. .45 Revolver specifications and that since the proofing of revolvers at this plant during the present war, no failures of barrels or cylinders have occurred. In the opinion of the Hand Arms & Equipment Branch such proofing is not necessary . .*

## Patenting the New Hammer Block

U.S. patent no. 2,470,259, titled "Safety Device for revolvers", was applied for on April 2, 1946 and granted to Joseph W. Norman and Carl R. Hellstrom, assignors to Smith & Wesson, on May 17, 1949. The page of illustrations from the patent is shown in fig. 163, and the patent disclosure is excerpted on pages 147 and 148.

## Springfield Armory Has (Almost) the Last Word

Excerpts from a postwar report prepared for the Commanding Officer of the Ordnance Corps at Springfield Armory, dated 8 September, 1952, originally classified as Restricted, contain some interesting additional information concerning the hammer block issue, as follows:

*. . It is not recommended that the hammer block be eliminated. Although the rebound slide will effectively block the hammer from falling when struck ordinary blows, the additional strength afforded by the hammer block is necessary for resistance to unusually heavy blows. The rebound slide is hollow and can be crushed, as was the case in a Naval accident . .*

*With reference to the effect of the hammer block on the action, it should be understood that there are two types:*

*a. That used on the "Victory Model" and the current "Short Action" model Cal. .38 revolvers. This is a long, slender member whose action is positively controlled in both directions by a cam in the side plate and a pin on the rebound slide.*

*b. A spring-actuated hammer block used on the Smith & Wesson, Cal. .38-200 model manufactured for the British during the war. This was an earlier type, later improved upon.*

*The hammer block (b, above) has been known to stick due to an accumulation of grit and gummy oil in the action. Frequent cleaning and oiling with very light oil will correct this situation. Hammer block (a, above) is an improvement in that it must move when the rebound slide moves. With this positive action, the only plausible reason, for interference with the hammer, is that an improper fit exists . .*

## Some Latter-Day Questions Remain

While taken directly from official records, some of the statements made in the above documentation appear ambiguous at best and falsely misleading at worst, and certainly beg further questions.

First, in the initial May 29, 1944 report we read that "The Block, Hammer, is harder than the Hammer and Frame of the Revolver", to which we might ask just how much harder the hammer block purportedly was, or could be, than Smith & Wesson's famous "glass hard" hammer (and trigger).

Second, concerning the statement made by Mr. Hellstrom, one might well question what a "raw recruit" was doing with a "loaded revolver" on a crowded "battleship".

Third, the postwar report from Springfield Armory contains the assertion that the "old" hammer block was only used in the British .38/200 model, which is not true. Previous documentation confirms that the fatal accident was caused by a U.S. Navy Victory Model, serial no. V 95139.

Finally, we are still not completely sure just exactly what caused the accident. The May 29, 1944 report states that "When the Hammer spur is struck a sharp blow, the hardened Block, Hammer causes a sufficient indent of both hammer face and frame to permit firing the weapon", and speaks of the "inherent weakness of this device." The Naval Ordnance report on the further tests that were conducted following the accident states that "Some of these failures have been due to the hammer block spring becoming inoperative due to dirt, sand or metal filings becoming wedged between the hammer block and the sides of the plate groove in which it operates"; while the postwar Springfield Armory report states that in response to unusually heavy blows, "The rebound slide is hollow and can be crushed, as was the case in a Naval accident." It also opines that the old hammer block "has been known to stick due to an accumulation of grit and gummy oil in the action."

## Summing Up the Hammer Block Saga

We have already discussed and described the "side-swing" hammer block, which was patented in 1915. No doubt many hammers on prewar loaded M&Ps had been struck by steering wheels, pavement, and similar hard objects, and did not fire. But the "side-swing" hammer block did require that the weapon be kept marginally clean and, more critically, free of internal grease. When the M&P went to war during WWII, no doubt many were first dipped in heated Cosmoline to deter rust. When they were finally issued out, the thick Cosmoline would remain internally unless the guns were carefully (and laboriously) cleaned, a relatively complicated operation which was certainly beyond the capability or remit of the average soldier (or sailor). This thick grease, especially when cold, could keep the hammer block from springing out of its recess in the sideplate to block the hammer. Heavy dirt could also do it, but my guess is that it was basically a Cosmoline problem—unless, of course, the fatal revolver was defective. We recall Mr. Franklin's December, 1942 report, excerpted above, wherein he warned that "This can only result in the Navy getting about 25% of their guns in such poor shape that the Army would have rejected them."

The new hammer block, cam-operated by the rebound slide, used positive mechanical force to block the hammer, so as long as the rebound slide could move, heavy grease or dirt would not tie up the safety and prevent it from moving into the blocking position. As noted, this was designed in 1944, but according to Major Snyder's report, excerpted above, it was not installed until the beginning of 1945 in Victory Models and not until March, 1945 in British .38/200 revolvers.

The point to note here is that as long as your pre-war M&P is *not* clogged up with heavy grease or dirt, you can safely carry it with six rounds in the cylinder. A lot of people seemed not to understand this, and when I was in the Army, some people thought that only our C-prefix Military and Police revolvers (made in the 1950 - 1960 timeframe) could be safely carried with all six chambers loaded. Gun ignorance is all too common, especially institutional gun ignorance, I find.

# Wrapping Up the Wartime M&P

Wartime production of the Victory model ended on August 27, 1945, with serial number SV 811119, five months after the last .38/200 had rolled off the line.

As to the total production of both models, John Henwood records that

> . . *Sources at Smith & Wesson place the number of .38/200 and Victory Model revolvers manufactured during World War II at 1,110,392: 542,190 Victory Models in addition to the 568,200 .38/200s.*

As McHenry and Roper confirmed, "[The .38/200] is undoubtedly the most extensively used military revolver ever made."

# Part II: The Golden Age

*Chapter Thirty-One*

# Early Postwar Demand Surges

## America After WWII

In America, the post-WWII era was different from any period which had existed before. First, of course, the Depression, which had gripped the country from 1929 to 1940, had ended, and everyone had more money. Also, unlike the aftermath of WWI, when the rural areas had gone into an economic tailspin, this had not occurred in the immediate post-WWII period. Additionally, coming out of the war as one of the few countries that had not experienced the crippling devastation to their infrastructure that modern wars bring, and actually suffering very light casualties in comparison to those of the other major powers, the U. S. was poised to become a pre-eminence in the world, both politically and economically. Indeed, the years from 1945 onward can be classified to a great extent as the "American Period".

Further, unlike the 1920s, no crime wave followed the war, thanks to the lack of such things as Prohibition.

We still tend to look back fondly at the 1950s as a relatively crime-free decade, with people known for leaving their doors unlocked and keys in the ignition of their car. While younger people will find it hard to believe that such times existed, I am certain that many readers will remember just as I do as a kid in the 1950s leaving doors unlocked, windows open, and your father never taking the key from the ignition of the family motor vehicle. It does almost seem hard to believe as I write it. And glass-fronted gun cabinets or open gun racks in the kids' bedrooms, for that matter.

# The Legacy of the Wartime M&P

## No Repeat of the Post-WWI "Dumping" of Model 1917s

Reference was made in Chapter Twenty-Seven to the post-WWI sell-off of surplus S&W Model 1917s through the DCM and the NRA, with John Henwood concluding, "The firm neither forgot nor forgave what they considered to be "dumping"."

Later excerpts from Henwood's account pick up the post-WWII story, as follows:

> *While it performed admirably during the war, once hostilities ended a decision was made not to retain the Victory Model as a standard sidearm of the U.S. Armed Forces, although it was retained as "limited standard" for a number of years. A large number were declared surplus, only a few remaining on active duty, mostly with Naval and Marine aviators. The rest posed a disposal problem, since Smith & Wesson felt that the selling of Model 1917 revolvers by the U.S. Government following World War I had cost them a good deal of business [and] they saw to it that a clause was inserted in their new wartime contracts enjoining the U.S. Government from selling Victory Model revolvers . .*
>
> *Government agents oversaw the destruction of the greater part of these arms, once they were declared surplus . . The remains of the flattened revolvers were sold as scrap . .*
>
> *. . Although not allowed to sell them, nothing prevented the Government from giving them away*

*[and] some Victory Models did escape, and eventually reached the commercial market . .[S]ome were exported as part of various military assistance programs, as well . .*

## British Commercial Conversions of .38/200 Revolvers

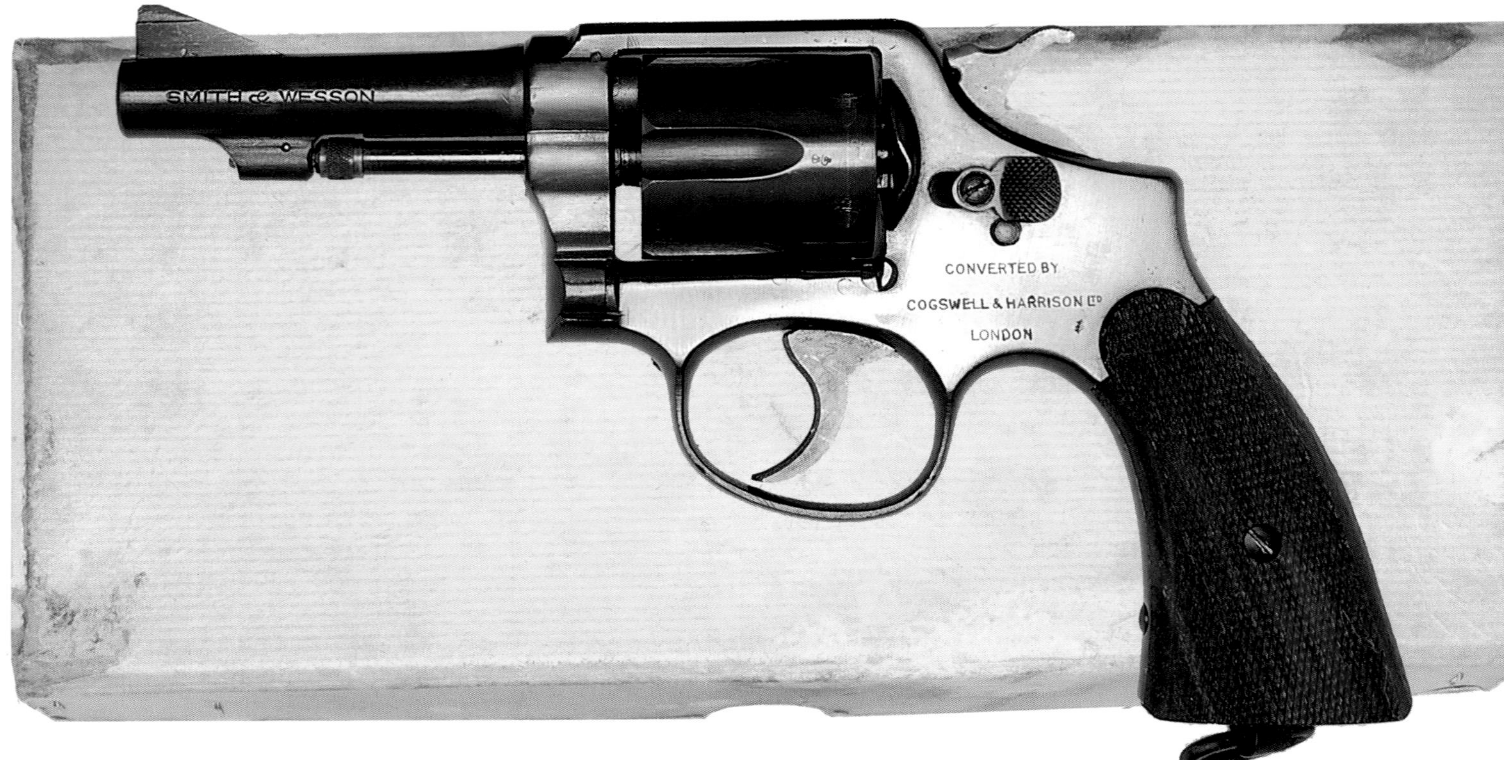


382. Left side view of a wartime British .38/200 revolver, serial no. V 73945 on its original plain cardboard shipping box. The date "8-43" is stamped on the backstrap.

This example was converted after the war by Cogswell & Harrison Ltd. of London. The caliber remains .38 S&W (.38/200), but the barrel has been shortened to 4", a new ramp style front sight has been fitted, the stocks finely checkered, and the entire gun has been refinished and engraved as shown. Each chamber of the cylinder bears British BNP proofs. Dave Terbrueggen collection

After the war, a number of ex-wartime .38/200 S&W revolvers were reconditioned by such long-established British gunsmithing firms as Cogswell & Harrison and Parker-Hale and then re-sold on the commercial market, most back into the United States. These conversions could involve merely shortening the barrel and refitting a ramp front sight, while more detailed work involved a caliber conversion to .22 rimfire by lining the bore and chambers with small-bore tubes.

The proprietary name for this process as used by Parker-Hale was "Parkerifling", and the .22 rimfire conversion was described in the 1955 (and later) Parker-Hale catalogs as follows:

### *Parker-Hale S&W Conversion*

*The basis for the conversion of this revolver to .22" calibre rim fire will be readily recognised as the famous Smith & Wesson .38" calibre Military and Police model of which quantities were issued to the R.A.F. during World War II.*

*When fitted with target sights these revolvers made excellent competition weapons with which the R.A.F. Teams have in the past scored signal successes at Bisley. We, therefore, adopted this weapon as the most suitable available choice for conversion of its calibre and by the addition of [an] adjustable backsight . . we have produced an inexpensive .22" calibre Target revolver of the highest degree of accuracy that will function reliably with short, long or long rifle cartridges of regular or high velocity. Each weapon is subjected to Birmingham Proof before sale. The barrels are Parkerifled—"for accuracy." The six chambers are bushed so as to encase the cartridge heads in accordance with modern practice. The inserted hammer noses are replaced to a shape more suited to rim fire striking and correct detonation of the rim fire cartridge, by a substitution of the trigger return spring the pull-off is reduceable near the minimum permitted without intereference with the main-spring or the engagement of the trigger and hammer. Each revolver is completely refinished and remarked with its new calibre and is subsequently tested for group and sighting accuracy.*

## Conversion to .38 Special for Resale in the U.S.A.

383. Right side view of another converted Lend-Lease .38/200 revolver, serial no. V 268957, which was shipped to England with "UNITED STATES PROPERTY" stamped on the top strap. After the war the barrel was chopped to 3" and a new ramp front sight was mounted. The chambers were reamed out to accept .38 Special cartridges, and the arm received new British proofs in 1955 before being re-imported into the U.S.

These .38 Special conversions were commonly sold by mail order in the 1950s and 1960s, before the passage of the 1968 Gun Control Act.

As discussed in Chapter Thirty-Five, Lee Harvey Oswald owned a similar converted .38/200 revolver.

private collection

Other than the distribution of stock .38/200s to the police forces of occupied Germany, discussed in detail below, John Henwood records the additional methods that were adopted for the disposal of wartime stocks of British S&W revolvers as follows:

*The British determined that they were still in possession of a rather large number of revolvers for which they felt no further need. One disposal scheme consisted of using them as reinforcing steel in concrete construction projects; another involved selling them off. . . mainly to U.S. dealers. A great number were returned to the United States in this manner. Some were sleeved, both barrel and cylinder, for the .22 Long Rifle cartridge [while] some were rechambered for the .38 Special, and most returned just as they left, in .38 S&W caliber . .*

*This .38 Special conversion was not a good idea, since the .38 S&W case was fatter than the .38 Special. (This is no longer true, the dimensions of the .38 S&W case have been altered to facilitate production; as currently made it resembles a short .38 Special case.) Badly bulged cases, and even ruptured cases, have been reported resulting from the use of one of these conversions with any of the more potent .38 Special loadings. It was economical, though, and . . proved very popular with those desiring a quality arm at a bargain price, but having no knowledge of firearms.*

## Police Use of Wartime Victory Models and .38/200s in the U.S. Zone of Occupied Germany

John Henwood's account continues to introduce the postwar military assistance programs whereby thousands of wartime M&P revolvers, both .38/200s and .38 Special Victory Models, were provided to the police in the U.S. zone of occupied Germany:

> *[S]ome Victory Models were furnished to civilian police establishments in the U.S. zone of occupied Germany at war's end, [although] in view of the rather limited presence of U.S. Naval aviation in Europe, as well as the restricted Army use of this arm, it would appear unlikely that there were enough Victory Models immediately available for this purpose. It is more probable that, in the interests of standardization, .38/200s were acquired from the British for issue to German police in the U.S. zone . .*

James Mock, well known to collectors of the U.S. carbine for his expertise regarding the postwar distribution and use of U.S. military carbines in foreign lands, has kindly provided the following information that deals specifically with the issue and marking of S&W M&P revolvers of wartime manufacture by the various police units in the U.S. zone of occupied Germany. As John Henwood correctly guessed, both ex-British .38/200s and .38 Special U.S. Victory Models were involved.

## The Potsdam Conference - Dividing Up a Defeated Germany

Nine weeks after the unconditional German surrender on May 8, 1945 (V-E Day), a high-level conference was convened at Cecilienhof, the home of Crown Prince Wilhelm Hohenzollern in Potsdam. The conference lasted from July 17 to August 2, 1945. Initially the chief delegates were Joseph Stalin from the USSR, Winston Churchill from the United Kingdom, and U.S. President Harry Truman, although Churchill was replaced during the conference by Clement Atlee, who had been elected Prime Minister in the first postwar British election.

Among the items on the agenda were the division of Germany and Austria respectively into four occupation zones; the redrawing of Germany's eastern border along the Oder-Neisse line, which effectively reduced Germany's land area by about 25% from its 1937 borders; war reparations; and the destruction of Germany's industrial war potential.

Prior to the Potsdam conference the U.S. had been allocated Bavaria, Hessen, all the states of Baden and Württemberg, as well as the American Sector of Berlin. It was decided at the conference that the French should control two-thirds of the merged states of Baden and Württemberg, with the U.S. retaining the upper third, which they named the new state of Württemberg-Baden.

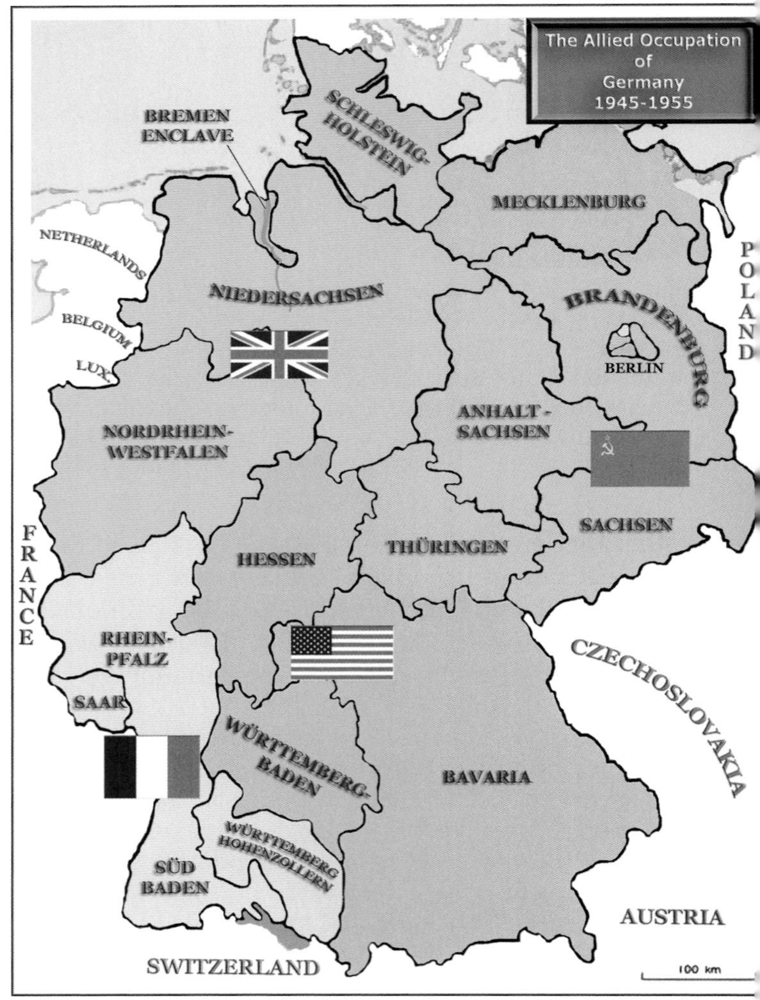


384 (right). A map of Germany, showing the boundaries of the Allied Occupation Zones, 1945 - 1955.
courtesy James Mock

In addition, at Potsdam the U.S. negotiated for and was granted its own port, which they called the Bremen Enclave. This area was received from the Canadians, who had occupied the port after the end of the war.

## The Structure of OMGUS

The military governor of the Office of Military Government, American Occupation Zone (OMGUS) was the U.S. Commander-in-Chief - Europe. He appointed a military governor for each of the five areas of the American Occupation Zone, which were as follows:

- Bavaria
- Berlin Sector
- Bremen Enclave
- Hessen
- Württemberg-Baden

# Marking of Weapons for German Police Use

Allied Control Council Directive #16, dated October 10, 1945, allowed the occupation governments in each of the four occupation zones (British, French, Russian and American) to arm the city police with pistols, and the "rural" police and the new "frontier" police with carbines. This directive also stated that all weapons provided to the German police in all occupied zones had to be of non-German origin, and marked to identify the agency to which they were assigned. However, neither the exact manner in which the arms were to be marked, nor the location of the markings on each weapon, was specified, leaving this up to each occupying nation's military government.

In the OMGUS area of control the decision regarding the makeup and location of the markings was passed on to the military governors in each of the five districts, and each, predictably, ordered something a little different. OMGUS named the new German police agencies using American law enforcement terminology, not the names the Germans themselves had chosen for their police.

All of the German states later purchased the weapons provided to them by the Western Allies, and eventually sold them to other German states or to private gun brokers.

## OMG Bavaria

OMG Bavaria (OMGB) ordered the word "Bavaria", followed by either "Municipal Police" or "Rural Police", to be marked on the left side of the frame of each of their revolvers. Bavaria was the only jurisdiction in West Germany to use these names on their weapons.

On January 7, 1946, the *Chef des Sicherheitswesens, Polizeipräsidium München* (Chief of the Security Branch, Munich Police Department), not the *Waffenamt* (Weapons Office), was ordered to do the actual marking on the weapons. After they were marked, the *Waffenamt* distributed them to the various branches and districts throughout Bavaria.

During the U.S. occupation, if one agency within Bavaria had no further need for a revolver, it was issued to another agency, and the markings were changed appropriately.

After the end of the occupation in 1955, the markings were no longer required.

385. Left side closeup of a Victory Model revolver, showing markings added by the Bavarian Municipal Police.
Reiner Herrmann collection

## The June, 1949 Inventory Report of German Police Personnel and Equipment

PERSONALSTÄRKE, -AUFGLIEDERUNG UND AUSRÜSTUNG,
(30. Juni 1949 in der US-Zone (ohne US-Sektor von Berlin)

| Land | BAYERN | | | | HESSEN | | | | BREMEN | WÜRTTEMBG.BADEN | | | US-Zone |
|---|---|---|---|---|---|---|---|---|---|---|---|---|---|
| Aufgliederung | Kommun. Pol. | Landpol. | Grenzpol. | Polizei insg. | Kommun. Pol. | Landpol. | Grenzpol. | Polizei insg. | Polizei insg. | Kommun. Pol. | Landpol. | Polizei insg. | |
| Bevölkerung i(in 1000) | 9.029 | | | | 4.280 | | | | 480 | 3.675 | | | 17.464 |
| Polizeidichte 1) | 1 : 476 | | | | 1 : 500 | | | | 1:185 | 1 : 435 | | | 1:470 |
| Personalstärke | 7.887 | 9.368 | 2.036 | 19.291 | 5.795 | 2.264 | 587 | 8.646 | 2.578 | 5.228 | 3.400 | 8.628 | 39.143 |
| davon Verw. Ang. | 632 | 293 | 38 | 963 | 784 | 105 | 11 | 900 | 349 | 420 | 373 | 793 | 3.005 |
| Bewaffng. Pistolen | | | | 8.864 | | | | 4.590 | 1.721 | | | 4.226 | 19.401 |
| Karabiner | | | | 11.721 | | | | 2.458 | 1.044 | | | 3.743 | 18.966 |
| Mobilität: Autos | | | | 1.132 | | | | 375 | 134 | | | 428 | 2.069 |
| Motorräder | | | | 2.300 | | | | 755 | 71 | | | 760 | 3.886 |
| Entlassgn. wegen Nazi-Verg. | (für die Periode 1.Juli 1948 - 30.Juni 1949) | | | 2 | | | | 9 | 2 | | | 18 | 31 |

1) ohne Grenzpolizei
Quelle: NA, RG 260, OMGUS, Adjutant General's Office, General Correspondence 1949, Box 13; hier: OMGUS-Civil Administration Division, Bad Nauheim, 8. September 1949, Semi-Annual German Police Personal & Equipment Report as of 30 June 1949 (Tabelle 2 ist eine Zusammenfassung verschiedener Tabellen dieses Reports)

386. The semi-annual inventory report of German Police personnel and equipment, including pistols and rifles, submitted to the OMGUS Civil Administration Division in Bad Nauheim in June, 1949. courtesy James Mock

On February 9, 1948, OMGB transferred control of all the U.S.-made firearms to the Bavarian government. On April 25, 1948, the *Waffenamt* conducted an inventory of their weapons which was included in the semi-annual inventory report as of June 30, 1949, submitted to the OMGUS Civil Administration Division in Bad Nauheim.

# OMG Hessen

OMG Hessen abbreviated the name Hessen to "HE", to be followed by either "M" for Municipal or "R" for Rural Police ("H-M" or "H-R") to be stamped on the backstraps of their revolvers.

By June, 1949, the Hessen *Polizei* had received 2,458 M1 carbines and 4,590 pistols from the U.S. Military Government (OMGUS), Hesse.

387 (right). Closeup of the backstrap of a Victory Model marked "HE – M" for the Hessen Municipal Police (*Stadt Polizei*).
James Mock collection

# OMG Württemberg-Baden

OMG Württemberg-Baden abbreviated the name Württemberg-Baden to "WB", followed by "S" for *Stadt Polizei* (Municipal Police) or "LP" for *Landespolizei* (Rural Police), also to be stamped on the backstraps. Revolvers marked "WB-LP" were also given a four-digit inventory number, reading for ex-

388. A German police .38/200 revolver, shown beside a wooden crate of 1,248 rounds of Canadian-made .380" DC MK IIZ (nitrocellulose) ammunition.

Note the partially obliterated paper label on top of the crate, which spells out the word "Canada" in English, Chinese and Russian. Reiner Herrmann collection

ample "WB-LP-0123", while the municipal police marking "WB-S" was followed by an abbreviation of the name of the city in which the particular revolver was issued, reading for example "WB-S-STG" (Stuttgart), with an inventory number.

By June, 1949, the German police in Württemberg-Baden had received 3,743 M1 carbines and 4,226 pistols from the U.S. Military Government (OMGUS), Württemberg-Baden.

389. Closeup of the backstrap of the above .38/200 revolver showing markings "WB—S—STG 323" (Stuttgart Municipal Police, inventory no. 323).

Reiner Herrmann collection

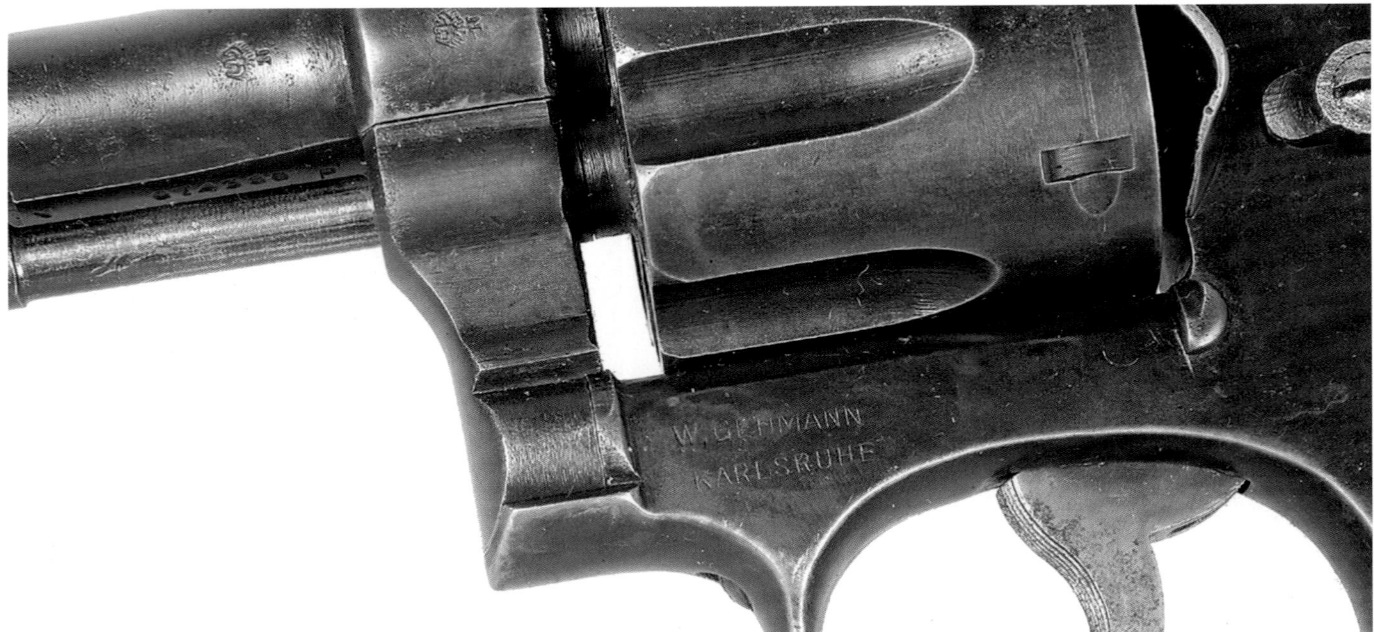


390. Left side closeup of a German police Victory Model, serial no. V 674386, showing markings applied after this revolver was released from police service and sold by the famed German target shooter Walter Gehmann in his gun shop Karlsruhe.

Note also the German commercial Eagle/N proofs on the barrel and frame at top. Reiner Herrmann collection

391 (right). Closeup of the backstrap of the above Victory Model, showing original police markings "WB–S–Kar 457" (Karlsruhe Municipal Police, inventory no. 457). Reiner Herrmann collection

## Stuttgart Police Target M&Ps

393. A group of three Stuttgart Police target .38 Special Victory Models, showing further details of the modified rear sights and the hammer "wings".
Reiner Herrmann collection

The Stuttgart police modified about five .38 Special caliber Victory Models in their weapons repair shop for use in target shooting. The modifications included a large square-bladed front sight pinned into a longitudinal slot cut in the forged sight base on the barrel, plus a bracket for a windage-adjustable rear sight, which provided an extended sight radius. Since this bracket hung out to the rear, obstructing the hammer and making it difficult to cock the revolver for single-action shooting, the hammer spur was cut off and fitted with a unique "wing" which protruded from each side, where it was easily grasped by the thumb of either hand.

## OMG Bremen Enclave

92 (previous page). Left side view of a .38 Special Victory Model, serial no. V 499143, one of about five modified by the Stuttgart Police shooting team for target use.
Note the high blade front sight, hammer "wings" and extended adjustable rear sight.
Inset: closeup of the backstrap showing the original police markings "WB–S–STG 705".
Reiner Herrmann collection

Revolvers in the Bremen Enclave were stamped "Pol. Br." on the left side of the frame, along with the added marking "L.u.S." (*Land und Stadt*; Rural and Municipal). The cities within the enclave were policed by the Bremen *Stadt Polizei*, while the surrounding countryside was policed by the Bremen *Landespolizei*.

By June, 1949, German law enforcement within the Bremen Enclave had received 1,044 M1 carbines and 1,721 pistols from the U.S. Military Government (OMGUS), Bremen.

394 (left). Left side closeup of a Bremen Police revolver showing markings "Pol. Br. L. u. S." Bremen Police *Land und Stadt*; Rural and Municipal).
NRA National Firearms Museum, courtesy James Mock

## Miscellaneous German and Austrian Police Markings

395. Left side closeup of Victory Model serial no. V 444417 showing original police markings milled out and legend "HEGE/SCH-HALL" (gunsmith Wilhelm Hebsacker, Schwäbisch Hall) added. Reiner Herrmann collection

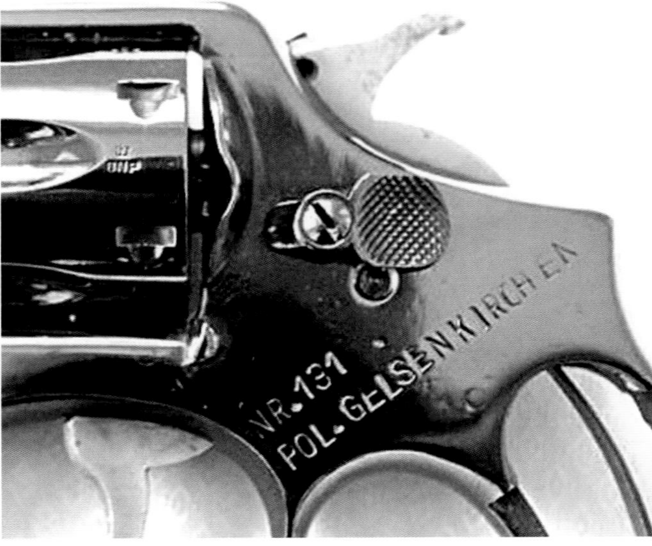


396. Left side closeup of reblued Victory Model marked "NR.131/POL.GELSENKIRCHEN".
courtesy James Mock

397 (right). Left side closeup of Victory Model showing stamped circular legend "ÖSTERREICH POLIZEI" (Austrian Police) and an inventory number, 1202.
courtesy James Mock

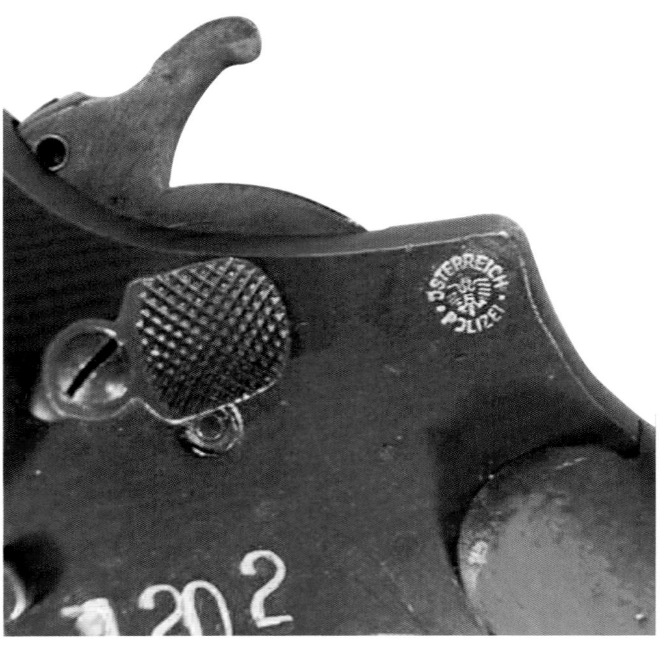

398. A typical sidearm set as issued to the postwar German police. The revolver is a .38 Special Victory Model.
Reiner Herrmann collection

## Arms in the American Sector of Berlin

The police in the U.S. Sector of Berlin are not known to have carried American revolvers. Berlin being considered a special case, they were issued FN pistols from 1945 to about 1958, at which time they switched to the French-made Manurhin P-1 (P38).

## Similar Activity in the British Zone

No detailed documentation has come to hand, but it appears from the image shown here that the British followed suit and issued their surplus .38/200 revolvers to the police in the British zone of occupied Germany.

399 (right). Closeup of the backstrap of a .38/200 serial no. V 759876 showing markings indicating issue to the Kiel Police, in the British zone of Occupied Germany.
Reiner Herrmann collection

# Summing Up the Wartime M&P

It is surprising to me how collectible (and expensive) these revolvers have become today, given the extremely high volume of production, their general sameness, and the rather lackluster dull wartime finish.

John Henwood's insightful comments on this subject are reprinted as follows:

*For many years the .38/200 and Victory Models were virtually ignored. Neither S&W collectors nor potential users showed any great amount of interest in these rough-looking arms; even those collectors specializing in WWII small arms paid them scant attention. Doubtless because of their unpolished exteriors and dull finish they were thought of primarily as "knockabout" or "tackle box" guns. This overlooked the fact that although the exterior was rough, the interior and the lockwork parts were as smooth and finely finished as ever. Even the firm disowned them: for many years the instruction and parts brochures furnished with each new S&W revolver contained a disclaimer to the effect that "No change of finish is offered on the Victory Model". Happily, this prejudice against the wartime M&Ps has dissipated in recent years, and they now figure prominently in any collection of either twentieth-century Smith & Wesson revolvers or World War II small arms.*

## The Postwar .38/200

*. . But that was not quite the end of the story. The .38/200 was retained in service by several British Commonwealth nations for some years following the war [and] S&W made an additional 10,000 for a Commonwealth nation in 1947. Although not listed in the catalog, this model was produced on special order for twenty years . .*

*Even after their military service with the Commonwealth was over, other users gladly accepted the [wartime versions]. The Israelis, for example, took all they could obtain, and even made their own copy [discussed below]. Various Commonwealth police organizations issued the .38/200 for a number of years after the military had abandoned the gun. For these users S&W continued to furnish the .38/200 (on special order) until 1965; after 1957 it was known as the "Model 11" [Chapter Thirty-Two]. Although no longer in first-line military service, several user nations stockpiled their .38/200s as a war reserve. These nations finally sold them off: as recently as the mid-1990s quantities of .38/200 revolvers were being imported and offered for sale in the U.S. . .*

# Meanwhile, Commercial Production Resumes

The factory was obviously well aware of the sales potential awaiting them in the commercial marketplace, and with the end of the war the military contracts were immediately terminated. The wartime "V" in the "SV" serial number prefix was dropped, and commercial production resumed on September 12, 1945, less than a month after V-J Day.

As an indication of its perennial popularity, the model chosen to restart commercial production was the square-butt M&P with a 4" barrel. The first example of an initial batch of 100 M&P revolvers was allocated the very next sequential serial number after the last Victory Model, no. S 811120, with the "S" indicating the continuing presence of the rebound slide-operated hammer block.

These were no doubt joyously received after a four-year dearth of new commercial Smith & Wesson products.

## The 1946 "All Model Circular"

While things were being put back to normal as quickly as possible, an immediate return to production of the full line of commercial handguns was simply not possible. It appears that for a number of years after the war (other than the later Centennial Catalog, issued in 1952), no booklet-style catalogs were issued after 1941, the company instead handing out two-color, four-page brochures known as "All Model Circulars". These combined a brief catalog depiction and description along with the retail price of each model. These circulars were released periodically as models were introduced or discontinued, and prices changed.

On the back page of the first of these circulars, with prices effective October 5, 1946, a frank assessment of just where matters stood as regarded production and delivery of the company's line of products, leading with the most popular model, the square-butt M&P, read as follows:

## *Anticipated Production Schedule*

*The square-butt M&P Revolver is in quantity production with shipments running from 16 - 20 weeks behind orders on blue finish guns—and slower on nickel finish.*

*We haven't been able to start general production on round-butt Military & Police Revolvers, and no definite schedule for this model has been set up.*

*The new K-22 Masterpiece is now in production, and we are making shipments in small lots against our earliest orders.*

*Since our file of orders went back to 1939, it is going to take a little time to bring deliveries up to date, particularly in view of the fact that this revolver is of advanced design and requires meticulous care in its production in order to meet the requirements of the target shooters.*

*In the meantime, we are tooling up for the K-32 and K-38 Masterpiece revolvers, and we believe it will be possible to start production on these some time during the last quarter of 1947.*

*Right now we have such a tremendous backlog of orders on file for these particular types that we doubt very much whether we will be able to undertake production of any other models before 1948 at the earliest.*

*However, when we eventually get the M&Ps and Masterpieces under control, we plan to produce our heavy-frame guns—the "357" Magnum, 38/44 Heavy Duty and Outdoorsman, 1926 Model 44 Military and Target, and the 1917 Army Model 45.*

*Our small-frame guns—32 Hand Ejector, 32 and 38 Regulation Police, 38 Terrier, 22/32 Kit Gun and Target—come last on our schedule, and as things are now developing, probably none will be made until some time during 1948.*

As another casualty of the war, prices for blue and nickel finish were no longer the same. The 1946 price for the 4" square-butt M&P was $56.50 in blue, and $62.00 in nickel.

## "Skilled Prewar Metal Finishers" Conspicuous in their Absence

Concerning the quality of the early postwar finish, John Henwood comments as follows:

*Early post-war revolvers have a finish which is noticeably "duller" than either pre-war guns or those produced since about 1957. This was a result both of the bluing process in use at the time and a lesser-quality polishing job, and reflected the extremely high level of skill required in the firm's polishing room; the skilled prewar metal finishers were no longer available, and several years were required to bring the finish up to the desired quality.*

## Prewar "Snubbies" with Early Hammer Blocks Straddle the War

As we have seen, to all intents and purposes, S&W products were simply unavailable commercially during the war years. As Walter Roper commented in his book *Smith & Wesson Hand Guns*, "At the present writing (1944) it is next to impossible to buy a new Smith & Wesson revolver of any kind, and just as hard to get ammunition."

Curiously, however, specialist prewar 2" M&P collector Mike Pacella has researched two interesting groups of "snubbies" which, while manufactured before the war, were not shipped until 1946. Being of prewar production, all these 2" M&Ps were fitted with the early long action and "side-swing" hammer block.

The first group are round butt blue guns, serially numbered in the wartime .38/200 series, which were not shipped until the late summer or fall of 1946. One must look under the left grip or on the barrel flat to note a hidden 'S', without which prefix the serial number will letter as a wartime .38/200.

The other group is a small series of round-butt nickel guns serially numbered in the range 625801 - 625820, with no hidden 'S' prefix, which were also not shipped until September, 1946. All the other serial numbers around this group were shipped from 1936 to 1940.

Four of these revolvers are shown in fig. 400, and the four letters covering them in fig. 401.

400. Four prewar "snubbies", varying in grip style and finish. All are fitted with the early long action and "side-swing" hammer block.

Above, left: serial no. 678890, blue finish and square butt, shipped on June 10, 1940.

Above, right: serial no. 676761, nickel finish, square butt, shipped on January 26, 1940.

Below, left: serial no. 625809, nickel finish, round butt, shipped on September 26, 1946.

Below, right: serial no. 626261, blue finish, round butt, shipped on August 14, 1934. Mike Pacella collection

401 (following page). Factory letters covering each of t four revolvers shown above, arranged in the same s quence.

Note the statement in the bottom left letter concerni serial no. 625809, which was not shipped until 19 which reads "The other serial numbers before and af this group were all shipped in 1936 to 1940. I can n explain why this group was shipped so far out of s quence." Mike Pacella collecti

Springfield Mass December 3, 2010

The revolver you inquired about is the .38 Hand Ejector, Military & Police Model. This model was introduced in 1899 and designed to fire the .38 S&W Special cartridge. It has been in continued production since it was originally introduced. However, during the past years, many design changes have been made to this model to improve the revolver's function. The collector has classified all of the improvements which occurred before 1945.

Your revolver is classified as the .38 Hand Ejector, Military & Police Model of 1905 Fourth Change. This modification occurred in 1915 and was produced until 1942 with a total production of 758,297 revolvers. These revolvers were produced between serial numbers 241704 and 1000000 of the .38 Hand Ejector series. The current production model of this series is known as the Model 10.

We have researched your Smith & Wesson .38 Military & Police Model of 1905 Fourth Change, caliber .38 S&W Special, revolver in company records which indicate that your handgun, with serial number 678890 was shipped from our factory on June 10, 1940, and delivered to Hershey's Co., Orrville, OH. The records indicate that this revolver was shipped with a 2 inch barrel, blue finish, and checkered walnut silver medallion square butt grips. This was a large shipment of various revolvers. There were 2 units in the above configuration in the shipment and they were bill at $20.68 each.

We hope that this information is helpful to you.

Sincerely,
SMITH & WESSON

Roy G. Jinks
Historian

SMITH & WESSON

Springfield Mass
October 30, 2008

The revolver you inquired about is the .38 Hand Ejector, Military & Police Model. This model was introduced in 1899 and designed to fire the .38 S&W Special cartridge. It has been in continued production since it was originally introduced. However, during the past years, many design changes have been made to this model to improve the revolver's function. The collector has classified all of the improvements which occurred before 1945.

Your revolver is classified as the .38 Hand Ejector, Military & Police Model of 1905 Fourth Change. This modification occurred in 1915 and was produced until 1942 with a total production of 758,297 revolvers. These revolvers were produced between serial numbers 241704 and 1000000 of the .38 Hand Ejector series. The current production model of this series is known as the Model 10.

We have researched your Smith & Wesson .38 Military & Police Model of 1905 Fourth Change, caliber .38 S&W Special, revolver in company records which indicate that your handgun, with serial number 676761, was shipped from our factory on January 26, 1940, and delivered to Oklahoma City Hardware Co., Oklahoma City, OK. The records indicate that this firearm was shipped with a 2 inch barrel, nickel finish, and checkered walnut square butt grips. This was a single gun shipment it was billed at $22.75. It was not inscribed at the factory and it appears the inscription was added well after the appointment of Deputy Rogers.

Sincerely,

SMITH & WESSON

Roy G. Jinks
Historian

Springfield Mass
December 17, 2007

The revolver you inquired about is the .38 Hand Ejector, Military & Police Model. This model was introduced in 1899 and designed to fire the .38 S&W Special cartridge. It has been in continued production since it was originally introduced. However, during the past years, many design changes have been made to this model to improve the revolver's function. The collector has classified all of the improvements which occurred before 1945.

Your revolver is classified as the .38 Hand Ejector, Military & Police Model of 1905 Fourth Change. This modification occurred in 1915 and was produced until 1942 with a total production of 758,297 revolvers. These revolvers were produced between serial numbers 241704 and 1000000 of the .38 Hand Ejector series. The current production model of this series is known as the Model 10.

We have researched your Smith & Wesson .38 Military & Police Model of 1905 Fourth Change, Special Post World War II Variation, caliber .38 S&W Special, revolver in company records which indicate that your handgun, with serial number 625809, was shipped from our factory on September 23, 1946, and delivered to Sports Inc., Chicago, IL. The records indicate that this handgun was shipped with a 2 inch barrel, nickel finish, and checkered walnut grips. This shipment was for 10 units all in the same configuration and serial numbered in a Pre-World War II serial number range. This group of revolvers is in a serial number range of 625801 - 625820 all shipped on 1946. The other serial numbers before and after this group were all shipped in 1936 to 1940. I can not explain why this group was shipped so far out of sequence.

Sincerely,

SMITH & WESSON

Roy G. Jinks
Historian

SMITH & WESSON

Springfield Mass
May 30, 2011

The revolver you inquired about is the .38 Military & Police Model. This model was introduced in 1899 and designed to fire the .38 S&W Special cartridge. It has been in continued production since it was originally introduced. However, during the past years, many design changes have been made to this model to improve the revolver's function. The collector has classified all of the improvements which occurred before 1945.

Your revolver is classified as the .38 Military & Police Model of 1905 Fourth Change. This modification occurred in 1915 and was produced until 1942 with a total production of 758,297 revolvers. These revolvers were produced between serial numbers 241704 and 1000000 of the .38 Hand Ejector series. The current production model of this series is known as the Model 10.

We have researched your Smith & Wesson .38 Military & Police Model of 1905 Fourth Change, caliber .38 S&W Special, revolver in company records which indicate that your handgun, with serial number 626261 was shipped from our factory on August 14, 1934, and delivered to Bolles Brendamour Co., Cincinnati, OH. The records indicate that this revolver was shipped with a 2 inch barrel, blue finish, and checkered walnut silver medallion round butt grips. This shipment contains only one unit having a two inch barrel and it was billed at $19.07.

We hope that this information is helpful to you.

Sincerely,
SMITH & WESSON

Roy G. Jinks
Historian

# The K-Frame Boom (1945 - 1980s)

402. Left side view of a postwar short-action .38 Special M&P, serial no. S 955141, blued finish with 5" barrel and aftermarket S&W Target grips modified for uniform carry.

Shipped on November 14, 1947 to the East Cleveland Police Department, for use in that small, rough area, which was entirely surrounded by the City of Cleveland.

Inset, left: closeup of rear grip strap showing factory roll-stamped marking reading "East Cleveland Police Department".

Guns with similar markings have been seen that date from the early 1920s, indicating that S&W had a long history of supplying this department. private collection

While not particularly noted as a high-crime period, the immediate post-WWII era was a time when new and expanding suburbs were being developed at a frantic pace. Each of these new little cities, out in what had been cornfields only a few short years earlier, needed a police department. All the officers needed to be armed, of course, and what better to arm them with than the S&W .38 Special Military & Police, which had become truly the definitive "service revolver".

Of course some departments used Colts, but they were both more expensive and heavier, so most of the police trade went to the Springfield product.

This expansion of the suburbs has continued from the last echoes of the first atomic bomb blast until recent times, much to the chagrin of urban planners who found it appalling that people, voting with their feet and wallets, were fleeing the old crowded cities in droves.

Up into the 1980s and later as these new police departments came into existence, Smith & Wesson K-frames were without doubt the dominant handguns. Many federal agencies also expanded in size, and this created an even greater demand for them. From 1945 to the present, for instance, the FBI has expanded tenfold or more. Similarly, other federal agencies have also expanded, and new ones have been created, thus increasing the demand for K-frames still more until, as discussed below, they began going out of fashion.

Of course, with the increase in money in the pockets of postwar consumers, the non-law enforcement types also began buying more handguns. Aside from true target shooting, always a rather expensive sport—not like golf, certainly, or racing cars; but definitely not for the economically straitened—plinking and other casual uses to which a handgun, available in a myriad of chamberings, can be put, also grew in popularity.

As more and more individuals owned their own homes, as opposed to living in crowded apartments in urban areas with multiple generations in the same unit, no doubt many a K-frame was purchased for home defense. Many men who had become familiar with weapons and comfortable around them, thanks to their exposure to them in the military, also bought a handgun (or a few). Had they never been in the service, perhaps many of them would not have thought about buying a handgun. Many of these men's sons and daughters, raised in a home with "Dad's revolver" handy would, in turn, themselves buy one when they became old enough.

The late 1950s saw the beginning of the Civil Rights Wars in the U. S., just as anti-colonial agitation had started all around the world in the late 1940s. Fortunately, in the U.S., the strife was not as violent as it was in many of the old European colonies, but this too created a demand for more handguns at all levels.

## The Rare "Mexican Model" - the .38 Special Target M&P of 1946

403. Left and right side views of a long-action M&P serial no. S 833542, with blued finish, Magna stocks, a 6" barrel and target sights.

According to the factory letter, serial no. S 833542 was manufactured in December, 1946, and was one of 2,091 .38 Military & Police postwar Target revolvers manufactured during that year. The majority (2,000) of these were delivered to the Mexican government, and the remainder were held in inventory. Less than 25 examples have surfaced in the U.S. over the last 40 years.

The interesting story of the "Mexican Model" as told by the importer, Col. Rex Applegate, is featured in Chapter Thirty-Five.

Inset, above left: closeup of the butt, showing serial number.

Inset, lower right: closeup of the S&W trademark logo on the frame, with extra line reading "Marca Registrada".

Chad Gripp collection

John Henwood's 'take' on the original postwar production of target-sighted M&Ps is as follows:

*As soon as production schedules allowed, production of the .38 Hand Ejector Target Model was restarted . . About 2,100 were assembled, probably mainly from prewar parts on hand, from November, 1946 through December, 1947; serial numbers ran between circa S 812000 and S 817000. The guns differed from the prewar version, having the micrometer click-adjustable rear sight devised for the Second Model K-22, as well as the new hammer block. Collectors know this model as the ".38 Military and Police Target Model of 1946"; it is believed that virtually all were exported to Mexico. All had 6-inch barrels, and were chambered for the .38 Special.*

As related by Col. Rex Applegate (beginning on page 561) who was living and working in Mexico at this time, the reason he was offered this lot of target-sighted M&Ps was because "the factory was proceeding to produce the new K ["Masterpiece"] Model and it was not deemed desirable to sell the older models in the U.S. domestic market."

## 1945 - 1948: 179,000 New M&Ps

John Henwood records that

*By mid-1948 the demand had slackened sufficiently that production runs of the round butt frame and barrels of other than 4-inch length were scheduled. The early postwar production amounted to just over 179,000 M&P revolvers in less than 2½ years, quite a production feat in itself, and a testimonial both to the consumer's faith in the quality of the gun and to their demand for it. It was America's "right arm", the most popular revolver for both police use and home defense purposes, and it seemed as though everyone wanted one, and wanted it immediately.*

## The .32 S&W Long Chambering, Briefly (1948 - 1950)

Among the interesting postwar M&P variations were some 4,813 examples made in the .32 Smith & Wesson Long chambering, shipped from January 19, 1948, until February 3, 1950 (fig. 660). They were available in 2-, 4-, and 5-inch lengths.

The .32 Smith & Wesson Long chambering is a little hard to understand, at least to me; but possibly a foreign order where .32 chamberings were common already or the law precluded the larger bore. I frankly would prefer a .22 Rimfire to a .32 Long in such a situation myself, but tastes will differ.

Clearly, all the social issues that manifested themselves in increased crime during the period from 1945 to the mid-1980s prompted the purchase of many a K-frame all over the world, and especially in the United States, but more likely the main reason for the tremendous production of the K-frame during this period was simply that it was largely one of sustained economic boom, with a very occasional setback. True, some people were laid off and unemployed, but certainly it is fair to say the economic lifestyle of most people, especially in the United States but actually throughout much of the world, with some obvious exceptions such as in Socialist/Communist countries, had improved. This economic betterment allowed and encouraged many people to buy and use a handgun, activities that they could not have afforded during the prior decades of economic depression. In response to these various demands, Smith & Wesson continued to produce better and better K-frame revolvers, both in design and materials.

# The Postwar "Masterpiece" Series

## The New Short-Action K-38 "Masterpiece"

The new short action, which had been developed and introduced briefly in the .22 Masterpiece in 1940, was adapted to the .38 Special chambering starting on February 11, 1948 at serial number S 990184, thus signaling the end of the old, long-action system so

404 (following page). A one-page flyer advertising the ne short-action K-38 Masterpiece revolver.

Note, below, a conversion kit was also available, convert "existing K-38s of late design" to the new sho action. Gaston Comeau collectic

# A PROVEN GUN... IN A NEW FORM

## THE K-38 MASTERPIECE

**now available with a Shorter, Faster, Single Action**

Long a favorite of the Champions, the K-38 Masterpiece is now offered with an even Shorter Action, Faster Lock Time, and in Single Action tuned to peak efficiency for three stage course shooting.

***This does not replace the standard model K-38 Masterpiece—It supplements it . . . . .***

—ALSO—

A conversion kit with which existing K-38's of late design may be converted to this new Short Throw Single Action.

Matched set of parts for installation by a competent gunsmith **$24.95**

Factory conversion, adjusted and tested **$33.40**

**SMITH & WESSON**

A Bangor Punta Company
Springfield, Ma. 01101, U.S.A.

beloved by many, including such notables as Ed McGivern, who had set his still unbeaten speed records with long-action Smith & Wesson K-frame revolvers.

John Henwood records that "The new action involved a redesign of the hammer and trigger, plus minor changes to other internal lockwork parts, and reduced the hammer travel by almost one-third." These adjustably sighted models also featured a distinctive full-length rib along the top of the barrel.

# Police Use of the "Masterpiece"

While these revolvers were aimed at the bull's-eye target shooter's market, they were also very popular with police shooters who wanted an accurate defense weapon that could be easily and precisely zeroed. While some were taken in the standard six-inch length, the more useful examples were ordered with their barrels cut to five or four inches by the factory Service Department.

As discussed below, these "custom" shortened Masterpiece models were so popular with defense shooters that a separate model called the Combat Masterpiece was introduced in 1952, factory-fitted with a 4-inch barrel, in two calibers: .38 Special for duty use, and .22 Rimfire for training.

Original Masterpiece barrels were tapered, while later models had straight, heavy barrels, which provided more weight and forward balance.

## The Missouri Highway Patrol, and the Illinois State Police

405. Left side view of a Missouri Highway Patrol K-38, ordered with the tapered barrel cut to 5" and a Baughman ramp front sight installed by the factory Service Department.

Many police agencies embraced the Masterpiece revolver as their official duty arm during the postwar era. In my home state of Missouri, the Highway Patrol (the premier law enforcement agency in the state, at least in their own minds), initially bought 5-inch-barreled versions of the K-38 Target revolver. The earliest examples of these were standard 6-inch K-38s with the tapered barrels cut to 5" by the factory Service Department, with a ramp front sight installed.

406. A later K-38 with three-screw sideplate, also with the barrel cut to 5" at the factory, as used by the Illinois State Police.

As shown below, this is the heavier straight-walled barrel with thicker rib.

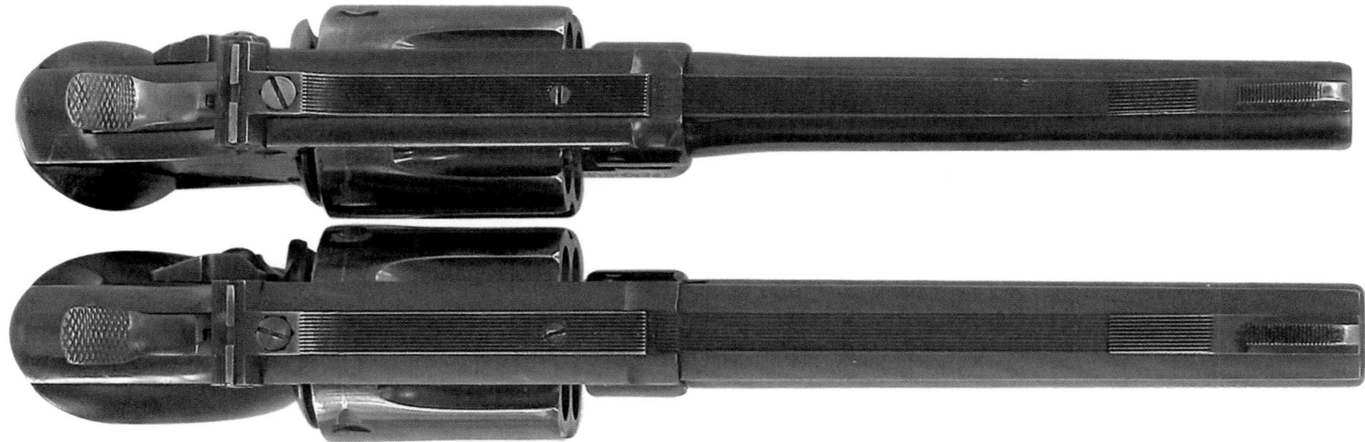

407. A top closeup comparison of the police K-38 revolvers shown in figs. 405 and 406.

Above: the "skinny barrel" version originally purchased by the Missouri Highway Patrol.

Below: the heavier, straight-walled barrel and wider rib on the Illinois State Police version.

When additional revolvers were needed, the Missouri Highway Patrol could no longer get 5-inch models, so they bought the four-inch Combat Masterpiece with its tapered barrel instead. Amusingly enough, they carried these in holsters meant for the 5-inch revolver, so everyone would look uniform. And yes, left-handed patrolmen carried right-handed holsters. After all, we must look uniform!

Over in Illinois, the Highway Patrol also went with the K-38 in the same 5-inch barrel length, but by then, the barrels were no longer tapered but straight-walled.

## The Kansas City, Missouri Police Department

On the far west side of the state, the Kansas City, Missouri Police Department, which as discussed beginning on page 89 had proudly boasted of being "100% Magnum Equipped" in 1939, later switched to K-38 Target revolvers with the barrels cut off to 4 inches, and used 4-inch holsters. A very fine weapon in every way, as long as it was loaded with good ammunition. No doubt it helped a lot of officers avoid back strain, with the 36-ounce K-38 replacing the 43-ounce .357 Magnum.

## The St. Louis Metropolitan Police Department

Meanwhile, in St. Louis, the standard fixed-sight M&P with a 4-inch barrel was the generally used duty weapon at the Metropolitan Police Department. The officer who killed more assailants than any other single man in the history of the Metropolitan Police carried a 4-inch M&P .38 tapered-barrel revolver.

## Popularity Continues After Stainless Steel Introduced in the 1970s

When stainless steel K-frames became available in the 1970s (Chapter Thirty-Two), many police agencies switched over to stainless Smith & Wesson models. While Ruger and even Colt ultimately offered mid-frame-size stainless revolvers, the best selection for many years was from Smith & Wesson.

# The New 'C' Prefix

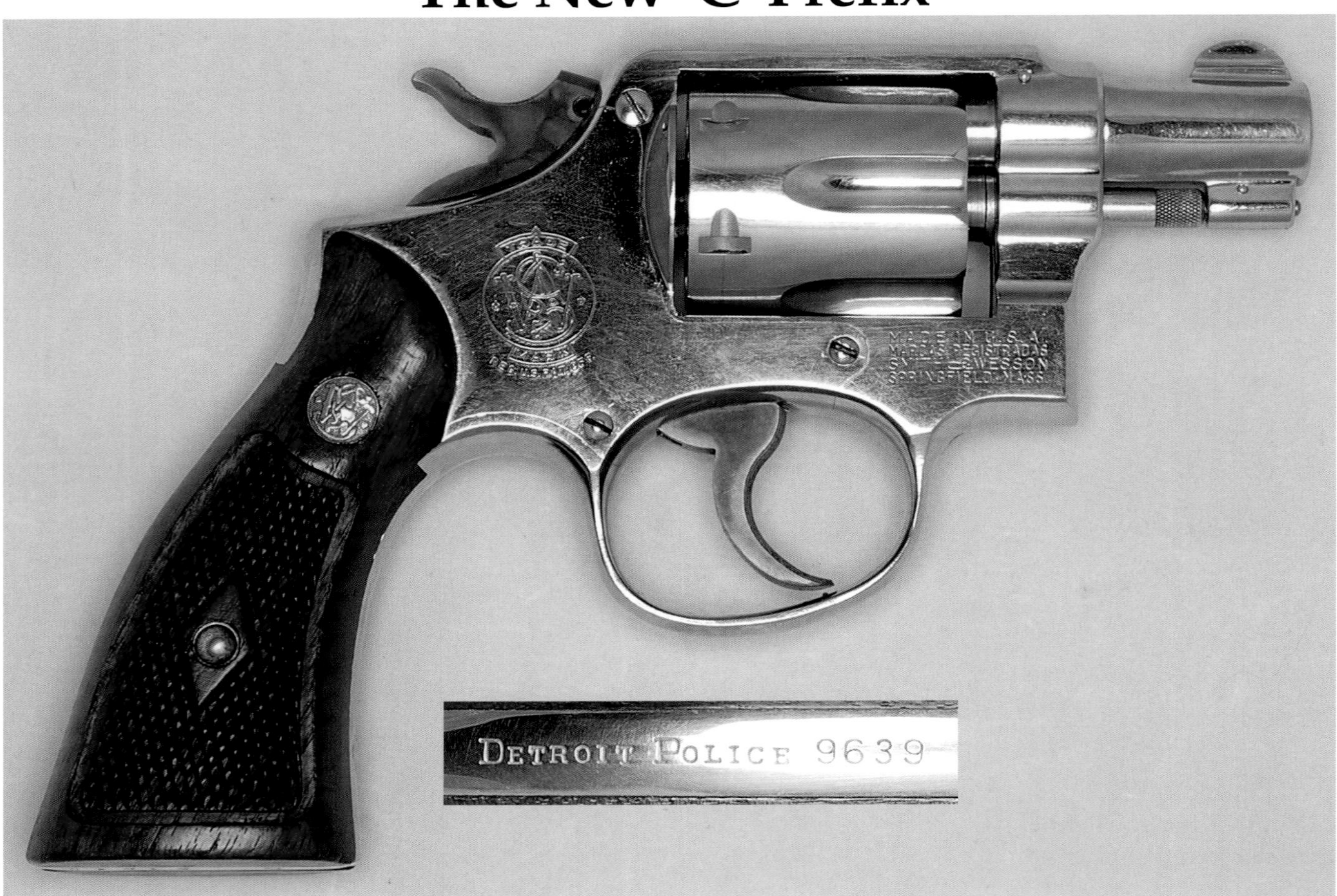


408. Right side view of a 2" nickel-plated M&P, serial no. C 91945, still with four-screw sideplate, one of 50 shipped to the Detroit Police Department in January, 1950.

Inset, below: closeup of the backstrap showing markings, roll stamped at the factory.

Dave Terbrueggen collection

## Completing the Second Million M&Ps (1948)

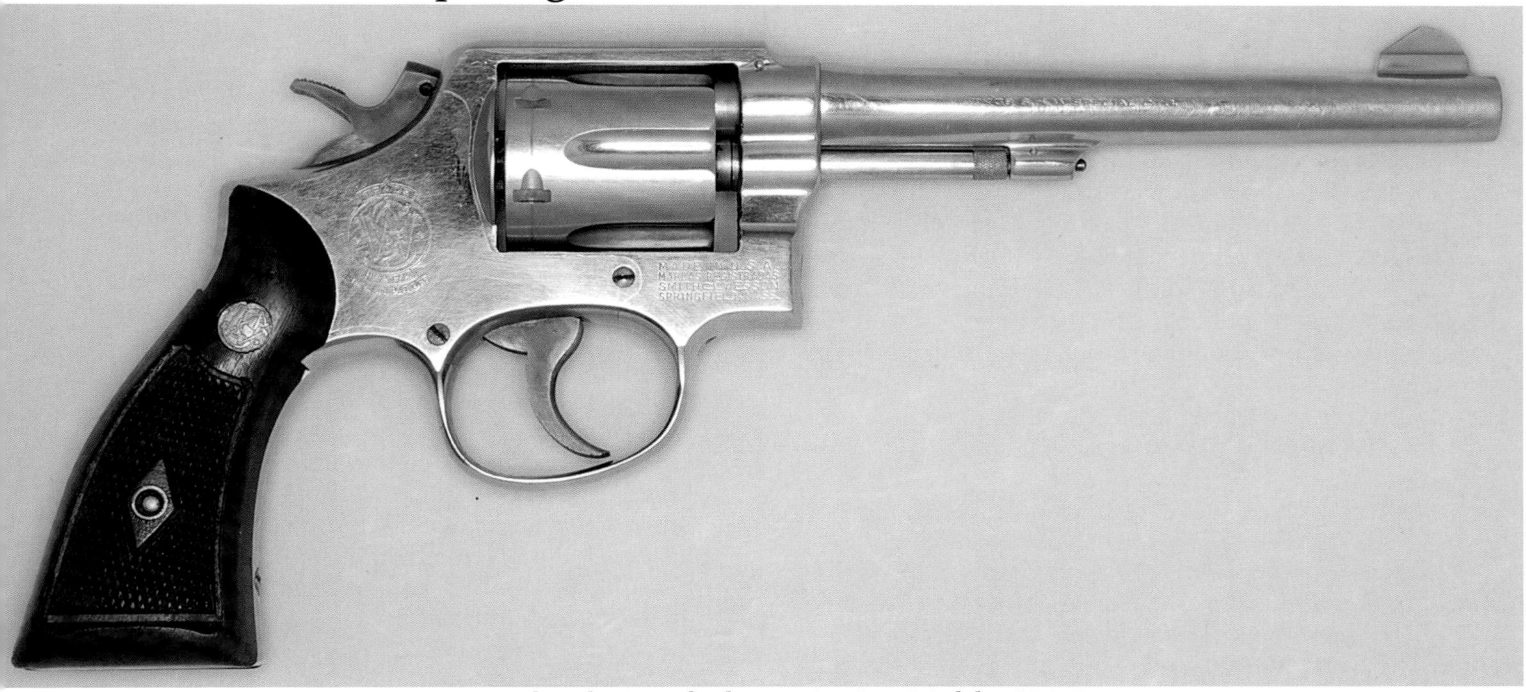

409. Right side view of a short-action "pre-Model 10" M&P in factory bright nickel finish with 6" barrel, serial no. C 331562. Dave Terbrueggen collection

It had taken 43 years to complete the first million M&Ps, from the introduction of the model in 1899 to April, 1942.

However, thanks to the consistent demand during the early postwar era, the second million M&Ps had been completed by March 22, 1948, a dramatically shorter span of only six years. The "S" serial number prefix was then discontinued, and the serial numbering of the fixed-sight K-frame guns began a new series using a "C" prefix, the first number being C1.

# The New S&W Plant

Writing in *Smith & Wesson, The Story of the Revolver*, then factory superintendent (and later company president) Carl Hellstrom described the situation as it had existed in the S&W plant at the outset of war production in 1942:

> *It soon became evident that our nearly 100-year old facilities on Stockbridge Street in Springfield could not stand a production load of twelve hundred guns per day. The old plant consisted of twenty-one mill type multistoried buildings, located in the heart of Springfield. Our drop forge hammers running twenty-four hours a day set up a vibration felt for blocks around, and for the safety of the plant, it was imperative to find another location for the forge shop . .*

A new site was purchased in 1942, although with the exigencies of war work and a lack of capital, the project lay largely dormant until October, 1946, when land preparation and building construction was resumed.

Finally, production was halted for a two-week period in 1949, as the entire operation of Smith & Wesson was transferred to the brand-new facility on Roosevelt Avenue, which remains the company's headquarters to this day.

# The Third Million M&Ps (1950)

The phenomenal popularity of the M&P revolver in the early postwar era was such that it took only a further two years for the third million fixed-sight models to be completed, in 1950.

Among the manufacturing changes introduced around this time, mostly to reduce costs while maintaining or enhancing the quality of the finished product, the pins and studs in the frame wall were mounted in blind holes, so that the ends were no longer visible through the finish on the left side of the frame.

John Henwood records further changes introduced during the early 1950s, as follows:

> *. . circa 1948 - 50, several other minor changes were introduced. The center pin bushing in the frame was dropped, the pin now locking into a hole in the frame itself . . The material now used in the frame was tough enough that the cylinder locking system could be used without the need for this hardened bushing. Somewhere about this time the hard-rubber round-butt stocks were discontinued, while the wood stocks were changed from Circassian to American walnut.*
>
> *The extractor rod head was reduced in diameter once again . . this time to .265", the same diameter as the rest of the rod. This also simplified production of the barrel, since a single straight flat could now be milled for extractor rod clearance, rather than the stepped cut formerly required . .*
>
> *In 1952 the plain "half moon" style [front] sight was altered so as to have the rear face flattened on an angle from the top edge to the top of the base. This flat face was rendered non-reflective by a series of horizontal grooves milled across it. Sights on 2-inch barrels were changed from the prominent "half-moon" to a long, ramp-style blade, grooved across the rear face.*

# The Centennial Catalog (1852 - 1952)

The preface to the S&W Centennial catalog, issued in 1952 over the signature of company president Carl R. Hellstrom, reads in part as follows:

> *In submitting this, our Centennial catalog, we are reaffirming our policy of producing only the highest quality products of proven designs. Behind us are 100 years of effort to make the safest and most dependable hand arms, and from this experience, our compilation is simply a listing of what has been proven the best of our many models and designs . .*

### *Double Safety Features*

It appeared that the wartime fatality which had led to the crash development of the rebound slide hammer safety in 1944 had not been forgotten, and the issue of safety was stressed on page 9 of the 1952 catalog under the above heading, as follows:

> *Unless the trigger is pulled intentionally, it is impossible to discharge a modern Smith & Wesson revolver, as the hammer nose or firing pin is pre-*

410 (right). The blue-and-red cover of the S&W Centennial Catalog, issued in 1952 to mark the 100th anniversary of the original partnership between D. B. Wesson and Horace Smith in 1852. Gaston Comeau collection

*vented from striking the cartridge primer by two independent and automatically operating safeties—the rebound slide upon which the lower end of the hammer rests, and the solid steel hammer block which lies between the hammer and the frame just below the hammer nose.*

*Even if the arm should fall and strike on the hammer with sufficient force to mutilate or smash the hammer, these two safety devices make accidental discharge of the arm impossible. The firing pin can hit the cartridge primer ONLY when the trigger is deliberately pulled back to its full-release position. No manipulation or slipping of the hammer during cocking can result in accidental firing at any time, since the falling path of the hammer will be mechanically blocked at all times except when the trigger is held in full-release position.*

## The New Masterpiece Line

### Most Modern Target Revolver Ever Designed

Several pages were given over to a complete description of all models of the new short-action Masterpiece line, which began with an interesting descriptive history of the K-22 model, as follows:

## The K-22 Masterpiece

*This 22 caliber heavy frame revolver, truly a masterpiece of the gunmaker's art, has a background worthy of this brief mention.*

*On January 3, 1931, we first produced a revolver in 22 rimfire caliber built on the frame of that favorite police veteran—the 38 Military & Police model. We had been making the 38 Military & Police in both police and target type weapons, and there had been for some time a request from law enforcement circles for a training gun in a sub caliber which could be used economically on the target range.*

*The answer was the original K-22, and that model was produced until 1940, when an improved model known as the original K-22 Masterpiece made its bow to the handgun fraternity. This Masterpiece model had a somewhat shortened action, micrometer click sights, a built-in anti-backlash trigger, and other improvements which made for greater accuracy and ease of handling . .*

*This K-22 Masterpiece was used until after World War II, at which time it was discontinued in favor of the new K-22 Masterpiece depicted and described herein. This new revolver has just about everything that the target shooter could ask for . . The fact that over 3,000,000 38 Military & Police revolvers are in the hands of satisfied users is indicative of the sturdy construction and perfect design of this type of revolver, and our following comments will be directed towards outlining the improvements which have been made on this already well known revolver in the most recent period.*

*First, it has a ribbed barrel for more rigidity, and a little more weight out front. The front sight has a ramp base of which the sight blade is an integral part, and the whole [is] firmly pinned in to the barrel rib. The bore is as usual precision reamed and rifled, after which it is lapped to a mirror-like finish . . The cylinder charge holes we continue to roll burnish for precision of diameter and ease of extraction. Hammers and triggers remain case-hardened for a lifetime of smooth and unchanging trigger pull. The rear sight is the same micrometer click sight which we first installed on our target models in 1940, and which has not seen the need of a single change in the last 12 years. The lockwork of this gun has been entirely redesigned so that this revolver is truly of the type known as a "short action" target weapon.*

*The hammer fall has been reduced to the minimum requirement consistent with good ignition of the cartridge primer and maintenance of accuracy . . The rearward action of the trigger is controlled by a built-in trigger stop which prevents all rearward motion of the trigger after disengagement from the hammer notch. The standard stocks supplied with the K-22 are of walnut, Magna style, [and] the tangs, both front and rear, are grooved, as is the trigger, to prevent slipping in the handling of this weapon . .*

## The K-32 and K-38 Masterpiece Revolvers

The 1952 catalog continued on to describe the other Masterpiece models, as follows:

*The new K-32 Masterpiece and the new K-38 Masterpiece revolvers are practically the same gun as the new K-22 model . . These three revolvers are of short action, and they are identical in external dimensions. The only differences are the facts that the K-22 is of 22 Long Rifle caliber, and the lockwork of the gun is designed for rim-fire ignition.*

*The K-32 and K-38 Masterpiece are of their respective [calibers and] center-fire ignition. Thus . . these three revolvers . . constitute as well-matched a trio as is possible to achieve . .*

*. . Where interest is centered on having these arms of equal weight irrespective of slight differences in external specifications, then the perfect set of guns will be the K-22 Masterpiece, the K-32 HEAVY Masterpiece, and the K-38 HEAVY Masterpiece. All three of these last-named guns will weigh 38 1/2 ounces if loaded with 5 target cartridges of approved type.*

The 1952 catalog then went on to describe the slight modifications which had been made to the "heavy" models in the two larger calibers in order to achieve weight parity with the smaller-bored (and thus heavier) K-22 Masterpiece, as follows:

## *The K-32 and K-38 Heavy Masterpiece Revolvers*

411. Left and right side views of a K-38 Heavy Masterpiece, serial no. K 224475, fitted with target hammer and target stocks.

Inset, above left: serial number as marked on the flat under the barrel.

Inset, below right: serial number as marked on butt.

As discussed on page 413, the lack of skilled metal polishers meant that the finish of these postwar products had not yet regained the excellence shown in prewar years.

Gaston Comeau collection

*Were it not for differences of opinion this would indeed be a very dull world in which to live, and believe us there ARE differences of opinion among those rabid enthusiasts who gather on the target ranges. There are those who prefer their revolvers matched as to size, and there is another school who prefer that their guns be matched for weight. It is for this latter group that we have produced the K-32 and the K-38 Heavy Masterpiece revolvers . .*

*These guns have a greater mass of steel in the forward part of the gun to compensate for the larger diameters of barrel and cylinder charge holes. In the final analysis the K-32 Heavy Masterpiece will be seen to have a larger barrel in external diameter as well as having a somewhat wider rib, but the gun when placed on the scales with 5 target cartridges in the cylinder will weigh exactly the same as the K-22 weighed under the same circumstances. Similarly, the K-38 Heavy Masterpiece will be seen to have quite a larger diameter barrel and an even wider rib, and changed frame specifications, but here again . . you have the weight of the loaded K-22 reproduced. The end result is obvious—3 guns to somewhat different external dimensions, but weighing each 38 1/2 ounces when loaded with 5 target cartridges . .*

412. Top closeup of the K-38 Heavy Masterpiece serial no. K 224475, showing details of micrometer rear sight and target hammer. Gaston Comeau collection

## *The Combat Masterpiece*

The 1952 catalog then introduced the new Combat Masterpiece, which was essentially the standard K-38 as described above but with a 4" barrel and Baughman type ramp front sight:

*The progression of the new Masterpiece Line of modern target revolvers would be incomplete if confined to use on the target range and barred from the field of law enforcement.*

*For many years we have been converting policemen's revolvers so that they might have adjustable sights and be otherwise better suited for target use. At the same time these officers have been purchasing target revolvers and having our Service Department shorten the barrels, modify the sights, and make the guns adjustable to the double purpose of competitive shooting and carrying in the holster while on duty.*

*With this custom work in the background and the Masterpiece target revolvers in production, it was only natural that we fall into the design of the most obvious combination which has ever presented itself to our Engineering heads.*

*It had been suggested that such a gun could be called the "Combat Masterpiece", and finding the title* apropos *we adopted it. Since the gun was obviously for use on the field of duty in both police and military circles it had to be of extremely durable and rugged construction, so we used the basic design of our Military & Police revolver which is a proven police weapon. Since the gun would also double for target range use and competitive shooting we added to it all the refinements of our Masterpiece target revolvers—the ribbed barrel, micrometer click sight, short action, swaged hammer spur, grooved tangs, etc., and out in front we fitted the long, graceful Baughman Quick Draw Ramp front sight which has already earned its spurs on thousands of Magnums in the hands of law enforcement officers.*

*The end result proved to be one of the most popular revolvers which we have placed before the trade in many years, and it is not only finding its way into the holsters of entire police departments, but also being used in increasing numbers in the firing of police matches where the use of holster weapons is specified.*

*The Combat Masterpiece is aptly described in our catalog as a "SHORT ACTION, TARGET GRADE GUN". The weapon is completely in keeping with the needs of the officer who is on combat assignment or operating under service conditions, and the gun is equally at home in the field of competitive target shooting.*

*For training purposes, and without additional cost, the Combat Masterpiece revolver is supplied in 22 rim-fire caliber for use with the popular and economical 22 Short, Long, or Long Rifle cartridges. This is an identical gun except for calibration and ignition specifications.*

The new short-action "Masterpiece" series, including the K-22, K-32, K-38, Combat Masterpiece and the later Combat Magnum, were serially numbered in a separate series using the "K" prefix, beginning with no. K101.

## A *Caveat* on the Use of the Different Sizes of .22 Caliber Ammunition

While the last paragraph of the 1952 catalog, quoted above, states that the .22 Combat Masterpiece is "for use with the popular and economical 22 Short, Long, or Long Rifle cartridges", John Henwood provides the following interesting comment on the use of .22 caliber rimfire ammunition in these revolvers:

*. . Note that the caliber marking on all .22 rimfire S&W K-frame models indicates that they are rifled and chambered for the .22 Long Rifle only, and are not intended for use with .22 Short or .22 Long cartridges. (The 29-grain bullet used in the .22 Short and .22 Long cartridges requires a different rifling twist for optimum results than does the 40-grain bullet of the .22 Long Rifle.)*

# Introducing the "Airweight" M&P

413. Right side view of an early "Airweight" M&P, introduced in September, 1952 at around serial no. C224000, in a round-butt model with a 2" barrel and an aluminum alloy frame and cylinder.

It appears that this early Airweight qualifies as having a unique "five-screw" sideplate - note the tiny lock screw securing the "Bug" screw at top.

The alloy-framed "Airweight" K-frame revolver was introduced in September, 1952, at around serial no. C224000, in a round-butt model with a 2" barrel.

John Henwood further describes the "Airweight" .38 Special M&P as follows:

*. . The weight was reduced to 14 3/8 ounces (a weight saving of 11 ounces over the steel 2-inch M&P), through the use of an aluminum alloy frame (.080" narrower than the steel version) and cylinder. These early guns had a hammer and trigger which were only .240" wide (the standard parts had a width of .265"). They also used a flat, serrated rectangular cylinder latch thumbpiece; these became known as "flat latch" guns. The flat latch proved unpopular, being somewhat more difficult to operate, and was replaced with a standard-design thumbpiece, made of aluminum, in 1966.*

*Smith & Wesson discontinued the use of the aluminum cylinder in 1954, fitting the lightweight round-butt frame with a steel cylinder which raised the weight to 18 ounces.*

A Smith & Wesson brochure dated May, 1953, while the aluminum cylinder was still being fitted, introduced the .38 M&P "Airweight" as follows:

*This weapon should find favor among those who seek a large, hand-filling gun for concealed carry, yet who wish the weight factor to be kept at an absolute minimum.*

Since the .38 Special cartridge was not a "big kicker" to begin with, the alloy-framed Airweight had a lot to offer for the truly weapon sophisticated. The Airweight concept proved popular, and was later produced in both round- and square-butt commercial versions with 2" and 4" barrels, as well as the U.S. Air Force "M13 Lightweight" version, which is discussed in Chapter Thirty-Six.

The "Airweight" concept was later expanded to include several smaller models. In addition to the Airweight K-frame M&P, the 1957 All-Model Circular lists lightweight versions of the J-frame .38 Special Chiefs Special and the hammerless Centennial, as well as the adjustably-sighted .22 caliber Kit Gun in a modifed square-butt version with a 3½" barrel.

# The Little-Known Israeli 9mm "Model 1952"

Until recently, very little information was available concerning the Israeli 9mm copy of the S&W M&P, although fortunately, as discussed below, new material has recently come to light from several sources.

John Henwood's account, from the section in his 1997 book headed "Imitations", reads in part as follows:

*In 1952 Israeli authorities directed that a M&P-type revolver . . be adapted for production in Israel. An almost-exact duplicate of the Smith & Wesson .38/200 furnished to the British, it was not for civilian or military use, but was intended for the police. Furnished with a 6½ inch barrel, a lanyard swivel, and uncheckered wooden Magna-style stocks, it was chambered for the 9mm Luger cartridge. The use of a rimless cartridge required that "half-moon" clips be used, and these were provided. Apparently all of these arms went to the Israeli internal security forces, it appears that none were made for sale or export . .*

Henwood concludes with the following empirical "guesstimate" of production:

*Judging by serial numbers, in excess of 19,000 were manufactured by Israeli Military Industries (IMI).*

The only other sources previously available added somewhat to the brief amount of knowledge Henwood had gleaned, but both—correctly, as it turns out—refuted his estimate of the production total as wildly optimistic.

The first of these is a brief but remarkably well-informed mention in the 1965 reference *International Armament Volume I*, by George B. Johnson and Hans Bert Lockhoven, which reads as follows:

*The Israeli copy of the Smith & Wesson Military and Police model is chambered for the 9mm Luger cartridge, and uses half-moon clips for this rimless automatic pistol ammunition. Only a very few were made by hand for gift purposes in 1952 - 1953; the manufacturer was "Israeli Military Industries", Israel.*

Another source is a single page from an article published in the January, 1989 issue of *GUNS* Magazine. This is also well researched, and although the author's name is not mentioned on the copied page that has come to hand, the style is reminiscent of that of the founder of *GUNS* Magazine himself, the late William B. (Bill) Edwards.

Fortunately, two other major sources of information have recently been made available. One of these is the coming to auction of the cased revolver presented by Israeli Prime Minister David Ben

Gurion to General Walter Bedell Smith. This historic arm is discussed and depicted below, but in a rare stroke of luck, among the documents accompanying this revolver are none other than the two letters referred to in the January, 1989 *GUNS* Magazine article. These are reproduced here, to accompany the following excerpts from the article:

> . . *One of the best examples of Israeli innovation is a revolver so rare that some senior staff people at IMI didn't even know of its existence. My 1969 edition of Smith and Smith's standard reference,* Small Arms of the World, *describes it briefly. I was unable to find anything about the gun elsewhere so I contacted IMI. Their initial reaction [fig. 414] was "Never heard of it." Further research on their part proved successful, however, and I was provided with more information [fig. 415].*
>
> *The gun in question is a revolver that is very nearly an exact copy of Smith & Wesson's great old workhorse, the Military & Police, now known as the Model 10. In 1951, IMI planned to produce 3,500 of them but, for a number of reasons, only 50 were actually made. Each was hand-made, half being fitted with 6-inch and the other half with 5-inch barrels. It would appear that these guns were put together individually over a two- or three-year period.*
>
> *S&W revolvers have been copied many times in many different countries. What is so unusual about these guns is the caliber. They were chambered for the 9mm Parabellum cartridge and intended to be used, as was our Model 1917, with half-moonclips.*
>
> *The initial concept was sound. It was a proven design, it was possible to get tooling and know-how from the U.S. quickly and economically, and the ammunition was readily available as it was already being manufactured in quantity by IMI for use in the Sten and other submachine guns already in service with the Israeli Defense Forces.*
>
> *The whereabouts of only three or four of these revolvers is known today, but it seems that at least one managed to find its way to the United States. Prime Minister David Ben Gurion presented revolver number 19519 to Lt. General Walter Bedell Smith, former head of the CIA, who later gave it to his chief assistant, W. H. Jackson. I learned recently that the gun was last known to be in the hands of a Connecticut dealer* . .

ISRAEL MILITARY INDUSTRIES

DATE: 13 December 1978

OUR REF.: 4093-6100

Dear Sirs:

In reply to your letter of 10/11/78 we must admit that we do not recall having manufactured a pistol which fits the description given by you.

However, if you could send us a photograph of the weapon, from both its sides, we may try to assist you in identifying the origin of the weapon.

Yours truly

I M I

JC/aj

HEAD OFFICE: HAKIRYAH, TEL-AVIV 61070, ISRAEL · P. O. B. 7055 PHONE 03-26 41 11 · TELEX: 03-3719 · CABLES: MISBIT TELAVI

414. The original IMI letter written in response to the initial inquiry from the *GUNS* Magazine researcher for information on the Israeli 9mm revolver, denying all knowledge of the project. courtesy Rock Island Auction Co.

ISRAEL MILITARY INDUSTRIES

DATE 27 February 197

OUR REF.: 726- 61

Dear Sirs:

In reply to your letter of 3rd January 1979 and after having checked our records, we are glad to inform you that, indeed, in the years 1951/52 we manufactured 50 pistols according to the attached photocopy taken from the book:

International Armament Volume I
by
George B. Hohnson
and
Hans - Bert - Lockhoven

Furthermore, we acknowledge having manufactured the pistol No. 19519 which was eventually presented as a gift by Mr. Ben Gurion to Lt. General Walter Bedell Smith.

We hope that the above information is satisfactory and will be of help to you.

Yours truly,

ISRAEL MILITARY INDUSTRIES

JR/aj

HEAD OFFICE: HAKIRYAH, TEL-AVIV 61070, ISRAEL · P. O. B. 7055 PHONE 03-26 41 11 · TELEX: 03-3719 · CABLES: MISBIT TELAVIV

415 (right). The second IMI letter, admitting that production of 50 revolvers did indeed take place, in 1951/52, and referring the researcher to the photo in *International Armament* which accompanied the brief mention quoted above. courtesy Rock Island Auction Co.

# The *Real* Story of the Israeli Model 1952

The other major new source of information is an article written by retired Lt. Col. Matti Chemed, one of the curators of the light weapons collection at the Israel Defense Forces (IDF) Museum in Jaffa/Tel Aviv. The original of this article appeared in Hebrew in the Israeli magazine *Caliber* (*Caliber kravi*), Vol. 18, winter issue, 2011. This magazine is no longer being published.

The following is a translation of Lt. Col. Chemed's article, kindly prepared for us by Lt. Col. (ret.) Bernie Schecter, former head of the Weapons Identification Lab at Israel Police HQ in Jerusalem, and his daughter Mara:

## *The Short Episode of the 9mm Revolver*

### *Matti Chemed, Lt. Col. IDF (ret.)*

***For a while the IDF toyed with the idea of manufacturing its own revolver which would fire a 9mm Parabellum cartridge. Once everything was ready, it was called off due to lack of funds and only a small number of weapons were manufactured, for use by the Chief of Staff***

*The history of an Israeli manufactured 9mm revolver is similar to the creation of the Dror LMG. The procurement was done before the establishment of the IDF and the declaration of statehood. Even though I don't have on hand (actual) testimony or documents pertaining to an intent to manufacture a weapon by Taas (IMI) underground, one can assume that the initiative to purchase the knowledge and manufacturing tools for a weapon to be produced in Israel was carried out by the delegation that purchased U.S. war surplus materiel. The delegation included Slavin, who resigned in 1944 from the underground management of Taas (IMI), and Yaakov Dostrovsky (Dori) as the Hagana Chief of Staff, who headed the delegation. The role of the delegation, which went to the U.S. at the end of 1945, aside from PR, was to collect monies for the purchase of ships to aid in the 'illegal' immigration of mainly machinery and equipment to manufacture weapons and ammunition for Taas (IMI). The American company Smith & Wesson responded to the representatives' request to prepare manufacturing plans and manufacturing equipment in order to produce an Israeli-made revolver, which would fire the 9mm Luger (Parabellum) cartridge. IMI was already making ammunition in caliber 9mm P for the Sten SMG. The ammunition specifications of the SMG and the self-loading pistol (Luger) were completely identical. The only difference between the loadings was that those intended for the SMG were more powerful. The difference between the 9mm P and a .38" [revolver] cartridge is, among other things, the fact that the first is rimless and the second is rimmed. The significance of this is that a .38" cartridge inserted into the cylinder of a revolver stops at the rim, while the 9mm, which is rimless, falls into the chamber of the cylinder, unless the cartridges are placed in half-moon clips which 'replaces' the rim, and prevents the cartridges from falling into the chambers of the cylinder.*

### *Kegs Filled with Parts*

*The idea of using a self-loading revolver cartridge was adopted from S&W's revolver called the 0.45" Hand Ejector Model 1917, which was used by the U.S. Army and manufactured from 1917 through 1919. The .45 ACP cartridge was in use by the U.S. Army in the self-loading Colt pistol Model 1911A1. The chosen model, or the one which the company offered the delegation, was the Hand Ejector Military & Police. In this model, the fixed rear sight is in the frame of the weapon, while the other first model provided by IMI to the IDF for testing in 1949 possessed an adjustable rear sight, held in a "dovetail" cut into the frame. The barrels fitted into the first models, which were manufactured only in Israel, were 6" (15.2cm) in length.*

*According to the IMI report dated August 8, 1951, plans were made in the U.S. to manufacture S&W revolvers. The revolver contained 73 parts, and to manufacture it, 450 processing activities were required, such as soldering, milling, machining and so on. 350 of these steps were required to produce the 24 main parts of the weapon. In preparing the manufacturing equipment, the gauges, etc., 1,500 sketches were made. Together with the manufacturing sketches, they also prepared the manufacturing equipment, and a certain*

# האפיזודה הקצרה של

## במשך זמן קצר השתעשעו בצה"ל ברעיון לייצר בארץ אקדח תופי מתוצרתו, שיירה כדור 9 מ"מ לוגר פרבלום. לאחר שהכל כבר היה מוכן, העניין בוטל בגלל העדר תקציב ומספר קטן בלבד של אקדחים יוצר לשימוש הרמטכ"ל

**סא"ל (מיל.) מתי חמד**

תולדות ייצור אקדח תופי 9 מ"מ מתוצרת ישראל דומות בעיקרן לסיפורו של מקלע ה"דרור" (ראו כתבה במגזין **"קליבר קרבי"**, גיליון מס' 13). הרכישה בוצעה לפני הקמת צה"ל והכרזת המדינה. אם כי אין בידי עדויות או מסמכים על המגמה ליצור אקדח על ידי תע"ש במחתרת, יש לשער שהיוזמה לרכישת ידע ומכשירי ייצור של אקדח שייוצר בארץ נעשו על ידי המשלחת לרכישת מכשירים מעודפי המלחמה בארה"ב. המשלחת כללה את **סלבין**, שהתפטר בסוף 1944 מניהול תע"ש במחתרת, **ויעקב דוסטרובסקי (דורי)** כרמטכ"ל ההגנה, שעמד בראש משלחת זו. תפקידה של המשלחת, שיצאה לארה"ב בסוף 1945 היה, בנוסף לפגישות הסברה, לאסוף כספים לקניית אוניות להעפלה ורכש נשק, בעיקר רכש מכונות וציוד לייצור נשק ותחמושת עבור התע"ש.

חברת Smith & Wesson מארה"ב נענתה לפניית נציגינו להכין תוכניות ייצור ומכשירי ייצור, על מנת לייצר בארץ אקדח תופי מתוצרתה, שיירה כדור 9 מ"מ לוגר פרבלום. בתע"ש ייצרו כבר כדור 9 מ"מ לתת-מקלע סטן. מידות הכדור 9 מ"מ לאקדח מטען ולתת-מקלע הן זהות לחלוטין. ההבדל בין הכדורים הוא בעוצמת ההדף החזקה יותר של הכדור המיועד לתת-המקלע. ההבדל בין כדור 9 מ"מ לכדור "38. של האקדח המקורי הוא, בין היתר, בזה שהראשון הוא ללא כרכוב (rimless) והשני הנו בעל כרכוב (rimfull). משמעות הדבר היא שכדור "38. המוכנס לתאו בתוף האקדח נעצר בכרכוב, ואילו כדור 9 מ"מ ללא כרכוב "נופל" לתוך התא בתוף, אלא אם כן הכדור נכנס לאטב "המחליף" את הכרכוב, והאטב מונע מהכדור 'ליפול' לתוך התא בתוף (ראה תמונה).

### חביות מלאות חלקים

הרעיון של שימוש בכדור של אקדח מטען באקדח תופי אומץ מהאקדח של Smith & Wesson הנקרא 0.45 Hand Ejector M 1917, שהיה בשימוש הצבא האמריקאי, ויוצר משנת 1917 עד 1919. כדור ה-ACP45 היה בשימוש בצבא ארה"ב באקדח המטען קולט מודל 1911A1. הדגם שנבחר, או זה שהחברה הציעה למשלחת היה Hand Ejector Military Police Model 10. בדגם זה, הכוונת האחורית בצורת אתנח חרוצה בגוף הכלי, ואילו הדגמים הראשונים שמפל"ן סיפק לצה"ל לבחינה (ב-1949) היו בעלי כוונת אחורית מתכווננת, שבנויה על "זנב דרור" הנכנס לשלד האקדח. הקנים שיוצרו רק בארץ היו לדגמים הראשונים, באורך של "6 (152 מ"מ).

אקדח סמית אנד ווסון אמריקאי מודל 1917 נטען בכדור 0.45 ACP

שלושה כדורים מוחזקים באטב מלאי המיועד לאקדח סמית אנד ווסון מודל 1917

46 קליבר קרבי

416. Page 1 of the original article as it appeared in Hebrew in the Israeli magazine *Caliber* (*Caliber kravi*), Vol. 18, winter issue, 2011, translated on pages 431 and 433.
courtesy Lt. Col. Bernie Schecter

*number of the simple weapon parts - those which required mainly automatic machining or milling, were made in the U.S.*

*The S&W historian, Mr. Roy G. Jinks, confirmed on February 10, 2000 that the company produced a small amount of the needed tooling, although according to the testimony of the IMI veterans, most of the tools were produced in Israel. They remember kegs full of processed parts for the revolver. It turns out that the two main parts of the weapon – the cylinder and the barrel – were not made in the U.S., only in Israel. The barrel, which had 4-groove rifling, like the Sten, was copied from the British production, as only the British produced barrels with 4 grooves. According to the S&W historian, they never produced a 4-groove barrel for their weapons, only 5- [and 6-] groove barrels. The fledgling underground manufacturing operation, and then IMI, after the State was established, made 4-groove barrels for the Sten and the Uzi SMGs.*

## *Complications in Manufacturing the First Series*

*At the end of 1948, Mr. Slavin set up the machines and manpower needed to produce the revolvers, and gave the order to implement this program. Only then it turned out to be impossible, because of the need to fix and change the manufacturing equipment, and the many incompatible aspects between the sketches of the weapon's parts and the tools. The sequence of activities and the sketches of the tools themselves became incompatible. These incompatibilities caused great complications in the production of the first series.*

*Since the proper and orderly activation of the manufacturing was impossible, it was decided that preparing three handguns would suffice; their parts to be fitted individually. The revolvers were given to the Army for testing in August, 1949. The revolvers were checked by the Technicians' Corps from a technical standpoint, and by Operations Research Division from an operational standpoint. The first technical experiment was carried out on March 22, 1949.*

*The results of the testing produced a report detailing a few fixable glitches. The Technical Corps advised against producing the adjustable rear sight, recommending instead the permanent notch sight in the frame (similar to the American M&P model). They also suggested to make do with a 5" (12.7cm) length barrel. Also, the report of the Operations Research Division detailed some glitches, and concluded that they would not recommend manufacturing the revolvers until the defects were corrected.*

*In response to these reports, the director of IMI accepted the majority of the recommendations, but then ordered the manufacture of a 50-weapon series, in accordance with the planned use of the manufacturing equipment without the need for individual fitting of separate parts. In order to do this the dimensions shown on the manufacturing plans and in the tools themselves had to be brought into agreement, but at the time this task was above and beyond the budgetary allowances. The budget allocations for light arms were designated for the development and production of sub-machine guns, and the purchasing of rifles and machine guns. The handgun therefore had a low priority, and even in 1950 a self-loading pistol was preferred to a revolver.*

## *Given Out as Gifts to VIP Guests*

*Before the eventual shut-down of the 9mm revolver program, the IDF ordered 30 pistols (within the framework of the 50 pistols) which IMI decided to assemble with individually-fitted parts, selected from the large numbers of pistol parts previously manufactured. The revolvers for the IDF order included some with 6" (15.2cm) barrels, some with adjustable rear sights fitted in a dovetail in the frame, and some with a 5" (12.7cm) barrel and a fixed rear sight notch in the frame. On the right side of the frame they stamped the IMI symbol, which included the Hebrew acronym standing for "Israel Weapons Manufacturing Factories", and underneath this a 5-digit serial number, starting with "195".*

*These revolvers were not handed over to the IDF, but were designated according to the Chief of Staff's order as gifts, per his decision. We do not have a list of who received the revolvers, but to the best of my memory, they were intended for VIP guests who visited the Chief of Staff, and for several IDF Major Generals. These revolvers appear to this day in the catalogue literature as one of the weapons with which the IDF was equipped . .*

417. Rear closeup of the cylinder of the Israeli 9mm revolver shown below beginning in fig. 432, showing the internal shoulders on which the mouths of the rimless cartridges chamber. Gaston Comeau collection

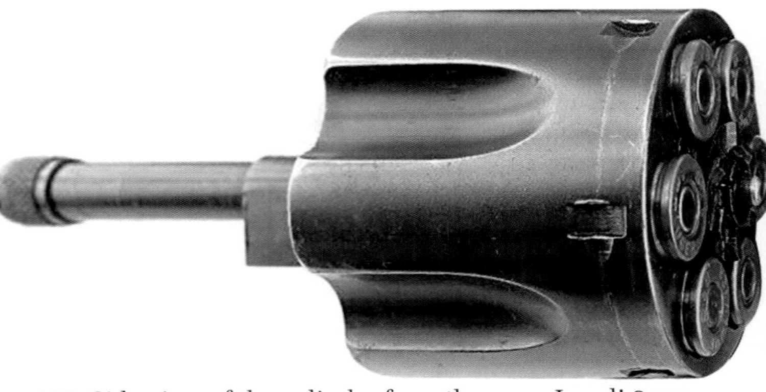

418. Side view of the cylinder from the same Israeli 9mm revolver, with cartridges inserted in the chambers.

These are correctly positioned for firing, but being rimless they cannot be grasped for extraction by the star ejector. Gaston Comeau collection

One comment might be added regarding Col. Chemed's assertion that unless the rimless 9mm cartridges are placed in half-moon clips, they will "fall" into the chambers of the cylinder. Rimless cartridges such as the 9mm and .45 ACP chamber on the mouth of the case, so that the problem in a properly dimensioned cylinder is not in chambering, but in extraction.

As shown in fig. 418, in the Israeli Model 1952 cylinder the cartridges will not "fall" in any further than necessary to position them for firing. The problem arises after they have been fired, because the normal star ejector is unable to grasp the rimless cases. Hence the need for half-moon clips, which also offer the advantage of faster reloading, in blocks of three cartridges at a time.

## Some Examples from the '195' Series

### The Bedell Smith Presentation, No. 19519

General Walter Bedell "Beetle" Smith (1895 - 1961), was General Eisenhower's Chief of Staff throughout most of WWII, the team becoming known as "Ike and Beetle". Winston Churchill nicknamed Smith "Bulldog" because of the tenacity with which he tackled problems.

After the war General Smith served as the Director of the CIA from 1950 to 1953, and during this period he visited Israel several times. One one such occasion Israeli Prime Minister David Ben Gurion presented him with revolver no. 19519, in a fitted wooden case with a silver plaque screwed onto the inside the lid, and General Smith's initials in a silver monogram on the outside of the lid.

419 (left). General Walter Bedell "Beetle" Smith (1895 - 1961), General Eisenhower's Chief of Staff throughout most of WWII, and Director of the CIA from 1950 to 1953. courtesy Rock Island Auction Co.

422 (left, following page). The silver initials "WBS" affixed to the lid of the case of the Walter Bedell Smith presentation revolver. courtesy Rock Island Auction Co.

420. Israeli Prime Minister David Ben Gurion, in a photograph taken around the time of the presentation and published in *LIFE* Magazine.

courtesy Rock Island Auction Co.

HONORARY CURATOR
WEST POINT MUSEUM
U.S. MILITARY ACADEMY

HONORARY CURATOR
WARMINSTER MUSEUM
BRITISH SCHOOL OF INFANTRY

JAC WELLER
Post Office Box 149
PRINCETON, NEW JERSEY 08540

GRADUATE AND LICENSED ENGINEER — FIREARMS CONSULTANT — EXPERT WITNESS COURT QUALIFIED — MILITARY HISTORIAN

1 November 1977
(Dictated 27 October 1977)

To Whom It May Concern:

Re: AN ISRAELI MANUFACTURED REVOLVER
SERIAL NO. 19519, CALIBER 9 MM
PARABELLUM
IN A PRESENTATION CASE WITH A
SILVER PLATE INSCRIBED
"TO LT. GENERAL WALTER BEDELL SMITH
IN APPRECIATION DAVID BEN-GURION
PRIME MINISTER OF ISRAEL

This weapon and case together with half moon clips in order to adapt it to the firing of rimless ammunition came into our possession from William Harding Jackson during the time that he lived in Princeton circa 1950 to 1960. He and Mary Jackson came out to the house with the case and revolver and sold them to us. Their reason was that the young Mrs. Jackson could not stand the presence of a firearm in the same home with her two boys who were just starting to handle things.

Mr. Jackson was Chief Assistant to General Smith during the time that they were both running the CIA. Smith was the director, but in poor health; we have heard it said that Jackson was responsible for the reorganization during the very last days of Truman's presidency.

Bill Jackson told us that Bedell Smith was not in any way a firearm's man and didn't like to accumulate personal possessions. He gave Jackson this revolver almost as soon as he received it himself, probably about 1950.

We are placing with this weapon in the same case a communication from Jehuda Wallach in connection with the make and model. Wallach is presently Professor and Head of Military History at the University of Tel Aviv. He is a former Division Commander in the Israeli Army during the 1957 War and has held half a dozen different semi-military positions in Israel since that time. He has been Weller's host on half a dozen occasions when he visited Israel. There is one revolver similar to that captioned above presently on exhibit in the Israeli Defense Forces Museum.

Cornelia Weller
CORNELIA WELLER

JAC WELLER

State of New Jersey)
County of Mercer )

BETTY S. ANDERSON
NOTARY PUBLIC OF NEW JERSEY
My Commission Expires May 21, 1980

On the 2nd day of November 1977, the subscriber, a Firearms Expert, appeared before me and acknowledge the above to be his signature.

Betty S. Anderson

421. Deposition from noted firearms writer Jac Weller, dated November 1, 1977, concerning the provenance of the 9mm Israeli revolver serial no. 19519, presented by Prime Minster Ben Gurion to General Smith.

courtesy Rock Island Auction Co.

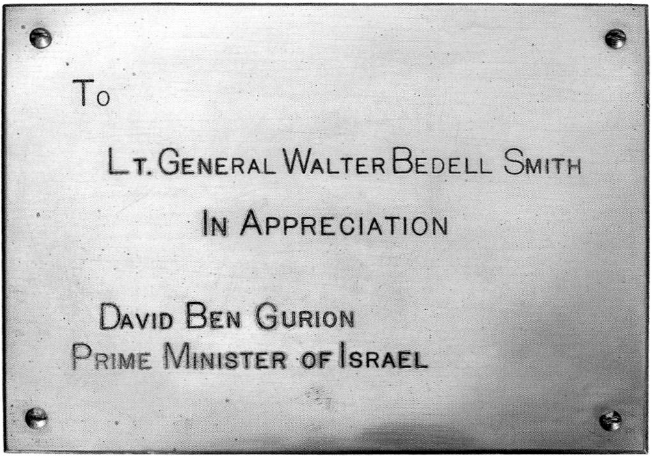


423. The silver plaque affixed to the inside of the lid of the case of the Bedell Smith presentation 9mm revolver.

cortesy Rock Island Auction Co.

424. The Israeli 9mm revolver, serial no. 19519, in its fitted case as presented to General Smith by Prime Minister Ben Gurion.

Note the label identifying "Ammunition for use in this revolver" and "Half-moon clips for accepting 9mm Luger". courtesy Rock Island Auction Co.

According to a later deposition from the noted firearms expert Jac Weller, dated November 1, 1977 (fig. 421), General Smith was "not in any way a firearms man and didn't like to accumulate personal possessions." He therefore gave the revolver to his chief assistant, William Harding Jackson, "almost as soon as he received it himself, probably about 1950." Jackson later sold the revolver to Mr. Weller.

425. Left side view of the Bedell Smith presentation revolver, serial no. 19519.

Note the "half moon" front sight, which appears integral with the barrel forging, the Magna-style stocks, and the lanyard swivel. courtesy Rock Island Auction Co.

426 (left). Right side closeup of the Bedell Smith presentation revolver, showing IMI crest and serial number. courtesy Rock Island Auction Co.

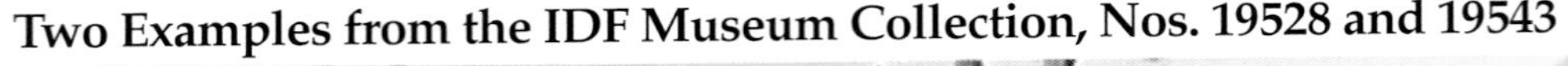

## Two Examples from the IDF Museum Collection, Nos. 19528 and 19543

427. A portion of a display panel at the IDF Museum in Jaffa/Tel Aviv, showing a right side view of 9mm "Smith & Wesson" (Israeli Model 1952) revolver serial no. 19528, which appears to be fitted with a 6½" barrel.

This example also features Magna-style stocks and a lanyard swivel. courtesy Lt. Col. Bernie Schecter

428 (right). Closeup of the IMI crest and serial no. as marked on the above revolver.
courtesy Lt. Col. Bernie Schecter

429. Right side closeup of Model 1952 revolver serial no. 19528. The rear sight is windage-adjustable in a dovetail in the receiver, as mentioned in Col. Chemed's article.

Note at upper left the two half-moon clips full of 9mm cartridges with nickeled primers, as manufactured by IMI in the 1950s. courtesy Lt. Col. Bernie Schecter

430. Another portion of the display panel featuring Model 1952 revolver serial no. 19543, with 5" barrel and fixed rear sight. courtesy Lt. Col. Bernie Schecter

431 (right). Closeup of the IMI crest and serial no. as marked on the above revolver. courtesy Lt. Col. Bernie Schecter

## Two Early Examples of the Model 1952 Pose Further Questions

As is so often the case, while many of the questions concerning this program are answered by Col. Chemed's informative article, the presence of two Model 1952 revolvers not numbered in the "195" series pose several further questions.

### The "Zero-Series" Target Model

432. Left and right side views of Model 1952 "0 Series" revolver serial no. 1008, with 6½" barrel, pinned-in square blade front sight, screw-adjustable target rear sight, coarsely-checkered Magna-style stocks with Star of David motif around the grip screw escutcheons, and no lanyard swivel. Gaston Comeau collection

An early hand-assembled example of a 6½-inch barreled version of the Israeli 9mm Model 1952 revolver resides in the Gaston Comeau collection. It is fitted with a screw-adjustable rear sight resembling the version used on prewar Smith & Wesson target models, and a fixed half-moon front sight blade, pinned into a block on the barrel.

Several features of this particular revolver indicate that it preceded the "195" series. The serial number, located on the bottom of the butt, is "1008" and the butt is marked with a "0", as are all the other components. This emulates the practice followed at Smith & Wesson, where all the components of initial toolroom production and experimental guns were

433. Top closeup of the receiver, showing details of the screw-adjustable target sight.

The rear screw (fig. 438) is the later "bottom-headed" type, which fits in a dovetail in the rear of the sight cutout. Curiously, however, no screwdriver slot has been cut in the top of the screw, rendering the sight effectively non-adjustable for elevation. Gaston Comeau collection

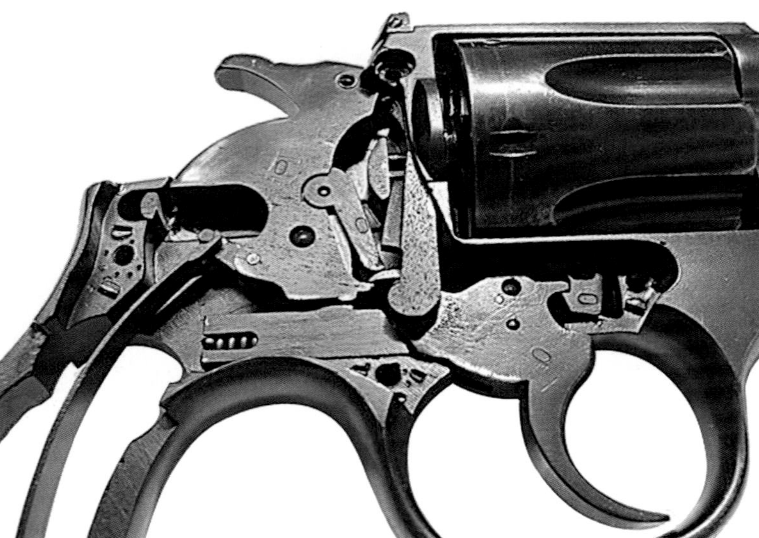

435. Right side closeup with the sideplate removed to show details of the action.

Note that each component is marked with a '0'. Gaston Comeau collection

437. Closeup of the sideplate, showing hand-engraved IMI logo and no serial number. Gaston Comeau collection

434. Closeup of the bottom the butt, showing serial number and absence of lanyard swivel.

Note the '0' at right, presumably indicating that this is no. 8 of the pre-production "0 series".

Gaston Comeau collection

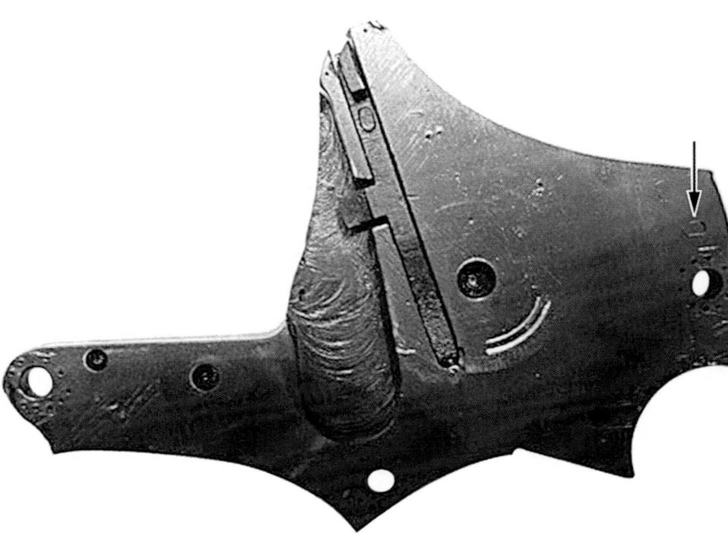

436. Interior view of the sideplate, showing details of "side-swing" hammer safety.

Both the safety arm and the sideplate itself (arrow) are marked with a '0'. Gaston Comeau collection

438. Underside view of the screw-adjustable rear sight, also marked '0', showing "bottom-headed" adjustment screw, which does not have a screwdriver slot in its top end. Gaston Comeau collection

439 (left). A closeup view down the barrel of the "0 series" Model 1952 revolver, showing 4-groove rifling, which the Israelis copied from the British Sten gun.

S&W rifling was always 5 grooves. Both are right-hand twist.

Gaston Comeau collection

440. Right side closeup of the front sight. Note that the square-sided "half-moon" blade is pinned in place.

Gaston Comeau collection

marked with a "0". These S&W "zero guns" are highly sought-after collectibles.

Furthermore, on no. 1008 the IMI logo on the sideplate is hand-engraved, indicating that this was a prototype, possibly no. 8 of an initial "zero" series numbered in a four-digit range beginning with "100".

## Another Israeli Target Model, Held in a British REME Museum

441. Right side view of another Israeli Target Model, with pinned front sight on 6½" barrel, highly polished Magna-style stocks, and no lanyard swivel.

The serial number "500107" is located at the front of the sideplate.

Note the variant recoil shield, a feature seen on all the Israeli Model 1952 revolvers.

REME Museum, Arborfield, photo by Richard Jones

Another early specimen of the Israeli Model 1952 is held in the REME Museum in Arborfield, U.K. This example is also fitted with the screw-adjustable target sight, and may be of somewhat later production than no. 1008 but still not part of the 30-gun "195-" series.

The grips are dark, smooth Magna-style wood, and the IMI logo appears machine-stamped. The serial number, reading "500107" plus two Hebrew characters, which appears ahead of the logo on the sideplate, suggests a further series numbered beginning with "500", of which this might be gun no. 107. The trigger (and presumably other components of the action) is marked with a "3".

# A Review of Sideplates and Screws

With K-frame revolvers, as with all post-1898 S&W side ejectors, the way many collectors distinguish among the various versions produced over the years is by the number of screws in the sideplate, and the presence (or absence) of a further screw in the frame in front of the trigger guard.

A person gains access to the mechanism of a Smith & Wesson side-ejector revolver by removing the sideplate, located on the right side of the frame. This is a carefully and tightly fitted component, designed to protect the mechanism from the ingress of dirt. Anyone who has ever looked at one, removed and refitted it, then considered the issue, will agree they are a wonder of fine precision workmanship.

Today, the advent of clever design modifications and CNC machining has reduced the amount of hand-fitting needed on a Smith & Wesson revolver to a minimum, but such was not the case in the early days.

In the beginning, sideplates were initially fitted in the "soft fitting" department, then disassembled, sent out for hardening and finishing, and returned for a final fitting in the "hard fitting" department. Later the first step was omitted, but even so, the fitters at Smith & Wesson were generally considered at the highest skill level of all employees. It was these men who had over the years mastered the hardest tool to use in any metal shop, the file. Keeping in mind what is involved in achieving the desired level of perfection, it is really quite amazing how quickly they turned out the volumes of revolvers being produced.

## How to Remove the Sideplate

The S&W 80th Anniversay catalog, undated but issued in conjunction with a retail price list dated June, 1935 stapled inside the rear cover, contains the following instructions on sideplate removal:

> *. . to do this without marring the frame, proceed as follows:*
>
> *1st. Remove the screw holding the stocks in place and take off the stocks.*
> *2nd. Take out the four screws holding the side plate in place, using a screw-driver of correct size. Then, holding the revolver flat in the left hand, side plate on top, strike the tang a few sharp blows with a piece of wood which has been covered with a soft cloth. This will loosen the side plate which can then be lifted off.* Do not attempt to pry *the side plate as the frame will certainly be marred . . Replace the side plate carefully.*

Today this operation is best performed using a non-marring plastic hammer. Holding the revolver as instructed above, a couple of sharp raps on the tang will lift the sideplate right off the frame.

## From Four Sideplate Screws to Three (1955)

Interestingly, in the catalog images of the initial side-opening Hand Ejector, the .32 caliber Model of 1896 (fig. 228, etc.), the sideplate is shown held by only three screws, although all the actual examples we have seen of this early model have a total of four sideplate screws.

The four-screw sideplate remained the norm for many years, as illustrated throughout the early chapters of this book. Naturally this meant drilling and tapping four holes to a precise depth, and then fitting screws to those holes so the heads were properly flush with the surface.

The top screw hole in the sideplate held what was referred to at the factory as the "bug" screw. According to Roy Jinks, this screw was so named "because it was a bugger to put in." This may well have been due to the fact that the other three sideplate screws have short reduced-diameter unthreaded end sections, called the "pilot", which make aligning them with the threads in the frame comparatively easy, while the "bug" screw is threaded all the way

442. The four sideplate screws, as used up to September, 1955 when the "bug" screw (left) was eliminated. The unthreaded top portion shown on the three rightmost screws was known at the factory as the "pilot".

Note the top of the front screw (right) has been hand-filed in assembly so that it will secure the shaft of the cylinder crane (fig. 555) without binding.

Gaston Comeau collection

down, and requires care in positioning it and starting it into the frame.

It might also be noted that, except on the wartime .38/200 and Victory Models, the rearmost sideplate screw is flat-headed, rather than dome-headed, as are the other screws. Further, as shown in fig. 442, the front screw, which started out identical to the lower screw, was hand-fitted in assembly so as to secure the crane shaft without binding.

By September, 1955 the designers had figured out a way to eliminate the "bug" screw, substituting a tongue on the top of the sideplate (fig. 454). The amount of handwork necessary was thus reduced, but the product itself was none the worse for it, being equally as robust and dependable today as it was when flappers were all the rage.

The "three-screw" sideplate (the gun itself being referred to by collectors as a "four-screw" model) then became standard until January, 1962, when the cylinder stop plunger spring screw in the front of the trigger guard was eliminated.

# The K-Frame Combat Magnum (1955)

Today, with more effective cartridge designs, a good .38 Special revolver is a fine thing, but this was not always the case. The standard round-nose 158 gr. Police Service .38 Special loading was always a little marginal in the opinion of many. As a consequence, demand arose for a more powerful chambering in the K-frame.

Once it became apparent that a K-frame could be made to handle, if not a limitless supply but at least a reasonable number of .357 Magnum rounds, the result was a new adjustable-sighted model called the Combat Magnum, which was introduced in November, 1955. The Combat Magnum featured an encased ejector rod, a full-length rib on the barrel, a longer cylinder with enclosed case heads, and, most importantly, it was chambered for the .357 Magnum cartridge.

As discussed in Volume I, this combination was created to meet the suggestion of famed Border Patrolman Bill Jordan (fig. 179), who had advised Smith & Wesson president Carl Hellstrom about year earlier that he thought a K-frame Magnum would be "the peace officer's dream" weapon.

As noted on page 166, Roy Jinks stated that the first example, serial number K260001, was shipped to Bill Jordan on November 19, 1955. It appears that this is incorrect. Bill Cross, who has researched this issue in depth, states that the Combat Magnum Bill Jordan received was not the first one made but the one with the lowest serial number, K 260001. This was actually the second gun made, and it was shipped to him on January 5, 1956. Major General Julian Hatcher of the NRA received the third gun made, which was shipped on January 20, 1956. Only one Combat Magnum, no. K 260003, was completed in 1955. It was kept in the factory collection and later engraved by Alvin White for presentation to President John F. Kennedy. This lavish gun is featured in the Engraving section of Chapter Thirty-Eight.

To the trivia fans among our readers, I should like to point out that this project was first made known to the public when Bill Jordan appeared on the old Skippy Peanut Butter-sponsored TV show "You Asked For It".

The Combat Magnum (fig. 443) also generated a lot of publicity in the gun magazines of the day. By that time, thanks largely to the increase in the general population and the corresponding increase in the number of "gun nuts", arms-oriented periodicals had begun to proliferate, and soon *GUNS*, *Guns & Ammo*, *Shooting Times* and other such publications were competing with *The American Rifleman* for attention. Of course there were other magazines which also published the occasional article about S&W revolvers, some of very short duration and little distinction, others with wider appeal such as *True* and *Argosy*.

443. Left and right side views of a typical pre-Model 19 Combat Magnum, serial no. K 261345, with nicely-figured Goncalo Alvez target stocks. It appears that by this time the S&W metal finishers had regained their prewar expertise, as evidenced by the lustrous, deep blue-black metalwork.

This revolver was shipped from the factory on June 15, 1956 to Seattle Marine and Fishing Supply Co., in Seattle, Washington. Bill Cross collection

*Chapter Thirty-Two*

# New Models and Modifications, 1957 - Today

## Numbers Replace Names

In 1957, Smith & Wesson decided to replace the model names of all their existing handguns with numbers, and to issue new numbers as and when new models were introduced.

In this chapter the model numbers assigned to fixed- and target-sighted K-frame revolvers are discussed, in numerical order.

# The Model 10 (.38 Special M&P)

The classic fixed-sight, .38 Special Military & Police revolver was given pride of place as the first in the new series, becoming the Model 10. As John Henwood recorded,

> *Effective June 10, 1957, the latest chapter in the Military and Police story began. On that date Smith & Wesson announced that the M&P would henceforth be known as the "Model 10". However the firm, realizing that the old "Military & Police" name had inspired a certain brand name loyalty, continues to use it in their advertising, calling the revolver the "Model 10 Military and Police". No changes were immediately made, other than stamping "MOD. 10" on the frame inside the yoke cut . . Today the Model 10 is still in production, and the end is not in sight . .*

### The Thorny Issue of "Dash" Changes

John Henwood explains the "dash" method used beginning in 1957 to indicate the introduction of minor modifications or alterations to the mechanisms of the various numbered models, as follows:

> *We are talking about a considerable period of time here, from 1957 to 1997 [the year Henwood's book was published]. During this time a number of minor alterations have been made to all (or at least to all the older variations) of the various models . . It is not really possible to keep them all straight, nor to discover exactly when these changes were introduced.*
>
> *The difficulty in keeping the changes straight arises from the fact that when new models were offered they already incorporated all the applicable modifications made to the older models. Consequently the "-2" on a Model 10-2 indicates different modifications than the "-2" on a Model 13-2. On the other hand, the "-2" on a Model 12-2 indicates the same changes as the "-2" on the Model 10-2. Thus the "dash" changes for each model must be considered in relation to that model only, even though they might apply to other models.*
>
> *. . eventually a whole series of "dash numbers" would appear. These did not signify new models, but design and mechanical changes in existing models. These changes were put into production on all models to which they were applicable. [For example,] Model "X-1" was introduced in 1960, as a change to the basic "X" model. In 1962*

*more improvements were made and the designation was changed to Model "X-2". But in 1963 a new variation on the basic "X" model was introduced, the "Y". When introduced the "Y" would include all the changes already made in the "X-2". Moreover, when more changes were made, in 1964, the "X-2" would become the "X-3", while the "Y" became the "Y-1" . .*

## "Dash" Changes as Applied to the Model 10

With the proviso that models which were introduced after the Model 10 may have fewer "dash" numbers while still incorporating all the earlier changes, the series of dash changes made to the Model 10 provide a basic list of all the modifications made since the model numbering system was instigated in 1957.

John Henwood further describes these "dash changes" as follows:

*. . Other than stamping the model number in the yoke cut on the frame . . no changes were immediately made to the former M&P revolver . . ; it was offered only in .38 Special with 2-, 4-, 5-, and 6-inch barrels, round or square butt with walnut Magna stocks, and either blue or nickel finish . .*

*Gradually a series of minor modifications began. Since the presence of each change was signified by a change in the "dash number" (a number following the basic model number), we can examine them in turn.*

## The Model 10-1: the "Heavy Barrel" Model 10 (1959)

The first "dash" change to the Model 10 was authorized in April, 1959, and resulted in the designation "Model 10-1". This was the same as the standard Model 10 square-butt revolver, with the exception that the 4" barrel was heavier, almost cylindrical throughout its length, with an integral rib and a small ramp front sight cross-pinned in place. The frame contour, in the area surrounding the barrel, also differs from that of the Model 10.

John Henwood comments on the Model 10-1 as follows:

*. This heavy 4-inch barrel added 3 ounces to the weight of the arm, and helped tame the additional recoil of those extra-power "+P" loads which were being popularized by law enforcement agencies . .*

## The Models 10-2 and 10-3 (1961)

The Model 10-2 was the traditional light-barreled Model 10, with the sight width changed from 1/10 inch to 1/8 inch. John Henwood continues,

*. . in addition the threads in the extractor and on the extractor rod were changed from right- to left-hand. This cured the recurring problem of the cylinder locking in place due to the extractor rod unscrewing itself. The Model 10-2 was announced in February, 1961.*

The Model 10-3 was also introduced in February, 1961. This was simply the heavy-barrel Model 10-1, updated with the Model 10-2 changes.

## The Model 10-4 (1962)

The Model 10-4, introduced in January, 1962, signalled a return to the 1/10-inch sight width, some having complained that the 1/8" sights were too wide. John Henwood continues,

*. . In addition, a redesign of the cylinder stop eliminated the need for the plunger and screw in the front of the trigger guard [discussed further below]. Model 10-4s all have the light barrel. Both the Model 10-2 and the Model 10-4 were manufactured concurrently for some time; the 1/10-inch sights were finally dropped circa 1975.*

## Eliminating the Cylinder Stop Plunger Screw

In the Model 1905, as part of an improved cylinder stop design, which moved slightly back-and-forth as it operated, a cylinder stop plunger and spring had been installed through a hole in the front of the frame and held in place by a screw, immediately above and in front of the trigger guard, first seen in figs. 262 and 263. This screw remained a feature from 1905 until January, 1962, when a new design of cylinder stop spring alleviated the need for this screw, and S&W revolvers produced after this change have been known as "three-screw" models.

This is yet another example of clever engineering allowing the factory to maintain the same quality, while reducing the cost associated with machining and fitting the parts to the frame. Certainly it made no difference in the actual functioning of the weapon. For the average user the main benefit seems to be in avoiding an unsightly screw head which could easily be damaged by using the wrong size screwdriver to tighten it should it ever become loosened due to recoil forces.

This type of design change illustrates a point well worth noting concerning Smith & Wesson revolvers. Over the years they continue to look and function the same, yet thanks to excellent engineering they have become increasingly more reliable, easier to make, and actually less expensive for the consumer. In fact, when relative values are taken into account, firearms and ammunition are cheaper today than ever before.

## The Models 10-5 and 10-6 (1962)

444. Left side view of a Model 10-5, serial no. C 723169, in original factory nickel finish with 5" barrel, shipped on January 15, 1965 to International Distributors, Inc. of Miami, Florida for direct shipment to Wackenhut Services Inc. at Las Vegas, Nevada. Note the marking "TWC 5924" on the side of the frame, enlarged in the inset. 'TWC' stands for The Wackenhut Corporation, which for many years held the security contract for Nevada nuclear test sites, and preferred 5" nickel-plated M10s for their uniformed guard force. private collection

The Model 10-5 was the light-barreled Model 10-2 with 1/8" sights, but without the cylinder stop screw in front of the trigger guard. It was introduced in January, 1962, at the same time as the Model 10-4.

The Model 10-6, also introduced in January, 1962, was the Model 10-1 (with 4" heavy barrel), without the cylinder stop screw.

# The Canadian-Assembled(!) Model 10

## Smith & Wesson Law Enforcement Equipment (Canada) Ltd. (1972-1979)

445. The modest premises of Smith & Wesson Law Enforcement Equipment (Canada) Ltd., located in an industrial mall area at 2249 Dunwin Drive, Mississauga, Ontario. photo by Gaston Comeau

The Canadian operation run by Smith & Wesson during the 1970s in Mississauga, Ontario was a modest but interesting (and previously unknown, to me at least) commercial venture.

The Canadian branch plant, officially known as "Smith & Wesson Law Enforcement Equipment (Canada) Ltd.", was originally established as a warranty repair depot for S&W products purchased by various Canadian law enforcement agencies. All necessary repairs were to be handled, except reblueing and frame replacement, by Josef Rothmuller, an Austrian master gunsmith who had emigrated to Canada some years before, and who had graduated from the Smith & Wesson Armorer School in Springfield.

However, due to the inherent quality of the product, few revolvers required adjustment, and apart from examining a few disastrously blown-up revolvers resulting from over-enthusiastic handloads, Joe had very little to do. At a meeting in early 1972 with L. J. Deters, S&W Senior Vice President in charge of manufacturing in Springfield, Joe persuaded Deters to allow him to assemble revolvers for Canadian police sales, the plan being to ship unassembled kits of components from Springfield to the Mississauga plant for assembly, inspection and test-firing.

With some financial support from the Ontario Ministry of Industry and Tourism an apprentice program was established, and three gunsmiths were

446. Master gunsmith Josef Rothmuller, in a photo taken in 1972. courtesy Gaston Comeau

This is to certify that JOSEF ROTHMULLER
has completed the prescribed Program on The Care and Maintenance of Smith & Wesson Revolvers & AUTOMATICS.

SMITH & WESSON, INC.

Foreman

General Superintendent

1-26-73
Date

446a. Official certificate dated January 26, 1973, attesting that Josef Rothmuller had completed the S&W armorer's course. courtesy Gaston Comeau

447. A view of the interior of the S&W (Canada) workshop at 2249 Dunwin Drive in Mississauga. All specialized tooling, etc., was supplied from Springfield. courtesy Gaston Comeau

hired and trained to assemble the components into finished revolvers, acting under the supervision of master gunsmith Joe Rothmuller.

Thus, during the period from April, 1972 through December, 1979, Smith & Wesson Model 10 revolvers, with either standard 6-inch or 4-inch heavy barrels, were assembled in Canada for sale to Canadian police agencies. Some of these guns were also sold commercially through police sales agencies.

The parts were shipped to the Canadian assembly plant in Mississauga with the barrels and sideplates pre-fitted, in standard blue boxes (with hand-lettered labels in those pre-computer print-out days). The other parts, which were unnumbered and

448. A closeup of some racks of partially finished Canadian-assembled Model 10s. courtesy Gaston Comeau

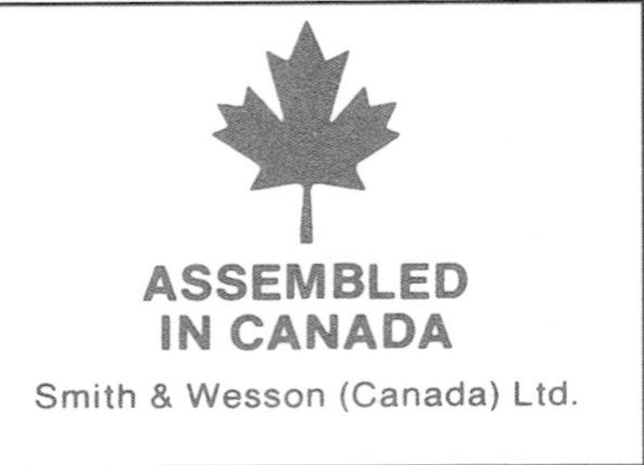


449. The peel-and-stick label indicating Canadian assembly, which was affixed to the blue boxes of early production. Gaston Comeau collection

450. Closeup of a typical box label from a 4" Model 10-6, serial no. 2D46455, assembled in Canada. Gaston Comeau collection

shipped separately in bulk, were then fitted in Canada.

In contrast to the batch-system operation in Springfield, each Canadian gun was assembled by a single person, meaning that assembly numbers were not needed, and since the parts were already hardened before being supplied in bulk, no serial numbers were applied to the cylinders.

Each finished revolver was double-checked by another assembler. Upon final assembly, inspection, and approval by the master gunsmith, the guns were replaced in the standard S&W blue boxes of the period, which already had hand-printed labels on them. A little sticker printed with a red Maple Leaf and the legend "Assembled in Canada/Smith & Wesson (Canada) Ltd." was then applied to the boxes of some early production, but this was soon discontinued as unnecessary, as a complete record was being kept of all the serial numbers of the Canadian-assembled revolvers. The guns were then test-fired at a nearby police range before being shipped to the ordering agency - Model 10s with standard-weight 6-inch barrels to the Royal Canadian Mounted Police (RCMP), and with heavy 4-inch barrels to the Ontario Provincial Police (OPP).

The Model 10 had become the standard-issue official revolver of the RCMP starting in the mid-1950s, when it replaced the Colt New Service. A friend who was a member of the force at the time commented they were a lot more comfortable to carry, and were consequently much favored by the "Mounties".

Other than the absence of the serial number on the cylinder and the usual assembly numbers in the crane area, nothing was stamped or otherwise marked on the revolver itself to indicate that it was assembled in Canada, only the sticker on the boxes of some early examples.

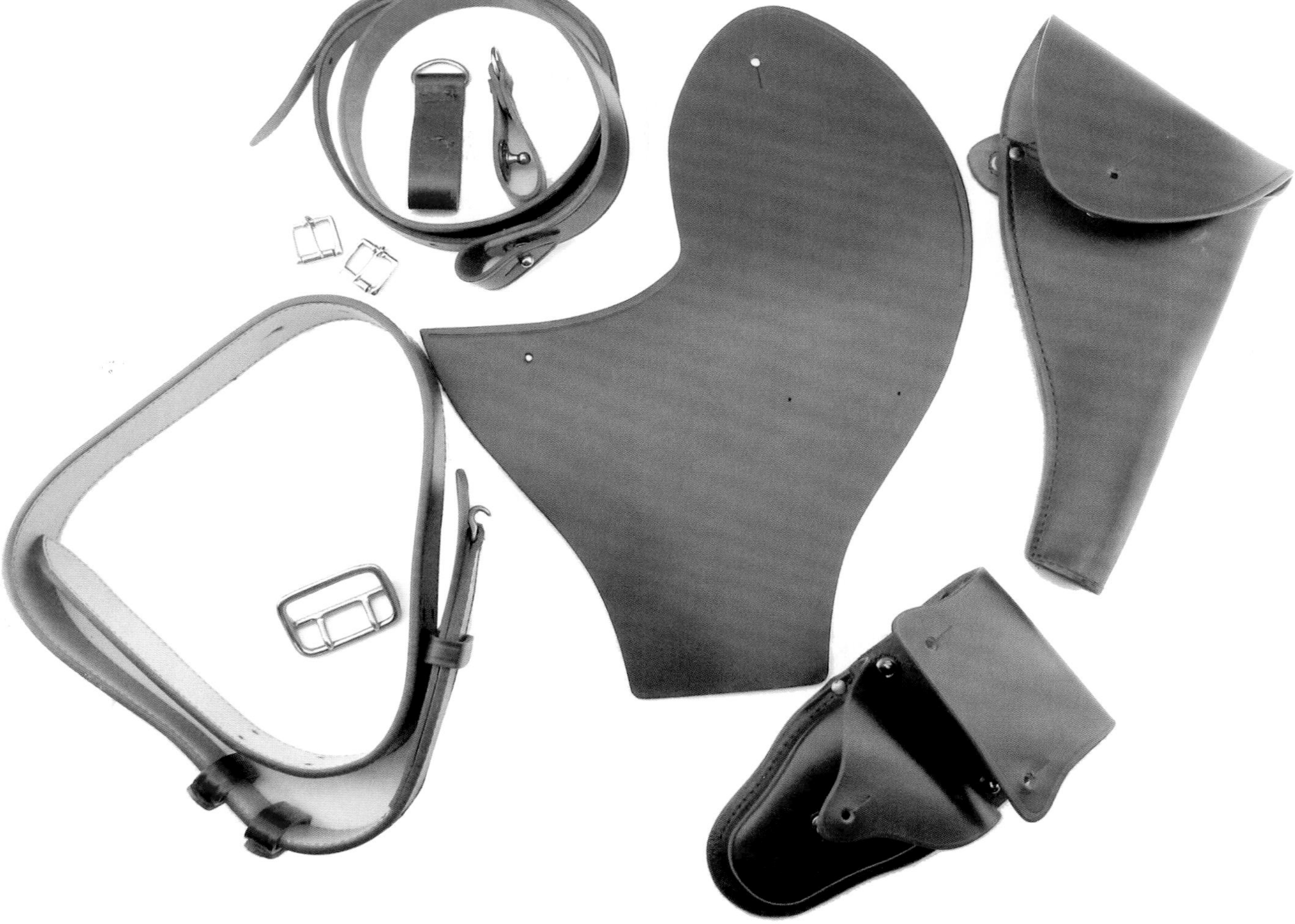

451. Unassembled and assembled russet leather components as received from the S&W Leather Co. for assembly in Canada as part of the RCMP contract. The brass buckles are gold plated.

Under the upper flap of the handcuff case (below right) are stitched leather loops for six .38 Special cartridges.
Gaston Comeau collection

Other revolver models assembled in Canada included a few Model 14s and some Model 36s (J-frame Chiefs Specials) with 3" barrels, the latter being purchased by the Canadian Forces Military Police. In addition, russet leather Sam Browne belts and covered flap holsters, both with gold-plated brass fittings, were assembled as part of the RCMP contract.

In the end, the effects of the late-1970s recession, plus the termination of the Canadian Excise Tax credit resulted in fewer sales, which were once again handled directly from Springfield, and this led to the closure of the Canadian plant in December, 1979.

As noted, some commercial sales were also made, although the police-contract guns themselves are quite a rarity in private hands, as neither the RCMP nor the OPP allowed retiring officers to purchase their handguns, and none were sold onto the surplus market.

452. Closeup of a size 36 RCMP Sam Browne belt assembly.
Note the S&W logo, stamped into the leather.
Gaston Comeau collection

## Joe Rothmuller's Personal Model 10-5

453. Left and right side views of Joe Rothmuller's personal 6" Model 10-5, serial no. C 142595, assembled by him on a reclaimed frame and fitted with a 6" RCMP barrel, target hammer, target trigger, and target stocks.

Inset, above left: detail of the 1/8" wide fixed front sight.

Inset, below right: closeup of the butt with stocks removed, showing serial no. and assembly markings on the underside. Gaston Comeau collection

At least one Canadian-assembled Model 10 was retained in non-governmental hands, this being the one which Joe Rothmuller put together for himself. In a 1983 letter to his friend, the S&W collector Gaston Comeau, Mr. Rothmuller described how he had purchased the frame in damaged condition from a customer, had it remanufactured at the Springfield factory, and then rebuilt the gun himself in Mississauga.

# The Iranian National Police Model 10

In *Small Arms Today*, author Edward C. Ezell states that a direct sale of 3,000 S&W Model 10 revolvers in caliber "9x29mmR" (.38 Special) was licensed to the Iranian National Police in Tehran by the U.S. State Department in 1977, although such revolvers had been an item of police issue there since 1974 or earlier.

In addition, U.S. FMS (Foreign Military Sales) of 3,021 Model 10s (NSN 1005-00-937-5839) were provided to the Iranian military in 1975, along with a further 800, under NSN 1005-00-937-5840, in 1975 - 76. Some Model 15s (.38 Special Combat Masterpieces) were also purchased.

454. The 3-screw sideplate from an Iranian Model 10, showing Farsi marking reading *shahrbonnie Keshvar* (National Police Force). Gaston Comeau collection, marking identification courtesy Arastou Rafizadeh

# The Latest Dash Changes

## The Models 10-7 and 10-8 (1977)

As John Henwood records,

> *The Model 10-7 . . , introduced during 1977, was the light-barreled Model 10-5, altered to remove the gas ring from the cylinder yoke, and place it in the cylinder itself. (The gas ring is the small spacer which protects the yoke and cylinder from gas and powder fouling during firing . .) The Model 10-7 was available with 2-, 4-, 5-, or 6-inch tapered barrels. (The 5- and 6-inch barrels were discontinued by 1988.)*
>
> *. . The Model 10-8 . . was the heavy-barreled Model 10-6, with the same gas ring change as the Model 10-7. It was also introduced in 1977, with a choice of 3- or 4-inch heavy barrels . . The 3-inch barrel length did not prove popular and was discontinued by 1988.*

## Deleting the Barrel Pin (1982)

John Henwood records that "In 1982 the barrel pin was deleted. The firm now relies on precision machining (and friction between barrel and frame shoulders) to hold the barrel in place."

# The Model 10-9 for the Royal Hong Kong Police

455. Left side view of a 4" Model 10-9, serial no. AHT 7976, as purchased by the Royal Hong Kong Police.

Note the modified square butt and "P.C." (Plain Clothes) stocks.

According to *The Standard Catalog of Smith & Wesson*, about 1983 "some 13,000 of these revolvers were traded in toward the purchase of new guns. Many were then purchased by AcuSport of Ohio for resale on the used gun market."

Inset, above: "C & E" (Customs & Excise) marking, found on some backstraps.

Inset, below: RHKP (Royal Hong Kong Police) marking on backstrap. Dave Terbrueggen collection

456 (left). Underside closeup of the above Hong Kong Police Model 10-9, showing serial number.

Note the lanyard ring is offset, so as not to obscure the serial number. Dave Terbrueggen collection

# The Peruvian Police Model 10

457. Right side view of a 2" Model 10 with no barrel pin, serial no. AEV 7997, manufactured in 1986 for the *Policia de Investigaciones del Peru,* the Peruvian equivalent of the FBI, and marked as shown with their crest on the sideplate.
Dave Terbrueggen collection

## The Models 10-9 and 10-10 (1988)

These were the last Model 10 "dash" changes to be discussed in John Henwood's book *America's Right Arm*, which as noted was published in 1997.

Some excerpts from his comments on these final changes read as follows:

> *The Model 10-9 (with light, tapered barrel) was introduced in 1988; only 2- and 4-inch barrels were available. Changes included a new yoke retention system (the yoke is now retained by a pointed, spring-loaded plunger, housed in the front sideplate screw, which engages a "V" groove in the yoke stud); a "radius stud package" (improvements to the hammer and trigger studs); a "floating" hand (involving changes to the trigger as well); and alterations to the hammer nose (firing pin) and hammer nose bushing. (A "hammer-nose spring", similar to the one already used in N-frame guns, was added.) . . Since 1995, only round butt frames have been furnished on S&W revolvers [and] Stocks are now black plastic Uncle Mike's Combat grips.*
>
> *Also introduced in 1988, the Model 10-10 has the same improvements as the 10-9 and is identical, except it has a 3- or 4-inch heavy barrel. (3-inch guns have round butts, this barrel length*

*was discontinued in 1988. Circa 1994, the 3-inch barreled round-butt guns were reintroduced for export only.)*

*. . During 1993 minor changes were made in both the 10-9 and 10-10; the extractor was modified by eliminating its guide slot, a flat along the side of the shaft now serving to keep the extractor aligned; the extractor pins were eliminated at the same time.*

# The Model 10-10 for Brazil

458. Left and right side views of a Model 10-10 with full lug 3" heavy barrel, made for the Brazilian market in .38 Special during the period when the .357 Magnum cartridge was prohibited for civilian sale.

This is basically the same as the Sasia fixed-sight variation of the M19 (fig. 595), and uses the longer .357 cylinder.

459. Left side view of a late M10 sold to the U.S. Marshal's Service.

Note the low ramp front sight, needed to zero with the 110-gr. JHP +P+ .38 Special loads that were issued at the time these revolvers were purchased.

### The Models 10-11 and 10-12 (1997)

According to *The Standard Catalog of Smith & Wesson*, four further "dash" changes have been introduced for the Model 10.

Introduced in 1997, the Model 10-11, fitted with the standard-weight tapered barrel, now contains a hammer and trigger made by the MIM (Metal Injection Molding) process, and a floating firing pin.

Also introduced in 1997, the Model 10-12 is the heavy barrel version, fitted with the same changes as the Model 10-11.

## The Limited Production Lew Horton Model 10

There are two schools of thought regarding the various "Limited Production" series of revolvers which have been offered, some feeling they are well worth acquiring while others see anything marketed intentionally as a "collectible" to be not nearly as desirable as the models made in truly limited numbers because they did not sell well for one reason or another.

Examples of such true rarities would include the prewar First Model K-32, which was introduced in 1938 and made for only two years, with only 94 sold (figs. 338 - 340); and the Second Model prewar K-22 (fig. 369), which was introduced in 1940 and discontinued in March, 1942 in favor of full-out wartime production after only 1,067 examples had been manufactured.

In any case this Model 10 with its fully color-case-hardened receiver, which was marketed in truly limited numbers by Lew Horton Distributing (80 in square-butt versions and another 70 in the round-butt configuration shown in fig. 460), is undeniably attractive. The square-butt guns were shipped first, beginning in May, 2001.

460. Left side view of a round-butt Model 10 with fully color-case-hardened receiver, unusual 4¼" barrel and laminated Magna-style stocks, marketed in limited numbers by Lew Horton Distributing. This model was first shipped in May, 2001. Dave Terbrueggen collection

# The 1899 Commemorative (Model 10-13, 2002)

1 (previous page). Left side view of the Model 10-13, the 99 Commemorative M&P. Note the 4" pinned barrel, and lack of a front extractor lug under the barrel.
Manufactured in extremely limited numbers: estimates ge from 34 to 38. Most were shipped to J&G Rifle Ranch Arizona.
Michael Wozniak collection, photo by Paul Goodwin

462. Right side view of the cased Model 10-13, the 1899 Commemorative M&P, showing details of wood presentation case and four-screw sideplate.

Only a limited number of these cases were made, and all were auctioned off—without guns—at the 2003 S&WCA annual meeting.

The circular indentation in the velvet lining was intended to hold a silver medallion (fig. 464), but none of these were officially produced.

Michael Wozniak collection, photo by Paul Goodwin

463. The presentation case for the Model 1899 Commemorative with lid closed, showing details of the laser engraving. Michael Wozniak collection, photo by Paul Goodwin

464. The 1899 - 1999 M&P Commemorative medallion.
As noted in the owner's display panel, "A handful of special Model 10s with no barrel lugs were made up for the 100th M&P Anniversary in 1999.
"Cases for these guns have a recess for a special commemorative medal, but only one lead proof is known. 4 silver copies were made from this lead proof. This is one of those 4." Michael Wozniak collection

The Model 10-13, introduced in 2002, is a special 100th Anniversary model called the 1899 Commemorative. Emulating the appearance of the original Model 1899, the Model 10-13 was produced on a four-screw frame with a 4" barrel without the front extractor rod lug. Apparently this was released in a very limited run of only 34 - 38 examples, and most were shipped to J&G Rifle Ranch in Arizona.

## The Model 10-14 (2002)

As discussed at the end of Chapter Thirty-Three, the Model 10-14, also introduced in 2002, began the era of S&W revolvers fitted with the patented Saf-T-Hammer internal key-lock system.

# The Model 11 (.38 S&W M&P)

With the advent of model numbering in 1957, the basic fixed-sight M&P in .38 S&W chambering became the Model 11.

John Henwood describes the Model 11 as follows:

> *. . Otherwise identical to the Model 10, it was chambered for the .38/200 (.38 S&W) cartridge, and was usually fitted with a 5-inch barrel (4- and 6-inch barrels were also offered, but are not often seen) and a lanyard swivel. The Model 11 was produced only on special order through 1965. In excess of 10,000 were made; probably all were exported to various British (and Commonwealth) police (notably the South African Police, who bought a quantity of Model 11-4s circa 1962) and military users. Post-1961 Model 11s incorporate all the applicable Model 10 "dash" changes through Model 11-5.*

465. Left and right side views of a Model 11-2, serial no. C 569259, with 4" barrel, modified square butt with P.C. stocks and lanyard swivel, as produced for the U.S. Post Office. The Model 11 was essentially the commercial version of the .38/200 revolver, in .38 S&W chambering.

The barrel markings on the right side read "38 S & W CTG. 178 GR." Dave Terbrueggen collection

| 11-2 | B | 4 | S | | |
|---|---|---|---|---|---|
| MODEL NO. | FIN | BARREL | STOCK | TH | TT |
| INS | PKR 5 | SPECIAL FEATURES: Swivel | | | |
| SER. NO. | C 256 004 | | FRONT SIGHT | | WO |

SMITH & WESSON

466 (left). The end label on the blue Bangor Punta box for another Model 11-2, serial no. C 25604. Note under "Special Features" the notation "Swivel".

Dave Terbrueggen collection

# The Model 12 (M&P "Airweight")

After 1957 the alloy-framed "Airweight" was designated the Model 12. A description of this model and the dedicated USAF version, called by them the M13 "Aircrewman", which shared slightly thinner components, appears in an excerpt from a 1965 article by Roy Jinks in Chapter Thirty-Six.

John Henwood records the chronology of the "dash" changes applied to the Model 12 as follows:

> *Engineering changes to the Model 12 resulted in models through "-4". The 12-1 was introduced during January, 1962, and called for the extractor rod being changed to left-hand threads, and the incorporation of the new cylinder stop. The 12-2, introduced at the same time as the 12-1, was furnished with these changes, plus 1/8" sights. The Model 12-3, introduced in 1977, resulted in a change in the gas ring location, from the yoke to the cylinder itself. The Model 12-4, which was authorized in 1984, had a thicker frame, making it the same thickness as all other K-frame guns .*

## A 2" Model 12-2 for the Winnipeg Police Department

467. Left side view of a 2" Model 12, serial no. D823649, in its original box, as sold to and marked by the Winnipeg, Manitoba Police Department.

Note the police marking "WPD/A724" stamped on the side of the aluminum frame. Gaston Comeau collection

468 (left). The label from the end of the blue box in which the above 2" Model 12 was originally shipped. It was returned with the gun when it was traded in years later.

Note the box is marked with the same police number as the gun. Gaston Comeau collection

469. Right side view of a 4" barreled M12 Airweight - a very fine but underappreciated defense weapon.
The grips were made by Fuzzy Farrant to the author's design.

470. Right side view of an M12 Airweight with an M10 heavy barrel installed.
The grips, made by Don Collins to the author's design, are ideal for concealed carry and duty use.

# The Model 12 with Safety Catch, for the French National Police

471. Right side view of the Model 12 revolver with 3" heavy barrel - marked "Airweight" - and manual safety catch on the sideplate, made up circa 1966 for the French National Police. The frame is typically set up for the "skinny" barrel, so the edges of the frame are beveled to reduce the gap.

Note the markings on the barrel are not centered, indicating that the factory used 4" barrels cut down to 3".

The safety lever, shown here in the "OFF" position, looks the same as the normal "flat latch" cylinder release, positioned upside down. courtesy Jean Huon

A special order of Model 12 Airweight revolvers with 3-inch heavy barrels and a sliding safety catch on the right side of the frame, was produced for the *Préfecture de Police* in Paris. Called the *Sûrété PN* ("Safety National Police") revolver, this arm was critiqued by John Henwood as follows:

> *Circa 1966 a special production run of Model 12s was made for the French police . . equipped (for some reason) with 3-inch heavy barrels. They also had a sliding manual safety catch thumbpiece on the right side, in the middle of the sideplate. (This is certainly an unusual combination: a lightweight frame fitted with a heavyweight barrel, and having an unnecessary manual safety located on the wrong side of the gun for right-handed users.)*

This is a rare arm in the U.S., with apparently only 20 examples known.

472. Four views of the 3-screw sideplate as fitted to the French National Police Model 12 revolvers, showing details of the safety catch.

Above: outside views, with safety OFF (left) and ON (right).

Below: inside views, with safety OFF (left) and ON (right). The safety functions exactly like the cylinder release, which automatically engages when the cylinder is open to block the hammer from moving back. The only difference is that the safety is located on the other side, and is manually operated.

forensics collection IRCGN, France

## Some Insights into the French Bureaucratic Mindset

The French researcher and author Jean Huon has kindly provided some insight into the rationale for the unusual combination of light frame, heavy barrel, and manual safety featured in this French Police model, which we have paraphrased as follows:

When a French member of the administration is put in charge of a project, he brings to it a very peculiar attitude which would never be tolerated in a private company. Two things are uppermost in his mind:

1. What can I do to put my own particular mark on this project?
2. Why should we adopt a simple solution, when a more complicated one can be found?

Of course this typically French "Administrative Handicap Spirit" would be a serious drawback if the end product were to be subjected to the harsh realities of the commercial marketplace, but these revolvers were officially acquired for police use only, and paid for out of the public purse.

Jean concludes that this type of bureaucratic mindset remains alive and well in the French public sector.

# The Swedish Air Force m/58 K-Frame Revolvers

473. Left and right side of two 2" Model 12 Airweight revolvers with steel cylinders, as used by Swedish forces.
Above: the "m/58", as carried by Air Force pilots flying jet fighter aircraft.
Below: the "m/58 D", used by some Inspection officers in the Swedish Coast Guard.
Note the three Swedish Crowns property mark, on the receiver above the trigger guard.
Per Dahlen collection

According to Per Dahlen, the technical consultant for Saab Arms Engineering, Land Division, in the post-WWII period the Swedish military used three Smith & Wesson K-frame models: the Model 10, Model 12 "Airweight", and the Model 14. (It might be said that these represented unusual choices for a military organization, especially one that had otherwise moved away from revolvers over 50 years earlier!)

The Swedish Air Force used two main S&W revolvers, the Model 10 and the Model 12. The Model

M7786-000490

# Revolver m/58

**Beskrivning**

BOKFÖRRÅDET

**FÖRSVARETS MATERIELVERK**
**Armématerielförvaltningen**
**1969**

474. The cover of the Swedish handbook for the Revolver m/58, issued in 1966. Per Dahlen collection

475. A box of 50 rounds of full-patch 9mm m/58 (.38 Special) ammunition, with a sample round shown in front. Per Dahlen collection

476 (below). An open spread of two pages from the handbook shown above, describing the m/58 (Smith & Wesson Model 12) revolver. Per Dahlen collection

## Allmänt

Revolver m/58 är ett kortpipigt repetervapen med roterande trumma rymmande sex patroner. Ammunitionen utgörs av 9 mm sk ptr m/58, vilken ej får förväxlas med annan 9 mm ammunition.

Riktmedlen utgörs av korn på pipan och siktskåra i stommen.

Yttre säkringsanordningar saknas.

Tillbehör: Revolverfodral m/58 med två bärremmar, läskstång, borstviskare.

## Handhavande

**Laddning**

Tryck fram det lättrade greppet, hanspärrgreppet, på stommens vänstra sida och tryck trumman åt vänster ur stommen. Fyll trumman med ammunition och för den åter i läge. Den spärras automatiskt. Hanens tändspets hålls då bakom stötbotten av en säkringsslid.

**Avfyring**

När man för avtryckaren tillbaka vrids hanen bakåt. Härvid spänns slagfjädern och samtidigt förs trumspärren ur spärrläge. Genom att trumman samtidigt vrids ett steg förs en patron till avfyringsläge. Efter matningsrörelsen spärras trumman och hanen frigörs. När avtryckaren släpps återförs den automatiskt till utgångsläget.

Hanen kan också spännas direkt utan att avtryckaren påverkas. Den hakas då upp i spänt läge.

**Patron ur**

För trumman åt sidan på samma sätt som vid laddning. Tryck därefter utkastaraxeln bakåt så att kvarvarande patroner eller hylsor kastas ur trummans patronläge.

Vid blindavfyringar kan stommen skadas genom hanens anslag vid tändstiftsurborrningen. Vid avfyringsövningar skall därför trumman vara laddad med tomhylsor.

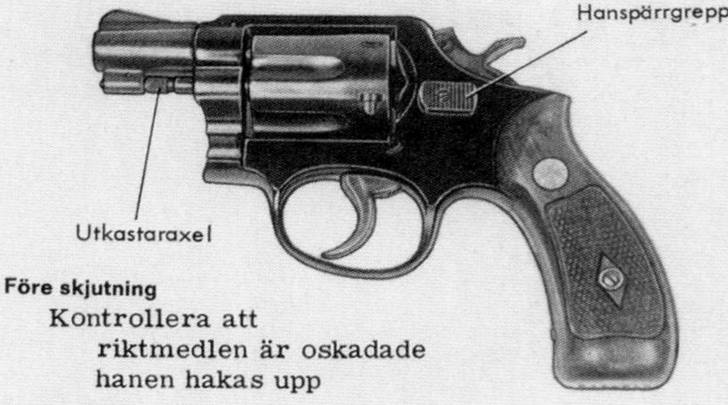


**Före skjutning**

Kontrollera att
riktmedlen är oskadade
hanen hakas upp

**Under skjutning**

Kontrollera att
rätt ammunition används (9 mm sk ptr m/58)
projektilen följer med då hylsa avlägsnas
efter klick

**Efter skjutning**

Kontrollera att patron ej finns kvar i vapnet.

Efter daglig tillsyn skall slagfjädern vara slappad. Detta görs genom avfyring varvid hanen bromsas med tummen.

477. The original black leather belt holster, used with the m/58 by Air Fiorce jet pilots.
Note the loops to carry six spare rounds inside the flap.
Per Dahlen collection

479. An experimental black leather ankle holster for the m/58 revolver, which was never purchased in quantity and never used in service. Per Dahlen collection

478 (left). The black leather open-ended Sickinger belt holster used with the m/58 D revolver by the Swedish Coast Guard. Per Dahlen collection

10, with steel frame and 4" barrel, called the "Revolver m/58 C", was used by the Air Force military police on the ground. The Model 12 "Airweight", called the "Revolver m/58", with its aluminum frame and a 2" barrel, was carried by pilots flying jet fighter aircraft.

In the 1980s some m/58 revolvers were "modified" by being fitted with wraparound Pachmayr rubber grips, the resulting gun being called the "m/58 D". Along with the open-ended black leather Sickinger holster shown in fig. 478, these were used by some Inspection officers in the Swedish Coast Guard.

The Model 14 with 6" barrel, called the "Revolver m/58 B", was purchased in small quantities only, and was used mostly for competition shooting and by the Armed Forces military police.

## Discontinuing the Model 12 "Airweight"

As John Henwood concludes,

> *The Model 12 was finally discontinued in 1986, a victim of those "+P" extra-high-powered cartridges, plus the never-solved problem of the anodized finish wearing off rather quickly . .*

# The Model 13 (.357 Magnum M&P)

480. Left side view of a typical Model 13-1 with 4" pinned barrel, modified to double action only (DAO) with hammer spur removed. The cylinder is recessed for the case heads.

The grips are non-factory wraparound plastic with molded finger grooves.

The fixed-sight, heavy-barrel Model 10 in .357 Magnum caliber, which was cheaper to make than the target-sighted M19, eventually became the Model 13.

The .357 Magnum Model 13 was described in an article about the USAF M13 "Aircrewman" by Roy Jinks, the S&W Historian, which appeared in the May, 1975 issue of *Arms Gazette* magazine. Portions of this article which describe the Air Force M13 "Aircrewman" appear in Chapter Thirty-Six, and excerpts describing the rationale for the S&W-assigned nomenclature "Model 13" to the .357 Magnum M&P are as follows:

*The Smith & Wesson Model 13, .357 Military & Police, is a fixed-sight, four-inch heavy barreled K-frame (medium frame) .357 Magnum revolver [which] was first developed as a service revolver for the New York State Police. When it was first placed into production in 1973, it was manufactured as a variation of the Model 10-6, which is the heavy-barreled .38 Military & Police. The only difference . . was that it was designed to withstand the higher pressures of the .357 cartridge. These early .357 Military & Police revolvers were stamped as Model 10-6, with a .357 Magnum barrel marking. As the popularity of this model grew and the demand increased, the factory realized the .357 M&P should become a standard model and added to the handgun line.*

*The decision was made to assign a model number to prevent confusion between the Model 10, .38 Special and the specially built .357 Magnum; but what number should be used? A review of unassigned model numbers showed that the model number 13 had never been assigned to any Smith & Wesson revolver. Therefore, the new fixed-sighted .357 was officially assigned the model number 13-1. This may seem rather straightforward but to the Smith & Wesson collector it presents a problem, for he now has two Model 13s to consider since there has been another Model 13 associated with Smith & Wesson's handgun line since 1953. The earlier Model 13, however, is not a Smith & Wesson assigned model number. It is a model number assigned by the U.S. Air Force to identify the lightweight Aircrewman model [described in Chapter Thirty-Six]. The Air Force assignment of M13 to this lightweight revolver was done before Smith & Wesson had considered the use of model numbers for identification . .*

## Starting with the Model 13-1 - No "Model 13"

John Henwood briefly records the history and the "dash" changes made to the Model 13 .357 Magnum revolver as follows:

*Introduced late in 1974, as a square-butt gun with a 4-inch barrel, the Model 13 remains in production today. Square butt Model 13 revolvers were fitted with the rounded Plain Clothes ["P.C."] service walnut stocks until 1995, when Uncle Mike's combat grips were introduced.*

*A round-butt version, having a three-inch barrel . . and Magna walnut stocks is also available. (The three-inch barrel is the shortest which will allow the full-length extractor rod to be fitted [which] is necessary to ensure the ejection of the .357 Magnum cartridge cases. This barrel length was originally made at the request of the FBI in 1981; it proved popular enough that it was added to the catalog.)*

*. . Model 13 revolvers also have several "dash" changes. There is no "Model 13": the Model 13-1 is the original version. (The basic "Model 13" designation was not used to avoid confusion with the USAF's M13 "Aircrewman" revolver.) The Model 13-2 designator indicated the relocation of the gas ring from the yoke to the cylinder itself; it was introduced in 1977. The Model 13-3 was introduced when the firm stopped counterboring the rear face of the Magnum-caliber cylinders for the cartridge heads in 1982 . .*

The Model 13-4 was introduced in 1988, fitted with the new yoke retention system and other changes described above under the Models 10-9 and 10-10. In 1994 the extractor rod was changed from grooved to flat-sided. Since 1995, as with all S&W revolver models, only round-butt frames have been produced.

## The 3" M13 - the Last Duty Revolver of the FBI

Although I'm sure they would hate to acknowledge it, when the FBI went to their last official duty revolver in 1981, they followed the lead of Raymond Sasia and the French police (both the FBI and Raymond Sasia are discussed under "Famous Users" in Chapter Thirty-Five) and chose the 3-inch, round-butt Model 13 in blued finish, chambered in .357 Magnum (although typically shot with .38 Special loads). These were supplied with pinned front sights so they could be replaced by FBI armorers, and each one was carefully sighted-in for the duty load of

481. Right side view of a Model 13-1 with 3" barrel, blued finish and round butt. This was the last duty revolver bought and issued by the FBI. A left side view is shown in fig. 185.

Note the pinned barrel and pinned ramp front sight,which allowed FBI armorers to alter the height of the blade easily to change zero as needed by individual agents. The pin holding the ramp sight is polished flush with the rib, and can only be seen under close examination.

482 (below). Right side view of a Model 13-3, manufactured in 1982 or later with non-pinned barrel and non-counterbored chambers in the cylinder.

The combat grips were made to the author's design.

158-gr. lead hollow-point .38 Specials while the new agent was at Quantico.

Some favorable reports were seen when the FBI adopted the three-inch M13 revolver as their last duty revolver, as in the opinion of everyone it was a pretty good choice, although I always thought it odd that the stainless Model 65 version was not chosen instead, and that a double-action-only variant was not adopted.

Having said that, most men at the Bureau (and they were all men then) who were "gun guys" put away their M13s (along with issued S&W M10 or Colt Official Police four-inch revolvers, depending on when they left Quantico) in the office safe, and carried an M19 with a 2½- or four-inch barrel.

When I worked as a federal law enforcement officer I left my federally-issued M10 four-inch skinny-barrel in the weapons room and carried a .45 Colt Commander, backed up with my .38 Smith & Wesson Bodyguard revolver, so I understand completely.

For the non-gun person, the 3" Model 13 is best known for being the weapon used by Jodie Foster, starring as a newly-minted FBI Agent in *Silence of The Lambs.*

# After the Third Million M&Ps

## The New "D" Series Serial Numbers

A new "D" serial number prefix was introduced on November 27, 1967, signaling that a third million revolvers had been produced since the "C" prefix had been introduced in March, 1948. These of course were only the fixed-sight examples, as the target models all used "K" prefix serial numbers.

# Numbers on Target-Sighted K-Frames

## Masterpieces - Technically Different from the M&P

Not only were the Masterpiece models serially numbered in various series of "K"-prefixed numbers (discussed below) but, as John Henwood points out,

> *Technically, these are not "M&P" revolvers, since the frames differ slightly (usually at the front of the top strap and around the barrel hole; the adjustable rear sight requires some changes in the frame top strap, as well), but they are almost the same . . The firm, of course, called [them] all "K-frame" guns . .*

### *[Stocks]*

> *At the start of this period (1957) . . "target" guns were furnished with walnut Magna stocks. Gradually these models came to be shipped already fitted with "target" stocks, [t]heretofore an extra-cost add-on option. In recent years, the firm has taken to fitting many of these same models with "combat" (smooth, with finger grooves) stocks made of some sort of fancy-grained hardwood such as Goncalo Alves, Pau Ferro, or Morado.*
>
> *In 1995, following a survey which showed that about 80% of buyers changed the stocks, the firm dropped the traditional wood stocks; all adjustable-sighted models now have soft black plastic stocks of the style manufactured by firms such as Michaels of Oregon or Hogue. To simplify this change, all current guns are made on round-butt frames. The wood stocks (combat, Magna service, and target) remain available as an accessory.*
>
> *. . Since it was possible to order a revolver fitted with whatever style stocks were desired, made in a variety of materials, there are many different combinations to be found. Unlike the Model 10, target-sighted K-frame guns have grooved front and back straps on the frames.*

### *[Sights]*

> *. . The Combat Masterpiece and .357 Combat Magnum revolvers fitted with 4-inch or shorter barrels started out with a plain ramp front sight, of the quick-draw "Baughman" type; this has been changed (at least in the stainless steel models), to a similar sight, but one having a red sighting insert.*

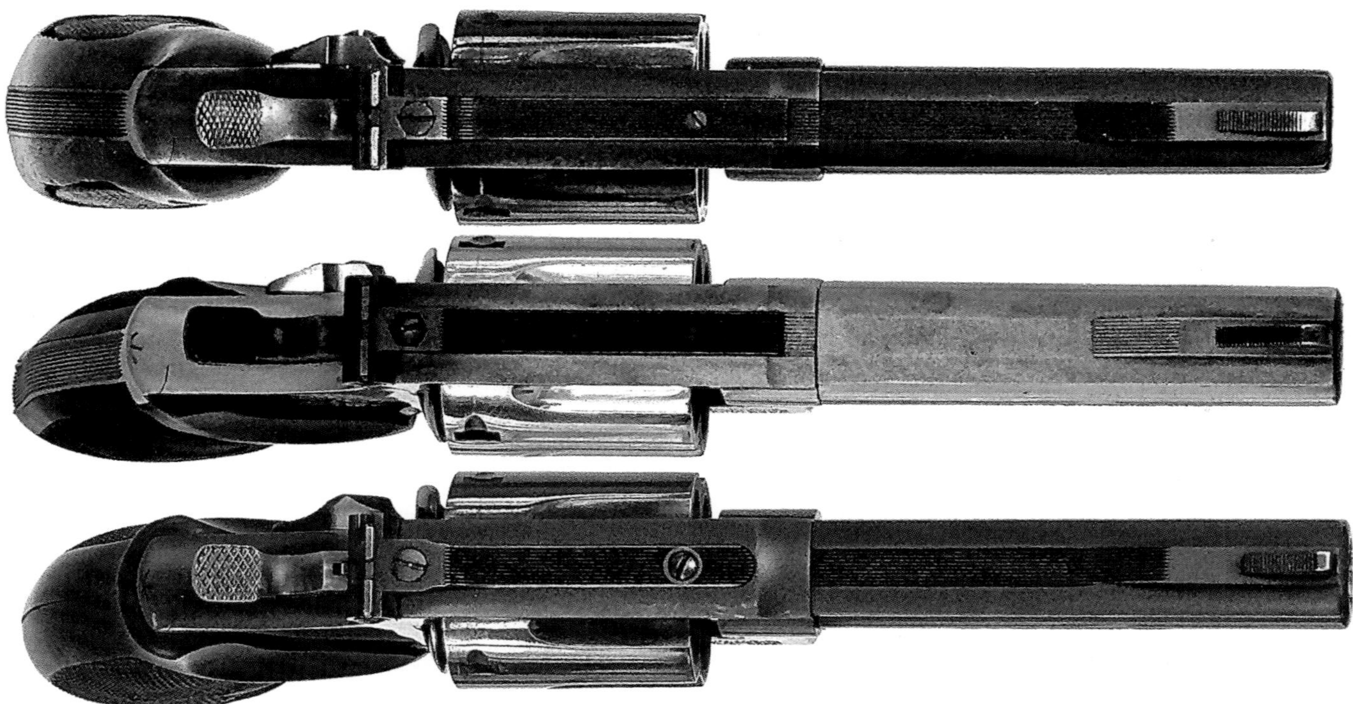

483. Top views of three target-sighted revolvers with special-order 4" barrels, showing differences.
Above: ex-Kansas City, MO Police Department M14, with pinned heavy barrel factory-cut to 4".
Center: special nickel-plated M15 variation for Dayton Gun. Note the extra-heavy, straight pinned barrel.
Below: ex-Illinois State Police M15 with factory-cut heavy non-pinned 4" barrel. Note the later form of the rear sight leaf and screw (Model 15-7, 1994).

*All use the micrometer-adjustable rear sight . . but from time to time some will have a white outline around the sighting notch. Since the sight slide was available as a replacement part, one cannot be sure that this feature is original to any particular gun. Four different heights of rear sight slides are used, depending on model and barrel length: .106", .126", .136" and .146" . .*

## [The Trigger Stop]

*Unlike the Model 10, many of the "target grade" guns had a trigger stop . . . , a small block of steel protruding from the frame behind the trigger. Intended to limit trigger overtravel (movement after the hammer is released) these were a source of problems, since if the single mounting screw loosened they might shift sufficiently to prevent the revolver's firing. In 1979 the firm recommended that this stop be removed from revolvers used for law enforcement and personal defense purposes, and mounted a recall program to accomplish this. Most police (and ex-police) guns have had the stop removed, civilian guns mostly still retain it. Later guns have a trigger stop consisting of a short rod inside the rebound slide spring, a system long used on the larger "N" frame guns.*

## Serial Numbers, 1957 - 1994

*[As mentioned in Chapter Thirty-One,] Adjustable-sighted guns, starting with the K-22 and K-38, were assigned their own numbering series immediately following World War II. The numbers started with "K101", and ran to K999999 by 1970. A new series, beginning with "1K1" started in 1970; it reached 1K999999 in 1971 and the prefix number changed to "2K" (which actually started in 1970), the series starting with 2K1. "K" series serial numbers do not flow in a smooth progression. During some years several different sequences were used simultaneously. The serial number is stamped only on the frame and sideplate; an "assembly number" of four or five digits is stamped on the frame, sideplate, yoke, and occasionally on the cylinder. This is used to assure that these hand-fitted parts are assembled together after polishing and finishing . .*

## ["Dash" Changes]

*. . Once model numbers were assigned, a series of "dash" changes were incorporated in the target models (those having adjustable sights), similar to those made in the fixed-sight models. "-1" indicates the change to left-hand threads on the extractor rod; it was adopted in December, 1959. "-2", adopted late in December, 1961 indicates the change to the later-style cylinder stop, eliminating the screw in the front of the trigger guard. "-3" from December, 1967, indicates the relocation of the rear sight leaf screw hole. Circa [sn] K260000 the top sideplate screw was dropped; this was done at the same time as this change was made to the [M&P]: September, 1955. Since this was before the change to model numbers, it went unremarked.*

*. . as each model was introduced it started out equipped with all the "dash" improvements already authorized. Thus (for example) in 1971 when the [stainless steel] Model 66 was introduced, it incorporated all the appropriate changes made through "-5" on the Model 10 . .*

# The Model 14 (K-38)

After 1957 the adjustable-sighted, 6" barrel K-38 "Masterpiece" target model was designated the Model 14. The Model 14 was dropped from the catalog in 1982, but a later version (still known as the "Model 14 K-38 Masterpiece" was reintroduced in 1991, as the Model 14-5.

## The "Single-Action Only" Model 14-2

485. The Model 14-2 shown in fig. 484, in its blue factory box with all accessories. Gaston Comeau collection

486 (left). Closeup of the receiver markings inside the crane area of Model 14-2 serial no. K764881.
Gaston Comeau collection

John Henwood records some general comments regarding various facets of the target-sighted K-frame models, as follows:

> *A seldom-seen variation is the "single-action only" Model 14, which has no double-action capability; in addition to furnishing the complete revolver, the parts necessary to convert a standard Model 14 to the single-action gun were available as a kit from the factory. No gunsmithing was required, the conversion was simply a matter of replacing parts*

487 (right). Closeup of the action of the single-action-only Model 14-2 with sideplate removed and hammer cocked. Note the absence of the double-action sear, the sear recess in the hammer, and the sear pin hole.
Gaston Comeau collection

4 (previous page). Left and right side views of single-ac-n-only Model 14-2, serial no. K764881, factory-fitted th target hammer, trigger and stocks.
Gaston Comeau collection

*. . This . . was somewhat less than satisfactory since it had one major flaw: a pull on the trigger would rotate the cylinder to the next chamber, but without firing, since the hammer did not move. This variation was only available from 1961 through 1982 [but] could be had, on special order, as late as 1984 . .*

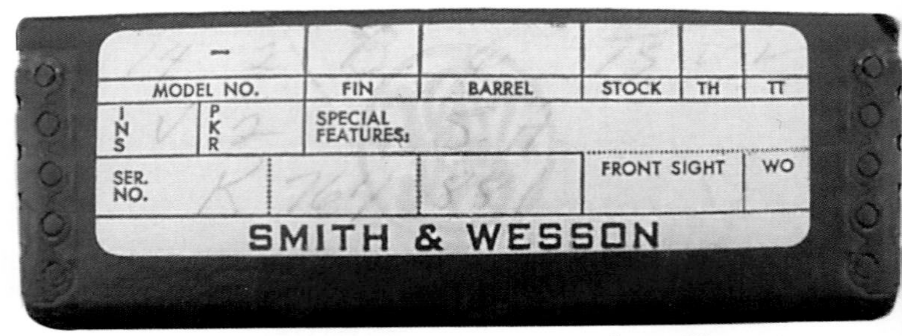


488. The box label for Model 14-2 serial no. K764881, marked "S.A." under Special Features.
Gaston Comeau collection

# The Model 15 (.38 Special Combat Masterpiece)

490. Left side view of a post-1982 Model 15 with non-pinned bull barrel.
The checkered Magna stocks no longer have the plain diamond around the grip screw escutcheon.

After 1957 the duty-oriented but target-sighted 4" model previously known as the .38 Special Combat Masterpiece became the Model 15.

As John Henwood comments, the Model15 was

*. . one of the most successful M&P variations. [It] is essentially a Model 10 with adjustable sights.*

*. . The latest change (15-7, 1994) involves changes in the rear sight assembly and extractor, plus the drilling and tapping of the frame [under the rear sight slide] for scope mounts.*

## The Model 15-8 in the Lew Horton Heritage Series

A special run of popular models were made up by the S&W Performance Center beginning in 2001 for Lew Horton Distributing. Called the Heritage Series, ten models were produced in all, each shipped in a special gold-color antiqued box depicting Horace Smith and Daniel Wesson plus a view of the original S&W factory, and marked "Heritage Series" on the front edge (fig. 802).

The Heritage Series version of the .38 Special Model 15-8 (fig. 491) features a color case-hardened frame with the Performance Center logo under the cylinder release, and a bright blue 4" barrel with ramp front sight. The top of the frame under the micrometer rear sight slide is drilled and tapped for scope mounts.

89 (previous page). Two early Model 15s, both with pinned tapered 4" barrels and early "diamond" Magna stocks.
Above: blue finish.
Below: nickel finish. Tyler 'T' grip fitted.

491. Left side view of a Model 15-8, serial no. GSC0104, produced in August, 2001 as part of the Lew Horton Heritage Series.

Note the round grips with laminated Magna stocks, the S&W Performance Center logo under the latest style cylinder release, the color-casehardened frame, and bright blue tapered non-pinned barrel.

Dave Terbrueggen collection

# The Model 16 (K-32)

John Henwood comments on the history of the .32 S&W Long caliber Model 16 (fig. 492) as follows:

> *This was the model number assigned to the ill-fated K-32 revolver in 1957. Designed as a target gun, it never proved popular with competitors, only 3,630 being produced between 1947 and 1973. The reason generally given was that the .32 bullet did not "buck" the wind as well as the .38 wadcutter used in target competition at that time. The K-32/Model 16 was essentially the same as the K-38/Model 14, except that it was chambered for the .32 S&W Long cartridge . .*
>
> *The Model 16 was discontinued in 1973, but was re-introduced in 1989 (as the Model 16-4), chambered for the .32 H&R Magnum cartridge. . . The Model 16 . . was discontinued once again in 1995.*

492. Right side view of a Model 16-2, serial no. 485868, produced in 1961 in .32 S&W Long caliber with a 6" tapered, pinned barrel. Dave Terbrueggen collection

# The Model 17 (K-22)

John Henwood continues as follows:

> *The Model 17 bears the same relationship as the Model 14 does to the K-38; it is simply a continuation of the earlier [K-22] model . . Always a popular arm, it remained in continuous production from the end of World War II through 1994. Initially available only in .22 Long Rifle caliber with a 6-inch ribbed barrel and target sights . . . over the years it received other barrel lengths, plus the same internal changes as the rest of these models. . . Although discontinued in 1995, the Model 17 was brought back in 1996. Now the Model 17-7, it features a .312" smooth combat trigger, .375" semi-target hammer, 6-inch barrel with full-length underlug, round-butt frame, and Hogue plastic stocks. The major change, however, was in the cylinder: its capacity was increased from six cartridges to ten . .*

493 (right). The author's Model 17 6" K-22 with Herrett Jordan-style stocks.

The target was shot offhand at 25 yards, using .22 shorts. Notwithstanding Henwood's *caveat* on the use of only .22LR cartridges (page 428), .22 shorts still perform acceptably.

494. Left and right side views of Model 17-8 (K-22) serial no. CA13422, with 6" full-lug barrel and 10-shot alloy cylinder.

Note the custom 2-piece stippled rubber grips, with molded S&W logos. Dave Terbrueggen collection

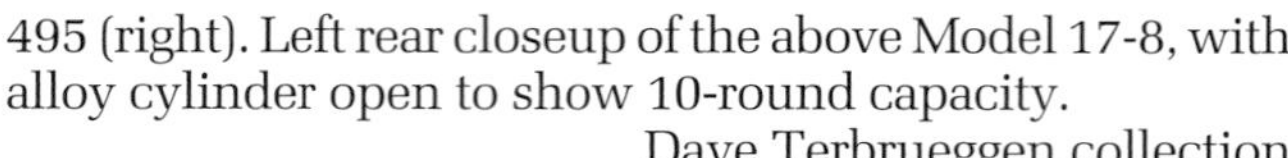

495 (right). Left rear closeup of the above Model 17-8, with alloy cylinder open to show 10-round capacity.

Dave Terbrueggen collection

# The Model 18 (.22 Combat Masterpiece)

496. Left and right side views of Model 18-2 serial no. K641493, with later target hammer and trigger installed by Metropolitan Toronto Police armorer Nick Chometa, and modified target stocks. editor's collection

*[The Model 18] is essentially the Model 17, fitted with a 4-inch barrel having the lighter exterior contours of the [tapered] barrel used in the Model 15. Initially intended as a training arm for police, it soon developed quite a following among outdoorsmen. Available only in .22 Long Rifle caliber, it incorporates the same changes as the Models 14 and 15. Introduced in 1950 [and] discontinued in 1986 . .*

# The Model 19 (.357 Combat Magnum)

497. The Model 19 (.357 Combat Magnum) with 2½" pinned barrel, shrouded ejector rod, and encased cartridge head cylinder, in a collage featuring a Secret Service shirt and holster.

This was the standard sidearm of the Secret Service for many years, well known from the Reagan attack.

The short ejector rod makes removing stuck cases difficult, which is why the FBI always picked 3- or 4-inch barreled revolvers. Leroy Thompson photograph

John Henwood has some interesting comments about the Model 19, which are excerpted as follows:

*Originally known as the ".357 Combat Magnum", this revolver is similar to the Model 15, except that it has a longer cylinder chambered for the .357 Magnum cartridge, and the barrel has a shrouded ejector rod similar to those found on the larger "N" frame guns . . Introduced in November, 1955, . . it was immediately popular with both sportsmen and peace officers. The Model 19 remains in production today (1997) with either 2½ or 4" barrels.*

498. Right side view of a post-1982 Model 19 with non-pinned barrel, in a .38 Special version made for Brazil while the .357 Magnum was prohibited for civilian sale.
Note the higher front sight.

499. Right side view of a Model 19 with fixed sights, originally made for Peru.
The modified square butt is fitted with a Tyler 'T' grip.

500. Right side view of a Model 19 with 4" non-pinned barrel and smooth factory grips fitted with a Tyler 'T' grip adapter.

This is an ex-State Department Security variation, also used by U.S. Naval Investigative Services and the FBI, which made a nice concealed-carry package.

*. . A few model 19s were made in 9mm Luger caliber for export. (Unlike the Model 547 [discussed below], these required the use of special "half-moon" clips.) Also a few in .357 Magnum caliber were made with fixed sights, on special order for the Peruvian National Police [fig. 499].*

*. . All the .357 Magnum variations, both blued and stainless steel, differ from the .38 Special guns in having longer cylinders, with the butt end of the barrel being correspondingly shortened.*

*"Dash" changes to the Model 19 mostly parallel those to the other models . . "-5" (1982) showed that the rear face of cylinder was not counterbored for the cartridge rims [and] "-7" (1994) shows that the frame is tapped for scope mounts . .*

*. . Over the years the Model 19 has been a favorite for use as a commemorative gun, appearing in at least eighteen issues . .*

# The Model 45 (.22 Caliber M&P)

John Henwood describes the Model 45 as follows:

*This model number was assigned to the .22 Long Rifle caliber Military and Police revolver. Produced from 1948 through 1957, it was re-introduced [as the Model 45] in 1963, at about [serial no.] C622700, and was made until 1965 (and possibly even as late as 1978). Only about 500 of the total production were sold through regular retail channels, the majority going to police departments and the U.S. Post Office Department. Details of barrel lengths, stocks, etc., are not known . .*

# The Model 48 (K-22 in .22 WRM)

502. Right side view of a Model 48-4 with 8⅜" barrel in .22 WRM caliber, with its spare .22LR rimfire cylinder.
Dave Terbrueggen collection

1 (preceding page). Right side view of a late Model 19-7 ith Performance Center top ported 3" barrel, late rounded ar sight leaf, and Hogue grips.
Dave Terbrueggen collection

The Model 48, chambered for the .22 Winchester Rimfire Magnum cartridge, is otherwise identical to the Model 17 (K-22).

A complete cylinder assembly in .22 LR caliber was available as an accessory option. "Dash" changes are the same as for the Model 17.

SMITH & WESSON
SPRINGFIELD 4, MASS.

PLEASE ADDRESS ALL COMMUNICATIONS TO THE COMPANY

August 26, 1959



Mr. B. D. Munhall
H. P. White Laboratory
Box 331
Belair, Maryland

Dear Burt:

This will acknowledge and thank you for your letter of August 4, requesting information on our K-22 Masterpiece Model 48, chambered for the 22 Magnum Rim Fire cartridge.

Incidentally, please excuse this rather belated reply to your letter, the reason being that the factory has been closed for two weeks for annual inventory, and I have been out to Camp Perry for a couple of weeks, and then took a little time off myself to get rested up from the Perry trip.

We are currently producing the gun described above, and have had it in production for some time. As a matter of fact I believe, or rather I am sure, we were the first on the market with this gun, having made deliveries even before Camp Perry time, and the guns are flowing out of here at a great rate at the present time.

The gun which we are using is the K-22 Masterpiece, which lends itself admirably to the purpose, and we are allowing an option of 4, 6, or 8 3/8-inch barrel length, with no change in price, and the price of the K-22 Masterpiece ($81.00) prevails on the over-all picture.

We are enclosing our latest all-model circular, which will give you the basic specifications of the gun, and here is the other information that you desire for your files.

Model Designation of Gun..........Model 48
Bore Diameter......................219"to .220"
Groove Diameter....................224"to .2257"
Width of Land...................... .040"
Width of Groove....................074"
Twist Direction....................R. H.
Rate of Twist......................10.00" Lead R. H.

We are always glad to furnish you with this type of information, with, of course,

SMITH & WESSON

(2)

Mr. B. D. Munhall August 26, 1959

the understanding that it is confined to your use in the laboratory, or the preparation of reports that are to be released in your firearms information service which you issue to police departments.

The one thing that we do not wish to do is have figures of this type published in, for example, sporting magazines, if we can avoid it, since this leads average Mr. John Doe to measuring up his own individual gun with the family yardstick, and then berating us because his gun does not meet with specifications.

You would be surprised at how many people will bring or send guns in here to us that meet the guages perfectly and within tolerances, but with their demand for new guns because of failure to meet specifications. Usually the measurements are taken with a steel rule, or sometimes, as in the case of bore diameters, with a micrometer sighting through the micrometer and the bore of the gun.

I don't believe I have to enlarge on the subject as you have probably encountered this problem many times, and it is for this reason that we are rather reluctant to have our manufacturing specifications published openly.

Another reason is because of the handloaders who are prone to size to the figure shown in a magazine with a complete disregard for manufacturing tolerances-- and this is always bad.

Regardless of the above, here's the information that you seek, and I sincerely hope that it will be of assistance to you.

With the writer's very kindest personal regards, as always, and I hope this finds you at your very best.

Sincerely yours,

SMITH & WESSON, INC.

F. H. Miller
Sales Manager

503. A two-page letter dated August 26, 1959 from Fred Miller, S&W Sales Manager, to Burton D. Munhall, manager of the prestigious H. P. White Laboratories, giving confidential details of the .22 Magnum cartridge.
Page two of this letter is also interesting.
Gaston Comeau collection

# The Model 53 (.22 Magnum/.22 Jet)

When the Model 53 was first released in .22 Jet caliber an example was naturally sent to Elmer Keith, the foremost gun writer of the mid-20th century. Keith tested it and immediately noted problems with the tapered case design, which were to be the cause for the later withdrawal of this model. In the Supplement added to the second edition of his famous book *Sixguns by Keith*, he noted,

> *. . The new [.22 Magnum] cartridge is made by swaging down the .357 Magnum case and has much the shape of a common milk bottle. I would have preferred more parallel sides and a sharper shoulder instead of the long gradual taper of the new case . .*

John Henwood describes the unsuccessful Model 53 as follows:

> *This was the Model 19 [Combat Magnum] but chambered for the .22 Remington Jet cartridge [and introduced in March, 1961]. (Barrels are roll-marked ".22 MAGNUM".) . . The cartridge was essentially the .357 Magnum, tapered down to .22 caliber. Adapters were furnished to allow the use of .22 Long Rifle cartridges in the gun, and the hammer had a moveable striker in its face. This allowed it to hit either of the two firing pins in the frame, one for the center-fire Jet cartridge, and one for the rim-fire .22 Long Rifle. As an option, a complete cylinder assembly in .22 Long Rifle caliber could be furnished . .*
>
> *The Model 53 was not successful, being plagued with a cylinder rotation problem. Upon firing those sharply tapered cases . . "set back" in the cylinder, eventually jamming it and preventing opera-*

504. A Model 53-2 with 4" barrel in .22 Remington Jet caliber, shown in the smaller of two sizes of box made for this model, which came with barrel lengths to 8⅜."

Note the spare .22 rimfire cylinder, and the adapters for using .22LR cartridges in the Magnum cylinder.

Dave Terbrueggen collection

*tion. While spotlessly clean chambers were a partial relief, as soon as the gun was fired the trouble started again. At the end of 1961 the Model 53 received the new style cylinder stop [and] the model number was changed to 53-2. The Model 53 was discontinued in 1974; about 15,000 were produced . .*

## The One-Off, Experimental Model 53 in .256 Winchester Magnum

In a further excerpt from the Supplement to the second edition of *Sixguns by Keith*, Elmer Keith commented on the release of the short-lived .256 Winchester Magnum cartridge as follows:

*Both Winchester and also Smith & Wesson have announced that they have produced a new .256 caliber center fire cartridge throwing a 60-grain soft-point bullet at 2,200 feet velocity from a sixgun. Ironically the Winchester announcement claiming the highest velocity Magnum revolver cartridge in the world came to me two weeks after Remington had sent me their pictures and brochure on the new .22 center fire Magnum [Jet] at 2,460 feet velocity. The new Winchester case is to my notion much better shaped than is the .22 Remington center fire Magnum, because it has nearly parallel sides and a good abrupt shoulder. Also the 60-grain .256 caliber bullet is a much more powerful and effective load than is the .22 center fire Magnum, even at its 360 feet [per second] higher velocity. I only hope that this new Winchester load, which I have only seen pictures of, is the same bullet diameter as the old .25 Stevens long rim fire. If such is the case, then I see no good reason why S&W and Colt and Ruger cannot bring out extra cylinders for the .25 Stevens to be used in the same gun . .*

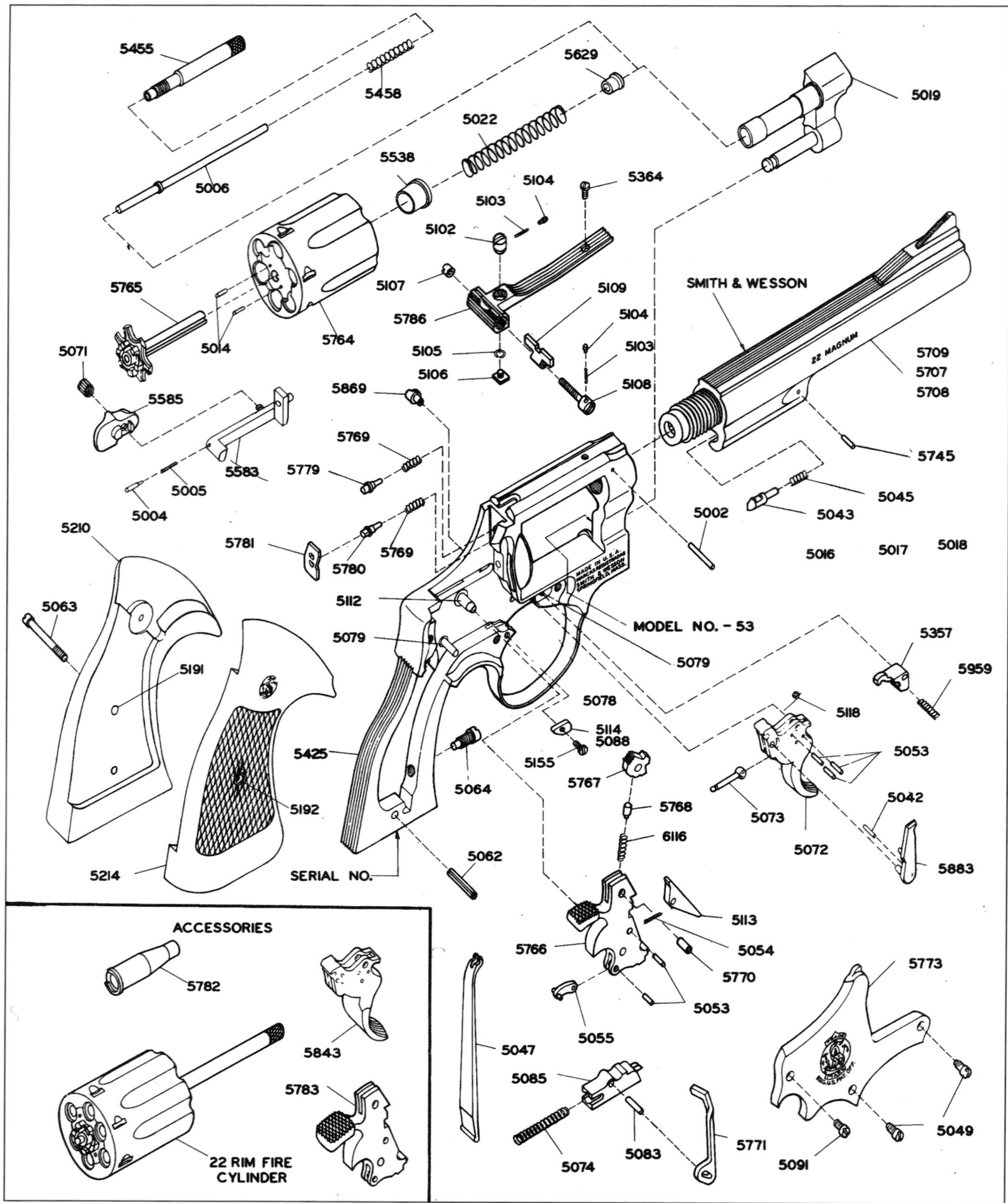


505. An exploded view of the .22 Magnum Model 53, as found in the Parts List folder included with each new Model 53 revolver. The special components needed for the double firing pin system are as follows:

In the frame: 5769 (2), firing pin spring; 5779, firing pin, upper; 5780, firing pin, lower; 5781, firing pin retainer. In the hammer: 5767, hammer nose; 5768, hammer nose plunger; 6116, hammer nose plunger spring.

Gaston Comeau collection

506. Left and right side views of the Model 53 chambered for the .256 Winchester Magnum cartridge, serial no. K438857, with $8\frac{3}{8}$" barrel. Manufactured circa 1961, this was the only example produced in this chambering.
Ray Cheely collection, photos by Paul Goodwin

*Smith & Wesson . . informs me that they will bring out the gun on the K frame as soon as Winchester gets enough ammunition to them for proper tests and development work . .*

*The new .256 Winchester cartridge will also be chambered in Colt and Ruger Single Actions, we understand . .*

Alas for Elmer, it was all not to be. As shown in fig. 506, Smith & Wesson did indeed produce a single example of the Model 53 in .256 Winchester Magnum caliber, but there the project stalled, never to be revived.

According to Geoffrey Boothroyd in his excellent book *The Handgun*, Sturm, Ruger & Co. briefly produced a single-shot Hawkeye revolver, built on the .44 Magnum Blackhawk frame, in .256 Winchester Magnum caliber. The Hawkeye remained in the catalog only from 1963 through 1967.

## Notes on the Short-Lived .256 Winchester Magnum Cartridge

In the 2nd Edition of his excellent reference *Ammo Encyclopedia*, author Michael Bussard summed up the .256 Winchester Magnum cartridge as follows:

> *American sportsmen have had a long-running love affair with .22 caliber centerfire varmint calibers ever since the .22 Hornet was developed. However, there was no room in American shooters' hearts for a .257 caliber varmint cartridge, and the .256 Win. Mag. quietly disappeared.*

507 (right). An example of the .256 Winchester Magnum cartridge, shown on top of a box of 50 rounds made by the Western Cartridge Co.

Like the .22 Jet, this rimmed cartridge was derived from the .357 Magnum case. It was introduced in 1960, but did not find favor and was soon discontinued.

Dave Terbrueggen collection

# Stainless Steel K-Frames (1970)

John Henwood describes the history, and some of the pitfalls, of stainless steel as a material from which to make revolvers, as follows:

> *. . For years the nickel-plated carbon steel revolver was a police favorite in those areas having a hot and humid climate. In such environments the blue steel revolver is prone to rust [and] the nickel-plated gun, while not immune to rust, corroded somewhat more slowly. The advent of the stainless steel firearm has reduced this problem even further, although not alleviating it completely.*
>
> *. . Until 1970 all . . "K" frame revolvers were of carbon steel or aluminum-with-steel-parts construction. The advantages of a corrosion-resistant gun had been obvious for many years, but there were problems to be solved. Most of the suitable stainless steels are difficult to machine, and are very difficult to heat treat; nevertheless the firm continued development work on a stainless steel M&P, finally putting it into production in 1970. Stainless steel models have the number "6" as the first digit of their model number. Several finishes are used, ranging from "mirror polished" through "highly polished" to "satin" and finally "matte", depending on model. All stainless steel guns receive some sort of passivation treatment to retard the formation of surface oxidation, which leads to dulling of the polished surfaces.*
>
> *The larger stainless steel parts are each stamped with a small letter "s", to identify the material. (This holds true for all S&W stainless steel models.)*
>
> *. . The stainless material originally used proved unsuitable for high-stress applications (hammer, trigger, coil springs) and was eventually replaced . . by matte chrome plated carbon steel (springs are not plated). Plated parts used in stainless guns are not marked; neither are the screws, the very smallest parts, nor those stainless steel parts without flat surfaces, such as the extractor rod . .*
>
> *. . Early stainless steel guns had stainless rear sights [fig. 523]. These proved to reflect too much glare, and were dropped in favor of the blued sight around 1973.*

# The Model 64 (Stainless Model 10)

508. Right side view of an early Model 64 (no dash) with 4" pinned, tapered barrel.

When this model appeared in September, 1970, the gun-oriented press started to perk up after decades of ignoring the plain steel M&P/Model 10.

The tradition of ignoring the Plain-Jane M&P in the gun-oriented press remained alive and well, except that when stainless steel models became available, the stainless version of the Model10, now labeled the Model 64, did at least get some reviews, as it meant that "the ideal police revolver" had been made even better in the eyes of many.

John Henwood's account of the Model 64 is excerpted as follows:

*In September, 1970, at about serial number D224000, the firm introduced a stainless steel Model 10, the Model 64. Initially available only as a .38 S&W Special square-butt gun having a standard-weight 4-inch barrel . . , within a few years it was offered with a four-inch heavy barrel as well [and] by 1978 the light-barreled version had vanished. Also available at about the same time were round-butt guns with either 2-inch standard barrels . . or three-inch heavy barrels . . A few early guns with 4-inch heavy barrels were chambered for the .357 Magnum . .*

*When introduced the Model 64 incorporated all the "dash" alterations adopted up until that time; changes therefore started with "-1". The 64-1 was the designation for the heavy barrel model, introduced in 1972. The 64-2 introduced the two-inch standard barrel Model 64, and the change in location of the gas ring from the yoke to the cylinder. The 64-3 was the heavy barrel version of the 64-2; both were introduced in 1977. In 1982 the barrel pin was deleted. In 1988 the Model 64-4 (2-inch barrel) and 64-5 (3- and 4-inch heavy barrels) were introduced; changes included a new yoke retention system [and other improvements, described in the section on the Models 10-9 and 10-10].*

# NYPD-1: the Last Duty Revolver of the New York City Police Dept.

509. Side views of two 4" heavy-barrel stainless Model 64 revolvers, both in the double-action-only (DAO) NYPD-1 configuration.

Above: with combat grips made by Fuzzy Farrant to author's design.

Below: with combat grips made by Don Collins to author's specifications. This is an excellent police revolver which has fired at least 40,000 rounds with no problems.

When the New York City Police Department went to their last official duty revolvers in the 1980s, they authorized the stainless Model 64 in 4-, 3-, and 2-inch barrel lengths, converted to fire double-action only and with the hammer spurs removed.

While they did not use the 158-gr. hollow-point loads, they did use a very similarly-shaped bullet, less the hollow point, with surprisingly good results, it appears. As long as your revolver was zeroed for your carry loads and your hold, it was pretty hard to beat one of these round butt revolvers in either the 3- or 4-inch lengths, although the 2-inch has always seemed rather silly to me if holster carry was anticipated.

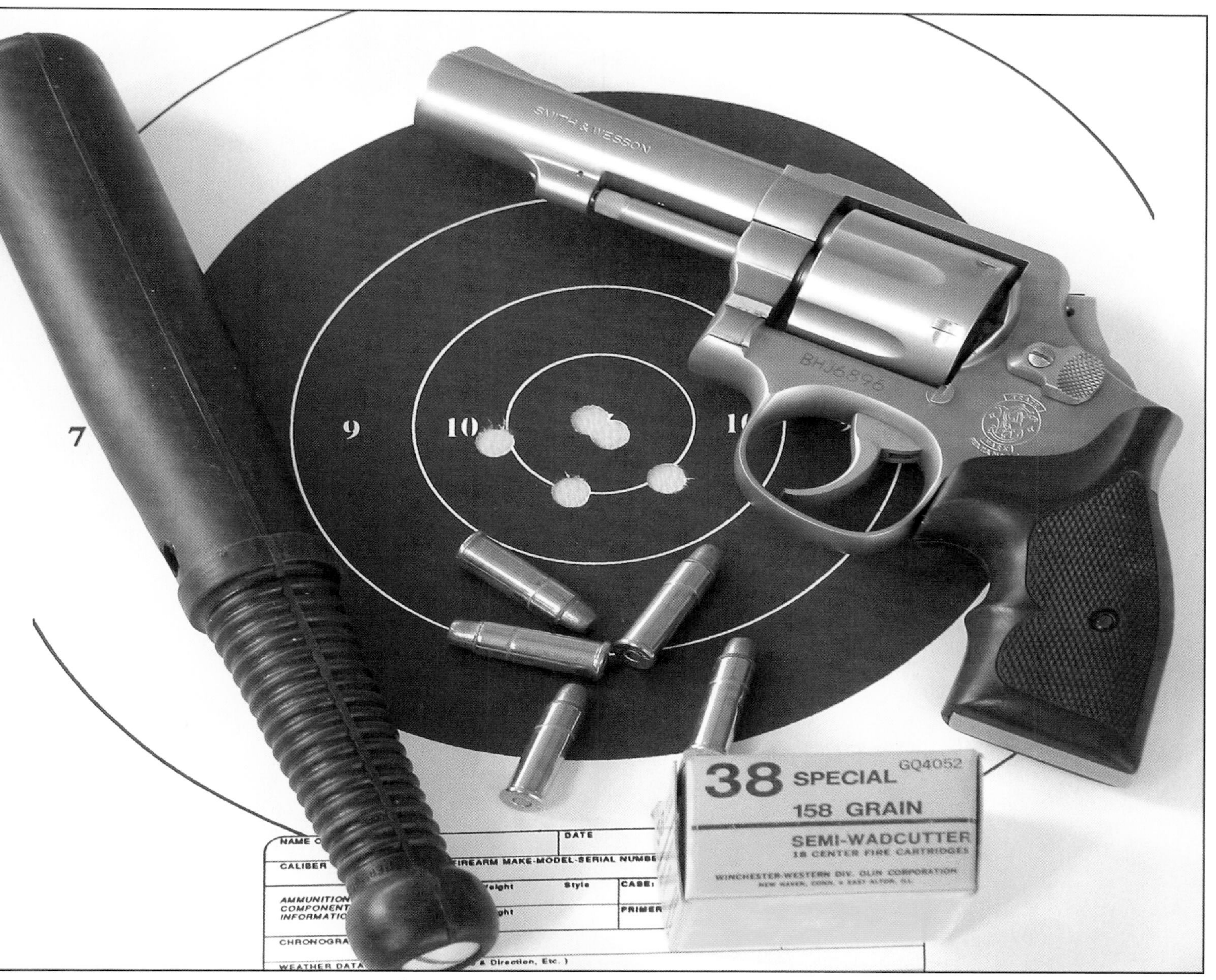


510. The New York City Police Department's last official revolver was a special DAO variation of the Model 64.

Here a square-butt example with a 4" heavy barrel poses alongside the "daylight" issue club and some special NYPD 158-gr. SWC (not hollow point) loads, which proved much more effective than earlier round-nosed loads.

As of 2012 a few revolvers were still authorized for police use in the "Big Apple", but as discussed in Chapter Forty, by then most had been replaced with high-capacity S&W polymer-framed 9mm autos.

511. Left side views of two round-butt stainless steel Model 64 revolvers with 2" barrels.
Above: the standard version, double- and single-action.
Below: NYPD-1 DAO version. Note the serial number, "BBY8730", stamped into the frame below the cylinder. The NYPD insisted that supervisors could see the serial number even when the butt was covered by rubber grips.

# The Model 65-1 (Stainless Model 13-1)

## The Model 64-1: Prototype of the Model 65

Portions of a Smith & Wesson factory letter which explain the genesis of the Model 65 are as follows:

*. . the revolver in question is one of the prototypes of the original Model 65.*

*The Model 65 was originally designed for various law enforcement agencies and was manufactured on the same frame as our Model 64 heavy barrel, which is called the 64-1. Because of the popularity of this particular model, with law enforcement agencies, the demand increased to such a point that it could no longer be just a special model manufactured for specific law enforcement agencies. Therefore, we decided to add it as a*

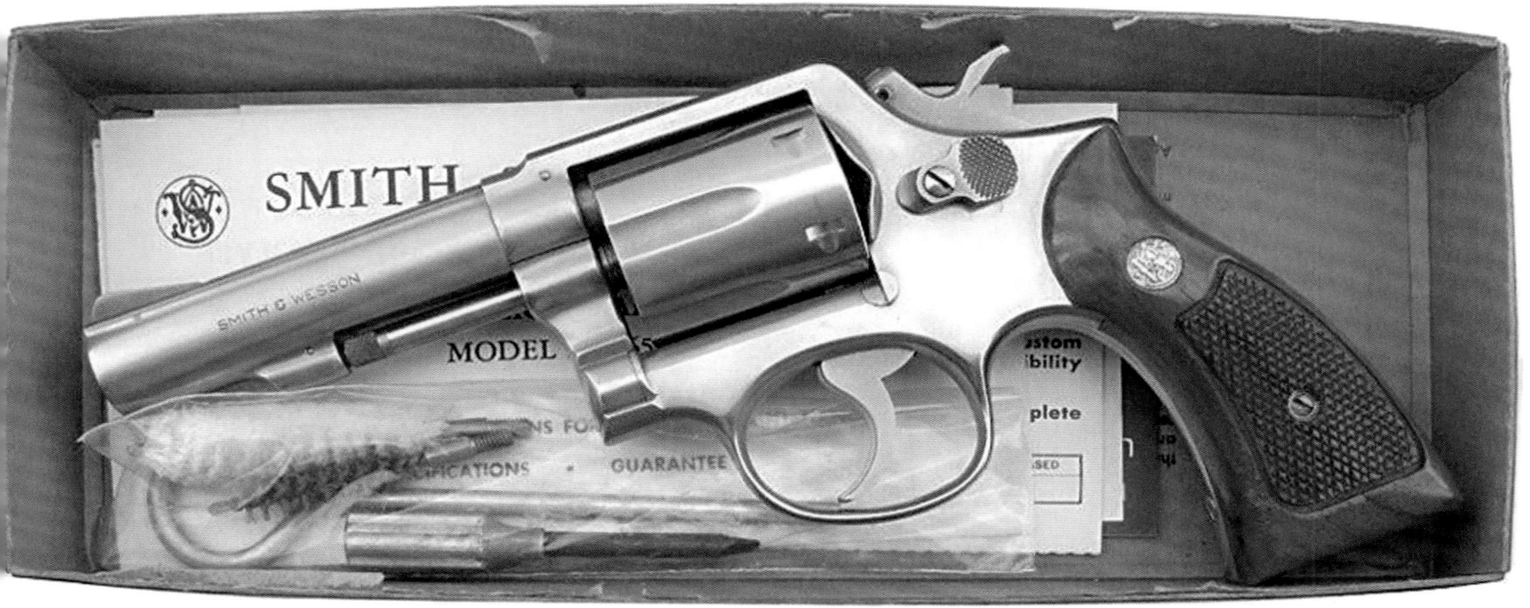


512. A Model 64-1, serial no. D759026, with 4" pinned heavy barrel, shown nestled in its blue Bangor Punta box complete with all the factory accessories.

As noted in the factory letter, below, the Model 64-1 was in fact the prototype of the Model 65, with approximately 1,200 made. Gaston Comeau collection

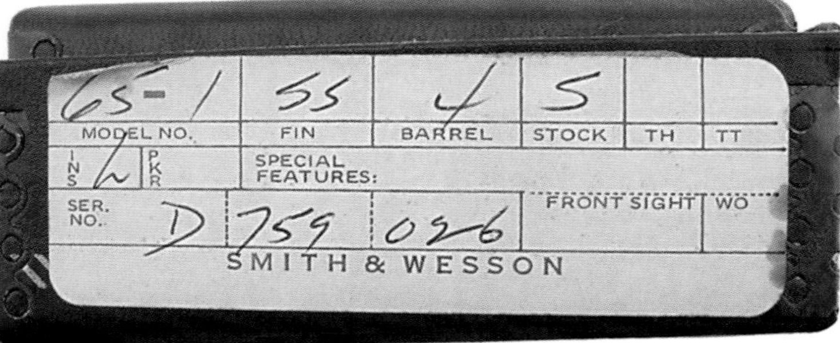


513. The box label for the above Model 64-1, described as a Model 65-1. Gaston Comeau collection

*separate model to our production line. It was at this time that we assigned the Model 65 designation.*

*However, we did have many guns in production which had already been designated to be completed as .357 fixed sighted Military & Police revolvers. These guns were completed and do carry the Model 64-1 barrel stamping. In reality they are the original Model 65. Production on this particular variation of the Model 65 is limited to about 1,200 units.*

515 (left). Above: closeup of the "MOD. 64-1" marking on the frame inside the crane area.

Below: closeup of the serial number on the butt.

Gaston Comeau collection

514. Rear view of the cylinder of the above Model 64-1, showing the counterbored areas around each chamber for enclosing the cartridge rims. Gaston Comeau collection

516. Right side view of a Model 65-2 with factory-supplied rubber grips and a 3" barrel inside a late cast shroud.
This is the stainless steel version of the "Sasia" model, discussed in Chapter Thirty-Five, which was in fact the inspiration for the last duty revolver of the FBI, the Model 13-1 (fig. 481).

The Model 65-1 was the stainless steel version of the fixed-sight Model 13-1, in .357 Magnum caliber. John Henwood's description reads as follows:

*Here is another stainless steel version of an earlier model. Introduced in 1972, the Model 65-1 . . is identical to the Model 13-1, except for the material. (In the same manner as the companion Model 13-1, there is no "Model 65"; it was introduced as the Model 65-1.) [As noted above], Prior to the introduction of the Model 65, some Model 64s were produced in .357 Magnum caliber, probably all on special order.*

*Like the Model 13-1, the Model 65-1 uses a cylinder which is 1/10-inch longer than that of the Model 10; like the Model 64, the 65-1 incorporated the latest K-frame improvements when it was introduced. Subsequent changes include the Model 65-2 (1977), which has the relocated gas ring, and the 65-3 (1982) which introduced the cylinder without cartridge rim counterbores.*

*In 1988 the Model 65-4 (4-inch barrel, square butt) and 65-5 (3-inch barrel, round butt) were introduced. Changes [reflected those of the Model 64-2 and 64-5, described above].*

## The Model 65LS (Stainless .357 Magnum, Lady Smith)

John Henwood continues as follows:

*Beginning in 1992 a variant of the Model 65 was offered, the Model 65LS. Back in 1989 the firm, in an attempt to broaden their potential market, offered a series of "J" frame (Chiefs Special) revolvers with features aimed at the feminine purchaser. They have sold well, but some buyers wanted "more gun". Smith & Wesson's response was to*

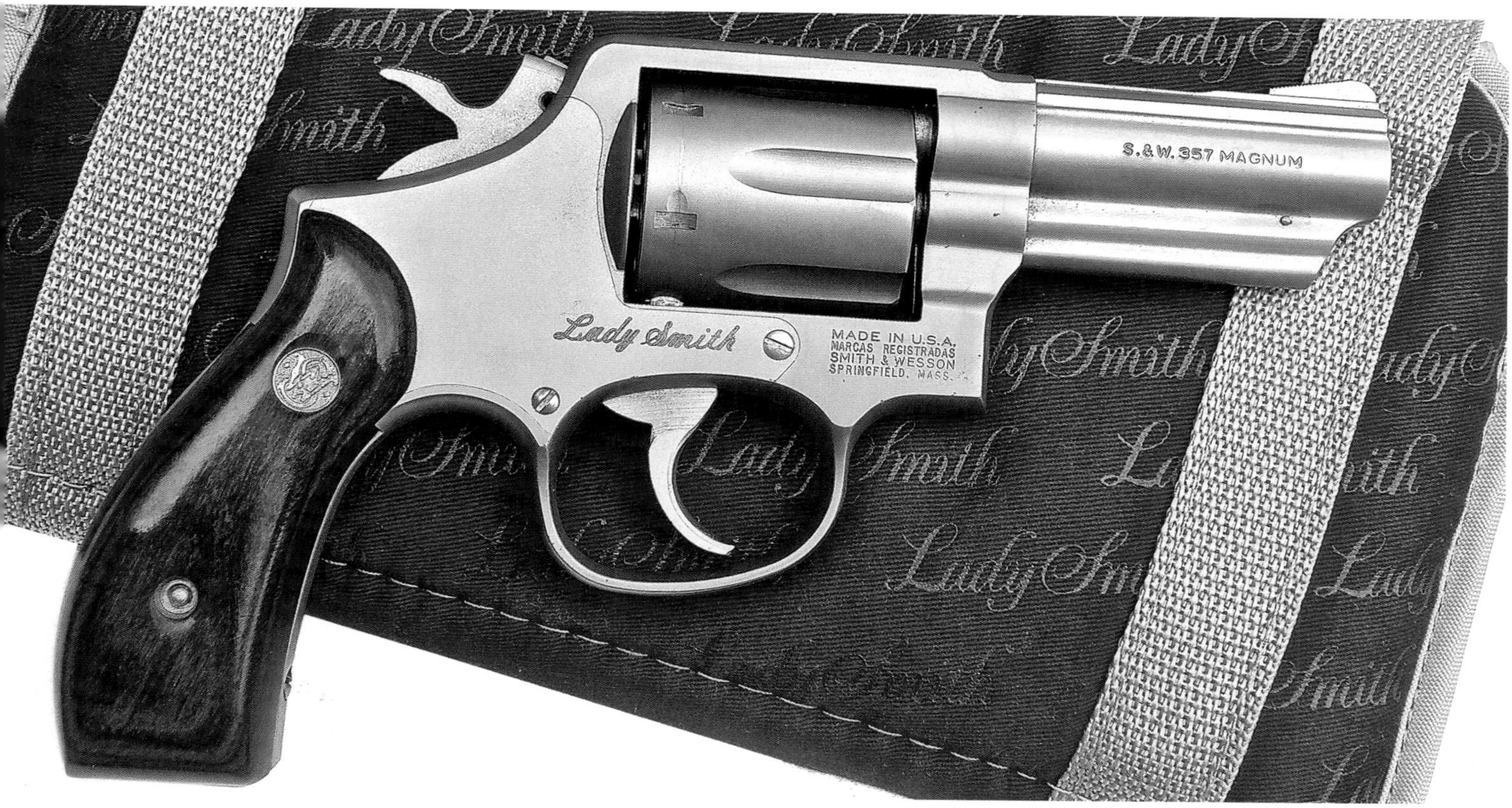

517. Right side view of a Model 65LS (Lady Smith), introduced in 1992, shown resting on its special soft case.

*introduce the Model 65LS, the initials standing for "Lady Smith" . .*

*Otherwise similar to the Model 65-5, the 65LS features a three-inch heavy barrel, a shrouded extractor rod (a feature not found on the standard Model 65); a non-glare "frosted" stainless steel finish; more rounded contours, particularly in the grip area; and thinner, uncheckered round-butt Magna stocks, made of laminated rosewood. The sideplate is rollmarked "Lady Smith" above the trigger. Caliber is .357 Magnum . .*

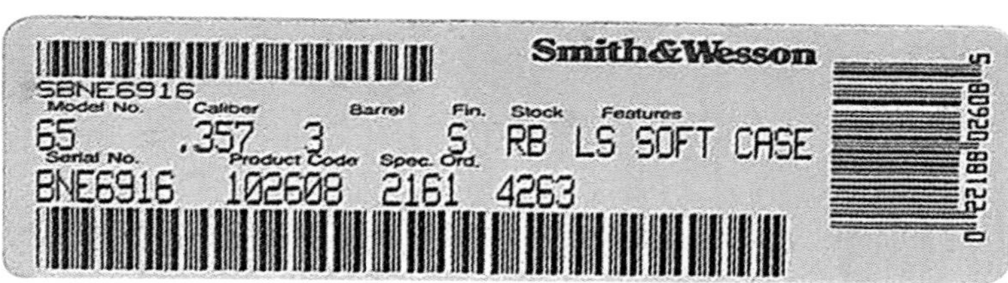


518. The case label describing the above Model 65LS (Lady Smith) revolver, serial no. BNE6916.

# The Model 66 (Stainless .357 Combat Magnum)

John Henwood provides the following description of the Model 66:

*This is the stainless steel version of the popular Model 19 Combat Magnum . . Introduced in 1971, it is available only in .357 Magnum caliber, as a round-butt gun with a 2½-inch barrel and a shortened extractor rod, a round-butt gun with a 3-inch barrel (not catalogued), or a square-butt gun . . with 4- or 6-inch barrels. A favorite with lawmen since its introduction, it remains available today . . Since 1995 all are equipped with Uncle Mike's "Combat Grip" stocks and round butt frames. The Model 66 is a favorite with those who issue commemorative revolvers; it has been used in at least nineteen issues.*

# The U.S. Border Patrol 50th Anniversary Commemorative Model 66

519. Left and right side views of the U.S. Border Patrol 50th Anniversary Commemorative Model 66, serial no. 7K5174G, one of 3,138 of this model manufactured in 1974.

In addition to the special markings on the barrel and the "USBP-0417" number on the frame, features include a recessed cylinder and pinned 4" barrel, red ramp front sight, white outline rear sight blade, and smooth Goncalo Alvez target stocks. Dave Terbrueggen collection

# "Dash" Changes to the Model 66

520. Left and right side views of an ex-factory collection Model 66, a DAO variation with blue/black finish applied at the factory.

John Henwood continues:

> *Changes include the Model 66-1, which involved the relocation of the gas ring from the yoke to the cylinder itself in 1977, and the 66-2 in 1982, which had a new cylinder without cartridge rim counterbores. In 1986 the 66-3 appeared [with changes mirroring those of the Model 10-9 and 10-10]. The latest model, the 66-4 appeared in 1994; changes include alterations to the rear sight assembly and extractor, plus the drilling and tapping of the frame [under the rear sight leaf] for scope mounts.*

521. Left and right side views of two Model 66 revolvers with 2½" barrels and round butts.

Above: pre-1982 manufacture with pinned barrel and recessed cylinder. This was the premier federal law enforcement weapon of the 1970s.

Below: post-1982 manufacture with non-pinned barrel and later cylinder with exposed cartridge heads.

522. Right side view of a Model 66 with 3" barrel and Tyler 'T' grip adapter.

The 3" barrel allows for the full ejector rod stroke to remove fired cases and is thus superior to the 2½" barrel, yet adds little extra overall length.

# The Model 67 (Stainless .38 Combat Masterpiece)

John Henwood continues with the description of the Model 67, as follows:

> *This is the stainless steel version of the Model 15 "Combat Masterpiece" . . Identical to the Model 15, except for material, it is made only with square butt and 4-inch barrel, chambered for the .38 S&W Special cartridge; flat-bottomed Magna stocks were standard, until 1995. Early (pre-1974) guns had stainless steel rear sight assemblies; later guns use the regular blued sight; all use a Baughman-style "red insert" ramp front sight. The Model 67-1 designation signified that the gas ring has been relocated . . The Model 67-2 (1988) has a new yoke retention system [and other modifications listed above under the Model 10-9 and 10-10]. The latest model, the 67-3 appeared in 1995 [with changes mirroring those of the Model 66-4, above]. An uncatalogued version, the 67-4 exists; it features a 3-inch barrel.*

523. Left and right side views of a consecutive pair of Model 67s, serial nos. 3K58737/8 with 4" barrels.

These revolvers are from the first year of issue: note the stainess steel sights, which gave way to blued sight assemblies after 1974. Dave Terbrueggen collection

524. Left side view of a Model 67 with two-piece 4" barrel and shroud, manufactured after the Saf-T-Lock was introduced in 2002. Note the blued sights.

This example was converted to DAO at the factory in a special order for the author.

# The Model 68 (Stainless K-38)

A special number of .38 Special stainless Model 66s with 6-inch barrels were assigned the nomenclature Model 68. (Interestingly, however, in later years when .357 Magnum revolvers such as the Model 19 were chambered for the .38 Special round to meet legal requirements in countries like Brazil, they remained cataloged as standard Model 19s.)

The Model 68 was described by John Henwood as follows:

> *This was a special run of Model 14s, in stainless steel, fitted with the Model 66-type [heavy] barrel having an extractor rod shroud, chambered for the .38 Special, and made for the California Highway Patrol. (And later for the Los Angeles Police; at the time neither of these agencies issued .357 Magnums.) Since the frames differ between this model and the Model 67, this arm was given its own model number. (The top front corners of the frame on the Model 67 are angled to match the contours of the narrow barrel rib; the wide rib on the 6-inch target barrel used on the Model 68 is the same width as the unaltered frame top.)*
>
> *Manufactured only in 1976 and 1983-4, it is believed that all went to the CHP (and the LAPD, in 1983), although it is possible that a few "contract overrun" guns may have been sold on the commercial market. In 1984 the Model 68 was reissued in a CHP commemorative model. The later guns are probably marked Model 68-2, with unpinned barrels and three letter-four number serial numbers.*

# Three-Digit Model Numbers (1980)

Smith & Wesson's new three-digit model numbering system was introduced in 1980. The first number indicates the material used as the basis of the arm, with 4 standing for aluminum, 5 for regular (carbon) steel and 6 for stainless steel.

# The Model 547

## A 9mm Revolver for the French *Gendarmerie*

525. Left and right side views of an early Model 547, serial no. 8D44998, with 3" pinned barrel. Markings on the right side of the barrel read "9MM CTG. PAT. 4127955"
Note the elongated round-butt grips, and the shortened hammer spur. Dave Terbrueggen collection

John Henwood introduced the Model 547 as follows:

> *. . the Model 547 . . is a blued-steel revolver. A curious arm, not at all common, it was the result of a large order placed . . by the French government in 1979.*
>
> *For reasons known only to themselves, the French police authorities had decided to rearm the French* Gendarmerie *with Smith & Wesson revolvers, chambered for the 9mm Luger cartridge. Long popular in Europe, and gaining popularity in the U.S. as a cartridge for auto pistols, the 9mm is about halfway between the .38 Special and the .357 Magnum in power. It seems a strange choice for use in a revolver, as it is rimless and must seat on the case mouth. In addition, there were problems involved in extracting the empty cartridge cases, since the regular extractor will not withdraw rimless cases.*
>
> *Among the specifications which gave S&W engineers headaches was a prohibition on the use of devices such as the "half-moon" clips used with the .45 ACP cartridge . . and the Model 1917 revolver . .*
>
> *The Model 547 is quite an interesting arm, having a number of unique features.*
>
> *. . The cylinder was chambered so that the case heads were flush with the rear face; it is also*

526. Left and right side views of another early Model 547, serial no. 9D37743, with square butt and 4" pinned barrel, marked the same as the 3" barrel shown in fig. 525.
Dave Terbrueggen collection

*slightly longer than that for the Model 10. The extractor head, or "star", is much thicker than is usual, and is cast from beryllium copper, an exceedingly tough and wear-resistant material. The pivot studs for both trigger and hammer are also made of this material, which has a very low friction coefficient.*

*. . The firing pin is spring-loaded, mounted in the frame, and is held in place with a retainer plate similar to the one used in the Model 53 (.22 Jet) revolver. Above the firing pin is a "limit pin", a spring plunger which lies flush with the breech face . . Upon firing, the hammer drives this pin forward against the cartridge case head. Since the limit pin is about .024" shorter than the firing pin, this limits the depth of the firing pin penetration into the cartridge primer.*

*This is intended to compensate for variable cartridge case lengths, and to reduce the number of punctured primers caused by excessive firing pin penetration . . This limit pin assures that all primers receive the same firing pin blow, regardless of case length.*

*Cartridge cases fired in this revolver show a round indentation in the case head where they were struck by the limit pin. The force exerted on the limit pin by recoiling cartridge cases is sufficiently violent that the hammer is thrust rearward far enough for the standard-length hammer spur to jab the shooter's hand, accordingly the hammer spur was shortened. A stronger mainspring and a longer strain screw were fitted in order to give a heavier hammer blow to fire the harder primers found in much foreign 9mm ammunition . .*

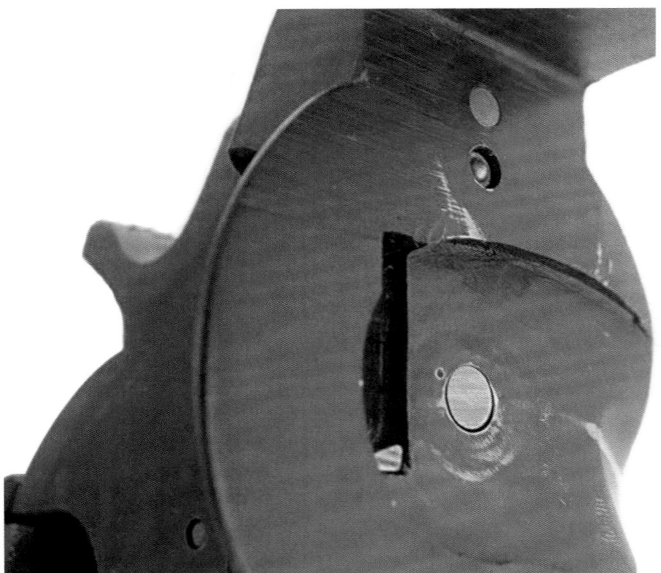

527. A closeup of the inside of the receiver of a Model 547 with the cylinder open, showing the spring-loaded limit pin above the firing pin. Gaston Comeau collection

528 (right). Another closeup inside the front of the receiver with cylinder open, showing serial number and "MOD. 547" designation. Gaston Comeau collection

*Legend has it that the Model 547 was placed in the S&W catalog only to sell off the French contract "overrun", the extra revolvers made to cover any guns which might be rejected by the French. Be that as it may, the 547 was only catalogued from 1980 through 1985, and U.S. sales were so slow that the firm declined to retain it as a regular part of their line . . The only change of any consequence during production was the elimination of the barrel pin, in 1982. For some reason this did not result in a new "dash" number . .*

According to an email from Roy Jinks in response to an enquiry from a collector, the factory manufactured a total of 10,270 Model 547s, of which 6,486 were round-

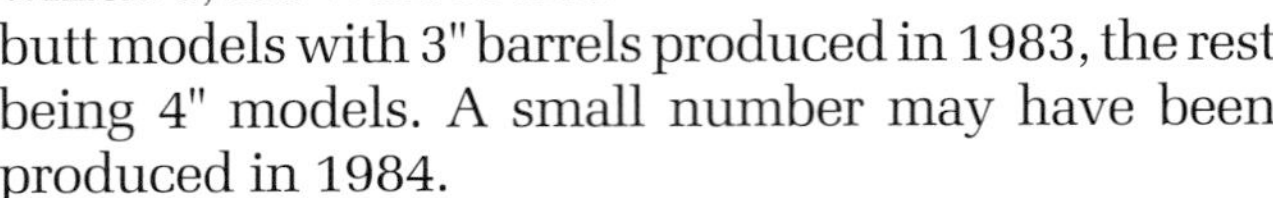

butt models with 3" barrels produced in 1983, the rest being 4" models. A small number may have been produced in 1984.

Many articles appeared in the gun-oriented press when the 9mm Model 547 revolver was introduced, but as John Henwood notes above, sales, once the first bloom was off the rose, were pretty slow. Not surprisingly, in my opinion, as no matter how clever the cylinder ejection system, one was always stuck with the question "why?", unless of course you had access to lots of free 9mm ammunition.

## S&W Describes the Rationale for the Model 547

Nevertheless, the Model 547 was given an enthusiastic writeup in the Summer, 1981 S&W *Bulletin*, and this is excerpted as follows:

### *S&W Solves the 9mm Revolver Problem*

*Smith & Wesson met the challenge of World War I by inventing a revolver that would shoot the .45 Auto cartridge used by the American military forces.*

*The company has met a new challenge by developing an entirely new revolver system that will handle the 9mm Auto, automatic pistol cartridge. This cartridge is extensively popular in Europe and is used in many automatic pistols in the United States.*

*But the task of designing a revolver for the 9mm is doubly difficult.*

*A revolver cartridge is headspaced on the rim. An automatic pistol cartridge is "rimless" so it can feed through a magazine. In 1917, S&W designers developed a half-moon clip, holding three cartridges, to provide the gripping surface for the extractor. In 1978, S&W developed a totally new kind of extractor system.*

*Revolver cartridges are generally straight-sided. The 9mm Auto cartridge is tapered—it is designed to move rearward on firing to function the action of a pistol. In a revolver, this "set back" could cause the firing pin to rupture the primer.*

*Earlier attempts to design a revolver extractor system for the tapered 9mm cartridge weren't successful. The short 9mm cartridge case can slip off and fall back into the charge hole. The extractor jams up on top of it and cannot seat fully closed. Or, the extractor hampered loading the cylinder with the extractor down.*

## EXTRACTOR ASSEMBLY INSTRUCTIONS

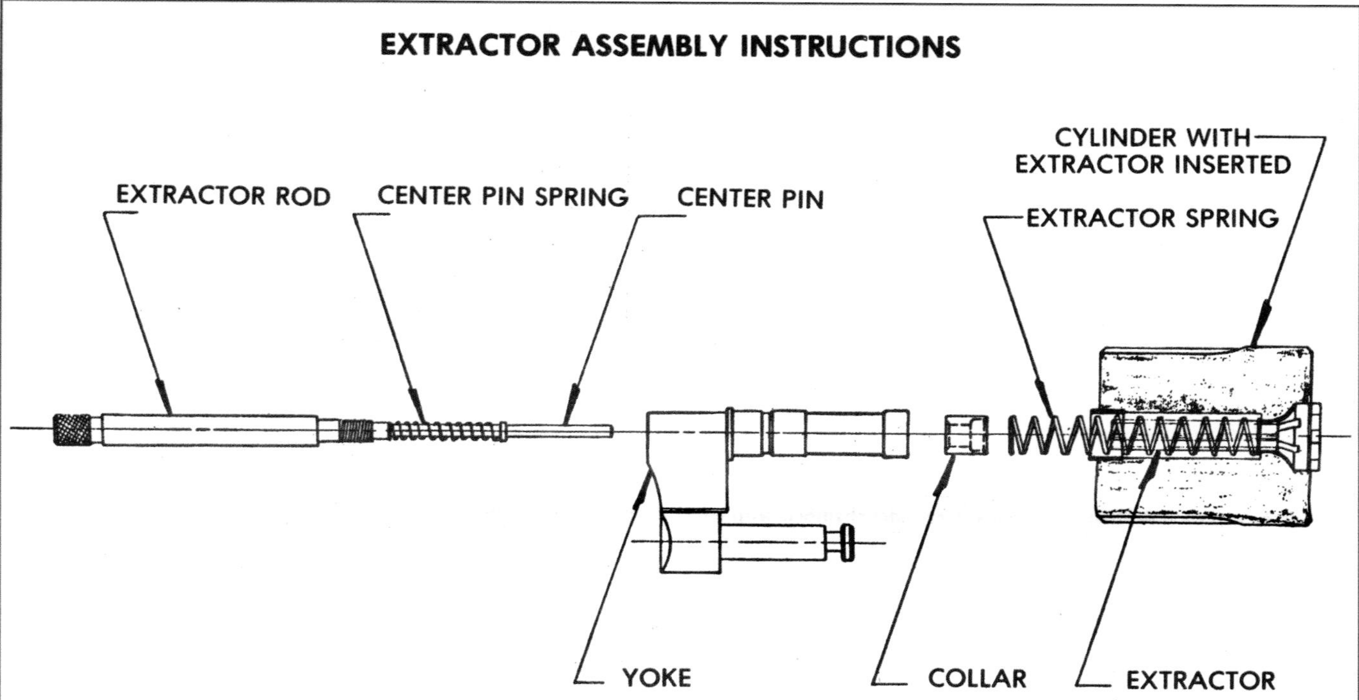


1. Insert extractor into the cylinder and line up VEE groves in stem with teeth in cylinder. Align dimple on extractor head outside diameter with notch in cylinder counterbore. Extractor will not seat to proper depth otherwise.
2. Insert collar into yoke arm hole followed by extractor spring. Then insert yoke with spring into cylinder with extractor.
3. While holding the yoke firmly against cylinder to keep the extractor spring compressed insert and tighten extractor rod with center pin and center pin spring pre-assembled as illustrated. *Note:* the rod has left handed thread and must be turned counter clockwise.
4. Once the rod is tight, back off clockwise one or two turns. Push rod forward to expose extractor head and stem.

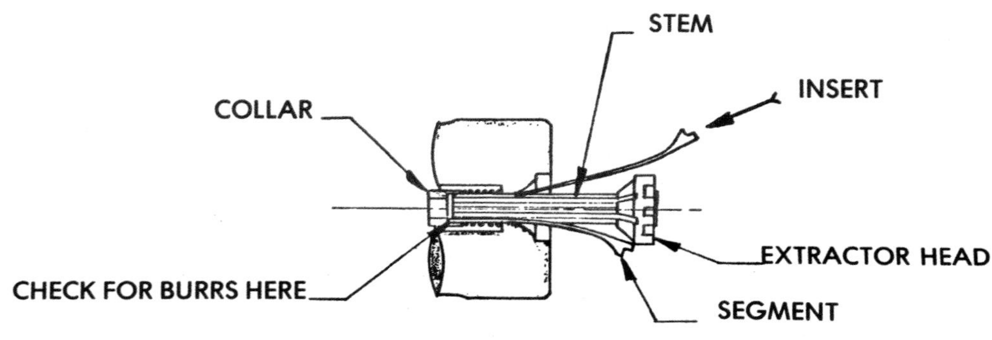


5. Insert segments into cylinder as shown. Head of segment should enter slot of extractor. Compress segment into slot to check for free activation. If segment will not compress into slot fully, back-off rod one more turn. (See #4). If segment does not insert disassemble and check for burrs on stem and or segments.
6. Once all segments are in release extractor rod to allow head to enter cylinder. Tighten rod firmly by turning counter clockwise with the rod clamped in a vise and turning the outside of the cylinder by hand.
7. Visually check activation of segments, keeping the yoke in the cylinder at all times so as not to bind the extractor mechanism.

529. The factory Extractor Assembly Instruction sheet, included in the box with each Model 547.

Two of the spring-steel segments which enter the cartridge cannelures are illustrated below.

Gaston Comeau collection

*The new Smith & Wesson Model 547, 9mm revolver solved both these problems.*

*The oval extractor is tapered with a spline groove facing each cylinder charge hole. There are retractable leaf extractors for each cartridge in the cylinder.*

*With the extractor fully seated, these leaf "springs" are cammed out of the way. You can load as easily as any other revolver. As you push the extractor rod, the leaves "pop out" to engage the rim of the cartridge case. Simple yet ingenious, a U.S. patent has been issued on the design. If a case slips off, just release the extractor. It returns home, retracted, and will pick up the case as you push the extractor rod again.*

*While these extractor leaves appear frail, in the assembly of extractor spring, head, collar, stem, yoke, barrel and cylinder, they are strong enough to rip right through the rim of a cartridge case.*

*The problem of "set back" is solved by using two pins under the hammer.*

*The normal firing pin floats under a flat-faced hammer. It is spring-loaded. Above the firing pin is a "limit pin" which rests against the base of the cartridge. This pin holds the cartridge in battery as it is fired.*

*The inertia of the hammer is overcome only after the peak of pressure is past. Then, as the case begins to move back, it pushes on the limit pin, raising the hammer and allowing the firing pin to retract at the same time.*

*This system of maintaining firing pin depth of indent into the primer is unique. A U.S. patent has been issued on this design.*

*There are advantages in having a revolver chambered for the popular 9mm Auto cartridge.*

*Because of the length of the cylinder, the bullet actually travels farther to get out of a four-inch barrel revolver than it does in a four-inch barrel automatic. Result, higher velocity.*

*Because the 9mm cartridge uses a fast burning powder, the pressure peak comes while the bullet is still in the cylinder. Thus, the gain achieved inside the cylinder is greater than the loss of pressure as the bullet jumps the cylinder gap.*

*This amounts to an increase in velocity of about 10 per cent and a gain in energy of some 20 per cent.*

*Ballistically, this S&W Model 547, 9mm revolver provides about 70 to 75 per cent of the energy you would get from a.357 Magnum, 125-grain JHP bullet. For comparison, a .38 Special +P bullet has only some 50 per cent of Magnum energy . .*

## A Better Mousetrap - from WWII?

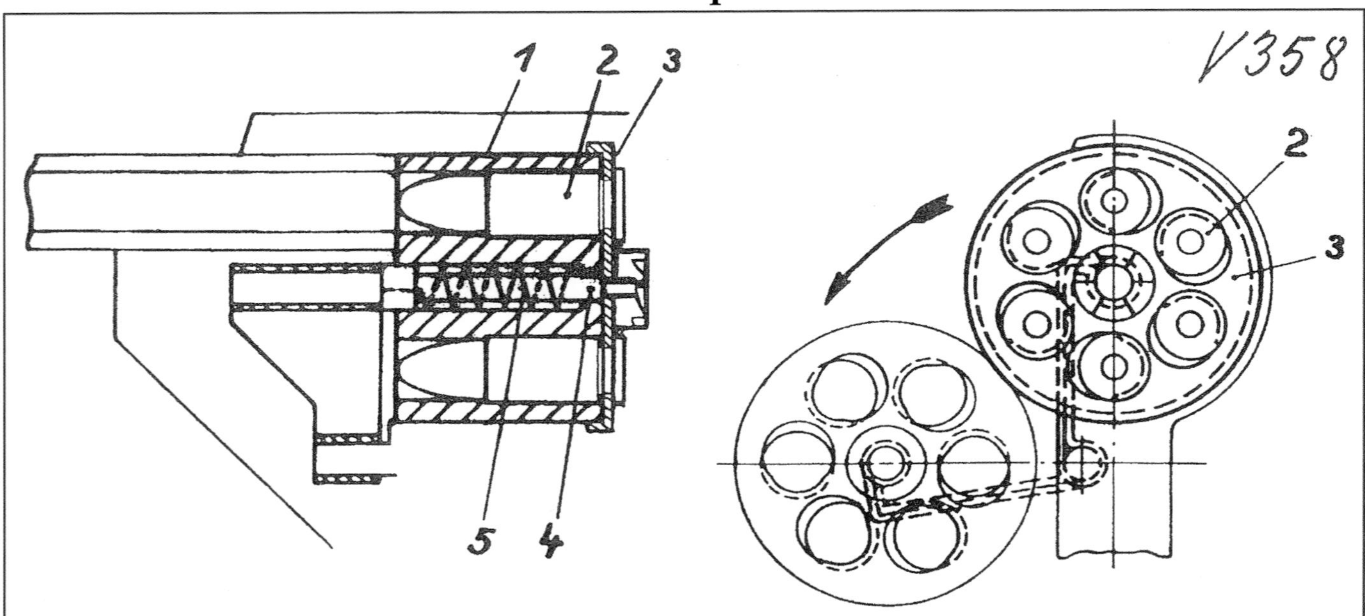


530. Late-WWII drawings from *Waffenfabrik* Mauser labeled V (*Versuch*; experimental) 358, of a swing-out cylinder for a proposed *Trommelrevolver,* incorporating an ingenious extractor for rimless 9mm cartridges.

A flat backplate with ovoid openings (3) is positioned on a spring-loaded central rod (4) over the rear of the cylinder (1). After the cartridges, positioned on the shoulder located in each chamber, are fired, the cylinder is swung out and the knurled edge of the backplate is turned slightly, locking it into each cannelure, then pulled to the rear to extract the spent cases. editor's collection, courtesy the late Walter Schmid

In the Summer, 1981 S&W *Bulletin* article it states that "Earlier attempts to design a revolver extractor system for the tapered 9mm cartridge weren't successful." However just such a device was made up experimentally at the Mauser *Waffenfabrik* during the latter part of WWII. Since no actual specimens of a revolver incorporating this device are known to have survived the war, this ingenious solution is not at all well known, and it is illustrated in fig. 530 as a matter of general interest.

## Excerpts from the Model 547 Cylinder Extractor Patent

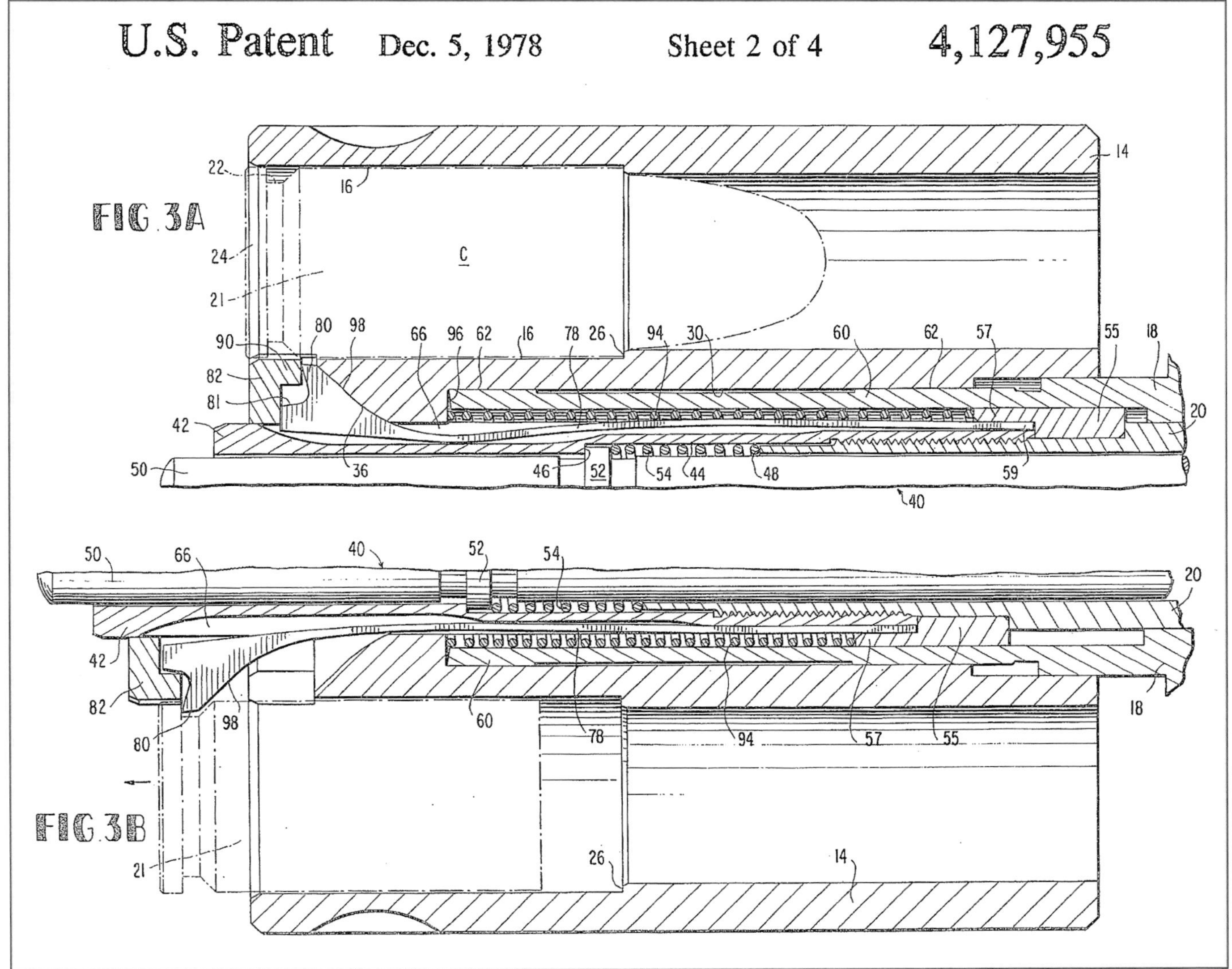


531. Two figures from sheet 2 of 4 sheets of drawings from U.S. patent no. 4,127,955 dated December 5, 1978, titled "Extractor Assembly for Rimless Cartridges".

Above: fig. 3A, showing the spring-steel extractor segment (98) fully seated within the revolver cylinder.

Below: fig. 3B, showing the segment moving rearwardly, with its tip (80) snapped into the cannelure of the chambered cartridge. U.S. Patent Office

As mentioned above, a patent was issued on the "simple and ingenious" extractor system used in the Model 547. U.S. patent no. 4,127,955 was granted on December 5, 1978 to Roger J. Curran of Stratford, Conn., and assigned to Bangor Punta Operations, Inc., of Greenwich, Conn.

Excerpts from the abstract read as follows:

*Disclosed is an extractor assembly including an extractor rod splined within a revolver cylinder and carrying spring leaf extractor segments in elongated grooves about its outer surface. The segments are prebent and biased in the assembly to displace extractor tips carried thereby radially outwardly. When the extractor assembly is fully seated within the revolver cylinder [patent fig. 3A], cam surfaces on the cylinder maintain the extractor tips spaced radially inwardly of the cylinder chambers. Upon axial displacement of the extractor assembly [i.e. when the extractor rod is pushed to the rear], the extractor tips, under the natural bias of the segments, move radially outwardly into the grooves of the cartridge casings [patent fig. 3B] whereby the tips displace the casings rearwardly from the cylinder chambers. Upon spring return of the extractor assembly into the cylinder, the extractor tips are cammed radially inwardly . . enabling the cylinder to be loaded.*

## Critiquing the Model 547

The frame-mounted "limit pin" of the M547 seems to work "flawlessly", as Jan Stevenson noted in his article on page 43 of the September/October, 1981 issue of his *Handgunner* magazine. I cannot say it better; but compared to a good .38 Special, it just strikes me as more expensive parts to make, install and get dirty.

In addition, the studs holding the hammer and trigger are thicker and stronger in the 547 than on the normal K-frame models, apparently to ensure compatibility with the hard military primers and high pressures of the French military-grade 9x19mm ammunition. Thus standard K-frame hammers or triggers will not interchange in a Model 547, and vice versa.

Furthermore, the stronger mainspring used in the 547 in order to give a heavier hammer blow results in a very heavy double-action trigger pull. According to Vito at the Smith & Wesson Performance Center, whose specialty is revolver action jobs, it is very hard to get a light trigger pull on this model. He has done up a few, and does not recommend it.

Back when the Model 547 was to be deleted from the catalog in 1985, it was planned to convert the remaining stock to .357 Magnum by simply recylindering them and selling them off, since the 9mm versions had not fared too well on the U.S. commercial market; although now, of course, they are desirable and expensive collectibles. This plan was scrapped, although a few 9mm Model 547s escaped; but had this plan been followed up, I feel the 547 would have made a dandy .357 Magnum.

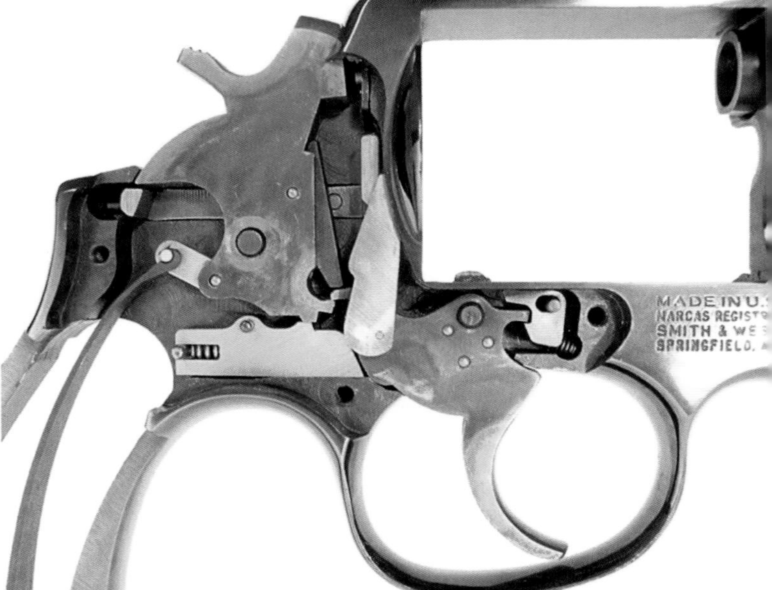

532. Right side closeup of a Model 547 with sideplate removed, showing the components of the action.

Note the flat-faced hammer, and the more robust hammer and trigger pins. Gaston Comeau collection

## Describing French-Loaded 9mm Military Ammunition

French 9x19mm ammunition was designed to work in the MAC 50 and MAS G1 (a French copy of the Beretta 92) self-loading pistols, and the MAT49 submachine gun. As with any such open-bolt-firing weapon, the cartridge must have sufficient power to blow the bolt far enough back so that, should the trigger be released, it will be caught on the sear. If it does not, and the bolt only goes back far enough to uncover a fresh cartridge, the weapon will continue to fire until the magazine is empty. This is distracting and annoying on the range, but positively dangerous and unacceptable in police service. Loading the cartridge to maximum power levels avoids this, as well as giving the submachine gun greater range and striking power, which is important for military weapons.

But with open-bolt guns where the firing pin is integral with the bolt, as it is in the MAT49, the

533 (following page). A sampling of some modern Frenc 32-round 9mm cartridge boxes *pour pistolets et pistole mitrailleurs* (for pistols and submachine guns), all wit brass cases unless specified.

Left column, from top: 1958; 1959; 1960 (steel case 1960; 1960 (with unheadstamped brass case).

Right column, from top: 1961; 1962; pilot lot 1965; 196 1969. Jean-Marc Grand collectio

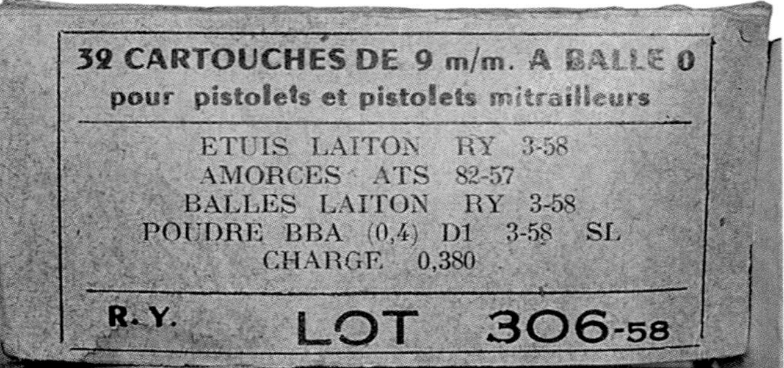


32 CARTOUCHES DE 9 m/m
pour pistolets et pistolets mitrailleurs

ETUIS : Laiton : 2 RY 61
AMORCES : Mle 1950 : 7 CF 61
BALLES : O : 2 RY 61
POUDRE : BBa (0,4) : 1 SL 61
CHARGE : 0,374 gr

LOT 721 RY 61

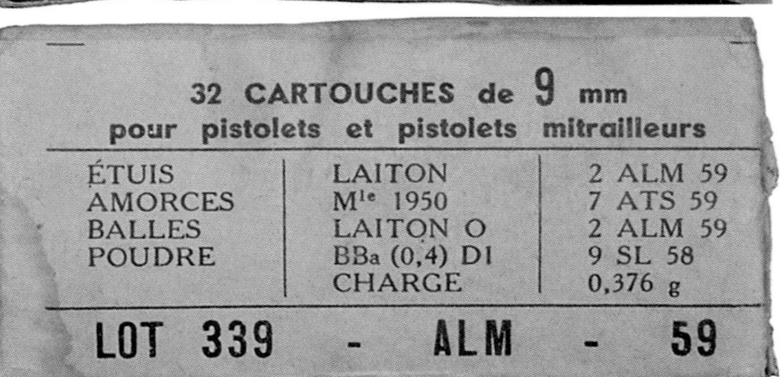


32 cartouches de 9 mm
pour pistolets et pistolets-mitrailleurs

ETUIS : Laiton : 2 - ATS-62
AMORCES : Mle 1950 : 32 - ATS-62
BALLES : O. Laiton : 2 - ATS-62
POUDRE BBa 0,4 : 7 - PB - 61
Charge : 0,377 g

LOT 240 - ATS 62

32 CARTOUCHES DE 9 mm.
POUR PISTOLETS
ET PISTOLETS-MITRAILLEURS

ETUIS Laiton : 2 ATS 65
AMORCES 4,5 Mle 1964 : 1 ATS 65
BALLES O. Laiton : 2 ATS 65
Poudre B BA 0,4 : 50 PB 64
Charge : 0,392

LOT PILOTE

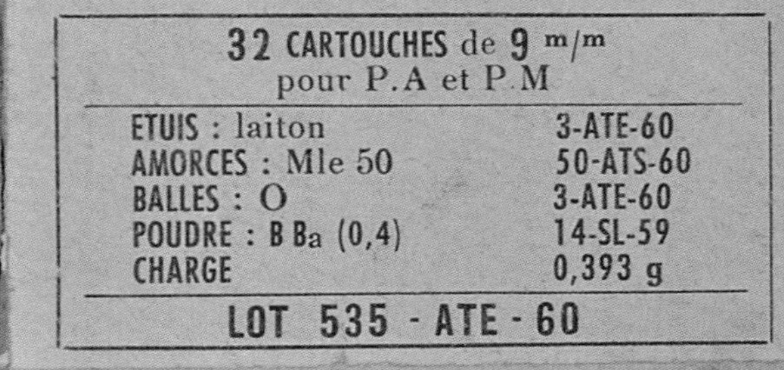


32 cartouches de 9 mm
pour pistolets et pistolets-mitrailleurs

ETUIS : Laiton : 3 - ATS-65
AMORCES : Mle 1950 : 40 - ATS-65
BALLES : O. Laiton : 3 - ATS-65
Poudre B B a 0,4 : 10 - PB - 65
Charge : 0,393 g

LOT 888 - ATS 65

32 cartouches de 9 mm
pour pistolets et pistolets-mitrailleurs

ETUIS : Laiton : sans marque
AMORCES : Mle 1950 : 36 - ATS-60
BALLES : O. Laiton : 2 - ATS-60
POUDRE BBa 0,4 : 9 - SL -59
Charge : 0,36 g

LOT 11 - ATS 60

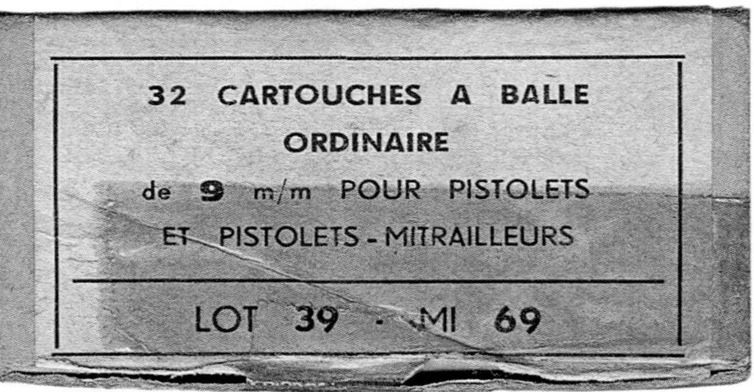

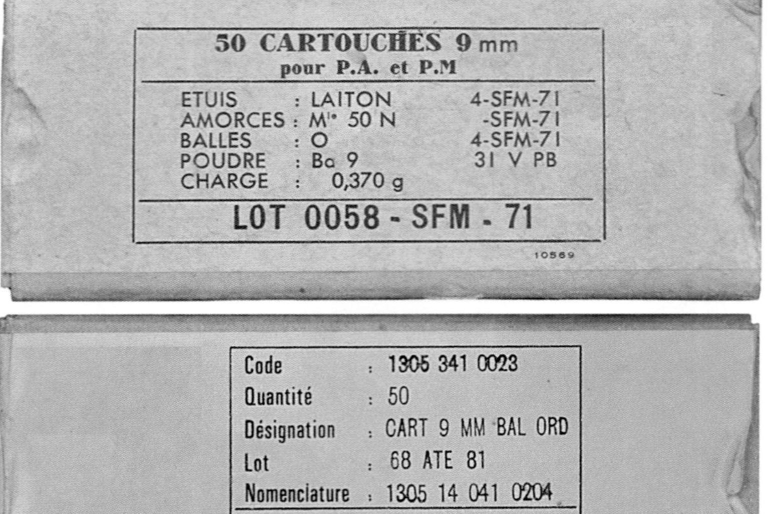

534. Four later 50-round boxes of French 9mm ammunition, from 1971, 1981, 1982 and 1988.
Jean-Marc Grand collection

535. A selection of French-made single 9mm rounds, the bullets they contain, and the steel or brass case bases with representative headstamps from 1948 through 1960.
Jean-Marc Grand collection

primer must be hard lest it fire too soon. This has engendered a typical problem today in the U.S. when commercial ammunition is used in M14s, AK47/74s, M16s and other arms which do not have a firing pin spring. The firing pin will routinely produce a small dent on the hard military primer upon chambering, but letting the bolt spring forward on a soft-primered commercial round can result in a catastrophic out-of-battery explosion.

Unfortunately, when you put these hard-primered, high-pressure cartridges in a revolver, it is difficult enough to get them to go off without risking pierced primers, and then, once fired, to keep them from backing up, tying up the cylinder and leaving hard extraction problems to be dealt with later. This is not generally a problem with .45 ACP revolvers such as the M1917 and its commercial counterparts, but the 9x19mm, especially in French and other military loadings, runs a lot higher in pressure.

# The Models 617 (Stainless K-22)

536. Right side view of a Model 617, serial no. BHP 7334, in satin finish with a special 4" barrel non-lug barrel, one of only 200 manufactured.

The two-piece light walnut stocks are fitted with silver S&W medallions. Dave Terbrueggen collection

John Henwood continues:

*This is the K-22 . . in stainless steel. Available only in .22 Long Rifle chambering, the 617 has square butt, and 4-, 6- or 8 3/8-inch barrels with full underlug, and smooth South American hardwood combat style stocks. This model was introduced in 1990, but was not catalogued for several years . . The 617-1, introduced in 1994, has the new rear sight, drilled and tapped scope mount holes, and the late-pattern extractor.*

*In common with the rest of the S&W line, in 1995 the 617 was fitted with a round-butt frame; at that time Hogue "Monogrip" black polymer stocks were fitted. Although the identical blued-steel version (Model 17) was reconfigured to a ten-shot capacity in 1996, the Model 617 retains its traditional six-shot cylinder.*

## The 10-Shot Model "617 Plus"

*Late in 1996 the firm announced a new model, the "617 Plus": the 617 outfitted with an aluminum alloy 10-shot cylinder. [The 617 Plus was] Available only with smooth combat trigger, semi-target hammer, a redesigned cylinder bolt thumbpiece, and a 6-inch barrel having a full underlug . .*

# The Model 647 (.17 HMR)

537. Left side view of a Performance Center Model 647, serial no. VAR 030X, manufactured in 2004 with 12" fluted Lothar Walther barrel in caliber .17 Hornady Rimfire Magnum (HMR). Dave Terbrueggen collection

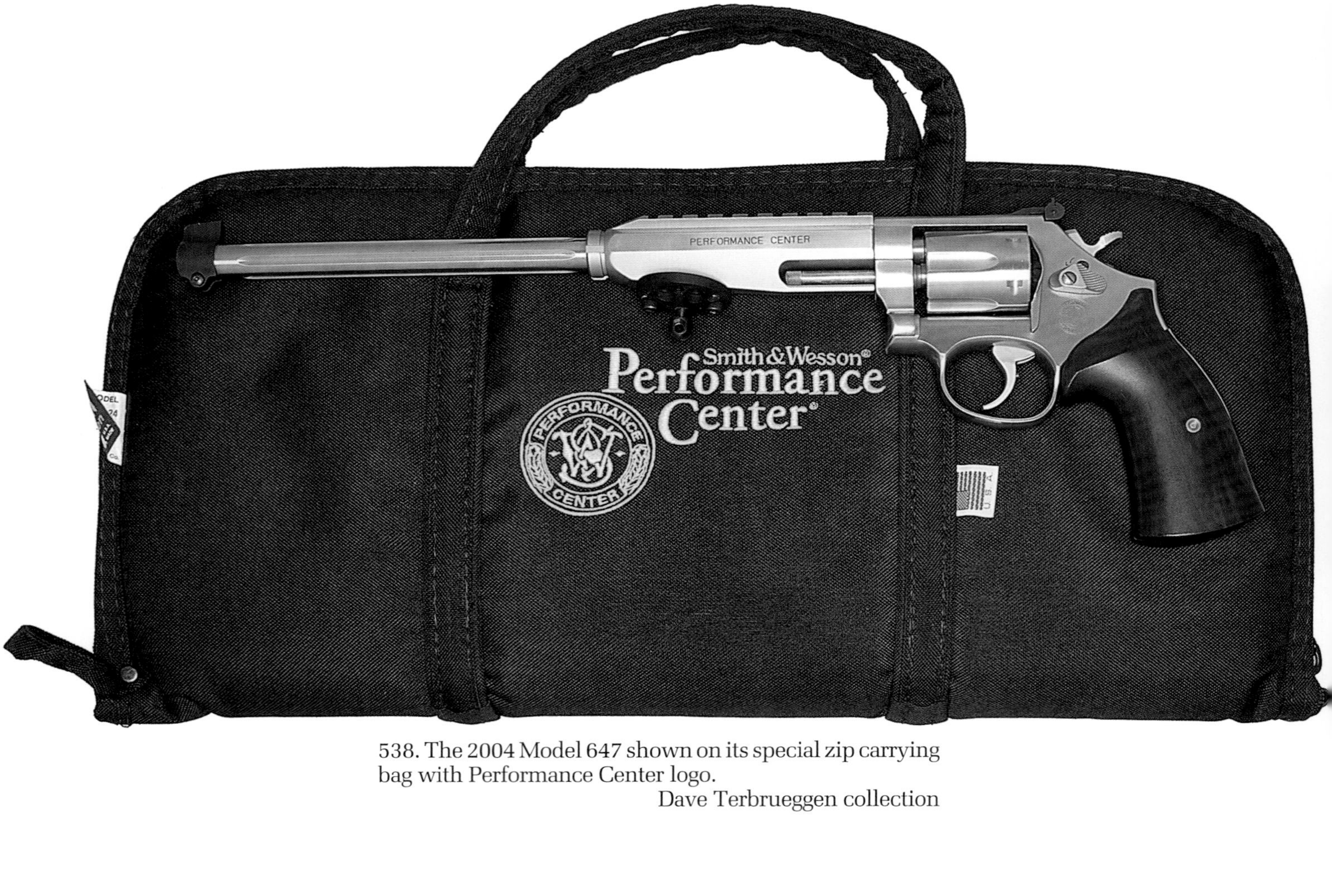

538. The 2004 Model 647 shown on its special zip carrying bag with Performance Center logo.
Dave Terbrueggen collection

539. Left side view of a later Model 647-1 in caliber .17 HMR, manufactured in 2013, serial no. CDE 6107.

The removable front sight is not shown, and the bipod mount is now built in and fitted with a rail. The factory two-piece walnut target stocks are laser-carved with S&W logos. Dave Terbrueggen collection

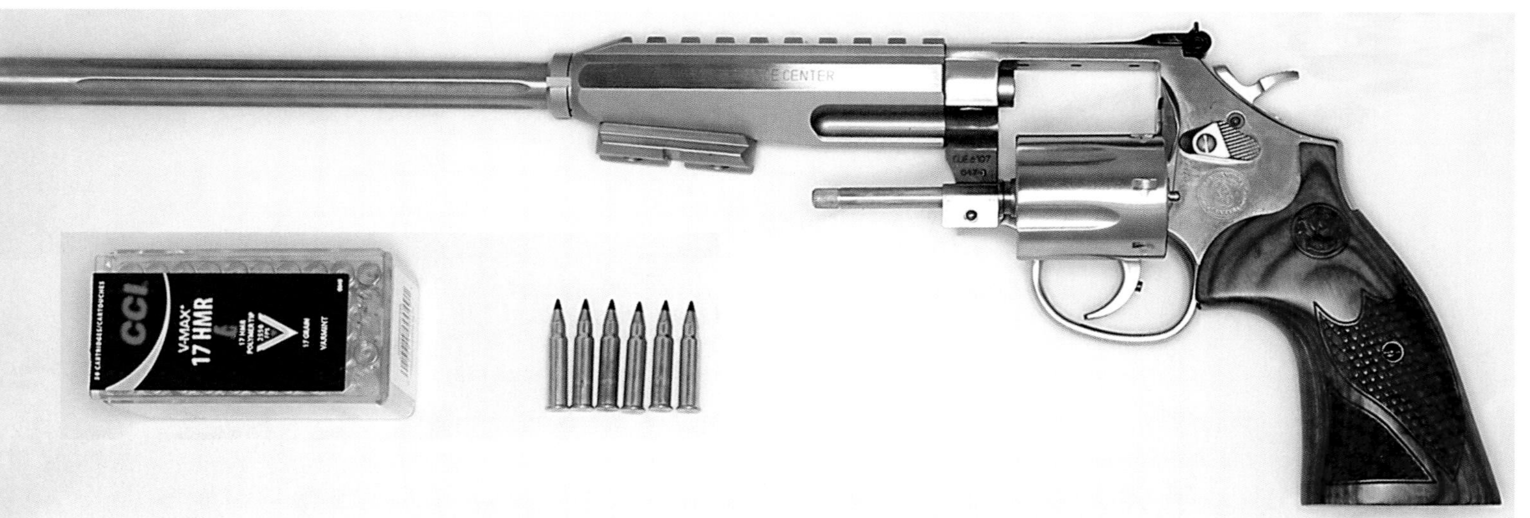


540. The Model 647 shown above, with cylinder open. Note the spring-loaded detent in the crane, which replaces the front extractor rod lock on this model.

Below is a plastic box of 50 rounds of CCI .17 HMR cartridges with polymer tips, and six loose rounds.
Dave Terbrueggen collection

This was a limited edition produced by the S&W Performance Center which, as discussed beginning on page 178, was established in 1990. The project to build a revolver chambered for the .17 Hornady Magnum Rimfire cartridge was originated in 2003, and the first guns were released in 2004.

The two examples in the Dave Terbrueggen collection, one from 2004 and the other from 2013, both have 12" fluted barrels supplied by the famous German barrel-making company Lothar Walther, and are equipped to take bipods and scopes on the integral top rail mount of the barrel sleeve.

541. The 2013 Model 547 fitted with a red- and green-dot adjustable Tachedge scope on the top rail, with a folding bipod clamped to the bottom rail.
Dave Terbrueggen collection

# The Model 648 (Stainless K-22, .22 WRM)

Introduced in 1990, the Model 648 is the stainless steel version of the Model 48 (fig. 502), chambered for the .22 Winchester Rimfire Magnum cartridge. It and the later Model 648-1, introduced in 1994, follow the same modifications noted above for the Model 617-1.

# The Model 686 CS-1

542. Left side view of a Model 686 CS-1 (previously the Distinguished Combat Magnum). The blued steel Model 585 is discussed and depicted beginning on page 175.

Built on the slightly larger L-frame, this is the weapon that replaced the K-frame in the U.S. Border Patrol. It will hold up indefinitely to full-power .357 Magnum loads, and is a dream to shoot with .38 Special ammunition, but it is quite a belt load.

Don Collins made the grips to the author's design for maximum concealment under clothing.

# "Triple Alpha - Four Numeric" Serial Numbers

John Henwood provides the following details on the serial numbering system currently in use on all models of Smith & Wesson revolvers:

> *In 1980 the present "triple alpha - four numeric" system was phased in, the process being completed (for the K-frame guns) in October of 1983. The new numbers started with AAA0001. A source at Smith & Wesson states that with this system (which is used on all models) it is not immediately possible to identify what models have which serial number blocks . .*

# John Henwood on "The K-Frame Juggling Act"

*By now it should be obvious that Smith & Wesson has spent the last 45 years juggling the "K"-frame guns. When the Model 14 was discontinued the Model 15, [t]heretofore made only with 2- or 4-inch barrels suddenly was supplied with the 6- and 8 3/8-inch barrels as well. At the time of the Model 14's re-introduction, the Model 15 instantly reverted to a single barrel length: 4 inches. The Model 67 was discontinued, then re-introduced. The Model 56 was dropped, but the Model 15 was immediately available with its 2-inch barrel. When the Model 18 was discontinued, the 4-inch barrel was added to the Model 17. And so on, and on. The more things change, the more they remain the same.*

*In addition to the regular-production models, the firm has manufactured several "limited edition" models (".357 Magnum K-Comp.", "Model PC-13", ".357 Magnum F Comp") in very small quantities on special order for some of their distributors. These have such exotic features as ported barrels, special stocks, "bobbed" hammers, or "double-action only" actions. All are basically minor alterations to existing models. The Smith & Wesson Performance Center has also issued hand-fitted and specially-accurized versions of several different models.*

# Part III: A K-Frame Retrospective

*Chapter Thirty-Three*

# Features of the K-Frame

As we entered the first decade of the 21st century, articles in the gun-oriented press noted and considered the latest versions of the century-old K-frame design, now retrofitted with such innovations as hammer/trigger locks, MIM (metal injection molded) parts, and two-piece barrels with shrouds slipped over them, the rifling being cut by the innovative electro-chemical machining process rather than a cutting tool; in all sorts of chamberings, barrel lengths, and materials. Many of these late models are discussed in Volume I.

Nevertheless, the impressions from the last article reviewed could easily echo the comments first made about the Military Model on March 9, 1899, when it was said:

> . . *The exquisite workmanship for which Smith & Wesson arms are noted is seen on the new model but it impresses one with its durability and strength, and will no doubt prove to be what it was intended for—a serviceable military revolver.*

In this chapter we offer comments on a number of the features found in and on K-frame revolvers from their inception in 1899 to today, which are shown in many of the illustrations in earlier chapters.

## Butts and Stocks

### Round Butt vs. Square Butt

When it was originally introduced in 1899, the M&P revolver was available in a round-butt configuration only. The round butt has always proven useful for those with small- to medium-sized hands, especially for double-action shooting.

However, as single-action target shooting became popular (and was used in police qualifications of the early period), the square-butt frame was introduced. Many people found this configuration easier to use when the weapon was fired in the single-action mode. As a consequence of this, the square-butt frame soon displaced the round butt in popularity until almost the end of the period during which the M&P was the standard for U. S. law enforcement use.

### Hard Rubber or Walnut Stocks

The earliest stocks available on the M&P revolver series were made of molded hard rubber or checkered Circassian walnut, the same size as the grip frame. These "service" stocks, as they were called, were narrower and did not extend up the frame like the later Magna-style grips. They were adequate if not great for use with the low felt recoil of the loads of the time, although they allowed the weapon to "jump" in the hand when fired, and this made the shooter have to reacquire his grip and sight picture before firing a second or follow-up round.

The hard rubber grips of course tended to crack when dropped or struck on hard objects. In the early days of the model, steering wheels on autos were rare (since cars themselves were rare) but during the 1920s and later, such things no doubt caused much of the damage seen so commonly today on surviving examples of this style of grip. They also tend to be slick, especially when wet with rain, sweat, or blood.

## Stocks of Other Materials

During the early period the factory offered pearl and ivory grips for the M&P series as extra-cost options, sometimes carved but generally plain in the same style as the standard "service" stocks.

The 1908 catalog included the following cautionary note regarding pearl stocks:

> *As inferior pearl stocks are sometimes fitted to Smith & Wesson revolvers after they have left the factory, it is necessary to caution the public in regard to them. These are thin, imperfect, ill-fitting, and in every way inferior to those supplied by us, and injure the appearance of the arm. In order to protect our reputation and the public, it has become necessary to use our monogram trade-mark in the usual place in the stocks . . This is inserted in gilt, and is a guarantee of quality.* .

Rarely stag grips are seen, and some may well have been factory-supplied. Interestingly enough in my experience, stag grips seem to be more uncommon on Smith & Wesson revolvers than on Colt handguns of similar style, like the Army Special/ Official Police, although exactly why this is so is unclear.

## Checkered vs. Smooth Wood Stocks

Checkered wood stocks were standard, with different patterns of checkering used over time. Originally hand-checkered, in later years this gave way to checkering done by machine.

Factory-made wooden stocks have typically been made out of either Circassian (early) or, later, American walnut, but occasionally other more exotic woods such as cherry, maple, and elm, are seen.

Smooth-finish walnut service stocks were standard during the WWII era, when the M&P revolver was supplied to the U.S. government and to British and Commonwealth forces. These plain, unchecked wood grips were designed to speed production and were a cheaper alternative to checkered wood stocks.

## Magna Stocks

In the 1930s the patented Magna stock design with its high shoulders was adapted to the M&P series with great success. The patent drawings appear in fig. 145, and the single-page descriptive S&W brochure is reproduced in fig. 156.

Such stocks made it less likely that the weapon would slip in the hand. Early examples were hand-checkered, with a plain diamond shape around the grip screw escutcheons and a fairly shallow border. Later examples deleted the diamond around the screw escutcheons, had a deeper border, and were machine-checkered.

Later, especially in the postwar years, plain, uncheckered Magna-style stocks of highly-figured exotic woods were frequently fitted to deluxe, factory-engraved guns. These are often the preferred style of stocks for the serious gun handler who needs the ability to shift the grip in the hand during presentation of the weapon from the holster, avoiding thusly the commitment to a hasty hold that checkered stocks provide.

## The Modified "P.C." (Plain Clothes) Square Butt

On the other hand, many plainclothesmen seem to prefer checkered stocks, as they keep the weapon from slipping in the hand. For these users modified square-butt Magna stocks were introduced, first on fixed-sight duty models circa 1965, with the bottom edges of the butt rounded over. These were intended to reduce wear on both clothing and the stocks when the gun is carried under a coat or jacket. These are known as "P.C." (Plain Clothes) stocks. John Henwood notes that

> . . *Sometimes the P.C. stocks are referred to as "Police Combat" stocks; this is not correct, according to the firm.*

Of course round-butt models were still offered, and while not as popular these were typically sought out by the more sophisticated users who had normal-size hands and who shot their revolvers in the double-action mode, both on the street and in routine practice sessions to keep their skill levels up.

It has always seemed odd to me why they did not just stick with round butts to please the more tactically aware (and smaller-handed), and offer larger grips for the single-action fans. I will note with some satisfaction that this was finally accomplished in 1995 when, realizing that most buyers would routinely change out factory-supplied stocks for something more to the user's preference, the factory discontinued making stocks altogether and installed aftermarket grips made of soft rubber, or occasionally wood, offering the K-frame in a round-butt-only configuration.

# Sights

## The Pros and Cons of Fixed vs. Adjustable Sights

Revolvers without sights are worthless except for close-range point-shooting. While point shooting can be surprisingly effective out to 25 - 35 yards, in my experience, once beyond that you really need to have some way to line up your weapon to get positive, consistent results.

Sights on the M&P revolver have varied over time, getting better as the years have gone by, both from the standpoint of visibility as well as sturdiness. Right from the beginning the M&P was offered as a service weapon with fixed sights, and as a target model with adjustable sights. It was clear to everyone that while the basic revolver was the same, and thus equally accurate in either configuration, obviously the target model could be zeroed more precisely. This is always an important consideration when the distances shot over may vary, the loads used might be different, plus lighting conditions as well as individual holding practices could cause a shift in the point of impact.

Fixed rear sights were originally 'U'-shaped, shallow and narrow. With good eyesight and good light, the narrow rear sight could yield good results, but as either vision or light dims, lining up the front sight in the narrow notch becomes increasingly difficult. My experience with such sights is that one is always raising the revolver up to spot the front sight in the narrow rear notch, and high shots can easily result. Widening the 'U' notch out to allow a good strip of light on either side of the front sight blade helps a lot, and deepening and squaring the notch helps even more. This is exactly what the factory did in 1925, leaving us today with a fixed rear sight with a square notch.

In comparison with the sturdy fixed sights, a target-sighted model might very well suffer damage, knocking the sights out of the zeroed position due to "groveling in the gravel" with a subject, hitting the steering wheel when exiting a car, or contacting any of the dozens of other hard objects a projecting-on-a-hip handgun will typically encounter in the career of a police officer. While I have always thought it was better to be able to properly zero your handgun for a given load and hold with adjustable sights, most times a handgun will be shot using the point system anyway, so if the sights were to be knocked out of position, it really would not make much if any difference. (Elmer Keith agreed with this position, by the way, so I am in good company).

Others have always felt that the rugged nature of fixed sights made them preferable for patrol or duty purposes. Since most police officers cannot shoot very well, I suppose it really does not matter much anyway. Fixed-sight revolvers, depending on the loads, the distances, the light, and the shooter's position/stance, will be within 12 inches of the point of aim at 25 yards, in my experience, and frequently hit quite a bit closer. Having said that, being two inches left and two inches down still bothers me, which I guess is why I always prefer adjustable-sighted models. Others who are not as concerned with perfect zeroes but who may have experienced more of the rough-and-tumble aspects of life, like the fixed sight models. Experience leads to expectation, I suppose.

Early fixed-sight M&P revolvers had the front sight forged in a "half-moon" shape as an integral part of the barrel. Naturally, being rounded at the top, such sights would not snag in holsters upon withdrawal. They were smooth in finish, however, which frequently caused light to glance off the surface, yielding a changing point of aim. Similarly, since it was a rounded surface and not flat toward the eye, getting a perfect sight picture could be difficult.

The fixed front sight was originally quite knife-like and narrow, but today it is 1/8 inch wide and serrated to break up any light hitting it. Typically ramped in shape, it will not snag on the holster yet presents a good straight face to the shooter's eye.

# Three Early Types of Adjustable Sights

543. Underside view of the original style of K-frame adjustable rear target sight, with single screw which passes through the unthreaded hole in the sight leaf from above and threads into the top of the frame.

Note the sight leaf bears the revolver serial number, that of the .32-20 target model serial no. 96878.

Gaston Comeau collection

544. Underside view of the second type of adjustable rear sight, from the prewar K-22 Outdoors-Man's revolver serial no. 638567 (fig. 326).

Note the threaded hole. As shown in fig. 545, this took a different type of elevation screw.

Gaston Comeau collection

546 (right). Rear closeup of top of frame with adjustable sight leaf removed, showing T slot dimensioned to accept the flange of the rear sight elevation adjustment screw shown in fig. 545.

Gaston Comeau collection

545. Right side closeup of the second style of adjustable rear sight leaf, showing special elevation screw with flange on bottom and slot in top. Gaston Comeau collection

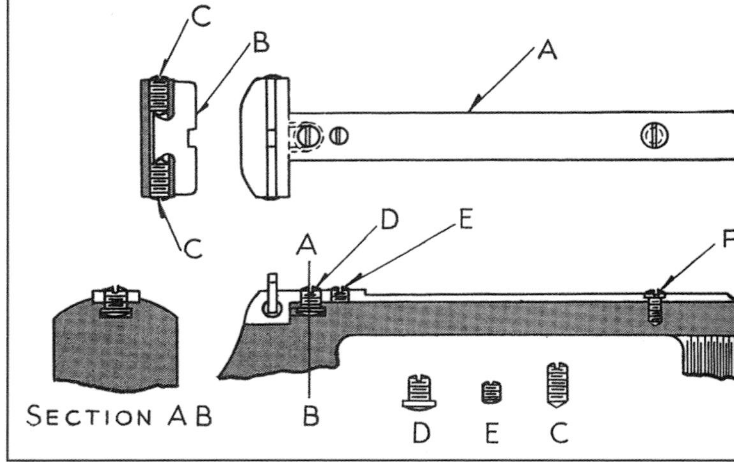



547. A diagram of the third type of adjustable rear sight, from the 1938 edition of *Burning Powder*.

The labeled features are explained as follows:

*Note head of elevating screw "D" works in undercut in frame (section A-B). Blocking screw "E", when set draws head of "D" up against top of undercut, thus locking sight leaf against change of elevation. Windage screws "C" and "C" are opposed and lock each other against change in windage.*

Gaston Comeau collection

The windage adjustment capability in the original screw-adjustable units was described in the 75th Anniversary catalog, issued in 1931, as follows: "Lateral motion of the notch slide is accomplished by loosening the screw on the side to which it is desired to move the slide—then binding the slide in position by tightening the screw on the opposite side."

As far as the elevation adjustment was concerned, however, these early sights actually came in three different configurations, as follows:

1. In addition to the screw which affixed the front of the sight leaf to the top of the frame, the initial type of adjustable rear sight (figs. 281 and 543) featured a single elevation screw which entered from the top and, passing through a plain unthreaded hole in the sight leaf, screwed into the frame. Adjusting this screw up or down raised or lowered the spring steel sight leaf to produce the required change in elevation.

2. The second type of adjustable rear sight (figs. 544 and 545) also featured a single adjustment screw for elevation, but this was configured differently, and the hole in the sight leaf was threaded. As described in the 75th Anniversary catalog, "The screw governing the vertical adjustment has a flange head which enters a T slot in the top [rear] of the frame, so that both up and down movement of the sight is controlled."

3. As described in the 80th Anniversary catalog, issued in 1935/6, the third type of adjustable rear sight (fig. 547) resembled the second type, above, but in addition to the flange-headed elevation screw a second, "blocking" screw was added. This sight was further described on pages 38 and 39 of the 1938 edition of *Burning Powder* as follows:

> *With the present Smith & Wesson target sight the matter of elevation is somewhat less simple owing to the addition of a blocking screw which was done recently to insure a positive and non-changing adjustment. To raise or elevate the rear sight, it is first necessary to release the locking screw, as shown in [fig 547], and then secure the elevation by turning the elevating screw in a clockwise direction the desired amount. When this is done, the blocking screw is then set firmly, and then to make sure that the sight is positively locked, attempt to lower the rear sight by turning the elevating screw counter-clockwise. It will be noted that as there must be a slight amount of lost motion between the head of the elevating screw and the undercut slot in which it works, the effect of firmly seating the blocking screw will be to take up this lost motion, thereby slightly elevating the sight. For that reason we advocate getting the final elevating adjustment by use of the blocking screw, with the elevating screw free, and then drawing down with the elevating screw as firmly as can be done with the Smith & Wesson target screw driver which we supply with each of our target arms.*

## Introducing the Micrometer-Click Rear Sight

The micrometer rear sight found on the current models was first introduced on the K-22 Masterpiece model in 1939. The 1941 catalog described this new sight as having "Positive, two-point click adjustments for both windage and elevation. Once click moves the point of impact 1 inch at 50 yards - 1/2 inch at 25 yards." Previously, instead of these easily and clearly felt adjustments, one windage screw was moved a bit, then the sight blade was locked into position by tightening the other screw into it, with an empirical test then undertaken. Time-consuming as this was, it was certainly easier to accomplish a sight adjustment with a Smith & Wesson revolver than it was with a Colt, where the "guess and by golly" school of adjustment reigned supreme (and the screw heads were really, really tiny and hard to use).

Rear sight blades have changed over time, with the factory basically adopting the various types of blades offered initially by commercial sight manufacturers such as D. W. King of San Francisco, a championship shooter in his own right who led the way in developing a complete line of excellent front

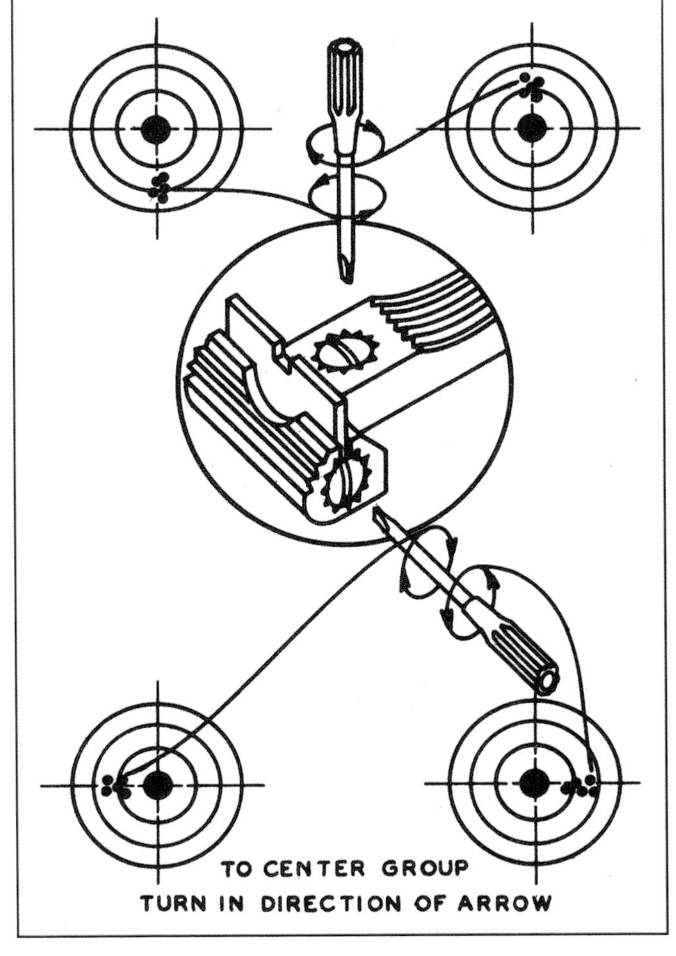


548 (right). A small piece of card stock labeled "S&W Micrometer Click Sight", with a dry-fire practice target on the reverse, as included in the boxes of target-sighted K-frames during the Bangor Punta era.

The micrometer sight patent, granted on January 16, 1940, is shown in fig. 121 and described on pages 117 and 118, with an exploded view shown in fig. 122.

Gaston Comeau collection

and rear sights to be installed on all manner of revolvers, including Smith & Wessons. King also developed lots of fine front sights as well, all designed to help achieve the goal of giving the shooter a more visible and readily aligned set of sights in order to deliver bullets consistently on target. As these sights became more popular, they could be ordered installed by the factory, and then eventually they were actually made at the factory, effectively cutting out the aftermarket sight maker who had led the way.

Rear sight blades were available in a wide variety of patterns from the standard square notch (always a good choice) to a white-outlined 'U'-shaped rear notch, and almost anything in between. Front sights also went from a standard front blade of the Patridge design to the same sights with both flat-surface gold or silver beads in them, to rounded gold beads, ramped Baughman-style sights, either plain or in a red-ramped style, along with a lot of other variations.

## Supply and Demand

Such out-of-the-ordinary sights could be ordered installed on the revolver originally, but were for the most part, I think, installed when an owner sent his revolver back to the factory for extra sight work. Before WWII no doubt Smith & Wesson accepted individual orders for factory-made revolvers fitted with special sights, but after the war was over, the demand for revolvers was quite high, and I think such individually-placed orders must have been quite few in number. Then, about the time the postwar demand slackened, Korea, then the boom times of the '50s kicked in, and just when all that was petering out, along came Vietnam and the Civil Rights wars, again fueling demand. When I got my first new-in-the-box Smith & Wesson in 1965, you took what came in and were happy to get it. No one I ever knew even dreamed of ordering something special direct from the factory.

Of course, after the 1968 Gun Control Act was passed, such direct orders and shipments were for the most part legally impossible. True, an individual could place an order with his dealer, who would then in all likelihood go through his distributor, although some dealer-direct orders were made—but such an approach was pretty awkward. A few really well connected individuals like H. H. Harris of Chicago could place such an order for you and you could reasonably expect to get your weapon delivered as ordered, but this was an exceptional approach. I wish I had thought more about this prior to 1968!

What all of this means, at least to me, is that any revolver you see with a set of unusual sights on it was likely done up at the request of someone who was pretty serious about their firearms. While you may not agree with their conclusions about what was best, it is always interesting to encounter such a revolver about which someone thought enough to be willing to spend extra time and money in order to get something special.

## S&W Sights Today

Currently applied (or available) front and rear sights on the K-frame Smith & Wesson revolvers are the best they have ever been from the standpoint of seeing them and holding their positions once the weapon is properly zeroed. Such sights have always been better than those installed on Colt firearms, and certainly today continue to be the superior choice. With good, sturdy, easy-to-see-and-zero sights, a fine trigger pull and a well-rifled barrel fitted to a cylinder where the alignment is well done, if you do not shoot good groups with your revolver it is either poor ammunition or the shooter, and ninety-nine times out of 100 it is the shooter. Certainly today's sights are unlikely to provide the excuse you are looking for to explain away poor performance on the range or in the field.

# Long and Short Actions

Over the years two basic action types have been used on the K-frame Smith & Wesson: the early "long" action and the later type, commonly called the "short" action. While it is generally thought that the short action was not introduced until after WWII, the first short actions actually appeared on the .22 Masterpiece target models in 1940 (fig. 369). However, with the closing down of the commercial line in 1942 to devote the factory to war production, all further applications of the newly-developed short action had to wait until the war was over and commercial production could be resumed.

The initial postwar models were built using old-stock components and thus still featured the long action, but in 1947 the short action appeared once again, and was soon installed across the line. Thus the fine old long action, so well liked by such notable double-action shooters as Ed McGivern and Bob Nichols, became another casualty sacrificed in the name of progress.

The long action, of course, required the hammer to be pulled further back on a longer arc to be cocked, or to release the sear if shooting double-action. The long action gave the hammer more momentum, and was possibly intended to insure that primers of late 19th century vintage, which sometimes suffered from quality control issues, would ignite reliably. The speed with which several rounds could be fired might have been slightly slower, but Ed McGivern had no trouble using a stock long-action M&P Target .38 Special revolver to achieve his astounding world speed records for double-action shooting, which probably still stand today.

The new short action became the standard in the early postwar years, and remains so to this day. A one-page factory brochure describing the new short action K-38 Masterpiece, plus a kit to convert "K-38s of late design", is shown in fig. 404. The short action made single-action cocking easier, because the hammer only had to be pulled back roughly 60% of the previous distance. This spelled the demise of the "hump back" hammer, discussed below under "Hammers".

Additionally, since the weapons were mostly being fired in the single-action mode, even that shortened arc was sufficient to provide more than enough momentum to insure reliable ignition, primer quality control having been much improved during the quarter-century between the introduction of the M&P revolver in 1899 and the arrival of custom short-action target revolvers created by the likes of King and Buchanan.

By the end of the 1930s, except for the likes of Bob Nichols and Ed McGivern (and their followers), people tended to shoot their K-frames in the cocked single-action mode since mostly they shot at bullseye targets (or tin cans at the dump, or perhaps pine cones atop a log when camping), so it was only natural that those who had an opportunity to shoot a K-frame fitted with such a custom short action would like it, and want to have one made that way at the factory. One thing to rely on about capitalism is that if people want something, someone will supply it—even if it may not be needed or even useful. This is what freedom is all about, after all.

The short-action K-frame could thus be said to fulfill a useful purpose for target shooters (formal or informal), if that was the use to which you put your revolver. Certainly the double-action aspect of the new short action might not be quite as smooth as the old long action, but it seems safe to say that the vast majority of users will achieve no better results with one over the other. Those who are better trained and experienced might well prefer the old system, but such individuals could also get good results with a short action, and of course it gave them something to gripe about when the shooting was over and the coffee mugs came out.

# Triggers

Initial triggers on the M&P were smooth-faced, but as target shooters started to migrate to the K-frame revolver, demand for a grooved trigger arose, which would avoid slippage and keep the finger in the proper position. When single-action fire was the norm for sport or even qualification work, these grooved triggers actually could prove useful. However for practical or defense-oriented shooting where the shooter is firing his weapon in the double-action or trigger-cocking mode, grooves on the trigger are actually a hindrance, as you want your finger to have the ability to shift along the trigger as it is being moved rearward. The grooved Masterpiece trigger is shown in fig. 330.

Target shooters are also to blame (or credit, depending on how you view K-frame revolvers) for the introduction of the wide grooved target trigger. A wide trigger will give the feeling of a lighter trigger pull, even though the actual weight of the pull is the same. Target shooters initially created the demand by popularizing aftermarket trigger shoes, which could be bolted onto the standard trigger to widen it. But these would sometimes come loose, and certainly looked unartful, and the telltale circular marks made by tightening the tiny Allen screws to secure the shoe remained on the trigger long after the accessory was discarded. Thus demand centered on the wide, grooved, factory-made target trigger. However such triggers further slow up fast double-action work and, while useful for target shooting, they are a real drawback for practical applications.

## Trigger Stops

549. Left and right side views of a DAO .357 Magnum Model 19, issued in a limited run by the S&W Performance Center with a 3" Magnaported barrel, bobbed hammer, and checkered walnut finger grips.

Note the non-adjustable trigger stop, permanently installed at the factory in the back of the trigger.

Dave Terbrueggen collection

Once the trigger "breaks", i.e. releases the sear, a trigger that continues to move to the rear, now under no pressure, can typically cause "dipped" shots. This can be very annoying in target work, and the way to prevent it is to install a stop to prevent further rearward movement of the trigger. Aside from the trigger stop designed and included on postwar Masterpiece revolvers at the factory, the pros and cons of which are discussed by John Henwood in Chapter Thirty-Two, this can be done in a variety of ways.

One non-factory method commonly encountered is done by drilling and tapping the trigger and installing a set screw into the back edge. This would be fine, except that occasionally the screw will loosen, and when it does, it can prevent the trigger moving back far enough to release the sear, effectively rendering the weapon unfireable. Since this can happen without the shooter's being aware of it until he attempts to fire a shot, it can spell disaster for practical or defensive purposes.

## Trigger Designs for Target vs. Defense

None of this of course would be an issue if such target-oriented items would be rigorously restricted to the firing range. Unfortunately they are not, and many people will add these target aids to the defense revolver under the mistaken impression that items which will help make the revolver capable of yielding greater scores on targets, will prove equally useful in helping the defense-oriented shooter place his shots on his assailants. Equally unfortunate is the fact that these items, all commanding extra cost, of course, are often present on the higher grades of revolvers, so when a person wants to get the best possible revolver of a given type, making the selection based on price (generally not a bad method of determining what is the best, given the nature of free-market capitalism), he will end up with such target accessories even though the weapon is intended for more practical applications.

Fortunately for the practical users of K-frame revolvers, the factory recognized these issues and now offers a smooth-faced "Combat" trigger, slightly wider than a standard trigger but much narrower than a target trigger. While not as good for formal single-action target shooting, for those who plan on a more practical use for their K-frame, this is clearly the one to have installed.

# Hammers

550. A selection of hammers from center-fire K-frame revolvers of different vintages.

From left: early long action hammer with "chafing pins"; long action hammer marked "REG. U.S. PAT. OFF." on rear curve; short action hammer with swaged spur; later semi-target hammer with lower, wider, deeply checkered spur; full target hammer with extra-wide spur, heavily checkered; flash-chromed hammer for use in stainless steel revolvers. Gaston Comeau collection

The hammer does two things in a revolver. The most obvious one is that it carries the firing pin and, when the trigger is pulled, it directs the firing pin into the primer with sufficient force to ignite it and fire the chambered cartridge.

The other thing it does is to allow the shooter to cock the weapon manually if it is to be fired in the single-action mode. Generally hammers are cocked with the thumb, either of the hand holding the weapon or the non-shooting hand.

## The "Hump Back" Hammer

Early Smith & Wesson M&P hammers were checkered on top, but of a shape that really was not especially fast or certain to cock. For those who shot single-action on the target range, the early long action did of course take slightly longer to cock, and more critically their thumbs might well slip off the hammer when cocking it through the long arc. For such individuals the patented "hump back" hammer was introduced during the latter 1930s, designed specifically to make rapid cocking of the hammer more certain. Drawings from the "hump back" hammer patent appear in fig. 53, and the descriptive pamphlet issued by the factory is shown in fig. 54.

John Henwood memorably and correctly described the "hump back" hammer as follows:

> *It was ugly as sin, but anyone who tried a hump-back hammer became an instant convert. It reduced the apparent effort required to cock the revolver appreciably, and fell more naturally under the thumb when trying to cock the gun rapidly. Available in both rimfire and centerfire versions, the humpback hammer was first listed in the mid-1930s; it was listed in the catalogs for a few years after World War II, but apparently was not actually produced after about 1941.*

However the "hump back" hammer was an option, meaning that the weapon either had to be ordered that way or sent back to the factory for fitting and installation. Most people did not special-order items from the factory in those days, but bought what was on display at their local retail outlet. Since such places got their weapons from distributors who got the most common models from the factory, such special hammers rarely showed up on the local retailers' countertops.

Sending a handgun back for installation of such a hammer was a task. After the 1920s, you could not mail firearms to the factory, and there was no UPS or FedEx. Instead it had to be sent via Railway Express or some similar commercial shipper. I recall sending something as a kid by Railway Express, and it was a big job: you had to get it to the railway station in order to ship it. They did not come and pick it up, like UPS or FedEx will do at my office today. Nor was it inexpensive. Then, as now, if you wanted to send a handgun back for extra work, you had to be pretty serious about your guns. Few people then were any more serious about their shooting than they are today, which is no doubt the reason such special hammers are seen more on adjustable-sighted target models than fixed-sight duty-oriented K-frames.

Also, no matter how useful and practical, to many the hump back hammer just "didn't look right". However if you did a lot of single-action shooting under close time restraints, or were out where your thumbs were likely to be either really cold or wet with sweat, snow or rain, it might well be worth the price of admission.

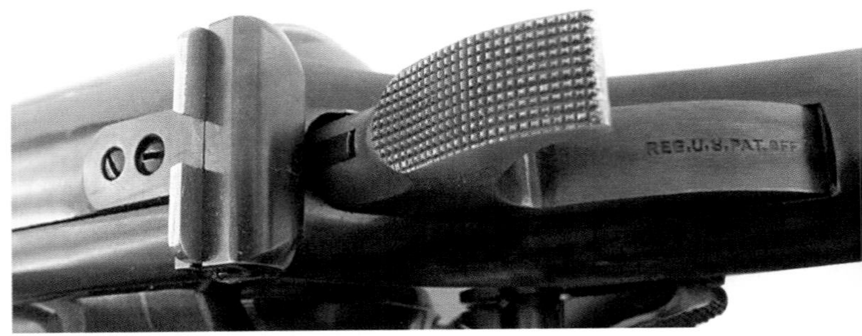


551. Rear closeup of the "hump back" hammer on a post-1926, pre-K-38 .38 Special target revolver, serial no. 670727. Note the locking screw in the rear sight leaf.

While not particularly attractive, the hump back hammer is surprisingly convenient and pleasant to use, as John Henwood states at left.

As discussed in page 4 of the factory .357 Magnum brochure (fig. 43), the patent office marking refers to the exclusive "glass hard, tough cored hammer and trigger . . that have been accepted by the United States Patent Office as *a recognized trade-mark*".

Gaston Comeau collection

## Target Hammers in the Modern Age

For some purposes, such as timed rapid-fire shooting on the target range, bigger, wider and rougher hammer spurs are thought to make the cocking motion faster and more certain. With that in mind, hammers took on a new look in the postwar era, modeling themselves after the hammers offered by D. W. King, Buchanan, and other custom gunsmiths who specialized in helping the target shooter achieve better scores with better equipment. As shown in fig. 550, postwar hammers had larger spurs with coarser checkering on them, making them easier to cock with slippery thumbs and, thanks to the new short action, the arc of the hammer in cocking was also shorter. Of course, such hammers tended to get caught on coat linings and what not, but for the type of person who was manually cocking his revolver, that was not likely a concern. Instead a demand was created for an even wider hammer spur, to which the factory responded by designing the target hammer, with a lower and wider platform.

Interestingly, the wider platforms on these hammers sometimes tend to break off over time. My late friend Kent Lomont told me of many of his target hammers breaking off after putting 20,000 or more rounds through the revolver. I suppose the extra weight was such that the constant slamming home would set up metal fatigue. I have never encountered this problem myself, but all my high-volume K-frame revolvers are typically shot double-action only, and have had their spurs removed. Those that are not removed are standard-size spurs.

## "Bobbing" a Hammer

Many people who carry K-frame revolvers under clothing of some type will remove the hammer spur. Some go further and also remove the single action cocking notch, so that allegations about cocking the hammer to reinforce street commands which have in the past prompted unintentional shootings can be successfully countered. Some people of course do not go that far, keeping the single-action capability and merely removing the hammer spur to avoid snagging. Such people will typically checker the top of the remaining portion of the hammer, and then train themselves to start the hammer rearward with their trigger finger, then grasping the checkered area on top of the shortened hammer and pulling the hammer backwards until it cocks on the single action sear. Bill Jordan and Skeeter Skelton both recommended this approach, so it is not something that is outside the range of sensibility by any means. But it is something I believe best reserved for the well-trained and cool-headed individual, for use preferably when the target is not another human being. Having said that, however, men like "Packer Jack" Newman used slip hammers on their single action M1873 Colt revolvers, and were known to cock them when approached by strangers. Frankly this has always seemed a little over the top to me, and I am not totally certain about the Jordan/Skelton approach either, at least on a defense weapon.

When setting out to "bob" a hammer, many do not realize is that there is more to the issue than just getting out your saw, file, and grinding wheel. Over the years, most Smith & Wesson hammers have been case-hardened—"glass hard" is the phrase used by the factory to describe their hammers and triggers. This makes them very wear-resistant, but unlike Colt hammers it makes them difficult to modify and usually impossible to repair if they get damaged.

Mentioning removing the spur from the K-frame hammer leads us almost seamlessly back to the initial purpose of a hammer, which is giving enough weight and momentum to the firing pin to consistently ignite the primer, causing the chambered cartridge to fire reliably. The amount of metal removed from a hammer when the spur is taken off will reduce the hammer's weight and consequently its momentum, and hence the striking force of the firing pin on the primer. Combining this with the shorter hammer throw on short-action K-frames, and primers that might be a little thick and heavy, such as in some high-pressure .357 Magnum loadings (or some brands generally, like Winchester), or the firing pin nose being slightly short, or any combination of these and other factors will produce misfires.

When the New York City Police Department adopted its last official revolver, the Model 64 in 2-, 3-, and 4-inch lengths, a bobbed-hammer double-action-only trigger system was mandated. Getting them to fire every time without having a trigger pull that was so heavy as to be difficult to use was found to be quite a technical challenge. It was finally achieved, however, and my M64 NY-1 M&P style revolvers have never misfired, although I have used the same low-grade reloads in other Smith & Wesson K-frames that will not fire them due to the thick primers used by the reloader who did the work.

The bottom line for bobbed hammers is "don't try this at home"—best send it back and let the men at the factory set it up correctly so you can benefit from their hard-won experience, obtained thanks to the New York City Police Department contract.

## Hammers in Stainless Steel - Briefly

For a brief period after K-frame revolvers first appeared in stainless steel, in 1970 and thereafter, the hammers were also made out of stainless steel, so the factory could claim that the entire weapon, except for the stocks, was stainless. But such hammers were not as hard as the case-hardened carbon steel hammers, and they quickly lost their ability to hold proper trigger/hammer tolerances, which resulted in changing trigger pulls. They were soon replaced with flash-chromed hammers made out of case-hardened steel in the traditional way, which looked the same as the rest of the stainless steel components in the revolver. An expensive solution no doubt to what was really mainly a cosmetic issue, but then unplated case-hardened hammers are prone to rusting, unlike the rest of the weapon if made of stainless steel.

# Barrels and Barrel Pins

Initially the barrels on Military & Police revolvers were threaded into the frame and pinned in place by means of a small-diameter pin driven transversely through a hole in the frame and top of the barrel. Thus, unlike a Colt product, removal of the barrel required that the pin first be taken out - a difficult task for most modestly equipped would-be gunsmiths, especially as the pins were thin, requiring a drift thinner than those normally encountered in a handyman's toolbox, as it was the one in the set that had snapped off the first time it had been used. The pins were also tightly fitted, and often corroded into position after years of misuse and/or neglect. Backwoods and kitchen-table gunsmiths would try to drive the pins out, and such handiwork is often evidenced by multiple imprints of the misaligned drift (or nail) on the frame when these attempts came to no avail.

Sometimes such people overlooked the barrel pin altogether and attempted to remove Smith & Wesson barrels by just applying torque, like they would with a Colt revolver. This of course would twist the frame, effectively ruining the weapon. All of these amateurish efforts are generally doomed to failure, leaving a disfigured if not ruined revolver in their wake. (Guess which would-be gun book writer wanted a two-inch rather than a four-inch M&P when he was 12 years old and had an extra two-inch barrel to install, if he could only get that four-inch barrel out, and you will know how I can write with such authority on this issue!)

## Deleting the Barrel Pin

In later years, starting in 1980 or so with the development of the L-frame revolver but later applied to the entire line, the barrel pin was deleted, and the barrel was simply screwed in without further fanfare. While originally most of us thought that this was an attempt to cheapen the product (it no doubt did result in a slight cost saving) and that the barrel would screw loose in time (some reportedly did – none in my experience, however, or that of anyone I know), in the end it has made little difference to the quality of the revolver. It did help keep the cost down, and thus availability up, for individuals who bought their own weapons, thus permitting them to use the money saved to buy practice ammo (or something frivolous like kids' shoes) while still getting a Smith & Wesson, the world standard for revolvers since 1856, as you will recall. It takes a strong commitment and a lot of practice to make a good revolver, I think.

## The Modern Way - Barrels in Cast Shrouds

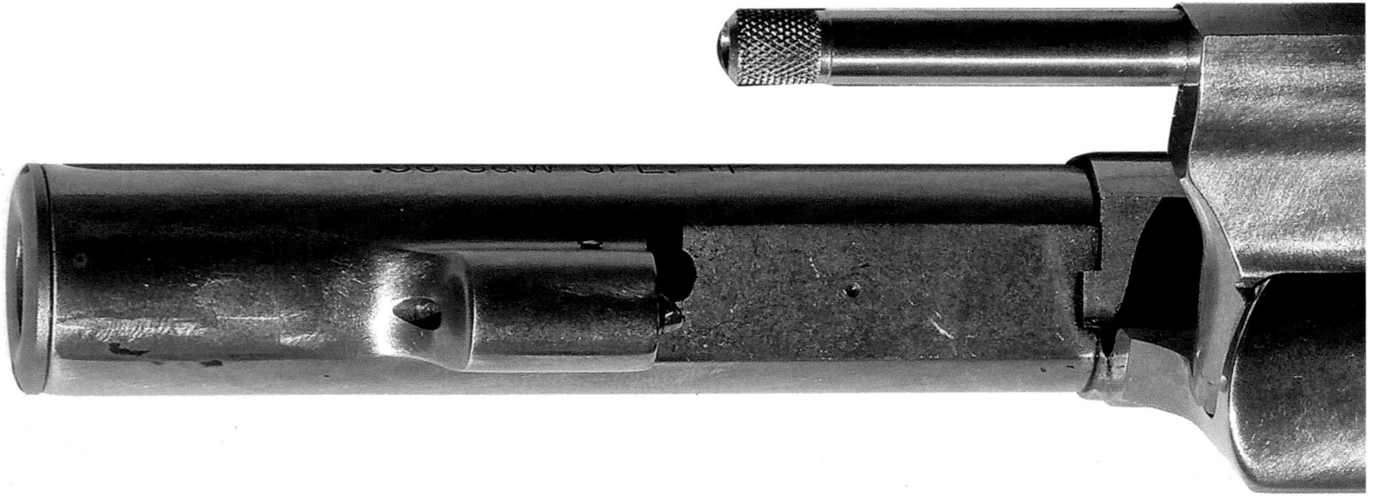

552. Underside closeup of a modern K-frame Model 67-6 revolver with cylinder open, showing the barrel sleeve which is slipped on over the plain tubular barrel and secured with a threaded end cap. Note the square projection on the front of the receiver, right, onto which the sleeve is positioned to keep it from turning.

553. Left front three-quarter closeup of a sleeved barrel showing the threaded end cap and markings ".38 S&W SPL. +P" on the side of the sleeve.

In the most recent years the system has been changed again, with a straight-walled barrel tube threaded into the frame and then a cast shroud, which matches the traditional contour of the appropriate model, being slipped on over the barrel and secured with an end cap or plug threaded onto the barrel muzzle.

Such barrels are not rifled in the conventional manner by cutting rifling in them, by the way, but by an electro-chemical machining process which etches the grooves by means of an electrode working with a conductive slurry.

While some people think the old cut rifling was better, the new method seems to yield results equal to the old, and is no doubt cheaper to produce. Perhaps at the very highest levels of shooting skill, and using ultra-precision ammunition, cut rifling might produce better results, but I would guess the difference would be slight, and certainly nothing that would be obvious for any practical purpose.

# A Discussion on Bore Dimensions

## The .38 S&W vs. the .38 Special

As discussed in Chapter Thirty, when World War II broke out in 1939, Britain was caught short on handguns just as it had been in 1915, and once again Smith & Wesson began a crash program to produce revolvers for the British, although this time the model of choice was the M&P in .38 S&W caliber rather than the larger .455 N-frame of WWI. The chambers for the tapered .38 S&W cartridge start out slightly larger in diameter, and the cartridge itself is shorter than the .38 Special, but that simply required the use of the appropriate chambering reamer. As Walter Roper notes in Chapter Thirty, providing the British with the M&P in that chambering was seen as an ideal solution for all concerned.

## Using .38 Special Barrels in .38/200s as a Wartime Expedient

Also according to Walter Roper, the lead bullets of the .38 S&W could be squeezed down to fire in a barrel bored for .38 Special with no ill effects, and thus the factory used the same barrels on these British revolvers as they were using on their standard .38 Special M&Ps. The fact that .38/200 revolvers were initially supplied in several different barrel lengths seems to indicate that a substantial number of .38 Special M&P barrels already existed in stock, probably as the result of "make work" projects designed to keep workers busy and on the payroll during the latter years of the Depression when sales were slow.

Of course by that time the British were using jacketed bullets in order to comply with the Hague Convention, but still it seems that no difficulty was envisaged. This is interesting when we consider that according to David Penn, the noted British military weapon specialist, firing military .38 S&W cartridges in rechambered .38 Special Colt revolvers sometimes left projectiles stuck dangerously in the bore, and the Colt barrels were often drilled out from the muzzle to remove two or three inches of rifling in order to alleviate this problem; although this counterboring has not been observed on any British-issue Smith & Wessons.

Nevertheless, actual measurements taken for us by the St. Louis Metropolitan Police Department Crime Lab confirm Walter Roper's assertion that the same bore dimensions were used for both the wartime British .38/200 revolvers and the U.S. .38 Special Victory Model.

So why did Colts have a problem with stuck bullets and not Smith & Wessons? The only thing I can think of is that they kept their tolerances closer; otherwise it is a mystery to me.

## Curious Comments from the Warren Commission

With this in mind, the official comments made about the ex-Lend Lease Canadian .38 S&W M&P revolver rechambered to .38 Special which was (allegedly) used by Lee Harvey Oswald to kill officer J. D. Tippet in 1963 are curious. According to the Warren Commission report, it could not be confirmed that the recovered bullets were fired from Oswald's weapon, due to excessive bore size allowing the bullets to 'skip' along the rifling. That has always made sense to me, knowing as I did that the .38 S&W cartridge normally required a bigger bore size than the .38 Special; but after reviewing Roper's comments, then David Penn's, and finally having the results of some real measurements, the statement is puzzling. I suppose the bore could have been excessively worn, either from cleaning or shooting full metal-jacketed loads, especially if by chance Oswald's M&P had previously happened to be a range gun, used repeatedly to train waves of recruits during the war. Would Oswald have checked the bore of his revolver when he got it, or, better yet, zeroed it at 25 yards and thereby discovered bullet tumbling? Certainly he must have zeroed his rifle, so why not his revolver also? This is all getting curious and leading us astray so I will stop here and let you, the reader, ponder about it—although another point: why go home to pick up your revolver after shooting the President? Why not bring it with you to begin with and save yourself a trip home; especially if you might anticipate encountering a little trouble leaving the Book Depository?

## Official S&W Bore Dimension Data from 1957

As discussed in Chapter Thirty-Two, after WWII Smith & Wesson made special-order runs of the M&P in the .38 S&W chambering from time to time to fill requests from Commonwealth countries, and it appears that these did have different bore dimensions, larger than those used in .38 Special barrels. This information comes from one of a series of cards prepared by the H. P. White Laboratory in Bel Air, Maryland, using data supplied directly from the S&W factory in response to a request from manager Burton D. Munhall. The covering letter, dated May 14, 1957, signed by S&W Assistant Sales Manager Fred H. Miller, appears here as fig. 554.

The official factory data for all calibers of revolvers and pistols then being manufactured by Smith & Wesson is as follows:

SMITH & WESSON
SPRINGFIELD 4, MASS.

PLEASE ADDRESS ALL COMMUNICATIONS TO THE COMPANY

May 14, 1957

REGISTERED MAIL

Mr. B. D. Munhall, Mgr.
H. P. White Company
Box 331
Bel Air, Maryland

Dear Mr. Munhall:

Here is the information that you requested, and this data has been taken directly from the drawings from which we work, and is correct as of this date.

As far as I can learn, and as I understand the situation, we use these same specifications for all guns in the same caliber.

That is to say, the Kit Gun has the same specifications as the 22/32 Target, 22 Combat Masterpiece, the K-22, and the new 22 Automatic as yet not released.

The same will apply in the other calibers, with apparently this one exception. In 45 caliber, for reasons as yet unexplained to me, we have a .001" difference in the land diameter between the corresponding specification in the target model.

I presume this is for reasons of accuracy, but at any rate I am giving you one card on the military specifications and another one on the target specifications.

I believe this will make it possible for you to make an accurate application of this data for your files and for the project that you outlined for us here at the office.

Trusting that the above will meet with approval, and with kindest regards as always, I remain,

Cordially yours,

SMITH & WESSON, INC.

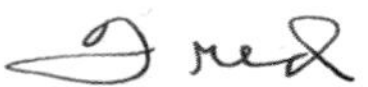

F. H. Miller,
Asst. Sales Manager

554 (right). Copy of a factory letter dated May 14, 1957, from S&W Asst. Sales Manager Fred H. Miller to Burton D. Munhall, manager of the H. P. White Labs in Bel Air, Maryland, supplying the official rifling specifications as used in S&W revolvers. Gaston Comeau collection

# Rifling Specifications

## .22 LR Caliber

| | | | |
|---|---|---|---|
| Direction | R. H. | Land Diam. | .2135 - .2147 |
| No. Grooves | 6 | Land Width | .0413 |
| Groove Dia. | .2225 - .2242 | Twist Rate - 1 turn in | 15 in. |
| Groove Width | .071 | | |

## .32 Caliber

| | | | |
|---|---|---|---|
| Direction | R. H. | Land Diam. | .303 - .3042 |
| No. Grooves | 5 | Land Width | .095 |
| Groove Dia. | .312 - .3137 | Twist Rate - 1 turn in | 18.75 in. |
| Groove Width | .095 | | |

## 9mm

| | | | |
|---|---|---|---|
| Direction | R. H. | Land Diam. | .345 - .346 |
| No. Grooves | 6 | Land Width | .071 |
| Groove Dia. | .353 - .3547 | Twist Rate - 1 turn in | 10 in. |
| Groove Width | .115 | | |

## .38 Special Caliber

| | | | |
|---|---|---|---|
| Direction | R. H. | Land Diam. | .346 - .3472 |
| No. Grooves | 5 | Land Width | .1034 |
| Groove Dia. | .3555 - 3574 | Twist Rate - 1 turn in | 18.750 in. |
| Groove Width | .114 | | |

## .38 - 200 Caliber

| | | | |
|---|---|---|---|
| Direction | R. H. | Land Diam. | .350 - .3512 |
| No. Grooves | 5 | Land Width | .1034 |
| Groove Dia. | .3595 - .3614 | Twist Rate - 1 turn in | 18.750 in. |
| Groove Width | .114 | | |

## .44 Caliber

| | | | |
|---|---|---|---|
| Direction | R. H. | Land Diam. | .4170 - .4182 |
| No. Grooves | 5 | Land Width | .1335 |
| Groove Dia. | .4290 - .4307 | Twist Rate - 1 turn in | 20 in. |
| Groove Width | .1285 | | |

## .45 Caliber (Military)

| | | | |
|---|---|---|---|
| Direction | R. H. | Land Diam. | .444 - .4452 |
| No. Grooves | 6 | Land Width | .072 - .075 |
| Groove Dia. | .450 - .4517 | Twist Rate - 1 turn in | 15 in. |
| Groove Width | .154 - .157 | | |

## .45 Caliber (Target)

| | | | |
|---|---|---|---|
| Direction | R. H. | Land Diam. | .443 - .4442 |
| No. Grooves | 6 | Land Width | .072 - .075 |
| Groove Dia. | .450 - .4517 | Twist Rate - 1 turn in | 15 in. |
| Groove Width | .154 - .157 | | |

## An Appeal for Confirmation

Post-WWII M&P (and, after 1957, Model 11) revolvers chambered in .38 S&W were only made up to fill foreign orders. Examples to be found in collectors' hands in the U.S. are typically overrun guns from postwar production, and are few in number. I have not been able to convince any Model 11 owners to let me check the above measurements, as the guns are all in unfired condition. While I toyed with the idea of buying one just to confirm the information, I found the prospect of then trying to justify continuing to own a revolver in this caliber—now in fired condition—so depressing that I passed on the idea. If you own one, and are willing to slug the bore and measure it carefully, please let me have the results.

In conclusion, I would note that Ruger made a run of .38 S&W caliber Security Six revolvers for the Indian Police a number of years ago. I would bet the bore dimensions were the same as for the standard .38 Special models, but I do not know for certain.

# Cylinders

Although they look the same as ever, cylinders on the K-frame S&W have changed over time. Originally the cylinder was made of soft steel, with hardened steel inserts in the stops, but this was discontinued early on around the 20,000 serial number range. Thereafter, in the post-WWI era, the cylinders were heat-treated to improve their strength.

Interestingly enough however, it does not appear that Smith & Wesson ever limited their revolvers to black powder use only, even prior to the introduction of the heat treating process. While the .38 Special cartridge was originally a black powder loading, it very rapidly became available loaded with smokeless powder, and the M&P proved more than capable of handling such loads. Of course today, high-pressure loads such as +P or +P+ might very well "jug" a non-heat-treated cylinder, and even the early heat-treated cylinders are not to be used with high-pressure loads. Fortunately I do not suppose many of these pre-WWI veterans are being used on a daily basis anymore, or at least not used by the type of people who will buy high-performance ammunition. Having said that, I am certain that as I write these lines someone, somewhere, has his trusty pre-1915 era M&P, with its nickel plate flaking and hard rubber grips broken and cracked, loaded up with 110-gr. JHP +P+ loads that his brother-in-law got from a friend of a friend who used to be a cop for some agency which used them in the early 1980s. Fortunately for that individual, if not the collector, such loads may well "jug" his chambers, making it difficult to extract the fired brass, but they will not blow up the weapon, which is a testimony to the design and strength of these century-old revolvers.

The only other major change in K-frame cylinders came with the development of the K-frame Magnum, when cylinders were initially counterbored to allow the cartridge rims to be recessed, thus providing full support for the cartridge base. This had been thought useful in 1935 when the .357 Magnum was introduced in the N-frame line, and while the process was continued in the K-frame Magnums for about 25 years, by 1982 recessed chambers had been discontinued.

I do not believe there is any real difference between the .357 Magnum cylinder and the .38 Special cylinder currently, except for depth of chambering. Certainly the factory descriptions of models that are otherwise identical, except for chambering, do not indicate any difference in cylinder heat treating or material.

The two most interesting K-frame cylinders are those fitted to the Model 53, chambered for the .22 Magnum (or Jet) cartridge, and those made in 9x19mm, used in the Model 547. Both of these models are described in Chapter Thirty-Two.

The M53 cylinder was standard in every way except chambering, but if any oil was left in the chambers, thanks to the steep taper of the cartridge cases they would set back upon firing, thus tying up the cylinder. No other chambering ever had this problem, although sometimes you had to beat out empty .357 Magnum cases, depending on the loads, but at least the cylinder would open to permit you to do so!

The Model 547, chambering the rimless 9x19mm Parabellum (or Luger) cartridge, employs a very clever system of spring-steel "fingers" which snap into the cannelures of the cartridges and push them out as the extractor rod is depressed. Despite a lot of parts and fancy engineering, it worked just fine, although the Model 547 was not nearly as popular as might have been desired, due mainly, I believe, to the time it came out coinciding with the adoption by the

U.S. military of a high-capacity, double-action 9x19mm self-loading pistol, which concept was also embraced by many U.S. police forces. In Europe also, except in France, they jumped from simple blowback 7.65mm (.32 ACP) and 9mm short (.380 ACP) autoloaders to locked-breech 9x19mm pistols, most by then considering the revolver to be obsolete.

By the late 20th century, even in France, those who had embraced the revolver had retired from positions of authority, and the Model 547 with its unique and clever extraction system became a footnote in the history of police weapons.

## Yokes and Yoke Screws

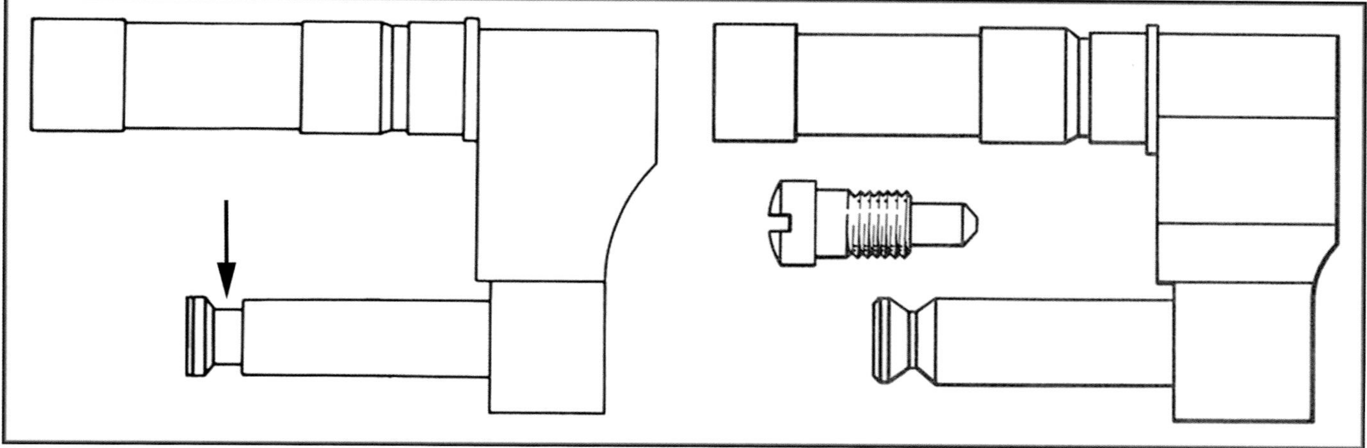

555. Comparison drawing of two styles of cylinder yokes. Left: early style, with flat recess for front sideplate screw (arrow). As shown in fig. 442, the pilot of the front screw was filed during assembly to insure that it retained the yoke without binding.

Right: later style, introduced in 1988, wherein the yoke is retained by a pointed, spring-loaded plunger housed in the front sideplate screw, which engages a 'V' groove in the yoke stud. Gaston Comeau collection

## Cylinder Releases

Being a side-opening hand ejector revolver, the M&P of course needs some type of device to release the cylinder. The cylinder release, originally called the "bolt thumb piece", has been a feature of the M&P revolver ever since the very first .38 Military Model was announced in 1899. Pushing forward on the cylinder release button frees the cylinder so that it may be pushed outward from the locked position.

The release button has changed in appearance over the years, while still performing the same function. Early release buttons were checkered and concave in appearance. They worked fine, except for occasionally coming loose, although if the thumb was held high, the recoil of the weapon would drive the release into the thumb, often scraping away flesh.

In later years, especially on alloy-framed models, a simple flat release button was used. This is merely grooved instead of checkered and, being thinner, tends not to abrade the thumb upon recoil. This is an especially good feature, considering that such alloy-framed revolvers naturally will exhibit greater felt recoil forces. However this same thinness that helps avoid conflicts with the thumb also means that it is harder to slide the button forward, making the cylinder release less rapid and certain. Still, it is not necessary for you to open the cylinder until you are ready to reload, and since most gunfights are over long before a cylinder is empty of loaded cartridges, the benefits to be had by not striking the thumb joint outweigh the deficiencies imposed with the thinner release button.

In the latter years of the 20th century, a new release button design was installed, modeled on the release levers seen on many custom revolvers, which often had the lower portion of the standard release removed, or at least the rough checkering removed, so that damage to the thumb was avoided or minimized. Late-model factory cylinder releases likewise removed this material from the lower portion of the button, while still offering a deeper button than the flat releases commonly found on the alloy-framed revolvers. At first glance these new releases look a little odd to eyes long used to the full-sized, traditional release, but as one who has frequently scraped the skin off my thumb and who has also ground some of the checkered metal off the button, they do tend to grow on you as being nice-looking as well as practical and useful.

## Extractor Rods

The M&P revolver, being a Hand Ejector, needed an extractor rod to permit the shooter to push all the fired cases from the cylinder with one motion.

Over the years, the front tip of the extractor rod, which of course is what the shooter pushes, either with a finger or more properly the palm of the hand, has changed. Originally it was a separate threaded piece, knurled on the outside, and larger in diameter than the rod itself, which made jamming the palm of the hand onto it to forcefully eject the fired cases a reasonably comfortable operation. I suppose when the M&P originally came out, shooting black powder cartridges where residue would build up quickly, it would have been common for fired cases to stick to the walls of the chambers, making them difficult to remove with anything less than a firm push on the extractor rod. This larger diameter end piece then no doubt made it easier to use, and more comfortable when the palm was struck smartly on it. But, after the adoption of the barrel lug into which the extractor rod head fitted, the larger size rod head required more involved machining and fitting. In today's world of CNC machining it would not be as difficult, but in the early 20th century, this was something that required careful and time-consuming setup and machining.

As black powder faded from the scene, at least as far as duty loads were concerned, and the cylinder chambers were routinely burnished, and the quality and dimensions of the brass cartridge cases became more standardized, the need for a serious pounding on the extractor rod must have diminished. As a consequence the diameter of the end of the rod was gradually reduced, and eventually the rod was made all in one piece, allowing the area behind the barrel lug to be simply cut straight on the bottom of the barrel.

The extractor rod assembly was thus made simpler and cheaper to manufacture, yet it still accomplished its task just as well as the original. True, with some high-pressure .357 Magnum loads it becomes difficult to remove the fired cases with a simple push of the palm and they need to be pounded out, using a wooden block on the rod. Such ammunition simply should no longer be used for any practical purposes. If you cannot remove your fired cases with a firm push of the palm on the extractor rod, you definitely need to change loads!

## Special-Order Models with Encased Ejector Rods

Special runs of what were typically adjustable-sighted, encased ejector lug models have been made, especially for overseas sales, with a few overruns being released domestically in fixed-sight versions. The Peruvian M19P (fig. 449) and the French Police 3-inch "Sasia" versions of the M19, discussed in Chapter Thirty-Five, are examples of this breed. Both have encased extractors, but fixed sights.

Revolvers that typically do not have the fully-enclosed ejector lug have also had them installed for certain foreign orders, such as the Brazilian M10 3-inch models in .38 Special, which while retaining their M10 model number are otherwise identical to the French Police fixed-sight 3-inch M19 .357 Magnum revolvers.

# Chamberings

The K-frame Smith & Wesson first appeared at the end of the black powder era, initially being chambered for the .38 Long Colt, which was then the official U.S. service cartridge, as well as the new longer Smith & Wesson-designed .38 Special cartridge. Both of these were originally loaded with black powder, but the weapon was capable of taking the higher pressures of the smokeless loads that soon followed in these same cartridges.

The other chambering available right from the outset was the .32 WCF (Winchester Center Fire) or .32-20 cartridge. This loading has occasionally been the source of some problems, since it was also available as a high-velocity load intended for use in the Winchester Model 92 rifle. Once out of the box, it is generally impossible to determine whether you have a rifle-power loading or a handgun cartridge. Often the jacketed-bullet loads were for rifles, with flat-topped plain lead for revolvers, but not always. Firing a rifle cartridge in a K-frame revolver is unpleasant at best and may even lead to damage, which is not a good thing.

Despite this potential difficulty, the K-frame .32-20 has always had something of a following. Those who used this revolver out-of-doors for vermin removal found that the flat-shooting capability of the .32-20 gave a longer more effective range. Some people also like the .32-20 as a defense weapon, either because of restrictive laws where they live which might well ban a .38 but permit a .32, a common situation in some British colonies, or because of the light recoil of the cartridge. For not only were the bullets of less weight, typically 115 grains versus 158 grains for the .38 Special, but the diameter of the bore and chambers was smaller, so that the revolver weighed more, particularly in the front end, and hence produced even less felt recoil.

Skeeter Skelton often told the wonderful story of a Mexican police officer of his acquaintance who carried a four-inch, round-butt .32-20 M&P as his defense weapon, using it to kill his .45 ACP-armed attacker, as he could quickly shoot several rounds from his little .32-20 while his assailant was still recovering from the heavy recoil of the first shot from his .45. Hitting and placement are the keys, after all, in hunting and gunfighting both, not making a noise; although in my experience the four-inch .32-20 M&P always produced a lot of muzzle blast and not an inconsiderable amount of muzzle flame.

The K-frame was also briefly made in .32 Smith & Wesson Long, to meet the demands of the target shooting crowd who had to shoot a minimum of .32 caliber in centerfire contests. But such chamberings have always been pretty rare, since the demand from that market was slim, and relatively few of these models were sold. For law enforcement, except for some portions of the world, .32 is pretty passé if you use U. S.-made revolvers.

The .38 Special of course has long been and remains the standard, while the .38/200 version of the .38 Smith & Wesson round is another chambering that was common in guns sold to Britain and the Commonwealth during WWII. The postwar version, the Model 11, was largely exported and is only rarely encountered.

The .357 Combat Magnum K-frame, which first appeared in 1955, has remained quite popular with many law enforcement agencies and individuals. The former were organizations which anticipated their officers or agents needing greater power and penetration than could be achieved with the .38 Special, and the latter were individual buyers who wanted to get the benefit from the power level of the .357 Magnum while still permitting them to practise with cheaper and less powerful .38 Special ammunition.

In a rare revolver made originally for the French police and later sold to an extent in the U.S., the K-frame was chambered for the 9x19mm, a surprisingly powerful cartridge when loaded in revolvers. The Model 547 was available in three- or four-inch barrel lengths and, as discussed above, had a special cylinder with a patented extractor to permit extraction of the rimless 9x19mm cartridges. It also had bigger and stronger studs in the frame to insure that the revolver would hold up using these high-pressure loads, many of which abroad were typically used in open-bolt-firing submachine guns.

There have been K-frame prototypes made in five-shot capacity chambered for .44 Special and .41 Magnum, but alas no quantity production of K-frame models in such chamberings has taken place. More is the pity; but I assume the factory was concerned about the long-term effects of these high-pressure loads being used in K-frames, even when only five cartridges were contained in the cylinder.

Other cartridges that have been chambered include the commonly encountered .22 Rimfire, the .22 Rimfire Magnum and its offshoot the .17 Hornady Magnum Rimfire (described in *Ammo Encyclopedia* as "a true 200-yard rimfire hunting cartridge"), and the .22 Jet or .22 Magnum. The latter of course is the .357 Magnum cartridge necked down to .22 caliber, shooting a 40-grain bullet at some 2,100 - 2,200 fps. As discussed above, with its rapidly tapered case, this chambering was doomed from the outset since with even small traces of lubricant in the chamber the fired case would set back, binding the cylinder. However, these Model 53 revolvers, using the supplied rimfire chamber inserts and especially if accompanied by the factory-available .22 Rimfire auxiliary cylinder, made a dandy understudy for the Model 19 in .357 Magnum.

Despite Elmer Keith's enthusiastic writeup, excerpted in Chapter Thirty-Two, there was only ever one single example of a S&W Model 53 chambered in .256 Winchester Magnum, which was another even shorter-lived offshoot of the .357 Magnum. This revolver, fitted with an 8⅜" barrel, fired a 60-grain, .257"-diameter bullet from a rimmed, necked case 1.281" long, producing a maximum breech pressure of 43,000 psi.

To sum up, while it cannot be said that the K-frame was available for any cartridge a person might possibly need or want, since it was never chambered for the big-bore heavy loadings so useful for big game—although other, larger-framed models shooting these rounds were always available in the line—certainly a sufficiently wide range of chamberings were available in the K-frame to handle most of the needs of the vast majority of shooters. With proper placement, some of the available loadings could take extremely large and dangerous game, but more to the point really the K-frame revolver was of a size and weight that the average person could carry it on a daily basis and shoot it with sufficient accuracy and power to accomplish the tasks set for that combination of cartridge, revolver and shooter.

# Finishes

Smith & Wesson has supplied a variety of finishes for K-frame revolvers over the years. Most commonly seen, of course, is blue, whether high- or low-gloss. For military revolvers made during wartime, a proprietary dull phosphate coating known as Parkerizing was applied, which hides a multitude of sins left over after a bare minimum of surface smoothing and polishing.

Other more exotic finishes such as nickel, silver, chrome, and even gold plate are also encountered, frequently in the case of nickel and much less so in the case of the other three. Before WWII the factory price was the same for either blue or nickel finish.

No doubt some other exotic finishes have been made available from time to time, but if bought as a collector's item, such unusual things obviously need to be verified by factory letter.

As the finish depends on the expertise of the underlying polishing, finishes will exhibit a more or less shiny appearance, depending on what was ordered by the purchaser, or the period of production at the factory.

## A Factory Chrome-Plated M&P

556. Left side view of the prewar .38 Special long-action M&P serial no. 611108, with 6" barrel and factory chrome plated finish, standing in front of the gold and blue box in which it was shipped from the factory. Note the S&W medallion in the checkered walnut service stock, which is noticeably larger in diameter than the standard size. Chad Gripp collection

557. Underside view of the grip of the above chrome-plated M&P, showing serial number.
Chad Gripp collection

559. Closeup of the end of the gold and blue box in which this revolver was shipped, showing small paper label reading "CHROME" pasted over the standard "Blue" wording. Chad Gripp collection

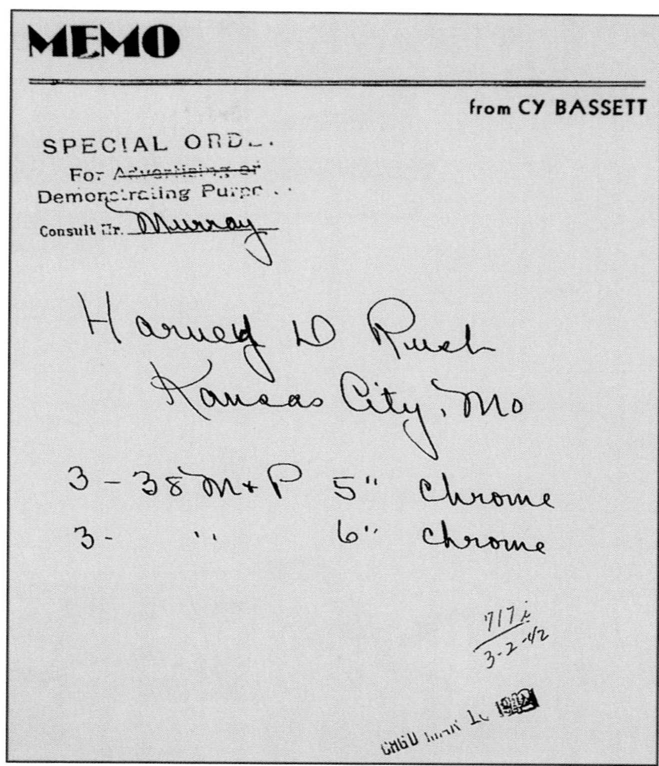
MEMO

from CY BASSETT

SPECIAL ORD...
For ~~Advertising or~~
Demonstrating Purp...
Consult Mr. Murray

Harvey D Rush
Kansas City, Mo

3 - 38 M+P 5" Chrome
3 - " 6" Chrome

3-2-42

558. The notation in the S&W Memo account of a Special Order of 6 M&Ps, 3 with 5" barrels and 3 with 6" barrels, all chrome plated, to be delivered to salesman Harvey D. Rush of Kansas City, Missouri "For Demonstrating Purposes".

The handwritten notation at bottom would seem to indicate that these were shipped on March 2, 1942, just days before all commercial production was halted in favor of war work. Chad Gripp collection

Portions of a factory letter explain the history of this unusual revolver as follows:

> *Smith & Wesson .38 Military & Police Model of 1905 Fourth Change Special Production revolver . . with serial number 611108, was shipped from our factory on September 23, 1960, and delivered to Charles Greenblott, New York City. This revolver is one of a group of 10 revolvers that were produced with 6 inch barrels and chrome plate finish rather than Smith & Wesson's standard nickel finish. These revolvers were originally assembled in 1937 and were used as samples from that date forward. Approximately 6 of the handguns have been recorded to date with the last ones being sold to Mr. Greenblott's company in 1960. From examining the records it appears as these revolvers were originally requested by Smith & Wesson salesman H. D. Rush of Kansas City, MO. Several of these chrome plated samples were shipped to Mr. Rush [in 1938] and then delivered for test and returned to the factory [where they] remained . . until [they were] finally sold in 1960.*

560. Closeup of the bottom of the gold and blue box in which this chrome-plated revolver was shipped, showing serial number written in grease pencil.
Chad Gripp collection

# A Factory Nickel .357 Combat Magnum, with Rare 5" Barrel

561. Left and right side views of a .357 Combat Magnum, serial no. K594899, with target hammer, target trigger, target stocks and rare 5" barrel, in bright nickel finish.

This was a special-order revolver, shipped to Gil Hebard Guns, Inc. of Knoxville, Illinois on August 16, 1965 for delivery to Bob Loveless, the famous knife maker.

Bill Cross collection

# "Pinto" K-Frames

562. Right side view of a Model 65-5 "Pinto", with stainless steel 3" barrel (with full ejector rod shroud) and frame, with the hammer, trigger and cylinder made of conventional steel, the hammer and trigger casehardened and the cylinder blued.

A view of the left side of this revolver appears as fig. 189. Leroy Thompson collection

Occasionally a person will encounter a revolver exhibiting a mix of finishes. These have become known among collectors as "Pintos", after the horse of a similar mix of dark and light. For revolvers, "Pintos" typically have a cylinder and barrel of one finish, say nickel, and the frame of another, usually blue. Some people call a revolver with the nickel frame and blued barrel and cylinder a "reverse Pinto", while others simply lump them all together. Of course you can also have other finishes on "Pintos", another common one being a gold cylinder with a silver-plated barrel and frame.

Some people really like "Pintos", thinking that they are unusual and exotic looking, while the combination of finishes strikes others as gauche and tasteless.

I have always suspected that these actually represent an attempt by the factory to use up a surplus of one type of part. For instance, the factory will frequently use parts that have cosmetic flaws in their nickel-plated revolvers, since the plating can conceal some types of these. If a large supply of such nickeled barrels and cylinders were to become available, rather than scrapping them, something a Yankee concern like Smith & Wesson is unlikely to do at the best of times, they might assemble them into blued frames, thus creating a small series of "Pintos". This also explains why their "reverse Pinto" of blue barrel and cylinder assembled on a nickeled frame is seen much more rarely. (You will note I said these are more rare, not more desirable.)

That gets back to exactly why "Pintos" have such a limited appeal, for to many they seem to represent the worst of everything. After all, until stainless steel revolvers became common, the way to avoid rust and corrosion was to order your revolver nickel-plated overall. As a side issue, for defense guns especially, "Pintos" seem very big when you point them at people, and this can sometimes help encourage your opponent to back down. After all, a gunfight avoided is always better than one chanced, even if won. But if you are worried about your cylinder and barrel corroding, don't you have the same concerns for the frame of your revolver, which holds all those moving parts? I would think so, for rain water, snow and sweat dribbling onto and into your frame is not good for it, and a full-nickel finish will help avoid the problems that can arise due to such exposure.

Similarly, on the "reverse Pinto", where you have a nickeled frame, the same corrosion issues apply, only now on your barrel and cylinder. A little rust on the outside of your revolver frame would actually seem preferable to me than on the inside of your barrel, although obviously neither is good.

Mixing gold- and silver-plated parts seems to me to be more of a cosmetic issue than one associated with preservation, and perhaps standard "Pinto" revolvers likewise represent a matter of appearance rather than reflecting any practical usefulness. As noted, some people simply like the way they look, or like something different from that embraced by the rest of the herd. These individuals seek out "Pinto" revolvers, and have even been known to buy a fully blued and a fully nickel-plated revolver and send them both back to the factory to have the parts swapped out, making one into a "Pinto" and the other into a "reverse Pinto", even though that seems to me to be taking a lot of time and trouble to get the worst of both worlds.

As a collector of K-frames, a person should at least consider having a few "Pintos" in his or her stable. As a practical user, however, whether for self-defense, hunting, or target work (of greater or lesser formality), I would say it's best to pass on them, unless you get a really good deal on the price, as will occur when an example that offers little in the way of practicality is put on the block and there is no one about to bid on it who simply loves them in that irrational fashion that effects us all from time to time, whether with firearms, other things, or other people.

# More on the Saf-T-Lock Mechanism

As noted in the Introduction, shortly after the Saf-T-Hammer Corporation acquired Smith & Wesson in May, 2001, the basic design of most S&W revolvers was modified to include their proprietary internal key-operated safety lock mechanism, which when activated renders the hammer inoperable. As mentioned in Chapter Thirty-Two, the Model 10-14, introduced in 2002, began the era of S&W K-frame revolvers fitted with the internal key-lock system.

The patent for this device had been applied for on April 12, 2001 and granted as no. 6,523,294 on February 25, 2004, in the names of several inventors and assigned to Smith & Wesson.

Excerpts explaining the configuration and function of the mechanism, taken from this rather complex patent, which describes several versions of the basic safety lock and consists of a total of 22 claims and 5 sheets of drawings, read as follows:

> *. . The lockarm actuator **42** is mounted within a bore disposed in the sidewall **78** of the frame **12** adjacent the thumbpiece **28** . . The hammer **34** includes an arcuate slot **80** disposed in the side surface **82** of the hammer **34** positioned adjacent the lockarm **40**. The lock slot **74** . . extends off of*

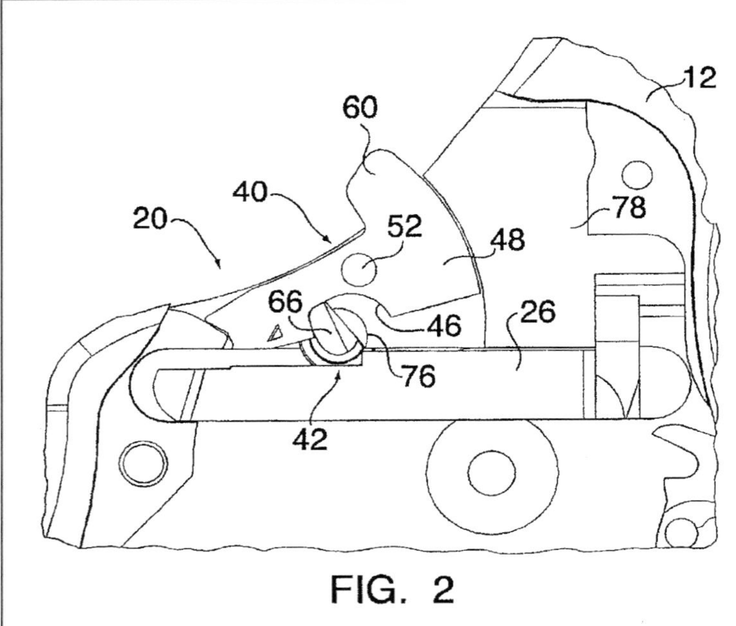


563. Fig. 2 from U.S. patent no. 6,523,294, granted on February 2, 2003, showing the numbered components of the Saf-T-Lock system. U.S. Patent Office

564. Left side closeup of a late DAO Model 67-6, with barrel marked ".38 S&W SPL. + P" (fig. 553). The key for the Saf-T-Lock system is shown lying on the frame.

Note the flag (**60**, fig. 563), is up, and the word "LOCKED" is visible. The flag can be felt by the shooter's thumb, which is helpful in the dark.

The cylinder is loaded with a full six rounds of +P ammunition, but with the Saf-T-Lock mechanism in the locked position as shown, the revolver cannot be fired.

*the arcuate slot **80** of the hammer **34** and the flag **60** resides within the revolver frame **12** adjacent the hammer **34**, out of sight . . When the hammer **34** is drawn back in this condition, the hammer **34** pivots relative to the lockarm **42**, rotating past the hammer post **52** that is disposed within the arcuate slot **80**. In this condition, the revolver can be fired without obstruction from the lockarm **40**.*

*To actuate the safety lock mechanism **20** into the safety-on condition (as shown in [patent] FIG. 2), the operator rotates the lockarm actuator **42** clockwise using a [key]. When the lockarm actuator **42** is rotated clockwise, the cam lobe **66** engages the cam surface **46** of the lockarm **40** causing the lockarm to pivot about the pivot post **56**. The cam **66** rotates the lockarm **40** an amount sufficient to move the hammer post **52** out of the arcuate slot **80** and into the aligned lock slot **74**. At the same time, the rotation of the lockarm **40** causes the flag **60** to rise out of the revolver frame **12** into a visible position. In the safety-on condition, the cam **66** and cam surface **46** cooperate with each other in such a way that the lockarm **40** is prevented from being moved into the frame **12**; i.e., pushing downward on the flag **60** binds the cam lobe **66** into contact with the cam surface **46**. In the safety-on and -off positions, this . . safety lock mechanism **20** does not interact with or obstruct the cylinder release bar **26**. As a result, the cylinder **14** can be opened and closed, thereby allowing the operator to inspect the cylinder for ammunition cartridges . .*

*Chapter Thirty-Four*

# Competition for the M&P

## Other U.S. Armsmakers

### Colt's, of Course

565. Left side view of a Colt Official Police, the main M&P competitor before WWII.

For many years the Colt Army Special, introduced in 1908 and later renamed the Official Police, constituted the main competition for the Smith & Wesson M&P revolver, but there have been many other competitors, both of American and foreign origin, and a brief review of these serves once again to underscore the remarkable "staying power" of the M&P.

### Harrington & Richardson

From U.S. makers other than Colt's, some early competition came from Harrington & Richardson, with their line of inexpensive top-break revolvers. However these shot only .38 Smith & Wesson loads, not Specials, so it seems their competitive impact was pretty minimal. No doubt some watchmen and homeowners would buy them, taking the position that they were .38s, after all, and cheaper than a Smith & Wesson, much less a Colt, which always seemed to be slightly more expensive; but at least such buyers were not being misled about what they were buying.

# Sturm, Ruger & Co.

566. Left and right side views of the Ruger Security Six with 6" barrel, in .357 Magnum caliber, a main competitor of the S&W M19/M66 series in the 1970s.

In the postwar era, competition from Colt's continued, but with less impact as the years went by, but then a new major U. S. armsmaker, Sturm, Ruger & Co., came to take their place.

William Ruger, one of the company's founders and a very savvy designer, had never shown much interest in self-defense weapons initially, but in the late 1960s, Ruger finally got into producing weapons for defensive work. Their first such revolver was called the Security Six or Speed Six, depending on the type of sights fitted – adjustable or fixed. These were clearly designed to compete with the K-frame, being about the same size.

Designed for cost-effective manufacture by making extensive use of quality investment castings, Rugers were relatively cheap to produce, perhaps a bit thick, with grips that were not too good. Still, they were strong and accurate, and no doubt provided stiff competition to the Smith & Wesson K-frame line. Later their GP series, which was even thicker and heavier, if perhaps stronger, was less competitive against the K-frames except in terms of price.

As discussed in Chapter Thirty-Six, military versions of .38 Special Ruger double-action revolvers called the "Service Six" (with square butt) and the "SS84-L (with semi-round butt), and the .357 Magnum caliber "GS32-N", were used by the U.S. military, and were featured alongside 2" and 4" S&W Model 10s in the Army TM 9-1005-206-14&P-1, issued in August, 1985 (fig. 624).

Ruger revolvers still offer competition and they are a little cheaper, perhaps, but they are "so heavy and so thick" that they lack the nimble feel you get with a K-frame Smith & Wesson.

# The Legacy of the Spanish Counterfeits

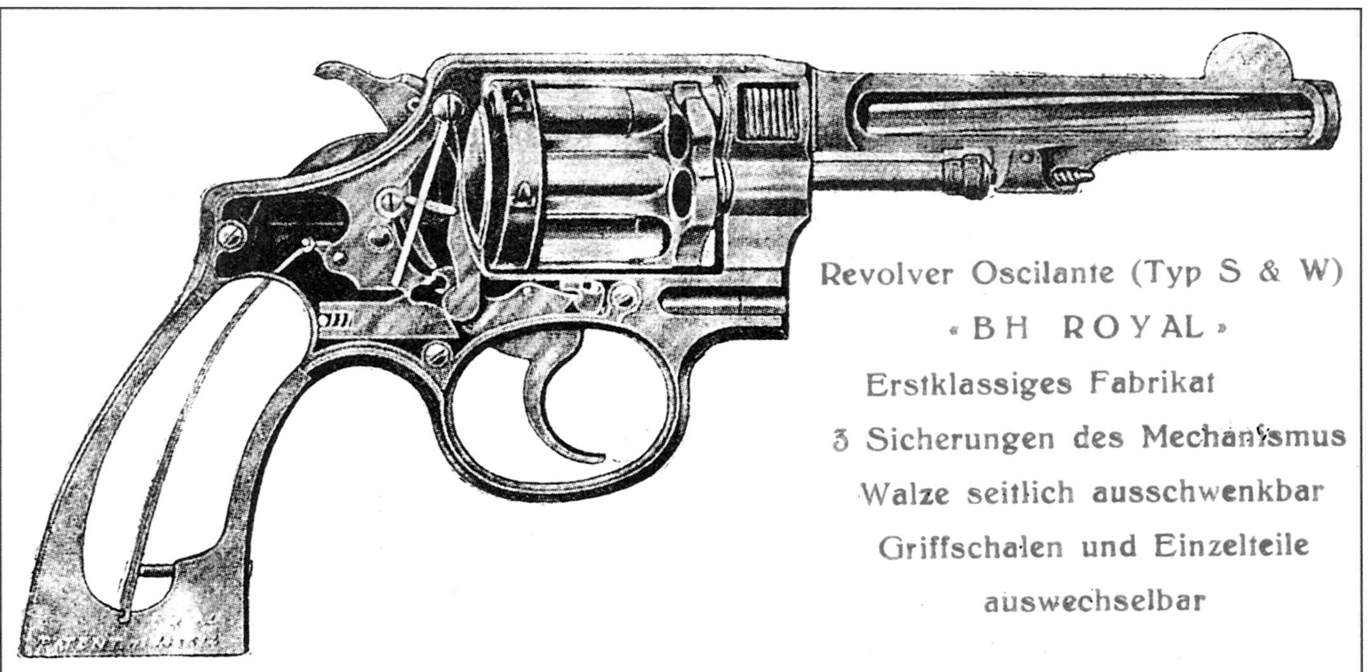


567. A cutaway drawing of the action of the "Type S&W Royal" revolver as made and marketed by Beistegui Hermanos of Eibar, Spain. Received by the H. P. White Laboratories on March 26, 1931.

The German legend reads "First class manufacture, 3 mechanism safeties, side-swing cylinder - stocks and single parts interchangeable". Gaston Comeau collection

Most competitors were content to let their products stand on their own merits, unlike the Spanish arms industry which, under the urging of several unscrupulous U.S. importers, did their utmost to copy the S&W product as exactly as possible in the years after WWI. This story is told in detail in Chapter Twenty-Eight.

These cheap counterfeits were popular with many, despite the efforts of Smith & Wesson to stem the tide, and Spanish copies of M&P revolvers are still commonly seen to this day. A friend of mine who runs a local gun store always has stories of the countless old ladies who keep bringing in their deceased husbands' revolvers to sell. Many of these men had only one revolver, and most of these are Spanish M&P copies, now almost 90 years old. They are typically still loaded with lead bullets, growing

TELEGRAMMES: BEISTEGUI-EIBAR

CODES: ABC 5th Ed. impr.d / BENTLEY / RUDOLF MOSSE

MAR 26 1931

MARQUES DEPOSÉES:
ROYAL
LIBIA
BULWARK
PARAMOUNT

BEISTEGUI HERMANOS

FABRIQUE D'ARMES
DE GRANDE PRÈCISION

EIBAR (ESPAGNE)
APARTADO 33

RECEIVED
H.P. WHITE LABORATORY

LISTE D'EXPORTATION N.° 30

568 (right). The cover of Catalog No. 30 from Beistegui Hermanos of Eibar, Spain, makers of the Royal line of S&W copies as well as arms marketed under various other brand names. Gaston Comeau collection

569. The letterhead of J. L. Galef & Son, Inc., of New York City.

The distinctive helm-and-target crest at left, which as noted here was registered as a trademark with the U.S. Patent Office, is seen on the side of a Spanish import (fig. 300) and in a U.S. catalog listing (fig. 299).

Despite the ruling against them in the S&W lawsuit of 1922 (Chapter Twenty-Eight), Galef continued to do business for many years thereafter. This letter is dated August 27, 1957, while Galef was acting as importers of the BSA Royal Line of high-powered bolt-action hunting rifles.

Gaston Comeau collection

green with age, and may or may not work properly. Frequently clicking them a few times will snap the mainspring, which has crystalized over the years. Such revolvers are worthless for any legitimate purpose and are likely not worth $10.00 even to someone who wants to commit a crime with an untraceable weapon. Most people I know buy them and keep them around until the next sponsored "weapon buyback", when they get $100 for each one they turn in, which they then donate to the NRA Institute for Legislative Action to fight anti-gun laws.

The Spanish maker Astra made revolvers in the postwar era which provided more legitimate competition. While a lot better than they had been in 1920s, these were still not up to the Smith & Wesson standard, so unless you just had to have a new low-cost revolver that looked a lot like a Smith & Wesson, but did not plan on shooting it much, you would likely pass on the Astra.

# Belgian Revolvers

The Belgian manufacturers were initially much like the Spanish, although they were not so blatant in their efforts to deceive, and the metal and workmanship were better. However, most of their pre-WWII designs were obviously foreign, and did not really offer any serious competition to Smith & Wesson. I have no doubt they sold well in Latin America and other areas of the world, but certainly no one would confuse them with a Smith & Wesson.

Most were offered in odd European chamberings or at best .38 Smith & Wesson (not Special), so few were sold in the United States. A lot of those seen today are pocket pistols, not the belt gun size of the M&P, and were imported prior to 1914. They were cheaper than equivalent U.S.-made products, and were aimed at the man or woman who wanted an inexpensive, small-sized handgun to carry with them.

The bigger belt-sized Belgian revolvers might have been used by some watchmen who wanted to buy the cheapest possible weapon but, at least in the United States, it seems these weapons are pretty rare. I think those who fell into this category of buyer tended to go with the Spanish imitations previously discussed.

In more recent years Fabrique Nationale Herstal (FN), which had been marketing Browning-designed semi-automatic pistols since 1899, introduced their Barracuda revolver (fig. 208), designed to compete for police sales in Europe during the time when the revolver (especially a three-inch .357 Magnum version) was considered the ultimate police weapon, thanks to the influence of Raymond Sasia and the French police. While it was in production the FN Barracuda was undoubtedly a fine revolver which would undersell a comparable Smith & Wesson in Europe.

# French Revolvers

## A Trio of "Sasia Guns"

570. A trio of .357 Magnum caliber "Sasia guns", all with 3" barrels and fixed sights.
Left: the Manurhin MR 73. A sectioned drawing of the action of this revolver appears in fig. 210.
Right: the later Manurhin MR88 (fig. 211). Both of these are excellent police revolvers.
Below: an S&W Combat Magnum (Model 19) with fixed sights, the arm that Raymond Sasia acquired for élite units of the French police.

571. Left side view of a Manurhin MR73 with 5¼" barrel and full underlug, adjustable sights and ergonomic grip, as used by the French counterterrorist unit GIGN.

The French revolver business was pretty much a government monopoly, although it seems that commercial *Modèle* 1892 revolvers were also made. However it would not appear that these offered any real competition to the M&P, their sales being aimed at the French-speaking market around the world. Excellent revolvers in themselves, and quite innovative in many aspects, the cartridge was pretty dismal and unlikely to attract anyone in the United Sates except as a souvenir of their time in France.

More recently, however, the French had become very taken with the revolver. While it is true that followers of French Police Commissioner Raymond Sasia bought fixed-sight three-inch .357 Magnum Smith & Wessons (fig. 595), they soon wanted to get French-made revolvers of a similar type. They did so with the excellent Manurhin MR73 and later MR88 revolvers, which were well made, and designed every bit as well as a Smith & Wesson.

The only thing that saved the day was that their production capacity was low, and it seems they did not know how to market their products successfully in the U.S.

# The British Webleys

The British firm of Webley & Scott Ltd. made excellent weapons, and marketed them all over the world. Prior to the turn of the century, Webley revolvers of the R.I.C. (Royal Irish Constabulary) class were well known and well regarded in the United States, although not inexpensive. Offering a short barrel, double-action trigger pull, and chambered for .45 caliber projectiles, these were small but pretty serious weapons. Even the late expert Jeff Cooper, as few as 40 years ago, thought the Webley R.I.C. was a "great gun", far superior to a .38 Chiefs Special for a pocket gun. General Custer carried a pair of them at the Little Big Horn (a lot of good they did him), and many others also liked Webley products, which were well made out of good materials.

No doubt they initially offered serious competition to Smith & Wesson products in the United States and all over the world, but the English determination to stay with a top-break design when after the mid-1890s it was obvious that the solid-frame side-ejector was the wave of the future, no doubt impacted on the Webley's ability to compete.

In addition, the top-break .38 revolver could not take the longer .38 Special cartridge, and even though the advent of smokeless powder meant it was not really necessary to have such a long case, I think it would have been a hard sell to convince a lot of people that a top-break was strong enough to handle the pressure levels of the more powerful .38 Special ammunition. No doubt this would have been done but Webley, exhausted by two World Wars and harassed by new restrictive laws that ultimately destroyed their home market, chose not to compete in the belt gun market as far as the United States was concerned. They of course continued to produce lots of .38 caliber top-break revolvers for law enforcement and personal defense use all over the British colonial world throughout the period of the M&P, until they finally succumbed to English trade unionism and socialism and went out of the revolver business completely in the late 1960s. Until then, however, Webley was a serious competitor to the Smith & Wesson M&P revolver, except in the United States.

## Surplus Webleys and Enfields Popular with U.S. Watchmen

As an aside, .38 caliber English revolvers of Webley or Enfield make became very popular in the security guard field in lots of places in the United States in the post-WWII era. Many watchmens' organizations were limited to .38 revolvers for arming their officers. Whether purchased by the company or the individual watchman, war-surplus .38 Webley or Enfield revolvers which sold for $14.95 in the late 1950s and early 1960s qualified as .38s, and could be used. A friend of mine who ran such a business bought 50 of them just for this purpose. Surplus ammunition was also cheap, and so he saved a lot of money over buying new Smith & Wesson M&P .38 revolvers, or even surplus ones that cost $29.95 at that time. I will admit that the first time I saw his officers armed with Enfield double-action-only .38 revolvers, I was a little surprised.

Similarly, these surplus English revolvers were serious competitors for the M&P with many homeowners and grocery store and gas station operators, who just wanted a cheap .38 revolver for the cash drawer or bedside table. At least they were a lot better than the Spanish revolvers that had filled that role 30 to 40 years earlier, even if the loadings were not great.

# Surplus European Ordnance Revolvers

Speaking of the 1950 - 1960 time frame, many other European ordnance revolvers came into the United States as surplus during that time which offered competition to the Smith & Wesson M&P. While most were bought by collectors of military weapons, some no doubt were purchased in lieu of an M&P revolver. Many of these were well made, in great condition, and were in chamberings which, if odd, could be used with surprising effectiveness. I tested most of these revolvers in my book *The 100 Greatest Combat Handguns*, and found that many are really quite good. If you were stuck in some backwater area or during a period when it might be difficult to get current-production American-made weapons, you could certainly find such things as Dutch 9.8mm, Italian 10mm, German or French 10mm Ordnance revolvers, or even 7.5mm Swedish or 7.62mm Russian service revolvers. Many of these were easily obtained due to various legal issues, and curiously none of them seems to have posed much of a threat to the so-called "lawful authorities", who are often inclined to allow the sale of such oddities even while devoting themselves to violating many civil rights. No doubt when they were available via mail order in the U.S. prior to 1968, people who might well have been better served with a heavy-barrel M10 bought them as their home or business defense gun in order to save money. And I have no doubt that even today in some places where a pre-1898 "antique" revolver can be obtained without the government "permission slip", they still offer some competition to the whole K-frame line. Such buyers are likely to be few in number in the 21st century, but the number of sales lost prior to 1968 to these imported former military revolvers might well have been substantial, given my recollection about how hard it was to buy new Smith & Wesson K-frame revolvers, at least of the more interesting variations (not bread-and-butter M10s) in the 1960 - 1968 period. Good Smith & Wesson revolvers were always hard to locate, and always brought list price or more in my neck of the woods.

# Competition from Rossi and Taurus

572 (below). Left side view of a modern Taurus revolver, chambered for hot .38 Special +P ammunition.

The late Kent Lomont,who routinely shot hundreds of thousands of rounds every year from his many handguns, certainly got more than his money's worth under the Taurus "unlimited lifetime warranty" policy.

In more recent times it seems the Latin American revolver manufacturers are becoming the major S&W competitors, only this time they speak Portuguese, not Spanish. Rossi and Taurus, both Brazilian manufacturers, started out making fairly poor-quality copies (but at least obviously marked – those 1920s lawsuits were still doing some good, it seems).

During this period Taurus and Rossi introduced lines of Brazilian-made K-frame competitors. Early examples were not much and represented little real challenge except at the lowest level of buyers, but while Rossi never got very good, Taurus improved and managed to turn out some pretty good products. Maybe not quite up to Smith & Wesson standards, but likely 90% as good at perhaps 75% of the cost, which represented a real saving for many, especially if they needed to buy a lot of weapons and did not intend to shoot them a lot.

# Other Modern European Competitors

Competition also came from Germany, where some revolvers, such as the Korth, were incredibly expensive and well-made while others were much cheaper and often of low quality. Similar Italian-made competitors were found not to be of sufficient quality to compete with Smith & Wesson. Over in Czechoslovakia (later the Czech Republic), K-frame competitors were also made, although these were also not really of a quality to go toe-to-toe with the Smith & Wesson product. Further, until the fall of communism, they could not be imported into the U.S. without a high duty on them, rendering them little threat to Smith & Wesson for domestic sales, although elsewhere in the world they could be competitive.

# Summing Up: the Competition Today

Today, in the early years of the 21st century Colt's is pretty much gone, of course, and competition from Europe is pretty thin, it seems to me, since the French are mainly out of the revolver business, as are the Germans, except for some very high-end products which remain prohibitively expensive.

Revolver production continues in the Czech Republic, but these are not inexpensive, while Astra has closed its production line and so has FN, as regards revolvers.

If price is a determining factor, a person is better to look to something in the Taurus line from Brazil. I would prefer a used but not abused Smith & Wesson to a new Taurus, myself, but some people do not like to buy used handguns or used cars, and for them a new, lower-priced Taurus might well be a good choice. However, on the resale market you will no doubt get out of your Smith & Wesson at least what you put into it, and get it faster.

As they used to say in years past in the Packard automobile advertisements, "ask the man who owns one", and so it is with the Smith & Wesson K-frame revolver.

*Chapter Thirty-Five*

# Famous Users

As might be expected with a weapon made in the millions that has been popular for over 100 years, during which time many wars were fought and much exploration done, target shooting with handguns blossomed into a very popular sport, and crime reached heights unknown in prior centuries, the Smith & Wesson M&P has been used by many interesting individuals. Some of these people are more well-known than others: some are famous for deeds that they performed with their revolvers, while others may have simply been armed with an M&P when something momentous occurred nearby. Some may be well known only for the ill deeds that they perpetrated, or because they were associated with others even more infamous than themselves.

It is of course impossible to discuss all of these noted individuals, and readers would no doubt differ if asked to make their own selection, meaning that someone I might consider an interesting user you might not.

Similarly, someone who was well known in a certain locale might be virtually unheard of a few hundred miles away, while someone famous at one time may long ago have faded into obscurity, and today's well-known M&P users (should many remain) may be forgotten before this book goes into a second printing.

Still, there were some famous people whose reputations have become inextricably associated with the mid-frame Smith & Wesson revolver, and it may be interesting just to consider this issue and see where and in whose hands this famous Smith & Wesson product has shown up over the years. After all, you are known by your companions, as mothers often say, and so it is to a degree with your choice of weapon.

## Elmer Keith

In his classic book *Sixguns* Elmer Keith tells the wonderful "Chink Noodle Shop" story, which involved an M&P carried by a police officer named Martin. The year seems to have been 1924. The young Elmer was riding his horse along the main drag in Helena, Montana, the state capital, when he was hailed by his friend Officer Martin, a policeman on the local force, who wanted to show Elmer his new M&P Target model 6-inch .38 Special revolver. When asked what Keith thought of his new acquisition, Keith replied that he thought the caliber too light for defense work.

Just as it was handed back to Martin a young man ran up, breathlessly reporting "a holdup at the Chink Noodle Shop". Officer Martin announced, "Well, I guess this is it", and ran to the shop while Keith followed along. Keith sat outside the shop on his horse as Martin went in, and shots were fired. A bullet from the bandit (wielding a top-break .32) came through the window. Another hit Officer Martin in the shirt, and was stopped by his notebook. Martin emptied his M&P into the bandit's chest, who was carried alive but injured from the shop.

Keith noted that the poor stopping power of the M&P .38 was confirmed by the outcome of this incident, concluding that one shot from a heavily-loaded .44 or .45 would have terminated the whole affair.

## J. Henry Fitzgerald

As everyone knows, "Fitz" was a staunch Colt man, and the only reason he appears here is because of the following story he relates in the book he self-published in 1930 entitled *Shooting*. The story concerns a gunfight wherein the make of the arm used by the lawman involved is not mentioned (inferring that it might well have been a Smith & Wesson, because had it been a Colt, Fitz would probably have included this detail).

The story, in Fitzgerald's own words, is as follows:

> . . *An old friend of mine, in relating a gun fight which he had with a colored man whom he was trying to arrest, said: "Well, Fitz, you know I never could hit one of those darn targets, but I hit this bird three times and that's the first three shots I ever fired that were all in the black."*

Actually, Fitzgerald says quite a number of things about guns and gunfighting in his interesting and informative book that are well worth keeping in mind, regardless of the make of gun used. The following brief excerpt is just one example among many:

> . . *It is true that the men who settled the West were not target shots and the eastern standard seems to measure all men by their ability to hit a target. The old gun fighter would give a sorry exhibition at this kind of shooting, and sadder still would be the story of a target shooter meeting one of the quick-draw artists at a distance of six to ten feet. There is only one answer to this; the target man would be killed before he knew what it was all about. In target work men shoot for pleasure and in quick draw and protection work they shoot for keeps . . When guns are used the fastest man wins; single or double action, the loser is dead just the same . .*

# A. L. A. Himmelwright

About the same time Elmer Keith was evaluating Officer Martin's M&P, a book on handguns titled *Pistol and Revolver Shooting* by one of the leading firearms writers of the early 1900s, A. L. A. Himmelwright, was already going into multiple printings. In this book Himmelwright recognized that the M&P was an excellent target revolver, noting with enthusiasm that it was capable of 10-shot 1 ½ -inch groups at 50 yards.

He also expressed appreciation for it being an excellent police revolver, far superior to the various top-break .32s and .38s commonly in use by many urban police officers in the pre-WWI era. Himmelwright's endorsement of the M&P continued in various editions of his book from 1904 through the last printing in the late 1930s.

# Ed McGivern

As discussed beginning on page 62, the most interesting user of the M&P revolver during the 1930s was undoubtedly Ed McGivern (fig. 61). He of course needs no introduction to readers even today, famed as he was for awe-inspiring feats of speed- and aerial-shooting, mostly conducted with target-sighted M&P revolvers with which he set many multiple target records that remain unbroken to this day, and in fact are unlikely ever to be broken.

## A Letter to Doug Wesson

From his home in Lewistown, Montana, Ed McGivern wrote a letter to S&W vice-president Douglas B. Wesson dated May 25, 1932, right in the worst part of the Depression, which is interesting on a number of levels. The handwritten original has been overwritten and is rather hard to read, so the text is reproduced as follows:

> *Dear Doug:*
>
> *Please find enclosed $146.46 for Six Revolvers at $24.41 each for my shooting class - This extra equipment makes the whole department fully armed with S&W .38 spl target revolvers. As they had 4 of the .38 revolvers, we are adding 4 more and we now have K-22s for practice and we are adding 2 more, so the list calls for*

573. A photograph captioned "Ed McGivern's Lewistown Montana Police Shooting Team". These were the men for whom McGivern was ordering the revolvers mentioned in his letter to Douglas Wesson.

Officer Frank Barrow is at far right, but the names of the other members of the team are not available.

574. Left and right side views of one of Ed McGivern's .38 Special target model M&Ps.

Note the King gold bead front sight, and the special carved target stocks with his name incorporated in the oak leaf design on the right grip.

NRA National Firearms Museum collection

575. Right side view of a .38 Special M&P target model, serial no. 642741, with 6 inch barrel and McGivern gold bead front sight. As described in the factory letter, below, this was one of the revolvers shipped to Ed McGivern in response to his letter to Douglas Wesson, which is reproduced here. Jim Fisher collection

*2 - K-22 target revolvers with McGivern sights*
*4 - 38 Special M&P square butt target Revolvers McGivern Sight and 6-inch barrels*

*Making the 6 guns for which the money orders are inclosed. Send them as soon as you can get them inspected and ready. I am trying to develop a real five-man police team and believe I have some excellent material.*

*Now I owe your firm yet for one K-22 on my own account that I have not been quite able to take care of yet so I want your consideration just a little further.*

*I need one more K-22 for myself. Will you send it C.O.D. separate from above order or will you trust me to send you the money for it immediately after receipt of it. In that case it could be shipped with the others if sent on open account. I have quite a little money coming in during June with which I'll clear up the old K-22 charge and clean the slate.*

Mr. Jim Fisher
Box 474
Vaughn, MT 59487-0474

Springfield Mass December 26, 2012

Dear Mr. Fisher:

The revolver you inquired about is the .38 Military & Police Model. This model was introduced in 1899 and designed to fire the .38 S&W Special cartridges. It has been in continued production since it was originally introduced. However, during the past years, many design changes have been made to this model to improve the revolver's function. The collector has classified all of the improvements which occurred before 1945.

Your revolver is classified as the .38 Military & Police Model of 1905 Fourth Change. This modification occurred in 1915 and was produced until 1942 with a total production of 758,297 revolvers. These revolvers were produced between serial numbers 241000 and 1000000 of the .38 Hand Ejector series. The current production model of this series is known as the Model 10.

We have researched your Smith & Wesson .38 Military & Police Model of 1905 Fourth Change Target, caliber .38 S&W Special, revolver in company records which indicate that your handgun, with serial number 642741 was shipped from our factory on June 2, 1932, and delivered to Ed McGivern, Lewistown, MT. The records indicate that this revolver was shipped with a 6 inch barrel equipped with a McGivern gold bead front sight, adjustable rear target sight, blue finish, and checkered walnut grips. This shipment was for 4 units of the .38 M&P targets serial number 642715, 642736, 642749 & 642741. Also included in this shipment was 2 K-22 Outdoorsman serial numbers 639539 & 639607. All these revolvers were in the same configuration and they were billed at $22.19 each. Enclosed is a copy of the original invoice.

We hope that this information is helpful to you.

Sincerely,
SMITH & WESSON

Roy G. Jinks
Historian

576 (right). Factory letter authenticating the above .38 Special M&P target model as being shipped to Ed McGivern on June 2, 1932, and listing the other .38 and .22 revolvers that were shipped on the same date. Jim Fisher collection

*Doug I want two pair of Ivory Handles, one pair for K-22 and one pair for 38 M&P square butt target revolver. You could send me a bill for these or send them C.O.D. just as you wish - would like them by middle of June at latest. If possible put S&W medallions on them. Just like you did in the other pair, they look swell, and I want the medallions on all guns that I have and use. I'm just a little proud of them.*

*The new 38 gun came to hand and promises some excellent results. I put in a stronger trigger spring and it promises to be pretty fast.*

*I don't want to impose on you old Pal, but I'll surely appreciate it if you'll send that other K-22 and let me send you the money later, I just don't have the $24.41 to spare just now for a few days.*

*Hathaway of Am. Rifleman wrote me some time ago that he felt quite sure my article would come out in July issue, you might get in touch with him about the advertising, if any, you wish to run in the same issue.*

*By the way Doug how about getting out a small booklet on flying target shooting with revolvers and super speed revolver work. Double action shooting etc. I have some wonderful material on hand and Outdoor Life is going to give me the culs used in the article, so perhaps you and I could cooperate and get this out as an advertising feature for your guns. I've had hundreds of calls for such a book. I'd like to help you out with the material for the booklet and I'll guarantee you I'll be very reasonable with you with the entire matter as I very much appreciate your cooperation. The shooting public will grab it up and S&W arms will be a real topic of conversation at all points, let me hear from you promptly please.*

*Sincerely Yours, Ed McGivern*

## More on Ed McGivern's Amazing Feats

Perhaps McGivern's most famous feat involved using serial no. 640792, a standard 6-inch M&P Target .38 Special revolver, to fire 5 shots into a group easily covered by a man's hand in 2/5ths of a second. A truly amazing performance, and a fine illustration of what the M&P, any M&P, was capable of doing.

McGivern frequently wrote of his experiences and techniques, making it clear that he used "stock" M&P revolvers, and attributing his successes to their superior double-action pull. He could do amazing things with his M&P revolvers, and the clear message was that anyone who wished to do the same could at least get the same equipment with which to start on their quest to equal his feats. If you had an M&P and could not get at least close to his level of performance, it was not the weapon that kept you from your goal – it was your skill level.

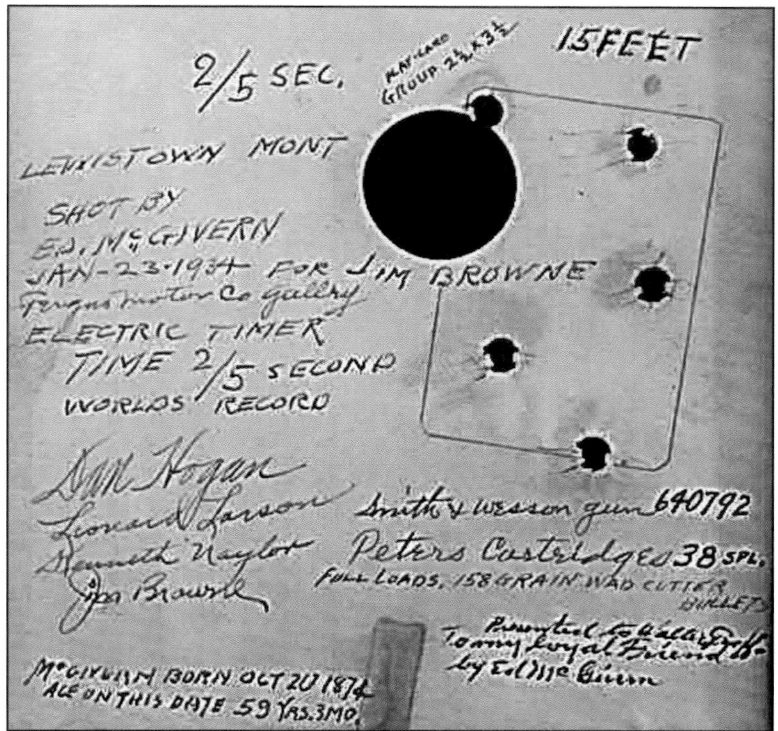


577. The actual target, covered with eyewitness attestations, shot by Ed McGivern in his amazing feat of firing five rounds into a group the size of a playing card in 2/5ths of a second, using Peters .38 Special cartridges fired in S&W target M&P serial no. 640792.

As noted, this was, and remains, a world's record.

578. Left and right side views of a 2" M&P modified for pocket carry, with gold bead front sight and bobbed hammer, checkered on top, owned by Ed McGivern.
NRA National Firearms Museum collection

# Smith & Wessons in Hollywood

During the later 1930s, movie stars in Hollywood were frequently known for their hunting trips and the arms they carried and used. Smith & Wesson .357 Magnums were of course the prestige weapons, and it is known that Gary Cooper, James Stewart, and Clark Gable all owned them. But Clark Gable was truly a hunter, and not just going through the motions to improve his image. He also owned a K-22, serial no. 126131, a 6-inch blued example. Anyone serious about shooting handguns should have a K-22 or its equivalent. Perhaps he taught Carole Lombard to shoot with it!

# Hermann Göring

During WWII, of course, hundreds of thousands of M&P revolvers were put to use. Perhaps the most interesting wartime user of the M&P was *Luftwaffe Reichsmarschall* Hermann Göring. Fat and decadent-looking, addicted to drugs and a fanatical follower of the morally bankrupt political, ethical and economic policies of Adolf Hitler, Göring had nevertheless been a much-decorated flying ace during WWI, and had taken over as the last commander of von Richtofen's Flying Circus after the Red Baron was killed in action in 1918. Göring was also an avid hunter and shooter.

Interestingly, with all of the German weapons available to him, Johnson and Lockhoven report in Volume I of their excellent two-volume reference *International Armament* that when Göring surrendered to troops of the American 36th Division at

579. Left side view of the 4-inch blued M&P revolver, serial no. 642357, which Herrmann Göring surrendered to troops of the American 36th Division at Radolstadt, Austria, on May 9, 1945.
West Point Museum collection, photo by the author

Radolstadt, Austria, on May 9, 1945, he was armed with a 4-inch blued M&P revolver, serial no. 642357, which had been shipped to a dealer in Germany in 1934.

This revolver, along with Göring's Marshal's baton and some other personal artifacts, is today on display at the West Point Museum.

# Col. Rex Applegate

During WWII, then-Captain Rex Applegate developed close-quarter battle courses in armed and unarmed combat for the U.S. Army. He was recruited by "Wild" Bill Donovan to run the OSS "School for Spies and Assassins" at a secluded location in Maryland, which is now known as the Camp David Presidential Retreat. During the war he also served for a time as the personal bodyguard to FDR.

As shown in fig. 336, Smith & Wesson thought so highly of Col. Applegate that in 1946 they gave him the only K-22 target revolver ever produced with fixed sights and a 2" barrel, serial no. 657624.

Later he was the source and inspiration for several of the characters used by Ian Fleming in his highly successful series of James Bond novels.

One of Applegate's own books, titled *Kill or Get Killed - A Manual of Hand-to-Hand Fighting*, first published in 1943, was reprinted in 1976 as Fleet Marine Reference Publication (FMFRP) 12-80.

After the war, Applegate wrote an interesting account detailing his involvement with the Mexican arms industry, which is excerpted as follows:

## *The Smith & Wesson Mexican Connection*

*My association with Smith & Wesson goes back to my boyhood some 65 years ago. During my teens I had a .22/32 Kit Gun. My father, a Deputy Sheriff, carried a .32 Hand Ejector. My uncle Gus Peret, the famous Remington-Peters Exhibition Shooter, favored S&W Model 3, single-action revolvers. I have four of his Model 3 revolvers in my collection. The rarest is a .38 Special, made on order for him by Douglas Wesson, who was a good friend. After entering the regular Army in 1940, I maintained my interest in Smith & Wessons and was fortunate by means of my assignments to become closely associated with officials at the Smith & Wesson plant during the WWII period.*

*In my capacity as Chief of the Combat Section at the Military Intelligence Training Center, Camp Ritchie, Maryland, I became very well acquainted with Dave Murray who was the sales manager; C. R. Hellstrom who was the plant superintendent; Harold Austin, who later became sales manager; and Fred Miller, who succeeded Austin during the sixties . .*

*Due to my "factory connection" I was able to secure several special handguns that I treasure. One was an M&P [sic] Model with a 2 inch barrel in .22 caliber that is still in my collection [fig. 336].*

*. . While in Europe I acquired a combat associated disability which forced my retirement from the regular Army in 1945. It was recommended by the military surgeons that I retire to a high, dry, warm place. Fortunately, I was able to do so in Mexico because of friendship with another Colonel, who had previously lived in Mexico City and was also about to retire. This particular Colonel was well connected. His father-in-law was one of the wealthiest Mexican bankers and he secured the rights to assemble Nash automobiles in the country. I was invited to participate in this venture in the capacity of service manager.*

*In the fall of 1945, I left for Mexico City, established residence and helped in the organization of this new venture. However, my first love was still firearms and I was hopeful that, by some means, I would be able to get into the Mexican firearms business. Fortunately, due to my connections with [Dave] Murray, I was offered the opportunity to sell, in Mexico, 2,000 Military & Police revolvers. This was the .38 Hand Ejector, 6 inch barrel Target Model with a high front sight and a gold bead (since called the Mexican Model). Dave Murray advised me that I could have the first option to sell these revolvers. The factory was proceeding to produce the new [short action] K Model and it was not deemed desirable to sell the older models in the U.S. domestic market.*

*. . In Mexico, as in the U.S. and everywhere else, there was a great scarcity of commercial model firearms due to the wartime shortages [and] it seemed that selling them was not going to be a problem.*

580. Col. Rex Applegate, in a photograph taken after his return from Mexico to the United States in 1963.

While living in Mexico, Applegate imported 2,000 S&W "Mexican Model" long-action, target-sighted M&P revolvers (fig. 403) for sale in that country.

*. . The Mexican War Dept. was in charge of the issuance of import licenses of firearms. As is inevitable in Latin countries and certainly in Mexico at that time, it was necessary . . to be sure that the Mexican General issuing the license was also remunerated.*

*. . In any event, the 2,000 revolvers were subsequently imported in lots and distributed throughout the country [and] the final importation of all these arms resulted in a very sizeable commission as my share of the proceeds. This "stake" enabled me to get in the Mexican Arms business.*

*Shortly thereafter, I left Nash and entered into partnership with Frank Sanborn, a prominent American businessman in Mexico City. We formed a sales company called "Cia Importada Mexicana" to represent various U.S. arms and ammunition companies and allied lines. This company operated successfully representing S&W, High Standard, Remington, H&R, Peters and other al-*

*lied lines until the middle 1950s when a new Mexican government came into power and a 100% import duty was placed on all firearms. This resulted in my organization of an arms manufacturing and assembly company called "Armamex" which operated until the early 1960s. By this time, another regime and President had taken over and all gun stores were later permanently closed and their inventories confiscated by the Mexican government.*

*. . In 1962, due to the domestic turmoil taking place in the U.S., I was asked by the U.S. Army to act as a consultant in the riot control field. This factor combined with family matters caused a permanent change of residence back to the U.S. in 1963. I have always felt that S&W was the company basically responsible for my initial success in entering the arms business in Mexico and many subsequent favorable happenings during my somewhat varied career.*

# George H. W. Bush

Much more common and not nearly as interesting was the 4-inch Victory Model carried by George Herbert Walker Bush as an 18-year-old Naval aviator when he was shot down in 1945. He lost this revolver to a sailor aboard the submarine which rescued him, who later returned it to him after he became President.

# Bill Jordan

After the end of WWII, when civilian production was resumed, the M&P started to replace Colt revolvers as the police standard in many areas. In 1955, Bill Jordan, the noted U. S. Border Patrolman, met Carl Hellstrom, then the president of Smith & Wesson, at Camp Perry that year.

Jordan's concern about the M&P was the same one that Elmer Keith had mentioned so many years earlier to Officer Martin on the dusty streets of Helena, Montana – namely, lack of stopping power. Jordan suggested that the M&P be chambered for the .357 Magnum cartridge to get better stopping power in over-the-counter ammunition. He also suggested the encased ejector lug, to give a better forward balance to the weapon. Hellstrom embraced this concept, and presented K-frame "Combat Magnum" serial no. K260001 to Jordan in appreciation for his inspiration. Jordan in turn took the gun on the then-popular TV show *You Asked For It*, calling it "the answer to a peace officer's dream". And so it became for many in law enforcement over the next two or three decades.

# Eleanor Roosevelt

Eleanor Roosevelt, former First Lady (and left-wing troublemaker in the eyes of many), had a concealed carry permit authorizing her to carry her M&P revolver as she traveled, out of fear of attacks by members of the KKK or similar organizations who did not appreciate her political views. Certainly a much cheaper approach to ex-First Lady security for the taxpayers than we have today! Even if you do not appreciate her political positions, you cannot fault her choice of revolver.

# Dot Lind

Dot Lind, the distaff side of the famous Lind Exhibition Shooters who were well known in the 1950s, used an M&P in her act. She also trained actress Betty Hutton for her role as Annie Oakley in *Annie Get your Gun* with this same M&P revolver.

# The FBI

As discussed in Chapter Thirty-Two, the .357 Magnum M13 with round butt and a 3" barrel was the last duty revolver adopted by the FBI in 1981, but there was a long history of S&W revolver use in Federal law enforcement before that time. Some examples from a series of FBI Academy postcards in the collection of ex-FBI agent Larry Wack are depicted here to illustrate this.

## FBI Academy Postcards

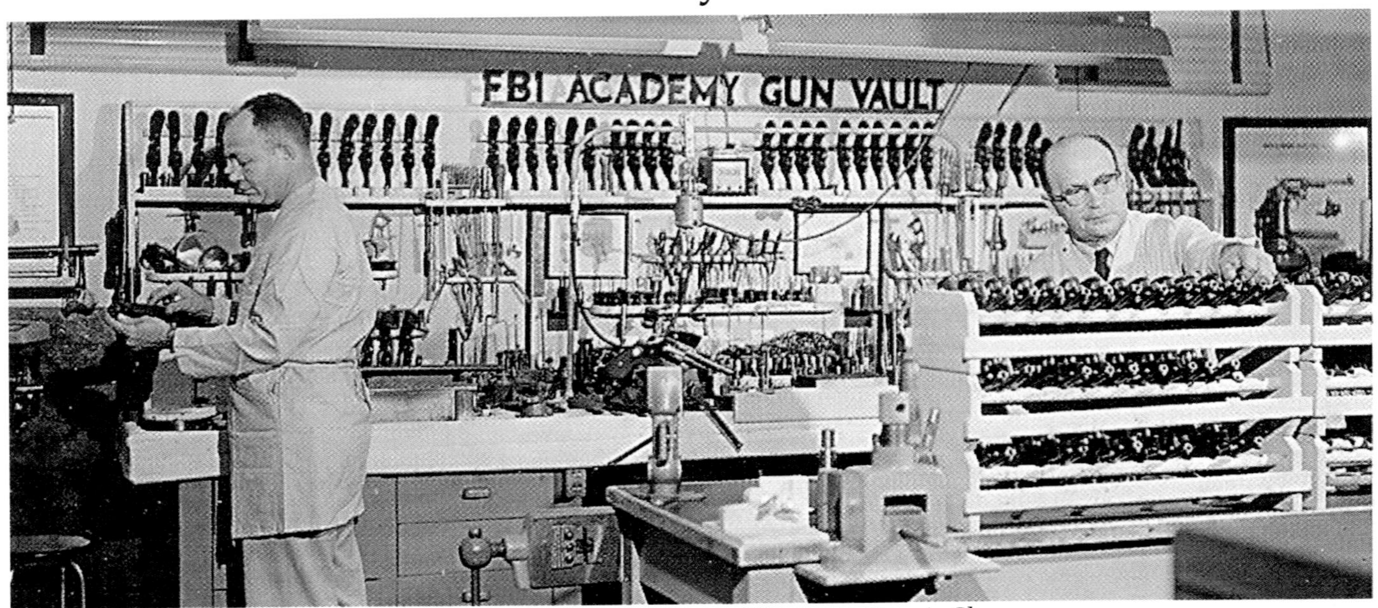


581. The original caption reads "Weapons Repair Shop, FBI Academy. Factory-trained employees maintain weapons in top condition."

Note the racks of duty revolvers, and the M&P training chart at far right. Larry Wack collection

582. "FBI Double Action revolver course. Special Agents firing .38 caliber revolvers from the 15-yard firing line on one of the Practical Pistol Course Ranges at the FBI Academy." Larry Wack collection

583. "Night firing, FBI Ranges, Marine Corps Base, Quantico, Virginia. Tracer bullets fired from .38 caliber revolvers." Larry Wack collection

## Another Presentation Magnum for J. Edgar Hoover

584. Left side view of the cased .357 Combat Magnum, serial no. K 333333, ornately engraved and inlaid with gold by master engraver Alvin A. White, as presented by William O. Sweet to J. Edgar Hoover on July 26, 1958. Chad Gripp collection

As noted on page 69, "On May 10, 1935, .357 Magnum revolver serial no. 45768, marked with registration no. 1 [figs. 68 and 69], was sent to Washington by S&W Sales Manager Cy Bassett for delivery to J. Edgar Hoover, the Director of the FBI."

585. Right side view of the cased Alvin White-engraved .357 Combat Magnum presented by William O. Sweet to J. Edgar Hoover on July 26, 1958.

Note the bust of Hoover inlaid in gold on the sideplate, and the gold numerals "1917/1924" on the front of the frame. These commemorate the period during which Hoover gained prominence within the Justice Department for his work on indexing "subversives" within the United States, cataloguing over 450,000 people. On November 7, 1919 Hoover rounded up over 10,000 American citizens suspected of being communists and anarchists, most of whom were eventually released. Eventually his case against Emma Goldman and her subsequent deportation (for her views on women's suffrage and birth control) led to Hoover's promotion to Assistant Director of the Bureau of Investigation. Chad Gripp collection

TO
J. EDGAR HOOVER
DIRECTOR - F. B. I.
FROM
BILL SWEET
JULY 26, 1958

586. Closeup of the gold plaque affixed to the blue velvet cloth inside the case of the Sweet presentation Combat Magnum. Chad Gripp collection

In way of thanks for this prestigious gift, Hoover wrote an inflammatory memorandum dated March 19, 1936, addressed to his immediate superior, the U.S. Attorney General, wherein he described the "menace" which the new Magnum revolver represented to the forces of law and order. This memorandum is reproduced in full on pages 70 - 72.

Some twenty years later, a well-connected businessman named William O. Sweet, whose grandfather had established a gold chain manufacturing concern in the late 1800s, and whose father was friends with then-S&W president Harold Wesson, presented a lavishly engraved and gold-inlaid cased .357 Combat Magnum revolver to Hoover. The precise reason for the presentation is not known, but an impressive photographic record of the occasion and the gun itself has survived and is presented here.

Excerpts from the factory letter detailing some facts about the revolver and the presentation read as follows:

*. . We have researched your Smith & Wesson Model 19 .357 Combat Magnum, Special Order Variation, caliber .357 Magnum revolver in company records which indicate that your handgun, with serial number K 333333 was shipped from our factory on May 19, 1958 and delivered to William O. Sweet, Sweet Manufacturing Co., Attleboro, MA. The records indicate that this revolver was shipped with a 4 inch barrel, polished but not blued and fit with plain rosewood grips. This revolver was prepared for engraving and was provided on a no charge basis and charged to the Advertising Account. It was for Mr. Sweet to present to Mr. J. Edgar Hoover. Mr. Sweet was a well known gun collector, but the records do not show his relationship to Mr. Hoover . .*

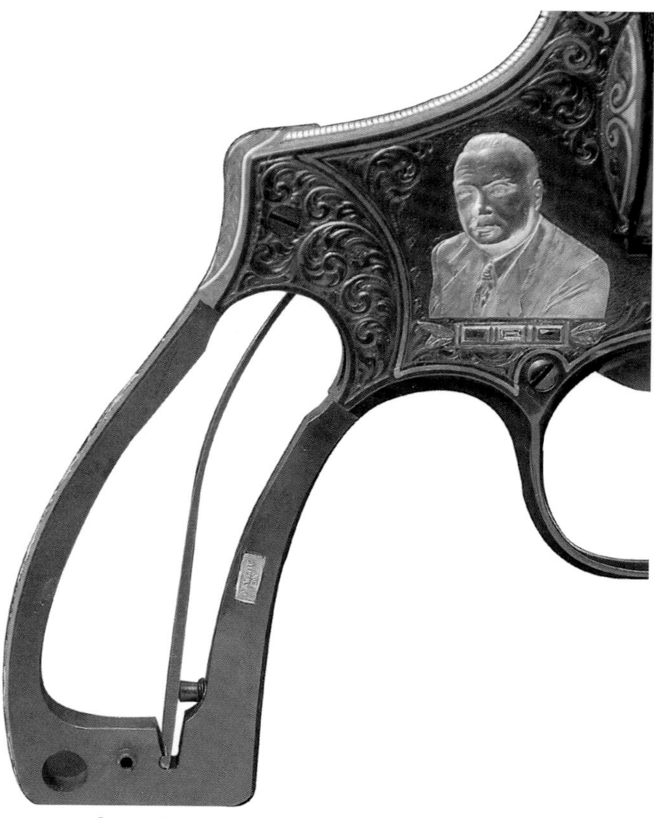

587. Right side closeup of the grip area of the Sweet presentation Combat Magnum with the rosewood stocks removed, showing Alvin White's personal gold cartouche reading "A A WHITE/ENG." affixed to the front grip strap.

Note the three jewels, a ruby, a diamond and an amethyst (red, white and blue), inlaid under the gold portrait of Hoover. Chad Gripp collection

588. Closeup of the ornately engraved FBI seal on the left side of the frame of the Sweet presentation Combat Magnum. Chad Gripp collection

589. Closeup of the underside of the trigger guard of the Sweet presentation Combat Magnum, showing a facsimile of Hoover's signature inlaid in gold.

Compare with fig. 71. Chad Gripp collection

590. Closeup of the underside of the butt, showing serial number "K 333333" inlaid in gold.

Chad Gripp collection

591. Rear closeup showing details of the engraving on the backstrap, with large no. "1" at top and the scrolled words Fidelity, Bravery, Integrity (FBI) inlaid in gold.

Note the beautifully checkered rosewood stocks, presumably also the work of Alvin A. White.

Chad Gripp collection

592. A photograph taken to commemorate the presentation of the revolver shown above by William O. Sweet to J. Edgar Hoover, in Hoover's office in the Justice Department building on July 26, 1958. Chad Gripp collection

# G. Gordon Liddy

Other famous users of the M&P during this same timeframe included former FBI Agent G. Gordon Liddy, the noted political commentator and Watergate burglar, who carried a K-38 Combat Masterpiece when he reported to his first office with the FBI.

As discussed on page 81, Liddy was later converted to a 3½-inch .357 Magnum N-frame revolver by the old-timers in the office who told him, echoing Keith's comments, that his .38 Special revolver lacked stopping power. This was before the Combat Magnum and the later M13 came out, no doubt; since when they did they tended to replace the heavier N-frame in the holsters of the period.

# White House Security

The standard M&P in the hands of White House policemen was sufficient to stop Puerto Rican terrorists and failed assassins who attempted to kill President Truman, who was staying at Blair House during his second term while the White House was being remodeled.

Either the Puerto Ricans had not been told about the lack of stopping power, or the White House police shot pretty straight (or were lucky). Sometimes it is better to be lucky than skillful, of course, but generally it seems the more skilled you are, the more lucky you are likely to get.

# Ian Fleming

The famous creator of James Bond, Ian Lancaster Fleming, who in his youth had attended Eton, Sandhurst and the Universities of Munich and Geneva, later had a career of his own in British Naval Intelligence during WWII.

Fleming's first James Bond novel, *Casino Royale*, was published in 1952. Several years later he received a letter from a reader - the well-known Scottish gun writer Geoffrey Boothroyd - complaining that there were no details about the firearms Bond used in Fleming's early novels.

At the time Fleming was working on his fifth Bond adventure, *From Russia, with Love*, the first edition of which was published in 1957. Writing later in 1962, Fleming himself took up the story as follows:

> *. . The volume I was working on at the time of my correspondence with Geoffrey Boothroyd was* From Russia, with Love, *and, with the correspondence in mind and remembering the excellent trompe-l'oeil jacket for Raymond Chandler's* The Simple Art of Murder *. . my idea for a jacket was a gun crossed with a rose. So I decided to approach Dickie Chopping, who is probably the greatest trompe-l'oeil painter in the world and for whose work I have a great admiration.*
>
> *Dickie Chopping having agreed in principle, the next requirement was a suitable gun. I at once thought of Geoffrey Boothroyd's favourite—the S&W .38 Special M&P whose barrel he had sawn to 2 [sic] inches, and whose trigger guard he had cut away for quicker shooting, and I wrote asking for the loan of the gun.*
>
> *Geoffrey Boothroyd agreed. His beautiful gun came down to me by registered post and was sent on to Dickie Chopping, who at once set to work, commenting in a letter around the middle of September, "It has been the very devil to paint, but fascinating."*
>
> *. . The Chopping jacket was a tremendous success, both in England and America . .*

593. The jacket front cover of the first edition of the popular James Bond novel *From Russia, with Love*, by Ian Fleming.

As discussed at left, this was painted by British *trompe-l'oeil* artist Richard Chopping to Fleming's design, and featured a modified S&W .38 caliber revolver loaned by Scottish gun writer Geoffrey Boothroyd.

courtesy Mark Terry, Facsimile Dustjackets LLC

In his own book *The Handgun* (1970), Geoffrey Boothroyd described his revolver as:

> *. . a conversion from .38 S&W Special to .380 [.38 S&W] which was subsequently modified by the writer. These modifications consisted of shortening the barrel from the original 5" to 2¾" and fitting a ramp sight block and ramp foresight. The top strap was altered to accommodate an adjustable rear sight, the front of the trigger guard was cut off and the butt rounded. New stocks were made, the action was polished and hammer and trigger were 'engine turned' . .*

# Lee Harvey Oswald

No doubt British .38/200 revolvers were used by lots of interesting people during WWII, but for some reason I have not been able to find any of their stories to share with you. When brought into the U.S. as surplus during the 1960s, these revolvers often had their barrels shortened to two inches and the front sights remounted by the importers, Seaport Traders, making them into rather crude concealment revolvers. They also had the chambers reamed out to accept .38 Special cartridges. This resulted in an arm really only suitable for being a "gas station gun" in the judgment of many. A "gas station gun" of course is a low-priced revolver kept by the cash register which would be left in place when the station closed each night, and was subject to all sorts of wear and tear and climate-induced misfortunes in environments where snow, salt, and similar finish-destroying things abounded.

However poor, such a cut-down surplus Canadian Lend-Lease M&P was good enough for alleged presidential assassin Lee Harvey Oswald, who used it to kill Dallas police officer J. D. Tippit in 1963. Stopped on the street after the Kennedy shooting, Oswald pulled his revolver and killed the policeman on the spot.

Oswald's revolver is today on display at the National Archives in Washington, D.C.

# Jim Cirillo, NYPD

A more uplifting example of the use of the M&P was by noted lawman Jim Cirillo, then of the New York City Police Department. He used his 4-inch Model 10 .38 Special in a famed shootout where he shot and killed two men in the space of a few heartbeats.

Jimmy always said that, try as he might thereafter, he was never able to duplicate his performance that day. Another example of good luck closely following the well-skilled, I suppose.

# Raymond Sasia - the French Connection

Many people in the United States think that after WWI, European police forces all went to carrying autoloading pistols. This is no doubt true to a great extent, as evidenced by the countless semi-autos typically in 7.65mm (.32 ACP) brought home as souvenir capture guns by returning GIs. It is thus surprising for many to discover that the combat revolver in .357 Magnum is not only alive and well among those at the hard edge in the police services in France, but is actually considered to be the prestige weapon there. The possession and use of one shows that the bearer is a member of an especially sophisticated group of gun-packers, and is a good illustration of how important an individual sidearm can be as a status symbol to a given position or field.

In the case of police armament in France, the person responsible for this development was Raymond Sasia. His past history has always been a little murky in parts, although his latest autobiography has shed more light on his life, as long as we recognize that as with any such effort over which the author has been able to exert personal discretion, many things might well have been deleted, minimized, or even inflated. It is probably impossible for anyone to write a completely true story when writing their autobiography, due to the effects of selective memory, some concern for others' feelings, and in the case of people like Sasia, the statute of limitations!

## Becoming de Gaulle's Chief Bodyguard

When the Fourth Republic collapsed in 1958 and Charles de Gaulle returned to power, he brought with him the Fifth Republic. Averting a civil war was not easy, for de Gaulle was confronted with the Algerian crisis which he solved by basically giving Algeria away. As Algeria had been considered an integral part of France for almost one hundred years by then, was populated by many Frenchmen, and even then was known to contain great wealth, this was not a popular decision with many, who felt betrayed. For several years a shadow war was fought between the government and the Secret Army Organization (OAS), a right wing para-military organization. The de Gaullist forces created strong-arm squads called *barbouzes* to counter the OAS, which traditional military and police forces seemed incapable of managing. Sasia was originally a member of such a strong-arm group, and gradually gravitated to being a de Gaulle bodyguard, then his chief bodyguard. As de Gaulle was the target of many attacks during the period, it says a good deal for Sasia's skills that de Gaulle died at peace in his own bed many years after leaving office.

As a bodyguard, Sasia transferred over to the police services from the murky world he had once inhabited, and over the next decades he became a dominant force in police circles, especially concerning police weaponry. At the end of his time in the police, before his retirement, he held the rank of *Controlleur General de la Police Nationale*.

## Sasia at the FBI Academy

During the de Gaulle crisis period in the 1960s, armed crime was once again on the rise in France, and no doubt to enforce his position as a police expert, rather than merely as a hired gun, Sasia was sent to the FBI Academy in 1962. As many know, the FBI offers courses to foreign police officials, not only to familiarize them with FBI techniques but also to influence them at a variety of levels.

Sasia proved to be an excellent example of the type on whom the courses made an impression, as he was very proud of this period in his life. Even in his most recent book, published fifty years after the fact, he included a photo of himself getting his attendance certificate from the hands of the master himself, J. Edgar Hoover. What Hoover thought of the Frenchman is unknown, but given his disdain for foreigners in general and people of loose sexual morals in particular (almost a given for any French cop, in my experience), I can imagine.

594. The jacket front cover of Raymond Sasia's memoir *Mousquetaire du Général* ("The General's Musketeer"), recalling his days as De Gaulle's chief bodyguard.

Nevertheless, for the next fifty years, Sasia obviously remembered and cherished the time he had spent with the FBI.

## Two Police Forces in France: the *Gendarmerie* and the *Police Nationale*

There are two police forces in France - the *Gendarmerie* and the *Police Nationale*, both of which are controlled by the Ministry of the Interior. The *Gendarmerie*, military in origin and normally in uniform, polices the countryside and small towns with fewer than 20,000 inhabitants, while the *Police Nationale* (National Police) operates in larger towns and cities.

At the time the French police typically carried hammerless blowback .32 ACP semi-autos such as the Unique Rr51 and similar low-end weapons, with no doubt some old 8mm revolvers thrown in as well. Sasia changed all that.

## The Origins of the French Model 12 "Airweight" with Side Safety

Originally he got the National Police to order Smith & Wesson "Airweight" (Model 12) M&P revolvers with three-inch barrels, equipped, at the request of some dimwitted bureaucrat, with a manual safety (figs. 471 and 472). Occasionally one of the overruns from this contract turns up in the U.S. and is eagerly snapped up by a collector, but naturally no serious gunman wants them. Neither did Sasia.

## Adopting the 3" Model 19 Combat Magnum, with Fixed Sights

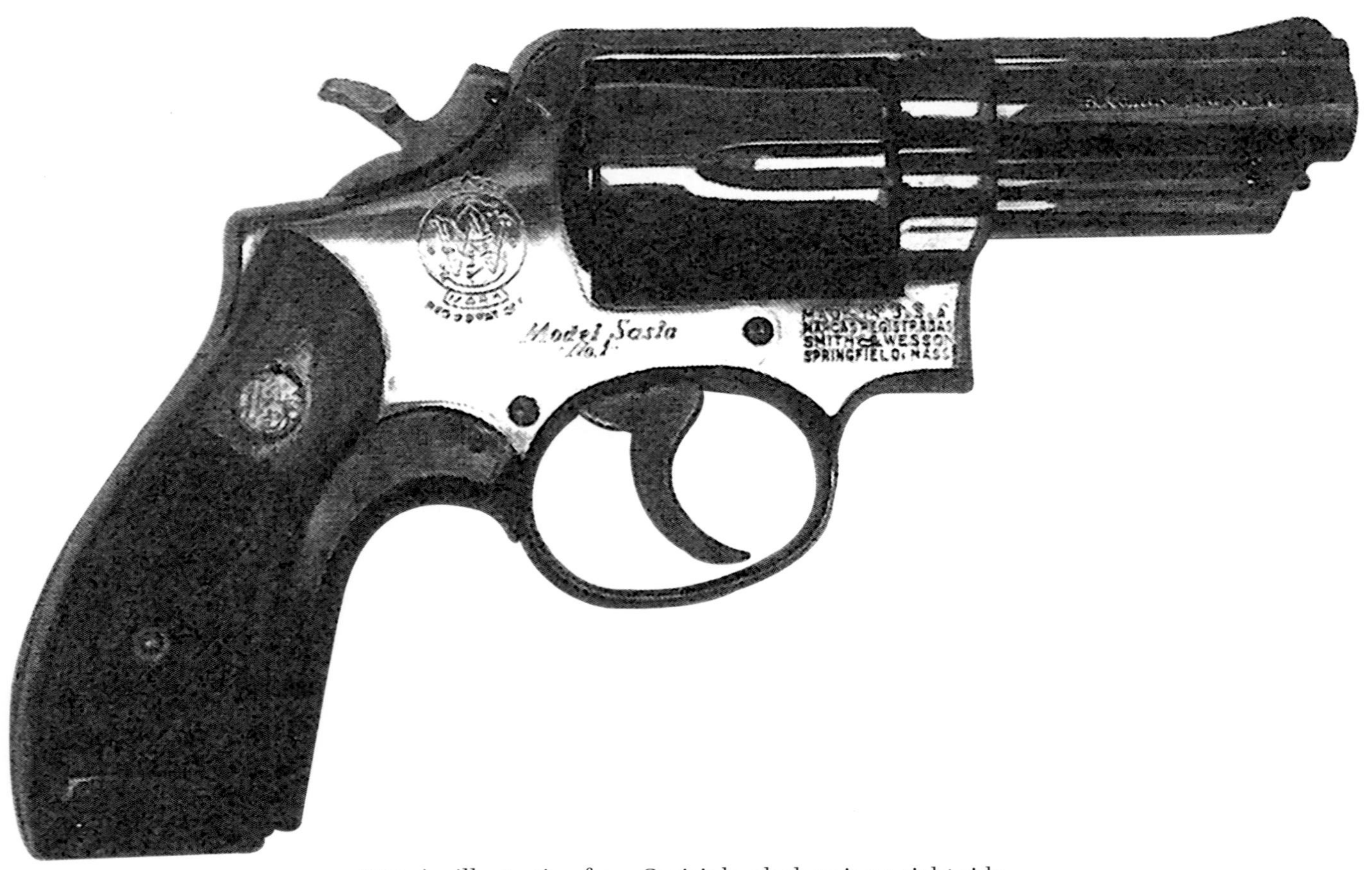


595. An illustration from Sasia's book showing a right side view of the first "Sasia" model S&W M19 with round butt, grip adapter, 3" underlugged barrel and fixed sights.
Note the engraving on the sideplate, reading "Model Sasia/No. 1".

As his authority increased, Sasia got the police to buy standard M&P .38 Special revolvers. But as his authority and prestige continued to rise, he was able to gain even more power, and examples in .357 Magnum were acquired, as were three-inch versions of the Smith & Wesson Model 19 Combat Magnum.

When exactly he got the idea to buy a fixed-sight version of the M19 is not clear. It would not have come from the FBI, as at the time they were issuing four-inch, steel-framed .38 Special caliber S&W M&P and Colt Official Police revolvers. Only in the 1970s did the Bureau follow the example of the French police, when they bought as their last standard-issue revolver the three-inch M13 .357 Magnum in blued finish. So Sasia did not follow the FBI example: they followed his!

My good friend, Alabama citizen, long-time English resident, and intellectual gunman, Jan Stevenson, thinks Sasia came up with the idea by becoming influenced by Chic Gaylord, the famous New York City holstermaker of the 1960s. This could well be, as no doubt Gaylord's shop would be worth a stop for any serious gunman coming through New York City at the time, as Sasia would have done on his way to the FBI Academy in Virginia.

Chic really liked three-inch guns. He always thought the three-inch made the ideal plainclothes carry length and believed, really believed, that the three-inch length gave better accuracy and penetration than a four-inch, basing this conviction on some obscure impossible-to-prove (or disprove) *wave theory*. Such theoretical approaches appeal to the French, also, it seems. Chic also was a great believer in fixed sights on defense guns, since he thought adjustable sights tended to get knocked out of alignment. Maybe he hit the steering wheel with his carry gun when climbing out of the driver's seat of his car, as Chic was pretty stout, and there was not much space there. He also liked the full ejector rod capability of the three-inch barrel over the shorter length rod/barrel combination, and even wrote an article about it in *GUNS* magazine in 1965. As to the encased ejector rod housing of the M19 versus the unprotected standard M&P approach, a lot of us, along with Elmer Keith, and no doubt Sasia, just found it more elegant.

The revolver that earned the Sasia stamp of approval was a blued-finish, round-butt, fixed-sight, three-inch version of the Model 19 in .357 Magnum caliber. It was not cheap to acquire, and was used only by those at the sharp end of the police stick, so it thus became the prestige weapon. If you saw anyone with one, you knew, just knew, they were likely to be pretty sharp or at least pretty well connected, as otherwise they would not have one. When the head of the French Intelligence Services committed suicide after being *outed* as a KGB mole, he did it with a Sasia Model Smith & Wesson (or at least that was what was found on the floor – you can never tell who actually pulled the trigger). Everyone I know thought it showed some real class in choice of weapon at least, if not companions.

## The Birth of the Model 547

As is typical in France, where they love to create an ornate and involved pedagogy for everything, the result often not being as important as the method (while in the U.S. we tend to care about only the result, and not how we got there), one of the things Sasia did as his influence increased in the French police service was to see to it that an equipment bureau for selecting new items was created. This was called the *Bureau de l'armement et des moyens de défense* (Office of Armament and Means of Defense), abbreviated as BAD. This group was responsible for re-equipping the French police at many levels with new revolvers. Obviously the expensive Sasia Model 19 would not be a good economic choice as a general-issue sidearm, and of course then it would no longer be a prestige weapon, either.

Somewhere along the line BAD decided that since the police were then using 9x19mm submachine guns (typically MAT 49 models – a really fine submachine gun by the way, only the single-feed magazine being a drawback), a revolver with a three-inch barrel, less the encased ejector rod and chambered for 9x19mm, would be just the ticket. "Save money on ammo, *n'est ce pas?*", was no doubt the theory, although chambering a rimless, high-pressure round in a revolver had been tried before without much success, and the situation was even more complicated by the fact that the French did not want to use half- or full-moon clips to hold the cartridges, which can bend and thus require a hard hammer strike, since primers are not always hit with sufficient force otherwise.

Of course, avoiding the use of pre-clipped cartridges effectively does away with the excellent speed-loading feature these offer and, given the typically hard primers found on French 9x19mm ammunition, the primers were going to have to be struck pretty hard anyway. But the French police represented a big market, and, as related in Chapter Thirty-Two, Smith & Wesson developed the 9mm Model 547 (figs. 525 and 526) to fit this demand.

When Raymond Sasia returned to France from the FBI Academy, I don't suppose anyone would have thought his attendance would have yielded a number of interesting variations on the K-frame Smith & Wesson. But it seems that it did so, with the exotic variation of the M19, later the similar-appearing (except for model stamping and depth of chambering) M10s for the Brazilian market, the M65 Lady Smith Models, perhaps even the FBI's last service revolver, the three-inch M13; and of course the 9mm Model 547 for the *Gendarmerie*.

The Model 547 was really quite an engineering feat, if somewhat dubious as regards its practicality as a revolver for self-defense purposes. I suppose if you have access to lots of free 9x19mm ammunition, or live someplace where you can get it but not much else, and the local powers that be will be okay if you own a revolver but not a *dangerous self-loader* –

places like New York and similar cultural backwaters.

Given the development by other manufacturers such as FN, Ruger, and of course Manurhin with their excellent MR73 and later MR88 models, all intended to capture a share of this European police market for three-inch barreled .357 Magnum revolvers (fig. 570), it is fair to say that Raymond Sasia was a very significant figure in the development of the K-frame as a fighting handgun during the 1960 to 1990 timeframe.

# Massad Ayoob

When Massad Ayoob, the noted firearms writer and instructor, had young children at home, he developed a four-inch Model 66 which he referred to as "Puffy". He had the cylinder modified to avoid the lockup issues which plagued early M66 revolvers when used with hot .357 Magnum loads, and replaced the stainless trigger and hammer with standard casehardened units in order to get and maintain the best trigger pull.

Lastly, he had a Magna trigger safety installed (fig. 699), so "Puffy" could not be fired by his young daughters (or their friends) when laid about.

# The Police-Issue M&P Fades Away

As the popularity of revolvers for police use started into its long decline in the late 1980s and 1990s, with duty revolvers being seen even less frequently now in the early decades of the 21st century, it follows that fewer famous users of the M&P remain.

Of course a lot of M&Ps are still carried every day, all over the world, and no doubt still do fine work. In fact, with roughly 6½ million (not to mention the 1½ million target-sighted models) made over five generations of users, it is likely that more than 50 million people have used the M&P revolver at one time or another. This means there were lots of famous users who are not mentioned here, and many people who got to grow old only because of the M&P, which is in itself quite a worthwhile accomplishment.

*Chapter Thirty-Six*

# Postwar U.S. Military Use

## A Retrospective on Earlier U.S. Military K-Frames

Speaking of famous users, in Chapter Twenty-Five we have discussed how the U.S. Navy and Army were quick to adopt trials quantities of the very first K-frame Hand Ejector, the Model 1899, followed by a similar purchase by the Navy of Model 1902s.

However the ineffectiveness of the .38 Colt service cartridge during the Philippine Insurrection, discussed in earlier chapters, compelled the Ordnance Department to consider a change in caliber. As quoted in *Colt .45 Service Pistols* by Charles W. Clawson, the conclusions of the Thompson-LaGarde Board's exhaustive study of various pistols and revolvers, released on March 18, 1904, stated clearly that "a bullet which will have the shock effect and stopping power at short ranges necessary for a military pistol or revolver should have a caliber not less than 0.45."

At the time this effectively ended any military interest in the medium-caliber K-frame, although as discussed earlier and in Volume I, quantities of larger N-frame revolvers, in caliber .455 for the British and in .45 ACP for U.S. service use, were adopted during WWI.

Then, as discussed in Chapter Thirty, .38 caliber revolvers were once again approved for military issue during WWII, and manufactured in vast quantities, in .38 S&W (.38/200) for the British and in .38 Special in the U.S. Victory Model.

## A Foot in the Door

As far as post-WWII U.S. forces were concerned, therefore, the .38 Special S&W K-frame revolver was already a familiar item of issue which was firmly ensconced in the military supply system. Further purchases of commercial K-frames were made as time went on, both to replace aging Victory Models and to expand the military arsenal with new models.

In order that the reader can appreciate the widespread use of S&W K-frame revolvers by the U.S. military after WWII, and to provide as complete an account as possible, we are also including coverage of military accessories (ammunition, training manuals, holsters, ammunition pouches, etc.) in this chapter.

We begin coverage of the postwar U.S. military K-frame models with excerpts from several sources in John Henwood's book, as follows:

# The Military M&P (Model 10)

*Aside from purchases of the M13 "Aircrewman" and the Combat Masterpiece [discussed below], the U.S. military also procured regular M&P revolvers. Chambered for the .38 Special, these were ordered with 2-inch barrels in both square- and round-butt styles, and with 4-inch barrels and square butt frames. Taken from regular production, all have a commercial blued finish. Early examples are known to have the new short action, Magna-style "diamond" stocks, "half-moon" front sights, and the inscription "U.S. ARMY" rollmarked on the left side of the frame, below the cylinder. Later guns have Magna P.C. stocks, and are stamped "U.S." on the frame backstrap.*

*. . Evidently most post-1961 acquisitions had 1/8-inch sights. Lanyard swivels were not provided. These military guns were furnished in the basic Model 10 pattern, plus the 10-2, 10-5, 10-7 and (probably) 10-9 versions, as well as the pre-1957 M&P style.*

596. Left side view of .38 Special M&P serial no. C 264074, with 4" barrel, square butt and lanyard swivel.

Inset, right: closeup of the government acceptance "P", stamped on the frame ahead of the hammer.

Inset, left: closeup of the backstrap showing roll stamped marking "U S PROPERTY".

According to the factory letter (fig. 598), this revolver was shipped on October 20, 1953 to the Marine Corps Supply Annex at Camp Lejeune, N.C.

Jeff Moeller collection

597. Underside closeup of the barrel of the above M&P with cylinder open, showing the serial number.

Jeff Moeller collection

*The latest examples (circa 1985) were catalogued by the military under National Stock Numbers 1005-00-937-5839 (4-inch round butt), 1005-00-937-5840 (2-inch round butt), and 1005-00-214-0934 (4-inch square butt, P.C. stocks). All were known to military users as the "Revolver, Caliber .38 Special, Smith & Wesson, Military and Police, Model 10".*

*. . Eventually over 133,000 M&P/Model 10 revolvers are thought to have been ordered, from the 1950s through the 1980s . .*

598 (right). Factory letter dated April 14, 1989, covering the disposition of M&P serial no. C264074, shown here.

Jeff Moeller collection

No. 048929

OFFICE OF
SMITH & WESSON
REVOLVER Manufacturers

Springfield Mass April 14, 1989

We received your letter of recent date regarding your Smith & Wesson .38 Military & Police revolver and requesting information.

The .38 Military & Police revolver was originally introduced in 1899 and has been in continuous manufacture since that date. To date, we have produced over five million of this model.

The .38 Military & Police model was the proper name for this revolver prior to Smith & Wesson's assigning model numbers. When Smith & Wesson assigned model numbers to their revolvers in 1958, this .38 Military & Police became known as the Model 10.

We have researched your Smith & Wesson .38 Military & Police revolver in company records which indicate that your handgun, with serial number C264074, was shipped from our factory on October 20, 1953 to the Marine Corp., Supply Annex, Camp Lejune.

We trust that the information furnished will be helpful as well as of interest to you.

Sincerely,

SMITH & WESSON

Roy G. Jinks
Historian

RGJ/dsg

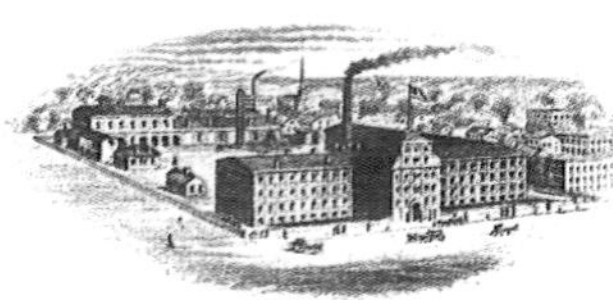

599. Left side view of another Model 10, serial no. C263711, with 4" barrel, modified square butt and lanyard swivel.

Inset, top right: enlargement of government "P" stamp.

Insets, below left: closeup of modified square butt showing serial number, and "U.S. PROPERTY" on backstrap.

Springfield Mass July 9, 200

Dear

We received your letter of recent date regarding your Smith & Wesson .38 Military & Police revolver and requesting information.

The .38 Military & Police revolver was originally introduced in 1899 and has been in continuous manufacture since that date. To date, we have produced over five million of this model.

The .38 Military & Police model was the proper name for this revolver prior to Smith & Wesson's assigning model numbers. When Smith & Wesson assigned model numbers to their revolvers in 1958, this .38 Military & Police became known as the Model 10.

This famous model has been assigned to five different serial number series. The original series started with the number 1 and continued to 1,000,000, in 1942 a second series was started beginning with serial number V1. The "V" prefixed was used only during World War II in 1946 at approximately serial number 811000 of the original "V" series the "V" was dropped and an "S" was used until 1948 when the serial number reach S1000000. From 1948 to 1968 a "C" prefix was used and this was followed by a "D" prefix which was continued until 1983 when the serial number series was merged into the new Triple Alpha Four numeric series.

We have researched your Smith & Wesson .38 Military & Police Pre-Model 10, United States Marine Corp. Contract, caliber .38 Special, revolver, with serial number C263711, in company records. Our records show this handgun was shipped from our factory on December 28, 1953, and delivered to United States Marine Corp., Marine Corps Supply Annex., Camp Lajeun, NC. The records indicates that this revolver was shipped with a 4 inch barrel, blue finish, checkered walnut grips, and United States Markings.

Sincerely,

SMITH & WESSON

Roy G. Jinks
Historian

600 (right). Factory letter covering the above M&P ("pre-Model 10") seral no. C263711, confirming that it was produced under a contract for the United States Marine Corps.

Notwithstanding its earlier serial number, according to the factory letter this revolver was shipped to the USMC at Camp Lejeune on December, 28, 1953, two months after the M&P shown in fig. 596.

601. Training Marine Corps Security Police at the USMC Security Guard School - a 1980s period photo of a female member aiming a 4" Model 10.

Judging by the lack of ear or eye protection, this is probably a dry-firing exercise.

602. Left side view of a round-butt M&P with 4" barrel and no lanyard swivel.

Note the flattened rear face of the front sight, a feature introduced in production in 1952.

This example was delivered to the U.S. Army Boston Procurement District in 1967 or 1968, and was a popular model in the military for many years.

Inset: closeup of the backstrap, stamped "U.S."

Jeff Moeller collection

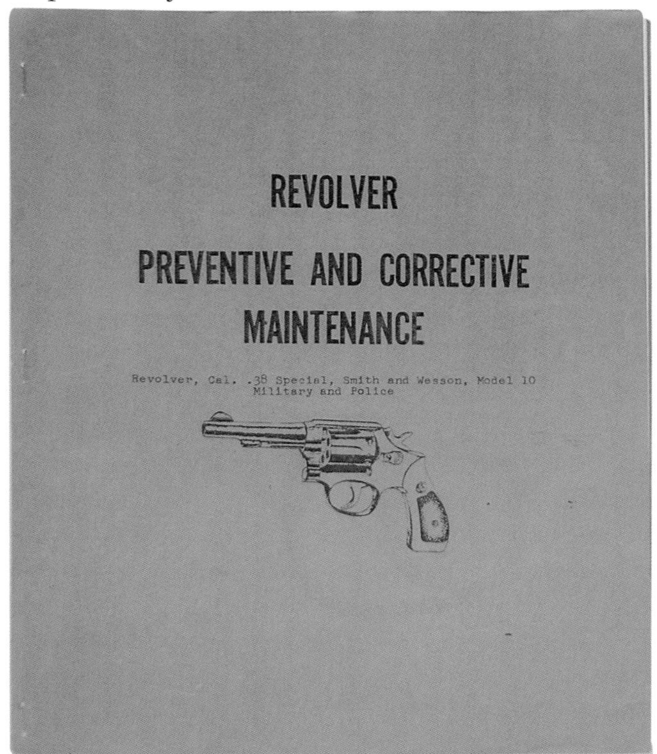


603. A 24-page military handbook from the late 1960s, subtitled "Revolver, Cal. .38 Special, Smith & Wesson, Model 10 Military and Police", depicting the popular round-butt, 4" M&P. This was issued to U.S. forces in Vietnam. Jeff Moeller collection

REVOLVER PREVENTIVE AND CORRECTIVE MAINTENANCE

Revolver, Cal. .38 Spec., Smith and Wesson, Military and Police Models

LESSON OBJECTIVES: Upon successful completion of this lesson, you will be able to:

(1) Identify the general characteristics of the Revolver, Cal. .38 Spec., Smith and Wesson.
(2) Identify the revolver's special and improvised tools and their uses.
(3) Identify the revolver's operational controls and their functions.
(4) Identify the revolver's clearing procedures, fieldstripping sequence, and assembly sequence when fieldstripped.
(5) Identify the revolver's organizational (2d echelon) maintenance, intermediate (3d echelon) maintenance disassembly/assembly procedures.

WRITTEN ASSIGNMENT:

A. Multiple Choice: Select the ONE answer which BEST completes the statement or answers the question. After the corresponding number on the answer sheet, blacken the appropriate box.

Value: 1 point each

1. What type of weapon is the revolver, cal. .38 special?

a. Six-shot, breech loading, hand weapon
b. Seven-shot, cylinder loading, hand weapon
c. Six-shot, hand actuated, breech loaded, hand gun

2. What is the cylinder assembly mounted on?

a. Frame assembly b. Yoke assembly c. Extractor assembly

3. How many manually operated safeties are there on the revolver, cal. .38 special?

a. Five c. One
b. Two d. None

4. How wide is the front sight blade of the Model 10 revolver?

a. 1/8 inch c. 1/4 inch
b. 3/16 inch d. 3/8 inch

5. How wide is the front sight blade of the Victory Officer's and the Victory Service Model revolvers?

a. 1/16 inch c. 1/8 inch
b. 1/12 inch d. 1/4 inch

6. What kind of rear sight is common to all three models of the military and police revolver?

a. Adjustable notch c. Machined notch
b. Mechanical notch d. Smooth frame notch

7. The serial numbers of the Victory Officer's Model are preceded by the letter

a. "SV." c. "B."
b. "C." d. "A."

p. 1

604. One of six pages of text in the handbook shown in fig. 603, posing a number of multiple-choice questions concerning the Model 10 "Victory Officer's and the Victory Service Model revolvers". Jeff Moeller collection

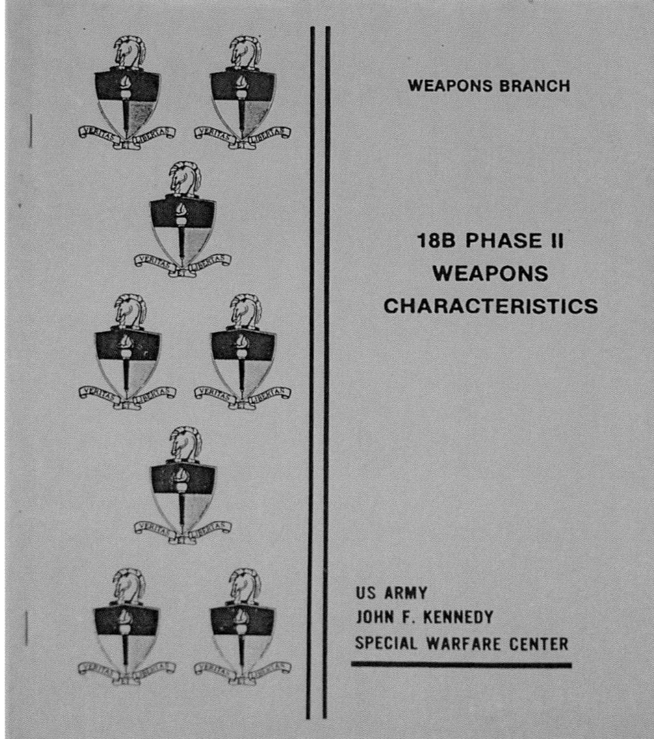


605. A 48-page U.S. Army instructional handbook from the 1970s, depicting and describing various allied and foreign weapons. Jeff Moeller collection

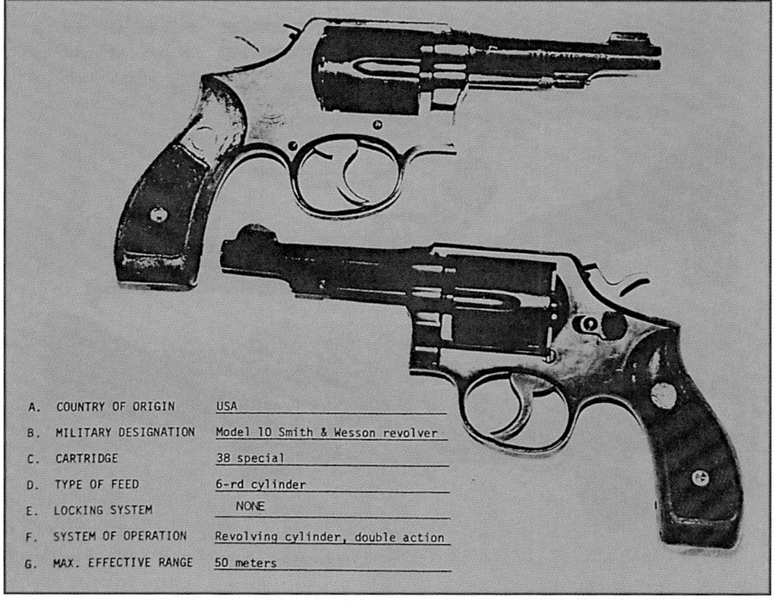
A. COUNTRY OF ORIGIN USA
B. MILITARY DESIGNATION Model 10 Smith & Wesson revolver
C. CARTRIDGE 38 special
D. TYPE OF FEED 6-rd cylinder
E. LOCKING SYSTEM NONE
F. SYSTEM OF OPERATION Revolving cylinder, double action
G. MAX. EFFECTIVE RANGE 50 meters

606. A sample page from the JFK Special Warfare handbook shown in fig. 605, depicting and describing the round-butt Model 10 revolver. Jeff Moeller collection

# The USAF M13 "Aircrewman"

607. Left and right side views of the U.S. Air Force M13 lightweight "Aircrewman" revolver, with aluminum alloy frame and cylinder.
Inset: closeup of the U.S. Air Force property marking on the backstrap. John Miller collection

John Henwood describes the Smith & Wesson version of the lightweight "Aircrewman" revolver used by the USAF as follows:

> *From 1952 through 1957 the U.S. Air Force bought a quantity (said to be about 40,000) of airweight revolvers having a blue black (black anodized frame and cylinder) finish and 2-inch barrels, for use by air crew members. Basically the same as the commercial "Airweight" model, they had the same narrow frame and flat cylinder latch as the early "Airweight". They were called the "Revolver, Aircrewman, .38 Caliber, M13" by the Air Force. Having walnut Magna stocks (some with S&W medallions, others with medallions bearing the Air Force emblem), they may be recognized by the "Revolver, Lightweight, M13" marking on the top strap (several variants are known, including the absence of a marking), together with "Property of U.S. Air Force" on the backstrap, and AIRCREW-MAN/.38 S.&W. SPL." (2 lines) on the right side of the barrel. M13s carry commercial serial numbers in the "C" series, ranging from circa C 247000 to about C 405600. Some early guns have special "AF-prefix" serial numbers.*
>
> *The M13 was not successful, the aluminum cylinder proving insufficiently strong; most were scrapped . . although a very few escaped destruction to become prime collector's items. (A surprising number of collector's variations [at least nine] exist in this one model; most consist of minor differences in rollmarkings.) Many collectors feel*

608. Left side closeup of the U.S. Air Force M13 "Aircrew-man", showing marking on top strap.

Note also the government acceptance "P" on the frame below the cylinder. John Miller collection

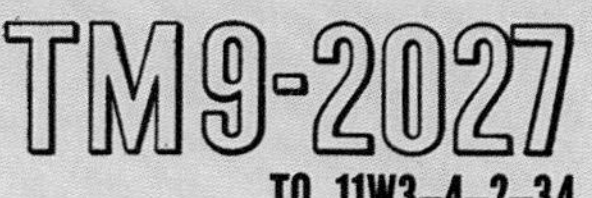

TM9-2027

TO 11W3-4-2-34

DEPARTMENT OF THE ARMY TECHNICAL MANUAL

ORDNANCE MAINTENANCE

CAL. .38 SPECIAL
LIGHTWEIGHT
REVOLVER M13
(COLT AND SMITH
AND WESSON)

DEPARTMENT OF THE ARMY • JULY 1956

610. Left side closeup of an S&W M13 Lightweight "Air-crewman" revolver, showing U.S. Air Force medallion which appeared in the walnut Magna stocks of some examples. Rick Nahas collection

609 (left). The cover of TM9-2027, the Ordnance Maintenance Technical Manual for the Colt and S&W M13 lightweight revolvers, dated July, 1956.
Gaston Comeau collection

*that this model has been rather extensively counterfeited over the years, since it differs from the standard Airweight only in the markings which are machine-engraved . . .*

A similar 2" lightweight model, also called the M13, was supplied by Colt's.

## An In-Depth Description of the S&W M13 "Aircrewman"

The USAF M13 was described in an article by S&W Historian Roy Jinks, which appeared in the May, 1975 issue of *Arms Gazette* magazine. Portions already excerpted in Chapter Thirty-Two explain the difference between the Air Force-assigned "M13" nomenclature for these lightweight revolvers and the later .357 Magnum version of the fixed-sight M&P, which was called the "Model 13" by the factory.

The portions of the article describing the lightweight "Aircrewman" revolver are excerpted as follows:

*The Aircrewman revolver was the Smith & Wesson .38 Military and Police Airweight, having a round butt and two-inch barrel. This . . was the lightest weight six-shot revolver available, weighing only 14½ ounces. It was first produced . . on September 23, 1952 as a copy of the steel framed .38 M&P round butt, two-inch revolver except for the frame and cylinder, which were made of a high tensile strength aluminum alloy. To further lighten the weight . . the barrel diameter was reduced. The hammer and trigger width was also trimmed, thus allowing the total weight of the frame to be reduced. This modified frame was referred to as the KA frame. It resulted in the need for the factory to produce special hammers, triggers and rebound slides which were only for the lightweight model, thus making interchangeability of the standard .38 M&P and lightweight M&P impossible.*

*The new lightweight revolver was designed to fire the standard velocity low pressure .38 Special cartridge since the alloy cylinder could not withstand pressures developed by high velocity cartridges or heavy handloads. To identify this model . . the barrel was stamped .38 Special Airweight, with Smith & Wesson receiving a trademark patent for the name "Airweight".*

*In late 1952 the Air Force became interested in this revolver for use by Aircrewmen. The Air Force contract, issued in late 1952, called for Smith & Wesson to manufacture the alloy frame revolver which carried the Air Force marking. [The grips were fitted with a special Air Force medallion, although the standard S&W grip medallion was used on a limited basis.]*

*Thus the Air Force created what for years has been referred to by the collectors as the Smith & Wesson Model 13.*

*The Air Force Aircrewman 13 was manufactured . . from 1952 until October, 1958, with the factory receiving* several *procurements to cover the 39,545 revolvers produced . .*

## The Rationale for the M13

John Henwood provides the following interesting explanation of why the USAF chose the ultra-light M13 for aircrew issue:

*Concerns about ejecting from a damaged aircraft at supersonic speeds prompted the Air Force to obtain the lightest possible revolvers for air crew use; this requirement for extreme lightness accounts for the aluminum cylinder. The fear at the time was that a standard-weight revolver might inflict injuries during a high-speed bailout, since it was carried in a special breast pocket holster on the issue flying suit.*

## The M13's Achilles' Heel

### The .38 Special M41 Cartridge - Not Always Used

However, as Roy Jinks' 1975 article continues,

*. . The Aircrewman revolver program became a problem to the Air Force when reports of blown cylinders became numerous. The Air Force ammunition issued for this handgun had been a low-pressure M41 .38 Special cartridge. However, individuals did not restrict themselves to low velocity cartridges, and began to use high velocity cartridges which caused pressures which were suffi-*

*cient to cause the cylinder to rupture. The Air Force investigated the problem and a decision was made to recall all issued Aircrewman revolvers, destroying them as well as all existing stocks. These revolvers were destroyed by crushing in a large press, thus crushing barrel and cylinder. After destruction . . they were sold as scrap for parts. Many of these parts have in recent years been reassembled and sold to collectors. It is important to note that, if you own one of the original Aircrewman or Smith & Wesson Airweight .38 M&P revolvers, it not be fired with the high velocity cartridges.*

# The Military Model 14 (K-38)

611. Left side view of a military .38 Special Model 14 (K-38) with target hammer, as delivered to the USMC at Quantico.
Inset: closeup of frame marking "USMC PROPERTY".
Jeff Moeller collection

John Henwood briefly describes the military use of the Model 14 (K-38) as follows:

> *. . A number of Model 14s were purchased by both the U.S. Army and Air Force during the early years of [the] period [from 1965 through 1978]. Known as the "Revolver K-38 (Masterpiece)", they were used both for training and competition.*

# The Model 15 (.38 Combat Masterpiece)

John Henwood continues to briefly describe the military use of the Model 15 (.38 Combat Masterpiece) as follows:

> *. . In 1962 the U.S. Air Force ordered a number of Model 15s with heavy 2-inch barrels. Smith & Wesson catalogued this gun as the "Model 56" from 1962 through 1963 [see below]; later guns are marked "Model 15". The 2-inch barrel was discontinued circa 1978 . . The Air Force also acquired a quantity of regular four-inch barreled Model 15s, as did the U.S. Marine Corps and the U.S. Navy's elite UDTs (Underwater Demolition Teams) . . Some of those Model 15 revolvers supplied to military customers may have smooth grip straps, permitting the backstrap to be rollmarked . .*

612. Left side view of a military .38 Special Model 15 (Combat Masterpiece) with tapered, pinned barrel and modified square butt with no lanyard loop. Note the frame marking "U.S.A.F." and what is presumably an inventory number.

These were originally supplied with standard blued finish as shown, and were Parkerized if and when rebuilt.

Jeff Moeller collection

## Army and Marine Corps Use of the Combat Masterpiece in Korea

As John Henwood records,

> *During the Korean war purchases of the .38 Combat Masterpiece were made by both the U.S. Air Force and the U.S. Marines. Both services issued the revolver to flight personnel, as replacements for aging Victory Models.*

613 (right). The cover of TM9-1005-206-14P/1, the 39-page Department of the Army Technical Manual dated February, 1971, covering the 2" Colt Detective Special, the 4" Colt Police Positive, the 6" S&W Model 14 and the 4" Model 10 in both square and round butt versions.

Jeff Moeller collection

**TM 9-1005-206-14P/1**

DEPARTMENT OF THE ARMY TECHNICAL MANUAL

OPERATOR'S, ORGANIZATIONAL, DS, AND GS MAINTENANCE REPAIR PARTS AND SPECIAL TOOLS LISTS

REVOLVER, CALIBER .38 SPECIAL: COLT, DETECTIVE SPECIAL, 2-INCH BARREL (1005-726-5786)

REVOLVER, CALIBER .38 SPECIAL: COLT, POLICE POSITIVE, 4-INCH BARREL (1005-716-2938)

REVOLVER, CALIBER .38 SPECIAL: S AND W, K-38 MASTERPIECE, M14, 6-INCH BARREL (1005-830-2497)

REVOLVER, CALIBER .38 SPECIAL: S AND W, MILITARY AND POLICE, M10, SQUARE BUTT, 4-INCH BARREL (1005-214-0934)

REVOLVER, CALIBER .38 SPECIAL: S AND W, MILITARY AND POLICE, M10, ROUND BUTT, 2-INCH BARREL (1005-937-5840)

REVOLVER, CALIBER .38 SPECIAL: S AND W, MILITARY AND POLICE, M10, ROUND BUTT, 4-INCH BARREL (1005-937-5839)

HEADQUARTERS, DEPARTMENT OF THE ARMY
FEBRUARY 1971

614 (left). An early female member of the U.S. Air Force "Air Police" directs traffic at an airbase guard gate in the early 1970s, armed with her M15 revolver.

615 (below). Left side view of a later U.S.A.F.-marked M15 with target hammer, on a background of an Air Force tunic, an Air Force Security Police badge, a military issue strap holster (fig. 650), and three rounds of military full-patch 158-grain .38 Special ammunition.

Compare with fig. 612: this revolver has been Parkerized as part of a rebuild program.

Leroy Thompson collection

616 (left). A recent photo of a U.S. Marine team in training shows the M15 still in use in the 21st century.

# The Model 18 (.22 Combat Masterpiece)

# The USAF Model 56 (2-Inch K-38)

618. Left and right side views of the seldom-seen Model 56, a pragmatically finished version of the finely polished Model 14, fitted with a 2" barrel. Procured by the USAF and never sold commercially, most Model 56s were later destroyed.

Inset, left above: closeup of crane area showing marking "MOD./56".

Inset, below: closeup of "U.S." stamping on smooth backstrap. Leroy Thompson collection

The Model 56 was a short-lived Masterpiece-type revolver, with target sights and a 2" barrel, made for issue to the USAF. It bears the same sort of resemblance to the more finely finished Model 14 as the Highway Patrolman (Model 28) does to the .357 Magnum (Model 27). The Model 56 was intentionally cheaper to produce than the Model 15, and in addition to a less finely polished finish has no grooves on the sight leaf, rib or backstrap. The Model 56 was never sold commercially.

John Henwood records the brief saga of the Model 56 as follows:

> *Originally furnished to the U.S. Air Force, the Model 56 can be described as a Model 15 with a 2-inch heavy barrel; more accurately it is a Model 14 with its barrel shortened to two inches. Here is another model number introduced only because of differing contours where the barrel and frame join . . The Model 56 barrel had the same wide-rib contour as the Model 14; this is not compatible with the Model 15 frame, which is contoured to match the narrow rib on its barrel.*

17 (previous page). Left side view of a commercial Model 8 (.22 Combat Masterpiece) with modified square butt, s used by the Atomic Energy Commission.

Inset: closeup of crudely handstamped "US GVT" ıarking. Jeff Moeller collection

619. Top closeup of the above Model 56. Note the top strap is not grooved. Leroy Thompson collection

> *[The Model 56] was offered from 1962 through 1963, about 15,200 were made for the U.S. Air Force; most were later destroyed. After the Model 56 was discontinued, the 2-inch barrel was transferred to the Model 15 series, where it remained until it was dropped, circa 1978.*

# The U.S. Navy Model 19 (Combat Magnum)

As John Henwood records,

> *In 1965 the U.S. Navy bought about 150 Model 19-2s [Combat Magnums] having 4-inch barrels and round butts, for use by their elite SEAL forces.*

## S&W Production Lags Behind Demand During the Vietnam Era

Starting in the mid-1960s, the U.S. initiated the "War on Drugs", which continues today, a half-century later, with no end in sight. This "war" has engendered a number of very unfortunate side effects, making a lot of criminals fabulously rich and corrupting many in high places, all of which has created a bigger demand for defensive handguns. As the K-frame revolver was perhaps the main law enforcement defense sidearm of the period, it is not surprising that demand, already very high, continued to grow.

At the same time, however, the Vietnam War (1959–1975, as it involved U.S. forces) took a lot of the production capacity of Smith & Wesson, so that from about 1964 to 1975 the war, combined with the domestic "Drug Wars", made it very difficult to find new or used Smith & Wesson revolvers of any type available on the commercial market. Even a "common as dirt" K-frame, fixed-sight, four-inch, blue .38 Special, square-butt M10 revolver was so scarce than any that came into local stores in my home town of St. Louis during the period were immediately grabbed up as soon as they were put in the showcase. Even if you did not need another one, it was good trading stock.

It was even worse for anything unusual or really desirable. For myself and a few friends, this drought of good Smith & Wesson revolvers would continue until Joe Desay of the J & G Rifle Ranch in Turner, Montana, (now of Prescott, Arizona, where it is not so cold) started buying them up and reselling them at a premium via *Shotgun News*. Many people resented his selling them at a price well beyond factory list, but I was always happy to get what I wanted, and viewed it as a great example of free market capitalism at work. During that time I bought a bunch of good Smith & Wesson revolvers, paid more than list for them, and still have them now four decades later.

# Ruger Military Revolvers

620. Right side view of two double-action .38 Special revolvers purchased by the military from Sturm, Ruger & Co. during and after the Vietnam War era, both with 4" barrels and lanyard swivels. Both are unfired, and still have the neoprene spacers in the cylinders as shipped from the factory.

Above: the square-butt "Service Six" model, one of 6,500 ordered in December, 1977 by the U.S. Army Armament Material Development and Readiness Command at Rock Island Arsenal for the Navy and Marine Corps.

Below: the semi-round-butt SS84-L model, purchased in a 1980 contract.

Note both bear official "U.S." property stamps.

Jeff Moeller collection

621. A familiar orange-and-black commercial Ruger box, showing how the military-contract Model SS84-L .38 Special revolver was shipped. Jeff Moeller collection

622 (left). Closeup of military markings on the bottom of the box, showing details of NSN identifier, contract and serial number. Jeff Moeller collection

1005-01-094-7045
REVOLVER, CAL. .38 SPECIAL
1 EA.
DAAA09-80-C-2041
SERIAL NO. 156-82372

TM SS84-L

TECHNICAL MANUAL
FOR
RUGER®
SS84-L
MILITARY MODEL
DOUBLE ACTION REVOLVERS
Caliber .38 Special

NATIONAL STOCK NUMBER:
1005-01-040-8989
MANUFACTURER'S CATALOG NUMBER:
SS84-L

STURM, RUGER & Company, Inc.
Southport, Connecticut 06490 U. S. A.
ALL RUGER FIREARMS ARE DESIGNED AND MANUFACTURED IN RUGER FACTORIES IN THE UNITED STATES OF AMERICA

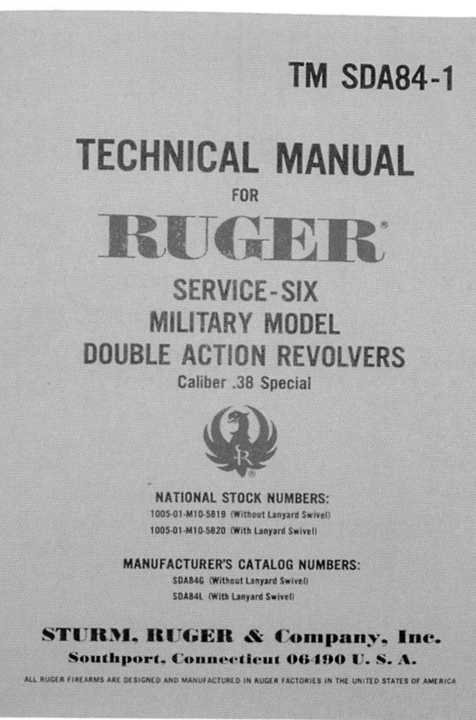

TM SDA84-1

TECHNICAL MANUAL
FOR
RUGER®
SERVICE-SIX
MILITARY MODEL
DOUBLE ACTION REVOLVERS
Caliber .38 Special

NATIONAL STOCK NUMBERS:
1005-01-M10-5819 (Without Lanyard Swivel)
1005-01-M10-5820 (With Lanyard Swivel)

MANUFACTURER'S CATALOG NUMBERS:
SDA84G (Without Lanyard Swivel)
SDA84L (With Lanyard Swivel)

STURM, RUGER & Company, Inc.
Southport, Connecticut 06490 U. S. A.
ALL RUGER FIREARMS ARE DESIGNED AND MANUFACTURED IN RUGER FACTORIES IN THE UNITED STATES OF AMERICA

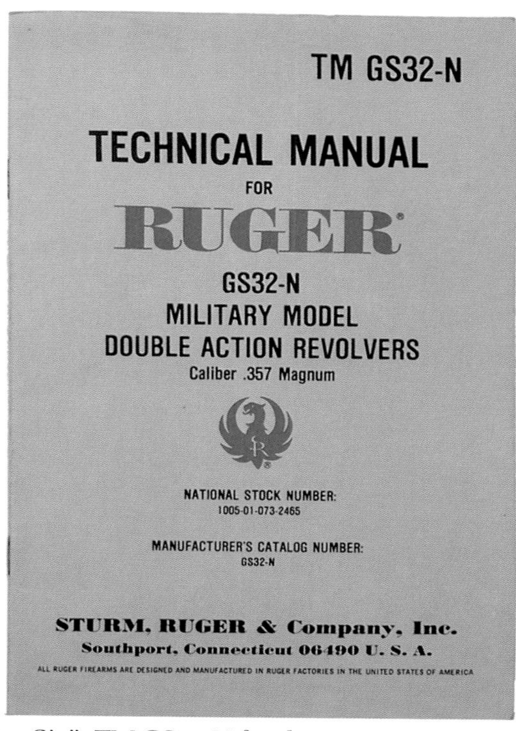

TM GS32-N

TECHNICAL MANUAL
FOR
RUGER®
GS32-N
MILITARY MODEL
DOUBLE ACTION REVOLVERS
Caliber .357 Magnum

NATIONAL STOCK NUMBER:
1005-01-073-2465

MANUFACTURER'S CATALOG NUMBER:
GS32-N

STURM, RUGER & Company, Inc.
Southport, Connecticut 06490 U. S. A.
ALL RUGER FIREARMS ARE DESIGNED AND MANUFACTURED IN RUGER FACTORIES IN THE UNITED STATES OF AMERICA

623. The covers of three Technical Manuals describing Ruger double-action revolvers.

From left: TM SS84-L, for the .38 Special model SS84-L with semi-round-butt; TM SDA84-1, for the .38 Special square-butt "Service Six"; TM GS32-N for the .357 Magnum caliber GS32-N, as used by the Naval Investigative Service (NIS). Jeff Moeller collection

Possibly due at least partly to the heavy demand and consequent lack of availability of Smith & Wesson products during the Vietnam War era, the military also purchased and used three models of double-action revolvers manufactured by Sturm, Ruger & Co. Two of these are illustrated here.

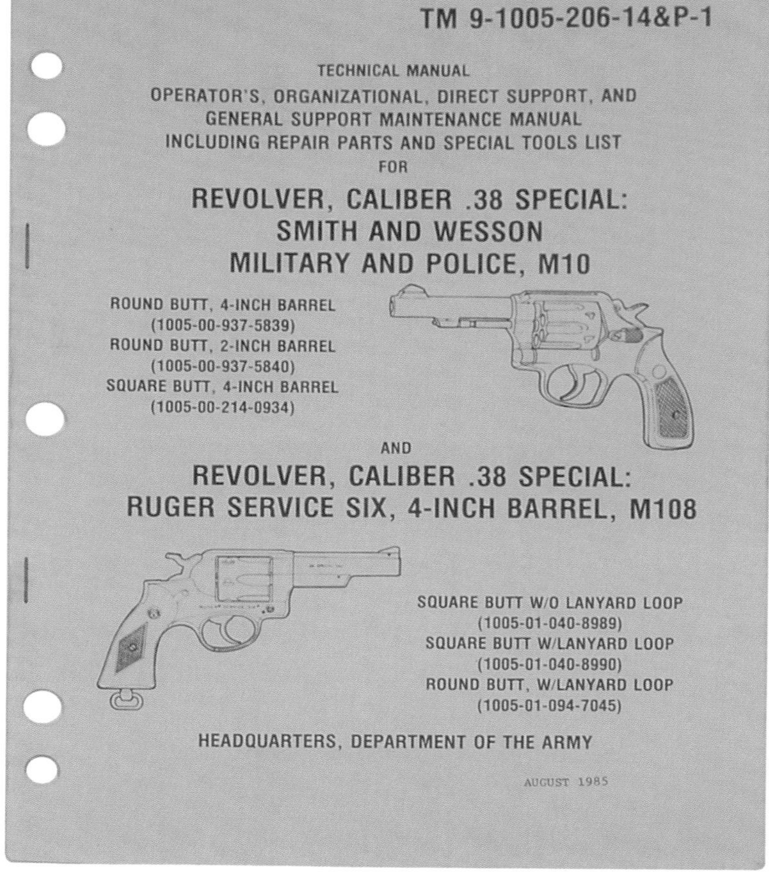

TM 9-1005-206-14&P-1

TECHNICAL MANUAL
OPERATOR'S, ORGANIZATIONAL, DIRECT SUPPORT, AND
GENERAL SUPPORT MAINTENANCE MANUAL
INCLUDING REPAIR PARTS AND SPECIAL TOOLS LIST
FOR

REVOLVER, CALIBER .38 SPECIAL:
SMITH AND WESSON
MILITARY AND POLICE, M10

ROUND BUTT, 4-INCH BARREL
(1005-00-937-5839)
ROUND BUTT, 2-INCH BARREL
(1005-00-937-5840)
SQUARE BUTT, 4-INCH BARREL
(1005-00-214-0934)

AND

REVOLVER, CALIBER .38 SPECIAL:
RUGER SERVICE SIX, 4-INCH BARREL, M108

SQUARE BUTT W/O LANYARD LOOP
(1005-01-040-8989)
SQUARE BUTT W/LANYARD LOOP
(1005-01-040-8990)
ROUND BUTT, W/LANYARD LOOP
(1005-01-094-7045)

HEADQUARTERS, DEPARTMENT OF THE ARMY

AUGUST 1985

624. The cover of TM 9-1005-206-14&P-1, the complete Technical Manual for the .38 Special 4-inch round- and square-butt S&W Model 10 and the round- and square-butt Ruger Service Six revolver, military designation M108. Jeff Moeller collection

# Military .38 Special Cartridges

## Types and Loadings Available in 1947

Before the adoption of the USAF lightweight M13 "Aircrewman" revolver there was no requirement for a special standard-velocity .38 Special cartridge which was safe to fire in alloy cylinders.

The several .38 Special loadings and types available in 1947 for military issue were listed in TM9-1990, titled "Small-Arms Ammunition", issued by the War Department in September, 1947. Pertinent sections of this TM are excerpted as follows:

### *134. Cal. .38 Special Cartridges*

***a. GENERAL***

*These cartridges may be fired from the following . . S&W caliber .38 special revolvers: . . S&W Military and Police, .38-44, Outdoorsman, and Magnum. The cartridges are 1.53 inches long, except the blank and mid-range wad-cutter cartridges which are 1.16 inches long. The rimmed cartridge case is 1.16 inches long. Diameter of the case head is 0.433 inch and of the case body is 0.378 inch.*

***b. CARTRIDGE, BALL, REVOLVER, CAL. .38 SPECIAL, 158-GRAIN BULLET***

*1. Cartridge*

*This cartridge is authorized for issue to the Counter Intelligence Corps on requisition by all Corps Areas, Departments (except the Philippines), Defense Commands, and Base Commands. The cartridge is 1.53 inches long.*

*2. Bullet*

*The S&W special 158-grain bullet has a round tip . . The bullet is of lead and its base end is cupped. The bullet is "inside lubricated", having one cannelure containing a lubricant which lies below the neck of the case in the assembled cartridge. The cartridge case is crimped in to a groove in the bullet . . The bullet is 0.74 inches long.*

***c. CARTRIDGE, BALL, REVOLVER, CAL. .38 SPECIAL, 158-GRAIN BULLET, STEEL JACKET (COPPER PLATED).***

*This cartridge is similar to that described in* b, *above, except for the bullet which has a copper-plated steel jacket . .*

***d. CARTRIDGE, BALL, REVOLVER, CAL. .38 SPECIAL, MID-RANGE, 146-GRAIN BULLET (WAD CUTTER)***

*This cartridge is used in target practice and contains a reduced charge of propellant for mid-ranges. The bullet is entirely enclosed in the cartridge case. It has three cannelures, a deep cup formation in the base of the bullet, and a flat front. Upon firing, it cuts a clean hole in the target . .*

***e. CARTRIDGE, BALL, REVOLVER, CAL. .38 SPECIAL, 200-GRAIN BULLET, NICKELED CARTRIDGE CASE (SUPER POLICE)***

*This cartridge uses the same case as the other caliber .38 special cartridges. The case, however, is nickel-plated. The bullet weighs 200 grains and is blunt-nosed and of lead alloy. It is an "inside lubricated" bullet having two cannelures below the case-to-bullet crimp groove. The base of the bullet is cupped. The bullet is 0.81 inches long . .*

***f. CARTRIDGE, TRACER, REVOLVER, CAL. .38 SPECIAL, 120-GRAIN BULLET, STEEL JACKET***

*This cartridge is for observation of fire, for incendiary purposes, and for signaling. It consists of the same case and primer as the other caliber .38 special cartridges, but differs in having a*

*120-grain copper clad steel bullet containing a tracer composition in its base. The tip of the bullet is painted red.*

***g. CARTRDGE, TRACER, REVOLVER, CAL. .38 SPECIAL, 158-GRAIN BULLET, STEEL JACKET***

*This cartridge is for observation of fire, for incendiary purposes, and for signaling. It consists of the same case and primer as the other caliber .38 special cartridges, but differs in having a 158-grain copper clad steel-jacketed bullet containing a tracer composition in its base. The tip of the bullet is painted red . . Average range of trace is 352 yards.*

***h. CARTRIDGE, BLANK, REVOLVER, CAL. .38 SPECIAL***

*This cartridge is used for simulated fire and signaling. It has no bullet. The mouth is crimped and closed by a wad. This cartridge is 1.16 inches long.*

***i. CARTRIDGE, TEST, HIGH-PRESSURE, CAL. .38 SPECIAL***

*This cartridge is for use only in inspection of weapons. The same components, except for the increased propelling charge, as those in the 158-grain lead bullet caliber .38 special cartridge are used. Since this ammunition develops dangerously high chamber pressures, 21,600 to 24,000 pounds per square inch, it will not be used for any other purpose. Due to the danger involved in firing this cartridge, it should only be fired from a fixed rest under a hood, by means of a mechanical firing device, and only by authorized personnel . . It may be identified by the cartridge case which has a mottled brownish black coating.*

## A Description of the M41 Cartridge from 1956

The Department of the Army Technical Manual TM9-2027 (Air Force Technical Order TO 11W3-4-2-34) dated July, 1956 (fig. 609) briefly introduces the cartridge type to be used in the lightweight M13 "Aircrewman" revolver as follows:

*Cal. .38 special, containing a 130-grain guilding metal jacketed lead bullet. Std. chamber pressure of 16,000 psi.*

## .38 Special Types and Loadings Available in 1961

A later edition of the manual titled "Small-Arms Ammunition", Army TM 9-1305-200/Air Force TO 11A13-1-101, dated June, 1961, begins with a full description of the M41 loading, which was for use with the M13 lightweight revolver. Relevant sections from this TM are excerpted as follows:

## *113. CARTRIDGES FOR CALIBER .38 SPECIAL REVOLVERS*

*These cartridges . . may be fired from the following . . S&W caliber .38 special revolvers: . . S&W Military and Police, .38-44, Outdoorman, and Magnum. These cartridges may also be fired in revolver, lightweight, caliber .38 special, M12 (aircrewman's).*

### *114. CARTRIDGE, CALIBER .38 SPECIAL: Ball, M41, 130-Grain Bullet*

***a. Cartridge***

*This cartridge is an item of issue for use in caliber .38 lightweight revolver M13. The cartridge is 1.53 inches long. Diameter of the case head is 0.433 inch and at the mouth is .379 inch. The total weight of the cartridge is approximately 203 grains.*

***b. Bullet***

*The bullet consists of a gilding-metal jacket and a lead-antimony slug. The bullet weighs 132 grains. The cartridge case is crimped into a groove in the bullet. The length of the bullet is .593 inch.*

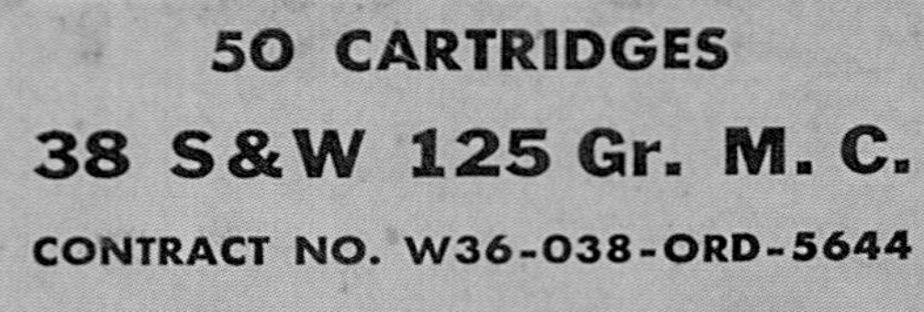


625. A selection of military 50-round cartridge boxes from various manufacturers and lot numbers. The top leftmost box holds .38 S&W cartridges, while the rest are for .38 Special, mostly the M41 loading approved for use in the lightweight M13 " Aircrewman" revolver.
John Miller collection

*c. Velocity*

*The basic velocity will not be less than 950 fps at 15 feet. The average velocity will not vary from the basic velocity by more than 25 fps.*

*d. Pressure*

*The average pressure will not exceed 16,000 psi.*

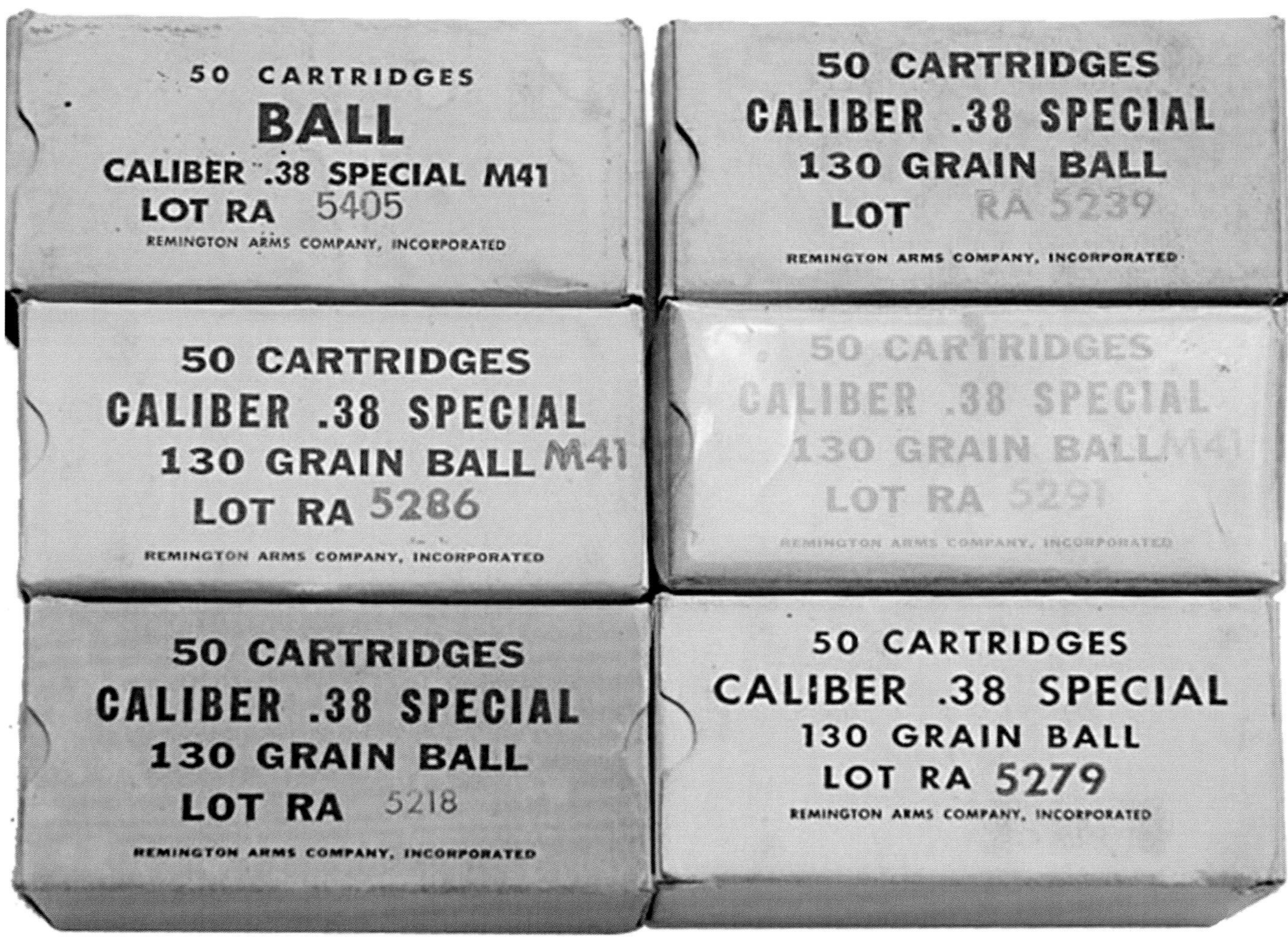


626. Six more military 50-round .38 Special cartridge boxes from various manufacturers and lot numbers, all of the 130-grain M41 loading. Jeff Moeller collection

*e. Accuracy*

*The average of the mean radii of all targets at time of acceptance at 50 yards is not greater than 2 inches.*

### *115. CARTRIDGE, CALIBER .38 SPECIAL: Ball, Lead Bullet, 158-Grain Bullet*

*a. Cartridge*

*This cartridge is authorized for issue to the Counter Intelligence Corps and Military Police only. It is for zone of interior training use. This cartridge is 1.53 inches long.*

*b. Bullet*

*This S&W special 158-grain bullet has a round tip . . The bullet is made of lead and its base end is cupped. The bullet is inside-lubricated, having one cannelure containing a lubricant which lies below the neck of the case in the assembled cartridge. The cartridge case is crimped into a groove in the bullet . .*

627. Six more military 50-round .38 Special cartridge boxes from various manufacturers and lot numbers, all of the 130-grain M41 loading. Jeff Moeller collection

## 116. CARTRIDGE, CALIBER .38 SPECIAL: Ball, 158-Grain Bullet, Steel Jacket (Copper-Plated)

### a. Cartridge

*This cartridge is similar to that described in paragraph 115 above except for the bullet which has a copper-plated steel jacket. This cartridge is for operational use by the Counter Intelligence Corps and Military Police . .*

## 117. CARTRIDGE, CALIBER .38 SPECIAL: Ball, Revolver, Midrange, 146- or 148-Grain, Lead Clean-Cutting Bullet, Western Super Match or Equivalent

### a. Cartridge

*This cartridge is used for target practice and contains a reduced charge of propellant for midranges.*

### b. Bullet

*The bullet is entirely inclosed in the cartridge case and it has three cannelures, a deep cup formation in the base of the bullet, and a flat front. The bullet weighs 146- to 148-grains and is of lead alloy. Blunt, but with a sharp shoulder or corner, the bullet will cut a clean hole*

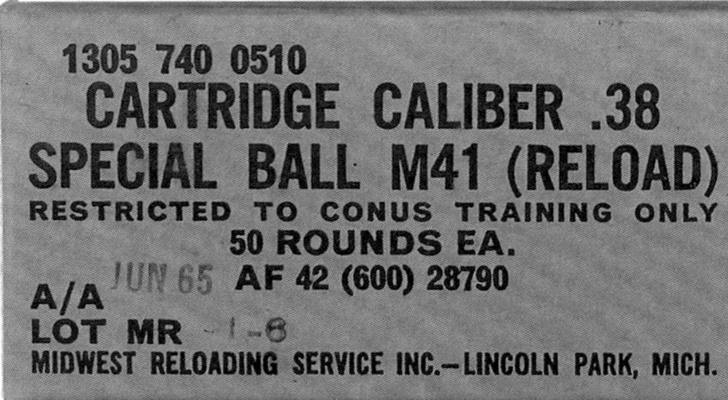






628. Two boxes of rare military M41 reloads, processed for the U.S. Air Force by Midwest Reloading Service of Lincoln Park, Michigan. These were for military training use only within the continental United States (CONUS).

Below: side of box with warning label.

upper box: John Miller collection
lower box: Jeff Moeller collection









629. Four 50-round boxes of military High Velocity loadings with 130-grain bullets, for Air Force use in their Model 15 and Model 56 S&W revolvers.

A sample round, with full copper jacket, is shown beside the second box.

first three boxes: Jeff Moeller collection
lower box: John Miller collection

630. A wooden crate stencilled on top "SMALL ARMS AMMUNITION" holding 2,500 rounds of .38 Special ammunition with 158-grain steel jacketed bullets (military code T2BFA), in Remington 50-round green-and-red commercial-type boxes from lot number R.A. 5033, as shown in fig. 631. From the almost illegible stencilling on top, it appears this crate was sent from the Naval Surface Weapons Center in Crane, Indiana to the Naval base in Corpus Christi, Texas. Jeff Moeller collection

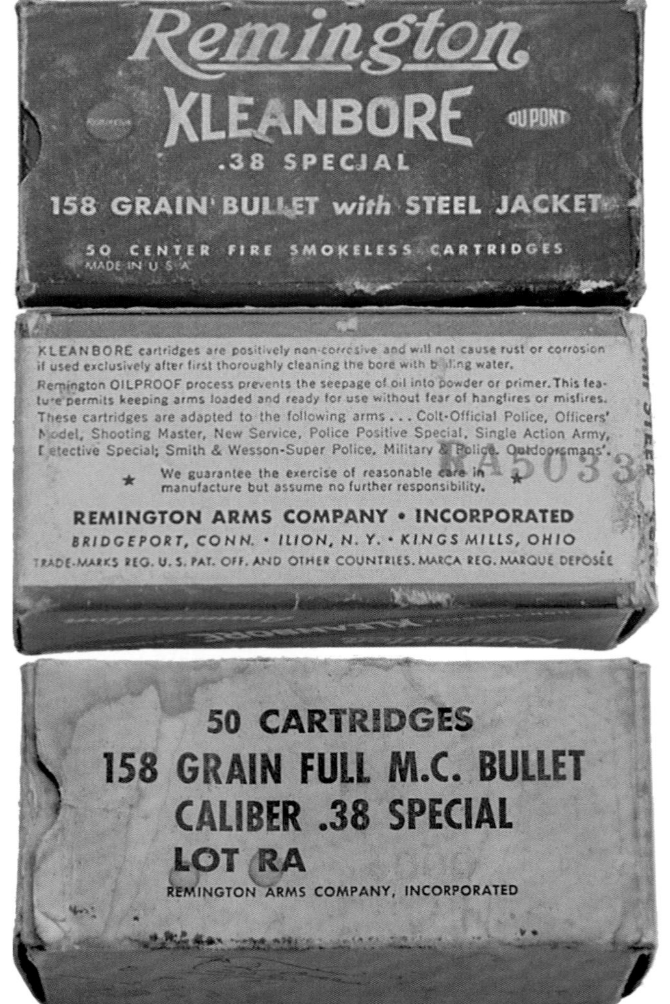


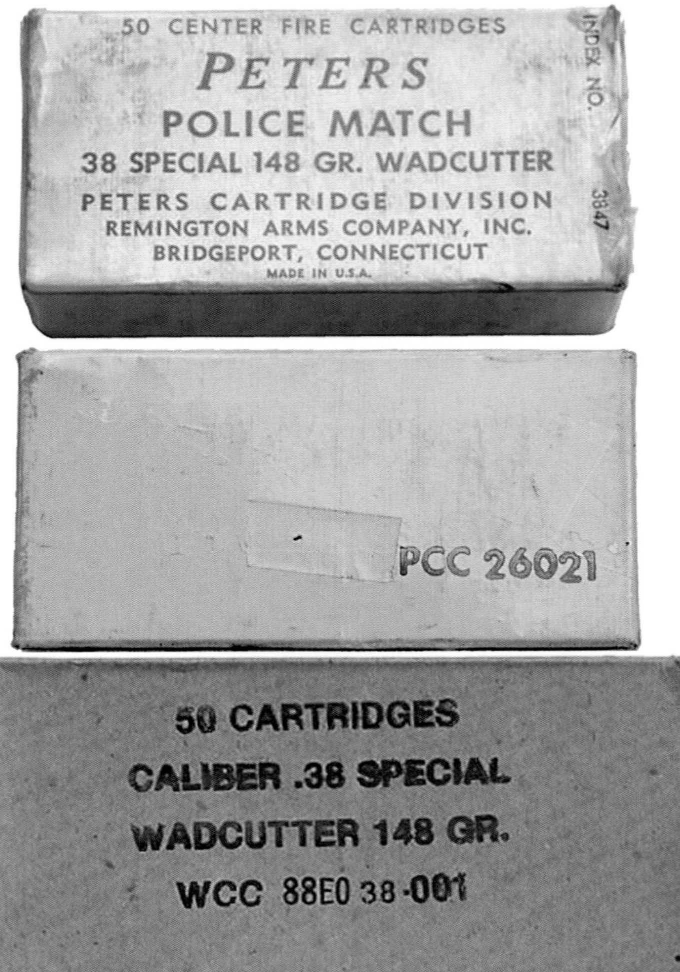

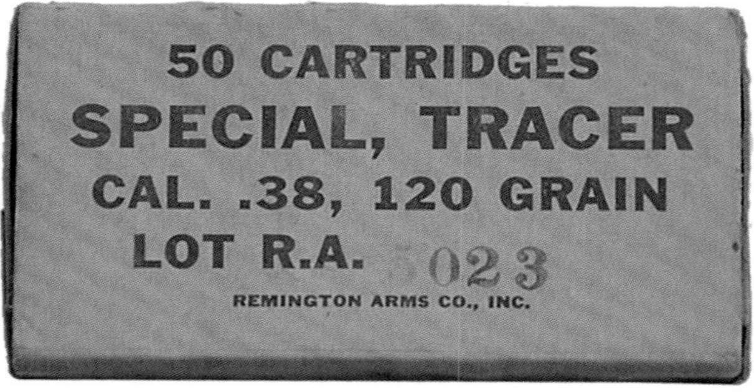




633. Four different boxes of .38 Special cartridges loaded with Tracer projectiles.

The box at bottom left contains "Red Signal" cartridges from the Naval Ammunition Depot in Crane, Indiana, dated February, 1968, as used by downed pilots in Vietnam to indicate their position. John Miller collection

*through target paper, thus making a hit easier to spot and score. It is sometimes called a wad cutter or clean-cutting bullet, and is inside-lubricated.*

### *118. CARTRIDGE, CALIBER .38 SPECIAL: Test, High-Pressure, 158-Grain Bullet*

*This cartridge is for use only in inspection of weapons. Except for the increased propelling charge, the same components as those in the 158-grain lead-bullet, caliber .38 special cartridge are used. Since this ammunition develops dangerously high chamber pressures, 21,600 to 24,000 psi, the HPT cartridge will not be used for any other purpose. Because of the danger involved in firing this cartridge, it should be fired only from a fixed rest under a hood, by means of a mechanical device, and only by authorized personnel. The cartridge is 1.53 inches long and can be identified by its case which has a mottled brownish black coating.*

31 (left, preceding page). Above: the top and bottom of a ommercial green-and-red box of 50 158-grain steel-jack-ed cartridges from Remington Arms Co. Inc. lot no. RA 033, as packed in the crate shown in fig. 630.

Below: a later plain cardboard box of 50 similar rounds, s packed for the military by Remington.

32 (right, preceding page). Above: the top and bottom of box of Peters .38 Special cartridges loaded with 158-gr. adcutter bullets, manufactured under military contract r target shooting. Note the government lot no. on the ottom.

Below: a later box of 50 .38 Special wadcutter cartridges aded for the military by Winchester, as packed in the etal ammo can shown at right in fig. 634.

Jeff Moeller collection

## A Pair of Ammo Cans for Military .38 Special Ammunition

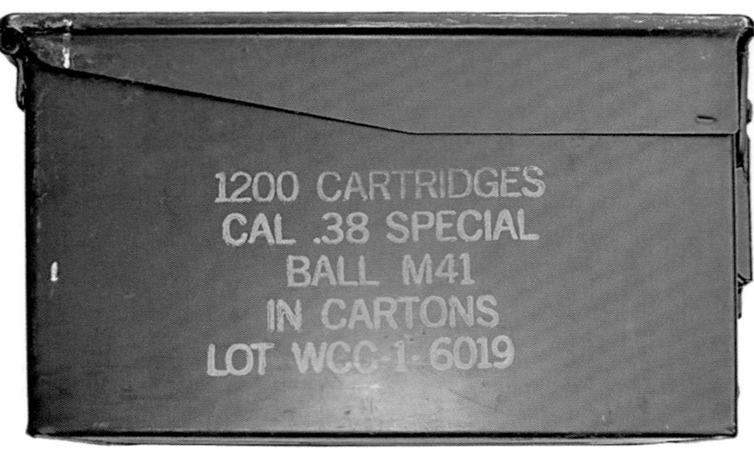


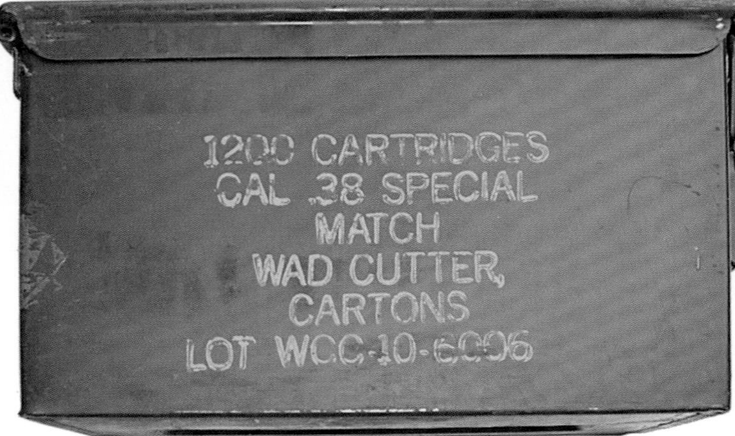


634. A pair of standard military ammunition cans, with markings indicating both contain 1,200 rounds of .38 Special ammunition, both loaded under military contract by Winchester.
Left: 130-grain M41 Ball.
Right: 148-grain Match wadcutter.
Jeff Moeller collection

# Military .22 Rimfire Ammunition

A brief excerpt concerning military use of .22 Rimfire ammunition, taken from Chapter 8 of the standard reference *History of Modern U.S. Military Small Arms Ammunition Volume II* are as follows:

*This type of ammunition, for the most part, was of commercial nature and procured primarily for training purposes . .*

635. Two early commercial boxes of .22 LR cartridges. The lot numbers indicate these were loaded for the military during WWII. Jeff Moeller collection

## The Little-Known WWII T42 and M24 Cartridges, with Jacketed Bullets

Further interesting excerpts from the *History of Modern U.S. Military Small Arms Ammunition Volume II* explain the development of the T42 and M24 .22 rimfire cartridges, both of which were loaded with metal-jacketed bullets:

*During the early part of 1944 the Ordnance Department was requested to procure a large quantity of cal. .22 Long Rifle hollow point hunting ammunition for use by the Air Force in a survival rifle. In the spring of 1944 a ruling by the Army canceled this order because of the possible violation of the Hague Convention. Accordingly, the Ordnance Department was requested to develop a jacketed bullet for the Cal. .22 Long Rifle ball cartridge that would satisfy the terms of the Convention . . and*

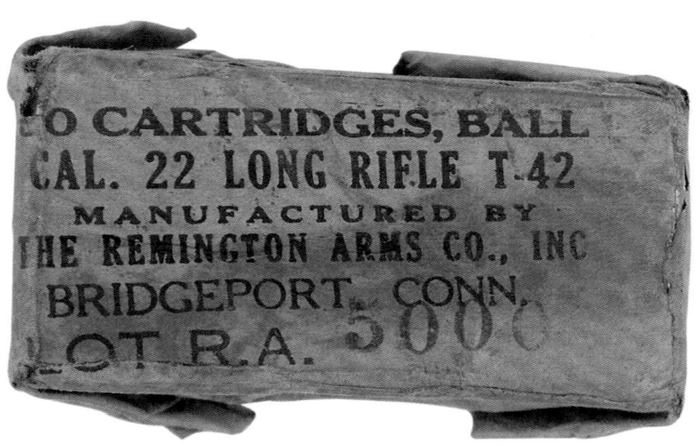


636. A packet of 50 rounds of T42 steel-cased cartridges with full-metal-jacket bullets, as loaded by Remington Arms Co. John Miller collection

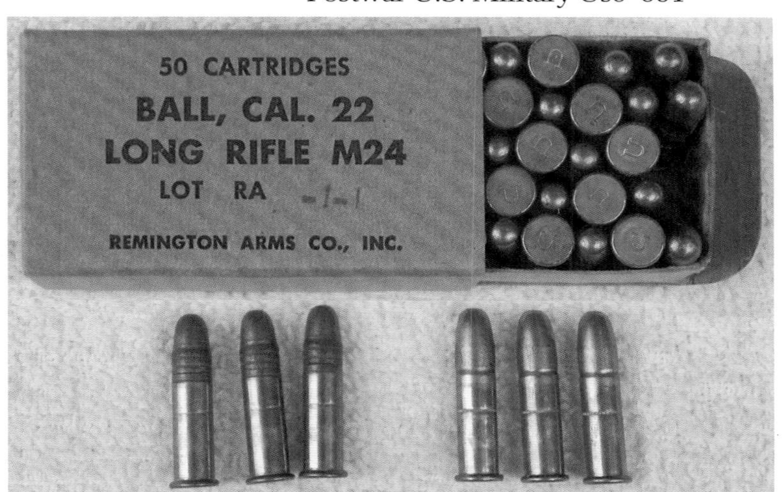


637. A box of 50 rounds of the later M24 cartridges with metal-jacketed bullets, also loaded by Remington. John Miller collection



638. A "brick" of 500 rounds of M24 .22 caliber rimfire cartridges, loaded with 40-grain metal jacketed bullets. John Miller collection

*the following nomenclature was assigned: Cartridge, Ball, Cal..22, T42. Remington Arms Co. was given a development contract for this round and started work in September 1944.*
*. . Because of the urgent requirement . . the T42 cartridge was placed on the critical list during January 1945 . . During May 1945, an additional 1,588,000 rounds of the T42 cartridge were procured from Remington for use by the Office of Strategic Services. This ammunition was for use in [High Standard] automatic pistols equipped with silencers. As a result of the satisfactory performance of the T42 cartridge and the continued use of this type of ammunition by the Air Force in E12 and E14 Survival Kits, the Ordnance Department adopted the T42 as the M24. This was confirmed by Ordnance Committee action in May 1945.*
*. . Both the T42 and M24 cartridges were packed in 50-round commercial boxes that may or may not be overprinted with the military designation . .*

A further quote from *High Standard Automatic Pistols 1932 - 1950* by Charles E. Petty adds the following interesting note concerning the military use of High Standard automatic pistols equipped with silencers:

639. Two views of a military ammunition can holding 5,100 rounds of standard velocity .22 rimfire ammunition. Left: side view, showing markings. Right: top view with lid removed, showing method of packing in 50-round boxes. Jeff Moeller collection



640. An assortment of 50-round boxes of .22 Long Rifle cartridges as loaded by various contractors for the military. The top two are the earliest. Jeff Moeller collection

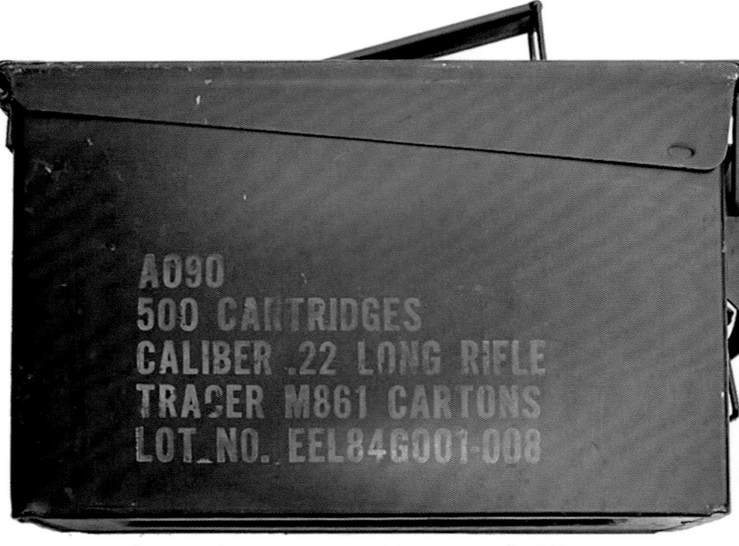


641. Another military ammunition can holding 500 rounds of M861 .22 rimfire Tracer ammunition. Jeff Moeller collection

*. . An interesting variant of the USA-HD is found in the USA-HD-MS. This is a silencer-equipped version made for clandestine use by the O.S.S. and other military agencies. Over 2,000 silencers were installed on guns taken at random from regular production. These guns were sometimes completely unmarked and were shipped in plain brown boxes . .*

# Military Holsters, Belts, and Cartridge Pouches

## A Belt and Holster Set for the U.S. Navy Model 1899

642. A covered flap holster and cartridge pouch as issued for use with the 1,000 Model 1899 First Model Hand Ejectors purchased by the U.S. Navy.
courtesy Rock Island Auction Co.

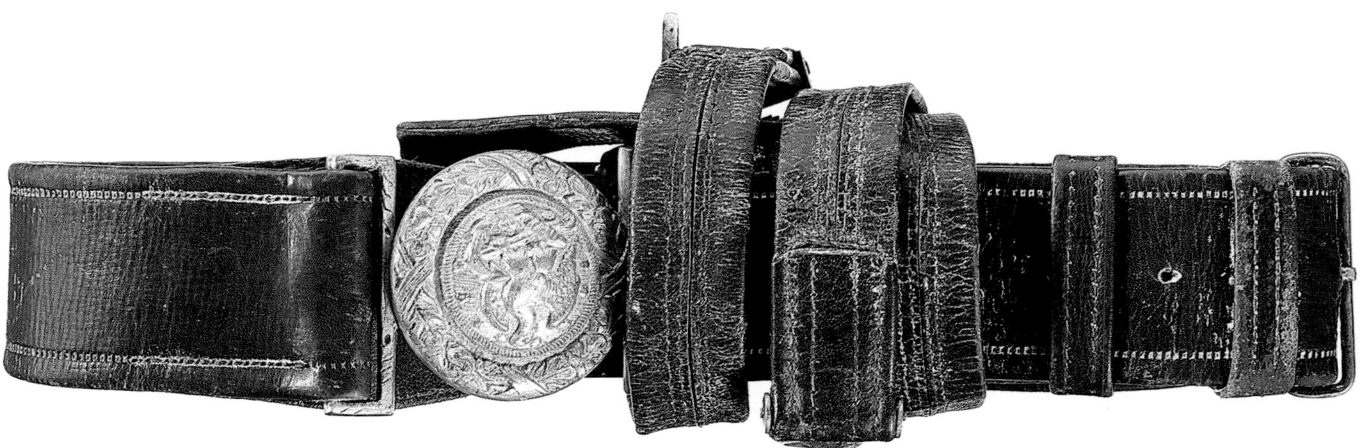

643. The brass-buckled belt, issued along with the holster shown above, for use with the U.S. Navy Model 1899 revolver. courtesy Rock Island Auction Co.

## A U.S.-Made WWII-Issue Holster and Lanyard

644. A brown leather U.S.-marked flap holster for use with the British .38/200 revolver, with 5" barrel.
courtesy Rock Island Auction Co.

645. A WWII-issue woven fabric lanyard with sewn leather end piece and metal hook for attachment to the lanyard swivel of a U.S. Victory Model .38 Special revolver. As shown at right, this item was made by Hickok in 1943.
Jeff Moeller collection

646. Closeup of the leather lanyard end piece, showing maker's name and date, 1943. Jeff Moeller collection

## A Vietnam-Era Advisor Holster and Belt Set, Locally Made

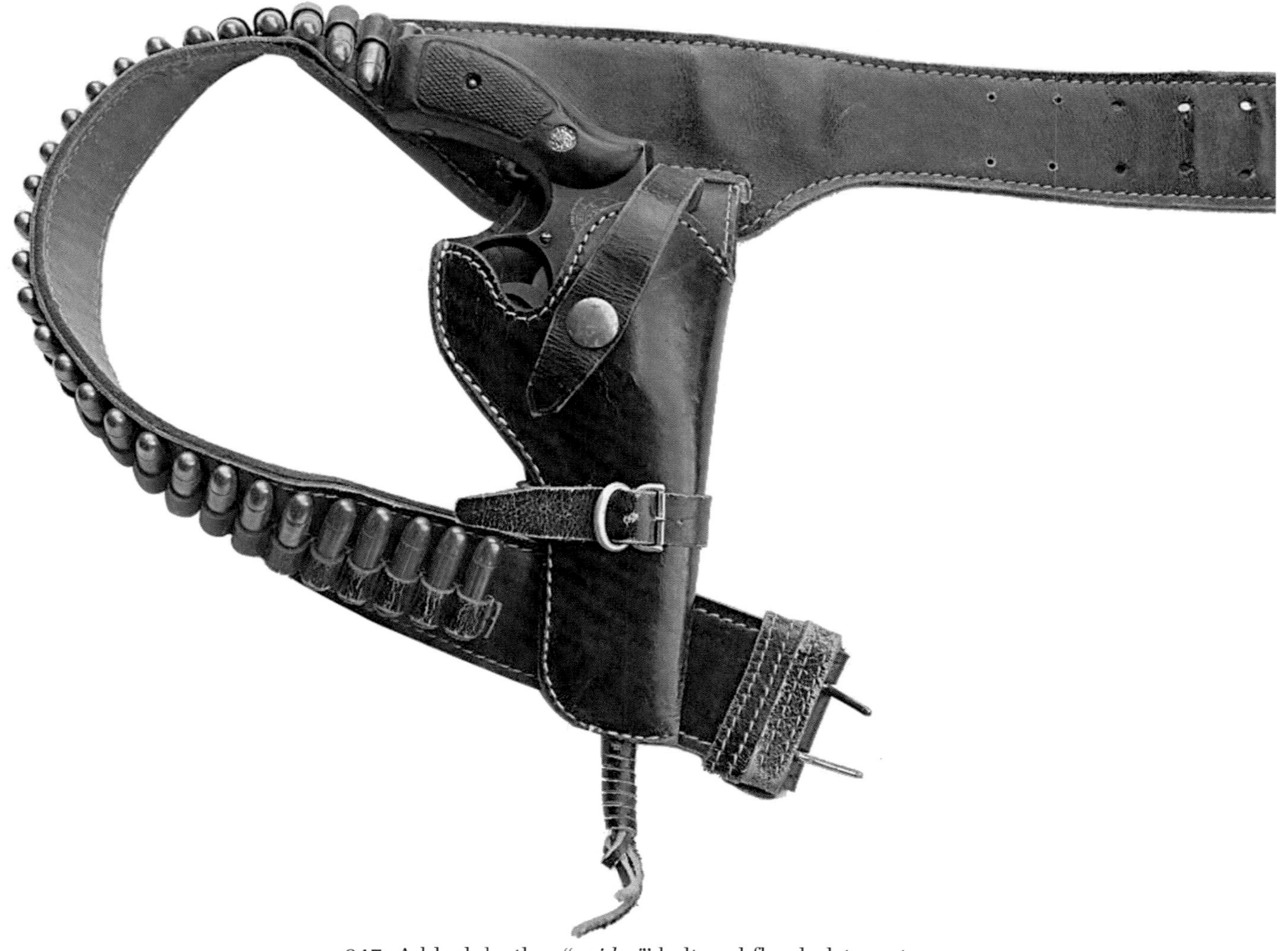

647. A black leather "*coi boi*" belt and flap holster set, as made in-country by local craftsmen for use by U.S. advisors and helicopter pilots in Vietnam. Note the belt loops, holding 30 rounds of .38 Special ammunition.

The revolver is the U.S.-marked, 4" round-butt M&P shown in fig. 602. Jeff Moeller collection

# A Vietnam-Era Survival Vest

648. A mesh survival vest as worn by Air Force pilots in Vietnam. The Camillus survival knife and M10 holster have been sewn directly onto the vest.

Inset, right: an unfinished leather version of the survival vest holster, with instructions. Jeff Moeller collection

## A USAF Flap Holster for Belt or Shoulder Carry

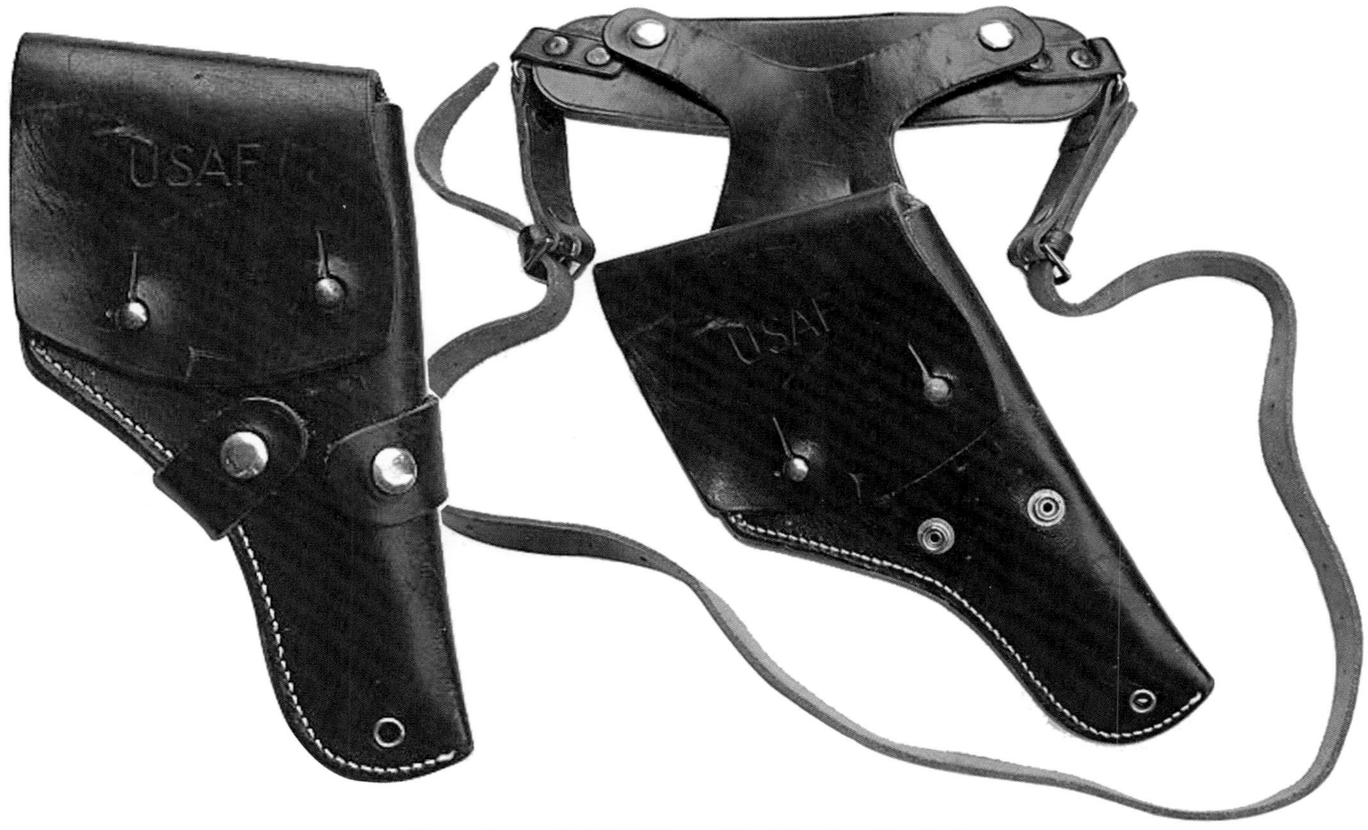


649. Two views of a USAF issue black leather flap holster.
Left: with snaps configured for belt carry.
Right: with snap portion swivelled for use with the extra flap and strap as a shoulder holster.
Jeff Moeller collection

## A Belt Holster for All Issue Army and Air Force 4" Revolvers

650. A new-in-the-box black leather belt holster made for use with all Army and Air Force issue 4" revolvers.

This holster, made under military contract by S&W Leather Co., is also shown in figs. 615 and 755.

Inset, right: box end label identifying this item as "Holster, Hip, RH". Jeff Moeller collection

# A USAF-Issue Swivel Belt Holster and Ammo Pouch

651. Front and back views of a USAF-issue "Holster Assembly" (swivel belt holster and ammunition pouch), both made and marked by the J. M. Bucheimer Co. in 1966.
Jeff Moeller collection

652. The above "Holster Assembly" as packed for shipment to the USAF Air Police.

Inset, right: the box end label of the Holster and Case, packed in September, 1977. Jeff Moeller collection

## A Post-Vietnam Shoulder Holster

653. Back and front views of a modern reissue of a WWII favorite shoulder holster, made by Hunter Corp. in black leather. Jeff Moeller collection

# A USAF Crewmember Shoulder Holster

654. A black leather shoulder holster with spring retention, for USAF-issue Model 15 revolvers.

The spare cartridge strip shown below was often attached to the shoulder strap. Jeff Moeller collection

655 (left). Front and back views of a black leather strip with six spare cartridge loops, designed to attach to the strap of the above shoulder holster. Jeff Moeller collection

# A Black Leather Belt Holster, Issued in the 1970s and 1980s

656. Back and front views of a black leather belt holster with studded flap and belt hanger, issued with 4" revolvers in the 1970s and 1980s. Jeff Moeller collection

## A 1980s Military Police/Air Police Holster

657. Back and front views of a 1980s-issue angled belt holster with inner flap for retention of the revolver, used by the Military Police and Air Police.

Jeff Moeller collection

# Two Air Police Revolver Ammo Pouches

658. Front and back views of two issue black leather ammunition pouches, designed for belt wear, each with two separate pockets closed by metal snaps.

Above: made by Atchison Leather Products Co.

Below: made by Oklahoma Leather Products Inc.

Jeff Moeller collection

659. A modern version of the WWII-era pistol lanyard shown in figs. 645 and 646, made of green nylon with plastic keepers and metal spring clip.

Issued for use with all later contract revolvers from Ruger and S&W, as well as with the Beretta M9.

Jeff Moeller collection

*Chapter Thirty-Seven*

# Unusual Variations, and Other Rarities

When I first suggested the K-frame Smith & Wesson revolver as the subject for a book to Blake Stevens, my editor and publisher, his response was typical of the initial impression I frequently get when mentioning these guns – they are so common that it would be a challenge to make a book about them seem interesting. When most people think of the M&P, they see merely ho-hum, Plain-Jane blued steel revolvers with square-butts, fixed sights, and four-inch tapered barrels. True, K-frames have enjoyed an unmatched production run and are still going strong today, and they have a lot of history behind them in law enforcement and the military, but "Seen one, seen 'em all" seems to be the response of many.

However when you go beyond the seemingly boring bread-and-butter models and start considering the variations the factory has offered over the years—those seen fairly commonly, then with increasing rarity, to the ultimate point of being really very exotic—if someone likes handguns at all, they will acknowledge that yes, indeed, there are a lot of interesting K-frames around, a lot more than you might normally think about, and taken as a whole they do make for a worthwhile and interesting book.

Here we will review some of the features that make for interesting examples, unusual variations, and even a few rarities. Naturally we cannot mention all the various oddities, but we will try to include weapons that are interesting (at least to me), and ones that we can illustrate. No doubt some readers will know of other examples that are not mentioned here but which are, in fact, every bit as interesting if not more so than the ones we have included.

### Describing the Common, or Garden, M&P

To get started, let's describe the "standard" K-frame so we know in which direction we are headed in our quest to find the non-standard examples.

I suppose the one I mentioned above—a square-butt, all-steel, fixed-sight, tapered-barrel, four-inch, blue-finish .38 Special—would be considered the most common example of the standard Military & Police revolver. Such guns have been manufactured nearly continuously for over a century now, and since 1957 they have been called by a model number, in this case the Model 10, instead of the earlier designation "M&P". The example in question might have an older long action or a postwar short action, but it would still pretty much be viewed as the classic or basic K-frame.

So with these characteristics in mind, let's expand our horizons in all directions to see what makes for interesting variations.

## Features That Make Interesting Variations

### Barrels

Barrel length and style, of course, readily come to mind. Two-, three-, five- and six-inch barrels are quite common, but barrels of 6½" and 8⅜" in length also exist on some K-frame models. Whereas the standard barrel was tapered to help keep down weight, a heavier, straight-walled barrel is found on

660. Left side view of what appears to be a common or garden variety square-butt, blued M&P, with a 5" barrel, but appearances can be deceiving.

This is actually the rather rare .32 Long variation. "S" and "C" serial number prefixes are found, mixed in with the .38 M&P series, with 4,813 manufactured from 1948 to 1950. Barrels in 2" and 4" are known, but only about 910 were built with 5" barrels. This is serial no. C 54341, which was shipped on October 2, 1950. Jim Fisher collection

more recent examples. This design helps shift the weight forward, which many prefer as an aid to weapon balance. It also helps to keep the muzzle down during recoil, since the extra forward weight dampens muzzle whip, thereby speeding up recovery for second and subsequent shots.

The early standard barrel was round with no rib, but ribs have long been a feature of many K-frame barrels to further increase forward weight, again shifting the weapon balance forward. Early ribs were narrow, later ones were wider and grooved to avoid heat build-up, always an issue with target shooters who often fire long strings in matches. The ribs can vary in width depending on the cartridge chambering since some cartridges, being small, will result in less steel being removed from the barrel and cylinder, hence the rib will be made narrower so that the weapon loaded will weigh the same as the larger-caliber revolvers in the same series, where more steel is removed from the barrel and cylinder yet the cartridges themselves are heavier.

On the front end of any of these barrels, one of a variety of front sights can be found that differs from the integrally-forged fixed front sights on our standard classic K-frame, whether the original "half-moon" or the later style with a flattened rear face.

The classic barrel does not sport the encased ejector rod so beloved by Smith & Wesson aficionados. However there are many K-frame models that do have encased ejector rods, and the elegance of these reinforces the comments of the late Elmer Keith, who often said that he thought such encased ejector rod housings should be a trademark on all Smith & Wesson revolvers.

## Sights

The classic example, of course, is a fixed-sight weapon. As shown in fig. 296, rear sights on early examples have a shallow U-shaped notch, while later examples have a deeper, clearly-defined square notch.

Adjustable sights have been featured on the many "target" K-frame models over the years. The three types of early screw-adjustable rear sights which have been provided over the years are depicted and described in Chapter Thirty-Three. These early target sights were comparatively difficult to adjust and the earliest versions did not always stay in position, whereas later model sights have quite rugged micrometer-click adjustments which are easily and precisely set.

### Chamberings and Finishes

As indicated in the sections about chamberings and finishes, there have been lots of different cartridges fired in these revolvers, and lots of different finishes applied. Conventional blued-steel .38 Special models are the classic, but nickel or chrome finish and alternative chamberings such as .357 Magnum and .32 WCF are not by any means uncommon, while others, like .38 Smith & Wesson, are normally seen only in military models like the WWII-vintage .38/200 and the postwar Model 11. In that same vein, gold-plated K-frames are very striking, in my judgment, but quite rare.

## Special Markings

### Property Stamps

The vast majority of examples feature only the factory-applied logos and legends, but the K-frame Smith & Wesson, especially the Military & Police fixed-sight version in .38 Special caliber, has always been a working gun, and it is not surprising that so many of them show up with the name of the department or agency that originally bought and used them roll-stamped or simply engraved on the metal surface someplace. Typically these appear on the backstrap or bottom of the grip frame, but occasionally they are located on the side or top of the frame.

Some of these markings are obvious, fully spelling out the name of the using organization, while others can be pretty obscure, especially if you do not live around the area where it was originally used. Often a hint as to what type of agency owned the revolver originally comes more from the number applied than the initials, since a high number will tend to indicate that it was larger organization. While many of these marks, especially the roll-marked or better engraved ones, were done at the factory as part of the order and can thus be documented in the letter you can request from the factory, others were often applied by the organization after acquisition. The latter tend to be hand-stamped, and frequently look pretty ugly. Still, these can be interesting to see and collect, as they do link the revolver to some history.

As a rule of thumb for collectors, the more mundane the organization, the more likely it is to be an honest revolver. For example, an M&P six-inch hand-stamped "WCSD 48" (standing for Wabash County Sheriff's Dept., Gun No. 48, if ever there was such a thing) is more likely to be what it purports to be than one stamped "Texas Dept. of Safety" (the source for the Texas Rangers in our timeframe). Similarly, an M&P marked "Dept. of Justice" may mean it went to the FBI, but maybe not—it could have been issued to the guard at the front door of the building.

Even if it did go to the FBI, it might well have sat in the Arms Room all its life, being used only as a replacement range gun in case someone's duty revolver went down. Or even if issued, it might have been immediately stuffed away, as a friend of mine did with his issue pre-WWII revolver, received in 1968 upon leaving Quantico for his first assignment, being replaced with a personally-owned (and hence unmarked) Model 19 four-inch Smith & Wesson.

Depending on the markings and how they were applied, such K-frames typically sell for less money than a similarly conditioned non-marked example. Unless they are verifiably from some really interesting agency or organization, or you have some unusual connection with such a group (you worked there, or your dad did, etc.), it seems to me most people view such markings rather like tattoos on girls, especially if they are of other guys' names: it diminishes their value.

### Retailer Markings

In that same manner, weapons marked with the names of retailers from Britain or any part of its old Empire bring a premium, at least among my friends. I enjoy looking at them, I will admit, but would not pay extra for them, as I think a handgun inscribed with the name of a British retailer about as interesting as one marked "Sears and Roebuck, Chicago", but obviously tastes differ. I am not a fan of notched grips or blood-spattered finishes either, but I know guys who really think these are exciting. Maybe they have a better imagination than I do, but these always remind me of bogus Nazi daggers made in 1946 and (chicken) blood-spattered Viet Cong flags made by Vietnamese ladies in Fenton, Missouri in 1978. I'll pass, thank you, on such things unless I or someone I know actually picked them up.

# Engraved K-Frames

## A Deluxe, Gold-Plated Engraved Model 1896

661. Right side view of a deluxe version of the first Hand Ejector, the I-frame Model 1896, with factory pearl grips.

While not a K-frame, this is too pretty an example to leave out.

The serial number would indicate that this was manufactured around 1902. It was subsequently gold-plated and engraved by a New York dealer. The cylinder pin was left bright, and the hammer and trigger are casehardened.

courtesy Rock Island Auction Co.

K-frame revolvers have been the canvas for many very fine engraving jobs over the years. These of course can vary from rather spartan examples to reaching the encrusted stage, but at whatever level, they are uncommon in comparison to their standard colleagues.

Many people do not want to use an engraved example as it is "too pretty to shoot". This has always seemed odd to me, absent gold inlays and what not that may fall out due to recoil forces. (Guess how I know not to shoot these anymore!)

Decoratively engraved examples of course fall into a different category from simple property- or retailer-marked examples. If done properly, and subject to documentation, these can be worth more than the value of the revolver without engraving plus the cost of the engraving.

In the following section we will discuss several basic categories of engraving and their relative values, assuming no other historical connection. (If the weapon also has some separate historical connection, then we are not just speaking about the engraving.)

# Factory-Engraved K-Frames

662. Left side view of a Model 1902 with 6½" barrel, serial no. 33267, with nickel finish, "style 3" factory engraving and factory pearl grips with gold medallions.

According to the factory letter, this revolver was shipped on January 13, 1904 to the Philip Bekeart Co. in San Francisco. courtesy Rock Island Auction Co.

## Roy Jinks on the History of Factory Engraving

On the subject of factory-engraved guns, which can be documented, S&W Historian Roy Jinks wrote an interesting article titled "Engraving is a Traditional Artform" which appeared in the Spring, 1982 issue of the Smith & Wesson *Bulletin*. This is excerpted as follows:

> *Decorating firearms is not a new form of art. It dates back to the invention of weapons. Kings, knights, landowners and even primitive Indian warriors decorated their weapons to show their status or [to] ward off evil spirits.*
>
> *During the Renaissance, as art became more refined, firearms decorating reached a pinnacle in high metal relief and elegant stock carving that equals the artistry of the great masters on canvas. . . The art of firearms decorating was introduced in the United States in 1700 with the decoration of the Pennsylvania rifle . . Once American gunmakers began to receive worldwide recognition, the need for high grade engraved firearms grew.*
>
> *The first high quality engravers were immigrants who came to the United States from Germany. L. D. Nimschke came to America in 1850. Gustave Young immigrated to the United States in 1846, but did not have a significant impact on the gun engraving industry until he joined Colt's.*
>
> *Although there were many other engravers working in the United States for various arms companies, Young and Nimschke were the two who set the styles that became the American style of scroll. Their influence is seen in the engraving being offered by the arms industry today.*
>
> *During the period from 1852 to 1878, Smith & Wesson used such independent engravers as Richard Bates Inshaw, L. D. Nimschke, and F. Martin. These artists generally cut an open style of scroll which had broad appeal, could be executed fairly rapidly and [thus] could be sold at a reasonable price.*
>
> *. . Nimschke developed a style of open scroll that was both attractive and gave good coverage. It was so appealing that it was copied by many*

663. Left and right side views of a round-butt Model 1905 First Change revolver, serial no. 108212, nickel plated and factory engraved, with factory pearl grips with gold medallions. The left side of the barrel reads ".38 S&W SPECIAL/& U.S. SERVICE CTG'S"

The factory letter confirms that this revolver was shipped on December 28, 1908 to a Harry M. Styner.

courtesy Rock Island Auction Co.

*independent engravers who worked for the large wholesalers in New York City [and] became known as the New York style.*

*Smith & Wesson [first] retained their own in-house engraver in 1867. At that time, D. B. Wesson hired Gustave Young, one of the finest engravers in the United States.*

*Young had executed some exquisite pieces for heads of state around the world during his tenure at Colt's. His expertise included the art of gold inlay and the similar, less costly open style scroll.*

*Gustave Young and his sons, Oscar and Eugene, dominated firearms engraving at Smith & Wesson until 1912.*

*. . After the era of the Young family ended in 1912, gun engraving at Smith & Wesson was given little attention. The factory hired Harry Jarvis, a good engraver but lacking the artistry of the Young family. His style was an open leaf type, even more open than that made popular by Nimschke . .*

*During the pre-World War II period, John Goodyear worked in-house. Contract engravers R. J. Kornbrath and Alvin White were used.*

664. Left and right side views of a Model 1905 Second Change revolver with target sights and a 6½" barrel marked ".32 WINCHESTER CTG", in a nickel-finish special factory engraved edition with factory rework star, made for an E. S. Ashley. The engraving on the bottom front of the frame features the intertwined initials "ESA".

The grips were checkered walnut when the gun was shipped on February 9, 1910, but were subsequently replaced with the pearl grips with carved steer head shown here. courtesy Rock Island Auction Co.

*After World War II, Harry Jarvis re-opened the S&W engraving department and worked as an engraver until his retirement at age 83.*

*Russell Smith was added to the engraving department in 1954. A number of engravers worked for him as the department grew, but this department took a back seat to production work.*

*In 1974 the question was asked, "Do we handle the back orders for engraving and give the customer what he wants, or do we get out of the engraving business?" Smith & Wesson decided in favor of the customer.*

*Russell Smith is now the "dean" of the custom engraving department, working with younger engravers Domingos Joaquim and Paul Piquette.*

*Smith & Wesson now offers a variety of engraving styles. They can do custom engraving to meet any description the customer wants. Less expensive but well executed standard engraving patterns follow the open style of American engraving developed by Nimschke and Young . .*

## Work by Noted Factory Engravers of the Past

Revolvers factory-engraved by noted engravers who are no longer with us will bring a substantial premium simply because they are no longer available, and some people will collect the work of certain well-known engravers. Smith & Wesson has frequently offered high-quality engraving from the factory, and as Roy Jinks discusses above, weapons engraved by Gustave Young and his sons, Oscar and Eugene, are perfect examples of what I am talking about. The Smith & Wesson M&P came out just at the

665. Left and right side views of a 4" fixed-sight M&P, serial no. 244788, factory-engraved by Oscar Young.
This revolver was shipped in 1915, likely as a gift to a law enforcement officer.

end of the period during which the Young brothers were engraving, so there cannot be many of them, and consequently a Young-engraved M&P revolver is quite the collectible.

The fixed sight four-inch example illustrated in fig. 665 is no doubt even rarer, since it was either a gift for a law enforcement officer, probably just beginning or ending his career, or a reward for a service well performed; possibly capturing a desperate criminal, saving a large payroll from bandits, or taking someone important home instead of to the station when found someplace where fancy ladies and alcohol existed side by side. Don't laugh! That is how one of the most important political families in my home town got started.

## Work by Recent Factory Engravers

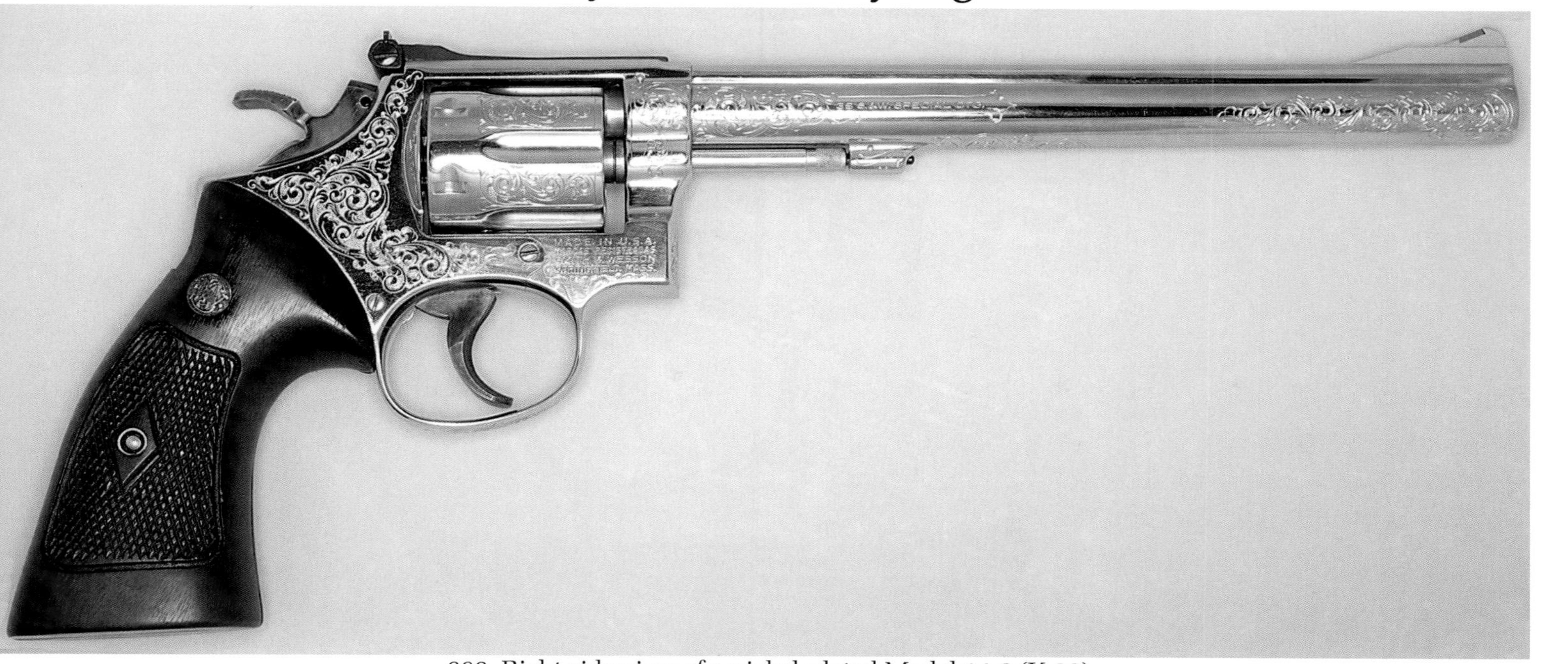

666. Right side view of a nickel-plated Model 14-3 (K-38) serial no. 6K67074 with 8⅜" barrel, target hammer, trigger and stocks, with full factory scroll engraving done circa 1980. This gun was probably returned to the factory for engraving and nickel plating.

Dave Terbrueggen collection

667. Right side view of a factory-engraved and nickel-plated Model 45 in .22 LR caliber.

The Model 45 is a rare piece in itself, and only a very few were so engraved and plated at the instigation of factory historian Roy G. Jinks.

668. Left and right side views of a .357 Magnum caliber Model 19-4 serial no. 32K9210, nickel-plated with full Class A factory engraving and smooth walnut round-butt stocks. Dave Terbrueggen collection

Engraving done at the Smith & Wesson factory has always been of good quality, and generally it has been excellent from the time of the Youngs to the examples done by Paul Piquette more recently. In the 1930s, it seems there were no house engravers on staff, and the weapons were sent out; and in the 1950s the work was not as well done as it was in earlier and later years.

Recent engraving jobs from the factory will typically bring slightly less or slightly more than the cost of the weapon, plus the current engraving cost. The market is always thinner the higher the price of a revolver, which tends to bring down the value of the engraved examples. However there are some people who hate to wait three to twelve months for a specially-ordered engraved example and want or

669. Left and right side views of a DAO Model 64 NYPD-1, factory engraved for the author in a bas-relief oak leaf pattern by master engraver Paul Piquette.

need it now, to serve as a gift or for some other reason, and are willing to pay a premium for an existing example in order to get immediate possession.

## Levels of Factory Coverage

Throughout the history of the K-frame revolver, factory engraving has been offered in differing levels of coverage, and priced accordingly. In recent times this has yielded levels A, B, and C, with A being about 90% coverage, B two-thirds, and C one-third. Of course, depending on the barrel length, this may seem like more or less work, since a six-inch K-frame with C-level engraving will seem to have less coverage than a two-inch model with the same level of coverage. Most people who order factory engraving tend to go to the highest level—after all, if they are going to do it, they might as well go "whole hog".

Interestingly, revolvers purchased and then sent back to be factory-engraved are not charged the

670. Left and right side views of a Model 66 DAO with 4" barrel, factory-Class A engraved and fitted with factory cut-down target stocks.

11% excise tax on the engraving, which is a good saving, especially when you are opting for full-coverage work.

On the other hand, weapons engraved at the factory not to order but just to keep the engraver busy will yield lots of B- and C-level engraved examples. A competent engraver working for inventory can do a C-level job on a K-frame in a couple of hours.

If at all possible, factory-engraved examples should have the factory box with them, for the box will document the serial number, the level of engraving, and the fact that it was factory-engraved. If sent back for the work, then a statement reflecting the work, the level done, and date needs to be included, as shipping records will not reflect the nature of the work undertaken at the factory. It is nice if the engraving job is signed also, as this helps to verify the work.

# Non-Factory Engraving

On a somewhat lower scale than the two classes of factory-engraved examples discussed above, we have non-factory jobs, although a few of these can also have some real value. For example, a revolver engraved by the legendary contract engraver Rudolph Kornbrath will be worth more than a similar factory-engraved example, and so it is with the work of the modern American master Alvin A. White, and maybe four or five other independent engravers. Examples of the work of both of these masters is included below.

But, if you really either want to get the money or want to pay it out for such examples, the accompanying documentation must be impeccable.

## Rudolph Kornbrath

Born in Austria, Rudolph J. Kornbrath became the most famous American gun engraver of the 20th century. His clients included kings, statesmen and famous sportsmen from around the world, and although he always remained independent, he was engaged to work on special projects by nearly every U.S. firearms manufacturer at one time or another. Mr. Kornbrath died in 1946.

### The Alf Landon Presentation Revolver

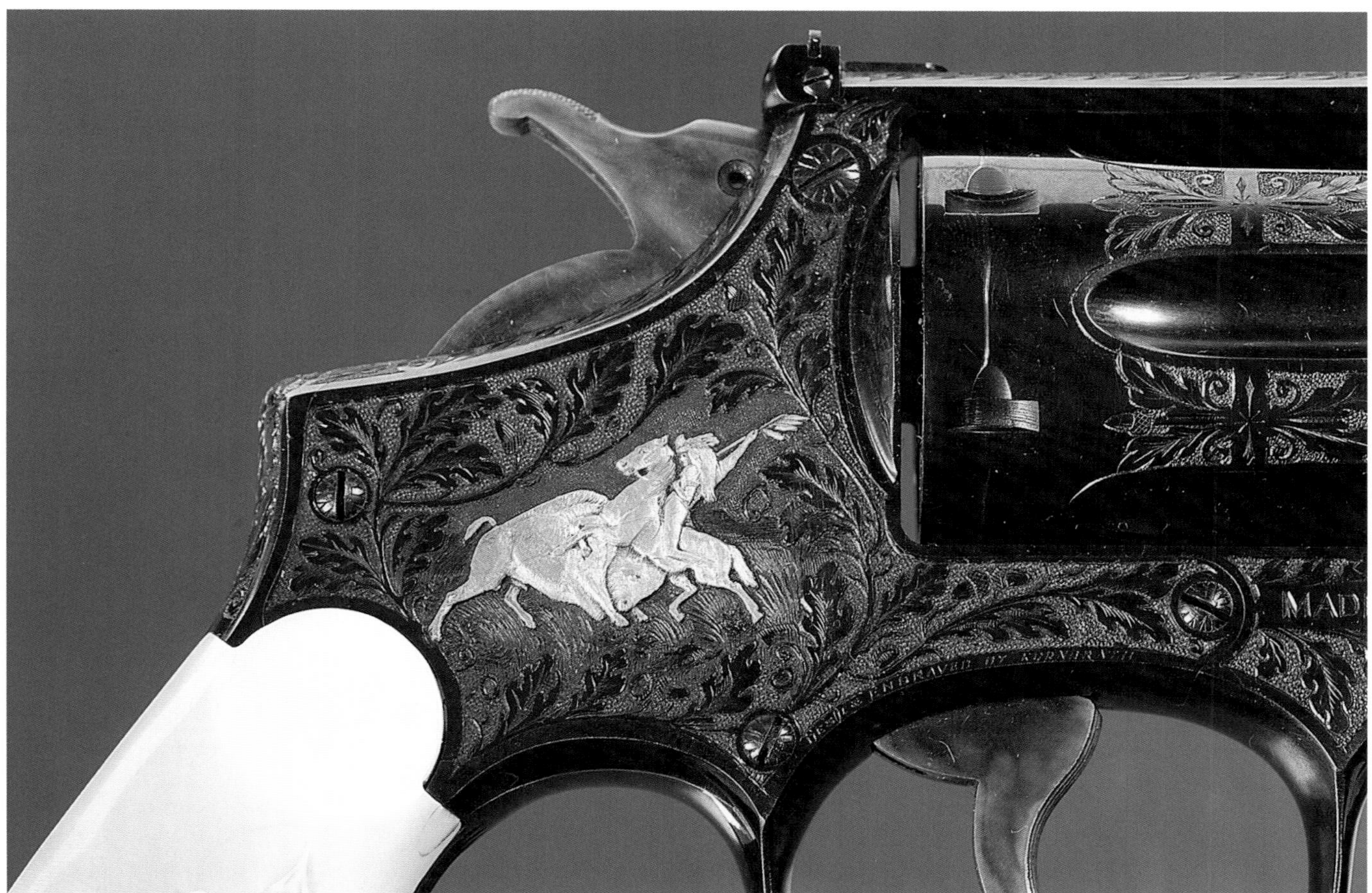

671. Right side closeup of K -frame target revolver, serial no. 649901, engraved in a vine and oak leaf pattern by Rudolpf Kornbrath. The scene is from the Beirstadt painting titled "The Last of the Buffalo", inlaid in 21-carat gold. courtesy Rock Island Auction Co.

In 1936 a K-frame target revolver, serial no. 649901, was lavishly engraved and gold inlaid by Kornbrath and fitted with carved ivory grips featuring an eagle and flag motif. This arm was intended for presenta-

672. Left side closeup of the Kornbrath-engraved presentation target revolver, showing a bust of "Buffalo Bill" Cody in postage stamp form, also in 21 carat gold relief.
courtesy Rock Island Auction Co.

673. Closeup of the right side view of the above Kornbrath-engraved target revolver, showing legend "DES'D & ENGRAVED BY KORNBRATH". This is the only known instance where he signed his work in this fashion.
courtesy Rock Island Auction Co.

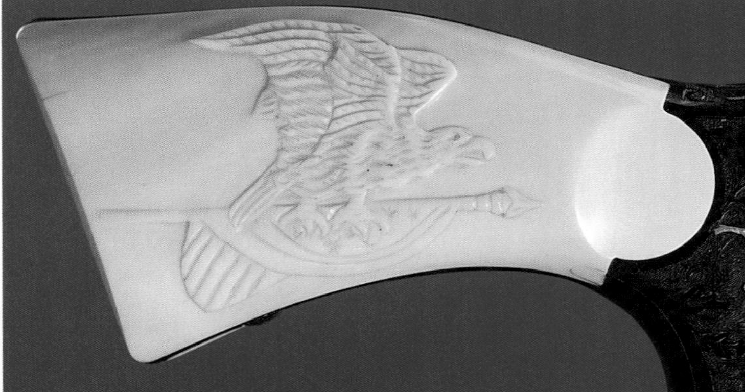

674. Closeup of the right ivory stock, showing carved eagle and flag motif, also done by Kornbrath.
courtesy Rock Island Auction Co.

tion to Alf Landon, who was a candidate for President of the United States that year. Mr. Landon did not win the election, however, and the revolver went on to be owned by several prominent collectors before coming to auction in 1991.

An appraisal of this Korbrath-engraved and gold inlaid K-frame target revolver, prepared and notarized by C. W. Slagle in 1991, evaluated it at $90,000.00.

# A Lavishly Engraved 'Snubbie' from 1950 - Still "On the Books"

675. Left side view of an ornately scroll-engraved 2" M&P with gold banding, serial no. C137309, a 5-screw, short-action round-butt .38 Special revolver "probably manufactured in November, 1950". Mike Pacella collection

Excerpts from the S&W factory letter concerning the above lavishly-engraved 2" .38 Special revolver, dated April 7, 2009, read as follows:

> *We are sorry to inform you that we cannot supply any information concerning [this firearm, which] is open on Smith & Wesson records with no disposition listed, therefore we are unable to trace the history of this firearm.*
>
> *. . Technically this firearm should still be in the Smith & Wesson factory as there is no record of it being shipped. However, these types of mistakes occur as a result of carelessness of the records clerk missing a number on an invoice. There is always the possibility that the revolver was used for a promotion and delivered to one of the company executives and shipped out on what is called a Memo Account. These accounts sometimes were not properly recorded . .*
>
> *We have researched . . in company records which indicate that your handgun, with serial number C137309, was probably manufactured in November, 1950 . .*

Since no further information is available, there is no way of ascertaining whether the engraving was done at the factory or not.

# Alvin A. White

An independent craftsman who began his career during the Depression of the late 1920s and early 1930s, Alvin A. White of Manchester, Connecticut, is the only prewar engraver of major rank who was still active in modern times. Known as the "Dean" of modern American arms engravers, Mr. White was considered one of the top ten men in the field in 1966.

He signed nearly all his own work, usually by adding an inconspicuous gold rectangle or cartouche marked "A A WHITE/ENG." (fig. 587).

White established the A. A. White Engravers company, employing several expert engravers during the years 1961 - 1973. A later article concluded, "[White] has no catalog or price list and is not seeking work."

## The *First* Combat Magnum, Engraved for Presentation to John F. Kennedy

676. Left and right side views of the first Combat Magnum, serial no. K 260003, masterfully engraved and gold inlaid by Alvin A. White and fitted with carved ivory stocks for a planned presentation to President John F. Kennedy, which never took place.

As described in the text, this arm features the Great Seal of the United States on the sideplate, and an anchor on the left side of the frame. Bill Cross collection

In an excerpt from a promotional bulletin dated May, 1981 (page 166), S&W Historian Roy Jinks stated that "The first Combat Magnum (Model 19) was presented to Bill Jordan . ."

However, as discussed on page 445, more recent research has shown that Bill Jordan actually received the Combat Magnum with the lowest serial number, K260001, which was the second one made. It was shipped to him on January 5, 1956.

Only one Combat Magnum, serial no. K260003, was made in 1955, meaning that no. K260003 was the *first* Combat Magnum manufactured by Smith & Wesson. It was completed on December 15, 1955, and was kept in the factory collection until September, 1962, when S&W sent it to Alvin White to be custom engraved and inlaid with gold and silver. It was intended that this factory commission should be presented to President John F. Kennedy, and the design features the Great Seal of the United States on the sideplate and an anchor, to commemorate Kennedy's WWII Naval service, on the left side of the frame. The stocks of ivory were also made by Mr. White, and feature an American eagle on the right panel. The S&W monograms, the escutcheon and stock screw are made of gold.

Whether it was completed before Kennedy was assassinated on November 22, 1963 is not known, but in any event the presentation never took place.

## Another Alvin White Masterpiece, for William O. Sweet

Portions of a factory letter describing Combat Magnum serial no. K331446 (fig. 678) read as follows:

> *We have researched your Smith & Wesson Model 19 .357 Combat Magnum, Special Order Variation, caliber .357 Magnum, revolver in company records which indicate that your handgun with serial number K 331446 was shipped from our factory on June 19, 1958 and delivered to William O. Sweet, Attleboro, MA. The records indicate that this revolver was shipped with a 4 inch barrel, polished but not blue, and Goncalo Alves round butt grips. This revolver was a special ordered and purchased by Mr. Harvey Foster, Special Agent In Charge, Federal Bureau of Investigation, 327 Federal Building, Indianapolis, IN, but shipped to Mr. Sweet for engraving.*

## The Hoover and Sweet Presentations - the Earliest Known Round-Butt Combat Magnums

It is interesting that the Hoover and Sweet presentations, produced in 1958, both have round butts, and precede the general release of the round-butt Combat Magnum by several years. The round butt was not introduced for general sale until the 2½" Model 19 was introduced in August, 1966.

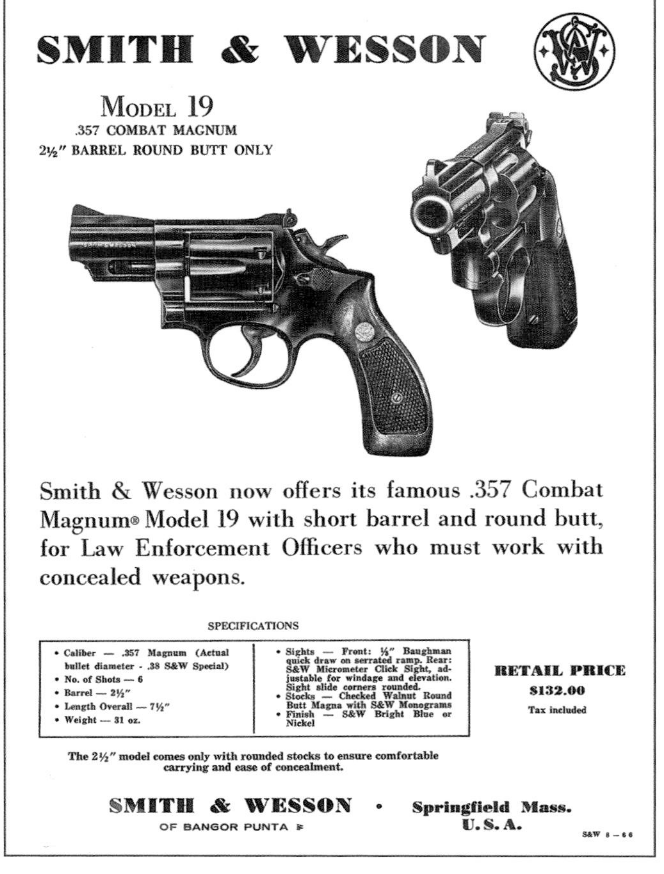


677 (right). The one-page factory brochure introducing the round butt Model 19 (Combat Magnum), dated August, 1966, also shown as fig. 184.

The Hoover and Sweet presentation Combat Magnums, both shipped in 1958, precede the general release of the round butt in this model by eight years.

Gaston Comeau collection

678. Left and right side views of the round-butt "mate" to the Hoover presentation Combat Magnum shown in figs. 584 - 591, which was ordered by the FBI and engraved by Alvin A. White for William O. Sweet (fig. 592). The sideplate is inlaid with a full moon over a log homestead in the pines, all in gold.

Inset, above left: the inlay of the Sweet Mfg. Co. logo, surrounded by a gold chain.

Inset, below right: closeup of butt, showing serial number inlaid in gold.

According to the factory letter, this revolver was shipped exactly one month to the day from the ship date of Hoover's gun. Chad Gripp collection

## A Gold-Plated Model 19, Engraved by Alvin White

679. Left and right side views of Model 19 with 4" barrel and target stocks, serial no. 2K7017, engraved and gold plated by Alvin A. White.

The hammer and trigger are also gold plated.

This example has a pinned barrel and full-length, counterbored cylinder.

# Other Non-Factory Engraved Guns

680. Left and right side views of a Model 65 with 4" barrel and ivory Magna-style stocks fitted with a Tyler 'T' grip, non-factory engraved.

This example also has a pinned barrel and full-length, counterbored cylinder.

Except for such exceptional artists as Rudolph Kornbrath and Alvin White, most other non-factory engraved examples, no matter how interesting in appearance, or how much area the engraving covers, are simply not worth paying much over the value of the unadorned revolver. A 20% increase over a plain example in similar condition is about all you would ever want to pay for it, if you think you will ever want to sell it to a legitimate person. If you are planning on being buried with it, giving it away as a gift, or have simply fallen in love with it, then naturally you can ignore my comments and pay through the nose for it. You will do better not to, however, as you will probably hate yourself tomorrow if you do. Buy the factory-engraved example, pay as indicated earlier, and you will always be happy with your purchase.

I like engraved handguns of all types, and especially K-frames that have been used but properly cared for. With use, not abuse, they take on a fine, noble appearance.

If you watch what you buy and get good items to begin with, when the time comes to pass on your treasures to the next generation, you should be able to get more than your money out of them, already having had your pleasure out of them many times over.

## Engraved Guns Including the Original Owner's Name

681. Right side view of a .38 Special Model 1905, serial no. 371688, shipped on March 15, 1921 to Foster Thornberg Hardware Co. in Huntington, West Virginia. It was owned by Elijah (Lige) Rose, who was the Deputy Sheriff of Carter County, Kentucky, and engraved as shown, featuring his title on the sideplate and his name on the grip strap.

Note that the grip frame is bent forward somewhat, toward the trigger guard. This resulted when Deputy Rose had to defend himself against a horse which was trying to bite him as he attempted to arrest the rider. He grasped the revolver around the cylinder and trigger guard, with the barrel pointing up, and struck the horse's head with the heel of the butt. The arrest was completed.

private collection

As an aside, many such engraving jobs, whether factory or non-factory, will include the original owner's name. Unless this is of a famous (or infamous) person, or you are related to them in some meaningful way, such revolvers bring less money than the non-named examples.

Rarely this may not be the case as the weapons get to the 75- to 100-year-old level, especially if it is indicated that the gun was used by a law enforcement official or military man. Some people like to buy such things named to an individual who might not be well known, and in such cases, they will bring a premium. This is especially so, it seems, with weapons showing British military connections.

# Further Factory Variables

## Hammers and Triggers

As discussed in the sections dealing with them, hammers and triggers are mainly of two common types, depending upon vintage, but non-standard examples are also seen. Hammers can vary from the wide target-style spur to the deadly serious and efficiently snagless "bobbed" type, usually installed on weapons which are destined (or at least intended) to live a life under coats of suit-jacketed agents, plainclothesmen, and citizen gun-toters.

Non-standard triggers likewise can be wide and grooved to help target shooters reduce the felt weight of the trigger pull and help control it, or the wide, smooth "Combat" type so favored by the double-action shooter, as it permits the trigger finger to smoothly move along the face of the trigger as it is being pulled.

## Materials

All components of the classic M&P are made of conventional steel, but early in the postwar era, the alloy-framed model was introduced, to help reduce the weight on the shooter's belt. Barrels remained steel, of course, but the earliest examples had alloy cylinders (fig. 413). With the advent of high-pressure .38 Special ammunition this soon became too much of a good thing, and the alloy cylinder went the way of the Dodo bird, but the alloy frame remained, making for a nice, lightweight revolver. Commonly found finished to resemble our classic blued-steel examples, two-inch and polished versions resembling a nickel finish are not rare.

Longer models with five- and six-inch barrels are rare, however, and the same lightweight frames now used in adjustable-sighted K-frames can safely be said to be rare. This has always seemed a bit odd to me, as a heavy four-inch barrel attached to an alloy frame cut for adjustable sights, as found on the K-frame Combat Masterpiece or K-38, strikes me as a highly desirable combination. Especially so if the barrel and cylinder were made of stainless steel, so that combined with the alloy frame, you would have a nice, low-maintenance revolver. I have never seen one like this, however.

## Butts and Stocks

The most common butt shape seen on our classic is square-bottomed, but many right from the beginning preferred the round butt commonly supplied on two-and three-inch-barreled weapons, while today, all K-frames are round-butt only. Some who liked the early round butt also liked longer barrels, and occasionally one of these will be found, although in my experience the longer the barrel the more uncommonly it is seen.

Lanyard rings or loops are occasionally found on the bottom of the butt. These were standard on some military-contract models, both the early (1899-era) Army models and the hundreds of thousands of .38/200s and Victory Models supplied during WWII.

Generally speaking, the farther away the revolver is from uniform duty use (by size, finish, and chambering), the more unusual a lanyard ring is, since it is something that typically appeals only to a certain type of buyer. Still, for years the factory would supply and install a lanyard ring upon request, for a slight extra charge. Thus it would be very unlikely to find one on a two-inch, nickel-plated, .32 WCF caliber K-frame with adjustable sights, while on a blued Combat Masterpiece it might well only merit the "interesting" level. Still, it makes for a variation.

Lots of different factory-made stocks have shown up over the years on K-frames. Our classic, depending on the vintage, might have standard thin walnut "service" grips that fit into the frame, while the postwar classic has wider, higher Magna-style stocks, either square-butt or modified square-butt with the bottom edges and corners beveled a bit to avoid wearing the linings of jackets. Stock materials can also vary substantially. A wide variety of woods other than walnut have been supplied, as well as pearl, ivory, and stag. The last is quite rare, with fewer than a half-dozen factory-supplied examples having been authenticated in over 100 years, according to my non-factory source. Pearl and ivory seem to have been more commonly used in the pre-1939 days than after the war, but any examples authenticated with such factory-installed grips are noteworthy.

### The Wesson Grip Adapter - Rarely Seen on K-Frame Revolvers

The Wesson grip adaptor, so commonly seen on pre-war .357 Magnum revolvers, was also available along with standard stocks on K-frames shipped during the pre-1940 period. The factory brochure for this accessory appears as fig. 141, and the patent drawing is shown in fig. 142.

The K-frame version must have been requested very infrequently, as I have seen at least 100 Magnum-size grip adaptors for every one on a K-frame. I recall seeing only one factory-lettered K-frame revolver where it was noted that the grip adaptor was factory-supplied.

682. Left side closeup of the .38 Special target revolver, serial no. 638567, shown in fig. 326, with grip panel removed to show details of the rare K-frame version of the Wesson grip adapter. Gaston Comeau collection

## Summing Up the Collectible K-Frame

To sum up, within the roughly six million K-frame revolvers which have been manufactured almost continuously over a period of more than a century, with many varied alternatives to the "standard" length, sights, grips, finish, and chambering being made available during that period, not to mention mechanical differences not so readily apparent from the outside, such as the various hammer safeties used over time, it should not be surprising that lots of interesting variations exist. However, until you start noticing them and knowing what to look for, this very obvious fact may not be apparent.

As stated at the outset, when you first think about the K-frame model, you think they are all alike and rather boring, but then as you consider the issue more closely, you soon realize that there really are a lot of interesting examples out there, and that given their relatively low price they make excellent collectibles.

### John Henwood on the Mathematics of Possibilities

John Henwood offers the following interesting comments on the astounding number of versions of the basic K-frame revolver which the factory has made available over the years, as follows:

> *[In addition to the various calibers and "dash" changes] a number of options have been offered, and the combinations are almost endless: made with square- or round-butt frames; manufactured from alloy (carbon) steel and stainless steel, as well as aluminum; there have been over a dozen different stock styles and materials; five different standard finishes (stainless steel, blue, and nickel, plus black and nickel anodized aluminum); five hammers (standard, bobbed, airweight, semi-target, and target); five trigger configurations (standard, narrow, airweight, smooth combat, smooth target, target); and six barrels (2-, 4-, 5- and 6-inch stand-*

*ard weight, plus 3- and 4-inch heavy barrels), over this time period. This adds up to 54,000 possible combinations, all different. And this is without including sighting equipment or any seldom-seen options such as lanyard swivels . .*

*Chapter Thirty-Eight*

# Custom Features

The Smith & Wesson K-frame, whether the fixed-sight duty or adjustable-sighted target model, is a wonderful revolver just as it comes from the factory—well made, with good power levels, highly accurate, and reliable. However, given its phenomenal popularity and longevity, it should come as no surprise that over the years it has been the subject of numerous modifications from top to bottom and front to back by clever, talented, highly-skilled gunsmiths. Certainly a review of some of these ex-factory modifications is interesting and useful. Some of them are really excellent, and most are useful for certain purposes for certain people.

Shooters have always been individuals, and some of them obviously wanted a weapon for some special purpose or one better suited to accomplishing a specific task, at least in that shooter's mind. When the M&P first came out in 1899, the Smith & Wesson No. 3, typically in .44 Russian but sometimes in .32 caliber, was their most popular target-grade revolver. However it was obvious to many right from the outset that the new M&P would make a fine target revolver, since the new .38 Special was clearly a very accurate cartridge, and only became more so as the years went by.

Also, while the gunsmiths at the factory have always been top-notch, it is only fair to acknowledge that the Smith & Wesson revolver, like any product, is necessarily built to a price point, and for those who demand the "extra mile" there are gunsmiths who have the talent and the time—for a monetary consideration, of course—to go beyond the standard of work that came out of the factory. It is also well worth noting that many fine design features which were developed by independent gunsmiths over the years have later turned up in factory-produced models.

In addition to custom gunsmithing, a variety of aftermarket accessories were offered by a number of companies, including Smith & Wesson themselves.

## Custom Stocks

The K-frame Smith & Wesson has been the subject for many fine aftermarket custom stocks. In the years before WWII, famed makers such as Roper and Sanderson made grips for a wide variety of users. Target shooters in particular seemed to be willing to pay extra for a special grip which they thought would give them an edge on the target range, with some hunters and practical gun men also being willing to buy such custom work, albeit in much fewer numbers.

In the postwar era new custom stockmakers have appeared, possibly the best known being Steve Herrett, who have provided all sorts of interesting and well-made custom stocks to fit Smith & Wesson K-frame revolvers, fabricated from a variety of exotic materials.

In addition, a lot of non-factory grips were offered over the years which basically duplicated the design of the factory stocks but were made of exotic woods, ivory, and pearl, not to mention non-natural materials such as plastic. While some of these had some interesting design features we will not deal with them in great depth, only mentioning them here to illustrate how popular and widely-used the K- frame Smith & Wesson has been for over 100 years.

## Factory Replacement Stocks

683 (left). A blister pack containing a factory replacement set of K-frame rosewood target stocks.

Such aftermarket items were routinely offered on racks in sporting goods stores and gun shops, and proved popular with many customers. Gaston Comeau collection

## Aftermarket Grip Adapters

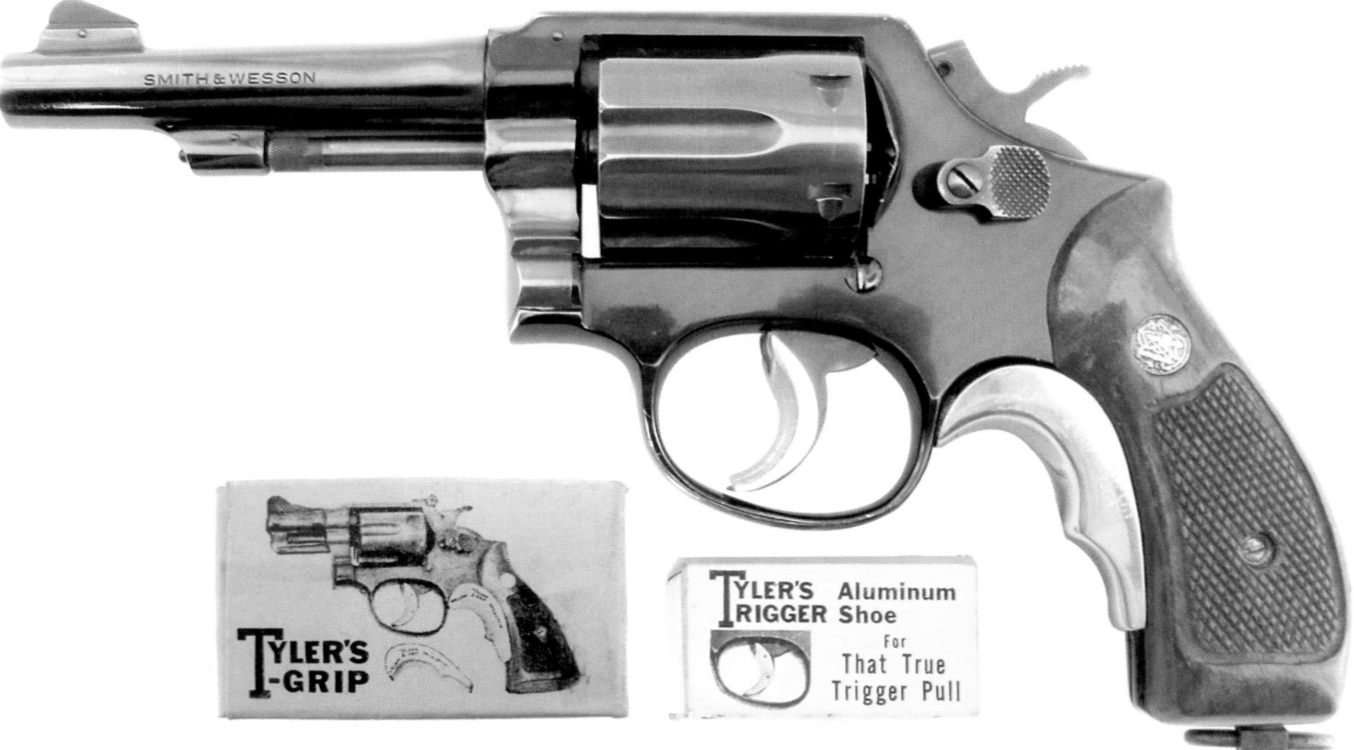

In addition to the Wesson grip adapter, a rarely seen K-frame accessory (fig. 682), other companies such as Tyler, Pachmayr, and even Smith & Wesson offered adapters which filled up part of the gap between the trigger guard and the butt.

685 (right). The original box for a genuine Smith & Wesson grip adapter, available in small, medium (shown here), and large sizes.

This pattern is quite similar to other plastic or rubber adapters such as those made by Pachmayr.

Gaston Comeau collection

# Sights

Target-grade revolvers were made by the same men and on the same machines as the standard models, so whether fixed- or adjustably-sighted, the barrel and cylinder as well as the lockwork were identical. But the target shooter might well be firing specialized loadings which may have produced lower velocities than normal, contained lighter bullets, or embodied some other change from the factory standard. These men were also possibly firing a course of fire at a different distance than that for which the factory had zeroed the weapon with standard ammunition. Naturally, as loadings and distances change, so will the point of impact of the bullet. Similarly, some people like to use a center hold, and others a six o'clock hold. Lastly, people all see their sights differently, and often adopt preferred holds on their revolvers, both of which will also result in differing points of impact.

All of these factors caused a demand for an adjustable-sight revolver over at the Colt factory, where side-ejector models had been made in target-grade formats prior to the development of the M&P.

The target-grade Colts had a front sight which was adjustable for elevation changes. Over time this moveable front sight idea proved to be all too moveable, especially if carried in a holster, unless and until the adjustment screw was rusted in place once the arm was properly zeroed—which is unsightly and of course renders any further adjustments for differing loads, ranges, lighting conditions or shooters' holds difficult or impossible. Thus the Colt approach of a movable front sight was rejected by Smith & Wesson.

Similarly, the Colt rear sight was adjustable for windage, but it also tended to shift unless the screws were rusted in place. The adjustment screws on these Colt rear sights have very tiny, soft heads, which tend to get marred as one attempts to tighten them firmly to keep the sight in place. Overall, both the front and rear Colt sights were capable of improvement, and one could but try to keep the screws in place with something similar to Loctite, (if not as effective in the early days of the Colt Target revolvers), then watch carefully for shifting points of impact, which could indicate slippage.

In Springfield, with the benefit of some hindsight, the S&W designers examined the existing Colt sights, noted their defects, and, quite simply, made better sights. The front sight was fixed in position. It might pick up leather from the holster, but it was not going to move. The rear sight provided adjustments for both elevation and windage. Early examples did not offer the precise, measured clicks later introduced in the micrometer rear sight, and also had really small heads on the screws. Fortunately the factory-supplied screwdrivers hold up well and, unlike the Colt sight screws, it seemed you did not have to tighten the S&W screws so forcefully. All in all a much better sighting solution, but almost as soon as they came out, specialist sight companies such as the D. W. King Company of San Francisco began marketing better rear sights. (An illustrated treatise on King front and rear sights begins on page 119.) Not only were the screw heads bigger, but also the sight adjustment gave definite clicks, each of which produced a measured amount of movement of the bullets on target.

In addition, the sight blades of the rear sight on the standard factory units were black and square-

684 (previous page). Left side view of an alloy-frame Model 12 with 4" barrel, round butt and lanyard swivel, (an unusual combination in itself), fitted with a Tyler 'T' grip. The Tyler grip adapter was made of aluminum, while most other such add-ons were made of plastic or rubber.

Also shown installed is a Tyler trigger shoe, both accessories complete with their original boxes.

Gaston Comeau collection

notched. Some people see their sights better if they are of a different shape and have such eye-catching things as white outlines surrounding the notch. Many of the features of the aftermarket sights developed by the specialist companies were later offered and installed by Smith & Wesson, and still later arrangements were made with their designers so that these sights could be completely copied by the factory at Springfield.

The specialists also offered alternatives to the factory front sights, which gave better definition for many. Again, these were developed and initially installed by customizers, later available on special order for installation at the factory, and still later copied by the factory.

## The Evans "Wondersight"

686. Right side closeup of an S&W K-frame revolver with the "Wondersight" attached by means of the supplied screw replacing the upper sideplate screw.
Gaston Comeau collection

687. Rear three-quarter closeup of the same revolver with the "Wondersight" attached, showing details of the sight aperture and windage adjustment knob.
Gaston Comeau collection

U.S. Army Lt. Col. Alonzo Gaidos (1896 - 1982) is perhaps most familiar to readers of the Collector Grade *WAR BABY* series, wherein we depict and describe several ingenious conversion systems, designed and patented by Col. Gaidos in the early years after WWII, which transformed the standard M1 carbine into a selective-fire weapon.

Another of Col. Gaidos' inventions was the "Wondersight", which he designed, patented and manufactured in the late 1940s. His company, Firearms Development Laboratories, also did other contract and speculative weapons-related work.

The "Wondersight" was described in a Dope Bag article that appeared in the November, 1991 issue of *The American Rifleman*. This interesting article is excerpted as follows:

> *In 1953 Firearms Development Laboratories of Duarte, Calif., announced its adjustable, low-mounted Wondersight designed for no-gunsmithing installation on fixed sight medium- and large-framed Smith & Wesson revolvers. The only tool required was a small screwdriver; the sight's mounting screw simply replaced the top sideplate screw present on all S&Ws at that time, and the gun's front sight needed no modification to accommodate it.*
>
> *. . The single sight mounting screw could be loosened and retightened to permit manual raising or lowering of the sight for elevation adjustment, and a stationary indicator point touched on the clearly marked graduation points on the side of the sight base. Each point move changed the point of impact approximately 3" at 25 yds. from a 5½" or 6"-barreled revolver.*
>
> *The windage adjustment was more refined; each distinct click of the knurled adjustment knob changed the lateral point of impact approximately 1/4" at 25 yds. from the same revolver.*
>
> *The sight was inexpensive and remarkably well designed, made and finished. It was also very well received, for it was introduced to the market at the right time.*
>
> *By the mid-1950s there were huge quantities of surplus revolvers being imported from many*

MOUNTING INSTRUCTIONS FOR THE F. D. L. LONG-RANGE MICROMETER REAR SIGHT FOR REVOLVERS

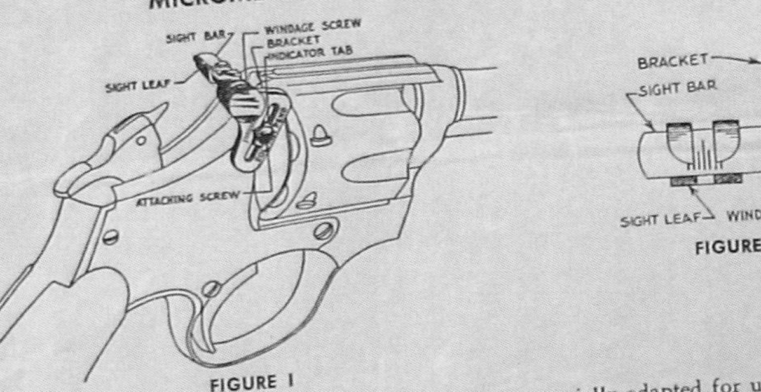


FIGURE I

BRACKET
SIGHT BAR
SIGHT LEAF
WINDAGE SCREW

FIGURE II

The F. D. L. Long-Range Micrometer Rear Sight is especially adapted for use on Smith & Wesson Revolvers since it is readily attachable with the aid of a small screwdriver. Modification of the existing front sight or any other component part of the revolver is not necessary.

FIGURE I illustrates the sight mounted on the Smith & Wesson Victory Model .38 Caliber Revolver. The same illustration will apply for all service models.

To attach the sight simply remove the upper screw from the side plate on the right hand side of the frame and attach the sight against the plate with the screw and indicator tab, making sure that the indicator tab is properly positioned with the lugs in the slot of the bracket. The bracket can be raised or lowered as desired and it is properly positioned when the aperture of the sight leaf is in line with the sighting groove on top of the frame. For long range the bracket should be raised the desired amount and since it is provided with graduations each representing 12 minutes of angle, moving the bracket upward a distance of one graduation will place the point of impact of the bullet 12" higher at each 100 yards of range. Lowering the bracket a distance of one graduation will place the point of impact 12" lower, etc.

The Sight Leaf on the Sight Bar is provided with a lateral adjustment governed by a micrometer windage screw. The Sight Bar is also graduated to represent 12 minutes of angle. The long graduation in the center of the Sight Bar represents the axis of the barrel and when aimed, it also represents the aiming point. Moving the Sight Leaf toward the long graduation in either direction will move the point of impact of the bullet closer to the aiming point so that if the Sight Leaf is moved a distance of one space toward the long graduation the point of impact of the bullet will be 12 inches closer to the aiming point at each 100 yards of range.

The micrometer is provided with interrupted stops or clicks, numbering six to one complete revolution of the windage screw. Twelve (12) clicks or stops or two (2) turns of the screw will indicate moving the sight leaf a distance of 12 minutes of angle, or one space between graduations, which likewise moves the point of impact of the bullet 12 inches at 100 yards in the direction the sight leaf is moved. Use of the F.D.L. sight is simplified since it is only necessary for the shooter to determine whether his shots are registering right or left of the target. If the shots are registering on the right of the target, the windage screw is rotated to the left which moves the sight leaf toward the long graduation mark on the sight bar, thus placing the point of aim closer to the target.

FIGURE II shows the graduations on the sight bar in relation to the sight leaf when the sight is set at zero. Moving the sight leaf in either direction toward the center graduation moves the point of impact of the bullet toward the target. The following table is provided to show the effects produced by rotation of the windage screw.

| No. of Clicks | Min. of A-gle | Point of Impact on Target | | |
|---|---|---|---|---|
| | | 100 yds. | 50 yds. | 25 yds. |
| 1 | 1 | 1 in. | 1/2 in. | 1/4 in. |
| 4 | 4 | 4 in. | 2 in. | 1 in. |
| 12 (or 2 rev.) | 12 | 12 in. | 6 in. | 3 in. |

FIREARMS DEVELOPMENT LABORATORIES, P.O. BOX 25, DUARTE, CALIF.

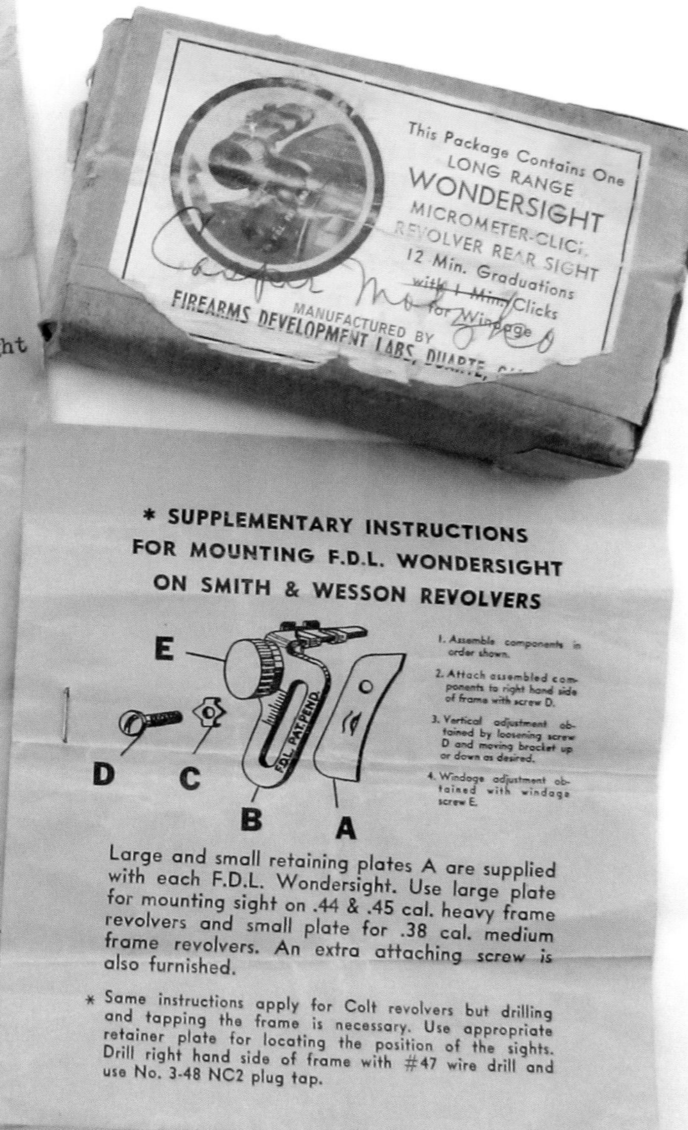


* SUPPLEMENTARY INSTRUCTIONS FOR MOUNTING F.D.L. WONDERSIGHT ON SMITH & WESSON REVOLVERS



1. Assemble components in order shown.
2. Attach assembled components to right hand side of frame with screw D.
3. Vertical adjustment obtained by loosening screw D and moving bracket up or down as desired.
4. Windage adjustment obtained with windage screw E.

Large and small retaining plates A are supplied with each F.D.L. Wondersight. Use large plate for mounting sight on .44 & .45 cal. heavy frame revolvers and small plate for .38 cal. medium frame revolvers. An extra attaching screw is also furnished.

* Same instructions apply for Colt revolvers but drilling and tapping the frame is necessary. Use appropriate retainer plate for locating the position of the sights. Drill right hand side of frame with #47 wire drill and use No. 3-48 NC2 plug tap.

688. The instructions and original box for the "Wondersight", developed by retired Ordnance Lt. Col. Alonzo Gaidos and now manufactured by Evans Precision Tooling, PO Box 1090, Philomath, OR 97370-1090.
Gaston Comeau collection

*sources, particularly from England . . Many [of these] gained Wondersights and benefitted from them.*

*The 1968 Gun Control Act, however, temporarily halted military surplus imports, and in the 1970s, with few surplus revolvers on the market at any price, we lost track of [the Wondersight].*

*Now with the receipt of a sample from the current makers [Evans Precision Tooling, PO Box 1090, Philomath, OR 97370-1090], the source is sure.*

*The sample was mounted on a Model 37 revolver in about one minute, and it seems no different from those made almost 40 years ago. Even the marking is the same. The price is higher (as are surplus revolver prices) but still reasonable in our view. The changes are in the form of "extras". Instead of supplying only a slotted 3-48 mounting screw, Evans gives two screws, one slotted and the other a more modern hex screw with wrench. The Wondersight purchaser can choose which to use, and this may well be the only problem the installer will face.*

# Other Custom Touches

Of course, modifications to factory revolvers were not limited to sights. Different finishes were a common if mostly cosmetic alteration. More critically, custom barrel and action work was offered, a simple example being breaking the edges of the chamber charge holes, making them easer to load (especially rapidly) with wadcutters. For bulls-eye targets this does not mean much, but when Practical Pistol Courses (PPC) are fired, this can be a useful modification. This is a good example of a specialty course of fire mandating a custom modification.

# Trigger Pull Modifications

The key to a good action is smoothness and minimal friction, and custom action work mainly involved making the trigger pull smoother and possibly lighter, bearing in mind that it is most critical that the weapon fire every time. But some courses of fire involve primers which are thin and easily ignited. Other primers are harder, and require a definite strike to ignite reliably. Most of these trigger pull issues are handled by smoothing the inside of action to reduce friction and felt pull.

The best way to get the action smooth yourself, assuming no burrs on parts, debris in the action or lack of lubrication, is to fire the weapon, or at least dry fire it a couple of hundred times a day (your precious revolver being fitted with a set of snap caps, of course, for this operation).

Even just clicking it repeatedly double-action while watching TV will do wonders. If you can do this while watching your sights and focusing on trigger control, it will help improve your shooting skills and your revolver's action at the same time.

# Mainspring Modifications

Another custom modification involved replacing the leaf mainspring with one of greater or lesser strength, either to get more certain ignition or a softer, lighter trigger pull. Some in the past have replaced the leaf spring with a coil spring assembly similar to that found in the smaller J-frame Smith & Wesson revolvers. One reason for this was the (very) occasional breakage of a leaf spring. The coil springs are almost unbreakable, but the trigger pull resulting from this modification is generally harder and heavier, and as a consequence this modification is rarely seen.

Replacing the mainspring occasionally can be of assistance, but turning back the strain screw is not a good idea. A Smith & Wesson revolver should never have the mainspring that powers the hammer backed off or reduced in strength. While a reduced-power mainspring will give less pressure for the finger to overcome in cocking the hammer, it will also give a less certain hammer strike, and may well result in misfires. Even if the primer ignites, it may do so in an erratic manner, and targets shot with revolvers fitted with such low-strength mainsprings typically show "stringing" up and down on the target. Two examples of groups obtained from a machine rest to illustrate the results of loosening the strain screw are shown on page four of the S&W factory brochure for the .357 Magnum revolver (fig. 43).

Absent some very specific course of fire, and restricting your revolver to that course of fire, I believe that any revolver should be capable of firing any standard factory ammunition. You can remove friction from your trigger action and still get reliable ignition if your gunsmith knows what he is doing.

# Custom Short Actions and Lightened Hammers

During the period when bulls-eye target shooting was a popular sport, say from 1920 through 1950, largely before the S&W factory offered its own short action, shorter actions were being developed and promoted by custom gunsmiths. Many other action modifications were also offered, all with the hope of reducing the "lock time" (the period after the hammer is released and until the firing pin hits the primer). The shorter this is, the less the handgun is likely to move, with the consequent alteration of where the bullet will strike being minimized. As shown in fig. 690, "skeletonizing" or drilling out the hammer to lighten it is but one example of such a custom modification intended to reduce lock time.

I rather doubt that any of these things really amounted to much in terms of practical value, but they certainly are distinctive, and guys who are gunsmiths love trying to offer clever mechanical solutions for human skill problems, especially when they can sell them.

*BUCHANAN SHORT ACTIONS*
(U. S. Patent #2324674)
*and BUCHANAN ACCURACY JOBS*

**The Ultimate in precision craftsmanship, as proven on the firing line from Coast to Coast.**

*J. D. BUCHANAN*

**1500 W. Verdugo Ave. Burbank, California**

689. An advertisement for custom short actions and accuracy jobs done by the famous gunsmith J. D. Buchanan, as it appeared on page 70 of the May, 1946 issue of *The American Rifleman*. Gaston Comeau collection

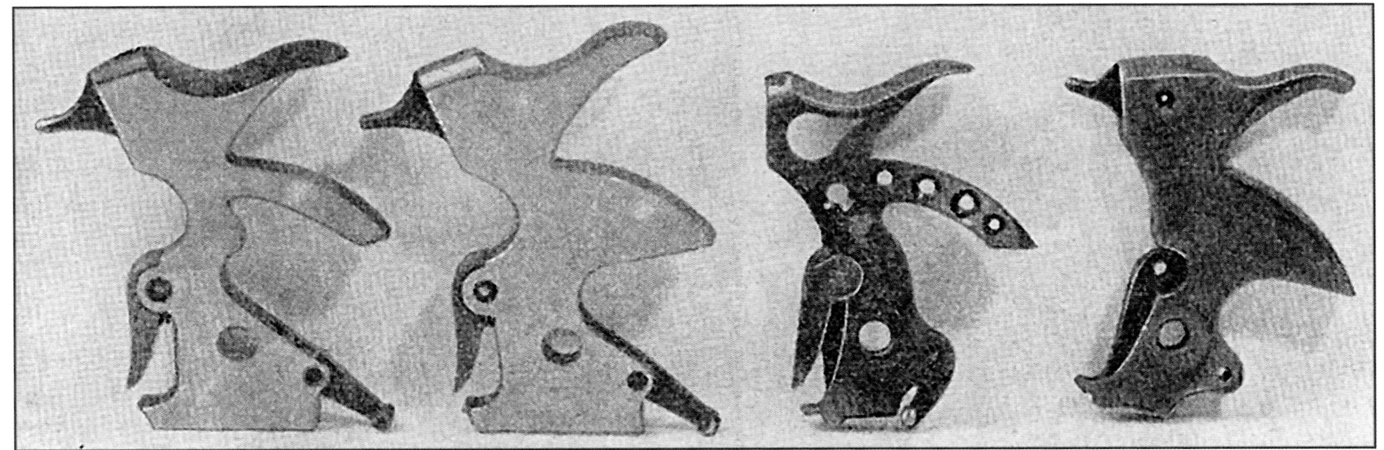

690. A comparison of altered and unaltered Colt (left) and S&W (right) hammers from an early *Rifleman* article, showing different ways of lightening them for faster action.

# Barrel Replacement

Besides trigger jobs, barrel replacement is another common modification. Some people think the barrel twist on factory barrels is not the best for wadcutter-type bullets, and that a non-factory alternative is a better solution. A person likely needs to shoot really well in order to tell the difference, but some people no doubt do have that skill level. Others replace the barrel to get a difference balance point, or to reduce felt recoil. For this reason large, thick pipe-like barrels are often seen on PPC type K-frame revolvers. Some people who want to use their revolvers at longer ranges will get longer barrels installed in order to reap the advantages of additional velocity and a longer sight radius. In the early 1960s, barrel change-outs for the PPC-type courses of fire became very common, but for normal bulls-eye target shooting, most found that the standard barrels were fine. Similarly, standard barrels were fine for defense and duty use, being convenient enough to be comfortably carried yet still delivering more than adequate accuracy.

691. Left side view of a customized .38 Special Model 64 revolver, used by a number of famed marksmen to fire over one million rounds in PPC matches. The massive bull barrel was made by Robert Jones of Jackson, Mississippi, and the sight rib is a top-of-the-line Bo Mar unit with adjustable rear sight and front sight protectors.

Inset: front view showing rebated barrel crown and method of inletting the sight rib into the barrel.

NRA National Firearms Museum collection

## Describing My Pope-Barreled M&P

Harry Pope was perhaps the most popular American barrelmaker of the pre-WWI era. Today weapons fitted with his barrels are viewed as cherished artifacts of a golden age in firearms. Although best known for the highly accurate barrels he installed on single-shot rifles, he also rebarreled some handguns, mostly single-shot .22 pistols, but it appears a total of six .38 M&P revolvers were also graced with his barrels. The revolver illustrated here is one of the six that passed through his magical hands.

It of course started out in life as a standard Target Model M&P, which is a pretty fine revolver right out of the box, but obviously its owner wanted something a little better. The first thing he did was to install a set screw in the rear of the trigger guard as an over-travel trigger stop. No one can shoot his best with a trigger that continues to the rear after releasing the hammer, as this oftens result in a dropped muzzle, causing low shots.

Next, the grip was modified. As everyone who has ever shot one knows, the standard "service" stocks on early M&P revolvers are not very good. They slip in your hand upon recoil, and can rap your knuckles with even mild loads at times. The owner here has added a platform at the rear of the grip that allows the weapon to be held firmly in the hand without shifting, and lengthened the grip to allow a full grasp on the weapon. The entire grip was then covered in rough buckskin, to prevent it slipping in the hand. With these modifications the weapon does not shift in the hand upon recoil, and thus the shooter does not have to try to re-obtain the same hand position after each shot.

692. Left side view of my early pre-1914 target model M&P, serial no. 129312, rebarreled by Harry Pope using barrel no. 208, measuring 8¼" in length.

A wood extension has been added to the back of the butt, and the entire grip is covered in rough buckskin. In addition, a trigger stop has been threaded into the bottom of the trigger guard.

693. Right side closeup of pre-1914 target model M&P no. 129312 with cylinder open, showing details of the ejector rod lug which Harry Pope made up and attached to the barrel.

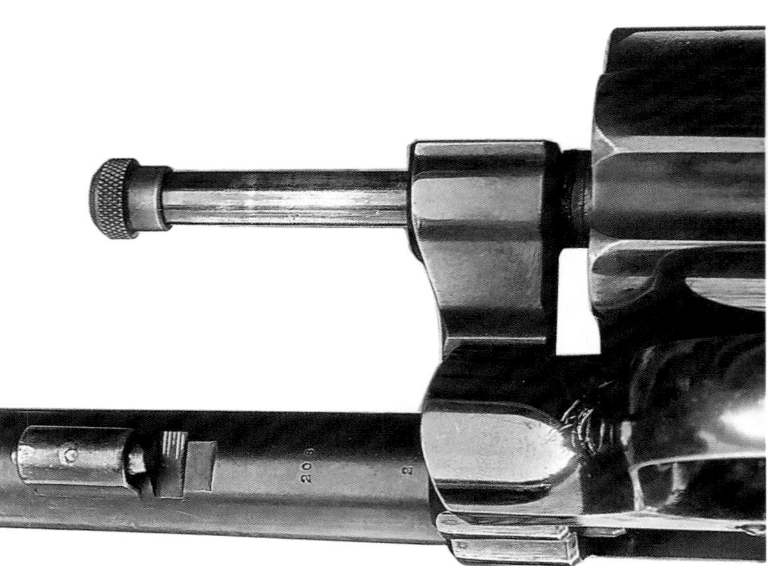

694. Underside closeup with cylinder open, showing marking on barrel no. 208.

695. Closeup of the barrel, showing maker's name "H. M. POPE" on the side.

696. Right side closeup of the front of the Pope barrel, showing Marble gold bead front sight.

Nothing was done to the hammer, but this is to be expected since this was well before D. W. King came up with his idea of making the hammer spur wider and easier to cock.

The entire action is glass smooth. It may have come from the factory that way, perhaps helped along a little by an outside expert, or, more likely, it is simply the result of thousands of rounds being fired through it over a century or more.

Obviously the shooter wanted the longest barrel possible which would still follow the rules for formal match shooting, and this barrel measures 8¼ inches in length. He wanted a fine, highly-accurate barrel, hence the barrel he chose was made and marked by Pope, and numbered '208'.

Of course, making a Smith & Wesson barrel is somewhat harder than making a barrel that merely screws into the frame, as it has the ejector rod locking lug at the front which must be precisely positioned. As can be seen in the photos, apparently Pope made a lug that looks a lot like a factory lug but not quite as rounded, welded or silver-soldered it in place, and fitted it with the ejector lock, pin and spring from the original barrel. Quite the project, I think, and no doubt one of the reasons Pope barrels on Smith & Wesson revolvers are so rare, as they entail a lot of extra work, and no Pope barrel was ever inexpensive.

The front sight was obviously installed by hand after being made up from stock, but with a Marble's gold bead topping it. These beads allow fine accuracy, and are designed to be centered over the bullseye.

The condition of this Pope-barreled M&P shows lots of use but no abuse. Considering that it was no doubt shot originally with corrosive-primed ammunition, the condition of the bore and cylinder chambers show that the owner used good maintenance procedures. No doubt long after the original owner found that he could no longer shoot it well enough to justify it due to declining eyesight, subsequent owners recognized it as a valuable piece of equipment and cultural artifact. The blue is worn and thin in many areas, with some minor pitting around the frame areas that may have contacted a leather holster or pouch in which it was stored, but it is just as capable of fine work today as it was when King Edward VII was alive and well.

Interestingly enough, while researching for this book, I encountered an advertisement in the September, 1937 issue of *The American Rifleman*, offering perhaps this very revolver for sale. The ad reads in part as follows:

*SMITH & Wesson Model 1905 .38 Special 8 inch Harry Pope barrel. Holster. Inside perfect, outside very good. Best offer.*

The results of a shooting trial with my Pope-barreled M&P are featured in Chapter Thirty-Nine.

# Frame Conversions

Other than offering round- and square-butt patterns, the frame of the K-frame revolver has rarely been changed by Smith & Wesson, although it has been subjected to some work by custom gunsmiths. Mostly this involves converting a square frame to the round butt configuration. Many people find the round butt better for certain types of work, especially concealed-carry purposes. This is not an incredibly involved machining job, and many people think it well worth the cost involved.

Some will also trim the front portion of the grip frame to make the length of the grip shorter. This allows a better grip feel for many. Fuzzy Farrant, a specialist grip maker in the 1960 – 1970 period, was well known for grips that required the toe of the frame to be removed. Doing so produced a much thinner grip, allowing the shooter to get a firmer grip on the weapon as it helped avoid the spreading of the fingers on the hand. Less spreading results in a firmer grip. Not so critical for target-loaded revolvers, but important for defense weapons or weapons used with defense power level ammunition.

# Revolver Safeties

A much more useful modification involves installing a safety on a revolver, and a variety of different designs have been developed over the years. For individuals whose revolvers are subject to seizure by assailants (the typical example being a uniformed officer attending a domestic disturbance call), this is a very helpful modification. These safety-equipped revolvers are also useful for someone who may need immediate access to his revolver yet may have lots of (typically little) unauthorized people on hand who might access the revolver while the owner was asleep or otherwise not actually carrying it on his person.

Some of these safeties involve installation of a catch on the weapon, much like those the factory installed on the 3" heavy-barreled Model 12 Airweights shipped to France for police use (fig. 471).

## The Cylinder Release Safety from Armament Safety International

Somewhat better was the “invisible” safety made in combination with the cylinder release, which an unauthorized user might not know existed and thus would not be inclined to flip off, as he might with a separate safety lever. Such a simple and ingenious device, offered by Armament Safety International of Hermosa Beach, California, is described in their self-explanatory brochure (fig. 697) and also in U.S. patent no. 3,978,603 (fig. 698), which is excerpted as follows:

### *Safety for Revolvers*

*. . Revolvers are generally not provided with any satisfactory safety. This presents a problem of accidental discharge of the revolver, while in a holster or otherwise . . when it is fully loaded and otherwise in a ready condition of use.*

*. . Known revolvers, such as Colt and Smith & Wesson, are provided with a thumbpiece for releasing the cartridge cylinder for loading. It has been found by the present inventor that if such thumbpieces could be held in certain positions, it would interfere with the movement of the hammer, as an operative safety.*

*Accordingly, it was another object of the present invention to provide an improvement of the structure of the thumbpiece, to provide a safety for locking the hammer in an operatively loaded position of the cylinder, yet with minor modifications to the revolvers without additional parts . . providing a new safety function not heretofore achieved in revolvers.*

*[With] reference to the drawings . . :*

- *FIG. 1 is a side elevation view of a conventional Smith & Wesson revolver partially broken away;*
- *FIG. 2 is a section along line 2 - 2 of FIG. 1;*
- *FIG. 3 is a section along line 3 - 3 of FIG. 2, showing the position of the thumbpiece . . as a safety when the gun is loaded;*
- *FIG. 3A is a view similar to that of FIG. 3 but showing the thumbpiece in the position to withdraw the cylinder for loading;*

# THE POSITIVE REVOLVER SAFETY THAT SAVES LIVES, ALWAYS WORKS, AND...

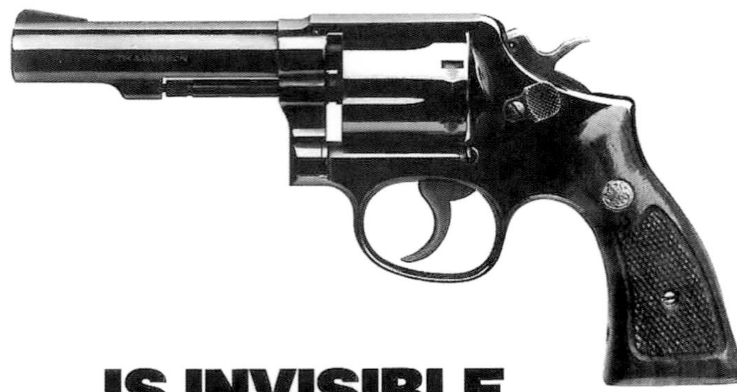

## IS INVISIBLE

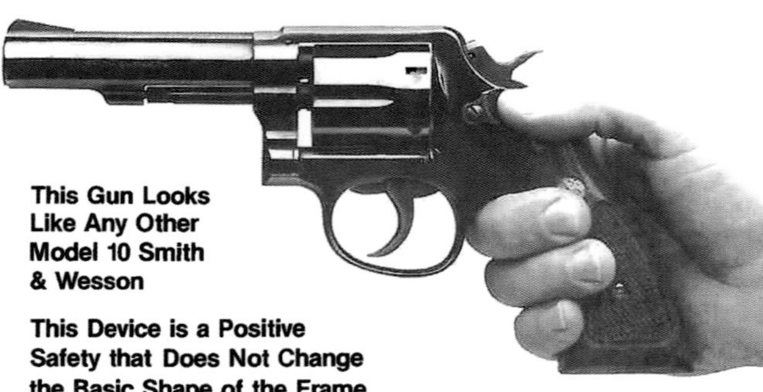

**This Gun Looks Like Any Other Model 10 Smith & Wesson**

**This Device is a Positive Safety that Does Not Change the Basic Shape of the Frame.**

Police officers, of necessity, carry sidearms exposed but are too "snatchable" during an altercation. This recently patented safety device is another piece of professional equipment of utmost importance to law enforcement officers, particularly patrolmen, or anyone who carries a weapon in their line of employment.
This safety can be installed on any Smith & Wesson, Colt or Ruger revolver.

### DID YOU KNOW

- Handguns are used to commit 69% of all police killings.
- The rate of officers having their own weapons used against them is over 8% higher in California than any other state.
- 68% of all officers fatally wounded are shot with their own guns.
- There is an 82% increase every five years in law enforcement officers being injured with their own guns.
- 54% of slain on-duty officers killed with their own guns were either a 2-man unit or assisted by other officers.
- California has experienced an 11% increase in officer slayings over the national figure.

These statistics compiled from Uniform Crime Reports, September, 1981, and California Specialized Training Institute, Camp San Luis Obispo, California, October, 1976.

## THE POSITIVE SAFETY THAT SAVES LIVES, ALWAYS WORKS, and IS INVISIBLE..................

### How It Works

A machined slot in the frame locks the hammer and cylinder without touching the mechanism. The screw is replaced with a special screw. By machining the thumbpiece and using a special bearing, the thumpiece is allowed to swivel freely. The safety is engaged by pressing the thumbpiece forward and upward, so the rear-end of the thumbpiece is angled toward the hammer. This effectively locks the trigger and hammer in the uncocked position. It leaves the top edge of the cylinder latch protruding slightly above the edge of the frame at hammer level. One releases the safety into "fire" mode by simply pushing it down into the normal thumbpiece position.

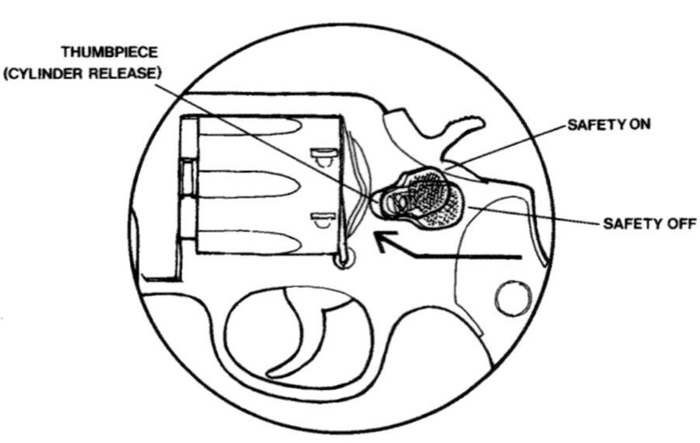


U.S. Patent Numbers 3,978,603 and 4,091,557

**A Positive Safety That Really Works...**

### DID YOU KNOW

- This safety child-proofs guns kept in the home.
- The release is natural and foolproof.
- The safety is designed for no loss in response time in a life-threatening situation.
- This safety buys one the time to recover the gun.
- The safety provides the revolver user a "locked and loaded" condition for the nightstand gun.

Any revolver can be modified by a qualified gunsmith within a matter of 15 minutes.

Within a short period of time, an entire police department can modify both on-duty and off-duty guns for a minimal cost (usually less than 15% of the cost of the gun).

For further information call or write:

ARMAMENT SAFETY INTERNATIONAL
420 Pier Avenue • Suite 109 • Hermosa Beach, CA 90254 • (213) 379-9992

697. A one-page brochure from Armament Safety International of Hermosa Beach, California, depicting and describing their patented "invisible" safety, built into the standard cylinder release thumbpiece. As stated at bottom right, "Any revolver can be modified by a qualified gunsmith within a matter of 15 minutes." courtesy Wolfhart Fritze

- *FIG. 3B is a section similar to that of FIG. 3A but showing the thumbpiece in position for firing the gun;*
- *FIG. 4 is a perspective view of the thumbpiece in accordance with the present invention . .*

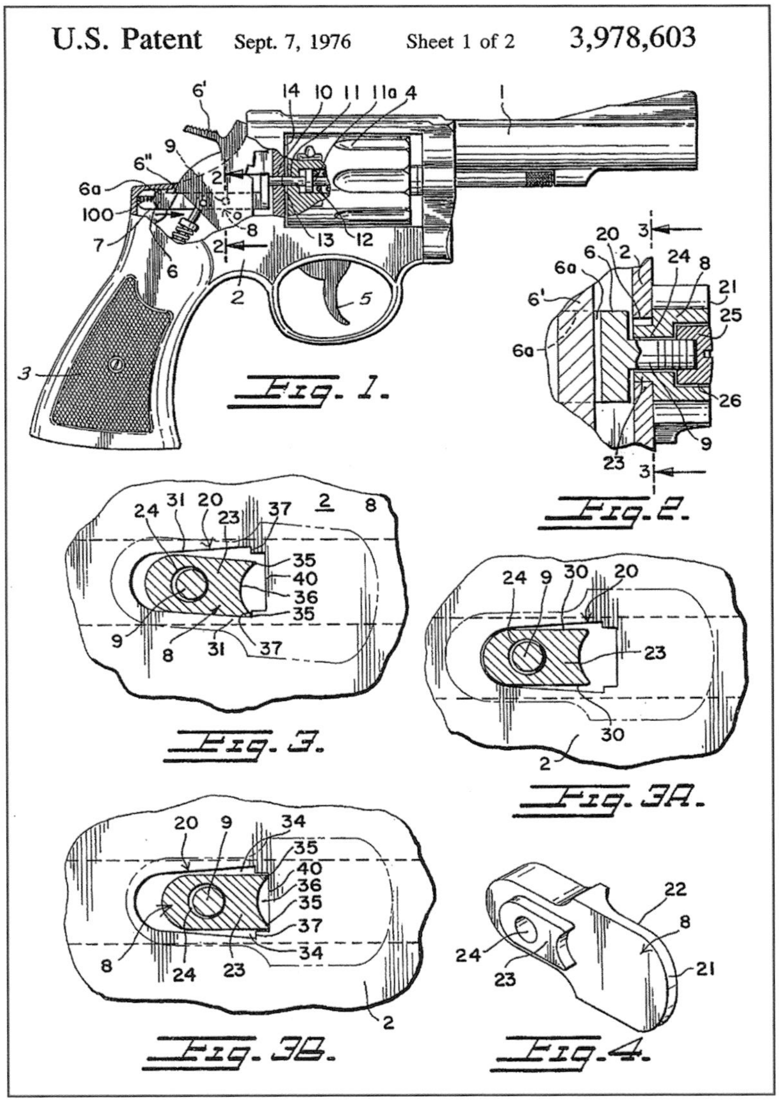

698 (right). Sheet 1 of 2 sheets of drawings from patent no. 3,978,603, granted on September 7, 1976, covering the "invisible" revolver safety conversion offered by Armament Safety International.

These drawings depict the conversion of a standard S&W revolver cylinder release thumbpiece, while Sheet 2 (not shown) describes the device fitted to a typical Colt revolver. U.S. Patent Office

U.S. Patent Sept. 7, 1976 Sheet 1 of 2 3,978,603

# The Magna Trigger Safety

## How It Works

In my opinion the best of the revolver safeties was the Magna Trigger Safety, developed to fit the police standard K-frame and patented by Joseph Smith in the 1970s. This required the front strap to be cut away and a module installed that contained a pivoting strut, which would prevent the rebound slide from coming back unless the strut was pivoted to the side. This strut gets pivoted due to a magnet contained in a ring worn by the shooter. The magnets are incredibly strong, and will activate the strut to be pivoted to the side even through wooden or rubber grips (with an aluminum, not steel, liner). If someone without this ring grabs the revolver, no matter how hard the trigger is pulled, it will not fire.

## Patenting the Magna Trigger Safety

Two patents were granted covering features of the Magna trigger safety. The earlier, U.S. patent no. 3,978,604, titled "Trigger Inhibiting Mechanism" was granted to Joseph E. Smith of Sunnyvale, California on September 7, 1976. The later patent, no. 4,067,132, titled "Safety Device for Preventing the Unauthorized Firing of a Weapon", was also granted to Mr. Smith on January 10, 1978.

Excerpts from the abstract of this second patent read as follows:

> *Trigger safety device for trigger-actuated devices is provided having a pivotally mounted magnetically responsive bar positioned on the inside of the handle or on the rear of the trigger. When the bar is oriented centrally, sufficient movement of the*

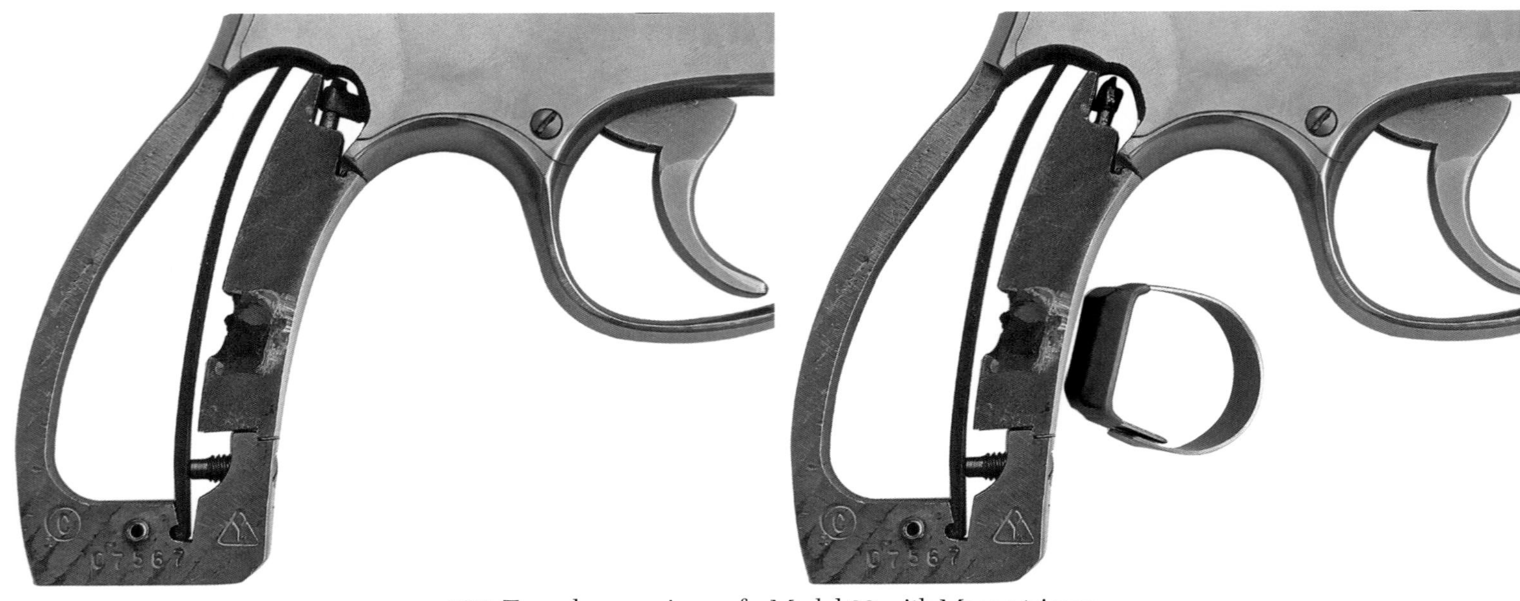

699. Two closeup views of a Model 66 with Magna trigger safety installed and stocks removed, showing details of the pivoting safety arm, installed in the modified front grip strap.

Note the key slots in the strap - the central section is held in place by the grips, and is removable sideways.

Left: safety strut at rest, with its head facing forward, preventing rearward movement of the rebound slide.

Right: safety strut pivoted by magnet in ring, permitting movement of rebound slide when trigger is pulled.

Leroy Thompson collection

*trigger is inhibited to prevent actuation . . The user of the device, by wearing a magnetic ring, displaces the bar from its central orientation and allows for sufficient movement of the trigger for actuation.*

## Practicality of the Magna Trigger Safety

Inventor Joseph Smith was awarded a $5,000 prize from the International Association of Chiefs of Police for his trigger safety, indicating its high level of official acceptance.

Unless a person snatching a revolver fitted with the trigger safety was extremely knowledgeable, and was thus capable of noticing the ring and understanding its significance, he would not know why the revolver could not be fired. Even if he knew it, unless the magnetic ring could be stripped from the owner's finger (and they are adjustable to fit snugly), the revolver still would not fire unless the grips are removed and the module removed. This of course is time-consuming and hardly likely during a typical domestic confrontation.

I think this is one of the best modifications ever made to K-frame revolvers. Back in the days before the advent of the Saf-T-Hammer internal key-lock system (fig. 564), when I carried a Model 66 and wanted to make certain that no one could fire my weapon except me, I had one fitted to my revolver, and added a round butt modification. This was when my daughter was little, and had her friends over all the time. I could sleep soundly knowing that my carry gun could be kept loaded and immediately accessed by me, but could not fired by anyone else.

My good friend, the noted Missouri lawman Chief Edward Seyffert, had a similar device installed in his three-inch Model 65 duty gun in response to concerns about weapon snatches, in the days before there was a computer in every police car.

700. Left side view of the Model 66 shown in fig. 699, assembled. There is no external evidence that the revolver cannot be fired by anyone not wearing the magnetic ring. A right side view of this revolver appears in fig. 188.
Leroy Thompson collection

## The Modern Age Catches Up - Problems with Computers

A problem associated with the Magna safety arose with the advent of computers in police cruisers, as the strong magnets proved capable of scrambling their hard drives. These magnets were so powerful that once, at Federal Court, when I asked the judge for permission to take a paper clip off his bench so I could attach some papers together to be submitted as an exhibit, I held my hand some twelve inches above the paper clip, causing it to jump up to my waiting ring. The judge caught this out of the corner of his eye and I know he was very puzzled by it, but he never did ask me how I performed my "magic trick".

In any case, by that time the rush by law enforcement users to self–loading pistols had effectively rendered the widespread use of the Magna Trigger Safety system much rarer than it would otherwise have been. However, if you have the need for extra security, do not have concerns about interference with computer equipment, and can be satisfied with a revolver (which you should be unless you plan on needing the extra rounds and speed of reloading that modern self-loaders supply), a K-frame revolver fitted with a Magna Trigger Safety makes a nearly ideal duty weapon.

# Summing Up Custom Modifications

On the whole, I feel that the time and money spent on much of the custom work discussed above would have yielded better results if it had been applied to practising shooting and buying ammunition. The famed J. Henry Fitzgerald summed up this same sentiment rather well in his 1930 book *Shooting*, by warning his readers not to become "the man who spends half his shooting time on whittling out different grips, changing the sights and in other ways trying to have the revolver or pistol do what he must do himself. Revolvers and pistols now on the market are so perfect in grip and balance that the shooter can easily adapt himself to the arm as issued."

Of course, one of the main reasons the latter part of this statement is true is thanks to the many good ideas which originated in the aftermarket and have over the years been incorporated into factory models.

"Fitz" agreed, asking rhetorically in a later section of his book, "But how else do improvements originate in firearms and ammunition except through the needs of the users. Actual use and experience bring forth our needs."

*Chapter Thirty-Nine*

# Proving the Pudding

## How Does the M&P Stack Up Against Earlier and Later Duty Guns?

When the Smith & Wesson Military and Police revolver was first released in 1899, it was not immediately apparent that it represented a potential breakthrough in terms of handgun design. It was by no means on the order of magnitude represented, say, by going from a percussion revolver to one with a bored-through cylinder firing self-contained cartridges. The latter had already existed for some time, although most of those offered by Smith & Wesson were top-break models.

A side ejector is certainly no quicker to operate than a top-break—in fact the top-break, which automatically ejects its empties, might even be slightly faster to use. The new M&P revolver was of course chambered for a more powerful cartridge, the S&W .38 Special, with a heavier bullet going faster than that of the standard service .38 Long Colt, thanks to its longer case holding a larger charge of black powder. Had smokeless rather than bulky black powder been in common use at the time, the extra length of the .38 Special cartridge case would not have been necessary, in which case it is entirely possible that a top-break model could have handled the increased power of the new cartridge. While we typically think of top-breaks as weak designs suitable only for low-pressure cartridges, no doubt with a little proper engineering a top-break could contain a cartridge with the stopping power of the standard .38 Special. After all, Webley did it in the 1920s with their Mark IV, chambered for the hemispherically-nosed 200-grain loading of the ".380 Revolver cartridge Mark I". However, if this course had been generally adopted, all of the subsequent loadings of the .38 Special cartridge that we have come to know and love might never have been developed—loadings which took it from being a fine target-puncher with poor stopping power to a load that has proven itself many times over the years to have excellent stopping power coupled with fine accuracy. A load such as the +P 158 gr. LHP, for many years the duty load in St. Louis, Chicago, and with the FBI, as well as numerous other law enforcement agencies around the world, clearly illustrates that with proper bullet design, the .38 Special revolver can be a very effective self-defense tool. Perhaps not the most powerful in the world, but easy to shoot, safe to use by people of varying skill levels, and inexpensive to operate.

Of course, the strength of the solid frame on the M&P and the length of the cylinder ultimately paved the way for a whole new series of even more powerful cartridges that would have been very unlikely candidates for use in a top-break revolver. These include the .357 Magnum, the .41 Magnum, and the .44 Magnum, all of which were developed thanks to the extra length and greater capacity of the old black powder .38 Special case allowing heavier charges of smokeless powder, which could be reliably contained by the strength of the Hand Ejector designs, first the K-frame M&P in 1899, and then the scaled-up N-frame New Century or Triple Lock in 1908.

Thus the M&P, while not originally being seen as a giant step forward in 1899, was rather like the small child who gradually fulfills his (or her) potential over time, to become an accomplished man (or woman).

But the question that is interesting to me, and hopefully to you also, is whether the M&P was actually superior to any marked degree over what was typically being carried at the time of its introduction for actual police use. Not what its potential was, or what it later became, but was an officer in, say, 1905, better off with his new M&P revolver than he had been ten years earlier with his top-break .38 Smith & Wesson? For that matter, is an officer today able to do things with his modern service weapon, let's say a Glock, or the Smith & Wesson equivalent, the M&P auto, that much better than his mid-century counterpart so as to not even be in the same league?

To determine the answers to these questions, I thought it best to dig out some firearms qualification courses from the periods mentioned (pre-1900, 1950s, and late 20th century) and, using a few shooters of differing skill levels, let them shoot all three courses of fire with a suitable top-break, a postwar K-frame with short action and adjustable sights, and then a state-of-the-art duty-style autoloader. Could the old top-break compete with the more powerful M&P? Does the modern officer's self-loader give him a greater advantage over his early-to-mid-20th century brothers? The only way to determine this was to try it out.

# Selecting Three Courses of Fire

The course of fire outlined by Captain K. K. V. Casey in the 1904 *Arms and The Man* magazine for revolver practice by police would seem to give us a good place to start. Then I thought we should go to the standard Practical Pistol Course developed by the FBI in the 1930s and used by many agencies through the 1970s, which would offer a good mid-point comparison.

Lastly, we have a qualification course of fire that is recommended for the officer of today. This last course was especially illuminating when used to determine whether the early revolvers could keep up with the modern self-loaders, or whether they would be left behind in the dust of history.

Certainly if we were evaluating the course of progress that has been made over the years in transportation modes, for example, the answer would be immediately apparent; and we could easily say that the modern 21st-century vehicle would overwhelm the horse-drawn paddy wagon of 1890, or even the 1950s model police car; but I was not so certain this would be true in the case of sidearms.

True, the late 20th century autoloaders are easier to reload, hold more rounds to begin with, and are much more resistant to the ravages of weather. But such things matter only if you anticipate missing your target a lot, contending with a lot more assailants at one time than really exist, except in the imagination of some, and are careless about maintenance involving your important personal safety gear. As weapons, however, is the M&P, the harbinger of a major step forward when it was released in 1899, so far behind in the first couple of decades of the 21st century as to be obsolete? The proof is in the shooting, as we shall see.

When performing these tests, we must take into account that the targets mandated for use with a given course of fire may well have an impact on the scores achieved. Thus it is misleading to evaluate the scores achieved on one target and the scores achieved on a different style of target, and conclude that the difference is due solely to the weapon or the shooter. What we did, therefore, was to compare the scores or results obtained by the same shooter on the same targets and course of fire, fired by three different weapons.

# Describing the Three Weapons and Loads

For the purposes of this evaluation, the weapons used were as follows:

1. Smith & Wesson 3rd Model top-break, five shot capacity, .38 Smith & Wesson caliber, four-inch barrel, serial no. 205876, manufactured between 1884 and 1895 (let's call it 1890);
2. Smith & Wesson Model 14 four-inch .38 Special, serial no. K338052, a target-grade Combat Masterpiece revolver, sent to the Kansas City (MO) Police Department in 1958;
3. Smith & Wesson M&P autoloader, .40 Smith & Wesson caliber, serial no. MPB4076. While not as popular as the Glock in modern police service circles, this is still quite a common duty weapon today, and is certainly the spiritual successor to the original M&P revolver on most levels, except as a target and hunting weapon, of course.

Loads used were all factory-fresh ammunition, the standard 146-grain round-nose for our top-break, 148-gr. Wadcutters for our Model 14, and 180-grain FMJ Federals for our late model M&P auto.

701. Right side view of the Third Model top-break 5-shot .38 S&W caliber revolver, serial no. 205876.

Made in the 1890s, this is still a surprisingly effective weapon today.

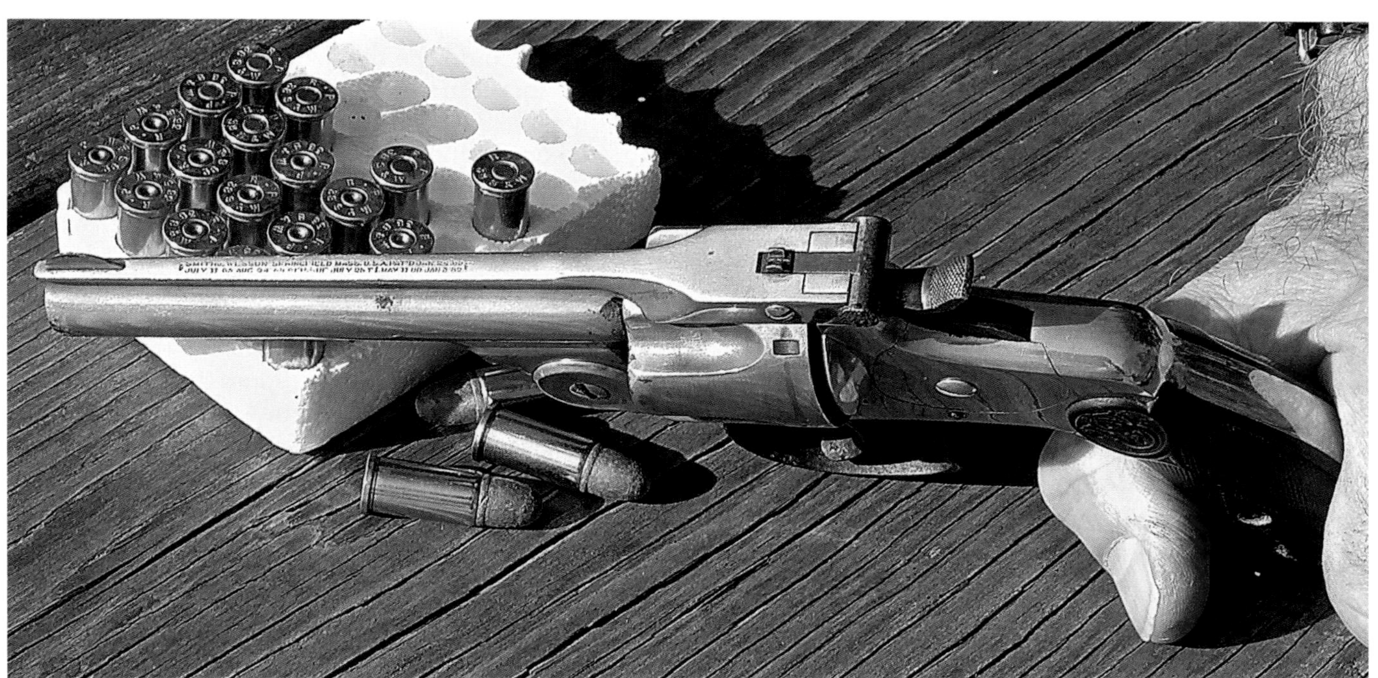

702. Top view of the above .38 S&W Third Model top-break revolver, showing details of the rudimentary sights and some of the factory-fresh 146-grain round-nose ammunition used in it on our "day on the range".

# On the Range

I am very familiar with shooting the Model 14 revolver, as well as the M&P auto, as were my other testers, but using the top-break was like venturing into a land long ago visited but currently unfamiliar. I suppose many if not most people reading this material are likely to have acquired such a top-break revolver at an early age when getting modern, current models was difficult due to legal issues or expense. My first carry gun at age twelve or so was a Hopkins & Allen .32, bought for ten dollars. It did have real pearl grips, and was listed for under three dollars in the 1904 Sears catalog, so right from the beginning I found that guns are a really good investment! I later went to a Smith & Wesson Safety Hammerless .38 three-inch, which had sights very similar to those on the 3rd Model top-break we tested. The last time I shot it (and used its sights) was in the basement of our family-owned laundry when I was fifteen. I remember that I had thought the sights were pretty slim there in that dark basement, and they still seemed pretty thin outside in Warren County, Missouri, on our late November and early December, 2012 test days.

703. The S&W Third Model top-break with action open, showing cylinder loaded to capacity with five rounds of .38 S&W ammunition.

Simply put, the sights on the top-break are rudimentary at best. The front sight is a mere sliver, about double the width of a razor blade. The test example was nickel-plated, but the nickel had peeled off the front sight, so a little white paint was daubed on to help improve its visibility. The rear sight was a small, narrow, short-in-height fixed 'U'.

Single-action pull was about six pounds, but fairly crisp, while the double-action pull was heavy and long, requiring much effort. Reloading the weapon was hindered by the tight fitting of the top latch, and the fact that the latch itself was not easily pushed upwards. Unlike some top-break models, the latch on the S&W 3rd Model does not extend much beyond the frame to allow easy access by the thumb. On the other hand, ejection was positive, and if opened vigorously the arm would eject the empties forcefully, allowing the shooter to reload readily.

The grip felt small in my hand. The other shooters also commented that the grip shifted in the hand, and did not allow a firm grasp to be taken. Of course the recoil of the cartridge is quite low, but the revolver is comparatively light, and the trigger guard did bounce against the knuckle joint with each shot.

The overall impression of the 3rd Model top-break was that this was a small, almost dainty weapon, but one which shot surprisingly well provided you could see the sights and fight the trigger into submission. I soon found that it was not zeroed for my eyes, but once that was made clear I was able to hold accordingly. I did fire a three-inch group of five shots at 25 yards with it off-hand when checking it out originally, so accuracy was certainly acceptable, despite what has to have been some lack of maintenance over the years which has affected the external appearance of the weapon.

I will not describe either the Model 14 or the M&P auto in any detail, as I suppose that they are well known to most readers, except to point out that the M14 had a modified square butt fitted with PC ("Plain Clothes") Magna-style stocks and a grip adapter, while the M&P auto was equipped with the small size grip insert. Both of these handguns felt much bigger in my hand, and much more solid. Smacking someone upside the head with either of them would be much more reassuring than trying the same thing with the early 3rd Model top-break, but it is as shooters that they were being evaluated here, not as blunt instruments. For that purpose, in the order of our weapons, a blackjack (1890), a baton (1950), or a Taser (today) were/are also carried.

# Comments on the Courses of Fire

704. The author firing the Third Model DA top-break at 25 yards on the 1890s course of fire.

In reviewing the various courses of fire that have been in vogue over the years, I could not help but note that the older courses always seem to involve shooting at greater distances. At first I found this puzzling, for surely people knew then, just as we know today, that most incidents involving attacks on police officers occur at close range. While it is true that some people think that if you can shoot accurately at a long range, you should be able to do so at close range (the opposite not being true, however), it dawned on me that these long ranges reflected the realities that those officers could encounter during the course of their duties.

Today, a review of police-involved shootings will typically show close-range encounters, since an officer is allowed to use deadly force only to protect himself or someone he is required to protect from grievous bodily injury or death, or if he is reasonably certain that the individual shot (or attempted to be shot) poses a substantial danger to the community. However, this policy has only been in effect since about 1975. Prior to that time, shooting fleeing felons was lawful, and more importantly, socially acceptable. What this meant for the officer on the beat in the 1890s when he turned a corner and saw an individual attempting to jimmy a window at night (a felony by any standard), he would call upon him to stop. If the individual turned, dropped his tool and ran, the officer could use deadly force to stop him. This means that the offender was likely moving away, at an increasingly greater distance. Certainly it would not be surprising to see a fleeing offender shot at 25 to 50 yards. Since the vast percentage of such pre-1975 shootings were likely to be at fleeing criminals rather than attacking criminals (even today more officers chase criminals than fight with them), it makes eminent sense that most shooting incidents will be those involving fleeing felons and great distances. Thus the shooting courses of the day were intended to test the skills the officers were most likely to use, i.e. hitting a man-sized target at a distance much greater than those we typically view as police shooting distances today.

I know of no survey of shooting incidents in the pre-1900 period for us to examine in order to determine the correlation between distances and results, but I imagine this would not really establish much, since even today if no body is discovered, often the incident is not noted. In an agency I am familiar with, for instance, an officer shot at a car that was attempting to run him down, but only after it had missed him and roared past, which seems a questionable decision at the federal level of law enforcement. The bullet apparently struck nothing of value, as no one seemed to be hit; and no one else was about, as it was around 3:00 a.m. The next day, once 12:00 noon had rolled around with no dead bodies or property claims being presented, the shooter was sent on his way with a suggestion that he not shoot at cars that had already passed him, and that he improve his skills. No report was ever prepared, submitted, or recorded.

If that was allowed to happen at the federal level in 1975 or so, I am certain that many earlier incidents involving burglars and robbers who did not fall down when shot at by officers with DA S&W .38 revolvers and K-frames were never noted in the records.

I selected the courses of fire as outlined herein after recognizing that they may not have been exactly what was shot when they were first introduced since, for instance, I did not have access to a suitable period holster for the 3rd Model top-break .38, and that our shooters all wore ear protection, which would have certainly not have been the case in the 1890s, nor probably during the 1950s. The shooters selected (which included the author as well as his shooting companion and fellow gun writer, Leroy Thompson) have many years of experience among them (well over 100 years just between myself and Leroy), so I suppose it is likely we had more experience than a typical officer of the 1890s period or even the 1950s, for that matter. But this was likely offset to a large extent by dimming eyes, but thankfully not shaky hands, yet. (I well remember a friend of mine, Jack Soutiea, then in his 80s, an old Bureau of Investigation man (not FBI) who carried a .32-20 four-inch M&P, complaining to me one day that he had missed two individuals who attacked him due to shaky hands: "First time I missed when I shot at anyone since I went to France in 1917", he reported. But all is well that ends well: the muzzle blast caused them to flee, and Jack went on his way, with no police report being made.)

705. Firing the 4" Model 14 at 25 yards on the modified 1990s FBI Qualification Course of Fire.

# Results from the 1890s Course of Fire

The 1890s course of fire consisted of a man target, with the distances and the number of rounds fired noted. Scores are averages:

| | | | Results - 150 max - 30X | | |
|---|---|---|---|---|---|
| Distance | No. of Rounds | Type of Fire | 3rd Model | M14 | M&P Auto |
| 15 yards | 10 | SA - strong hand only | 34-0X | 50-5X | 49-2X |
| 25 yards | 10 | SA - strong hand only | 49-4X | 50-7X | 41-0X |
| 50 yards | 10 | SA - strong hand only | 5-0X | 36-1X | 42-3X |
| Totals | | | 88-4X | 136-13X | 132-5X |

In reviewing these scores, it is apparent that at the longer range of 50 yards, the better sights of the M14 and the M&P Auto allow for much better results. However I cannot help but point out that when the next course of fire was shot at the same distances, this gulf evened out dramatically. Perhaps the shooters were getting used to the sight picture of the top-break, or the intensity of the sunlight was different, since this experiment took two days to conduct; although the weather seemed about the same on both days. Painting the very thin front sight on the DA Smith, coupled with a little paint on the rear sight also, may have helped the shooters pick it up and maintain alignment. I imagine it was that, along with increasing familiarity, that allowed our averages to improve the next time this course was shot at 50 yards. Ammunition should not have been an issue, as the trials were shot throughout with factory-fresh 146-grain RNL rounds.

Had this 50-yard anomaly not existed, the scores would have been very close. If we ignore it and base the results on the first 20 rounds fired, we get the following percentages:

| | |
|---|---|
| DA Smith | 83% |
| Model 14 | 100% |
| M&P Auto | 90% |

The better trigger pull of the Model 14 likely contributed to the higher score for it, which I do not find surprising, although the similarity in scores between the 1890-period top-break and the latest M&P Auto is quite interesting, I think. I put it down to each having roughly equivalently poor trigger pulls. Of course, the autoloader holds more rounds, is quicker to reload, and will not look as bad in 100 years as the old top-break does now, I am certain, thanks to its excellent rust-resistant finish, but for the first five shots, they were almost identical in actual performance, at least as regards strikes on target.

# Results from the 1950s Course of Fire

The 1950s course of fire was shot on a man target at the distances noted, with the number of rounds indicated. Scores are averages:

| | | | Results - 250 max - 50X | | |
|---|---|---|---|---|---|
| **Distance** | **No. of Rounds** | **Type of Fire** | **3rd Model** | **M14** | **M&P** |
| 7 yards | 10 | high level DA strong hand only | 50-8X | 50-8X | 50-8X |
| 25 yards | 10 | off-hand DA two hands | 44-3X | 49-3X | 50-2X |
| 25 yards | 5 | off-hand DA weak hand only | 12-1X | 22-1X | 13-0X |
| 50 yards | 10 | prone SA two hands | 43-2X | 19-0X | 48-2X |
| 50 yards | 5 | sitting SA, two hands | 24-0X | 38-0X | 22-1X |
| 50 yards | 10 | off-hand SA two hands | 39-0X | 40-4X | 41-2X |
| Totals | | | 212-14X | 218-16X | 224-15X |

In reviewing these scores, it is apparent to me that the DA Smith & Wesson and the M&P .40 Auto were roughly equal at all distances. Their poor performances in comparison to the Model 14 at 25 yards off-hand, weak hand only, I put down to the smoother trigger pull of the Model 14 in comparison to the DA Smith and M&P Auto.

The 50-yard prone result for the Model 14 seems odd to me, but I am reporting this as I counted it. Perhaps the sun was hitting the front sight oddly when the target was shot in that prone position at 50 yards with the Model 14, as I frankly would have expected much better results; certainly the results of

706. Firing the .40 caliber M&P auto pistol at 25 yards on the modified 1990s FBI Qualification Course of Fire.

the sitting and off-hand targets shot at the same distances were much better.

What is quite clear here is how close all three weapons were overall, and how the 3rd Model top-break and M&P.40 Auto were both suffering from the same problem of poor trigger pull, causing scores to suffer as a result.

The top-break held the fewest rounds at five, and was the slowest to reload of the trio tested. So while you might have more rounds available to fire with the later models, and could also reload more quickly, for the first five shots at least, they are all pretty much alike so far as results are concerned.

Cartridge performance might well be superior with the .40 S&W, but the difference between a .38 Smith & Wesson and a standard round-nose, solid-lead .38 Special is not really much, in my judgment - maybe 10 to 15%. Certainly in the period when both the DA Smith and the early M&P revolver were likely to be carried by officers on the street, being shot by either one would have been a bad experience.

# Results from the Modified 1990s FBI Qualification Course of Fire

Proceeding on to the last course of fire we used, I took a somewhat modified version of the FBI pistol qualification course which was in use when auto pistols were first in general use by the Bureau. It is interesting that the distances have been shortened up to a maximum of 25 yards, with greater emphasis on the shorter seven-yard range.

I did modify this course, so it is not identical to the FBI standard but it at least retains the flavor of that course of fire. As modified, it consisted of the following. Scores are averages:

707. Results with all three weapons tested in the modified 1990s FBI Qualification Course of Fire.
Left: Third Model top-break: 173 - 13X.
Center: Model 14: 175 - 18X.
Right: M&P auto pistol: 173 - 18X.

| | | | Results - 175 max - 35X | | |
|---|---|---|---|---|---|
| **Distance** | **No. of Shots** | **Type of Fire** | **3rd Model** | **M14** | **M&P** |
| 7 yards | 5 | strong hand only DA | 25-4X | 25-4X | 25-2X |
| 7 yards | 5 | weak hand only DA | 25-0X | 25-2X | 25-5X |
| 7 yards | 5 | two-hand DA | 25-5X | 25-5X | 25-5X |
| 15 yards | 10 | two-hand DA | 50-6X | 50-4X | 50-5X |
| 25 yards | 10 | two hand DA | 50-4X | 50-3X | 48-1X |
| Totals | | | 174-19X | 175-18X | 173-18X |

The target used here was different than that used on the other courses, and had a much larger scoring area for the highest point of fire, however, the "X" ring area was roughly the same size.

What we see here is that each weapon was yielding very similar results. The poor sights on the top-break were not as big a handicap shooting double action when the distances were the shorter 25 yards and under, and the better trigger pull of the Model 14 was likewise not as great an asset when the distances were short. Good triggers and sights obviously help the most as the distance increases, when a small amount of error caused by poor trigger control or sight misalignment gets magnified many times, resulting in wide shots on target. As we get closer, these factors diminish in actual importance, so far as the qualification courses of whichever period are concerned.

# Conclusions

So, to return to our initial questions:

1. Was the M&P revolver a major improvement in the field when it was introduced in 1899?
2. Is the M&P type revolver so out-of-date that it cannot compete with our current self-loaders?

So far as stopping power is concerned, I really do not see that the M&P initially represented a major improvement. While the .38 Special as originally loaded was somewhat more powerful than the .38 Smith & Wesson, the increase was not so substantial as to be overwhelming, or even possibly a basis for buying a new weapon. However, the .38 Special has certainly been developed into a very effective cartridge for personal defense, and even the .38 Smith & Wesson, originally designed by Daniel Wesson and introduced in 1876, achieved a similar result when the 200-gr. bullet loading of the "Official Police" or "Super Police" version was introduced in the late 1920s. As we have seen, it appears that this latter version was actually originated by the British in their .38/200 round, which was adopted as the standard British pistol cartridge and used, with a somewhat lighter, jacketed bullet, in Enfield and S&W M&P revolvers during WWII.

Clearly the new M&P revolver was faster to reload—at least as regards getting the cylinder open—but once that is done, they are about the same. The M&P of course gives you six rounds instead of five, which is nice; but it is a bigger and heavier weapon also. The double-action top-break Smith could be readily carried in the front or rear pocket, while the four-inch or longer M&P needs a holster.

The sights, even on the early M&P, were better than those found on the 3rd Model top-break, being wider in front and easier to pick up. This better set of sights would no doubt prove useful in hitting fleeing felons at 50 yards or more, so for that purpose, clearly the M&P is a better weapon. However, overall if you had been carrying your top-break and were used to it, you certainly would not need to go out and replace it with a new M&P.

As to whether the general arrival of the self-loading pistol has rendered the many variations of the M&P revolver no longer viable, it seems to me the answer is "No". Clearly from our scoring on the above qualification courses, we see little real difference. For personal defense, equally good ammunition, whether shot in a revolver or self-loader, will yield equal results. The self-loader can certainly hold more ammunition and is quicker to reload with a large volume of ammunition than a revolver, even when a special speed loader is used, since you are shoving six small objects into six small holes versus one large object (a loaded magazine) containing 15 or so rounds into one large opening in the bottom of the grip.

Reliability of both weapons is roughly the same, although clearly the autoloader is easier to maintain under dusty and dirty conditions. If you plan on needing heavy volumes of fire, or think you are likely to encounter a substantial number of assailants at one time, the autoloader should be your selection. On the other hand, if you anticipate single targets at longer ranges, or smaller targets at close range (say, a portion of a body concealed behind a bullet-resistant wall or vehicle, not to mention a hostage), then the better, practical accuracy due to good triggers that the revolver will deliver should be your choice, although a "square" gun with a good trigger is also a good choice. Just make certain you can deliver your rounds onto the intended target the first time (or at least by the 6th time - not the 15th time).

To sum up: the arrival of the M&P did not make all the earlier revolvers obsolete, and you can still comfortably use your K-frame for police or defense work today and not be at any greater risk than your predecessors were in years past. It will still perform just like it did when gas lights lit the streets, horses pulled wagons, and hoop skirts were all the rage.

# Shooting My Pope-Barreled M&P

708. Firing my Pope-barreled target M&P at 25 yards offhand, using the classic one-hand hold.

In Chapter Thirty-Eight I described an early modified M&P in my collection which has had its factory barrel replaced by one made by the famed Harry Pope (figs. 692 - 696), who of course was well known for his fine, highly accurate barrels. No doubt it was made for a target shooter who a few years earlier would have shot a black powder No. 3 Smith & Wesson on a formal course of fire.

Since this revolver was most likely intended for one-handed, off-hand shooting at bulls-eye targets, I decided to report on my experience with it in its natural home environment on the range.

First, I noticed how nicely it balanced, despite the long barrel. Since it lacked a heavy rib and the barrel tapered nicely, it was not muzzle-heavy as you might expect with such a "long tom". This helped me fire a five-shot string without fatigue. The grip was also quite good, allowing me to maintain a proper hold. Of course the recoil of .38 Special Match loads is not particularly heavy, but unlike those loads when fired in a standard M&P revolver, I encountered no hand slippage upon firing which would force me to readjust my grip after each shot. The over-travel screw was set perfectly, and the pull did break like a glass rod, which is of course the standard, or at least the ideal.

However, I found the sights difficult to use. This was no doubt caused by two factors. First, having 60-plus-year-old eyes, I have my shooting glasses set up to provide optimum resolution on the front sights of four-inch K-frames, Glock M17/22s, and five-inch Colt Government Model pistols, and a front sight further away from that point simply goes out of focus. Additionally, I prefer a one-eighth inch front sight, flat-faced or ramped, and found this thinner bead sight difficult to master, as when the long barrel was extended in a one-hand traditional target shooting hold, it appeared quite small. I also found the rear sight notch very narrow. Firing from under cover, I had great difficulty in picking up and maintaining alignment. Moving out into direct sunlight on a cloudless day, I could pick up the sights finally but the sun hit the bead front, causing me to shoot away from the sun's reflection on it. Perhaps smoking it would have helped.

Nevertheless, I found that if I did my part and really worked at it, I could get good results with this revolver. The target illustrated was of course the best

709. The target I shot with my Pope-barreled target M&P, using factory 148-gr. WC match ammunition at 25 yards.

of the bunch, but it does show what this revolver is capable of, perhaps more than what I as the shooter can do on demand.

As well as being a pre-1914 time machine, this early M&P revolver is a true historical treasure, and I enjoyed my day at the range with it. I believe Harry Pope would be happy to see that this old six-gun that left his shop so many decades ago is still capable of fine work.

*Chapter Forty*

# Requiem for the K-Frame

710. Left and right side views of one of the very last of the postwar long-action M&Ps, serial no. S956091, shipped to the Shapleigh Hardware Co. in St. Louis, Missouri on November 10, 1947.

Even though the M&P revolver was back in production for civilian consumption within a few weeks after the end of WWII, lack of production from 1941 through September, 1945, coupled with light production in the years before the war due to the lingering effects of the Depression, meant that many men who had made a lot of money working extra hours during the war years, and now wanted to spend it on a new Smith & Wesson revolver, could not get one.

The first postwar commercial M&P revolvers were exactly like the later Victory Models except for a better finish and no lanyard ring, with the 'V' prefix generally missing from their serial numbers, although a few early surplus frames still bore the 'V' prefix. By 1948 the short action adapted to the K-frame, which had been first installed in the K-22 target models in 1939 and then shelved for the duration, began to appear in the postwar .38 target-sighted revolver, and this is still found in the models being made today.

Not surprisingly, standard four-inch blue-finish models were the first out the door, followed by other barrel lengths including two, five, and six inches. Nickel finish was once again an option, and these were being shipped also. The .32-20 WCF model went the way of "Lucky Strike green", never to reappear in the postwar world. If you wanted one you had to find a used one, although there were plenty around, as it had been a surprisingly popular model.

As production resumed on the standard M&P .38, the line was slowly starting up again on other commercial models, including the various K-frame .22 Rimfire and target models. Even a few leftover old stock long-action N-frame .357 Magnums, fitted with adjustable micrometer sights, were offered in the late 1940s (fig. 166).

# The Golden Age (1948 - 1980)

711. Left side view of a Model 15 with 2" barrel, nickel finish, and modified square butt with "P.C." Magna stocks. A popular choice for use as an undercover duty weapon before the advent of stainless steel.

It can truly be said that the golden age of the Smith & Wesson K-frame revolver ran for a little over 30 years - from 1948 to 1980. It was at the beginning of this period that Smith & Wesson effectively drove Colt's from the police self-defense and target-shooter market. Both Ruger and Taurus later carved out certain market shares, thanks to good designs and workmanship, but I daresay neither would have sold enough product to gain a serious foothold had not demand on the production capacity of Smith & Wesson been so great from military and civilian users alike that their revolvers were in short supply during much of the latter part of this period.

Over the next several decades, a variety of engineering changes appeared, involving the number and placement of screws in the frame, the width of the rib on the target model barrels, types of barrels, degree of polishing: high-gloss or brushed blue finishes; and grip styles. Some of the changes were intended to cut down on extra machining steps, while others were designed to make a more reliable revolver, such as when the thread on the extractor rod was changed from right- to left-handed to make it less likely that the rod would come loose and tie up the weapon. All of these are discussed in the earlier chapters of this book.

Throughout it all, however, the K-frame Smith & Wesson retained its familiar outline and performed in the same positive fashion.

Starting in the mid-1970s, as discussed in Chapter Thirty-Two, stainless steel was introduced as a construction material, which made the resulting weapons even more versatile and appealing for many users.

New chamberings were added to the line which more than made up for deleting the old .32-20 WCF. These were intended either to give the user more power, such as when the .357 Combat Magnum was introduced, or to give the shooter an additional hunting edge or more versatility, such as when the .22 Rimfire Magnum and the .22 Centerfire Magnum (.22 Jet) were incorporated into the K-frame line.

As we have seen the .22 Jet turned out to be a short-lived offering, while the Model 547, chambered for the rimless 9x19mm cartridge, necessitated some unique and interesting modifications.

## The M&P: Everyone's Ideal Police Revolver

By the mid-1970s, stainless steel had become widely accepted and was routinely offered alongside identical models made of conventional blued steel, and most people seemed to agree that the K-frame four-inch Smith & Wesson, in either blue or stainless steel, was the ideal police revolver. Some might prefer the versatility of adjustable sights, while others preferred the simplicity of fixed sights which could not get banged out of alignment. And some still liked conventional metal (or at least a dark finish) as opposed to bright stainless.

Some reservations remained about the effectiveness of the .38 Special cartridge, although with the advent of loads such as the 158-grain LHP +P, this became much less of an issue.

There were those who liked the three-inch models as easier for plainclothes officers to carry. Although with a proper holster a four-inch was actually no problem, the three-inch was undeniably different, which is always a good thing to many.

True, quality control became an issue at times, but defective arms could be returned to be properly adjusted, although obviously they should never have left the factory in less than perfect condition in the first place.

More critically, supply was often short due to the combined effects of the Vietnam War, the Civil Rights movement, and the rise of the drug culture, but supply issues are only a concern if you are looking for something, not when you have one already.

# The Advent of the "Square" Gun

But while the mid-1970s found the K-frame Smith & Wesson at the top of the heap as regards defense weapons, it was soon to see its position under attack, and it was ultimately to be displaced by an Austrian polymer-framed upstart.

The U.S. military had been discussing replacing the .45 caliber M1911A1 pistol since the end of WWII, when officers had been fascinated by the double-action 9mm P38 pistol used by the Germans. Today of course we recognize that DA/SA triggers are not very efficient, but in the late 1940s, many people firmly believed they were the coming thing. U.S. manufacturers started making double-action 9mm autoloading pistols, and some initial trials were held with a view to possible military adoption. However these first tests were inconclusive, and interest turned cold for a variety of reasons, leaving us with alloy-framed Colt Commanders in 9mm, .38 Super, and more importantly .45 ACP, as well as the Smith & Wesson double-action 9mm Model 39 autoloader.

## The S&W Model 39 - the First U.S. Double-Action 9mm Auto Pistol

712. Left and right side views of a double-action 9mm Model 39, serial no. 63037. In the 1957 circular the Model 39 was also available in a single-action-only version.

This example is built on a steel frame, which is much less commonly seen than the alloy-frame version.

The Smith & Wesson Model 39 engendered some interest in the general use of autoloading pistols when it was introduced. The Warwick, Rhode Island, Police Department adopted it in 1962, and when the Illinois State Police adopted it in 1966, the beginning of a new wave was felt throughout the entire self-defense field. Despite this, the K-frame revolver remained dominant.

# The Beretta Model 92 - Adopted in 1984 as the U.S. Army M9

713. Left side view of a 9mm Beretta Model 92D, serial no. BER287658. The Model 92D is the DAO version of the Model 92, and has a bobbed spur hammer.

The Beretta 92 was adopted by the U.S. Army in 1984 as the M9. The M9 is a fine weapon until it breaks without warning, which it does, and for those with small hands.

But in the 1980s, the U.S. Army decided to take another look at high-capacity DA/SA self-loaders in 9x19mm. Further tests were conducted, and the result was the adoption of the Beretta M9 in 1984. The U.S. Army had said it was okay to adopt a foreign-designed weapon—albeit only after a domestic manufacturing facility was established in the U.S.—but a lot of other foreign-made autoloaders had also been tested, and some of these also looked good.

Two other critical elements were then added to the mix, namely better 9mm ammunition that was not only more effective against human targets but also functioned perfectly in these modern autoloaders, coupled with growing concerns about the drug wars that were creating a lot of violence. Police officers, who began to voice their fears that they were "outgunned" by their criminal opponents, considered that a high-capacity autoloading pistol would do much to "level the playing field". As regards safety concerns for street officers, chiefs of departments could issue DA/SA pistols more comfortably than they could weapons such as the single-action Colt Government Model.

## The Glock 22 - the Golden Age Ends

714. Right side view of the Glock 22, a "square" gun if there ever was one.

By the late 1980s the polymer-framed Glock had very largely replaced the M&P revolver in law enforcement circles.

Thus the sea change began, and whereas a few years earlier only a very few officers were carrying autoloaders, within ten years after the adoption of the Beretta M9 by the U.S. military the trend had become irreversible, so that today, in the second decade of the 21st century, the K-frame revolver is rarely seen in law enforcement holsters in the United States.

The golden age of the K-frame Smith & Wesson revolver as the law enforcement weapon of choice had ended, its place largely taken by the Glock, typically in .40 Smith & Wesson caliber—a fine weapon indeed, but perhaps with a little less soul and finesse to it.

# Autoloaders Take Over On the Range

## The .38 Special Clark Model 61-S

715. Left and right side views of the Clark Model 61-S, a Colt .38 Super Model 1911A1 modified to fire .38 Special wadcutters by James Clark, a gunsmith and shooter in Shreveport, Louisiana.

The Clark Model 61-S was popular with many target shooters in the late 1950s and early 1960s for use in bulls-eye matches.

All of the custom revolver modifications have pretty much died off now, thanks to the development of semi-automatic handguns that shoot .38 Special wadcutter ammunition. At first these were gunsmith-converted Colt .38 Super automatics modified to fire .38 Special wadcutters, such as the Clark Model 61-S shown above.

## The Purpose-Built S&W Model 52 "Master"

716. Left side view of the S&W M52-2, serial no. A 105630, a purpose-built .38 Special autoloader designed to fire mid-range wadcutters only. Introduced in 1971 as the .38 "Master", the M52-2 was an improved version of the original M52, fitted with an adjustable trigger stop, serrated hammer spur, and beefed-up extractor.

Soon after its introduction in the early 1960s, the Smith & Wesson Model 52, designed and purpose-built as an autoloader firing .38 Special flush-face wadcutter ammunition, effectively removed the K-38 target revolver from firing lines around the world.

## Advantages of the Target Autoloader

The serious target shooter of course has long ago replaced the target-grade revolver with a self-loading pistol, as such weapons are inherently more accurate. Not having to contend with the "jump" from the mouth of the cartridge case through the smoothbored front portion of the revolver chamber, then past the cylinder gap and through the forcing cone into the rifling, such pistols are of course almost always more accurate than a revolver, and, being self-cocking, do not have to be manually cocked, thereby avoiding the necessity to break your grip while thumbing the hammer spur back. They also offer a trigger pull which is as good, or nearly so, as that of a good target-grade revolver.

One might think that novices would still flock to the double-action revolver as being both easy and safe to shoot and manipulate, but my experiences in meeting a number of new shooters at the ranges I frequent tell me this is not the case, for I rarely see a K-frame revolver, although there are lot of black polymer-framed weapons with big butts that hold about a third of a box of ammunition, and fat slides that are difficult to carry comfortably in an inside-the-waistband holster.

## Requiem for the Target Revolver

One still sees them occasionally on offer at gun shows, typically still in the deceased shooter's box complete with spotting scope, a few old targets (kept due to being really good!), and a few loose patches never sewn onto his shooting jacket.

Grandpa has been dead now 20 years, the revolver was last fired in 1972, and grandma is going into a home at age 88, but those old revolvers will still shoot just as finely as the last time they appeared on the range, and they make great pine cone and tin can poppers with low-recoil, low-noise .38 wadcutters. You might want to try one!

## The Stainless Steel Model 5946

717. Left and right side views of the S&W Model 5946, a DAO 9mm autoloader in satin stainless steel which replaced the K-frame revolver in the NYPD and the RCMP.

# The Future of the M&P

On one hand, we could say that the nomenclature of the Smith & Wesson Military and Police model ended in 1957, when the factory began assigning model numbers to their revolver line and the .38 Special M&P became the Model 10. But while that is how the factory referred to it, for most users it continued to be known as the "M&P".

## The S&W Polymer-Framed M&P Auto Pistol

718. Right side view of an M&P autoloading pistol, serial no. MPA 2007, S&W's 21st century replacement for the K-frame revolver.

Built on a Zytel polymer frame with stainless steel elements in calibers 9mm, .40 S&W and .357 SIG, the M&P features a 4½" stainless steel barrel and stainless steel slide with a black Melonite finish.

Note the "universal accessory rail" molded into the front of the frame.

On the other hand, we could also say that the future of the "M&P" model seems assured, because when Smith & Wesson created their own version of the polymer-framed Glock—not a bad one, by the way, although not quite as good—at least they remembered its professional predecessor and named it the "M&P", and so the old traditional name continues to have a presence in the holsters of law enforcement officers on U.S. streets.

This is the pistol on which Smith & Wesson has pinned its hopes as being able to re-establish the firm's prominence as the leading supplier of police handguns in the world. While I have some reservations as to whether the new M&P autoloader is as rugged as a Glock in terms of standing up to long-time use, it is only fair to say it is quite good. Further, the factory has shown a willingness to modify their product to meet the demands of individual users, while Glock has stood firmly against any such flexibility; so who knows? The mid-21st century may well prove to be the Golden Age for the Military & Police model, albeit a bit square instead of round in shape, just as the mid- to late-20th century was for its ancestor of the same name.

However, leaving aside the "square" guns that now bear the honored M&P name, what does the future hold for the K-frame revolver?

As I have indicated elsewhere, thanks to savvy corporate directorship that has overseen various engineering changes and invested heavily in computer-aided machinery, a product that everyone acknowledges is difficult to make continues to be made and sold at very competitive prices. The latest models coming off the line are actually made of stronger, better materials, typically have better sights, and with today's loads are more powerful and at least as accurate as any M&P revolver turned out in the 20th century. In fact, as stated in Chapter Thirty-Two, when relative values are taken into account, firearms and ammunition are cheaper today than ever before, which is a pretty amazing accomplishment.

And yet, while I like these revolvers, and like being able to empty out the fired cases into my bag to be taken away to be reloaded, and appreciate the excellent trigger pull that a good revolver can give to permit better on-target results, I have to acknowledge it is unlikely that law enforcement will ever turn back to the revolver as their main duty weapon.

# Goodbye to All That

Although time and preference have seen to it that no revolver, even the M&P, could remain the main U.S. law enforcement sidearm forever, during its "Golden Age" it was certainly a remarkably durable and long-lasting police, target, and self-defense revolver, and frequently a military revolver as well, through force of circumstances.

The K-frame is too large for pocket or ankle carry, those being the areas where J-frame revolvers shine, even today. And, if you are looking for a revolver for handgun hunting or silhouette shooting on steel animal targets, you will want to take advantage of the larger and more powerful chamberings available in the N-frame models.

To a great extent the role of the K-frame for nearly 100 years was as a belt gun for defense, but that role has now been usurped, and it is not likely to return. But that is acceptable, I suppose, as nearly ten decades of steady work may well entitle the K-frame revolver to an honorable retirement as it becomes, like the Colt Single Action before it, the weapon of the collector who appreciates fine workmanship, a sense of history, and a vast number of interesting variations. Yes, I suppose it might as well be said that the K-frame Smith & Wesson is well on its way to becoming a serious collectible rather than a user's weapon. Not quite there yet, of course, as some of us still pack them daily, but when we are gone in a couple more decades, only the collectors and re-enactors will remain to appreciate these fine Smith & Wessons.

The "sea change" that finally upset this pattern had nothing really to do with the K-frame revolver itself, but nevertheless, as discussed above, the time did come when the "round" gun simply went out of fashion, and the "square" gun replaced it.

As John Henwood recorded it,

> *[Smith & Wesson's] increasing emphasis on autoloading handguns (and especially in the emerging technology of "plastic" guns) has also had a negative effect on revolver sales in general. From a manufacturing and sales standpoint, the self-loading handgun (particularly when made largely of injection-molded plastic) is almost irresistible. Although both cheaper and simpler to manufacture, and requiring far less hand fitting than a quality revolver, it can be sold (for reasons which the author does not even pretend to understand) at a higher price!*

But was there ever a better overall service revolver than a stainless steel K-frame three- or four-inch Smith & Wesson? Some might prefer to carry or shoot other arms, but it is hard to argue honestly that they are truly better, just different.

Writing in 1997, John Henwood agreed, as follows:

> . . *Yet the old M&P continues on, toward the start of its second century of service to Americans. Not, however, without some changes. The traditional blue-steel pattern is slowly being phased out. In 1997 only one version of the basic Model 10 (the Model 10-10, with a 4-inch heavy barrel) was offered. But the remaining variations (the stainless steel models, and those chambered for the .357 Magnum or fitted with adjustable sights) are still selling satisfactorily, and doubtless will remain in production well into the next century.*

# Conclusion

I rather doubt that when he designed the .38 Special M&P, Daniel B. Wesson thought that it would become the most significant and popular revolver of all time. Nor did he even begin to think of it in terms of a cultural icon, but of course that is exactly what it has become.

The world of 1899 into which the Military & Police revolver was born is long gone. It was a world of horses, gas lights, gold coins, straight razors, coal furnaces, long skirts, primitive medicine, and cartridges filled with black powder. All of those have been replaced with things that are newer, if not necessarily better; and one might well ask, how many of the everyday products familiar in 1899 would even be recognizable in the second decade of the 21st century?

Within this atmosphere of relentless renewal, the Smith & Wesson K-frame revolver is still in production and remains one of the company's flagship products to this day. The newest examples are just as reliable as the first ones, and work just the same way. Put a brand-new K-frame in the hands of a man born in 1865, when the U. S. Civil War was just ending and The South was still full of slaves, and he would know how to use it without any hesitation. Put an early one in the hands of a man (or woman) born within shouting distance of the 21st century and, while the grips might feel a little small and the sights might be a little harder to see, everything else would feel pretty much the same, certainly on single action. Maybe the double action would feel a little longer, but still quite smooth. These two people, separated by five or six generations, would easily be able to relate to the situation in front of them, whereas teamsters, bank tellers, barbers, fashion designers, or physicians from the same two periods would find a much, much greater gap to cross in dealing with what has happened to the tools of their trades.

I think you will agree with me that the K-frame Smith & Wesson is a very interesting revolver. It offers an amazing number of variations for the collector, and it remains a very fine handgun for target shooting and for certain hunting applications. And if you cannot find a model among all the K-frame alternatives available today that is suitable for your defensive purposes, you likely have some very unusual needs.

I hope you have enjoyed this voyage as we have explored the history of the K-frame revolver over the last century or so. I know I have enjoyed bringing it to you.

# Part IV: Commercial Accessories and Ancillaries

*Chapter Forty-One*

# Commercial Ammunition

## A Retrospective of Ammunition Development

719. A lineup of cartridges for which the K-frame revolver has been chambered over the years, excluding experimentals.

From left: .17 Hornady Magnum Rimfire; .22 Long Rifle; .22 Rimfire Magnum; .256 Winchester Magnum; .22 Remington Jet; .32-20 (.32 WCF); .32 S&W Long; .32 H&R Magnum; 9mm Parabellum; .38 Long Colt; .38 S&W; .38 Special; .357 Magnum. Dave Terbrueggen collection

When the M&P first appeared, the metallic cartridge consisted of a copper (later brass) case as a container for the (black) powder, fitted with a primer in the base, either rim-or central fire, and capped with a bullet that, although typically an elongated, round-nosed lead cylinder, could have been fired in a percussion revolver. Jacketed-bullet ammunition was used in modern rifles like the U.S. Krag as well as numerous European rifles of the period, but for handguns, it was strictly a lead bullet thing. Since the bullets were cylindrical in shape, they generally weighed a bit more than the round balls loaded over loose charges of black powder ignited by a percussion cap, which had been the norm less than 35 years earlier.

The then-standard U.S. service cartridge for revolvers was the .38 Long Colt, loaded with a round-nosed, solid-lead bullet weighing 150 grains and producing a muzzle velocity of about 750 fps. The bullet was not likely to expand on impact, absent striking some very heavy bone, which even then was likely only to rivet the nose of the projectile.

First chambered in the First Model Hand Ejector of 1899, the .38 Smith & Wesson Special cartridge was slightly longer than the .38 Long Colt, although the .38 Colt round could also be used. With an overall cartridge length of 1.570", the S&W .38 Special contained more powder and a slightly heavier projectile, which accordingly produced slightly greater velocity

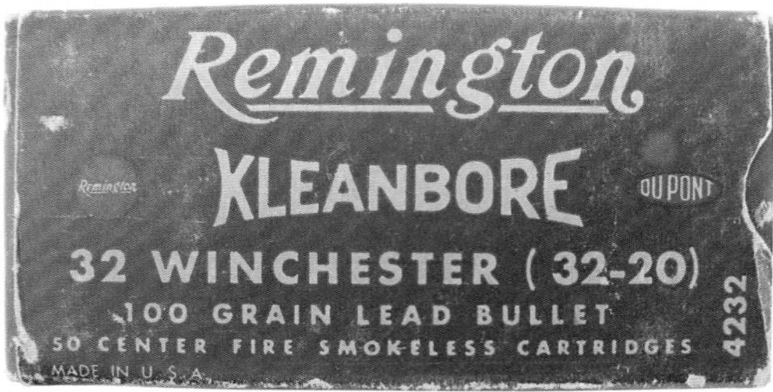


720. Four boxes, three early and one more recent, containing 50 rounds each of .32-20 (.32 WCF) cartridges.
The box at top left dates from before the 1910 merger of the Union Metallic Cartridge Co. with Remington Arms.
Gaston Comeau collection

than the .38 Colt service round. The first smokeless loadings appeared in September, 1899.

Right from the beginning the M&P was also available in the .32 WCF (or .32-20) chambering. Because this cartridge was also used in the Models 1873 and 1892 lever-action Winchester rifles, both of which had tubular magazines, the cartridge was always loaded with a flat-nosed projectile, lest the point of the bullet, no matter how rounded, set off the primer of the cartridge ahead of it in the magazine tube. The flat nose of the .32-20 bullets limited their ballistic potential in the Winchesters, but in fact made them much better in a handgun. When fired in the M&P revolver, the flat-tipped 115-grain .32-20 bullet produced a muzzle velocity lower than that in the rifle, but faster than the .38 Colt Long or .38 Special, which gave it surprisingly good stopping power. Many people over the years liked the M&P in .32-20 as a defense revolver, combining as it did good stopping power with light felt recoil. Outdoorsmen liked it due to the flat trajectory of the round, which made outdoor shots at an unknown distance easier to accomplish.

Other than the flat-nosed .32-20, bullets in the early 1900s were typically round-nosed, except for those used for target shooting purposes, which by 1905 or so were square-nosed lead "wadcutters", loaded to produce the same or slightly less velocity than the standard loads.

In the later 1920s, the 200-grain .38 S&W Super Police bullet appeared. This heavier bullet produced a lower muzzle velocity but, thanks in all likelihood to its longer, heavier bullet, it tended to tumble when it entered a body, with consequent better stopping power. The 200-gr. Super Police loading was apparently first used in a police shooting in 1927 near my home town, over in East St. Louis, Illinois, by Patrolman Robert Sweeney, who was said to have shot a burglar running from him at 75 yards. Struck in the kidney, the criminal dropped like a box of rocks. In an interesting sidelight, years later I had a client who had formerly been a Chief of Detectives in that same organization, who had come on the force in the 1950s. I asked him if he knew the famed officer and he replied in the affirmative, telling me of a couple of other miscreants he had shot (perhaps with his 200-gr. loads?) and noting that "Bob Sweeney was a hard man".

The British had already developed a similar heavy load, and used them to increase the stopping

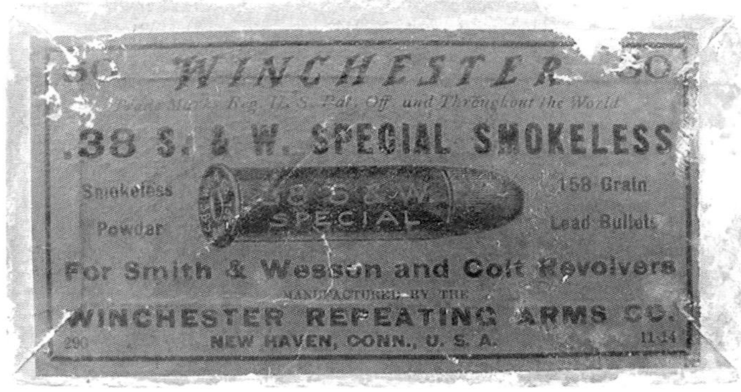

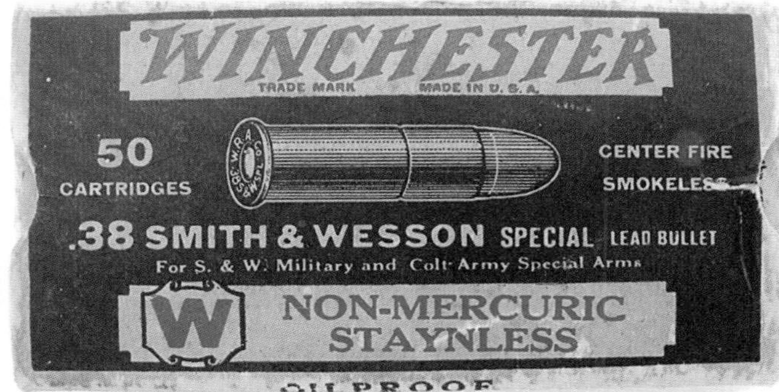

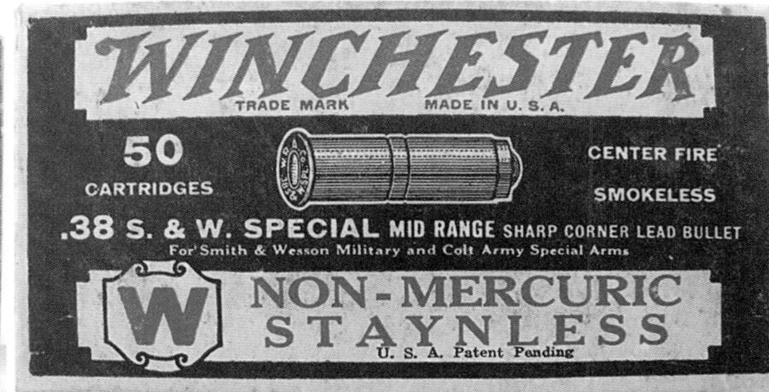

721. An initial sampling of a few of the very many box designs used to market .38 Special cartridges over the years.

The Winchester box at top left is old enough that it was deemed necessary to note that it contained rounds loaded with smokeless powder. Gaston Comeau collection

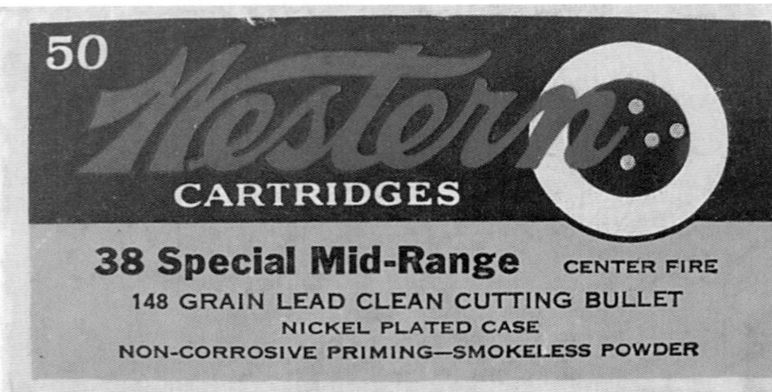

722. A further sampling of .38 Special cartridge boxes.
Gaston Comeau collection

723 (below). Boxes for the .38 Special 200-gr. Super Police loading, center, and the 150-gr. conical metal-piercing bullet, right.

724. Four representative sample boxes of commercial .38 S&W cartridges. Gaston Comeau collection

725. Four sample boxes of .32 S&W Long cartridges.

K-32 target revolvers were offered before and after WWII chambered for this cartridge, but as discussed in earlier chapters, the .32 never enjoyed anywhere near the popularity of the .38 Special and the .22 rimfire.
Gaston Comeau collection

power in their .38 S&W caliber Webley and Enfield revolvers, until it dawned on someone that a lead 200-gr. bullet might well violate the Hague Convention of 1907. They then went to a round-nosed fully-jacketed slug weighing 178 grains, although from all accounts this did not prove nearly as effective on humans shot with it during the war.

The biggest proponent of the 200-gr. Super Police .38 Special loading was the famed New York City holstermaker Chic Gaylord. He advocated a three-inch .38 Special Colt Police Positive, or a similar-length S&W Chiefs Special, loaded with such ammunition as being the ideal plainclothes self-defense handgun. Under Gaylord's influence, I bought a "skinny" barrel Model 36 three-inch nickel-plated Smith & Wesson, and used 200-gr. Super Police loads until switching off to Super Vel 110 gr. JHP ammunition in about 1966.

While the K-frame revolver has been made available in a variety of chamberings over the years, the .22 rimfire and .38 Special models are really the standard-bearers. These two cartridges have been made in hundreds if not thousands of different configurations over the years as manufacturers have attempted to make them accomplish all manner of things. It is, I think, safe to say that they are our two most versatile revolver cartridges, and a lot of development work by lots of brilliant minds has gone into making them so.

726. A brief but colorful sampling of 50-round .22 Long Rifle cartridge boxes.

Next to the .38 Special, the rimfire .22 remains a very popular chambering in K-frame S&W revolvers.

Gaston Comeau collection

# Beefing Up the .38 Special

727. Twelve modern special-use/high-performance .38 Special loadings, testifying to the incredible versatility and popularity of this cartridge. From left:

- Geco plastic training round;
- Thunderzap T.H.O.R. (Thermo Hydro-static Ordnance Round) +P+;
- DPX 110-grain +P;
- Federal Premium 129-grain jacketed hollow point +P;
- Winchester Ranger 130-grain bonded JHP +P;
- Gold Dot 135-grain +P;
- Federal 147-grain Hydro-Shok +P+;
- Super-X 150-gr. conical bullet metal-piercing;
- RWS 10.2g (158-grain) conical bullet metal-piercing;
- Winchester- Western 158-grain semi-wadcutter;
- Federal 156-gr. semi-wadcutter hollow point +P;
- Remington 200-grain Super Police.

In many ways, my experience with the .38 Special loadings commonly chambered in K-frame revolvers followed general ammunition developments. Beginning with the early round-nosed lead bullets, which were not especially effective, I graduated to jacketed bullets, first in handloads and later in store-bought commercial ammunition when these became readily available around 1966. Still later, when bullet designers became more experienced and skilled, I went back to all-lead projectiles with deep hollow points and good nose shapes with a little more velocity than the standard, earning them a "+P" power rating.

Later still, attempts by some to load the .38 Special up to .357 Magnum levels by using lightweight bullets and heavier powder charges yielded the "+P+" loadings, which soon proved to be destructive when fired in small J-framed revolvers and both loud and unpleasant to shoot in K-frames. More importantly, the actual stopping power achieved did not seem to be any better than that obtained with such loads as the old St. Louis Police, Chicago PD, or FBI standard of a 158-gr. lead hollow-point at +P pressure. The NYPD went to a very similar power load but declined to accept the hollow point bullet design, due to what I presume to have been "political correctness", and as a consequence, while the better bullet shape helped some, they did not get the really fine results that those other organizations did with the lead hollow-point version.

# The .357 Magnum in the K-Frame

Once the K-frame chambered for the .357 Magnum cartridge was announced, naturally all the load developments for that cartridge were applied to the K-frame. However when some of the loadings which used shorter than standard bullets were used, problems were encountered with flame-cutting on the top strap above the cylinder gap. The 125-gr. and 145-gr. loadings were especially bad for this. Some loads would also tie up some of the early stainless models due to the extreme heat they generated, and lastly the pressures generated by high-end .357 Magnum loads proved simply too much for the K-frame when used constantly over time. When only a few Magnum rounds were shot and the majority of practice was done with standard-pressure .38 Specials, there was no problem. But just about the same time that the standard non-target grade K-frame became available in .357 Magnum, police agencies began training with full-power loads all the time, in a move to counteract lawsuits filed against them for not giving their officers proper training programs. It was felt that because the difference between standard .38 Special ammunition and .357 Magnum defense loads was so great, unless trained to handle such high-power ammunition, both officers and the public could suffer the consequences. Bill Jordan, who was the creative genius behind the development of the Combat Magnum (the first K-frame Magnum, later called the Model 19), always said that it was meant to be shot only occasionally with Magnum ammunition and generally shot with .38 Special loads. He was correct. Given the drawbacks of using .357 Magnum ammunition all the time, and given the fine record of the 158-gr. lead hollow-point +P loading, many, including me, have determined that it is best to shoot good .38 Special ammunition in your K-frame, and reach for your L- or N-frame revolver if you just have to shoot Magnums all the time. For that matter, if hunting is the issue and you need more power, it is likely best to go to a bigger and heavier bullet. As my friend John Linebaugh (creator of the .475 and .500 Linebaugh line of cartridges) says, a big, heavy bullet does not get any lighter or smaller as it travels, although it may get slower; whereas a .357 Magnum bullet also gets slower but starts out lighter and smaller.

*Chapter Forty-Two*

# Carrying the K-Frame

## Commercial Holsters from Various Makers

728. A nickel-plated Model 1902 First Change revolver (1902 - 1905) with 6½" barrel and ivory grips, shown with a companion unmarked open-top leather holster and cartridge belt. courtesy Rock Island Auction Co.

Holsters in general have evolved over time, and so it is not surprising that holsters for the Smith & Wesson K-frame revolver have also changed, although some holsters of the type used in the early 20th century may still be found in use today.

For many, a holster may only be a convenient storage place, or a means of transporting a weapon to and from the range, or for carrying it while in the field. For such uses, almost any container will suffice, and a holster that was secure enough to allow safe carry in 1905 will be equally useful today.

Over the years many traditional U.S. holstermakers have offered products suitable for commercial purposes as well as duty use, with their catalogs depicting and describing both types.

To further illustrate the popularity of the K-frame revolver, a number of commercially-made holsters, designed for all types of users, are depicted throughout this chapter, in addition to some specialized designs intended for law enforcement use.

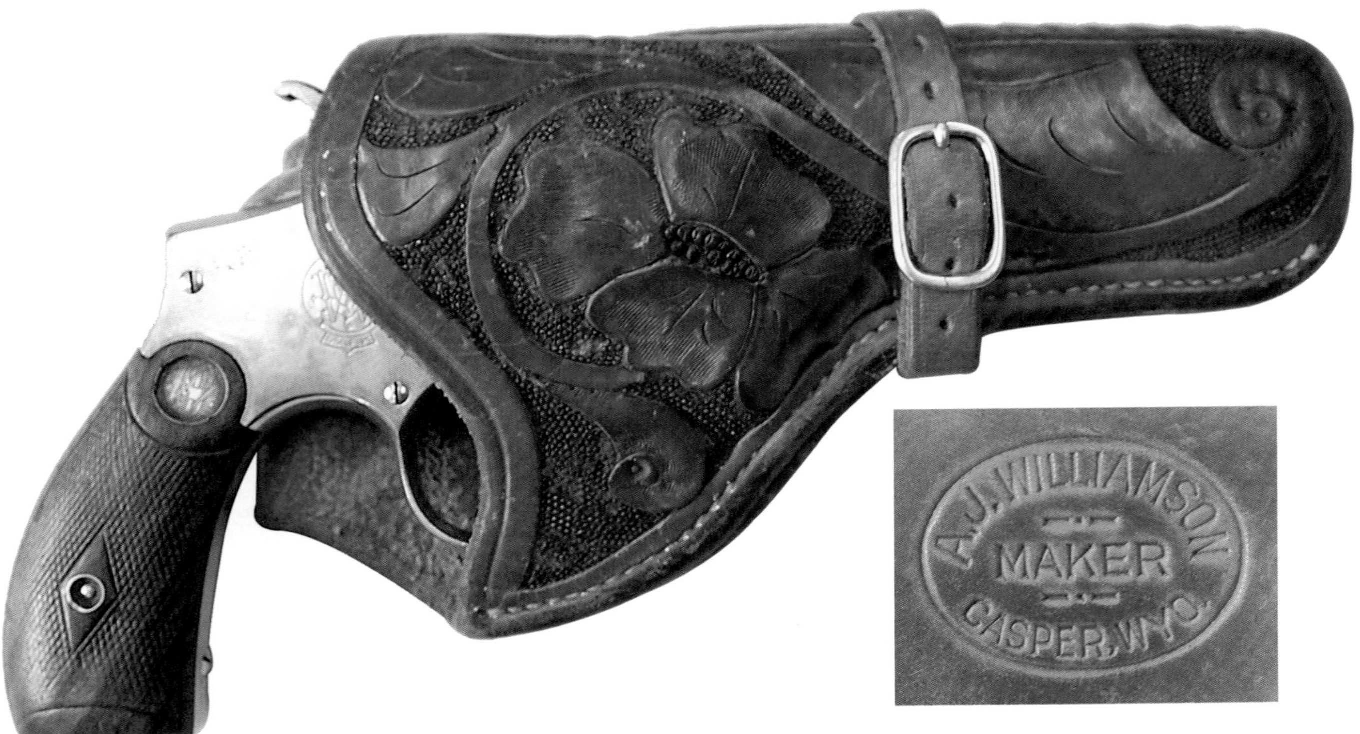


729. A .38 Special M&P Model 1905 Third Change, serial no. 179428, with 4" barrel.

Shipped to Simmons Hardware Co. of St. Louis, Missouri, on March 3, 1912, this was the personal duty gun of George J. Carroll, Deputy Sheriff (1908 - 1912), Sheriff (1921 - 1943) and later U.S. Marshal (1946 - 1949) for the District of Wyoming. Throughout his career in law enforcement he carried his revolver in this hand-tooled open-top holster.

Inset: closeup of back of holster showing name of maker, A. J. Williamson of Casper, Wyoming.

private collection

## Herrmann H. Heiser, Denver, Colorado

730. A floral-carved open belt holster with securing flap made for a 6" K-frame revolver by the Herrmann H. Heiser Saddlery Co. of Denver, Colorado.

Inset: rear of holster showing maker's name, trademark, and model no., 718. Gaston Comeau collection

**CATALOG**
**No. 30**

In respectfully submitting the following pages for your consideration, we hope for a careful perusal and will feel gratified if our efforts meet with your approval.

IF YOU want THE BEST IT IS POSSIBLE TO PRODUCE, we most particularly solicit YOUR patronage, as people who are critical and who may have been disappointed in the purchase of goods of this character in the past will recognize REAL CLASS and QUALITY as well as appreciate our careful endeavors to please.

Life Is Too Short to Take Chances

NO MAN EVER LIVED LONG ENOUGH TO WEAR OUT A HEISER HOLSTER

**The HERMANN H. HEISER SADDLERY CO.**
DENVER, COLORADO

IT PAYS TO HITCH TO THE HOUSE OF HEISER

THE
**Hermann H. Heiser**
**SADDLERY COMPANY**
DENVER, COLORADO

ESTABLISHED 1856 INCORPORATED 1916
"Pioneer Saddlers of the Great West"

SPECIALISTS
In the Manufacture of Custom Quality

Gun Scabbards, Pistol Holsters, Belts and Novelty Leather Goods

SEND US YOUR IDEAS AND SPECIFICATIONS

Anything you may desire will be made up for you at a price as reasonable as consistent with the best of workmanship and finest material. We solicit correspondence and will be glad at all times to make suggestions.

PERSONAL ATTENTION TO ALL DETAIL

To get the Genuine, INSIST upon seeing either this

OR

Heiser quality leather goods should not be compared or confused with the similar appearing goods carried in stock by most sporting goods or hardware stores in all parts of the country, since our goods are made to order especially TO PLEASE YOU and to give perfect satisfaction when used in connection with THE ONE PARTICULAR WEAPON that they were intended for, while the "hand-me-down" goods are made in large quantities from all kinds of material by machine and, as such, one type of holster is supposed to fit in a slipshod manner as many different kinds of guns as possible.

All descriptions are made brief to save you time, since the illustrations are all photogravures and consequently true to the article represented.

IT PAYS TO HITCH TO THE HOUSE OF HEISER Page 1

731. Front and back pages of the Heiser Catalog No. 30, dating from 1937. Gaston Comeau collection

732. A traditional loop style Heiser holster of plain leather for a 6" revolver, with full flap and thong-wrapped edge. Inset: a closeup of the snap, showing Heiser trademark. Gaston Comeau collection

733. A collage showing a standard long-action 4" M&P and a Heiser model 457 open belt holster, which was designed for the FBI, atop two targets illustrating the accuracy of which this fixed-sight revolver is capable.

The badge was carried by an agent of the Fish and Wildlife Service, U.S. Department of the Interior,

When the M&P was first released it was directed at military and police users, and thus the holsters first encountered for it reflect this "duty use" market orientation. It is well understood by most that a military handgun will typically get more wear in a year in the field than a police handgun will get in 20 years. A military man will be carrying his weapon through all types of hostile weather conditions, typically carrying lots of other gear as well on his belt or back, which can strike a holstered handgun, and in most cases he will not need his handgun too often. It may indeed only be viewed as a badge of rank by many, not a serious fighting implement; so immediate access to the weapon is not considered to be critical. This is especially so the further the soldier gets behind friendly lines.

Early military holsters for the M&P, such as are shown in figs. 642 and 644, tended to be flap holsters made of cowhide. Slow to permit withdrawal, they

735 (following page). The standard factory cutaway drawing of the early M&P with "side-swing" hammer block used as an advertisement by the George Lawrence Company, who as well as making holsters for S&Ws were for a time official distributors of Smith & Wesson products.
Gaston Comeau collection

did protect the revolver from the effects of weather and military campaigning, and when new and shiny they no doubt looked sharp as part of the uniform. With organizations more devoted to police functions on military bases, something other was occasionally seen, but for the most part during the entire pre-WWII period of U. S. military use of the M&P, the flap holster was what was used. It might vary in color, being brown originally and later black, and might be attached by hooks to the eyes of a GI pistol belt or with a rear loop threaded through a belt in the more common fashion.

In later conflicts and for specialized users such as air crew members, a variety of shoulder and belt holsters were fielded. These are discussed and depicted in Chapter Thirty-Six.

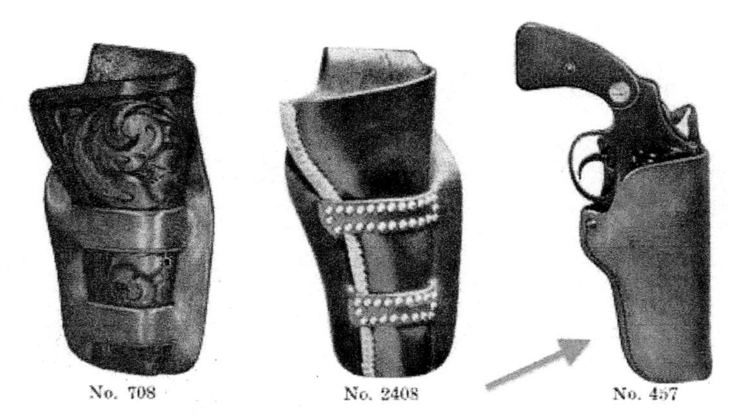


## Loop Style Belt Holsters for Revolvers

**For Revolvers Only, Not Made for Automatics**

These extra heavy holsters are made of the finest Oak Tanned California skirting leather and have what is known as the "Quick Draw" belt loop. Waxed thread sewed, open end, riveted at end of stitches, not lined. Design originated by one of the most expert gun men in the West.

| | Large | Medium | Small |
|---|---|---|---|
| No. 408—Plain smooth finish | $3.75 | $3.25 | $2.75 |
| No. 508—Hand basket stamped | 4.25 | 3.75 | 3.25 |
| No. 708—Mexican hand carved | 5.25 | 4.75 | 4.25 |

No. 908—Made of medium weight California Oak Tanned skirting leather, in plain smooth finish only; otherwise same as above.

| | Large | Medium | Small |
|---|---|---|---|
| No. 908—Plain smooth finish | $3.25 | $2.75 | $2.25 |

Following holsters are **Hand Thong Wrap Stitched** and ornamented with nickel ornaments as shown in illustration. Made of heavy leather, not lined, open end.

| | Large | Medium | Small |
|---|---|---|---|
| No. 2408—Plain smooth finish, fancy spotted | $5.25 | $4.75 | $4.25 |
| No. 2508—Hand basket stamped, fancy spotted | 5.75 | 5.25 | 4.75 |
| No. 2708—Mexican hand carved, fancy spotted | 6.75 | 6.25 | 5.75 |

Small holsters are made with one loop only, instead of two, as shown in cut.

Following holsters are made of heavy oak-tanned California skirting leather, closed end, unlined, waxed thread sewed, belt loop on back, there is a welt down the side but does not extend clear across bottom, welt permits a snug fit. A small hole is left in bottom to permit any dirt to sift out. Gun sets high exposing trigger guard and trigger. This holster was designed for the F.B.I. of Washington, D. C., who require holster for fast draw.

**Made for Revolvers Only.**

| | Large | Medium | Small |
|---|---|---|---|
| No. 457—Plain smooth finish | $2.00 | $1.75 | $1.50 |
| No. 557—Full hand basket stamped | 2.50 | 2.25 | 2.00 |
| No. 757—Full Mexican hand carved | 3.25 | 3.00 | 2.75 |

☞ Page 3 Shows How to Arrive at Price of Holster to Fit Your Gun ☜

IT PAYS TO HITCH TO THE HOUSE OF HEISER

Page 7

734 (right). A page from the 1937 Heiser catalog, illustrating and describing various types of holsters.

Note the arrow (above) pointing to the Model 547 holster, also shown in fig. 733, and arrow (below), pointing to the description stating "This holster was designed for the F.B.I. of Washington, D.C., who require holster for fast draw." Gaston Comeau collection

## The George Lawrence Company

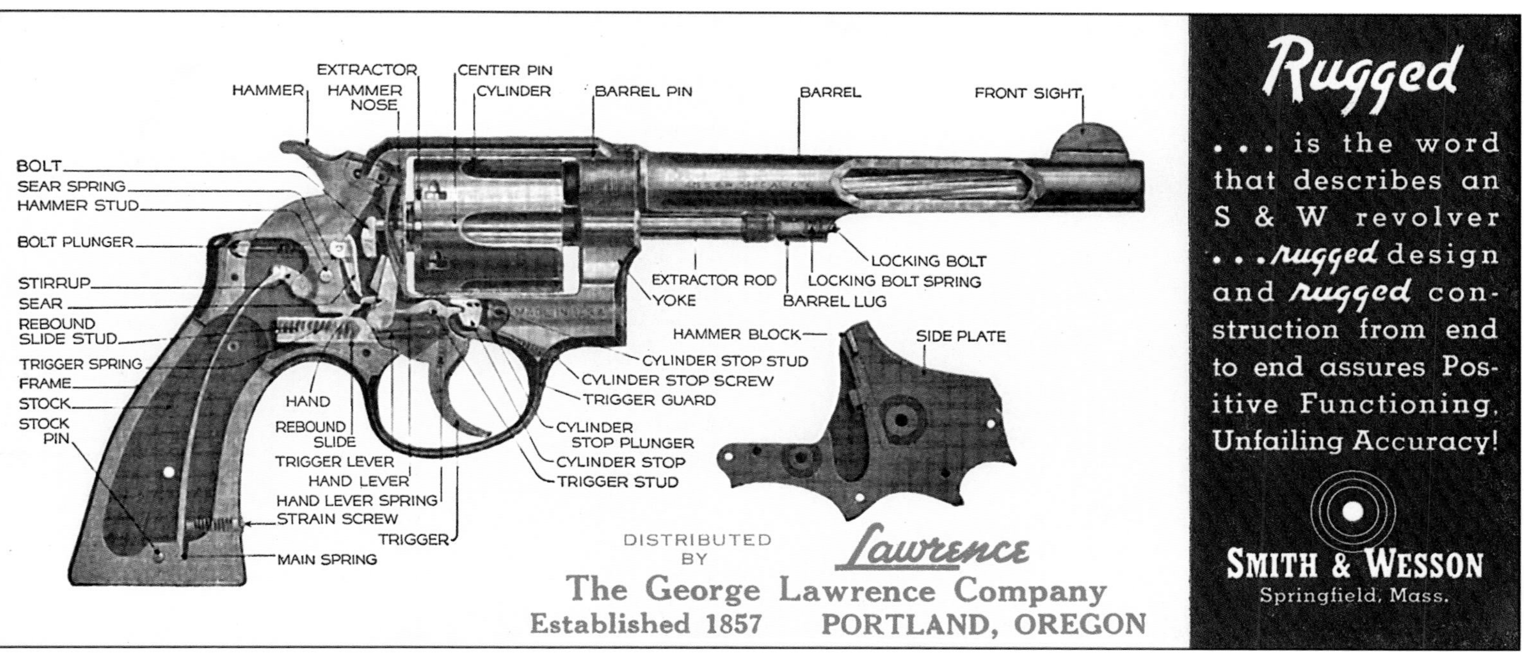

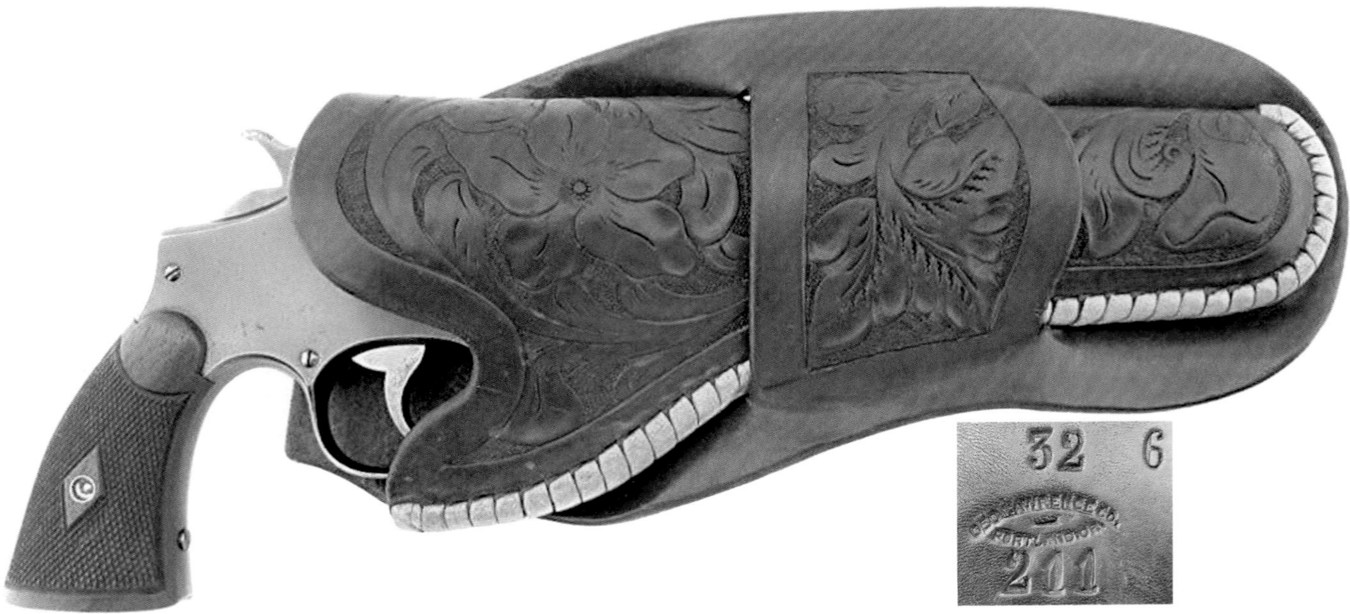

736. An open loop-style floral-carved holster for a 6" M&P with thong-wrapped edge, made by the George Lawrence Co.

Inset: closeup of back of holster showing Lawrence logo and holster type and style. Gaston Comeau collection

737. Lawrence open holster of plain leather, holding a 6" K target revolver.

As shown in the inset, this is the Lawrence model 120, which was designed by Elmer Keith.

Note the long strap. Gaston Comeau collection

738. Elmer Keith, in a photograph which appeared in the George Lawrence Company catalog no. 53 (1951), shown holding a Colt single action revolver in a Lawrence 120 holster of Keith's design.

A paraphrase of the catalog caption reads as follows: "Elmer Keith, nationally known gun editor, has had the George Lawrence Company produce a fast-draw holster of his own design, listed as the No. 120 'Keith' holster."

Gaston Comeau collection

739. A modified Keith holster, the 120S, in sewn plain leather, holding a 4" Combat Masterpiece. Note the shorter end on the strap.

Inset: closeup of rear of holster showing markings.

A 4" example of the original holster made to Keith's design is shown on the step beside him in fig. 738.

Gaston Comeau collection

## The S. D. Myers Saddle Co.

A brochure and catalog produced by the S. D. Myers Saddle Co. contained some interesting information regarding the holsters manufactured by this old-line company. This brochure is excerpted as follows:

### *Myers Leather Lore*

*Our skilled leather craftsmen have been with S. D. Myers for many years, and have undergone a rugged and demanding apprenticeship. Ninety percent of our work is done by hand, and this is what guarantees the Myers quality that our customers expect . .*

*S. D. Myers does not believe in mass production. Our custom hand-crafted process is designed to meet the needs of the individual order. We revolutionized holster building with the use of the welt and the blocking of each holster for a specific weapon. Because our work is done by hand, we are capable of modifying holsters to meet the customer's needs. For example: we can add safety straps, plug bottoms or sight protector plugs to any holster and make the belt loop either solid or snap-off. We can also change the hang and make most holsters in the crossdraw configuration . .*

*S. D. Myers leather products are made in three distinctive decorative designs to provide the finish desired by the customer. Our plain design is for rugged wear, where the equipment is exposed to the elements. Our basket weave provides an attractive design for both law enforcement equipment and the plain clothes group. S. D. Myers hand tooled, floral design, carved leather is most attractive and provides a product of rare beauty.*

**A STATEMENT FROM THE PRESIDENT**

The S. D. Myres Saddle Company was established in 1897 by my Father, S. D. "Tio Sam" Myres, and we have taken pride in earning the reputation for making quality merchandise and using the highest business ethics. Our **only** plant is located at 5030 Alameda, El Paso, Texas, and we market our products under the name of S. D. Myres Saddle Company.

We have through the years worked with those most qualified in the field of Law Enforcement, and received the help from such outstanding and nationally known Peace Officers as Tom Threepersons, Bill Jordan, Tommy Bock, Charlie Askins, Ed McGivern, D. A. "Jelly" Bryce, Bill Toney, and many others in developing the finest of holsters.

We wish to thank our many friends and customers for the opportunity to furnish them with their equipment in the past, and hope our products have merited their future business.

W. J. MYRES, President

740. A trade show exhibit of holsters and other leather products made by the S. D. Myers Saddle Co. of El Paso, Texas, fronted by the president, W. J. Myers, son of the original S. D. Myers who founded the company in 1897.
Gaston Comeau collection

# Holsters for Police Use

## An Historical Retrospective

As noted, the duty-oriented K-frame S&W is a belt gun, too heavy for pocket carry, and in instances where it was carried as an item of issue, a holster was required.

Over the last hundred years or so, police usage of the M&P revolver has involved a substantially more interesting issue of holster development and use. In the earliest days of the M&P revolver, the use of firearms by the police was something new. Most cities in the United States did not even have a police department in 1899. Instead a town constable, or a night watchman, coupled with the local sheriff's office, sufficed as a police presence. Of course bigger cities did have police departments, but even there it was very rare to have any standardized program of use or training with weapons. New York City was the first city to develop a firearm training program, when Theodore Roosevelt, then the Commissioner of Police, appointed shooting expert "Roundsman" Petty to the task. They had found that the officers at the time were incapable of hitting a 4 x 4-foot target at 50 feet, and that many of the weapons being carried were defective in one way or another.

Policemen in those cities that had departments in 1899 were typically politically-appointed ex-military people who were inclined to use their billy clubs to solve issues, not their firearms. In fact most citizens at the time were uneasy about seeing a uniformed armed group in their midst, fearing that it would lead to the diminuation of their civil rights (and they may well have been right). As a consequence of these concerns, and in keeping with the fashion of the day, police in 1899 tended to carry their weapons inside coat or hip pockets, and not in exposed belt holsters as we have all come to accept today. Being capable of being hidden under clothing was thus important, and this explains why all those small-framed .32 and .38 top-break Smith & Wesson revolvers were so common at the time. Certainly the stopping power of such cartridges left much to be desired, but in a day and age when antibiotics did not exist and medical care was rather rudimentary, being shot by a .32 or .38 round-nosed lead bullet travelling around 700 fps, which would not likely exit a person's stomach, was not something to fool around with. While the officer's skill level was such that he might not hit you, conditions were such that if he did, you were likely to die a painful, lingering death of blood poisoning or other infection.

By 1899, when the M&P came out, this issue of officers not exposing their weapons to public view was not just a prejudice restricted to the east coast, either. While it was common for men to have worn exposed belt guns in some areas 50 years earlier, the impact of the Civil War, the arrival of non-native immigrants along with their women and children and other deplorable aspects of "civilization" had made the practice less common. One will recall that even in Tombstone, Arizona, in 1881 when the famed OK Corral shoot-out took place, the dispute was over men openly carrying their weapons, and that the Earps, who were law enforcement officers at the time, carried their weapons under their clothing to conceal them from the community.

So it was in most places at the time, with officers carrying their revolvers concealed, with a billy club on their belt rather than a handgun.

Of course when it was introduced, the M&P represented a step up in both power level and size, compared to the common police revolvers of the day. Those weapons previously in common use we would today view as suitable for concealed carry, backup, or hold-out weapons, and I suppose in all actuality that is exactly what they were for the officer at the time, who was expected to rely on his fists or at worst his club to keep the peace. An officer who was forced to shoot someone was often looked upon as someone incapable of keeping order with his pugilistic skills.

741. A black-finish Model 66 (fig. 520) in the classic Jordan Trooper holster, as made by Don Hume.

The Jordan Trooper holster was commonly used in the last portion of the revolver era before safety holsters became common.

As a consequence of the arrival of the M&P revolver, the old system of hiding your "duty gun" in your inside coat or hip pocket did not work anymore. It was simply too big, and so it migrated to the belt, alongside the billy club. To avoid upsetting the "little old ladies" (and their psychological counterparts of all ages and sexes) who might be offended by the sight of a naked revolver, and to keep the rain off to protect such an expensive piece of equipment from rusting, and perhaps also to make for a nice "snappy appearance" in the eyes of those who set uniform standards, the flap holster was commonly used. These flap holsters became very popular, and were encountered right up to the very end of the revolver's common use by U.S. law enforcement. Often the use of flap holsters was justified as a security measure, since getting a revolver out of one was difficult. This naturally works both ways, since it not only inhibits the would-be snatcher but impairs the officer's ability to respond to sudden threats as well. But there has always been a school of thought that says the officer should have his weapon in hand when a threat is present, but that the threat of someone seizing his weapon is greater than the likelihood of the officer not recognizing a threat early enough to allow him to access his flap-holstered revolver.

## Problems with Flap Holsters

Once revolvers such as the M&P and the Colt Army Special became accepted as the standard for police use, and sidearms migrated from the inside pocket to the belt line, men almost immediately complained about the flap holster putting them at a severe disadvantage when they were surprised by an armed criminal. Open-top holsters were faster on the draw, even if they did expose the weapon to the weather and the gaze of passersby.

Straps to hold revolvers in place became commonplace as soon as open-top holsters were adopted, unless these were designed to put the revolver so deeply into the holster that it was unlikely to fall out. An example of this was the duty holsters issued for years in the New York City Police Department. For others however, the strap to hold the weapon in place to avoid it spilling out of the holster was common. These straps also helped keep assailants from pulling the weapon from the officer's holster.

Over the years straps or other containment devices changed position and type, but all worked on the theory that the officer had to release the snap on the retaining device before the revolver could be lifted from the holster.

## Innovative Methods of Retention - the Audley and "Clamshell" Holsters

742. A 6" M&P held securely in the Audley holster. Patented on October 13, 1914, the Audley featured a unique metal spring clip, just visible in front of the trigger. The revolver could not be drawn from the holster unless this clip was first depressed by the trigger finger.
Gaston Comeau collection

Of course there were some radical developments, such as the Audley holster, patented in 1916, and later the pop-open "clamshell" holster and the Berns-Martin front-break holster (figs. 159 and 160), which gave weapon security while at the same time being faster to operate and/or more secure from "gun grabs" than the common strap or retainer holster. Some of

743. Two views of the "clamshell" holster, another early safety holster used by the Los Angeles Police Department (and others) with K-frame revolvers.

Left: holster closed. Pushing the button behind the trigger allows the spring-loaded front to flip open, permitting withdrawal of the weapon.

these innovations were used as early as the 1920s, but never became common or general-issue.

While it was obvious that the problem of assailants grabbing an officer's weapon was resulting in many officers' deaths each year, no real breakthroughs in the prevention of this came until security holsters were introduced in the mid-1970s. Since by that time the K-frame Smith & Wesson in all its different variants was pretty much the *de facto* standard for police revolvers, these duty-style safety holsters were for the most part designed around them. Such safety holsters came with different levels of retention and in a variety of clever designs. Some were so positive in their retention that it was almost impossible for the officer to access his handgun unless he practised drawing it extensively. Since few police officers fall into that category, such "ultimate rigs" were often shunned, but the lesser ones could prove useful and still be practical.

Naturally such holsters were for external uniform duty use, but the retention concepts did flow over to plainclothes holsters to some degree.

The Smith & Wesson M&P series was available from the middle 1930s with a two-inch barrel, introduced in response to the two-inch Colt Detective Special revolver, first released in 1927; but in all honesty, the two-inch K-frame is simply not as good a pocket revolver as the smaller D-frame Colt. However, many people liked the two-inch .38 Special K-frame, as they are easier to shoot than the smaller-frame Colt revolver, and until 1949, when the Chiefs Special was introduced, all smaller-sized Smith & Wesson revolvers fired the substantially less powerful .38 S&W cartridge.

In my experience, however, plainclothes officers and "white shirts" who carried two-inch K-frames were not very serious gunmen. They might well have been excellent officers, but generally they were not very sophisticated regarding their firearms.

Over at the FBI, while individual agents could use personally-owned revolvers of differing types, the issue weapons were traditionally four-inch M&P or Colt Official Police .38 Specials, although as discussed in Chapter Thirty-Two, the last officially-issued FBI revolver was the famed three-inch Model 13 K-frame .357 Magnum. With proper holster selection, these could be conveniently carried without attracting attention. Hank Sloan, the long-time director of FBI firearm training, even designed a holster for general issue which, unlike many such institutionally-issued holsters, is actually a pretty good rig. Made of cowhide, it is true, but well proportioned, with the belt loop set at a good angle on your belt, and a shield to prevent snagging the hammer spur on your coat lining.

I have always thought my friend Jan Stevenson who wrote a wonderful article in a 1968 *Gun World* magazine entitled "Pistols For Plainclothesmen" was directly responsible for many people embracing full-size K-frame revolvers for non-uniformed self-de-

744. A Missouri Highway Patrol K-38 with thin 5" barrel (fig. 405), shown with issue shiny black patent leather duty holster, belt, cuff case, and ammo pouch, and shoulder patch and badge.

These old revolvers will still shoot well, as evidenced by the impressive 10-shot target.

fense work, shunning, except as backups, the J- and D-framed two-inch .38s previously so commonly bought by recently appointed detectives or agents. He made quite a clear and convincing case that a K-frame revolver with a four-inch barrel, if properly holstered, was every bit as easy to conceal as a two-inch model, and much easier to carry and shoot. This argument made good sense to sophisticated users, many of whom then went over to such four-inch models until the police revolver generally faded from the scene at the tail end of the 20th century.

As it is with the chicken and the egg, so it has been with K-frames and holsters. Right from its introduction it was clear that the M&P represented a superior choice for police work, in comparison to the underpowered top-breaks that preceded it. But it did require a new type of holster and a way to carry it to maximize the benefits of its design. Then, once the belt holster became popular, problems of access and security arose that previously did not exist, but needed to be solved in order to allow the K-frame to maintain its position of dominance in the field. Similarly, having gotten used to the accuracy and power

745. The M13, the last official FBI duty revolver, with issue russet leather holster and ammo pouch. These revolvers really shoot well, as evidenced by the five-shot target.

the K-frame brought with it, the plainclothes officer was reluctant to go backwards in those areas, and demanded holsters that would permit him to utilize these benefits. All the way, holstermakers sought to deliver a superior product to carry the K-frame Smith & Wesson. Had the K-frame not been so good in its role as a police firearm, the holstermakers would not have needed to be so creative; but then, had they not been so creative, the use of the K-frame might well have been more limited in scope. Both together made an excellent pair that only diminished in importance with the technological advances that brought in the "square gun", precipitating the retirement of the "round gun" which had served officers and agents so well for almost ten decades.

# The Hunter Corporation

Located in Westminster, Colorado, Hunter has been supplying premium-quality leather holsters, belts and accessories at an affordable price since 1952.

Many Hunter holster models are hand-boned, edge-dressed and form-fitted.

746 (right). Cover of the 1982 catalog of sporting goods from the Hunter Corporation.
Gaston Comeau collection

747 (below). A round butt .357 Magnum Model 19 with 2½" barrel (fig. 677) fitted with square-butt rosewood target stocks, in a form-fitted Hunter russet leather belt holster. Note the thumb release on the safety strap.
Inset: closeup of rear of holster, showing markings.
Gaston Comeau collection

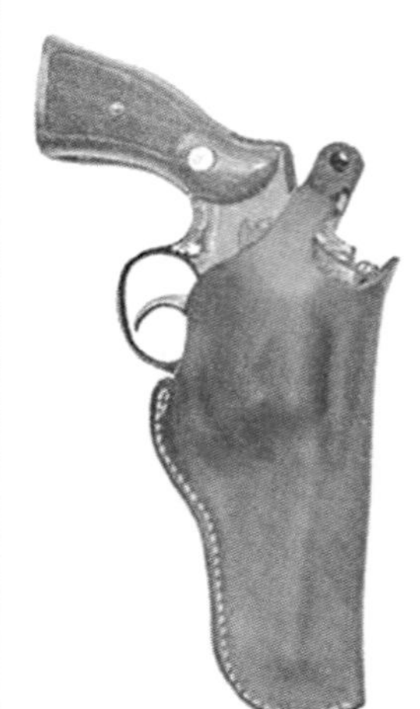

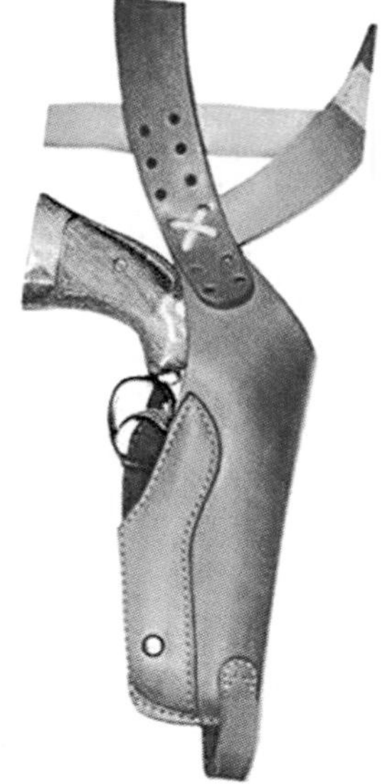

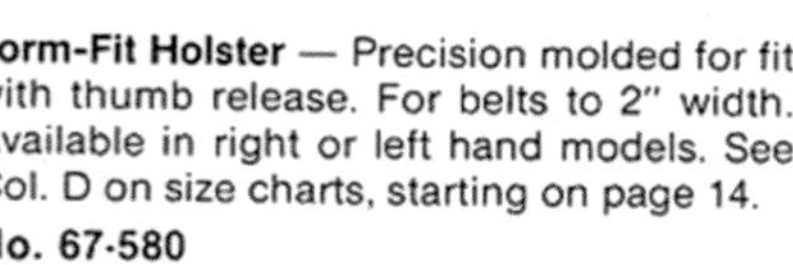


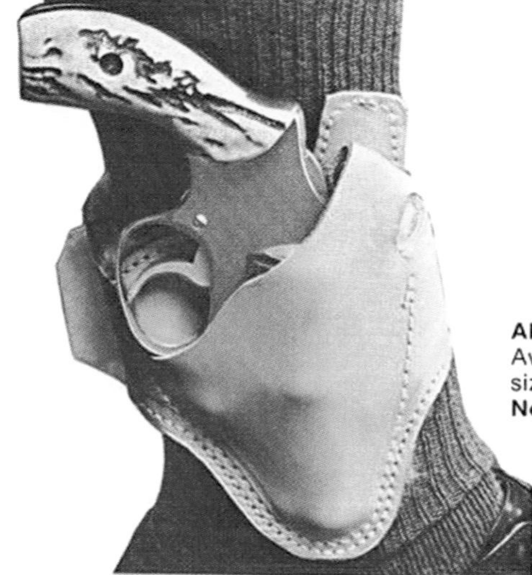


748. A composite of a page from the 1982 Hunter catalog, showing a few of the many models of holsters offered by the company.

As shown at top left, the form-fitted holster shown in fig. 747 is available for revolvers of different barrel lengths.

Gaston Comeau collection

## Smith & Wesson Leather Products, Inc.

Smith & Wesson Leather Products Inc. was founded in 1969 as a separate division of the company, with a stand-alone factory located in Lillington, North Carolina. By 1974 the division was issuing a complete Leather Products catalog, aimed specifically at lawmen and outdoorsmen. The foreword in the first edition of this catalog contains some interesting facts, and is excerpted as follows:

> *Since their origin in 1969, the Smith & Wesson leather products have become one of the major factors in the Leathergoods market. Our increased sales in each of these four years is directly attributable to our satisfied customers.*
>
> *In 1969, the Smith & Wesson Leathergoods line consisted of approximately 100 basic items. Today's products number over 300 items which are produced in a facility over three- and one-half times as large as the original . . This current Smith & Wesson holster catalog represents a continuation of both the Police Duty and Off Duty product lines as well as the Outdoorsman group and accessory products. The "Blazer" Holsters, for example, now accommodate almost three times as*

749. The front of a small fold-out holster catalog, issued by Smith & Wesson while the company was still owned by Bangor Punta. Gaston Comeau collection

750. A postal worker carrying a round butt K-frame revolver, likely an "Airweight" Model 12, in a Jordan-style holster, possibly of S&W manufacture.

The "diamondless" grip checkering pattern indicates the revolver was made post-1968.

*many handgun models as they did in 1972. The "Sportsman" Holsters now accommodate over 60% more handgun models than they did in 1972.*

*. . New products are already scheduled in each of the basic product lines which are presented as Duty, Off Duty and Outdoorsman for your convenience in selecting just the right style for your holster needs. Please note that some holsters appear in more than one basic category. We feel that some holsters cannot be classified exclusively as Duty or Off Duty because many hunters want safety or quick draw features which may be especially prominent in the Duty or Off Duty lines . .*

Robert Gould began working for S&W Leather Products Inc. in 1979, first as a product manager, and later as marketing products manager.

After the acquisition of the parent company by Lear Siegler Corp., and the subsequent leveraged buyout, the new management team at S&W decided to focus on firearms, and divest itself of the Leather Products division. Wishing to stay in the holster business, Gould and his partner John Goodrich bought the Leather Products subsidiary from S&W later that year. They have carried on operating the 50,000 sq. ft. Lillington, N.C. factory as Gould & Goodrich, and in the intervening years Gould & Goodrich leather products have been adopted by such prestigious outfits as the Saudi Arabian Royal Guard Regiment, the French National Police, the Puerto Rican State Police, the Hong Kong Police, and the Pennsylvania State Police.

752 (following page). Rear view of the spring clip duty holster, left, and the separate belt piece, right. To assemble, the holster is slid down over the tongue of the belt piece.

Note the tensioning screw in the back of the holster for adjusting the revolver retention spring.

Gaston Comeau collection

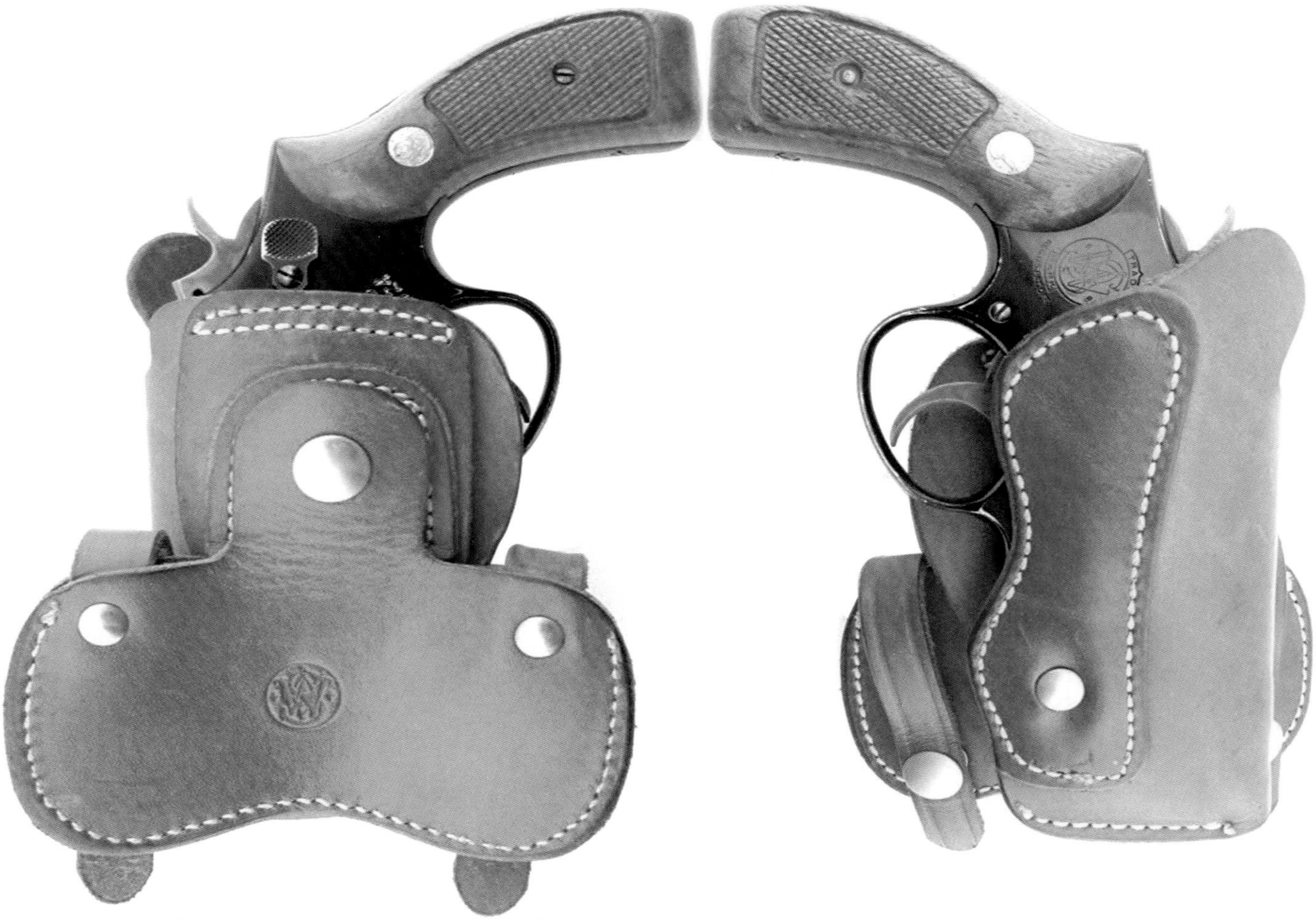

751. Back and front views of an S&W spring clip duty holster, holding a 2" M&P "Airweight" revolver.

As shown below, the belt section (left, with S&W monogram) is designed to remain on the wearer's belt while the holster itself can be snapped off with the revolver inside, for secure storage. Gaston Comeau collection

753. A Smith & Wesson Leather Company blue box from the Bangor Punta era, containing the spring clip holster assembly shown above. Gaston Comeau collection

## Smith & Wesson Holster Packaging

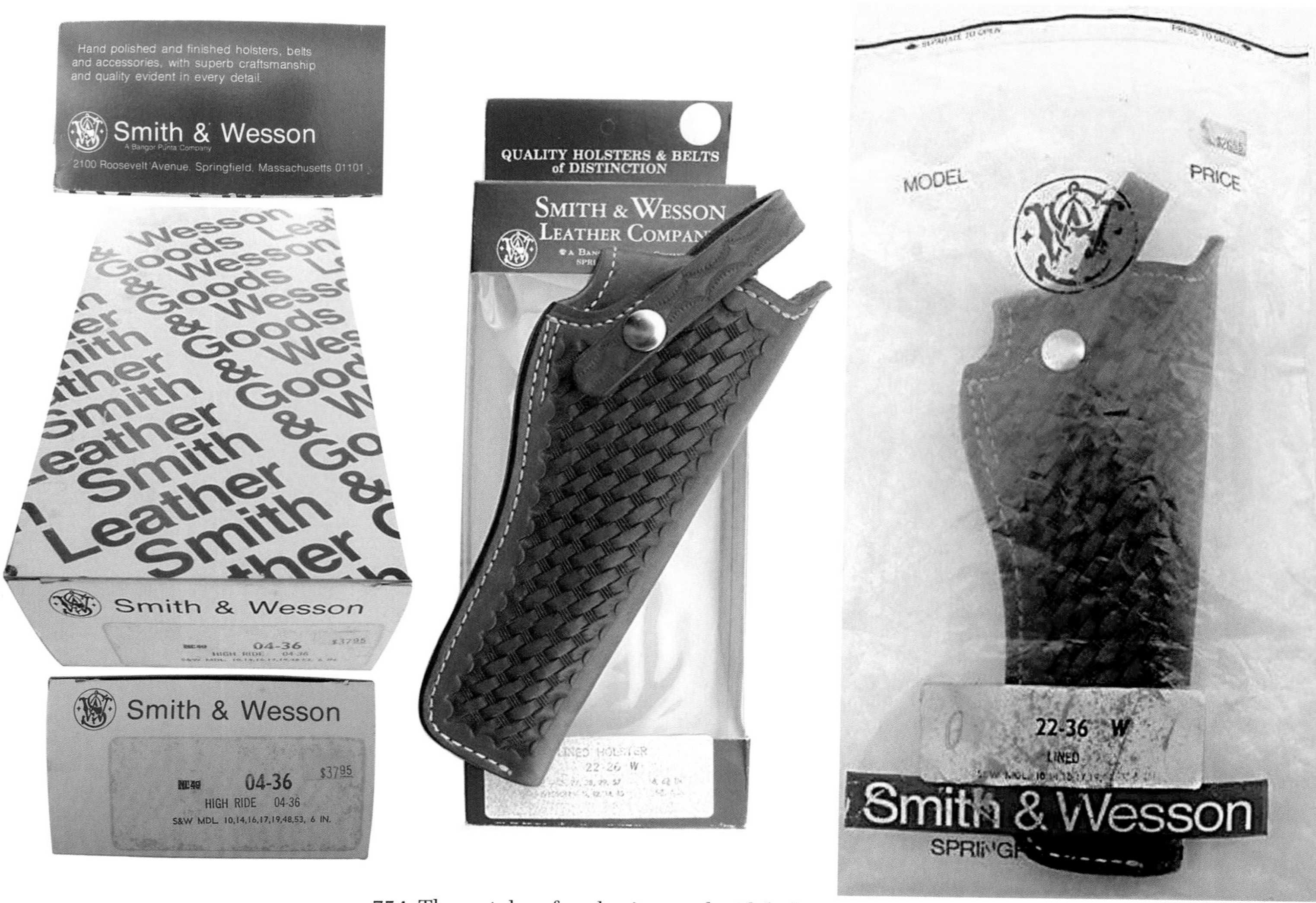


754. Three styles of packaging used with holsters made by Smith & Wesson Leather Products Co.

Left: original style cardboard box, showing markings on a portion of the side, above, and the end label on the flap, below.

Center: later style box with see-through plastic front, from later 1970s.

Right: last style, a simple zip-lock plastic bag.

Gaston Comeau collection

755. Front and back views of a late black leather belt holster with safety strap for a 4" revolver, made for the U.S. military by Smith & Wesson Leather Co.

This holster is shown in its military shipping box in fig. 650. Jeff Moeller collection

# Finale - Holsters Today

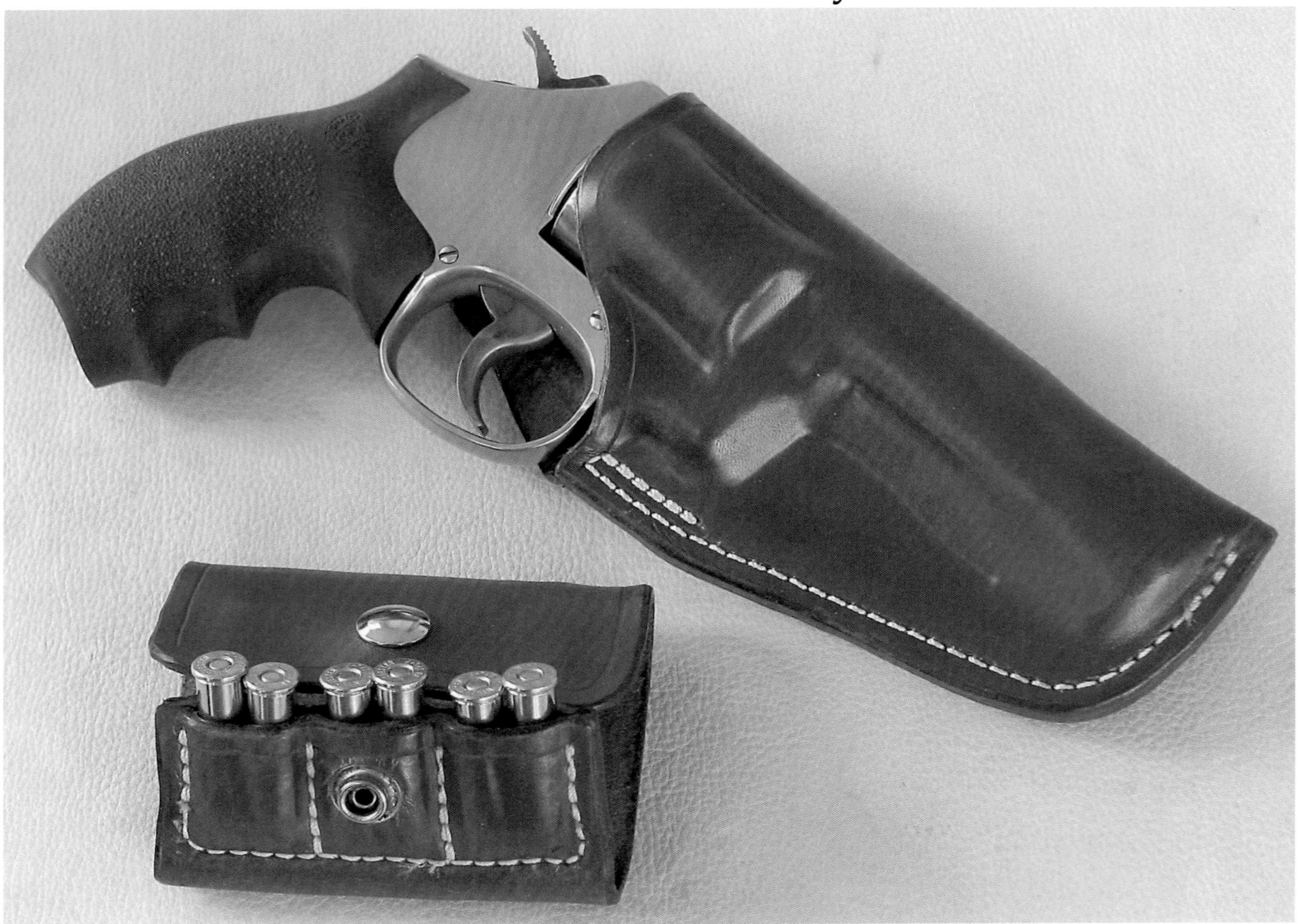

756. A late Model 64 (2012) in a holster originally designed by Chic Gaylord in the 1950s, but still made today.

In front is an ammo pouch of FBI design, holding 2X2X2 rounds.

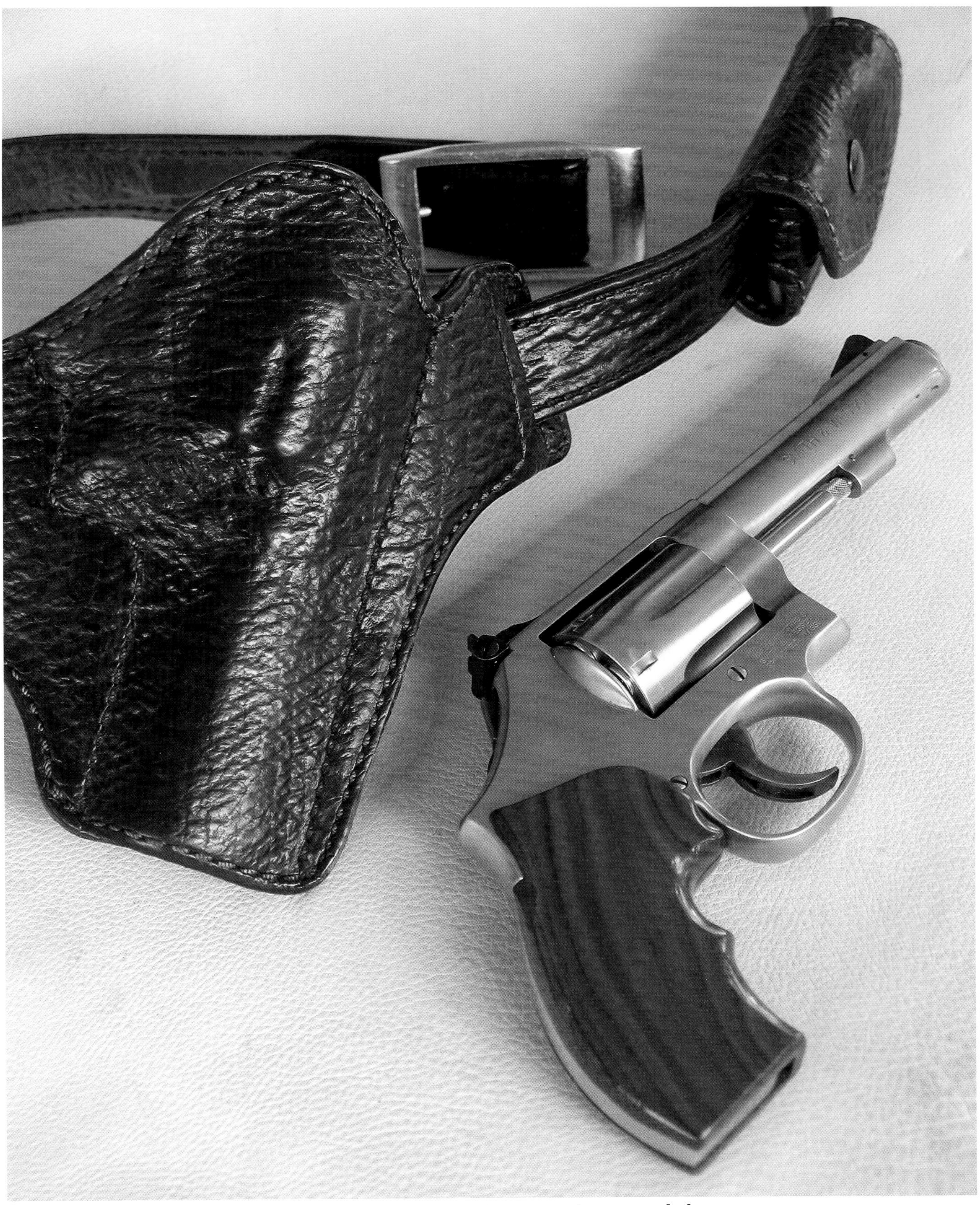

757. My 4" DAO Model 67 (fig. 524), with a custom holster and belt covered in black sharkskin. I have worn this rig for over 25 years.

*Chapter Forty-Three*

# K-Frame Boxes and Cases

## Early Cardboard Shipping Boxes

Historically, most owners of K-frame Smith & Wessons have had an unfortunate tendency to discard the boxes in which their revolvers were shipped. These were only made of cardboard, after all, and so even if they were not immediately thrown away, they got frayed or torn up at a much faster rate than their more durable contents. As a consequence, some of the various boxes used to ship Smith & Wesson revolvers over the years are rarer than the guns themselves. These boxes are highly sought-after by collectors today, and can bring surprisingly high prices. The foam-lined plastic "clamshell" cases used today are much more substantial and not as likely to be discarded as were their cardboard counterparts of times past but, given their awkward size, storing a number of them can be quite a challenge. These too have come in various configurations, and I would not be surprised to see them become rare collectibles 100 years or so from now. While much less durable, the cardboard boxes of yesteryear did tend to be more compact in size, so that storing your handgun in one of them (wrapped in moisture-resistant paper, of course) when putting it away in your safe (or stashing it in your rolled-up sleeping bag, as I did as a kid) was more convenient.

But whatever the type of box or its material, having the box in which the weapon was shipped will increase the collector value of the "package" and, if nothing else, increase the charm of the weapon. When you open a box for an M&P that was shipped in that box, you are repeating an activity and linking yourself to someone who, decades earlier, also appreciated the weapon enough to retain the box through the intervening years.

Since boxes have changed over time, and the correct box can add considerably to the value to the weapon itself, we will describe some of the various box types that have been used to ship K-frame revolvers over the years.

Of course, Smith & Wesson has always made handguns, not collectibles, and thus, as long as surplus stocks remained, they often used older-style boxes at later periods. Anyone who says of a company dedicated to making a profit—especially one with an operational history spanning over 150 years—that "they never did that" is bound to be caught out some of the time. What is to you and me a collectible was to the guys and gals in the S&W Shipping Department merely a container to be consigned to the not-so tender mercies of (take your pick, depending on your period of interest) the U.S. Postal Service, Railway Express, UPS/Federal Express, or even major trucking firms if you buy enough weapons. (Ask my friends Shawn McCarver and John Ross about getting truck-, and I mean real truck, not delivery-truck, shipments of product from Springfield!)

### The Hinged Orange Box

Shipping boxes of various patterns had existed for use with S&W products before the first K-frames were introduced in 1899, but at that time, and for some years thereafter, the revolvers were shipped in hinged-lid cardboard boxes which were covered in orange-colored fabric.

The pasted-on paper end labels describing the contents were green for blued weapons, white or orange for nickel-plated weapons. The serial number was often written on the bottom of the box in pencil or grease pencil (crayon).

758. An early 4" M&P, serial no. 279106, with gold medallions in service grips, atop its original hinged-lid orange-colored shipping box. Dave Terbrueggen collection

**S. & W. .38 MILITARY AND POLICE, 4 INCH**

DIRECTIONS FOR USE.—Grasp the stock of the arm with the right hand and with the thumb push the thumb piece forward, then with the other hand press the cylinder to the left. Place the charges in the chambers and return the cylinder to its place, when the arm is ready for use.

If it is desired to open the revolver with one hand, press the thumb piece forward with the thumb, and press the cylinder to the left ·ith the first two fingers of the same hand.

*To Eject the Empty Cartridge Cases.*—Swing the cylinder to the left as before, and while holding the muzzle elevated, push rearwards on the ejector rod with the disengaged hand. Release the ejector rod; the ejector will return to its former position, and the arm is ready to reload.

*To Remove an Exploded Shell.*—After having swung the cylinder to one side, as before directed, press upon the ejector rod sufficiently to start the cartridges from the chamber, when the exploded shell may be removed.

*To Remove the Cylinder.*—Loosen the forward side plate screw, and the yoke and cylinder may be withdrawn from the frame.

*In Ordering* parts for repairs, return the broken or damaged pieces.

Address **SMITH & WESSON, Springfield, Mass., U. S. A.**

**S. & W. MODELO—.38 MILITAR Y POLICIA. 4 PULGADAS**

*Para cargar.* Teniendo el arma en la mano derecha, empújese el pasador del tambor con el pulgar, y con la otra mano échese el tambor a la izquierda. Métanse los cartuchos en sus puestos y vuélvase el tambor a su posición primitiva.

*Para expelar cápsulas usadas.* Echese el tambor a la izquierda, como arriba mencionado, y, teniendo la boca del cañón por arriba, con la otra mano muévase hacia atras el piston del ejector. Sueltese el piston, entonces el extractor se vuelva a su propio puesto, y el arma quedará lista para recar[illegible]

*Para sacar [illegible] cápsula usada.* Echese afuera el tambor segun los direcciones anteriores, y empújese un poco el piston del extractor entonces se encontrará facil de quitar la cápsula usada.

*Para sacar el tambor.* Aflójese el tornillo delantero de la chapa lateral, y facilmente puede quitarse.

*Cartuchos.* Recomendamos especialmente para el uso en nuestros revólveres los cartuchos *con pólvora sin humo*, diseñados por nosotros, y fabricados por casas accreditadas, como U. M. C.—Remington, Winchester, etc.

**PEARL HANDLES**

All pearl stocks furnished by us bear our trade mark inserted as shown in cut; they are made from selected shells, the best obtainable, sound, perfect, and of good color, and are fitted and finished with care and accuracy.

As it is impossible at times to procure shells of suitable size and quality for stocks of our larger caliber revolvers we do not furnish them, preferring to use Circassian Walnut which, although simpl[illegible] in appearance, is much more appropriate.

We are aware of the fact that it often happens that the regular stocks which we furnish with our revolvers are removed and pearl stocks substituted. These latter are generally very thin, inferior shell, badly made and fitted, resulting in an unsatisfactory grip, and injuring the appearance of the arm.

We request our clients to always insist that the stocks whether of rubber, walnut or pearl, bear our registered trade mark which is a guarantee of quality and superiority.

**SMITH & WESSON**

**MANGOS DE CONCHA NACAR**

Todas las cachas de nácar suministradas por nosotros llevan nuestra marca de fábrica como se ve en el grabado; son hechas de conchas escojidas, las mejores que pueden consequirse, macizas, perfectas y de buen color; y son acabados y puestas con exactitud y cuidado.

Como a veces es imposible encontrar conchas del tamaño y de la consistencia adecuada para las cachas de nuestros revolveres de mayores calibres no las ofrecen, pref[illegible]do usar nogal circasiano; lo cual, aunque ma[illegible] sencillo en apariencia, es mucho mas a proposito.

Nos consta, sin embargo, que con frecuencia nuestras cachas originales son quitadas y reemplazadas por otras de nácar. Estas últimas generalmente son muy delgadas, inferiores, mal hechas y mal puestas; resultando que el agarro es muy poco satisfactorio, y que el arma pierde muchisimo en apariencia.

Rogamos a nuestros favorecedores insistir que las cachas—sean de goma, de nogal o de concha nácar—llevan siempre nuestra marca registrada cuya presencia es una garantia de superioridad.

**SMITH & WESSON**

760 (right). The green end label on the orange box for my factory Young-engraved M&P, serial no. 244788. which was shipped in 1915.

## The Hinged "Display" or "Patent" Box

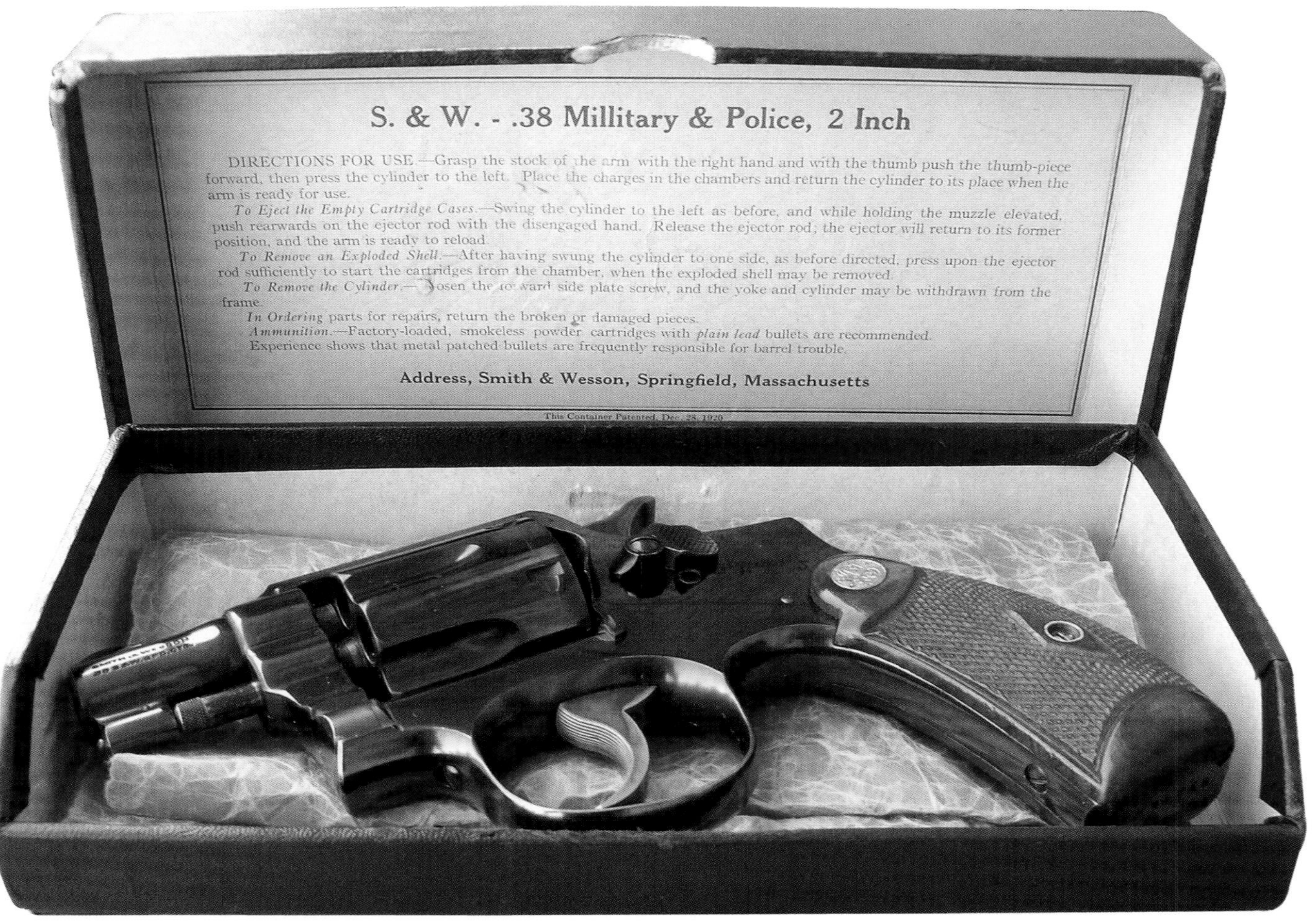


761. A blued M&P with 2" barrel, serial no. 676959, in its original hinged maroon-colored "Display" or "Patent" box dimensioned specially for the 2" barrel length. The tiny lettering at the bottom of the instructions printed in English only inside the lid reads "This Container Patented Dec. 28, 1920".

According to the factory letter, this revolver was not shipped until June 30, 1939. Mike Pacella collection

A new hinged box made of cardboard covered in paper with beveled front edges, known to collectors as the "Display" or "Patent" box, was patented on December 28, 1920. The color of the paper covering varies from a red-purple maroon shade to a dark blue-black.

A First Model Prewar K-32 in its Patent box with all accessories is shown in fig, 340.

As proud as they were of this new design, the old style continued to be used by the thrifty Yankee gunmakers of Springfield long after the new display box came out. I suppose it was the thing at the time for gun stores to display these, with their contents, in their glass showcases.

759 (previous page). The interior of the box that accompanied my factory Young-engraved M&P, serial no. 244788 (fig. 665), showing the operating instructions printed inside the lid, above, and a pasted-on label on the bottom describing pearl grips. Both are printed in English and Spanish.

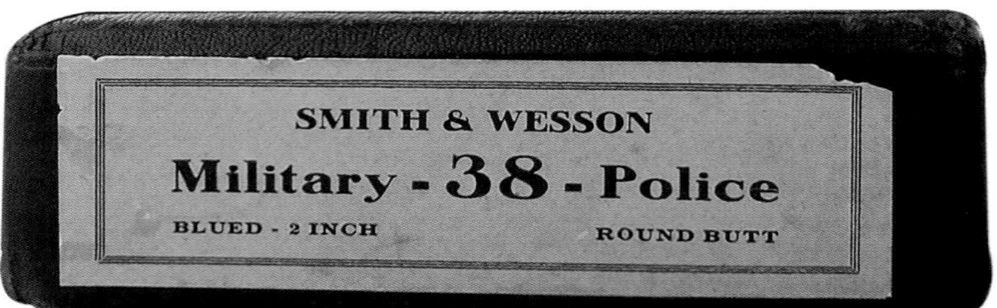


762 (left). The end of the maroon Patent box in fig. 761, showing pasted-on green paper label identifying the contents. Mike Pacella collection

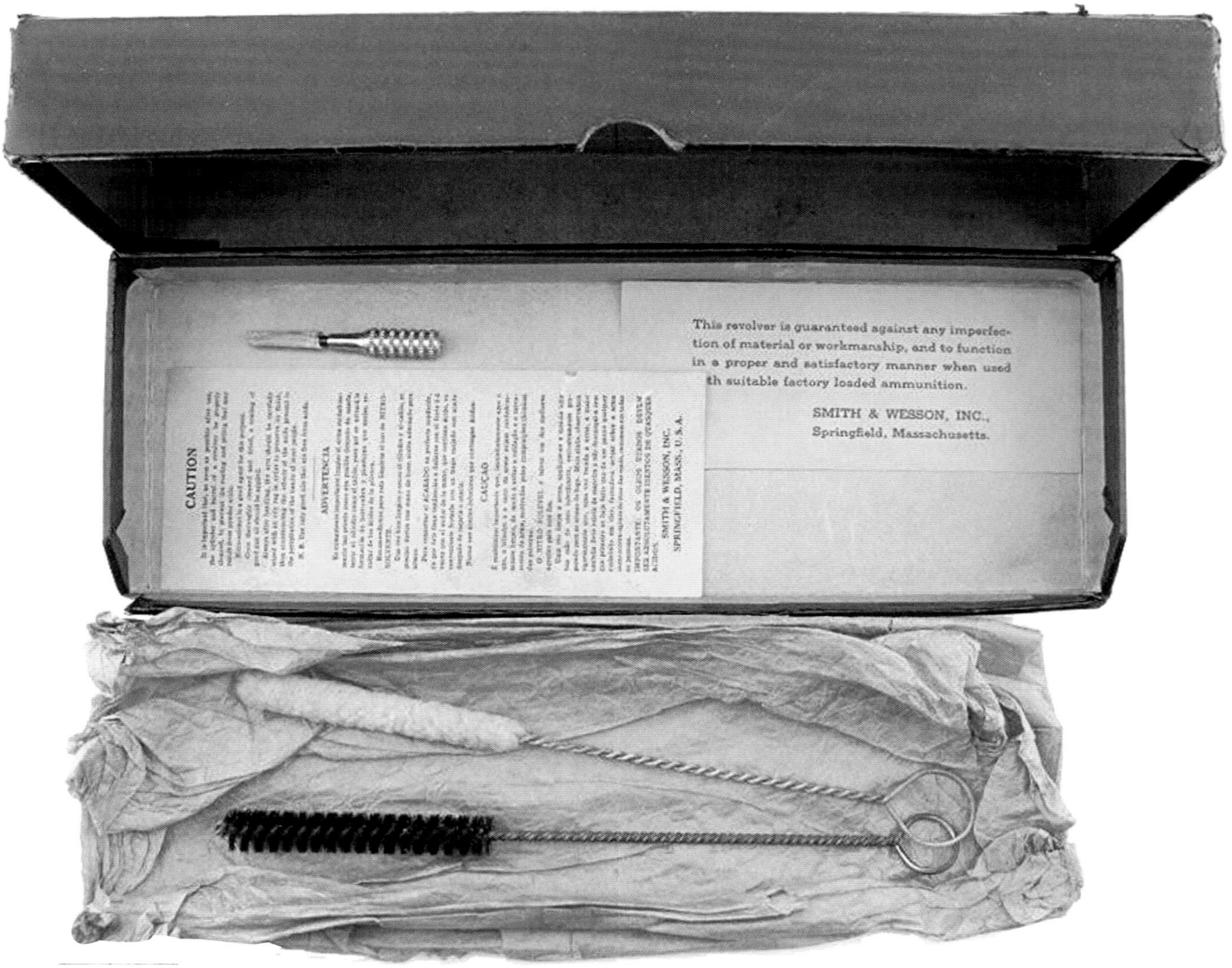

763. Interior of a hinged Patent box in black or dark blue with pale yellow-green interior, as used to ship the prewar K-32 revolver, serial no. 677296 in figs. 338 - 340, showing original contents, which included a screwdriver, a bore brush and mop, an instruction card in English, Spanish and Portuguese, and a guarantee card.

On the bottom of the box a faint two-line red rubber-stamped legend reads "K32/TARGET".

Gaston Comeau collection

764 (below). Closeup of the small screwdriver and its wax paper sleeve, included in the box above. By themselves, these original screwdrivers can be surprisingly valuable collectibles today. Gaston Comeau collection

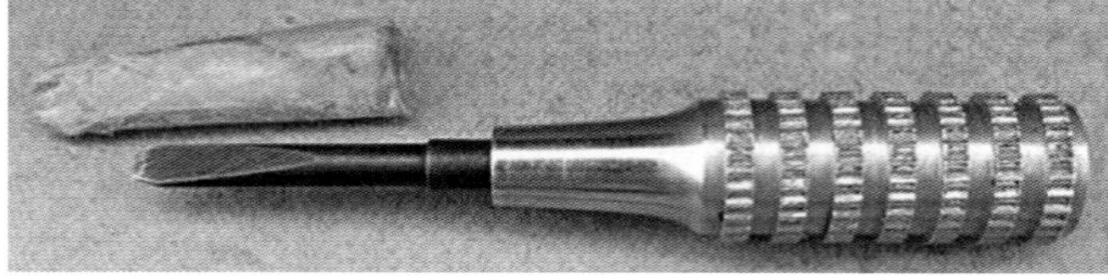

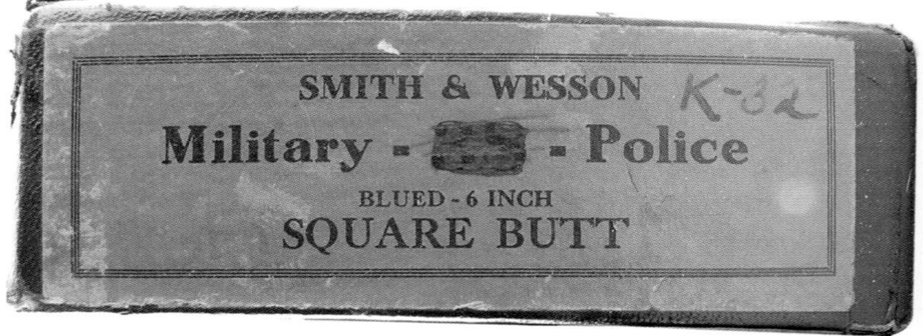

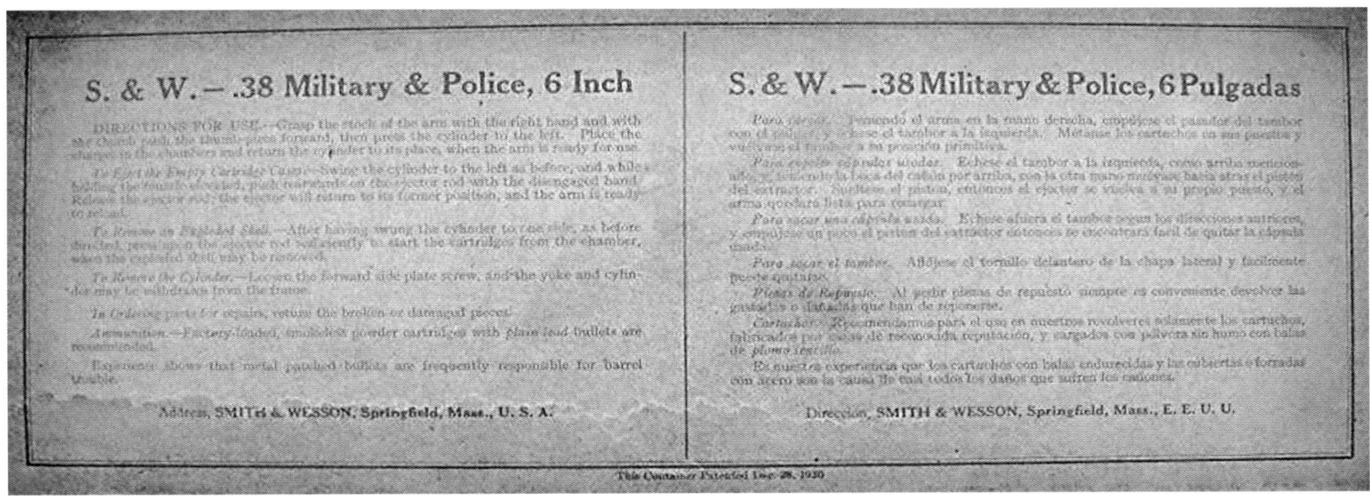


766. The inside of the lid of the black Patent box in fig. 763, showing English and Spanish instructions for the 6" M&P revolver. Compare with fig. 759: note the different type style.

This box actually contained a K-32, and as noted in fig. 765 the end label was so overmarked.

Gaston Comeau collection

The inside of many early box lids contained printed operating instructions, usually but not always in Spanish as well as English, which indicated the firm's appreciation of the strong market for their products south of the border.

On some early boxes information is printed or pasted on the inside of the bottom portion of the box, dealing with pearl grips. Today, thanks to the oft-quoted comment by General George Patton to the effect that only pimps in New Orleans bordellos carried guns with pearl grips, people tend to forget that pearl used to be the preferred grip material for serious target shooters like Walter Winans and Ira Paine, with ivory being a lesser choice. Obviously enough people liked pearl grips in those early days that Smith & Wesson sometimes found it difficult to find the raw material in a quality sufficient to meet their requirements.

## Prewar Red or Blue Two-Piece "Picture" Boxes (1933 - 1941)

Starting in the early 1930s and continuing up to WWII, red or blue boxes of two-piece design were used. The interior of the red box was also red, and a drawing of the weapon contained within appeared on the top of the box. Printing was in blue or gold, and information about the contents was on the ends of the box also.

Metal corner reinforcements, colored to match the cardboard color, first appeared with these boxes. While production of these boxes seems to have stopped in 1941, weapons are known to have been shipped in them as late as 1951. Again the serial number was typically written in pencil on a piece of paper pasted to the bottom of the box.

767. The end of the bright red "picture" box for a prewar K-22 Outdoorsman's revolver, preprinted in black. Four more views of this box appear in fig. 768.

This is the first appearance of the metal reinforcements, clamped in each corner of the lid.

Karlyn May collection

765 (previous page). The end of the K-32 black Patent box in fig. 763, showing pasted-on pre-printed green paper label.

The K-32 was not produced in sufficient quantities to warrant making up a special label for it. Note the ".38" has been inked out, and "K-32" written in at top right.

Gaston Comeau collection

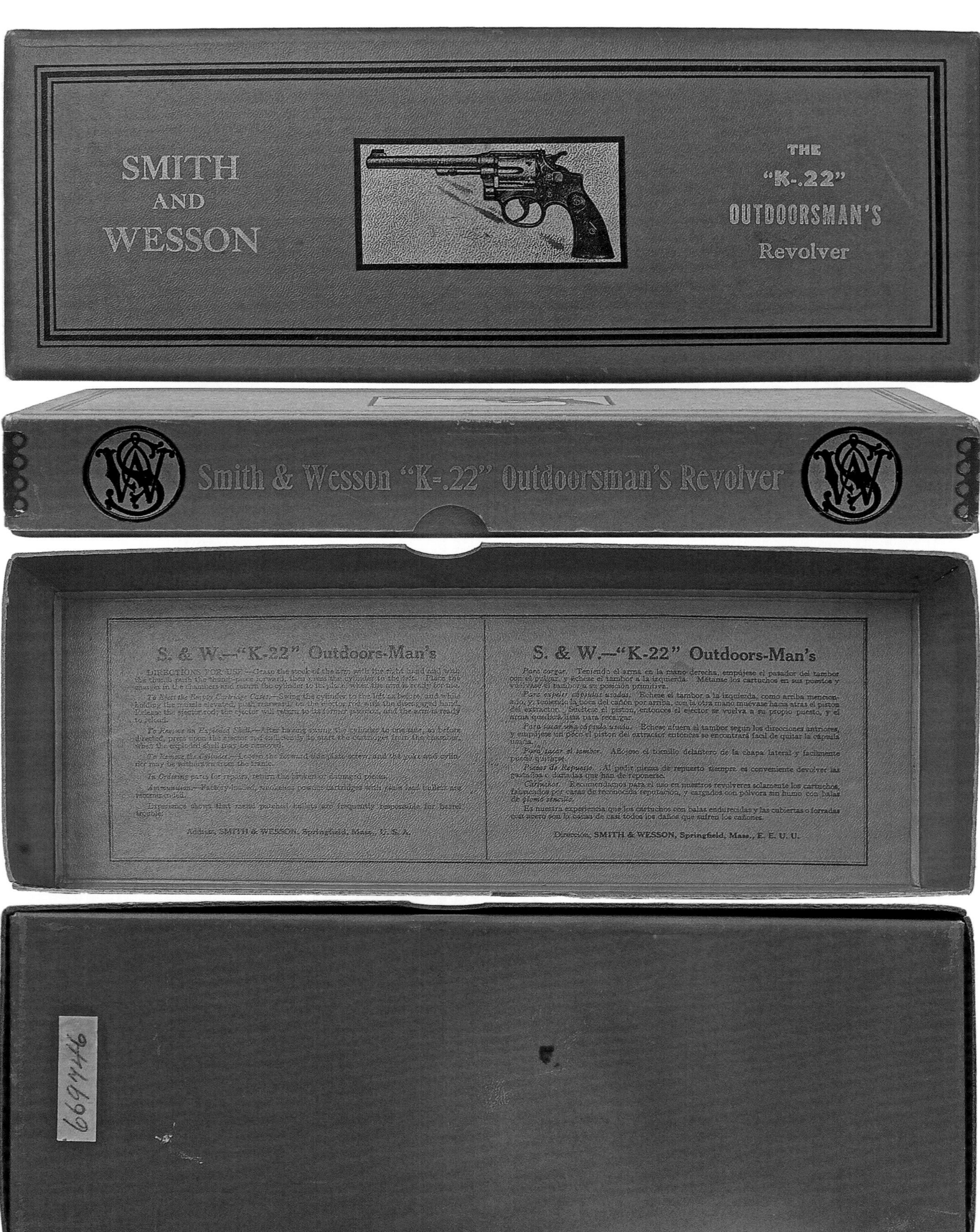
SMITH
AND
WESSON
THE
"K-.22"
OUTDOORSMAN'S
Revolver
Smith & Wesson "K-.22" Outdoorsman's Revolver
S. & W.—"K-22" Outdoors-Man's
Address, SMITH & WESSON, Springfield, Mass., U. S. A.
S. & W.—"K-22" Outdoors-Man's
Dirección, SMITH & WESSON, Springfield, Mass., E. E. U. U.
94699

## Wartime Plain Cardboard Boxes

During the war, the Victory Model and .38/200 boxes were simple plain two-piece cardboard containers, with no interesting markings or illustrations. Two such boxes are illustrated in figs. 374 and 382.

# Postwar Boxes (1946 - 1975)

## The Maroon or Black, Later Blue, Two-Piece Box

769. Right side view of the early postwar short-action K-38 Heavy Masterpiece, serial no. K224475 (fig. 411 and 412), which was shipped in this maroon two-piece box.
Gaston Comeau collection

A number of new box types appeared when commercial production resumed after the war. A rigid two-piece cardboard box covered in maroon or black, later blue, paper, was used for many revolvers that did not have a specific box designed for them. The serial number was penciled on the outside of the plain cardboard bottom, and an end label describing the contents was pasted on. These boxes were also used to return weapons for after-factory repairs, or if modifications were performed. These were blank inside, with no printed instructions on lid or bottom.

770. The end of the postwar two-piece maroon box above, showing pasted-on label pre-printed in blue to describe the contents, in this case a K-38 Heavy Masterpiece with target hammer and target stocks.

The interiors of these boxes were plain, with no printed instructions. Gaston Comeau collection

768. Four views of the bright red two-piece "picture" box for the prewar K-22 Outdoorsman's revolver serial no. 669746.

From top: top of box, with picture of the revolver; front of box, pre-printed in gold; inside of lid showing red color throughout, with printed instructions in English and Spanish; bottom of box, with handwritten serial number.
Karlyn May collection

771. Two more views of the bottom half of the maroon two-piece box shown in figs. 769 and 770.

Above: the plain interior, with the revolver sitting on the bore mop and folded "Helpful Hints" instruction sheet.

Below: the outside, showing the serial number handwritten in black grease pencil on the pale-green cardboard.

Gaston Comeau collection

772. An end label from a maroon two-piece box with no interior markings, identifying the contents as a 6" K-22 Masterpiece with target hammer and target stocks.

The serial number, penciled on the bottom of the box, reads K227164.

courtesy Karlyn May

773. Another end label from a maroon two-piece box, similar to the one for the K-38 Heavy Masterpiece shown in fig. 770, except this one confirms that the barrel has been modified at the factory to 4".

It was the demand for factory conversions like this from law enforcement users that led to the introduction of the Combat Masterpiece.

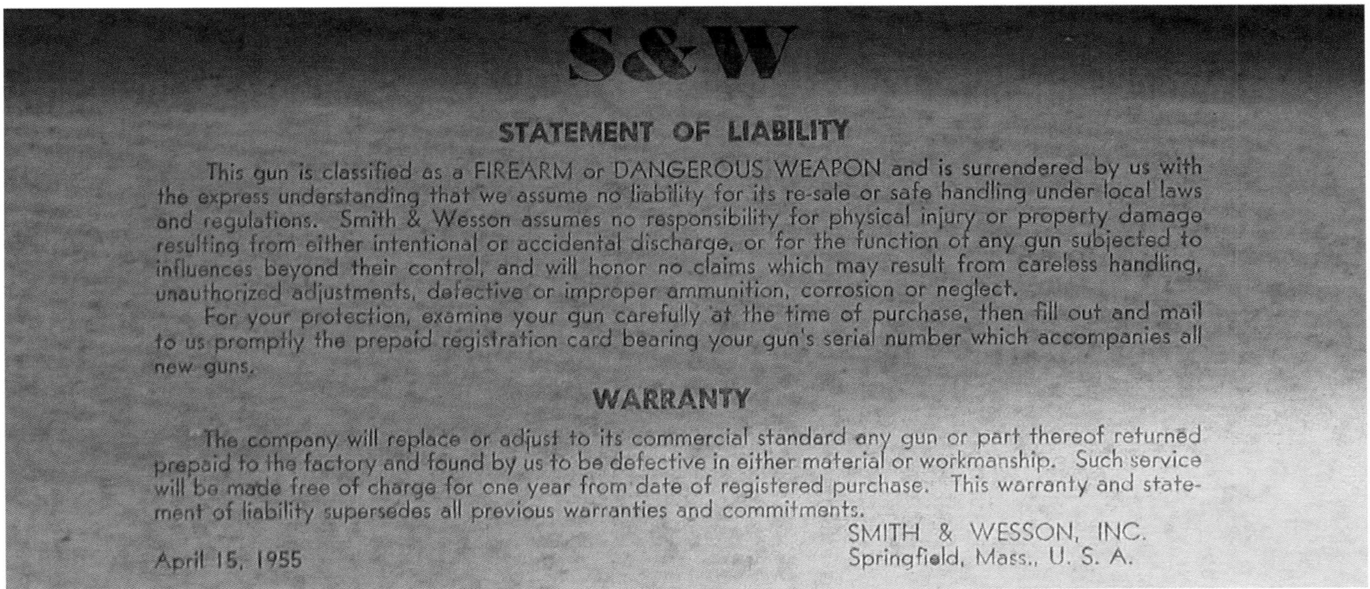

S&W

STATEMENT OF LIABILITY

This gun is classified as a FIREARM or DANGEROUS WEAPON and is surrendered by us with the express understanding that we assume no liability for its re-sale or safe handling under local laws and regulations. Smith & Wesson assumes no responsibility for physical injury or property damage resulting from either intentional or accidental discharge, or for the function of any gun subjected to influences beyond their control, and will honor no claims which may result from careless handling, unauthorized adjustments, defective or improper ammunition, corrosion or neglect.

For your protection, examine your gun carefully at the time of purchase, then fill out and mail to us promptly the prepaid registration card bearing your gun's serial number which accompanies all new guns.

WARRANTY

The company will replace or adjust to its commercial standard any gun or part thereof returned prepaid to the factory and found by us to be defective in either material or workmanship. Such service will be made free of charge for one year from date of registered purchase. This warranty and statement of liability supersedes all previous warranties and commitments.

SMITH & WESSON, INC.
Springfield, Mass., U. S. A.

April 15, 1955

774. The interior of the lid of the maroon two-piece box in fig. 772, showing Statement of Liability and Warranty dated April 15, 1955.

## Postwar Gold Boxes

775. The top of a two-piece gold box embossed with the image of an early postwar long action M&P with 4" barrel and half-moon sight.

Note the "Springfield 2, Mass." address: the timeframe for this early postal code was before 1963 but after 1943.

During the 20 or so years after the end of WWII, two-piece gold boxes were used for blued weapons and, as discussed below, silver for nickel-plated ones. I have always found these gold and silver boxes to be the most handsome of all the boxes Smith & Wesson used over the years. A picture of the model of the weapon enclosed was embossed on the lid, not merely printed, and the front and end of the box also contained the model information, including finish and barrel length, printed directly on the box with no pasted label.

Metal corner reinforcements in blue, silver, and gold color are seen, with no apparent rhyme or reason.

S & W 38 Military & Police Revolver

**Loading Directions:**—Grasp the stock of the arm with the right hand and push the thumbpiece forward. Press the cylinder to the left. Place the cartridges in the chambers and return the cylinder to its place. The arm is now ready for use.

**To Eject the Empty Cartridge Cases:**—Swing the cylinder to the left as above, and while holding the muzzle elevated, push rearward on the ejector rod with the disengaged hand. Release the ejector rod. The ejector will return to its forward position and the arm is ready to reload.

**To Remove a Single Shell:**—After having swung the cylinder open, press on the ejector rod sufficiently to start the cartridges from the chambers. The fired shell can then be drawn out by hand.

**Ammunition and Guarantee:**—This gun is guaranteed against any defects in material or workmanship when used exclusively with factory-loaded 38 Special caliber cartridges of standard velocity. It is primarily designed for ammunition with plain lead, lubricated bullets, and we recommend this type of cartridge to maintain utmost accuracy for the maximum length of time. Metal-jacketed bullets may be used, but have a tendency to cause greater barrel wear.

**In Ordering** parts for repairs, return the broken or damaged pieces.

Address, **SMITH & WESSON, Springfield 2, Mass., U. S. A.**

S & W 38 Military & Police Revolver

**Para cargar.** Teniendo el arma en la mano derecha, empújese el pasador del tambor con el pulgar, y échese el tambor a la izquierda. Métanse los cartuchos en sus puestos y vuélvase el tambor a su posición primitiva.

**Para expeler cápsulas usadas.** Echese el tambor a la izquierda, como arriba mencionado, y, teniendo la boca del cañón por arriba, con la otra mano muévase hacia atras el piston del extractor. Sueltese el piston, entonces el ejector se vuelva a su propio puesto, y el arma quedará lista para recargar.

**Para sacar una cápsula usada.** Echese afuera el tambor segun los direcciones anteriores, y empújese un poco el piston del extractor entonces se encontrará facil de quitar la cápsula usada.

**Para sacar el tambor.** Aflójese el tornillo dolantero de la chapa lateral y facilmente puede quitarse.

**Piezas de Repuesto.** Al pedir piezas de repuesto siempre es conveniente devolver las gastadas o dañadas que han de reponerse.

**Cartuchos.** Recomendamos para el uso en nuestros revolveres solamente los cartuchos, fabricados por casas de reconocida reputación, y cargados con pólvora sin humo con balas de **plomo sencillo.**

Es nuestra experiencia que los cartuchos con balas endurecidas y las cubiertas o forradas con acero son la causa de casi todos los daños que sufren los cañones.

Dirección, **SMITH & WESSON, Springfield 2, Mass., E. E. U. U.**

776. Inside the lid of the gold box in fig. 775, showing instructions and other information in English and Spanish.

777. The front of the gold box in fig. 775, showing preprinted S&W logo and model description.

778. The end of the gold box in fig. 775, showing preprinted information for a typical 4" M&P.

Even boxes for models as common as this are rare today, because so many were simply thrown away.

779. An as-new square-butt M&P with Magna stocks, short action and 2" barrel, serial no. C91662, atop its gold shipping box. Dave Tebrueggen collection

780. Another gold box for a short-action K-38 Masterpiece, a "Companion gun to the K-22 and K-32 Masterpieces", with features described.

781 (below). The front of the above K-38 Masterpiece gold box, with logo and model description.

### Gold Boxes with Altered Labels

782. The end of the above K-38 Masterpiece gold box, showing pre-printed information.

783. Another pre-printed box end for a K-38 Masterpiece with a paper label pasted over the original information identifying the contents as a 4" Combat Masterpiece.

Some models that were either just recently introduced or not in big production used boxes for a common variation with the end label altered, typically in grease pencil but occasionally in ink, or even with a paper label pasted over the original information, to reflect the correct identity of the contents. No doubt this was done for reasons of thrift then but it seems quite nice now, a human touch I suppose that is rapidly disappearing in our computer age. While this approach might seem to lend itself to aiding those individuals who fake rare variations of a revolver, this should not be much of a problem in the case of Smith & Wesson, since absolutely certain authentication is only a factory letter away.

## Blue and Silver Two-Piece Boxes

784. The top of a two-piece blue box used to ship a K-22 Masterpiece with 6" barrel. The name and address indicate that this was made prior to the Bangor Punta takeover in 1965.

785. The end label from the box shown above. The pre-printed M&P description has been overlaid with a pasted-on paper label specific to the K-22 Masterpiece.

786. The pasted-on end label from the blue box containing Model 14 serial no. K338052 with 4" heavy barrel, still marked "K-38".

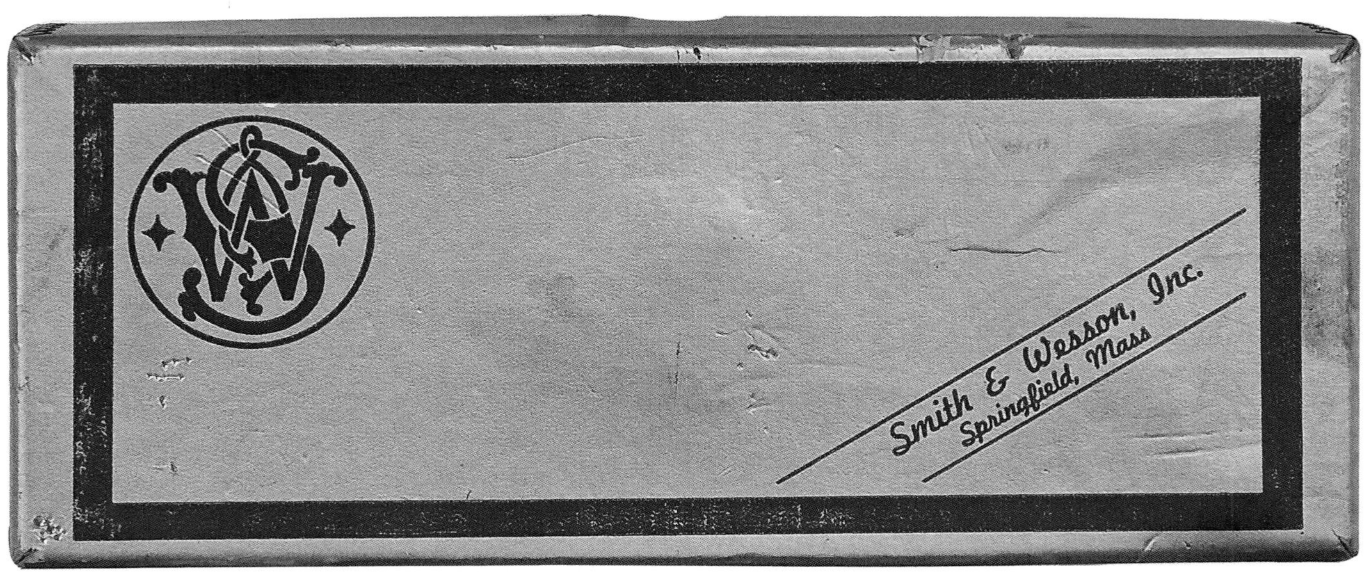


787. Top of the silver two-piece box for a nickel-plated Model 15-2 serial no. K578265, with a tapered 4" barrel.

788. Pre-printed label on one end of the silver box shown above, used to ship a nickel-plated Model 15 4" revolver.

789. Blank label on the other end of the silver box shown above, with handwritten description of the nickel-plated Model 15-2 revolver within.

Starting about the mid-1950s, the blue two-piece box appeared, with metal corners and silver printing for blued guns, while nickel-plated weapons came in silver-colored boxes.

There were several minor variations of these, the difference having to do with whether the silver border (on blue boxes) or blue border (on silver boxes) is solid or hatched.

Again the end labels contained information about the specific configurations of stocks, trigger, hammer, and barrel length. Serial numbers were penciled on the bottom.

I cannot tell whether or not "pinto" revolvers were always shipped in one style of box. Some are known to have been shipped in blue boxes. But for others, perhaps silver if the frame was nickeled; or maybe the lid was silver and bottom blued; or vice versa? I do not know, but it is an interesting question.

## Blue and Silver Boxes Reflect Changes in Corporate Ownership

When Bangor Punta took over in 1965, that name was added to the legend on top of the box, between the existing two lines reading "Smith & Wesson, Inc." and "Springfield, Mass.", and the logo "LSI" replaced the Bangor Punta name after Lear Siegler Corp. took over in 1984. Despite these changes in corporate ownership, older boxes continued to be used until they were gone.

About 1983, the blue one-piece box with tuck-in wings, the end containing a label with the weapon information, began to be used. Even those boxes can vary, however, with some including the Lear Siegler ownership information and some not. Also some have labels on both ends and others do not.

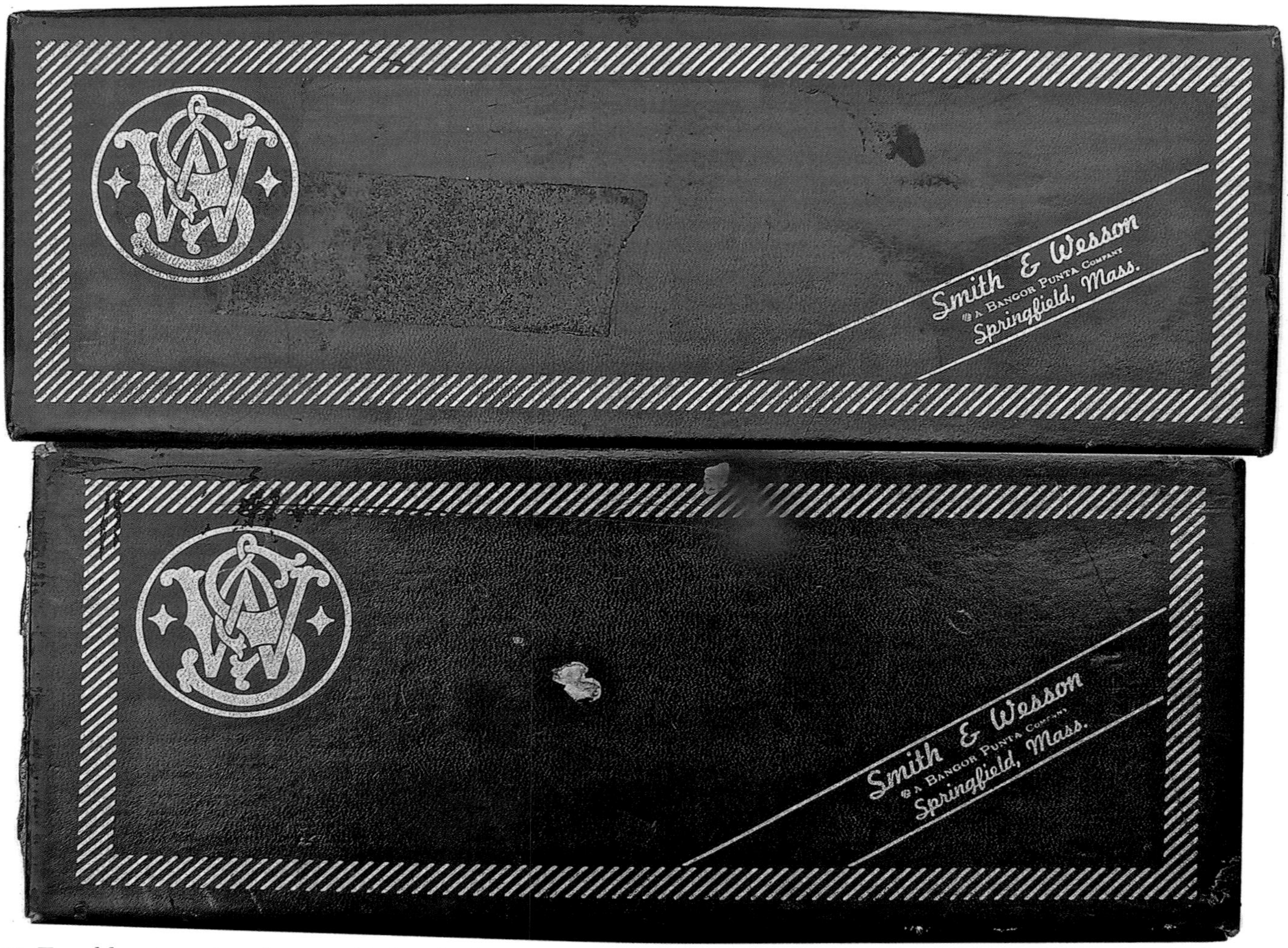

790. Two blue two-piece boxes with hatched silver borders, including the notice that Smith & Wesson was now "A Bangor Punta Company". The top box is for a 6" barreled revolver, and the slightly smaller one below is for my blued Model 66 with 4" barrel serial no. 4K94473 (fig. 520), from the factory collection.

791. End label for the 6" box shown above, with pre-printed description for a 6" Model 10 modified in white grease pencil.

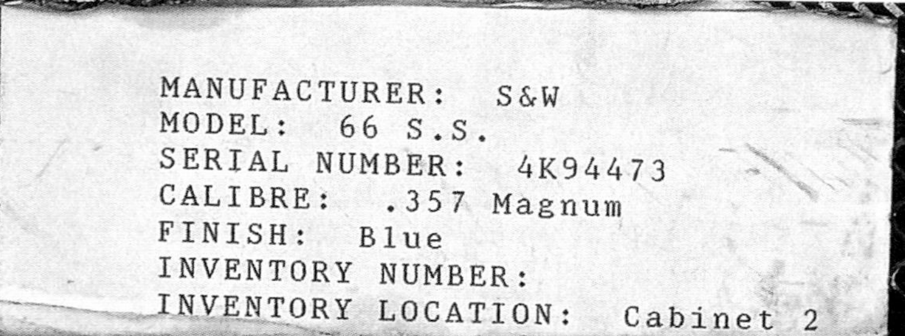

MANUFACTURER: S&W
MODEL: 66 S.S.
SERIAL NUMBER: 4K94473
CALIBRE: .357 Magnum
FINISH: Blue
INVENTORY NUMBER:
INVENTORY LOCATION: Cabinet 2

792. Special end label for above 4" box containing my blued-finish stainless Model 66 (fig. 520), indicating its location within the factory collection.

793 (right). Label on the other end of the box for my 4" Model 66, serial no. 4K94473. Note finish code "BSS" (blued stainless steel).

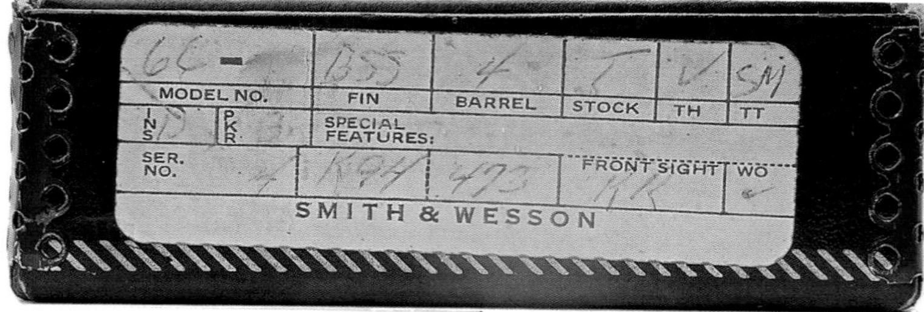

794. One of the first 100 stainless steel Model 66 revolvers made in 1970, serial no. K949140, in its silver Bangor Punta box.

This revolver was kept in the factory collection for five years before being shipped to G. T. Distributors in Rossville, Georgia, on November 7, 1975.

Bill Cross collection

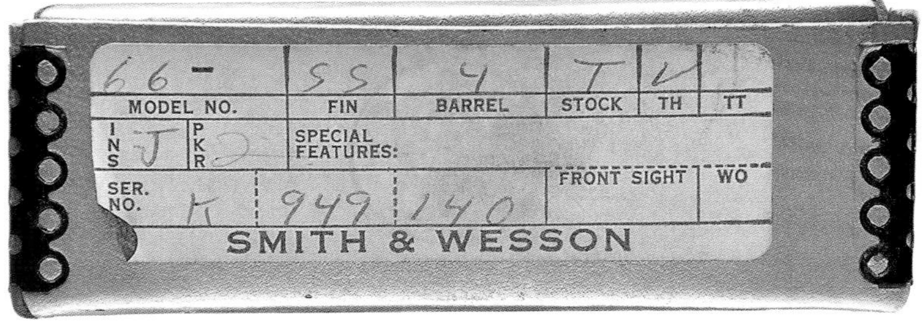


795 (right). End label for the above silver box containing Model 66 serial no. K949140, indicating that it is fitted with a target hammer. Bill Cross collection

# Box Sizes

In addition to the various colors and types of boxes, different sizes were available, since K-frame revolvers come in barrel lengths varying from 2 to 8⅜ inches, and boxes had to accommodate the length, yet not be oversized for the weapon contained.

Before the introduction of the 8⅜" barrel length a number of years ago, only three sizes were available, but with the addition of that barrel length, a fourth, longer box was mandated.

In addition to these four common sizes, a few other oddities exist, of which I was unaware until I started taking photos to illustrate this section of the book.

## Model 53 Boxes

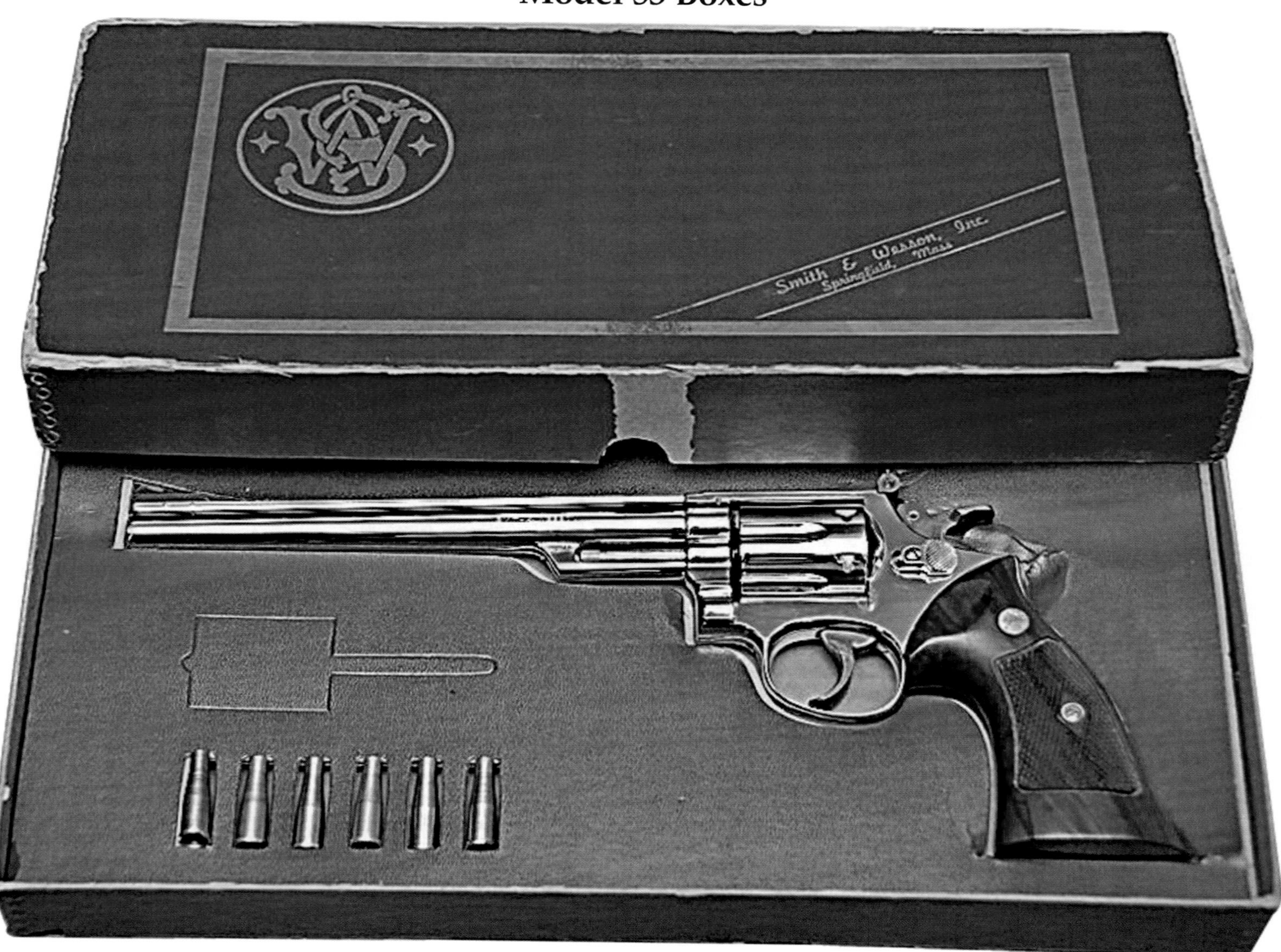


796. A nickel-plated .22 Magnum (Jet) Model 53 with 8⅜" barrel, in its special blue pre-Bangor Punta box.

Compare with fig. 504, which shows the shorter box used for Model 53s with 4 or 6" barrels.

Note the unused die cutting for the optional spare .22 RF cylinder, which was not included with this revolver.

The short-lived Model 53 .22 Magnum (or Jet) revolver came in three barrel lengths: 4", 6", and 8³⁄₈". These were shipped in special pre-Bangor Punta boxes die-cut to hold an optional spare .22 rimfire cylinder, as well as the cartridge inserts which allowed .22 rimfire cartridges to be fired in the cylinder chambered for the .22 Magnum. Since the spare cylinder was an extra-cost item, it would seem that few revolvers were actually shipped with spare cylinders, although the inserts were always included.

The resulting boxes were unique to this model, and came in two sizes - one for those with 4 or 6" barrels (fig. 504), and a larger size for revolvers with 8³⁄₈" barrrels.

As this weapon was made and sold at the time when silver boxes were commonly used for nickeled weapons, one would think that silver boxes would have been used for nickel-plated Model 53s, but I have never seen such a box. All the Model 53s I have seen came in blue boxes. The two I am familiar with, one blued with a 6-inch barrel and the other a 4-inch model in nickel, were obtained from J & G Rifle Ranch in 1971, and both came in blue boxes as described. I doubt many nickel M53s were made, so I imagine no specific silver or gray boxes were made for them.

## "Dayton Gun" Boxes in Different Sizes

797. Top views of two Model 14 pre-Bangor Punta blue boxes, both shipped in the same timeframe to distributor Dayton Gun. The box below is for a revolver fitted with target grips, and is slightly wider than the standard box, above.

The end labels for both appear in fig. 798.

The other interesting thing I learned most recently involves the blue boxes used to ship the famed "Dayton Gun" Model 14s. When I got a couple of these boxes out to photograph, I noticed when they were side-by-side that one was actually slightly wider than the other. That was because the wider one was for a weapon shipped with target grips, while the narrower box held a gun fitted with standard Magna-style stocks. Both were shipped from the factory direct to Dayton Gun, and the weapons were within 900 numbers of each other. The boxes are otherwise identical, but the wider box shows the target grips (an available option) on the label. I never realized this difference existed, and likely many others have not noticed it either unless they happen to compare the boxes for two otherwise identical handguns shipped to the same place at the same time. I know I would tend to overlook this, or if noticed simply think it a variation in manufacturing rather than a contract specification, but it appears to be an intentional difference in sizing, although it does seem to be a little more complicated than need be. But the photos are clear, and the one box did not shrink or the other one grow larger sitting on the shelf for the last 50 or so years. Both of these revolvers are unfired, and the boxes are in mint condition also.

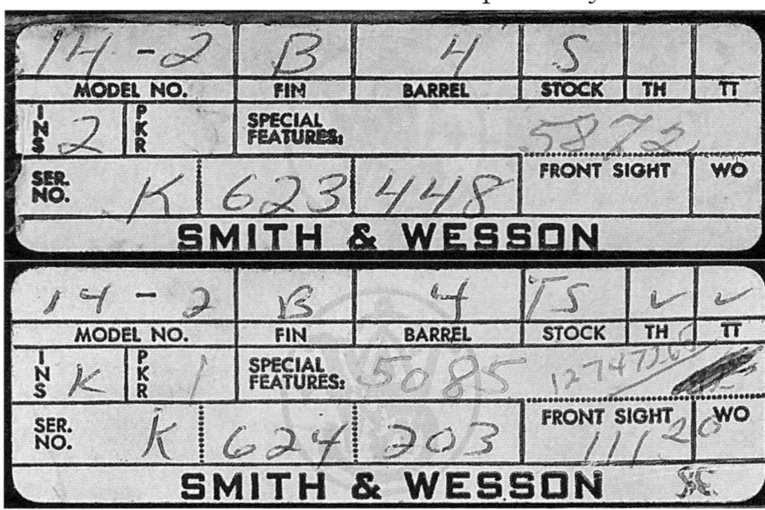


798. End labels for the two boxes shown in fig. 797.
Above: the slightly smaller box, for Model 14-2 serial no. K623448, with standard stocks.
Below: the slightly wider box, for Model 14-2 serial no. K624203, fitted with target stocks.

# One-Piece Blue Boxes

799. Top of the later style one-piece blue box with tuck-in wings, made of thinner cardboard and marked as shown.
This box contained a .38 Special Model 19 with 3-inch barrel and encased ejector lug as initially made for Brazil. The end label is shown in fig. 801.

In the mid-1980s a new one-piece box with tuck-in wings, appeared, made of thinner cardboard and marked "Revolver" repeatedly across the top. These came in four sizes, depending on barrel length of the revolver being shipped.

800. Front views of two late blue boxes as shown in fig. 799.

Above: with LSI logo and wording "A Lear Siegler Company".

Below: with wording reverted to the S&W logo.

The end labels for both these boxes appear in fig. 801.

801. End labels from the two late blue boxes shown above.

Left: describing the .38 Special Model 19 with 3-inch barrel and encased ejector lug, as initially made for Brazil.

Right: an NYPD DAO Model 64, with 4" barrel.

These were initially marked on the front to indicate corporate ownership by Lear Siegler, and later, after purchase by Tomkins PLC in 1986, the S&W logo was used again.

# The "Heritage Series" Antiqued Gold Box

802. The top and front of the special two-piece gold color antiqued box used with the 10 special models of the "Heritage Series", with color-casehardened frames.

The illustrations depict Horace Smith, left, the S&W Stockbridge St. factory, center, and Daniel Wesson, right.

Dave Terbrueggen collection

In August, 2001 the S&W Performance Center teamed up with Lew Horton Distributors to announce the "Heritage Series" of 10 special models, with color-casehardened frames and other features. A Heritage Series Model 15-8 appears in fig. 491.

These revolvers were shipped in special two-piece gold color antique-style boxes with blue metal corner reinforcements, with the top depicting Horace Smith on the left, the original S&W factory on Stockbridge St. (fig. 227) in the center, and Daniel Wesson on the right, with the legend "HERITAGE SERIES" on the front.

# Blue Plastic "Clamshell" Cases

803. Front view of the early, simplest style of foam-lined plastic "clamshell" hard case used by Smith & Wesson. All have holes in both handles for a padlock.

Foam-lined blue plastic "clamshell" hard cases were introduced starting in 1997. The shape of these varies, as indicated in the photos, from the plain early style to the more involved later models.

No doubt these are better for shipping, since they are stonger than the original cardboard boxes and contain foam padding to cushion the weapon. They can be locked if desired with a padlock, which some may find useful, I suppose. A label on one side or end contains information relating to the identity of the contents.

Thanks to the advent of improved computer technology, the days of the grease pencil modifications to a standard label are gone, and unique labels are now computer-generated, as illustrated here where a couple of fairly unique models are indicated.

While a factory letter for truly unique examples will still be desirable, I suppose these labels will

804. End label for Model 19 chambered in .38 Special especially for the market in Brazil.

As shown in fig. 805, this revolver was shipped with a Master Lock.

805. The first style plastic case with lid lifted, showing the foam-lined interior.

The Master Lock, which fills the trigger guard to render the weapon unfireable, is shown as shipped in its original plastic bag.

certainly make it easier for future collectors to verify that they have the "real McCoy" when viewing that nice, quaint, stainless steel, rubber-gripped revolver nestling in its foam-lined plastic case at the 2075 Tulsa Gun Show.

While the above comment will no doubt bring some smiles or even a laugh to readers of today, I am certain that a person who had a similar mindset would think the same about some M&P revolver in a cardboard box while reading about the latest shoot-out between beer smugglers, or applauding Henry Ford for introducing an electric starter on his 1928 Model A automobile.

806. The front of the newest style of plastic case, which is of much more involved construction than the earlier plain model.

807. The label side of the above current-style plastic case, showing computer-generated information about the contents.

The days of grease pencil notations are gone, but future collectors will cherish these cases, since the labels will confirm the correct contents.

809 (following page). Combat Magnum serial no. K260190 in its blue presentation case, with accessories.

This is one of only eight Combat Magnums known to have been shipped in presentation cases.

Bill Cross collection

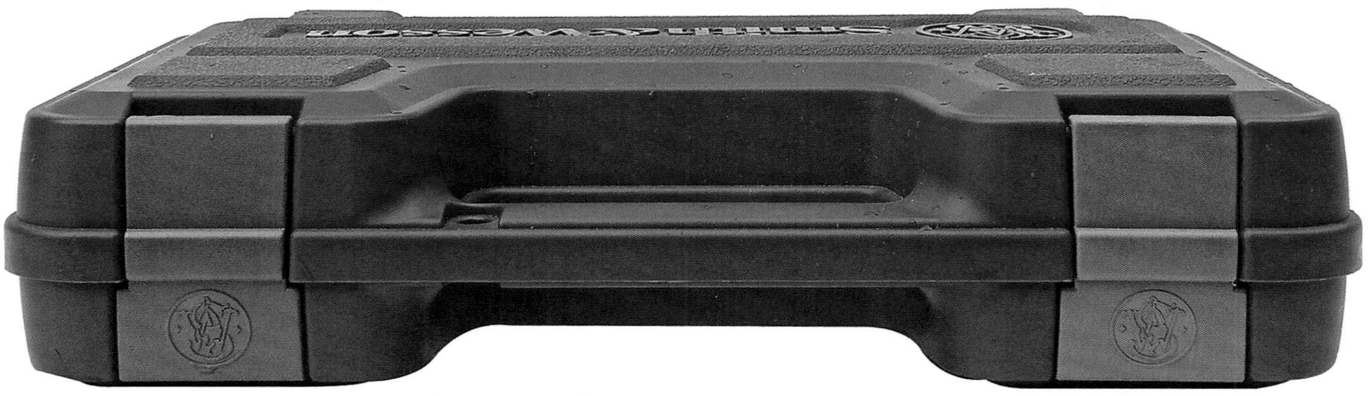

808. The top view of a current-style plastic case, with S&W logos on both closures.

# K-Frame Display Cases

In addition to the Model 10-13, (the 1899 Commemorative, fig. 461), the special wooden case for which is shown in figs. 462 and 463, it is known that a few rare Combat Magnums were shipped in special presentation cases. Two of these, from the Bill Cross collection, are discussed below.

## Combat Magnum No. K260190

810. The top of the lid of the blue presentation case for Combat Magnum no. K260190, showing "COMBAT MAGNUM" imprinted under the S&W logo.
Bill Cross collection

Most likely one of the first 100 Combat Magnums made, serial no. K260190 (fig. 809) was shipped on May 1, 1956 to Morley Murphy Co. in Green Bay, Wisconsin in a dark blue presentation case, which is numbered to the revolver on the bottom in white grease pencil.

This is one of eight Combat Magnums known to have been shipped in presentation cases. The case resembles those used for the .44 Magnum, except the bottom insert is made for a 4-inch K-frame revolver and the lid has "COMBAT MAGNUM" imprinted under the S&W logo.

811. Closeup of the bottom of the above Combat Magnum presentation case, showing serial number written in white grease pencil Bill Cross collection

## Model 19-3 No. K940639

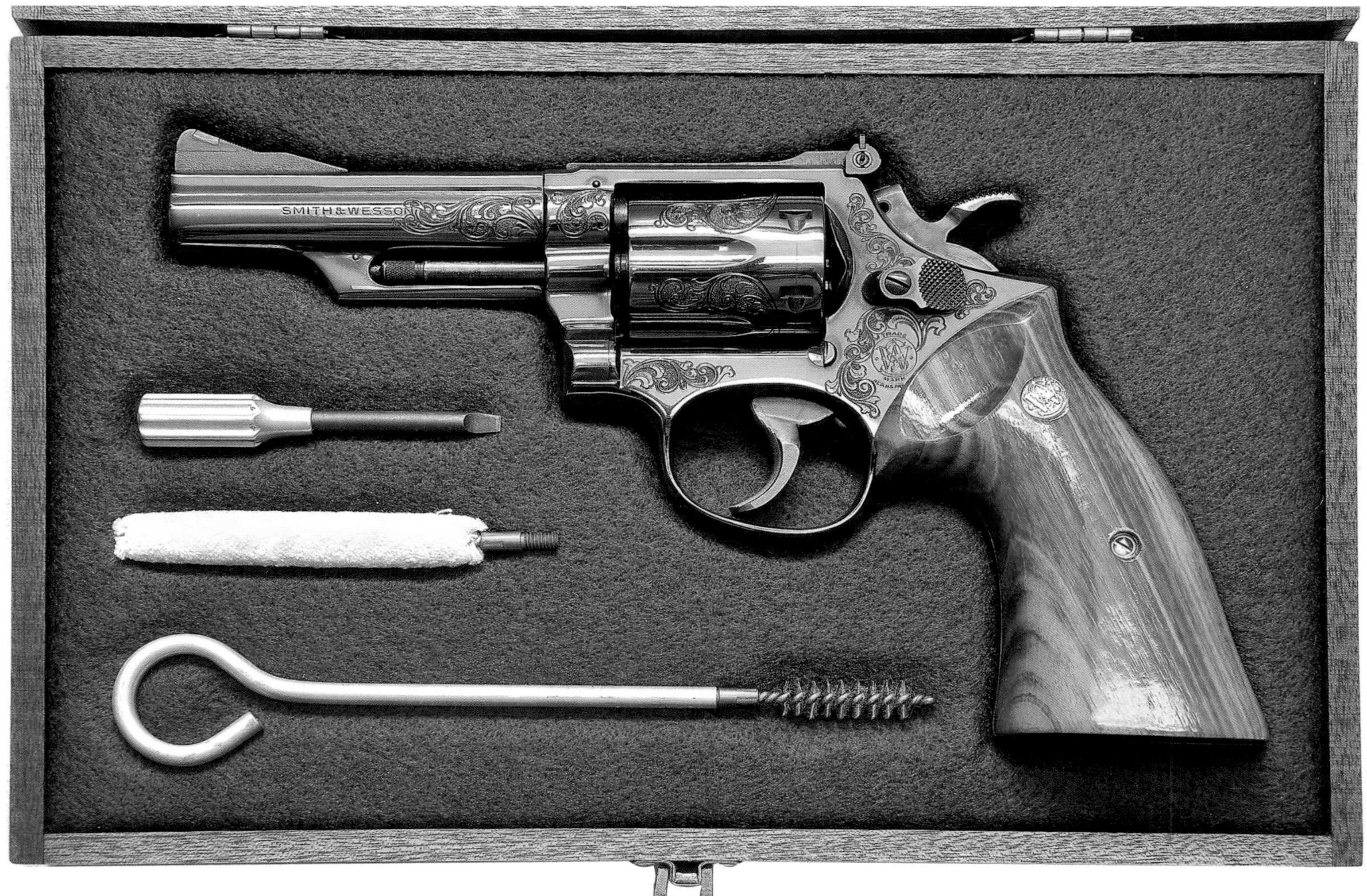


812. Class C engraved Model 19-3 serial no. K940639 in its mahogany presentation case, with accessories.
This is the only Model 19 documented to have been shipped in a presentation case. Bill Cross collection

Class C engraved Model 19-3 serial no. K940639 was shipped on October 21, 1971 to Rex Firearms in New York City. It is only Model 19 documented as being shipped in a mahogany presentation case, although there may be a few more.

The case resembles those used for the .41 and .44 Magnums, except the bottom insert is dimensioned for a 4-inch K-frame revolver.

# A Box Retrospective

To conclude this chapter on shipping containers, let me summarize by saying the following:

- A cardboard box can be rarer than the weapon it originally contained, due to the relative fragility of the box.
- The colors of the boxes and the styles of printing on them have changed over time, and the original colors have often faded with exposure to sun and air, so different shades are to be expected.
- No one can say that a box is "wrong" for a given weapon if it is close in time to the weapon's manufacturing date, due to the common practice of using up old stock for shipping purposes. Conversely, however, an early gun in a much later box is incorrect.
- A box that is "correct" will add considerably to the value of the weapon it contains, as it increases the charm and historical significance of the piece.
- The boxes are interesting, fun to view, and offer an insight into the past, adding to the "time machine" quality of the K-frame revolver.
- Even modern plastic cases, which themselves have come in different formats, may in the future become valuable collectibles for someone's great-grandchildren to appreciate.

813 (following page). Left and right side views of the Model 315 Nightguard, serial no. DBU41155, the first and (so far) only K-frame S&W manufactured on an "Sc" (Scandium/aluminum alloy) round-butt frame with internal key lock system, fitted with S&W-monogrammed rubber wraparound grips and provision for a lanyard pin (cutout and pin hole). S&W trademark under the thumbpiece in white against the all-black frame finish.

Caliber .38 Special, with a six-round stainless steel cylinder finished with a durable black PVD coating and a 2½" barrel with cast shroud, laser-burned "SMITH & WESSON" on the left side and "38 S&W SPL. +P" on the right.

Note the absence of the flame shield above the cylinder-barrel gap. Rick Nahas collection

# Finale

# The Model 351 Sc™ Nightguard

814. Top closeup of the Model 351 Sc™ Nightguard showing Trijicon "XS Sights 24-7 Tritium" front night sight and fixed "Cylinder & Slide" rear sight, unique in that it fits in the existing adjustable sight slot with no modification to the frame. Rick Nahas collection

With the release of the .357 Magnum caliber J-frame Model 360 Sc™ (fig. 204) and the .357 Magnum N-frame Model 327 Sc™ (fig. 203) in the early 2000s, the list of codes for receiver material shown on page 505—4 for aluminum, 5 for steel and 6 for stainless steel—required the addition of a new code, '3', for frames made of Scandium/aluminum alloy.

As well as the J-frame Model 360 Sc™ there are plenty of N-frame revolvers with Sc™ frames today, but the only K-frame made in the Sc™ material is the Model 315, shown here.

The developmental history of the rare element Scandium , taken from a 2001 factory brochure titled "The Weight of Things to Come", appears on page 189.

The Model 315 was introduced at the 2008 SHOT Show, too late for inclusion in the 3rd Edition of the *Standard Catalog of Smith & Wesson*. This model was produced in 2008 and 2009, and discontinued in 2010.

# *Bibliography*

## Books

*Advance Sheets of Biographical History of Massachusetts - Ideals of American Life - Containing Biography of Daniel Baird Wesson*. Boston Biographical Society, 1909

*America's Right Arm - The Smith & Wesson Military and Police Revolver* by John Henwood. Published by the author, 1997

*Ammo Encyclopedia, 2nd Edition* by Michael Bussard. Blue Book Publications Inc., Minneapolis, Minnesota, 2010

*Artistry in Arms* by Roy G. Jinks. Springfield, Massachusetts, 1991

*The Art of Handgun Shooting* by Charles Askins, Jr. A. S. Barnes Co., New York, 1941

*The Art of Revolver Shooting* by Walter Winans. G. P. Putnam's Sons, New York, Revised Edition, 1911

*Book of Pistols and Revolvers* by Joseph E. Smith. Castle Books, New York, 1968

*Burning Powder* Sixth Edition. Smith & Wesson, Inc., Springfield, Massachusetts, 1938

*Canadian Military Handguns, 1855 - 1985* by Clive M. Law. Museum Restoration Service, Bloomfield, Ontario, 1994

*Cartridges of the World* by Frank C. Barnes. Follet Publishing Company, Chicago, Illinois, 2nd Edition, 1969

*Centerfire American and British Pistol and Revolver Cartridges - Volume II of Cartridge Identification* by H. P. White and B. D. Munhall. The Combat Forces Press, Washington, D.C., 1950

*Colt .45 Service Pistols, Models of 1911 and 1911A1* by Charles W. Clawson, 1991

*Colt's New Service Revolver - "A Particularly Strong, Heavy Weapon"* by Timothy J. Mullin. Collector Grade Publications Inc., Cobourg, Ont., 2009

*Complete Book of Modern Handgunning* by Jeff Cooper. Prentice-Hall, Englewood Cliffs, New Jersey, 1961

*Complete Book of Shooting* by Jack O'Connor, Roy Dunlap, Alex Kerr, Jeff Cooper. Harper & Row, New York, 1965

*Cooper on Handguns* by Jeff Cooper. Petersen Publishing Co., Los Angeles, California, 1974

*Desperate Measures - The Last-Ditch Weapons of the Nazi Volkssturm* by W. Darrin Weaver. Collector Grade Publications Inc., Cobourg, Ont., 2005

*Ed McGivern's Book on Fast and Fancy Revolver Shooting and Police Training* by Ed McGivern. King Richardson Company, Springfield, Massachusetts, 1938

*Fighting Handguns* by Jeff Cooper. Trend Books Hollywood, California, 1958

*Gun Notes, Volume I: 1961 - 1970* by Elmer Keith. Stackpole Books, Harrrisburg, Pennsylvania, 1995

*Guns, Ammunition and Tackle* by Horace Kephart and A. L. A. Himmelwright. MacMillan Company, New York, 1904

*Guns & Shooting* by Lucian Cary. Arco Publishing Co., New York, 1960

*Handbook of Handguns* by Timothy J. Mullin. Paladin Press, Boulder, Colorado, 2001

*The Handgun* by Geoffrey Boothroyd. The Sportsman's Press, London, 1970/1988

*Handguns Afield* by Jeff Cooper. Trend Books, Hollywood, California, 1961

*Handgunner's Guide* by Chic Gaylord. Hastings House, New York, 1960

*Handguns for Self Defense* by Gerry Gore. MacMillan South Africa Publishers, Johannesburg, South Africa, 1979

*Handguns of the World* by Edward C. Ezell. Stackpole Books, Harrisburg, Pennsylvania, 1981

*High Standard Automatic Pistols 1932 - 1950* by Charles E. Petty. American Ordnance Publications, Charlotte, N.C., 1976

*Hints on Revolver Shooting* by Walter Winans. Knickerbocker Press, New York, 1904

*History of Modern U.S. Military Small Arms Ammunition Volume II: 1940 - 1945* by F. W. Hackley, W. H. Woodin, and E. L. Scranton. The Gun Room Press, 1978

*History of Firearms* by Hugh Pollard and Burt Franklin. New York, Reprint 1973

*History of Smith & Wesson* by Roy G. Jinks. Beinfeld Publishing, Inc., North Hollywood, California, 1977

*The History of Smith & Wesson Firearms* by Dean K. Boorman. Lyons Press, Guilford, Connecticut, 2002

*International Armament Volume I* by George B. Johnson and Hans Bert Lockhoven. International Small Arms Publishers, Cologne, Germany, 1965

*Le Tir Rapide* by Raymond Sasia. Lacer, Rambault, France, 1977

*MAGNUM - The S&W .357 Magnum Phenomenon* by Timothy J. Mullin. Collector Grade Publications Inc., Cobourg, Ont., 2012

*Mousquetaire du Général* by Raymond Sasia. Paris, France, Éditions Guéna, 2011

*No Second Place Winner* by Bill Jordan. Shreveport, Louisiana, 1965

*The 100 Greatest Combat Pistols* by Timothy J. Mullin. Paladin Press, Boulder, Colorado, 1994

*Ordnance Went Up Front* by Roy F. Dunlap. Samworth Publications, Plantersville, South Carolina, 1948

*The Peacemakers* by R. L. Wilson. Random House, New York, 1992

*Police Reserve & Home Defense Guard Manual* by William Dawkins. E. F. Dutton, New York, 1918

*The Pistol & Revolver* by A. L. A. Himmelwright. J. C. Little & Company, New York, 1908

*Pistol & Revolver Shooting* by A. L . A. Himmelwright. MacMillan Co., New York, 1920, 1922, 1923, 1927, 1928, and 1938 Editions

*Pistol and Revolver Shooting* by Walter F. Roper. The MacMillan Company, New York, 1945; Fifth Printing, 1957

*Pistols: A Modern Encyclopedia* by Henry Stebbins. Stackpole Co., Harrisburg, Pennsylvania, 1961

*The Pistol Shooter's Book* by Charles Askins, Jr. Stackpole Company, Harrisburg, Pennsylvania, 1953

*Pistols, Revolvers & Ammunition* by Michael Josserand and Jan Stevenson. Bonanza Books, New York, 1972

*The Redbook of Handguns* by Elmer Keith. Publisher's Develop. Co., Skokie, Illinois, 1961

*The Secrets of Double Action Shooting* by Bob Nichols. G. P. Putnam's Sons, New York, 1950

*Shooting* by J. Henry FitzGerald. The G. F. Book Company, Hartford, Connecticut, 1930

*Shooting For Ladies* by Walter Winans. G. P. Putnam's Sons, London, 1911

*Sixguns by Keith* by Elmer Keith. Stackpole Company, Harrisburg, Pennsylvania, 1961

*Sixguns & Bullseyes* by William Reichenbach. Samworth Publications, Plantersville, South Carolina, 1936

*Small Arms Today* by Edward C. Ezell. Stackpole Books, Harrisburg,PA, 2nd Edition, 1988

*Smith & Wesson 1857-1945* by Robert J. Neal and Roy G. Jinks. A. S. Barnes and Co. Inc., New York, Revised Edition 1975

*Smith & Wesson Hand Guns* by Roy C. McHenry and Walter F. Roper. Standard Publications Inc., Huntington, W.Va., 1945

*Smith & Wesson - The Story of the Revolver* by Martin Rywell and Carl R. Hellstrom, President, Smith & Wesson. Pioneer Press, Harriman, Tennessee, 1953

*The Standard Directory of Proof Marks* by Gerhard Wirnsberger, translated by R. A. Steindler. Jolex, Inc., 1975

*Standard Catalog of Smith & Wesson* by Jim Supica and Richard Nahas. Gun Digest Books, F+W Media, Inc., Iola, WI. 3rd Edition, 2006

*A Study of Colt's New Army and Navy Pattern Double Action Revolvers 1889 to 1908* © 2004 by Robert Best

*Textbook of Pistols & Revolvers* by J. S. Hatcher. Small Army Technical Publishing Co., Plantersville, South Carolina, 1935

*.380 Enfield No. 2 Revolver* by Mark Stamps and Ian Skennerton. Greenhill Books, London, 1993

*Training The Gunfighter* by Timothy J. Mullin. Paladin Press, Boulder, Colorado, 1981

*United States Martial and Collectors Arms* by Stephen L. Fuller. Military Arms Research Service, San Jose, California, 1977

*U.S. Cartridges and Their Handguns, 1795 - 1975* by Charles R. Suydam. Beinfeld Publishing, Inc., North Hollywood, California, 1977

*U.S. Handguns of World War II* by Charles W. Pate. Andrew Mowbray Publishers, Lincoln, Rhode Island, 1998

*U.S. Military Automatic Pistols, 1894 - 1920* by Edward Scott Meadows. Richard Ellis Publications, Inc., Moline, Illinois, 1993

*Webley Revolvers* (Revised from W. C. Dowell's *The Webley Story*) by Gordon Bruce and Christian Reinhart. Verlag Stocker-Schmid AG, Dietikon-Zürich, Switzerland, 1988

*The World's Submachine Guns [Machine Pistols] Volume I* by Thomas B. Nelson and Hans B. Lockhoven. International Small Arms Publishers, Cologne, Germany, 1963

## Catalogs

Catalog D-2 - "The Seal of Quality". Smith & Wesson, Springfield Mass., U.S.A., January 1, 1921, and Price List Catalog D-2, January 1, 1921

Catalog D-3 - "The Seal of Quality". Smith & Wesson, Springfield Mass., U.S.A., March, 1923, and Price List, Catalog D-3, December 20, 1923

Centennial Catalog - Smith & Wesson - Superior Revolvers - 1852 - 1952. Smith & Wesson Incorporated, Springfield, Massachusetts, 1952

Revolvers and Pistols - Catalog D-1, August 1, 1919 - "The Gun that Won". Smith & Wesson, Springfield, Mass., U.S.A.

*The Revolver for the Pocket, for the Military and for Target Practice*. Smith & Wesson, Springfield, Mass. U.S.A. (1909 - 1912 factory catalog)

Smith & Wesson Catalog "D" and Price List, Catalog D. Smith & Wesson, Springfield, Mass., March 1, 1917

*Smith & Wesson - Manufacturers of Superior Revolvers* undated, ca. 1925, with Retail Prices of Smith & Wesson Revolvers and Pistols, effective December 1, 1925

*Smith & Wesson - Manufacturers of Superior Revolvers* undated, ca. 1928

*Smith & Wesson Revolvers - Superior Revolvers, Pocket, Military, Target, Manufactured by Smith & Wesson Springfield Mass. U.S.A.* (1902). Reproduced by Jayco, 1962, with permission of Smith & Wesson

*Smith & Wesson - Superior Revolvers Since 1854.* Smith & Wesson Incorporated, Springfield, Massachusetts, 1941

## Articles

"A Criminal Stopper That Stops 'em" *The American Rifleman*, November, 1931

"A Full Hand" *Shooting and Fishing*, May, 1899

"American Handguns in British Service: Smith & Wesson and Their Competitors" by David Penn, Keeper of the Department of Exhibits and Firearms, Imperial War Museum. *Smith & Wesson Collector's News* Volume 26 No. 4, Winter, 1992

"A New Bullet" *Shooting and Fishing*, October, 1904

"A New Revolver of Advanced Design" by Maj. J. S. Hatcher. *The American Rifleman*, March, 1931

"A Policeman's View of Revolver Shooting" *Shooting and Fishing*, July, 1902

"A Stopping Charge for the .38" *Shooting and Fishing*, June, 1905

"A Tight Spot That's Safe" *The American Rifleman*, February, 1939

"A Trick That's Hard to Beat" *The American Rifleman*, July, 1938

"Accuracy Hangs on Align" *The American Rifleman*, December, 1938

"After Years of Service" *The American Rifleman*, February, 1939

"Another Important Ammunition Development by Western" *The American Rifleman*, January, 1927

"Better Sights" *The American Rifleman*, October, 1927

"Bye-Bye Bob Cat" *The American Rifleman*, August, 1930

"Caliber of Military Revolvers" *Shooting and Fishing*, May, 1905

"Chicago Revolver Shooting" *Shooting and Fishing*, April, 1902

"Colt New Army Revolver" *Shooting and Fishing*, October, 1904

"Company Tension!" *The American Rifleman*, April, 1939

"Engraving is a Traditional Artform" by Roy G. Jinks. Smith & Wesson *Bulletin*, Spring, 1982

"First Report of Military and Police Target" *Shooting and Fishing*, March, 1899

"Forging with Police Approval" *The American Rifleman*, June, 1938

"Headed for Rough Going" *The American Rifleman*, November, 1938

"Illustration: Target Group Shot with Military and Police" *Shooting and Fishing*, April, 1899

"Improved Ammunition for Revolvers" *Shooting and Fishing*, July, 1902

"In Command" *The American Rifleman*, July, 1930

"Life Insurance for Police Officers" *The American Rifleman*, January, 1931

"Long Range Revolver Shooting" *Shooting and Fishing*, April, 1900

"Luger Automatic" *Shooting and Fishing*, October, 1901, and May, 1902

"New Police Record at Camp Perry National Matches" *The American Rifleman*, October, 1931

"One for the Record Book" *The American Rifleman*, October, 1938

"Passing of the .45 Caliber Revolver" *Shooting and Fishing*, July, 1901

"Penetration of Pistol and Revolver Bullets" by Edwin Sturtevant. *Shooting and Fishing*, May, 1902

"Pickups – Manhattan and Elsewhere" *Shooting and Fishing*, March, 1899

"Police Revolver Practice St. Louis MO" *Shooting and Fishing*, April, 1903

"Post-War Models of Smith & Wesson: Model 13" by Roy G. Jinks. *Arms Gazette*, May, 1975

"Protection" *The American Rifleman,* April, 1927

"Queries and Replies" *Shooting and Fishing*, July, 1900, and October, 1900

"Report of Recalling .45s and Issuance of .38s" *Shooting and Fishing*, October 1901

"Revolver Shooting from Machine Rest" *Shooting and Fishing*, April, 1906

"S&W Solves the 9mm Revolver Problem" Smith & Wesson *Bulletin*, Summer,1981

"Shooting a Revolver" *The American Rifleman*, December, 1927

"Shooting Report with Smokeless Loads" *Shooting and Fishing*, March, 1899

"Smith & Wesson's Beanwheel Parabellum" by Jan Stevenson. *Handgunner*, September-October, 1981

Smith & Wesson Collector's Association, *The Smith & Wesson Journal*, Volume 1 - 26

"Smith & Wesson New Military Revolver" *Shooting and Fishing*, October, 1899

"Smith & Wesson Revolvers" *Shooting and Fishing*, March, 1899

"Smith & Wesson Revolvers with Fixed Sights" *The American Rifleman*, September, 1927

"Some Penetration Tests" by F. C. Ness. *The American Rifleman*, May, 1935

"Spring Anchorage" *The American Rifleman*, May, 1939

"Stands Up Under Shocking Treatment" *The American Rifleman*, September, 1938

"Stopping Power in Revolvers" *Shooting and Fishing*, April, 1905

"Sure Seat for Sure Shooting" *The American Rifleman*, August, 1938

"The Army Revolver" *Shooting and Fishing*, April, 1906

"The Bureaucrats' Belt Gun" by Jan Stevenson. *Handgunner*, July-August, 1981

"The Caliber of Military Revolvers" *Army and Navy Journal*, June, 1905

"The "K-22" Outdoorsman's Revolver" *The American Rifleman*, March, 1931

"The Officer's Model Colt Revolver" by Samuel J. Fort, M.D. *Shooting and Fishing*, November, 1904

"The Quantico Connection" by Jan Stevenson. *Handgunner*, May-June, 1981

"The Short Episode of the 9mm Revolver" by Lt. Col. (ret.) Matti Chemed. *Caliber* magazine (translated from the Hebrew *Caliber kravi*), Vol. 18, winter, 2011

"The Smith & Wesson Military Model 1905" *Shooting and Fishing*, December, 1905

"The Smith & Wesson .38/44 Super Police" *The American Rifleman*, November, 1931

"The .38 Caliber Military Revolver" *Shooting and Fishing*, June, 1905

"The ".38 Special" " *The American Rifleman*, August, 1928

"The .38 Special and Stopping Power" by R. E. Davis. *Shooting and Fishing*, January, 1935

"The .38 Special and Stopping Power" by R. E. Davis. *The American Rifleman*, January, 1935

"Tough Customers" *The American Rifleman*, May, 1930

"Toughest in the Block" *The American Rifleman*, March, 1939

"Woods Wisdom" *The American Rifleman*, March, 1930

## Manuals

Department of the Army Technical Manual TM 9-1305-200/Department of the Air Force Technical order TO 11A13010101, "Small Arms Ammunition". Departments of the Army and Air Force, June, 1961

Department of the Army Technical Manual TM 9-2027/TO 11W3-4-2-34 "Ordnance Maintenance, Cal. .38 Special Lightweight Revolver M13 (Colt and Smith and Wesson)". Department of the Army, July, 1956

War Department Technical Manual TM 9-1990, "Small-Arms Ammunition". War Department, September, 1947

## Monographs

*Smith & Wesson K-22, 1931 to 1961* by Charles L. Stellmacher, Seymour, WI, © 2003

# *Index*

## A



## B



## C

## D



## E



## F

# G



# H



# I



# J

## K



## L



## M



## N



## O

# P



# R

# S

# T



# U

## V



## W

# *A Compendium of Available Titles*

A complete list of all the titles published since Collector Grade was founded in 1979 appears on page *iv*. Not all of these are still in print. Those illustrated below were in stock when this book went to press, although some were in short supply and may have sold out since. Details on current availability may be obtained from our website:

**www.collectorgrade.com**

384 pages, 478 illustrations

416 pages, 441 illustrations

408 pages, 626 illustrations

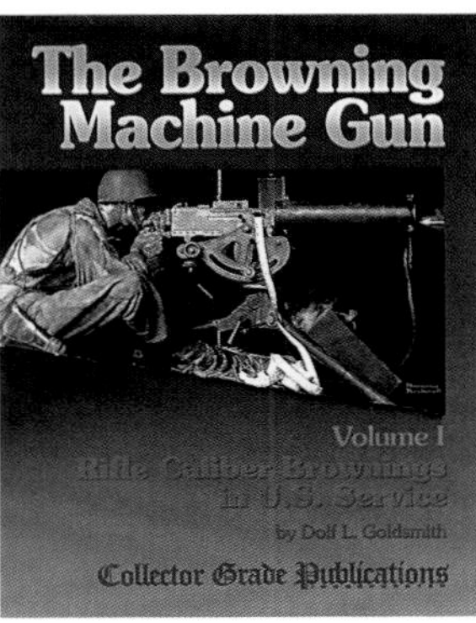


552 pages, 568 illustrations

392 pages, 486 illustrations

488 pages, 766 illustrations

448 pages, 510 illustrations

296 pages, 394 illustrations

228 pages, 278 illustrations

424 pages, 558 illustrations

584 pages, 819 illustrations

848 pages, 844 illustrations

256 pages, 361 illustrations

536 pages, 737 illustrations

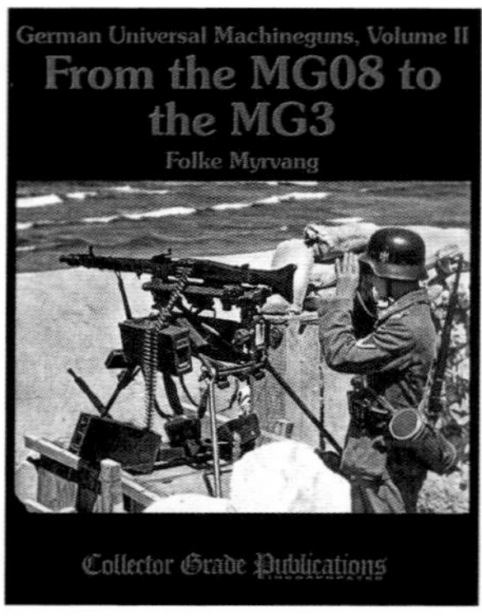


512 pages, 986 illustrations

304 pages, 291 illustrations

392 pages, 590 illustrations

227 pages, 244 illustrations

312 pages, 379 illustrations

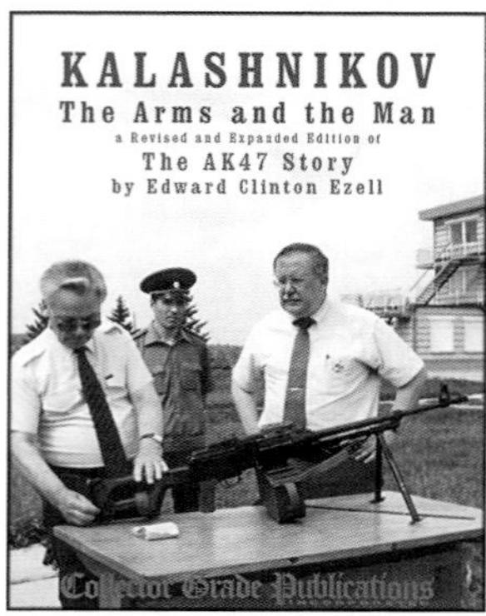


312 pages, 356 illustrations

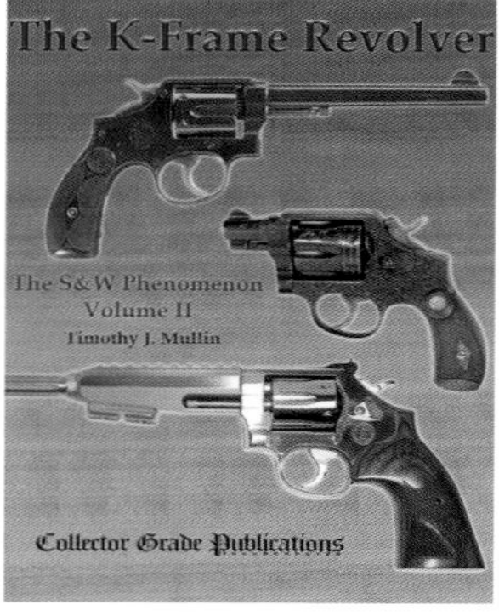


520 pages, 592 illustrations

360 pages, 382 illustrations

282 pages, 224 illustrations

576 pages, 870 illustrations

368 pages, 461 illustrations

496 pages, 646 illustrations

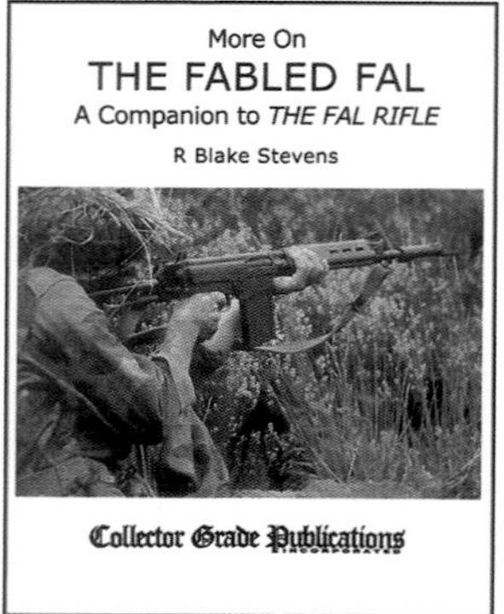


272 pages, 343 illustrations

2,014 pages,
1,917 illustrations

216 pages, 299 illustrations

500 pages, 751 illustrations

240 pages, 291 illustrations

404 pages, 368 illustrations

600 pages, 392 illustrations

872 pages,
1,201 illustrations

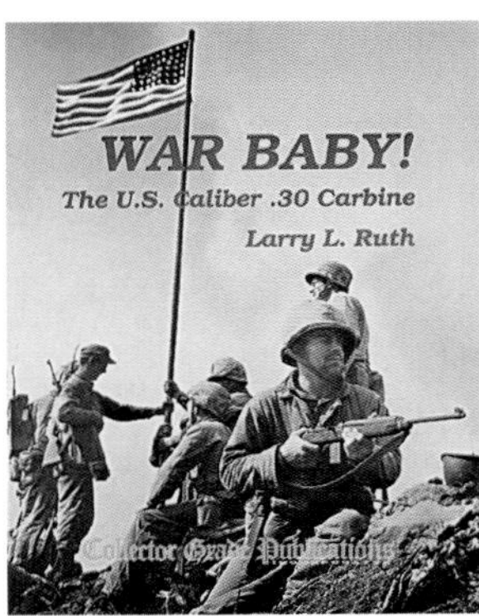


512 pages, 398 illustrations

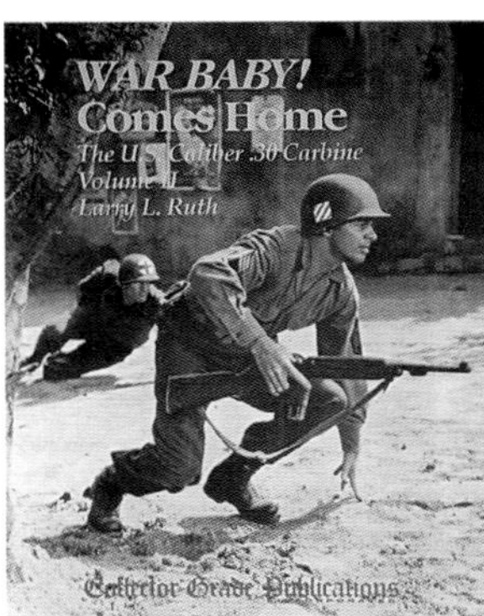


368 pages, 414 illustrations

952 pages,
1,328 illustrations

SMITH & WESSON
SECURITY POLICE
DEPARTMENT OF THE AIR FORCE
UNITED STATES OF AMERICA
N6499